PLUTARCH'S
MORALIA

X

PLUTARCH'S
MORALIA

IN FOURTEEN VOLUMES
VOLUME X
771E—854D

WITH AN ENGLISH TRANSLATION BY
HAROLD NORTH FOWLER

PROFESSOR EMERITUS,
WESTERN RESERVE UNIVERSITY

LONDON
WILLIAM HEINEMANN LTD
CAMBRIDGE, MASSACHUSETTS
HARVARD UNIVERSITY PRESS
MCMXLIX

FIRST PRINTED . 1927
REPRINTED . 1949

Printed in Great Britain

PREFACE

In preparing this volume I have tried to follow the methods and principles adopted by Professor Babbitt. The text is based upon that of Bernardakis's edition, but some departures from his readings have seemed unavoidable. The critical notes are by no means exhaustive, but I hope nothing essential has been omitted. All the essays contained in this volume are mentioned in the list of Lamprias except the two entitled *That a Philosopher ought to converse especially with Men in Power* and *To an Uneducated Ruler.* In that list one item (No. 52) is πολιτικῶν βιβλία β', *Two Books on Political Subjects.* No such title is found in the manuscripts of Plutarch's works, and the question arises whether our two brief essays may perhaps be intended, for their subjects are certainly political in the Greek sense of the word. In the list of Lamprias there is no indication that the *Comparison between Aristophanes and Menander* is a summary.

Additions to the bibliography given in Volume I. which have to do with the contents of the present volume are : *Plutarchi Libelli Duo Politici*, a dissertation by Ioannes Frerichs (Göttingen, 1929), containing the Greek text of the essays *That a Philosopher ought to converse especially with Men in Power* and *To an Un-*

PREFACE

educated Ruler with critical commentary and notes, and *The Manuscript-Tradition* (also reprinted as *The Text-Tradition*) of *Pseudo-Plutarch's Vitae Decem Oratorum,* by Clarence George Lowe, published in *University of Illinois Studies in Language and Literature,* ix. No. 4, 1924.

H. N. F.

Washington, D.C.
June, 1936.

CONTENTS OF VOLUME X

PAGE

THE TRADITIONAL ORDER OF THE BOOKS OF
    THE *MORALIA* ix

LOVE STORIES—
    Introduction 3
    Text and Translation 4

THAT A PHILOSOPHER OUGHT TO CONVERSE
    ESPECIALLY WITH MEN IN POWER—
    Introduction 27
    Text and Translation 28

TO AN UNEDUCATED RULER—
    Introduction 51
    Text and Translation 52

WHETHER AN OLD MAN SHOULD ENGAGE IN
    PUBLIC AFFAIRS—
    Introduction 75
    Text and Translation 76

PRECEPTS OF STATECRAFT—
    Introduction 156
    Text and Translation 158

CONTENTS OF VOLUME X

PAGE

ON MONARCHY, DEMOCRACY, AND OLIGARCHY—

    Introduction 303

    Text and Translation 304

THAT WE OUGHT NOT TO BORROW—

    Introduction 315

    Text and Translation 316

LIVES OF THE TEN ORATORS—

    Introduction 342

    Text and Translation 344

SUMMARY OF A COMPARISON BETWEEN ARISTO-
    PHANES AND MENANDER—

    Introduction 461

    Text and Translation 462

INDEX 475

THE TRADITIONAL ORDER of the Books of
the *Moralia* as they appear in practically all
editions since that of Xylander (1570), and their
division into volumes in this edition.

		PAGE
I.	De liberis educandis (Περὶ παίδων ἀγωγῆς)	1A
	Quomodo adolescens poetas audire debeat (Πῶς δεῖ τὸν νέον ποιημάτων ἀκούειν)	17D
	De recta ratione audiendi (Περὶ τοῦ ἀκούειν)	37B
	Quomodo adulator ab amico internoscatur (Πῶς ἄν τις διακρίνειε τὸν κόλακα τοῦ φίλου)	48E
	Quomodo quis suos in virtute sentiat profectus (Πῶς ἄν τις αἴσθοιτο ἑαυτοῦ προκόπτοντος ἐπ' ἀρετῇ)	75A
II.	De capienda ex inimicis utilitate (Πῶς ἄν τις ὑπ' ἐχθρῶν ὠφελοῖτο)	86B
	De amicorum multitudine (Περὶ πολυφιλίας)	93A
	De fortuna (Περὶ τύχης)	97C
	De virtute et vitio (Περὶ ἀρετῆς καὶ κακίας)	100B
	Consolatio ad Apollonium (Παραμυθητικὸς πρὸς Ἀπολλώνιον)	101F
	De tuenda sanitate praecepta (Ὑγιεινὰ παραγγέλματα)	122B
	Coniugalia praecepta (Γαμικὰ παραγγέλματα)	138A
	Septem sapientium convivium (Τῶν ἑπτὰ σοφῶν συμπόσιον)	146B
	De superstitione (Περὶ δεισιδαιμονίας)	164E
III.	Regum et imperatorum apophthegmata (Ἀποφθέγματα βασιλέων καὶ στρατηγῶν)	172A
	Apophthegmata Laconica (Ἀποφθέγματα Λακωνικά)	208A
	Instituta Laconica (Τὰ παλαιὰ τῶν Λακεδαιμονίων ἐπιτηδεύματα)	236F

THE TRADITIONAL ORDER

		PAGE
Lacaenarum apophthegmata (Λακαινῶν ἀπο-φθέγματα)		240c
Mulierum virtutes (Γυναικῶν ἀρεταί)		242e
IV. Quaestiones Romanae (Αἴτια Ῥωμαϊκά)		263d
Quaestiones Graecae (Αἴτια Ἑλληνικά)		291d
Parallela Graeca et Romana (Συναγωγὴ ἱστοριῶν παραλλήλων Ἑλληνικῶν καὶ Ῥωμαϊκῶν)		305a
De fortuna Romanorum (Περὶ τῆς Ῥωμαίων τύχης)		316b
De Alexandri magni fortuna aut virtute, libri ii (Περὶ τῆς Ἀλεξάνδρου τύχης ἢ ἀρετῆς, λόγοι β΄)		326d
Bellone an pace clariores fuerint Athenienses (Πότερον Ἀθηναῖοι κατὰ πόλεμον ἢ κατὰ σοφίαν ἐνδοξότεροι)		345c
V. De Iside et Osiride (Περὶ Ἴσιδος καὶ Ὀσίριδος)		351c
De E apud Delphos (Περὶ τοῦ ΕΙ τοῦ ἐν Δελφοῖς)		384c
De Pythiae oraculis (Περὶ τοῦ μὴ χρᾶν ἔμμετρα νῦν τὴν Πυθίαν)		394d
De defectu oraculorum (Περὶ τῶν ἐκλελοιπότων χρηστηρίων)		409e
VI. An virtus doceri possit (Εἰ διδακτὸν ἡ ἀρετή)		439a
De virtute morali (Περὶ τῆς ἠθικῆς ἀρετῆς)		440d
De cohibenda ira (Περὶ ἀοργησίας)		452e
De tranquillitate animi (Περὶ εὐθυμίας)		464e
De fraterno amore (Περὶ φιλαδελφίας)		478a
De amore prolis (Περὶ τῆς εἰς τὰ ἔκγονα φιλοστοργίας)		493a
An vitiositas ad infelicitatem sufficiat (Εἰ αὐτάρκης ἡ κακία πρὸς κακοδαιμονίαν)		498a
Animine an corporis affectiones sint peiores (Πότερον τὰ τῆς ψυχῆς ἢ τὰ τοῦ σώματος πάθη χείρονα)		500b
De garrulitate (Περὶ ἀδολεσχίας)		502b
De curiositate (Περὶ πολυπραγμοσύνης)		515b
VII. De cupiditate divitiarum (Περὶ φιλοπλουτίας)		523c
De vitioso pudore (Περὶ δυσωπίας)		528c
De invidia et odio (Περὶ φθόνου καὶ μίσους)		536e
De se ipsum citra invidiam laudando (Περὶ τοῦ ἑαυτὸν ἐπαινεῖν ἀνεπιφθόνως)		539a
De sera numinis vindicta (Περὶ τῶν ὑπὸ τοῦ θείου βραδέως τιμωρουμένων)		548a
De fato (Περὶ εἱμαρμένης)		568b

x

THE TRADITIONAL ORDER

		PAGE
De genio Socratis (Περὶ τοῦ Σωκράτους δαιμονίου)	.	575A
De exilio (Περὶ φυγῆς)	.	599A
Consolatio ad uxorem (Παραμυθητικὸς εἰς τὴν γυναῖκα τὴν ἑαυτοῦ)	.	608A
VIII. Quaestionum convivialium libri ix (Συμποσιακῶν προβλημάτων βιβλία θ') . . .	.	612c
I, 612c; II, 629B; III, 644E; IV, 659E; V, 672D; VI, 686A		
IX. VII, 697c; VIII, 716D; IX, 736c		
Amatorius (Ἐρωτικός)	.	748E
X. Amatoriae narrationes (Ἐρωτικαὶ διηγήσεις)	.	771E
Maxime cum principibus philosopho esse disserendum (Περὶ τοῦ ὅτι μάλιστα τοῖς ἡγεμόσι δεῖ τὸν φιλόσοφον διαλέγεσθαι) . . .	.	776A
Ad principem ineruditum (Πρὸς ἡγεμόνα ἀπαίδευτον)	.	779c
An seni respublica gerenda sit (Εἰ πρεσβυτέρῳ πολιτευτέον)	.	783A
Praecepta gerendae reipublicae (Πολιτικὰ παραγγέλματα)	.	798A
De unius in republica dominatione, populari statu, et paucorum imperio (Περὶ μοναρχίας καὶ δημοκρατίας καὶ ὀλιγαρχίας) . .	.	826A
De vitando aere alieno (Περὶ τοῦ μὴ δεῖν δανείζεσθαι)	.	827D
Vitae decem oratorum (Περὶ τῶν δέκα ῥητόρων)	.	832B
Comparationis Aristophanis et Menandri compendium (Συγκρίσεως Ἀριστοφάνους καὶ Μενάνδρου ἐπιτομή)	.	853A
XI. De Herodoti malignitate (Περὶ τῆς Ἡροδότου κακοηθείας)	.	854E
De placitis philosophorum, libri v (Περὶ τῶν ἀρεσκόντων τοῖς φιλοσόφοις, βιβλία ε') .	.	874D
Quaestiones naturales (Αἴτια φυσικά) .	.	911c
XII. De facie quae in orbe lunae apparet (Περὶ τοῦ ἐμφαινομένου προσώπου τῷ κύκλῳ τῆς σελήνης) .	.	920A
De primo frigido (Περὶ τοῦ πρώτου ψύχους)	.	945E
Aquane an ignis sit utilior (Περὶ τοῦ πότερον ὕδωρ ἢ πῦρ χρησιμώτερον) . .	.	955D
Terrestriane an aquatilia animalia sint callidiora (Πότερα τῶν ζῴων φρονιμώτερα τὰ χερσαῖα ἢ τὰ ἔνυδρα)	.	959A

THE TRADITIONAL ORDER

		PAGE
Bruta animalia ratione uti, sive Gryllus (Περὶ τοῦ τὰ ἄλογα λόγῳ χρῆσθαι) . . .		985D
De esu carnium orationes ii (Περὶ σαρκοφαγίας λόγοι β') . . .		993A
XIII. Platonicae quaestiones (Πλατωνικὰ ζητήματα) .		999C
De animae procreatione in Timaeo (Περὶ τῆς ἐν Τιμαίῳ ψυχογονίας)		1012A
Compendium libri de animae procreatione in Timaeo ('Επιτομὴ τοῦ περὶ τῆς ἐν τῷ Τιμαίῳ ψυχογονίας)		1030D
De Stoicorum repugnantiis (Περὶ Στωικῶν ἐναντιωμάτων) .		1033A
Compendium argumenti Stoicos absurdiora poetis dicere (Σύνοψις τοῦ ὅτι παραδοξότερα οἱ Στωικοὶ τῶν ποιητῶν λέγουσι)		1057C
De communibus notitiis adversus Stoicos (Περὶ τῶν κοινῶν ἐννοιῶν πρὸς τοὺς Στωικούς)		1058E
XIV. Non posse suaviter vivi secundum Epicurum ("Οτι οὐδ' ἡδέως ζῆν ἔστι κατ' 'Επίκουρον).		1086C
Adversus Colotem (Πρὸς Κολώτην) . .		1107D
An recte dictum sit latenter esse vivendum (εἰ καλῶς εἴρηται τὸ λάθε βιώσας) . .		1128A
De musica (Περὶ μουσικῆς) . .		1131A
Fragmenta.		

LOVE STORIES
(AMATORIAE NARRATIONES)

INTRODUCTION

THESE five short stories are interesting to the modern reader chiefly as examples of the kind of tale which appealed to the readers of Plutarch's time; for they were probably written during his lifetime, though not by him. In style and content they differ greatly from his genuine works. The elements of passion and of sentimental love are made to appear important in them rather on account of their dire consequences than for their own sake.

ΕΡΩΤΙΚΑΙ ΔΙΗΓΗΣΕΙΣ

A

(771)   Ἐν Ἁλιάρτῳ τῆς Βοιωτίας κόρη τις γίνεται
κάλλει διαπρέπουσα ὄνομα Ἀριστόκλεια· θυγάτηρ
δ᾽ ἦν Θεοφάνους. ταύτην μνῶνται Στράτων Ὀρχο-
F μένιος καὶ Καλλισθένης Ἁλιάρτιος.¹ πλουσιώτερος
δ᾽ ἦν Στράτων καὶ μᾶλλόν τι τῆς παρθένου ἡττη-
μένος· ἐτύγχανε γὰρ ἰδὼν αὐτὴν ἐν Λεβαδείᾳ λουο-
μένην ἐπὶ τῇ κρήνῃ τῇ Ἑρκύνῃ· ἔμελλε γὰρ τῷ
772 Διὶ τῷ βασιλεῖ κανηφορεῖν. ἀλλ᾽ ὁ Καλλισθένης
γε πλέον ἐφέρετο· ἦν γὰο καὶ γένει προσήκων
τῇ κόρῃ. ἀπορῶν δὲ τῷ πράγματι ὁ Θεοφάνης,
ἐδεδίει γὰρ τὸν Στράτωνα πλούτῳ τε καὶ γένει
σχεδὸν ἁπάντων διαφέροντα τῶν Βοιωτῶν, τὴν
αἵρεσιν ἐβούλετο τῷ Τροφωνίῳ ἐπιτρέψαι· καὶ ὁ
Στράτων, ἀνεπέπειστο γὰρ ὑπὸ τῶν τῆς παρθένου
οἰκετῶν, ὡς πρὸς αὐτὸν μᾶλλον ἐκείνη ῥέποι,
ἠξίου ἐπ᾽ αὐτῇ ποιεῖσθαι τῇ γαμουμένῃ τὴν
ἐκλογήν. ὡς δὲ τῆς παιδὸς ὁ Θεοφάνης ἐπυνθάνετο
ἐν ὄψει πάντων, ἡ δὲ τὸν Καλλισθένην προύκρινεν,
B εὐθὺς μὲν ὁ Στράτων δῆλος ἦν βαρέως φέρων τὴν

¹ Ἁλιάρτιος Wyttenbach : ἁλιάρτῳ.

4

LOVE STORIES

I

At Haliartus, in Boeotia, there was a girl of remarkable beauty, named Aristocleia, the daughter of Theophanes. She was wooed by Strato of Orchomenus and Callisthenes of Haliartus. Strato was the richer and was rather the more violently in love with the maiden; for he had seen her in Lebadeia bathing at the fountain called Hercynê in preparation for carrying a basket [a] in a sacred procession in honour of Zeus the King. But Callisthenes had the advantage, for he was a blood-relation of the girl. Theophanes was much perplexed about the matter, for he was afraid of Strato, who excelled nearly all the Boeotians in wealth and in family connexions, and he wished to submit the choice to Trophonius [b]; but Strato had been persuaded by the maiden's servants that she was more inclined towards him, so he asked that the choice be left to the bride-to-be herself. But when Theophanes in the presence of everyone asked the maiden, and she chose Callisthenes, it was plain at once that Strato found the

[a] Processions were common in Greek worship, and often young women, chosen usually for their good birth and their beauty, formed part of them, carrying baskets in which were offerings or utensils for use in sacrifices.

[b] A hero whose oracular shrine was at Lebadeia.

(772) ἀτιμίαν· ἡμέρας δὲ διαλιπὼν δύο προσῆλθε τῷ
Θεοφάνει καὶ τῷ Καλλισθένει, ἀξιῶν τὴν φιλίαν
αὐτῷ πρὸς αὐτοὺς διαφυλάττεσθαι, εἰ καὶ τοῦ
γάμου ἐφθονήθη ὑπὸ δαιμονίου τινός. οἱ δ' ἐπήνουν
τὰ λεγόμενα, ὥστε καὶ ἐπὶ τὴν ἑστίασιν τῶν γάμων
παρεκάλουν αὐτόν. ὁ δὲ¹ παρεσκευασμένος ἑταίρων
ὄχλον, καὶ πλῆθος οὐκ ὀλίγον θεραπόντων, δι-
εσπαρμένους παρὰ τούτοις καὶ λανθάνοντας, ἕως ἡ
κόρη κατὰ τὰ πάτρια ἐπὶ τὴν Κισσόεσσαν καλου-
μένην κρήνην κατῄει ταῖς Νύμφαις τὰ προτέλεια
C θύσουσα, τότε δὴ συνδραμόντες πάντες οἱ λοχῶντες
ἐκείνῳ συνελάμβανον αὐτήν. καὶ ὁ Στράτων γ'
εἴχετο τῆς παρθένου· ἀντελαμβάνετο δ' ὡς εἰκὸς
ὁ Καλλισθένης ἐν μέρει καὶ οἱ σὺν αὐτῷ, ἕως ἔλαθεν
ἡ παῖς ἐν χερσὶ τῶν ἀνθελκόντων διαφθαρεῖσα. ὁ
Καλλισθένης μὲν οὖν παραχρῆμα ἀφανὴς ἐγένετο,
εἴτε διαχρησάμενος ἑαυτὸν εἴτε φυγὰς ἀπελθὼν
ἐκ τῆς Βοιωτίας· οὐκ εἶχε δ' οὖν τις εἰπεῖν ὅ τι
καὶ πεπόνθοι. ὁ δὲ Στράτων φανερῶς ἐπικατ-
έσφαξεν ἑαυτὸν τῇ παρθένῳ.

B

D Φείδων τις τῶν Πελοποννησίων ἐπιτιθέμενος
ἀρχῇ, τὴν Ἀργείων πόλιν, τὴν πατρίδα τὴν ἑαυτοῦ,
ἡγεμονεύειν τῶν λοιπῶν βουλόμενος, πρῶτον ἐπ-
εβούλευσε Κορινθίοις· πέμψας γὰρ ᾔτει παρ' αὐτῶν
νεανίας χιλίους τοὺς ἀκμῇ διαφέροντας καὶ ἀνδρείᾳ·
οἱ δὲ πέμπουσι τοὺς χιλίους, στρατηγὸν αὐτῶν

¹ ὁ δὲ] Wyttenbach would add ἧκε.

slight hard to bear. But he let two days go by and came to Theophanes and Callisthenes asking that the friendship between him and them be preserved, even though he had been deprived of the marriage by some jealous divinity. And they approved of what he said, so that they even invited him to the wedding-feast. But before he came he got ready a crowd of his friends and a considerable number of servants, who were scattered among the others present and were not noticed ; but when the girl went, according to the ancestral custom, to the spring called Cissoessa to make the preliminary sacrifice to the nymphs, then his men who were in ambush all rushed out at once and seized her. Strato also had hold of the maiden ; and naturally Callisthenes and his supporters in turn took hold of her and held on until, although they did not know it at the time, she died in their hands as they pulled against each other. Callisthenes immediately disappeared, whether by committing suicide or by going away as an exile from Boeotia ; at any rate nobody could tell what had happened to him. But Strato slew himself in sight of all upon the body of the maiden.

II

A man named Pheidon, who was striving to make himself ruler of the Peloponnesians and wished his own native city of Argos to be the leader of all the other states, plotted first against the Corinthians. He sent and asked of them the thousand young men who were the best in vigour and valour ; and they sent the thousand, putting Dexander in

ἀποδείξαντες Δέξανδρον. ἐν νῷ δ' ἔχων ὁ Φείδων
ἐπιθέσθαι τούτοις, ἵν' ἔχοι Κόρινθον ἀτονωτέραν
καὶ τῇ πόλει χρήσαιτο, προτείχισμα γὰρ τοῦτο
ἐπικαιρότατον ἔσεσθαι τῆς ὅλης Πελοποννήσου,
E τὴν πρᾶξιν ἀνέθετο τῶν ἑταίρων τισίν. ἦν δὲ καὶ
Ἄβρων ἐν αὐτοῖς· οὗτος δὲ ξένος ὢν τοῦ Δεξάνδρου
ἔφρασεν αὐτῷ τὴν ἐπιβουλήν. καὶ οὕτως οἱ μὲν
χίλιοι[1] πρὸ τῆς ἐπιθέσεως εἰς τὴν Κόρινθον ἐσώθη-
σαν, Φείδων δ' ἀνευρεῖν ἐπειρᾶτο τὸν προδόντα καὶ
ἐπιμελῶς ἐζήτει. δείσας δ' ὁ Ἄβρων φεύγει εἰς
Κόρινθον, ἀναλαβὼν τὴν γυναῖκα καὶ τοὺς οἰκέτας,
ἐν Μελίσσῳ, κώμῃ τινὶ τῆς Κορινθίων χώρας· ἔνθα
καὶ παῖδα γεννήσας Μέλισσον προσηγόρευσεν, ἀπὸ
τοῦ τόπου θέμενος τοὔνομα αὐτῷ. τούτου δὴ τοῦ
Μελίσσου υἱὸς Ἀκταίων γίνεται, κάλλιστος καὶ
σωφρονέστατος τῶν ὁμηλίκων, οὗ πλεῖστοι μὲν
ἐγένοντο ἐρασταί, διαφερόντως δ' Ἀρχίας, γένους
μὲν ὢν τοῦ τῶν Ἡρακλειδῶν, πλούτῳ δὲ καὶ τῇ
F ἄλλῃ δυνάμει λαμπρότατος Κορινθίων. ἐπεὶ δὲ
πείθειν οὐκ ἠδύνατο τὸν παῖδα, ἔγνω βιάσασθαι
καὶ συναρπάσαι[2] τὸ μειράκιον· ἐπεκώμασεν οὖν[3]
ἐπὶ τὴν οἰκίαν τοῦ Μελίσσου, πλῆθος ἐπαγόμενος
καὶ φίλων καὶ οἰκετῶν, καὶ ἀπάγειν τὸν παῖδα
ἐπειρᾶτο. ἀντιποιουμένου δὲ τοῦ πατρὸς καὶ τῶν
φίλων, ἐπεκδραμόντων δὲ καὶ τῶν γειτόνων καὶ
773 ἀνθελκόντων, ἀνθελκόμενος ὁ Ἀκταίων διεφθάρη·
καὶ οἱ μὲν οὕτως ἀπεχώρουν. Μέλισσος δὲ τὸν
νεκρὸν τοῦ παιδὸς εἰς τὴν ἀγορὰν τῶν Κορινθίων
παρακομίσας ἐπεδείκνυε, δίκην ἀπαιτῶν παρὰ τῶν
ταῦτα πραξάντων· οἱ δὲ πλέον οὐδὲν ἢ τὸν ἄνδρα

---

[1] χίλιοι Meziriacus after Amyot: Φλιάσιοι.
[2] συναρπάσαι Leonicus: συναρπάσας.

8

command of them. Now Pheidon intended to make
an onslaught upon these young men, that Corinth
might be weakened and he might have the city in
his power, for he considered that it would be the
most advantageous bulwark of the whole Peloponnesus, and he confided this matter to some of his
friends, among whom was Habron. Now he was a
friend of Dexander and told him of the plot, so before
the onslaught was made the thousand young men
escaped safely to Corinth ; but Pheidon tried to
discover the betrayer of his plot and searched for him
with great care. So Habron was frightened and
fled to Corinth with his wife and his servants, settling
in Melissus, a village in Corinthian territory. There
he begot a son whom he called Melissus from the
name of the place. This Melissus had a son named
Actaeon, the handsomest and most modest youth
of his age, who had many lovers, chief of whom was
Archias, of the family of the Heracleidae, in wealth
and general influence the most outstanding man in
Corinth. Now when he could not gain the boy by
persuasion, he determined to carry him off by force.
So he got together a crowd of friends and servants,
went as in a drunken frolic to the house of Melissus,
and tried to take the boy away. But his father and
his friends resisted, the neighbours also ran out and
pulled against the assailants, and so Actaeon was
pulled to pieces and killed ; the assailants thereupon went away. But Melissus took his son's body
and exhibited it in the market-place of the Corinthians, demanding the punishment of the men who
had done the deed ; but the Corinthians merely pitied
him and did nothing further. So, being unsuccess-

---

³ οὖν added by Xylander.

(773) ἠλέουν. ἄπρακτος δ' ἀναχωρήσας παρεφύλασσε
τὴν πανήγυριν τῶν Ἰσθμίων, ἀναβάς τ' ἐπὶ τὸν τοῦ
Ποσειδῶνος νεὼν κατεβόα τῶν Βακχιαδῶν καὶ
τὴν τοῦ πατρὸς Ἄβρωνος εὐεργεσίαν ὑπεμίμνησκε,
τούς τε θεοὺς ἐπικαλεσάμενος ῥίπτει ἑαυτὸν κατὰ
τῶν πετρῶν. μετ' οὐ πολὺ δ' αὐχμὸς καὶ λοιμὸς
B κατελάμβανε τὴν πόλιν· καὶ τῶν Κορινθίων περὶ
ἀπαλλαγῆς χρωμένων, ὁ θεὸς ἀνεῖλε μῆνιν εἶναι
Ποσειδῶνος οὐκ ἀνήσοντος, ἕως ἂν τὸν Ἀκταίωνος
θάνατον μετέλθοιεν. ταῦτα πυθόμενος Ἀρχίας,
αὐτὸς γὰρ θεωρὸς ἦν, εἰς μὲν τὴν Κόρινθον ἑκὼν
οὐκ ἐπανῆλθε, πλεύσας δ' εἰς τὴν Σικελίαν Συρακούσας ἔκτισε. πατὴρ δὲ γενόμενος ἐνταῦθα
θυγατέρων δυεῖν, Ὀρτυγίας τε καὶ Συρακούσης,
ὑπὸ τοῦ Τηλέφου δολοφονεῖται, ὃς ἐγεγόνει μὲν
αὐτοῦ παιδικά, νεὼς δ' ἀφηγούμενος συνέπλευσεν
εἰς Σικελίαν.

Γ

Ἀνὴρ πένης Σκέδασος τοὔνομα κατῴκει Λεῦ-
κτρα· ἔστι δὲ κώμιον τῆς τῶν Θεσπιέων χώρας.
C τούτῳ θυγατέρες γίνονται δύο· ἐκαλοῦντο δ' Ἱππὼ
καὶ Μιλητία, ἤ, ὥς τινες, Θεανὼ καὶ Εὐξίππη.
ἦν δὲ χρηστὸς ὁ Σκέδασος καὶ τοῖς ξένοις ἐπι-
τήδειος, καίπερ οὐ πολλὰ κεκτημένος. ἀφικο-
μένους οὖν πρὸς αὐτὸν δύο Σπαρτιάτας νεανίας
ὑπεδέξατο προθύμως· οἱ δὲ τῶν παρθένων ἡττώ-
μενοι διεκωλύοντο πρὸς τὴν τόλμαν ὑπὸ τῆς τοῦ

---

^a The famous Isthmian games in honour of Poseidon, for
victors in which Pindar composed some of his odes.

10

ful, he went away and waited for the Isthmian festival,[a] when he went up upon the temple of Poseidon, shouted accusations against the Bacchiadae,[b] and reminded the people of his father Habron's benefactions, whereupon, calling upon the gods to avenge him, he threw himself down from the rocks. Not long afterwards the city was afflicted by drought and pestilence, and when the Corinthians consulted the oracle concerning relief, the god replied that the wrath of Poseidon would not relax until they inflicted punishment for the death of Actaeon. Archias knew of this, for he was himself one of those sent to consult the oracle, and voluntarily refrained from returning to Corinth. Instead he sailed to Sicily and founded Syracuse. There he became the father of two daughters, Ortygia and Syracusa, and was treacherously murdered by Telephus, who had been his beloved and had sailed with him to Sicily in command of a ship.

III

There was a poor man named Scedasus who lived at Leuctra; that is a village of the country of the Thespians. This man had two daughters, called Hippo and Miletia, or, as some say, Theano and Euxippê. Now Scedasus was a worthy man and friendly to strangers, though he was not very well off. So when two Spartan youths came to his house he received them gladly. They fell in love with the maidens, but were restrained from overboldness by

---

[b] The noble family which ruled Corinth in the eighth and seventh centuries B.C. Periander is its most famous member.

(773) Σκεδάσου χρηστότητος. τῇ δ' ὑστεραίᾳ Πυθώδε
ἀπῄεσαν· αὕτη γὰρ αὐτοῖς προύκειτο ἡ ὁδός· καὶ
τῷ θεῷ χρησάμενοι περὶ ὧν ἐδέοντο, πάλιν ἐπ-
ανῄεσαν οἴκαδε, καὶ χωροῦντες διὰ τῆς Βοιωτίας
D ἐπέστησαν πάλιν τῇ τοῦ Σκεδάσου οἰκίᾳ. ὁ δ'
ἐτύγχανεν οὐκ ἐπιδημῶν τοῖς Λεύκτροις, ἀλλ' αἱ
θυγατέρες αὐτοῦ ὑπὸ τῆς συνήθους ἀγωγῆς τοὺς
ξένους ὑπεδέξαντο. οἱ δὲ καταλαβόντες ἐρήμους
τὰς κόρας βιάζονται· ὁρῶντες δ' αὐτὰς καθ' ὑπερβολὴν τῇ ὕβρει χαλεπαινούσας ἀπέκτειναν, καὶ
ἐμβαλόντες ἔς τι φρέαρ ἀπηλλάγησαν. ἐπανελθὼν
δ' ὁ Σκέδασος τὰς μὲν κόρας οὐχ ἑώρα, πάντα δὲ
τὰ καταλειφθέντα εὑρίσκει σῶα καὶ τῷ πράγματι
ἠπόρει, ἕως τῆς κυνὸς κνυζωμένης καὶ πολλάκις
μὲν προστρεχούσης πρὸς αὐτὸν ἀπὸ δ' αὐτοῦ εἰς
τὸ φρέαρ ἐπανιούσης, εἴκασεν ὅπερ ἦν, καὶ τῶν
θυγατέρων τὰ νεκρὰ οὕτως ἀνιμήσατο. πυθόμενος
E δὲ παρὰ τῶν γειτόνων, ὅτι ἴδοιεν τῇ χθὲς ἡμέρᾳ
τοὺς καὶ πρῴην καταχθέντας ἐπ' αὐτοὺς Λακεδαιμονίους εἰσιόντας, συνεβάλετο τὴν πρᾶξιν ἐκείνων,
ὅτι καὶ πρῴην συνεχῶς ἐπῄνουν τὰς κόρας, μακαρί-
ζοντες τοὺς γαμήσοντας.

Ἀπῄει εἰς Λακεδαίμονα, τοῖς ἐφόροις ἐντευξό-
μενος· γενόμενος δ' ἐν τῇ Ἀργολικῇ, νυκτὸς κατα-
λαμβανούσης, εἰς πανδοκεῖόν τι κατήχθη· κατὰ[1]
τὸ αὐτὸ δὲ καὶ πρεσβύτης τις ἕτερος τὸ γένος ἐξ
F Ὠρεοῦ πόλεως τῆς Ἑστιαιάτιδος· οὗ στενάξαντος
καὶ κατὰ Λακεδαιμονίων ἀρὰς ποιουμένου ἀκούσας
ὁ Σκέδασος ἐπυνθάνετο τί κακὸν ὑπὸ Λακεδαιμονίων πεπονθὼς εἴη. ὁ δὲ διηγεῖτο, ὡς ὑπήκοος

---

[1] κατὰ added by Hirschig.

the worthy character of Scedasus, and the next day went away to Delphi, for that was the place for which they were bound. And when they had consulted the god about the matters which concerned them, they went back again towards home, and passing through Boeotia they stopped again at the house of Scedasus. Now he, as it happened, was not at Leuctra ; but his daughters, in accordance with their usual custom, received the strangers, who, finding the maidens unprotected, ravished them ; and then, seeing that they were exceedingly distressed by the violent wrong they had suffered, they killed them, threw their bodies into a well, and went away. When Scedasus came home, he missed the girls, but found everything that he had left in the house undisturbed, and so he did not know what to make of it all until, because his dog kept whimpering and often running up to him and from him to the well, he guessed the truth, and so drew up the bodies of his daughters. And finding out from his neighbours that on the previous day they had seen going into his house the Lacedaemonians who had been entertained there shortly before, he guessed that they had done the deed, because during their previous visit they had constantly been praising the girls and talking of the happiness of their future husbands.

Scedasus set out for Lacedaemon to see the ephors, and when he was in the territory of Argos night came upon him, so he put up at an inn, and at the same inn was another elderly man, a native of the city of Oreus in the territory of Hestiaea. Scedasus heard him groaning and uttering curses against the Lacedaemonians, so he asked him what harm the Lacedaemonians had done him. Then he proceeded to

13

μέν ἐστι τῆς Σπάρτης, πεμφθεὶς δ' εἰς Ὠρεὸν
Ἀριστόδημος ἁρμοστὴς παρὰ Λακεδαιμονίων ὠμό-
τητα καὶ παρανομίαν ἐπιδείξαιτο πολλήν. '' ἐρα-
σθεὶς γάρ,'' ἔφη, '' τοῦ ἐμοῦ παιδός, ἐπειδὴ πείθειν
ἀδύνατος ἦν, ἐπεχείρει βιάσασθαι καὶ ἀπάγειν
αὐτὸν τῆς παλαίστρας· κωλύοντος δὲ τοῦ παι-
δοτρίβου καὶ νεανίσκων πολλῶν ἐκβοηθούντων,
παραχρῆμα ὁ Ἀριστόδημος ἀπεχώρησε· τῇ δ'
ὑστεραίᾳ πληρώσας τριήρη συνήρπασε τὸ μειράκιον,
καὶ ἐξ Ὠρεοῦ διαπλεύσας εἰς τὴν περαίαν ἐπεχείρει
ὑβρίσαι, οὐ συγχωροῦντα δ' αὐτὸν ἀπέσφαξεν.
774 ἐπανελθὼν δ' εἰς τὴν Ὠρεὸν εὐωχεῖτο. ἐγὼ δ',''
ἔφη,[1] '' τὸ πραχθὲν πυθόμενος καὶ τὸ σῶμα
κηδεύσας παρεγενόμην εἰς τὴν Σπάρτην καὶ τοῖς
ἐφόροις ἐνετύγχανον· οἱ δὲ λόγον οὐκ ἐποιοῦντο.''
Σκέδασος δὲ ταῦτα ἀκούων ἀθύμως διέκειτο,
ὑπολαμβάνων ὅτι οὐδ' αὐτοῦ λόγον τινὰ ποιήσονται
οἱ Σπαρτιᾶται· ἐν μέρει τε τὴν οἰκείαν διηγήσατο
συμφορὰν τῷ ξένῳ· ὁ δὲ παρεκάλει αὐτὸν μηδ'
ἐντυχεῖν τοῖς ἐφόροις, ἀλλ' ὑποστρέψαντα εἰς τὴν
Βοιωτίαν κτίσαι τῶν θυγατέρων τὸν τάφον. οὐκ
ἐπείθετο δ' ὅμως ὁ Σκέδασος, ἀλλ' εἰς τὴν Σπάρτην
Β ἀφικόμενος τοῖς ἐφόροις ἐντυγχάνει· ὧν μηδὲν
προσεχόντων, ἐπὶ τοὺς βασιλέας ἵεται καὶ ἀπὸ
τούτων ἑκάστῳ τῶν δημοτῶν προσιὼν ὠδύρετο.
μηδὲν δὲ πλέον ἀνύων ἔθει διὰ μέσης τῆς πόλεως,
ἀνατείνων πρὸς ἥλιον τὼ χεῖρε, αὖθις δὲ τὴν γῆν
τύπτων ἀνεκαλεῖτο τὰς Ἐρινύας καὶ τέλος αὑτὸν
τοῦ ζῆν μετέστησεν.

Ὑστέρῳ γε μὴν χρόνῳ δίκας ἔδοσαν οἱ Λακε-

---

[1] ἔφη Bernardakis: ἔφθην (ἔφην Urb.)

tell that he was a subject of Sparta and that Aristodemus, who had been sent by the Lacedaemonians to Oreus as governor, had shown himself very lawless and cruel. " For," said he, " he fell in love with my young son and, when he could not gain him by persuasion, he tried to take him from the palaestra by force. But the teacher of gymnastics interfered, and many young fellows came out to help, so for the time being Aristodemus went away ; but the next day he manned a ship of war, seized the boy, sailed from Oreus to the opposite shore, and tried to rape him ; then when the boy would not submit, he cut his throat and killed him, after which he went back to Oreus and gave a dinner-party. But as for me," he said, " I learned of the deed, performed the funeral rites over the body, then went to Sparta and had an audience with the ephors ; but they paid no attention to me." When Scedasus heard this he was disheartened, for he suspected that the Spartans would pay no attention to him either ; and he in turn told the stranger of his own misfortune. Then the stranger advised him not even to go to see the ephors, but to turn back to Boeotia and build his daughters' tomb. Scedasus, however, did not take this advice, but went to Sparta and spoke with the ephors. They paid no attention to him, so he hurried to the kings, and from them he went up to every one of the citizens and told his tale of woe. And when nothing did any good, he ran through the midst of the city stretching up his hands towards the sun, and again he beat upon the ground and summoned up the Erinyes, and finally he put an end to his life.

Later, however, the Lacedaemonians certainly paid

(774) δαιμόνιοι· ἐπειδὴ γὰρ τῶν Ἑλλήνων ἁπάντων
ἦρχον καὶ τὰς πόλεις φρουραῖς κατειλήφεσαν,
Ἐπαμεινώνδας ὁ Θηβαῖος πρῶτον μὲν τὴν παρ'
αὐτῷ[1] φρουρὰν ἀπέσφαξε Λακεδαιμονίων· τῶν δ'
C ἐπὶ τούτῳ πόλεμον ἐξενεγκάντων, ἀπήντων οἱ
Θηβαῖοι ἐπὶ τὰ Λεῦκτρα, αἰσιούμενοι τὸ χωρίον,
ὅτι καὶ πρότερον ἐνταῦθα ἠλευθερώθησαν, ὅτε
Ἀμφικτύων[2] ὑπὸ Σθενέλου φυγὰς ἐλαθεὶς εἰς τὴν
Θηβαίων ἀφίκετο πόλιν καὶ Χαλκιδεῦσιν ὑπο-
φόρους λαβὼν ἔπαυσε τὸν δασμόν, Χαλκώδοντα
τὸν βασιλέα τῶν Εὐβοέων ἀποκτείνας. συνέβη δὲ
Λακεδαιμονίων ἧτταν παντελῆ γενέσθαι περὶ αὐτὸ
τὸ μνῆμα τῶν Σκεδάσου θυγατέρων. φασὶ δὲ πρὸ
τῆς μάχης Πελοπίδᾳ,[3] ἑνὶ τῶν στρατηγῶν τοῦ
D Θηβαϊκοῦ στρατεύματος, ἐπὶ σημείοις τισὶν οὐ
καλοῖς[4] κρινομένοις θορυβουμένῳ Σκέδασον ἐπι-
στῆναι κατὰ τοὺς ὕπνους, θαρρεῖν κελεύοντα· παραγίνεσθαι γὰρ εἰς Λεῦκτρα Λακεδαιμονίους, αὐτῷ
τε καὶ ταῖς θυγατράσι δώσοντας δίκας· πρὸ μιᾶς
δ' ἡμέρας ἢ συμβαλεῖν τοῖς Λακεδαιμονίοις, πῶλον
ἐκέλευεν ἵππου λευκὸν ἔτοιμον παρὰ τῷ τάφῳ τῶν
παρθένων σφαγιάσασθαι. τὸν δὲ Πελοπίδαν, ἔτι
τῶν Λακεδαιμονίων στρατευομένων ἐν Τεγέᾳ, εἰς
Λεῦκτρα πέμψαι τοὺς ἐξετάσοντας περὶ τοῦ τάφου
τούτου, καὶ πυθόμενον παρὰ τῶν ἐγχωρίων θαρ-
ροῦντα τὴν στρατιὰν ἐξαγαγεῖν καὶ νικῆσαι.

---

[1] αὐτῷ Bernardakis : αὐτῶ.
[2] Ἀμφικτύων] Ἀμφιτρύων Ricardus, cf. Paus. ix. 19. 3.
[3] Πελοπίδᾳ Bernardakis : Πελοπίδη.
[4] καλοῖς Bryan : καλῶς.

16

the penalty. For when they were rulers of all the Greeks and had placed their garrisons in the cities, Epaminondas the Theban first slaughtered the garrison of the Lacedaemonians in his own city, and when thereupon the Lacedaemonians made war upon the Thebans, the latter met them at Leuctra,[a] thinking it a place of good omen, because at an earlier time they had gained their freedom there, when Amphictyon, having been driven into exile by Sthenelus, came to the city of the Thebans and, finding them tributaries of the Chalcidians, freed them from the tribute by killing Chalcodon, king of the Euboeans. Now it happened that the utter defeat of the Lacedaemonians took place precisely in the vicinity of the tombstone of the daughters of Scedasus. And the story goes that before the battle Pelopidas, one of the generals of the Theban army, was disturbed by some omens which were considered unfavourable and that in his sleep Scedasus came and stood over him and told him to be of good courage, for the Lacedaemonians were coming to Leuctra to pay the penalty to him and his daughters ; and he enjoined upon him one day before fighting the Lacedaemonians to make ready a white colt and sacrifice it at the tomb of the maidens. So Pelopidas, while the Lacedaemonians were still in camp at Tegea, sent some men to Leuctra to find out about this tomb, and when he learned about it from the inhabitants of the place, he led out his army with confidence and was victorious.

[a] A village in Boeotia. The battle, which ended the Spartan hegemony, took place in 371 B.C.

Δ

E Φῶκος Βοιώτιος μὲν ἦν τῷ γένει, ἦν γὰρ
ἐκ Γλίσαντος,¹ πατὴρ δὲ Καλλιρρόης κάλλει τε
καὶ σωφροσύνῃ διαφερούσης. ταύτην ἐμνηστεύοντο
νεανίαι τριάκοντα εὐδοκιμώτατοι ἐν Βοιωτίᾳ· ὁ δὲ
Φῶκος ἄλλας ἐξ ἄλλων ἀναβολὰς τῶν γάμων
ἐποιεῖτο, φοβούμενος μὴ βιασθείη, τέλος δὲ
λιπαρούντων ἐκείνων, ἠξίου ἐπὶ τῷ Πυθίῳ ποιήσασθαι τὴν αἵρεσιν. οἱ δὲ πρὸς τὸν λόγον ἐχα-
λέπηναν καὶ ὁρμήσαντες ἀπέκτειναν τὸν Φῶκον·
ἐν δὲ τῷ θορύβῳ ἡ κόρη φυγοῦσα ἵετο διὰ τῆς
F χώρας· ἐδίωκον δ' αὐτὴν οἱ νεανίαι. ἡ δ' ἐν-
τυχοῦσα γεωργοῖς ἅλω συντιθεῖσι σωτηρίας ἔτυχε
παρ' αὐτῶν· ἀπέκρυψαν γὰρ αὐτὴν οἱ γεωργοὶ ἐν
τῷ σίτῳ. καὶ οὕτω παρῆξαν μὲν οἱ διώκοντες·
ἡ δὲ διασωθεῖσα ἐφύλαξε τὴν τῶν Παμβοιωτίων
ἑορτήν, καὶ τότε εἰς Κορώνειαν ἐλθοῦσα ἱκέτις
καθέζεται ἐπὶ τῷ βωμῷ τῆς Ἰτωνίας Ἀθηνᾶς
καὶ τῶν μνηστήρων τὴν παρανομίαν διηγεῖτο, τό
τε ἑκάστου ὄνομα καὶ τὴν πατρίδα σημαίνουσα.
ἠλέουν οὖν οἱ Βοιωτοὶ τὴν παῖδα καὶ τοῖς νεανίαις
ἠγανάκτουν· οἱ δὲ ταῦτα πυθόμενοι εἰς Ὀρχομενὸν
καταφεύγουσιν. οὐ δεξαμένων δ' αὐτοὺς τῶν
775 Ὀρχομενίων πρὸς Ἱππότας εἰσώρμησαν· κώμη
δ' ἦν παρὰ τῷ Ἑλικῶνι κειμένη μεταξὺ Θίσβης
καὶ Κορωνείας· οἱ δ' ὑποδέχονται αὐτούς. εἶτα
πέμπουσι Θηβαῖοι ἐξαιτοῦντες τοὺς Φώκου φονεῖς·
τῶν δ' οὐ διδόντων, ἐστράτευσαν μὲν μετὰ τῶν

¹ Γλίσαντος Xylander: κλείσαντος.

ᵃ i.e. by the disappointed suitors.
ᵇ The cult of Athena Itonia was brought to Boeotia by

IV

Phocus was by birth a Boeotian, for he was from the town of Glisas, and he was the father of Callirrhoë, who excelled in beauty and modesty. She was wooed by thirty young men, the most highly esteemed in Boeotia ; but Phocus found one reason after another for putting off her marriage, for he was afraid that violence would be done to him [a] ; at last, however, he yielded to their demands, but asked to leave the choice to the Pythian oracle. The suitors were incensed by the proposal, rushed upon Phocus, and killed him. In the confusion the maiden got away and fled through the country, but the young men pursued her. She came upon some farmers making a threshing-floor, and found safety with them, for the farmers hid her in the grain, and so her pursuers passed by. But she waited in safety until the festival of the Pamboeotia, when she went to Coroneia, took her seat on the altar of Athena Itonia,[b] and told of the lawless act of the suitors, giving the name and birthplace of each. So the Boeotians pitied the maid and were angry with the young men. When they learned of this, they fled for refuge to Orchomenus, and when the Orchomenians refused to receive them, they forced their way into Hippotae, a village lying on the slope of Mount Helicon between Thisbê and Coroneia. There they were received. Then the Thebans sent and demanded the slayers of Phocus, and when the people of Hippotae refused to deliver them, the Thebans, along with the rest of the

the Ionians when they were driven out by the Thessalians. Her sanctuary near Coroneia was the place of the Pamboeotia, the festival of the united Boeotians.

(775) ἄλλων Βοιωτῶν, στρατηγοῦντος Φοίδου, ὃς τότε
τὴν ἀρχὴν τῶν Θηβαίων διεῖπε· πολιορκήσαντες δὲ
τὴν κώμην ὀχυρὰν οὖσαν, δίψει δὲ τῶν ἔνδον κρατη-
θέντων, τοὺς μὲν φονεῖς ληφθέντας κατέλευσαν,
τοὺς δ' ἐν τῇ κώμῃ ἐξηνδραποδίσαντο· κατα-
B σκάψαντες δὲ τὰ τείχη καὶ τὰς οἰκίας διένειμαν
τὴν χώραν Θισβεῦσι[1] τε καὶ Κορωνεῦσι. φασὶ δὲ
νυκτός, πρὸ τῆς ἁλώσεως τῶν Ἱπποτῶν, φωνὴν ἐκ
τοῦ Ἑλικῶνος πολλάκις ἀκουσθῆναι λέγοντός τινος
" πάρειμι "· τοὺς δὲ μνηστῆρας τοὺς τριάκοντα
τόδε τὸ φώνημα γνωρίζειν, ὅτι Φώκου εἴη. ᾗ
δ' ἡμέρᾳ κατελεύσθησαν, τὸ ἐν Γλίσαντι[2] μνῆμα
τοῦ γέροντος κρόκῳ φασὶ ῥεῦσαι· Φοίδῳ δέ, τῷ
Θηβαίων ἄρχοντι καὶ στρατηγῷ, ἐκ τῆς μάχης
ἐπανιόντι ἀγγελθῆναι θυγατέρα γεγενημένην, ἣν[3]
αἰσιούμενον προσαγορεῦσαι Νικοστράτην.

E

C Ἄλκιππος τὸ μὲν γένος Λακεδαιμόνιος ἦν·
γήμας δὲ Δαμοκρίταν πατὴρ θυγατέρων γίνεται
δύο· συμβουλεύων τε τῇ πόλει κράτιστά τε καὶ
πράττων ὅτου δέοιντο Λακεδαιμόνιοι, ἐφθονήθη
ὑπὸ τῶν ἀντιπολιτευομένων, οἳ τοὺς ἐφόρους
ψευδέσι λόγοις παραγαγόντες, ὡς τοῦ Ἀλκίππου
βουλομένου τοὺς νόμους καταλῦσαι, φυγῇ περι-
έβαλον τὸν ἄνδρα. καὶ ὁ μὲν ὑπεξῆλθε τῆς Σπάρτης,
Δαμοκρίταν δὲ τὴν γυναῖκα μετὰ τῶν θυγατέρων

---

[1] Θισβεῦσι Bernardakis: Θηβεῦσι.
[2] ἐν Γλίσαντι Bernardakis: ἐγγίσαντι.
[3] ἣν added by Wyttenbach.

20

Boeotians, took the field under the command of
Phoedus, who at that time administered the government of Thebes. They besieged the village, which
was well fortified, and when they had overcome the
inhabitants by thirst, they took the murderers and
stoned them to death and made slaves of the
villagers; then they pulled down the walls and the
houses and divided the land between the people of
Thisbê and of Coroneia. It is said that in the night,
before the capture of Hippotae, there was heard
many times from Helicon a voice of someone saying
" I am here," and that the thirty suitors recognized
the voice as that of Phocus. It is said also that on
the day when they were stoned to death the old
man's monument at Glisas ran with saffron; and
that as Phoedus, the ruler and general of the
Thebans, was returning from the battle, he received
the news of the birth of a daughter and, thinking
it of good omen, he named her Nicostrata.[a]

V

Alcippus was a Lacedaemonian by birth; he
married Damocrita and became the father of two
daughters. Now since he was a most excellent
counsellor to the state and conducted affairs to the
satisfaction of the Lacedaemonians, he was envied
by his political opponents, who misled the ephors by
false statements to the effect that Alcippus wished
to destroy the constitution, and they thereby brought
about his exile. So he departed from Sparta, but
when his wife Damocrita, with their daughters,

[a] *i.e.* " She of the conquering host."

21

(775) βουλομένην ἕπεσθαι τἀνδρὶ ἐκώλυον, ἀλλὰ καὶ τὴν
οὐσίαν αὐτοῦ ἐδήμευσαν, ἵνα μὴ εὐπορῶσι προικὸς
D αἱ παρθένοι. ἐπεὶ δὲ καὶ ὡς ἐμνηστεύοντό τινες
τὰς παῖδας διὰ τὴν τοῦ πατρὸς ἀρετήν, ἐκώλυσαν
οἱ ἐχθροὶ διὰ ψηφίσματος μνηστεύεσθαί τινας τὰς
κόρας, λέγοντες ὡς ἡ μήτηρ αὐτῶν Δαμοκρίτα
πολλάκις εὔξατο τὰς θυγατέρας ταχέως γεννῆσαι
παῖδας τιμωροὺς τῷ πατρὶ γενησομένους. παν-
ταχόθεν δ' ἡ Δαμοκρίτα περιελαυνομένη ἐτήρησέ
τινα πάνδημον ἑορτήν, ἐν ᾗ γυναῖκες ἅμα παρθένοις καὶ οἰκείοις καὶ νηπίοις ἑώρταζον, αἱ δὲ
τῶν ἐν τέλει καθ' ἑαυτὰς ἐν ἀνδρῶνι μεγάλῳ δι-
επαννύχιζον· ξίφος τε ὑποζωσαμένη καὶ τὰς κόρας
λαβοῦσα νυκτὸς ἦλθεν εἰς τὸ ἱερὸν καιρὸν παρα-
E φυλάξασα, ἐν ᾧ πᾶσαι τὸ μυστήριον ἐπετέλουν ἐν
τῷ ἀνδρῶνι· καὶ κεκλεισμένων τῶν εἰσόδων, ξύλα
ταῖς θύραις πολλὰ προσνήσασα (ταῦτα δ' ἦν εἰς
τὴν τῆς ἑορτῆς θυσίαν ὑπ' ἐκείνων παρεσκευα-
σμένα), πῦρ ἐνῆκε. συνθεόντων δὲ τῶν ἀνδρῶν ἐπὶ
τὴν βοήθειαν, ἡ Δαμοκρίτα τὰς θυγατέρας ἀπέσφαξε
καὶ ἐπ' ἐκείναις ἑαυτήν. οὐκ ἔχοντες δ' οἱ Λακεδαιμόνιοι, ὅπῃ τὸν θυμὸν ἀπερείσωνται,[1] ἐκτὸς
ὅρων ἔρριψαν τῆς τε Δαμοκρίτας καὶ τῶν θυγατέρων τὰ σώματα. ἐφ' ᾧ μηνίσαντος τοῦ θεοῦ
τὸν μέγαν ἱστοροῦσι Λακεδαιμονίοις σεισμὸν ἐπι-
γενέσθαι.

---

[1] ἀπερείσωνται Bernardakis: ἀπερείσονται.

22

wished to follow her husband, she was prevented from doing so, and moreover his property was confiscated, that the girls might not be provided with dowries. And when even so there were some suitors who wooed the girls on account of their father's high character, his enemies got a bill passed forbidding anyone to woo the girls, saying that their mother Damocrita had often prayed that her daughters might speedily bear sons who should grow up to be their father's avengers. Damocrita, being harassed on all sides, waited for a general festival in which married women along with unmarried girls, slaves, and infant children took part, and the wives of those in authority passed the whole night in a great hall by themselves. Then she buckled a sword about her waist, took the girls, and went by night into the sacred place, waiting for the moment when all the women were performing the mysteries in the hall. Then, after the entrances had all been closed, she heaped a great quantity of wood against the doors (this had been prepared by the others for the sacrifice belonging to the festival) and set it on fire. And when the men came running up to save their wives, Damocrita killed her daughters with the sword and then herself over their dead bodies. But the Lacedaemonians, not knowing how to vent their anger, threw the bodies of Damocrita and her daughters out beyond the boundaries ; and they say that because the god was offended by this the great earthquake [a] came upon the Lacedaemonians.

[a] Probably the earthquake of 464 B.C. is meant.

THAT A PHILOSOPHER OUGHT TO CONVERSE ESPECIALLY WITH MEN IN POWER

(MAXIME CUM PRINCIPIBUS PHILOSOPHO ESSE DISSERENDUM)

INTRODUCTION

THIS brief essay was written in support of the contention that the philosopher should exert himself to influence the thought and conduct of men in power and should not shut himself away from the world. This view is consistent with Plutarch's own life. The essay is less carefully written than some of the others, and the text is somewhat uncertain in a few places, among which may be mentioned the very first sentence. In this the first word, Sorcanus, appears to be a proper name, but the name does not occur elsewhere, and therefore numerous emendations have been proposed. If the reading is correct, Sorcanus was some important personage and must have been well known to the person, whoever he was, to whom the essay is addressed; for although not written exactly in the form of a letter, the essay seems to be intended primarily for some one person's edification or entertainment.

ΠΕΡΙ ΤΟΥ ΟΤΙ ΜΑΛΙΣΤΑ ΤΟΙΣ ΗΓΕΜΟΣΙ ΔΕΙ ΤΟΝ ΦΙΛΟΣΟΦΟΝ ΔΙΑΛΕΓΕΣΘΑΙ

776   1. Σωρκανὸν[1] ἐγκολπίσασθαι καὶ φιλίαν τιμᾶν
B καὶ μετιέναι καὶ προσδέχεσθαι καὶ γεωργεῖν, πολλοῖς μὲν ἰδίᾳ πολλοῖς δὲ καὶ δημοσίᾳ χρήσιμον καὶ
ἔγκαρπον γενησομένην, φιλοκάλων ἐστὶ καὶ πολιτικῶν καὶ φιλανθρώπων οὐχ ὡς ἔνιοι νομίζουσι
φιλοδόξων· ἀλλὰ καὶ τοὐναντίον, φιλόδοξός ἐστι
καὶ ψοφοδεὴς ὁ φεύγων καὶ φοβούμενος ἀκοῦσαι
λιπαρὴς τῶν ἐν ἐξουσίᾳ καὶ θεραπευτικός. ἐπεὶ
τί φησιν ἀνὴρ θεραπευτικὸς[2] καὶ φιλοσοφίας δεόμενος; Σίμων οὖν[3] γένωμαι ὁ σκυτοτόμος ἢ
Διονύσιος ὁ γραμματιστὴς ἐκ Περικλέους ἢ
Κάτωνος, ἵνα μοι προσδιαλέγηται καὶ προσκαθίζῃ
C ὡς Σωκράτης ἐκείνῳ[4]; καὶ Ἀρίστων μὲν ὁ
Χῖος ἐπὶ τῷ πᾶσι διαλέγεσθαι τοῖς βουλομένοις
ὑπὸ τῶν σοφιστῶν κακῶς ἀκούων '' ὤφελεν,'' εἶπε[5],
'' καὶ τὰ θηρία λόγων συνιέναι κινητικῶν πρὸς
ἀρετήν''· ἡμεῖς δὲ φευξούμεθα τοῖς δυνατοῖς καὶ

---

[1] Bernadakis, following Pape, would prefer Σωρανόν.
[2] θεραπευτικὸς] θεραπεύσεως Duebner; πολιτικὸς Reiske; πρακτικὸς Bernardakis; cf. 777 A.
[3] οὖν Bernadakis: εἰ.
[4] ὡς Σωκράτης ἐκείνῳ Capps; ὁ Σωκράτης ὡς ἐκείνοις

28

PLUTARCH'S MORALIA

[776]   ...
...
...
...
...

THAT A PHILOSOPHER OUGHT TO CONVERSE ESPECIALLY WITH MEN IN POWER

1. In clasping Sorcanus to your bosom, in prizing, pursuing, welcoming, and cultivating his friendship —a friendship which will prove useful and fruitful to many in private and to many in public life—you are acting like a man who loves what is noble, who is public-spirited and is a friend of mankind, not, as some people say, like one who is merely ambitious for himself. No, on the contrary, the man who is ambitious for himself and afraid of every whisper is just the one who avoids and fears being called a persistent and servile attendant on those in power. For what does a man say who is an attendant upon philosophy and stands in need of it? " Let me change from Pericles or Cato and become Simo the cobbler or Dionysius the schoolmaster, in order that the philosopher may converse with me and sit beside me as Socrates did with Pericles." And while it is true that Ariston of Chios, when the sophists spoke ill of him for talking with all who wished it, said, " I wish even the beasts could understand words which incite to virtue," yet as for us, shall we avoid becoming intimate with

Wyttenbach : ὡς Σωκράτης, ἐκεῖνος Bernardakis : ὡς Σωκράτης ἐκείνοις.   [5] εἶπε Meziriacus : εἰπεῖν.

(776) ἡγεμονικοῖς ὥσπερ ἀγρίοις καὶ ἀνημέροις γίγνεσθαι
συνήθεις·

Οὐκ "ἀνδριαντοποιός" ἐστιν ὁ τῆς φιλοσοφίας
λόγος, "ὥστ᾽ ἐλινύοντα ποιεῖν ἀγάλματ᾽ ἐπ᾽
αὐτᾶς βαθμίδος ἑσταότα" κατὰ Πίνδαρον· ἀλλ᾽ ἐν-
εργὰ βούλεται ποιεῖν ὧν ἂν ἅψηται καὶ πρακτικὰ
καὶ ἔμψυχα καὶ κινητικὰς ὁρμὰς ἐντίθησι[1] καὶ
κρίσεις ἀγωγοὺς ἐπὶ τὰ ὠφέλιμα καὶ προαιρέσεις
D φιλοκάλους καὶ φρόνημα καὶ μέγεθος μετὰ πραό-
τητος καὶ ἀσφαλείας,[2] δι᾽ ὧν τοῖς ὑπερέχουσι καὶ
δυνατοῖς ὁμιλοῦσιν οἱ πολιτικοὶ[3] προθυμότερον.
καὶ γάρ, ἂν ἰατρὸς ᾖ φιλόκαλος, ἥδιον ὀφθαλμὸν
ἰάσεται τὸν ὑπὲρ πολλῶν βλέποντα καὶ πολλοὺς
φυλάσσοντα· καὶ φιλόσοφος ψυχῆς ἐπιμελήσεται
προθυμότερον, ἣν ὑπὲρ πολλῶν φροντίζουσαν ὁρᾷ
καὶ πολλοῖς φρονεῖν καὶ σωφρονεῖν καὶ δικαιοπραγεῖν ὀφείλουσαν. καὶ γὰρ εἰ δεινὸς ἦν περὶ
E ζήτησιν ὑδάτων καὶ συναγωγήν, ὥσπερ ἱστοροῦσι
τὸν Ἡρακλέα καὶ πολλοὺς τῶν πάλαι, οὐκ ἂν
ἔχαιρε φρεωρύχων ἐν ἐσχατιᾷ "παρὰ Κόρακος
πέτρῃ" τὴν συβωτικὴν ἐκείνην Ἀρέθουσαν, ἀλλὰ
ποταμοῦ τινος ἀενάους πηγὰς ἀνακαλύπτων πόλεσι[4]
καὶ στρατοπέδοις καὶ φυτείαις βασιλέων καὶ
ἄλσεσιν. ἀκούομεν δὴ Ὁμήρου τὸν Μίνω "θεοῦ
μεγάλου ὀαριστὴν" ἀποκαλοῦντος· τοῦτο δ᾽ ἐστίν,

---

[1] ἐντίθησι Reiske : ἐπιτίθησι.
[2] ἀσφαλείας] ἀφελείας Wyttenbach, Frerichs.
[3] πολιτικοὶ] πολῖται Hartman.   Perhaps φιλόσοφοι?
[4] πόλεσι Pohlenz : πόλει τε.

30

powerful men and rulers, as if they were wild and savage ?

The teaching of philosophy is not, if I may use the words of Pindar,[a] "a sculptor to carve statues doomed to stand idly on their pedestals and no more"; no, it strives to make everything that it touches active and efficient and alive, it inspires men with impulses which urge to action, with judgements that lead them towards what is useful, with preferences for things that are honourable, with wisdom and greatness of mind joined to gentleness and conservatism, and because they possess these qualities, men of public spirit are more eager to converse with the prominent and powerful. Certainly if a physician is a man of high ideals, he will be better pleased to cure the eye which sees for many and watches over many, and a philosopher will be more eager to attend upon a soul which he sees is solicitous for many and is under obligation to be wise and self-restrained and just in behalf of many. For surely, if he were skilled in discovering and collecting water, as they say Heracles and many of the ancients were, he would not delight in digging the swineherd's fount of Arethusa [b] in a most distant spot "by the Crow's Rock," but in uncovering the unfailing sources of some river for cities and camps and the plantations of kings and sacred groves. So we hear Homer [c] calling Minos "the great god's *oaristes*," which

---

[a] Pindar, *Nem.* v. 1 οὐκ ἀνδριαντοποιός εἰμ', ὥστ' ἐλινύσοντα ἐργάζεσθαι ἀγάλματ' ἐπ' αὐτᾶς βαθμίδος, loosely quoted. The translation is adapted from that of Sir John Sandys (in L.C.L.).

[b] Homer, *Od.* xiii. 404-410. The allusion is to the feeding-place of the swine tended by Eumaeus.

[c] *Od.* xix. 179.

ὥς φησιν ὁ Πλάτων, ὁμιλητὴν καὶ μαθητήν· οὐδὲ
γὰρ ἰδιώτας οὐδ' οἰκουροὺς οὐδ' ἀπράκτους
ἠξίουν εἶναι θεῶν μαθητάς, ἀλλὰ βασιλεῖς, οἷς
F εὐβουλίας ἐγγενομένης[1] καὶ δικαιοσύνης καὶ χρηστότητος καὶ μεγαλοφροσύνης, πάντες ἔμελλον
ὠφεληθήσεσθαι καὶ ἀπολαύσειν[2] οἱ χρώμενοι.
τὸ ἠρύγγιον[3] τὸ βοτάνιον λέγουσι μιᾶς αἰγὸς εἰς
τὸ στόμα λαβούσης, αὐτήν τε πρώτην ἐκείνην
καὶ τὸ λοιπὸν αἰπόλιον ἵστασθαι, μέχρι ἂν ὁ
αἰπόλος ἐξέλῃ προσελθών· τοιαύτην ἔχουσιν αἱ
ἀπόρροιαὶ τῆς δυνάμεως ὀξύτητα, πυρὸς δίκην
ἐπινεμομένην τὰ γειτνιῶντα καὶ κατασκιδναμένην.
καὶ μὴν ὁ τοῦ φιλοσόφου λόγος, ἐὰν μὲν ἰδιώτην
ἕνα λάβῃ, χαίροντα ἀπραγμοσύνῃ καὶ περιγράφοντα
ἑαυτὸν ὡς κέντρῳ καὶ διαστήματι γεωμετρικῷ
777 ταῖς περὶ τὸ σῶμα χρείαις, οὐ διαδίδωσιν εἰς
ἑτέρους, ἀλλ' ἐν ἑνὶ ποιήσας ἐκείνῳ γαλήνην καὶ
ἡσυχίαν ἀπεμαράνθη καὶ συνεξέλιπεν. ἂν δ' ἄρχοντος ἀνδρὸς καὶ πολιτικοῦ καὶ πρακτικοῦ
καθάψηται καὶ τοῦτον ἀναπλήσῃ καλοκαγαθίας,
πολλοὺς δι' ἑνὸς ὠφέλησεν, ὡς Ἀναξαγόρας
Περικλεῖ συγγενόμενος καὶ Πλάτων Δίωνι καὶ
Πυθαγόρας τοῖς πρωτεύουσιν Ἰταλιωτῶν. Κάτων
δ' αὐτὸς ἔπλευσεν ἀπὸ στρατιᾶς[4] ἐπ' Ἀθηνόδωρον·
καὶ Σκιπίων μετεπέμψατο Παναίτιον, ὅτ' αὐτὸν
ἡ σύγκλητος ἐξέπεμψεν

ἀνθρώπων ὕβριν τε καὶ εὐνομίην ἐφορώμενον[5]

---

[1] ἐγγενομένης Duebner: γενομένης.
[2] ἀπολαύσειν Coraes: ἀπολαύειν.
[3] ἠρύγγιον Herwerden: ἐρύγγιον.
[4] στρατιᾶς Coraes: στρατείας.

means, according to Plato,[a] "familiar friend and pupil." For they did not think that pupils of the gods should be plain citizens or stay-at-homes or idlers, but kings, from whose good counsel, justice, goodness, and high-mindedness, if those qualities were implanted in them, all who had to do with them would receive benefit and profit. Of the plant *eryngium* they say that if one goat take it in its mouth, first that goat itself and then the entire herd stands still until the herdsman comes and takes the plant out, such pungency, like a fire which spreads over everything near it and scatters itself abroad, is possessed by the emanations of its potency. Certainly the teachings of the philosopher, if they take hold of one person in private station who enjoys abstention from affairs and circumscribes himself by his bodily comforts, as by a circle drawn with geometrical compasses, do not spread out to others, but merely create calmness and quiet in that one man, then dry up and disappear. But if these teachings take possession of a ruler, a statesman, and a man of action and fill him with love of honour, through one he benefits many, as Anaxagoras did by associating with Pericles, Plato with Dion, and Pythagoras with the chief men of the Italiote Greeks. Cato himself sailed from his army to visit Athenodorus; and Scipio sent for Panaetius when he himself was sent out by the senate

to view the violence and lawfulness of men,

[a] *Minos*, 319 d. Generally regarded as spurious.

---

[5] ἐφορώμενον Xylander; ἐφορῶντες, Homer, *Od.* xvii. 487: ὑφορώμενον.

(777)
B   ὡς φησι Ποσειδώνιος.   τί οὖν ἔδει λέγειν τὸν
Παναίτιον; εἰ μὲν ἦς ἢ Βάτων[1] ἢ Πολυδεύκης ἤ
τις ἄλλος ἰδιώτης, τὰ μέσα τῶν πόλεων ἀποδιδρά-
σκειν βουλόμενος, ἐν γωνίᾳ τινὶ καθ' ἡσυχίαν
ἀναλύων συλλογισμοὺς καὶ περιέλκων[2] φιλοσόφων,
ἄσμενος ἄν σε προσεδεξάμην καὶ συνῆν· ἐπεὶ δ'
υἱὸς μὲν Αἰμιλίου Παύλου τοῦ δισυπάτου γέγονας,
υἱωνὸς δὲ Σκιπίωνος τοῦ Ἀφρικανοῦ τοῦ νικήσαν-
τος τὸν Ἀννίβαν τὸν Καρχηδόνιον, οὐκ οὖν[3] σοι
διαλέξομαι[4];

2. Τὸ δὲ λέγειν ὅτι δύο λόγοι εἰσίν, ὁ μὲν
ἐνδιάθετος ἡγεμόνος Ἑρμοῦ δῶρον, ὁ δ' ἐν προ-
φορᾷ διάκτορος καὶ ὀργανικός, ἔωλόν ἐστι καὶ
ὑποπιπτέτω τῷ

C   τουτὶ μὲν ᾔδειν[5] πρὶν Θέογνιν γεγονέναι.

ἐκεῖνο δ' οὐκ ἄν[6] ἐνοχλήσειεν, ὅτι καὶ τοῦ ἐνδια-
θέτου λόγου καὶ τοῦ προφορικοῦ φιλία τέλος ἐστί,
τοῦ μὲν πρὸς ἑαυτὸν τοῦ δὲ πρὸς ἕτερον. ὁ μὲν
γὰρ εἰς ἀρετὴν διὰ φιλοσοφίας τελευτῶν σύμφωνον
ἑαυτῷ καὶ ἄμεμπτον ὑφ' ἑαυτοῦ καὶ μεστὸν εἰρήνης
καὶ φιλοφροσύνης τῆς πρὸς ἑαυτὸν ἀεὶ παρέχεται
τὸν ἄνθρωπον.

---

[1] Βάτων Wyttenbach: κάτων.
[2] περιέλκων] περιπλέκων Meziriacus; περὶ ἐλέγχων φιλοσοφῶν
Xylander.
[3] οὐκ οὖν H.N.F.; οὔκουν Bernardakis; οὐκ ἀνεκτὸν ἄν
Pohlenz: οὐκ ἄν.
[4] διαλέξομαι] προσδιαλέξομαι Frerichs after some mss.
[5] ᾔδειν] ᾖδον Schadewaldt.
[6] ἄν added by Coraes.

as Poseidonius says.[a] Now what should Panaetius
have said ? " If you were Bato or Polydeuces or
some other person in private station who wished
to run away from the midst of cities and quietly in
some corner solve or quibble [b] over the syllogisms of
philosophers, I would gladly welcome you and consort
with you ; but since you are the son of Aemilius
Paulus, who was twice consul, and the grandson of
Scipio Africanus who overcame Hannibal the Carthaginian, shall I, therefore, not converse with you ? "

2. But the statement that there are two kinds of
speech, one residing in the mind, the gift of Hermes
the Leader, and the other residing in the utterance,
merely an attendant and instrument, is out of date ;
we will let it come under the heading

> Yes, this I knew before Theognis' birth.[c]

But that would not disturb us, because the aim
and end of both the speech in the mind and the
speech in the utterance is friendship, towards oneself
and towards one's neighbour respectively ; for the
former, ending through philosophy in virtue, makes a
man harmonious with himself, free from blame from
himself, and full of peace and friendliness towards
himself.

[a] Homer, *Od.* xvii. 487.
[b] περιέλκειν, literally " pull about." Plato (*Republic*, 539 B)
says that the young, when new to argument, find pleasure
ὥσπερ σκυλάκια τῷ ἕλκειν τε καὶ σπαράττειν τῷ λόγῳ τοὺς πλησίον
ἀεί, " like little dogs, in pulling and tearing apart by argument those who happen to be near them."
[c] By an unknown comic poet ; Kock, *Com. Att. Frag.*
iii. p. 495. *Cf. Moralia*, 395 E, Aulus Gellius, i. 3. 19, Marx
on Lucilius 952.

(777)   οὐ στάσις οὐδέ τε[1] δῆρις ἀναίσιος[2] ἐν μελέεσσιν,

οὐ πάθος λόγῳ δυσπειθές, οὐχ ὁρμῆς μάχη πρὸς
ὁρμήν, οὐ λογισμοῦ πρὸς λογισμὸν ἀντίβασις, οὐχ
ὥσπερ ἐν μεθορίῳ τοῦ ἐπιθυμοῦντος καὶ τοῦ μετα-
νοοῦντος τὸ τραχὺ καὶ ταραχῶδες καὶ τὸ ἡδόμενον,
D   ἀλλ' εὐμενῆ πάντα καὶ φίλα καὶ ποιοῦντα πλείστων
τυγχάνειν ἀγαθῶν καὶ[3] ἑαυτῷ χαίρειν ἕκαστον.
τοῦ δὲ προφορικοῦ τὴν Μοῦσαν ὁ Πίνδαρος "οὐ
φιλοκερδῆ," φησίν, "οὐδ' ἐργάτιν" εἶναι πρότερον,
οἶμαι δὲ μηδὲ νῦν, ἀλλ' ἀμουσίᾳ καὶ ἀπειροκαλίᾳ
τὸν κοινὸν Ἑρμῆν ἐμπολαῖον καὶ ἔμμισθον γενέσθαι.
οὐ γὰρ ἡ μὲν Ἀφροδίτη ταῖς τοῦ Προποίτου[4] θυ-
γατράσιν ἐμήνιεν ὅτι

πρῶται μίσεα μηχανήσαντο[5] καταχέειν νεανίσκων,

ἡ δ' Οὐρανία καὶ Καλλιόπη καὶ ἡ Κλειὼ χαίρουσι
τοῖς ἐπ'[6] ἀργυρίῳ λυμαινομένοις[7] τὸν λόγον. ἀλλ'
ἔμοιγε δοκεῖ τὰ τῶν Μουσῶν ἔργα καὶ δῶρα μᾶλλον
ἢ τὰ τῆς Ἀφροδίτης φιλοτήσια εἶναι. καὶ γὰρ τὸ
E   ἔνδοξον, ὅ τινες τοῦ λόγου ποιοῦνται τέλος, ὡς
ἀρχὴ καὶ σπέρμα φιλίας ἠγαπήθη· μᾶλλον δ' ὅλως
οἵ γε πολλοὶ κατ' εὔνοιαν τὴν δόξαν τίθενται, νομί-

---

[1] οὐδέ τε Xylander; ἦν οὐ Bergk: οὐ.
[2] ἀναίσιος Capps, cf. van Herwerden, Lex. Graec. Suppl.
s.v.; ἀναίσιμος Meziriacus; ἀπαίσιος Bergk: ἐναίσιμος.
[3] καὶ added by Reiske; τῷ added by Frerichs.
[4] Προποίτου Amyot; cf. Ovid, Metam. x. 221: προπόλου
or προσπόλου.
[5] μηχανήσαντο] μαχλήσαντο Bernardakis, Frerichs, and
some mss.   [6] ἐπ' Reiske: ἐν.
[7] λυμαινομένοις Reiske; διαδιδομένοις Frerichs: διαδεχομένοις.

---

[a] A verse of an unknown poet.   Ascribed to Empedocles
by Bergk.   [b] Isthm. ii. 10.

> Faction is not, nor is ill-starred strife, to be found in his members, [a]

there is no passion disobedient to reason, no strife of impulse with impulse, no opposition of argument to argument, there is no rough tumult and pleasure on the border-line, as it were, between desire and repentance, but everything is gentle and friendly and makes each man gain the greatest number of benefits and be pleased with himself. But Pindar says [b] that the Muse of oral utterance was " not greedy of gain, nor toilsome " formerly, and I believe she is not so now either, but because of lack of education and of good taste the " common Hermes " [c] has become venal and ready for hire. For it cannot be that, whereas Aphroditê was angry with the daughters of Propoetus [d] because

> First they were to devise for young men a shower of abominations, [e]

yet Urania, Calliopê, and Clio are pleased with those who pollute speech for money. No, I think the works and gifts of the Muses are more conducive to friendship than are those of Aphroditê. For approbation, which some consider the end and purpose of speech, is admired as the beginning and seed of friendship ; but most people rather bestow reputation altogether by goodwill, believing that we praise

[c] Κοινὸς Ἑρμῆς is a proverbial expression meaning " good luck should be shared " (cf. Menander, Arbitrants, 67 ; Lucian, Navigium, 12, p. 256 ; Theophrastus, Characters, 30. 7 ; Aristotle, 1201 a 20). But Hermes was god, not only of gain and luck, but also of eloquence, and here the meaning is that eloquence, which should be for the common good of all, has to be bought.

[d] See Ovid, Metam. x. 221 ff., especially 238 ff.

[e] From an unknown poet.

ζοντες ἡμᾶς μόνον[1] ἐπαινεῖν οὓς φιλοῦμεν. ἀλλ'
οὗτοι μέν, ὡς ὁ Ἰξίων διώκων τὴν Ἥραν ὤλισθεν
εἰς τὴν νεφέλην, οὕτως ἀντὶ τῆς φιλίας εἴδωλον
ἀπατηλὸν καὶ πανηγυρικὸν καὶ περιφερόμενον
ὑπολαμβάνουσιν.[2] ὁ δὲ νοῦν ἔχων, ἂν ἐν[3] πολιτείαις καὶ πράξεσιν ἀναστρέφηται, δεήσεται δόξης
τοσαύτης, ὅση δύναμιν περὶ τὰς πράξεις ἐκ τοῦ
F πιστεύεσθαι δίδωσιν· οὔτε γὰρ ἡδὺ μὴ βουλομένους οὔτε ῥάδιον ὠφελεῖν, βούλεσθαι δὲ ποιεῖ τὸ
πιστεύειν· ὥσπερ γὰρ[4] τὸ φῶς μᾶλλόν ἐστιν ἀγαθὸν
τοῖς βλέπουσιν ἢ τοῖς βλεπομένοις,[5] οὕτως ἡ δόξα
τοῖς αἰσθανομένοις ἢ[5] τοῖς μὴ παρορωμένοις. ὁ δ'
ἀπηλλαγμένος τοῦ τὰ κοινὰ πράττειν καὶ συνὼν
ἑαυτῷ καὶ τἀγαθὸν ἐν ἡσυχίᾳ καὶ ἀπραγμοσύνῃ
τιθέμενος τὴν μὲν ἐν ὄχλοις καὶ θεάτροις πάνδημον
778 καὶ ἀναπεπταμένην δόξαν οὕτως ὡς τὴν Ἀφροδίτην
ὁ Ἱππόλυτος " ἄπωθεν ἁγνὸς ὢν ἀσπάζεται," τῆς
δέ γε τῶν ἐπιεικῶν καὶ ἐλλογίμων οὐδ' αὐτὸς
καταφρονεῖ· πλοῦτον δὲ καὶ δόξαν ἡγεμονικὴν καὶ
δύναμιν ἐν φιλίαις οὐ διώκει, οὐ μὴν οὐδὲ φεύγει
ταῦτα μετρίῳ προσόντ' ἤθει· οὐδὲ γὰρ τοὺς καλοὺς
τῶν νέων διώκει καὶ ὡραίους, ἀλλὰ τοὺς εὐαγώγους
καὶ κοσμίους καὶ φιλομαθεῖς· οὐδ' οἷς ὥρα καὶ
χάρις συνέπεται καὶ ἄνθος δεδίττεται τὸν φιλόσοφον οὐδ' ἀποσοβεῖ καὶ ἀπελαύνει τῶν ἀξίων
ἐπιμελείας τὸ κάλλος. οὕτως οὖν ἀξίας ἡγεμονικῆς
καὶ δυνάμεως ἀνδρὶ μετρίῳ καὶ ἀστείῳ προσούσης,

---

[1] μόνον Meziriacus : μὴ μόνον.
[2] ὑπολαμβάνουσιν] περιλαμβάνουσιν Coraes.
[3] ἐν added by Coraes.
[4] γὰρ added by Bernardakis.
[5] βλεπομένοις Frerichs : μὴ βλεπομένοις. Bernardakis
would omit βλεπομένοις and παρορωμένοις.

those only whom we love. But just as Ixion slipped into the cloud when he was pursuing Hera, so these people seize upon a deceptive, showy, and shifting appearance in lieu of friendship. But the man of sense, if he is engaged in active political life, will ask for so much reputation as will inspire confidence and thereby give him power for affairs ; for it is neither pleasant nor easy to benefit people if they are unwilling, and confidence makes them willing. For just as light is more a blessing to those who see than to those who are seen, so reputation is more a blessing to those who are aware of it than to those who are not overlooked. But he who has withdrawn from public affairs, who communes with himself and thinks happiness is in quiet and uninterrupted leisure, he, " being chaste, worships afar off " [a] the reputation which is popular and widespread in crowds and theatres, even as Hippolytus worshipped Aphroditê, but even he does not despise reputation among the right-minded and estimable ; but wealth, reputation as a leader, or power in his friendships he does not pursue, however neither does he avoid these qualities if they are associated with a temperate character ; nor, for that matter, does he pursue those among the youths who are fine-looking and handsome, but those who are teachable and orderly and fond of learning ; nor does the beauty of those whom he sees endowed with freshness, charm, and the flower of youth frighten the philosopher or scare him off and drive him away from those who are worthy of his attention. So, then, if the dignity that befits leadership and power are associated with a man of moderation and culture, the philosopher

[a] Euripides, *Hipp.* 102.

B οὐκ ἀφέξεται τοῦ φιλεῖν καὶ ἀγαπᾶν οὐδὲ φοβήσεται
(778) τὸ αὐλικὸς ἀκοῦσαι καὶ θεραπευτικός·

οἱ γὰρ Κύπριν φεύγοντες ἀνθρώπων ἄγαν
νοσοῦσ᾽ ὁμοίως τοῖς ἄγαν θηρωμένοις·

καὶ οἱ πρὸς ἔνδοξον οὕτως καὶ ἡγεμονικὴν φιλίαν
ἔχοντες. ὁ μὲν οὖν ἀπράγμων φιλόσοφος οὐ φεύ-
ξεται τοὺς τοιούτους, ὁ δὲ πολιτικὸς καὶ περιέξεται
αὐτῶν, ἄκουσιν¹ οὐκ ἐνοχλῶν οὐδ᾽ ἐπισταθμεύων
τὰ ὦτα διαλέξεσιν ἀκαίροις καὶ σοφιστικαῖς, βουλομένοις δὲ χαίρων καὶ διαλεγόμενος καὶ σχολάζων
καὶ συνὼν προθύμως.

3. Σπείρω δ᾽ ἄρουραν δώδεχ᾽ ἡμερῶν ὁδὸν
Βερέκυντα χῶρον·

C οὗτος εἰ μὴ μόνον φιλογέωργος ἀλλὰ καὶ φιλάνθρωπος ἦν,² ἥδιον ἂν ἔσπειρε τὴν τοσούτους
τρέφειν δυναμένην ἢ τὸ ᾽Αντισθένους ἐκεῖνο χωρί-
διον, ὃ μόλις Αὐτολύκῳ³ παλαίειν⁴ ἂν ἤρκεσε⁵· εἰ δέ
σε ἠρόμην τὴν οἰκουμένην ἅπασαν ἐπιστρέφειν παρ-

---

¹ ἄκουσιν Reiske: ἀκούειν.
² ἦν added by Iunius.
³ Αὐτολύκῳ Wyttenbach: αὐτὸ (αὐτῷ) αὖ.
⁴ παλαίειν Bernardakis: πάλιν.
⁵ ἂν ἤρκεσε Wyttenbach: ἀνήρηκας; cf. Xen. Symp. 3. 8.

ᵃ See Euripides, *Hipp.* 115, and Stobaeus, *Flor.* 63. 3;
Nauck, *Trag. Graec. Frag.* p. 493.
ᵇ Aesch. *Niobe*, Frag. 153, Nauck, *Trag. Graec. Frag.*
p. 52. The speaker is Tantalus. The Berecynthian land is
near Mount Berecynthus in Phrygia.
ᶜ See Xen. *Symposium*, 3. 8, where Antisthenes says that

will not hold aloof from making him a friend and cherishing him, nor will he be afraid of being called a courtier and a toady.

> For those of men who too much Cypris shun
> Are mad as those who follow her too much ; [a]

and so are those who take that attitude towards friendship with famous men and leaders. Hence, while the philosopher who abstains from public affairs will not avoid such men, yet one who is interested in public life will even go to them with open arms ; he will not annoy them against their will, nor will he pitch his camp in their ears with inopportune sophistical disquisitions, but when they wish it, he will be glad to converse and spend his leisure with them and eager to associate with them.

3. The field I sow is twelve days' journey round ;
   Berecynthian land ; [b]

if this speaker was not merely a lover of agriculture but also a lover of his fellow men, he would find more pleasure in sowing the field which could feed so many men than in sowing that little plot of Antisthenes' [c] which would hardly have been big enough for Autolycus to wrestle in ; but if [he meant]: "I sow all this in order that I may subjugate the whole inhabited world," I deprecate the sentiment. [d]

his land is hardly enough to furnish sand to sprinkle Autolycus with before wrestling.

[d] The text is very corrupt, but the general course of the argument based upon the lines supposed to have been spoken by Tantalus may very well have been what is given in the translation. If the rich and powerful use their advantages for the common good of men, they are worthy of the philosopher's attention, but not so if they use their resources for purely selfish ends. See critical note, p. 42.

41

(778) αιτοῦμαι.[1] καίτοι Ἐπίκουρος τἀγαθὸν ἐν τῷ βαθυ-
τάτῳ τῆς ἡσυχίας ὥσπερ ἐν ἀκλύστῳ λιμένι καὶ
κωφῷ τιθέμενος τοῦ εὖ πάσχειν τὸ εὖ ποιεῖν οὐ
μόνον κάλλιον ἀλλὰ καὶ ἥδιον εἶναί φησι.

χαρᾶς γὰρ οὕτω γόνιμόν οὐδὲν[2]

ἐστιν

ὡς χάρις·

ἀλλὰ σοφὸς ἦν ὁ ταῖς Χάρισι τὰ ὀνόματα θέμενος
D Ἀγλαΐην καὶ Εὐφροσύνην καὶ Θάλειαν· τὸ γὰρ
ἀγαλλόμενον καὶ τὸ χαῖρον ἐν τῷ διδόντι τὴν χάριν
πλεῖόν ἐστι καὶ καθαρώτερον. διὸ τῷ πάσχειν εὖ[3]
αἰσχύνονται πολλάκις, ἀεὶ δ' ἀγάλλονται τῷ εὖ
ποιεῖν· εὖ δὲ ποιοῦσι πολλοὺς οἱ ποιοῦντες ἀγαθοὺς
ὧν πολλοὶ δέονται· καὶ τοὐναντίον, οἱ ἀεὶ διαφθεί-
ροντες ἡγεμόνας ἢ βασιλεῖς ἢ τυράννους διάβολοι καὶ
συκοφάνται καὶ κόλακες ὑπὸ πάντων ἐλαύνονται καὶ
κολάζονται, καθάπερ οὐκ εἰς μίαν κύλικα φάρμακον
E ἐμβάλλοντες θανάσιμον, ἀλλ' εἰς πηγὴν δημοσίᾳ
ῥέουσαν, ᾗ χρωμένους πάντας ὁρῶσιν. ὥσπερ
οὖν τοὺς Καλλίου κωμῳδουμένους κόλακας γελῶσιν, οὕς[4]

οὐ πῦρ οὐδὲ[5] σίδηρος
οὐδὲ χαλκὸς ἀπείργει[6]
μὴ φοιτᾶν ἐπὶ δεῖπνον

[1] εἰ δέ σε . . . παραιτοῦμαι] Bernardakis surmised that
beneath the corrupt text lurked a metrical version of what a
humane Tantalus might have said. . The translation assumes
a prose version of a prose explanation that a self-seeking
Tantalus might have said, as if Plutarch wrote, *e.g.*: εἰ δ'
εἶπε· Σπείρω (Bernardakis) ἵνα τὴν οἰκουμένην ἅπασαν κατα-
στερέφω, παραιτοῦμαι. See note *d* on preceding page.

And yet Epicurus, who places happiness in the deepest quiet, as in a sheltered and landlocked harbour, says that it is not only nobler, but also pleasanter, to confer than to receive benefits.

> For chiefest joy doth gracious kindness give.[a]

Surely he was wise who gave the Graces the names Aglaïa (Splendour), Euphrosynê (Gladness), and Thalia (Good-cheer); for the delight and joy are greater and purer for him who does the gracious act. And therefore people are often ashamed to receive benefits, but are always delighted to confer them; and they who make those men good upon whom many depend confer benefits upon many; and, on the contrary, the slanderers, backbiters, and flatterers who constantly corrupt rulers or kings or tyrants, are driven away and punished by everyone, as if they were putting deadly poison, not into a single cup, but into the public fountain which, as they see, everyone uses. Therefore, just as people laugh when the flatterers of Callias are ridiculed in comedy, those flatterers of whom Eupolis says[b]

> No fire, no, and no weapon,
> Be it of bronze or of iron,
> Keeps them from flocking to dinner,

[a] Probably an iambic trimeter. See Kock, *Com. Att. Frag.* iii. p. 495.

[b] From the *Flatterers*, by Eupolis; Kock, *Com. Att. Frag.* i. p. 303.

---

[2] οὐδὲν transposed by Kock *metri gratia*: γὰρ οὐδέν.
[3] εὖ πάσχειν Benseler.
[4] γελῶσιν οὓς Wyttenbach: λέγουσιν.
[5] οὐδὲ Meineke: οὐ.
[6] ἀπείργει Meineke: εἴργει.

43

κατὰ τὸν Εὔπολιν· τοὺς δ' Ἀπολλοδώρου τοῦ
τυράννου καὶ Φαλάριδος καὶ Διονυσίου φίλους καὶ
συνήθεις ἀπετυμπάνιζον, ἐστρέβλουν καὶ ἐνεπίμ-
πρασαν, ἐναγεῖς ἐποιοῦντο καὶ¹ καταράτους, ὡς
ἐκείνων μὲν ἀδικούντων ἕνα τούτων δὲ πολλοὺς δι'
ἑνὸς τοῦ ἄρχοντος· οὕτως οἱ μὲν ἰδιώταις συνόντες αὐτοὺς ἐκείνους ποιοῦσιν ἑαυτοῖς ἀλύπους
καὶ ἀβλαβεῖς καὶ προσηνεῖς, ὁ δ' ἄρχοντος ἦθος
F ἀφαιρῶν μοχθηρὸν ἢ γνώμην ἐφ' ὃ δεῖ συγκατευ-
θύνων τρόπον τινὰ δημοσίᾳ φιλοσοφεῖ καὶ τὸ κοινὸν
ἐπανορθοῦται, ᾧ² πάντες διοικοῦνται. τοῖς ἱερεῦσιν
αἰδὼ καὶ τιμὴν αἱ πόλεις νέμουσιν, ὅτι τἀγαθὰ
παρὰ τῶν θεῶν οὐ μόνον αὑτοῖς καὶ φίλοις καὶ
οἰκείοις, ἀλλὰ κοινῇ πᾶσιν αἰτοῦνται τοῖς πολίταις·
καίτοι τοὺς θεοὺς οἱ ἱερεῖς οὐ ποιοῦσιν ἀγαθῶν
δοτῆρας, ἀλλὰ τοιούτους ὄντας παρακαλοῦσι· τοὺς
δ' ἄρχοντας οἱ συνόντες τῶν φιλοσόφων δικαιοτέ-
ρους ποιοῦσι καὶ μετριωτέρους καὶ προθυμοτέρους
εἰς τὸ εὖ ποιεῖν, ὥστε καὶ χαίρειν εἰκός ἐστι μᾶλλον.

779 4. Ἐμοὶ δὲ δοκεῖ καὶ λυροποιὸς ἂν ἥδιον λύραν
ἐργάσασθαι καὶ προθυμότερον, μαθὼν ὡς ὁ ταύτην
κτησόμενος τὴν λύραν μέλλει τὸ Θηβαίων ἄστυ
τειχίζειν ὡς ὁ Ἀμφίων, ἢ τὴν Λακεδαιμονίων
στάσιν παύειν ἐπᾴδων καὶ παραμυθούμενος ὡς
Θαλῆς³· καὶ τέκτων ὁμοίως πηδάλιον δημιουργῶν

---

¹ καὶ added by Wyttenbach.
² ᾧ Iunius: ὡς.
³ Θαλῆς] ὁ Θαλῆς Bernardakis; Θαλήτας Frerichs.

ᵃ Cruel tyrants of Cassandreia, Acragas, and Syracuse
respectively.
ᵇ According to the legend, when Amphion played on his

but the friends and intimates of the tyrant Apollodorus, of Phalaris, and of Dionysius [a] they bastinadoed, tortured, and burned, and made them for ever polluted and accursed, since the former had done harm to one man, but the latter through one, the ruler, to many. So the philosophers who associate with persons in private station make those individuals inoffensive, harmless, and gentle towards themselves, but he who removes evil from the character of a ruler, or directs his mind towards what is right, philosophizes, as it were, in the public interest and corrects the general power by which all are governed. States pay reverence and honour to their priests because they ask blessings from the gods, not for themselves, their friends, and their families alone, but for all the citizens in common; and yet the priests do not make the gods givers of blessings, for they are such by nature; the priests merely invoke them. But philosophers who associate with rulers do make them more just, more moderate, and more eager to do good, so that it is very likely that they are also happier.

4. And I think a lyre-maker would be more willing and eager to make a lyre if he knew that the future owner of that lyre was to build the walls of the city of Thebes, as Amphion did,[b] or, like Thales,[c] was to put an end to faction among the Lacedaemonians by the music of his charms and his exhortations; and a carpenter likewise in making a tiller would be more

lyre, the stones of their own accord formed the walls of Thebes.

[c] Nothing is known of a musician or poet Thales. The musician Thaletas is said to have taught the lawgiver Lycurgus, but we do not hear of his putting an end to faction at Sparta.

(779) ἡσθῆναι, πυθόμενος ὅτι τοῦτο τὴν Θεμιστοκλέους
ναυαρχίδα κυβερνήσει προπολεμοῦσαν τῆς Ἑλλάδος
ἢ τὴν Πομπηίου τὰ πειρατικὰ καταναυμαχοῦντος·
τί οὖν οἴει περὶ τοῦ λόγου τὸν φιλόσοφον, διανοού-
B μενον ὡς ὁ τοῦτον παραλαβὼν πολιτικὸς ἀνὴρ καὶ
ἡγεμονικὸς κοινὸν ὄφελος ἔσται δικαιοδοτῶν,
νομοθετῶν, κολάζων τοὺς πονηρούς, αὔξων τοὺς
ἐπιεικεῖς καὶ ἀγαθούς; ἐμοὶ δὲ δοκεῖ καὶ ναυπηγὸς
ἀστεῖος ἥδιον ἂν¹ ἐργάσασθαι πηδάλιον, πυθόμενος
ὅτι τοῦτο τὴν Ἀργὼ κυβερνήσει τὴν "πᾶσι μέ-
λουσαν"· καὶ τεκτονικὸς οὐκ ἂν οὕτω κατασκευάσαι ἄροτρον προθύμως ἢ ἅμαξαν, ὡς τοὺς
ἄξονας, οἷς ἔμελλε Σόλων τοὺς νόμους ἐγχαράξειν.
καὶ μὴν οἱ λόγοι τῶν φιλοσόφων, ἐὰν ψυχαῖς
ἡγεμονικῶν καὶ πολιτικῶν ἀνδρῶν ἐγγραφῶσι
βεβαίως καὶ κρατήσωσι, νόμων δύναμιν λαμ-
βάνουσιν· ἦ καὶ Πλάτων εἰς Σικελίαν ἔπλευσεν,
ἐλπίζων τὰ δόγματα νόμους καὶ ἔργα ποιήσειν ἐν
C τοῖς Διονυσίου πράγμασιν· ἀλλ' εὗρε Διονύσιον
ὥσπερ βιβλίον παλίμψηστον ἤδη μολυσμῶν ἀνά-
πλεων καὶ τὴν βαφὴν οὐκ ἀνιέντα τῆς τυραννίδος,
ἐν πολλῷ χρόνῳ δευσοποιὸν οὖσαν καὶ δυσέκπλυ-
τον· ἀκμαίους² δ' ὄντας ἔτι δεῖ τῶν χρηστῶν
ἀντιλαμβάνεσθαι λόγων.

---

¹ ἂν added by Fränkel (or read κἂν for καὶ or ἐργάσασθαι
should be changed to ἐργάεσθαι, Bernardakis).
² ἀκμαίους Coraes: δρομαίους.

ᵃ Homer, *Od.* xii. 70.
ᵇ In his *Life of Solon*, xxv., Plutarch says that Solon's
laws were originally inscribed on revolving wooden tablets
(*axones*) in wooden frames. The *axones* were set up in the

pleased if he knew that it would steer the flagship of Themistocles fighting in defence of Hellas, or that of Pompey when he overcame the pirates. What, then, do you imagine the philosopher thinks about his teaching, when he reflects that the statesman or ruler who accepts it will be a public blessing by dispensing justice, making laws, punishing the wicked, and making the orderly and the good to prosper ? And I imagine that a clever shipbuilder, too, would take greater pleasure in making a tiller if he knew that it was to steer the Argo, " the concern of all," [a] and a carpenter would not be so eager to make a plough or a wagon as the *axones* [b] on which the laws of Solon were to be engraved. And surely the teachings of philosophers, if they are firmly engraved in the souls of rulers and statesmen and control them, acquire the force of laws ; and that is why Plato sailed to Sicily, in the hope that his teachings would produce laws and actions in the government of Dionysius ; but he found Dionysius, like a book which is erased and written over, already befouled with stains and incapable of losing the dye of his tyranny, since by length of time it had become deeply fixed and hard to wash out. No, it is while men are still at their best that they should accept the worthy teachings.

Royal Stoa. Toward the end of the fifth century, the wooden text having disintegrated and the laws having been modified, a new edition of Solon's laws was inscribed on both sides of a marble wall built in the Royal Stoa and of this a fragment has recently come to light in the Athenian Agora. See J. H. Oliver, *Hesperia*, iv. 5 ff., whose views are represented in the above statement.

TO AN UNEDUCATED RULER
(AD PRINCIPEM INERUDITUM)

INTRODUCTION

THE brief essay *To an Uneducated Ruler* may have formed part of a lecture, or it may, as its traditional title suggests, have been composed as a letter to some person in authority. There is nothing in it to prove either assumption. No striking or unusual precepts or doctrines are here promulgated, but the essay is enlivened by a few interesting tales and, considering its brevity, by a somewhat unusual number of rather elaborate similes. As usual Plutarch depends upon earlier writers for most of his material. The ending is so abrupt as to warrant the belief that the essay, in its present form, is only a fragment.

D   1. Πλάτωνα Κυρηναῖοι παρεκάλουν νόμους τε
γραψάμενον αὐτοῖς ἀπολιπεῖν καὶ διακοσμῆσαι τὴν
πολιτείαν, ὁ δὲ παρῃτήσατο φήσας χαλεπὸν εἶναι
Κυρηναίοις νομοθετεῖν οὕτως εὐτυχοῦσιν·

ουδὲν γὰρ οὕτω γαῦρον

καὶ τραχὺ καὶ δύσαρκτον

ὡς ἀνὴρ ἔφυ

εὐπραγίας δοκούσης ἐπιλαμβανόμενος. διὸ τοῖς
E ἄρχουσι χαλεπόν ἐστι σύμβουλον περὶ ἀρχῆς
γενέσθαι· τὸν γὰρ λόγον ὥσπερ ἄρχοντα παρα-
δέξασθαι φοβοῦνται, μὴ τῆς ἐξουσίας αὐτῶν
τἀγαθὸν κολούσῃ τῷ καθήκοντι δουλωσάμενος.
οὐ γὰρ ἴσασι τὰ Θεοπόμπου τοῦ Σπαρτιατῶν
βασιλέως, ὃς πρῶτος ἐν Σπάρτῃ τοῖς βασιλεύουσι
καταμίξας τοὺς Ἐφόρους, εἶτ' ὀνειδιζόμενος ὑπὸ
τῆς γυναικός, εἰ τοῖς παισὶν ἐλάττονα παραδώσει
τὴν ἀρχὴν ἧς παρέλαβε, '' μείζονα μὲν οὖν,'' εἶπεν,
'' ὅσῳ καὶ βεβαιοτέραν.'' τὸ γὰρ σφοδρὸν ἀνεὶς

ᵃ That Plato in his extensive travels visited Cyrene is
attested by Diogenes Laertius, *Vit. Phil.* iii. 6.
  ᵇ A quotation from some tragic poet ; see Nauck, *Trag.
Graec. Frag.* p. 617.
  ᶜ The five Ephors at Sparta, representing the five local

TO AN UNEDUCATED RULER

1. PLATO was asked by the Cyrenaeans [a] to compose a set of laws and leave it for them and to give them a well-ordered government ; but he refused, saying that it was difficult to make laws for the Cyrenaeans because they were so prosperous.

> For nothing is so haughty
> harsh, and ungovernable
> by nature as a man,[b]

when he possesses what he regards as prosperity. And that is why it is difficult to give advice to rulers in matters of government, for they are afraid to accept reason as a ruler over them, lest it curtail the advantage of their power by making them slaves to duty. For they are not familiar with the saying of Theopompus, the King of Sparta who first made the Ephors [c] associates of the Kings ; then, when his wife reproached him because he would hand down to his children a less powerful office than that which he had received he said : " Nay, more powerful rather, inasmuch as it is more secure." For by giving up that which was excessive and absolute in

tribes, were in charge of civil law and public order. Whether they were established by Lycurgus or by Theopompus (about 757 B.C. or later) is uncertain. In the sixth and fifth centuries B.C. they seem to have had more power than the kings.

καὶ ἄκρατον αὐτῆς ἅμα τῷ φθόνῳ διέφυγε τὸν
F κίνδυνον. καίτοι Θεόπομπος μὲν εἰς ἑτέρους τὸ
τῆς ἀρχῆς ὥσπερ ῥεύματος μεγάλου παροχετευσά-
μενος, ὅσον ἄλλοις ἔδωκεν, αὐτοῦ περιέκοψεν· ὁ
δ᾽ ἐκ φιλοσοφίας τῷ ἄρχοντι πάρεδρος καὶ φύλαξ
ἐγκατοικισθεὶς λόγος, ὥσπερ εὐεξίας τῆς δυνάμεως
τὸ ἐπισφαλὲς ἀφαιρῶν, ἀπολείπει τὸ ὑγιαῖνον.

2. Ἀλλὰ νοῦν οὐκ ἔχοντες οἱ πολλοὶ τῶν βασιλέων καὶ ἀρχόντων μιμοῦνται τοὺς ἀτέχνους ἀν-
δριαντοποιούς, οἳ νομίζουσι μεγάλους καὶ ἁδροὺς
φαίνεσθαι τοὺς κολοσσούς, ἂν διαβεβηκότας σφόδρα
780 καὶ διατεταμένους καὶ κεχηνότας πλάσωσι· καὶ γὰρ
οὗτοι βαρύτητι φωνῆς καὶ βλέμματος τραχύτητι
καὶ δυσκολίᾳ τρόπων καὶ ἀμιξίᾳ διαίτης ὄγκον
ἡγεμονίας καὶ σεμνότητα μιμεῖσθαι δοκοῦσιν, οὐδ᾽
ὁτιοῦν τῶν κολοσσικῶν διαφέροντες ἀνδριάντων,
οἳ τὴν ἔξωθεν ἡρωικὴν καὶ θεοπρεπῆ μορφὴν
ἔχοντες ἐντός εἰσι γῆς μεστοὶ καὶ λίθου καὶ μολί-
βδου· πλὴν ὅτι τῶν μὲν ἀνδριάντων ταῦτα τὰ βάρη
τὴν ὀρθότητα μόνιμον καὶ ἀκλινῆ διαφυλάττει, οἱ
B δ᾽ ἀπαίδευτοι στρατηγοὶ καὶ ἡγεμόνες ὑπὸ τῆς
ἐντὸς ἀγνωμοσύνης πολλάκις σαλεύονται καὶ περι-
τρέπονται· βάσει γὰρ οὐ κειμένῃ πρὸς ὀρθὰς
ἐξουσίαν ἐποικοδομοῦντες ὑψηλὴν συναπονεύουσι.
δεῖ δέ, ὥσπερ ὁ κανὼν αὐτός, ἀστραβὴς γενόμενος
καὶ ἀδιάστροφος, οὕτως ἀπευθύνει τὰ λοιπὰ τῇ
πρὸς αὐτὸν ἐφαρμογῇ καὶ παραθέσει συνεξομοιῶν,[1]
παραπλησίως τὸν ἄρχοντα πρῶτον τὴν ἀρχὴν
κτησάμενον ἐν ἑαυτῷ καὶ κατευθύναντα τὴν[2]
ψυχὴν[3] καὶ καταστησάμενον τὸ ἦθος οὕτω συν-

---

[1] συνεξομοιῶν Stobaeus (xl. 98 [100]); συναφομοιῶν Wyttenbach: συνεφομοιῶν.   [2] τὴν added by Reiske.

it he avoided both the envy and the danger. And yet Theopompus, by diverting to a different body the vast stream of his royal authority, deprived himself of as much as he gave to others. But when philosophical reason derived from philosophy has been established as the ruler's coadjutor and guardian, it removes the hazardous element from his power, as a surgeon removes that which threatens a patient's health and leaves that which is sound.

2. But most kings and rulers are so foolish as to act like unskilful sculptors, who think their colossal figures look large and imposing if they are modelled with their feet far apart, their muscles tense, and their mouths wide open. For these rulers seem by heaviness of voice, harshness of expression, truculence of manner, and unsociability in their way of living to be imitating the dignity and majesty of the princely station, although in fact they are not at all different from colossal statues which have a heroic and godlike form on the outside, but inside are full of clay, stone, and lead,—except that in the case of the statues the weight of those substances keeps them permanently upright without leaning, whereas uneducated generals and rulers are often rocked and capsized by the ignorance within them ; for since the foundation upon which they have built up their lofty power is not laid straight, they lean with it and lose their balance. But just as a rule, if it is made rigid and inflexible, makes other things straight when they are fitted to it and laid alongside it, in like manner the sovereign must first gain command of himself, must regulate his own soul and establish his own character, then make his sub-

---

[3] ψυχὴν Stobaeus and Reiske: ἀρχήν.

(780) ἁρμόττειν τὸ ὑπήκοον· οὔτε γὰρ πίπτοντός ἐστιν
ὀρθοῦν οὔτε διδάσκειν ἀγνοοῦντος οὔτε κοσμεῖν
ἀκοσμοῦντος ἢ τάττειν ἀτακτοῦντος ἢ ἄρχειν μὴ
C ἀρχομένου· ἀλλ' οἱ πολλοὶ κακῶς φρονοῦντες
οἴονται πρῶτον ἐν τῷ ἄρχειν ἀγαθὸν εἶναι τὸ μὴ
ἄρχεσθαι, καὶ ὅ γε Περσῶν βασιλεὺς πάντας
ἡγεῖτο δούλους πλὴν τῆς αὑτοῦ γυναικός, ἧς
μάλιστα δεσπότης ὤφειλεν εἶναι.

3. Τίς οὖν ἄρξει τοῦ ἄρχοντος; ὁ

> νόμος ὁ πάντων βασιλεὺς
> θνατῶν[1] τε καὶ ἀθανάτων,

ὡς ἔφη Πίνδαρος, οὐκ ἐν βιβλίοις ἔξω γεγραμμένος[2]
οὐδέ τισι ξύλοις, ἀλλ' ἔμψυχος ὢν ἐν αὑτῷ[3] λόγος,
ἀεὶ συνοικῶν καὶ παραφυλάττων καὶ μηδέποτε τὴν
ψυχὴν ἐῶν ἔρημον ἡγεμονίας. ὁ μὲν γὰρ Περσῶν
βασιλεὺς ἕνα τῶν κατευναστῶν εἶχε πρὸς τοῦτο
τεταγμένον, ὥσθ' ἕωθεν εἰσιόντα λέγειν πρὸς αὐτὸν
" ἀνάστα, ὦ βασιλεῦ, καὶ φρόντιζε πραγμάτων,
ὧν σε φροντίζειν ὁ μέγας Ὡρομάσδης[4] ἠθέλησε ''·
D τοῦ δὲ πεπαιδευμένου καὶ σωφρονοῦντος ἄρχοντος
ἐντός ἐστιν ὁ τοῦτο φθεγγόμενος ἀεὶ καὶ παρα-
κελευόμενος. Πολέμων γὰρ ἔλεγε τὸν ἔρωτα εἶναι
" θεῶν ὑπηρεσίαν εἰς νέων ἐπιμέλειαν καὶ σωτηρίαν ''· ἀληθέστερον δ' ἄν τις εἴποι τοὺς ἄρχοντας
ὑπηρετεῖν θεῷ πρὸς ἀνθρώπων ἐπιμέλειαν καὶ

---

[1] θνατῶν Pindar (Bergk-Schroeder, p. 458, no. 169 [151]):
θνητῶν. [2] γεγραμμένος Meziriacus: γεγραμμένοις.
[3] ἐν αὑτῷ Coraes: ἑαυτῷ or ἐν ἑαυτῷ.
[4] μέγας Ὡρομάσδης Kaltwasser: μεσορομάσδης; cf. Life of
Artax. chap. xxix.

jects fit his pattern. For one who is falling cannot
hold others up, nor can one who is ignorant teach,
nor the uncultivated impart culture, nor the dis-
orderly make order, nor can he rule who is under
no rule. But most people foolishly believe that the
first advantage of ruling is freedom from being ruled.
And indeed the King of the Persians used to think
that everyone was a slave except his own wife,
whose master he ought to have been most of all.

3. Who, then, shall rule the ruler ? The

> Law, the king of all,
> Both mortals and immortals,

as Pindar [a] says—not law written outside him in books
or on wooden tablets [b] or the like, but reason endowed
with life within him, always abiding with him and
watching over him and never leaving his soul without
its leadership. For example, the King of the Persians
had one of his chamberlains assigned to the special
duty of entering his chamber in the morning and saying to him : "Arise, O King, and consider matters
which the great Oromasdes [c] wished you to consider." But the educated and wise ruler has within
him the voice which always thus speaks to him and
exhorts him. Indeed Polemo said that love was
" the service of the gods for the care and preservation
of the young " ; one might more truly say that rulers
serve god for the care and preservation of men, in

---

[a] Bergk-Schroeder, p. 458, no. 169 [151] ; Sandys, p. 602,
no. 169 (L.C.L.). Quoted by Plato, *Gorg.* 784 B, *Laws*,
690 B.

[b] A reference to the original tablets of Solon's laws. See
Moralia, 779 B and note *b*, p. 46 above.

[c] Oromasdes is the Greek form of Ormazd, Auramasda, or
Ahura Mazdah, the great god of the Persians.

(780) σωτηρίαν,[1] ὅπως ὦν θεὸς δίδωσιν ἀνθρώποις
καλῶν καὶ ἀγαθῶν τὰ μὲν νέμωσι τὰ δὲ φυλάτ-
τωσιν.

ο´ρᾷς τὸν ὑψοῦ τόνδ᾽ ἄπειρον αἰθέρα,
καὶ γῆν πέριξ ἔχονθ᾽ ὑγραῖς ἐν ἀγκάλαις;

ὁ μὲν καθίησιν ἀρχὰς σπερμάτων προσηκόντων γῇ
δ᾽ ἀναδίδωσιν, αὔξεται δὲ τὰ μὲν ὄμβροις τὰ δ᾽
ἀνέμοις τὰ δ᾽ ἄστροις ἐπιθαλπόμενα καὶ σελήνῃ,
E κοσμεῖ δ᾽ ἥλιος ἅπαντα καὶ πᾶσι τοῦτο δὴ τὸ παρ᾽
αὐτοῦ φίλτρον ἐγκεράννυσιν. ἀλλὰ τῶν τοιούτων[2]
καὶ τηλικούτων ἃ θεοὶ χαρίζονται δώρων καὶ
ἀγαθῶν οὐκ ἔστιν ἀπόλαυσις οὐδὲ χρῆσις ὀρθὴ
δίχα νόμου καὶ δίκης καὶ ἄρχοντος. δίκη μὲν οὖν
νόμου τέλος ἐστί, νόμος δ᾽ ἄρχοντος ἔργον, ἄρχων
δ᾽ εἰκὼν θεοῦ τοῦ πάντα κοσμοῦντος, οὐ Φειδίου
δεόμενος πλάττοντος οὐδὲ Πολυκλείτου καὶ Μύρω-
νος, ἀλλ᾽ αὐτὸς αὑτὸν εἰς ὁμοιότητα θεῷ δι᾽ ἀρετῆς
F καθιστὰς καὶ δημιουργῶν ἀγαλμάτων τὸ ἥδιστον
ὀφθῆναι καὶ θεοπρεπέστατον. οἷον δ᾽ ἥλιον ἐν
οὐρανῷ περικαλλὲς εἴδωλον ἑαυτοῦ καὶ σελήνην
ὁ θεὸς ἐνίδρυσε, τοιοῦτον ἐν πόλεσι μίμημα καὶ
φέγγος ἄρχων

ὥστε θεουδὴς

εὐδικίας ἀνέχῃσι,

τουτέστι θεοῦ λόγον ἔχων, διάνοιαν,[3] οὐ σκῆπτρον
οὐδὲ κεραυνὸν οὐδὲ τρίαιναν, ὡς ἔνιοι πλάττουσιν

---

[1] καὶ σωτηρίαν added by Bernardakis. *Cf. Thes. and Rom.*
chap. ii.
[2] τοιούτων Bernardakis; *cf.* Stobaeus, xlvi. 99 (101):
τοσούτων.
[3] διάνοιαν] καὶ διάνοιαν Reiske; ἐνδιάθετον Frerichs.

order that of the glorious gifts which the gods give
to men they may distribute some and safeguard
others.

> Dost thou behold this lofty, boundless sky
> Which holds the earth enwrapped in soft embrace ? [a]

The sky sends down the beginnings of the appropriate seeds, and the earth causes them to sprout up ;
some are made to grow by showers and some by
winds, and some by the warmth of stars and moon ;
but it is the sun which adorns all things and mingles
in all things what men call the " love charm " which
is derived from himself. But these gifts and blessings, so excellent and so great, which the gods
bestow cannot be rightly enjoyed nor used without
law and justice and a ruler. Now justice is the aim
and end of law, but law is the work of the ruler, and
the ruler is the image of God who orders all things.
Such a ruler needs no Pheidias nor Polycleitus nor
Myron to model him, but by his virtue he forms himself in the likeness of God and thus creates a statue
most delightful of all to behold and most worthy
of divinity. Now just as in the heavens God has
established as a most beautiful image of himself the
sun and the moon, so in states a ruler

> who in God's likeness
> Righteous decisions upholds, [b]

that is to say, one who, possessing god's wisdom,
establishes, as his likeness and luminary, intelligence
in place of sceptre or thunderbolt or trident, with
which attributes some rulers represent themselves

[a] Euripides, unknown drama, Nauck, *Trag. Graec. Frag.*
p. 663. The following line is τοῦτον νόμιζε Ζῆνα, τόνδ' ἡγοῦ
Θεόν, " Believe that this is Zeus, consider this thy God."
Cicero translates this line in *De Natura Deorum*, ii. 25. 65.

[b] Homer, *Od.* xix. 109 and 111.

ἑαυτοὺς καὶ γράφουσι τῷ ἀνεφίκτῳ ποιοῦντες
ἐπίφθονον τὸ ἀνόητον· νεμεσᾷ γὰρ ὁ θεὸς τοῖς ἀπο-
μιμουμένοις βροντὰς καὶ κεραυνοὺς καὶ ἀκτινοβο-
781 λίας, τοὺς δὲ τὴν ἀρετὴν ζηλοῦντας αὐτοῦ καὶ πρὸς
τὸ καλὸν καὶ φιλάνθρωπον ἀφομοιοῦντας ἑαυτοὺς
ἡδόμενος αὔξει καὶ μεταδίδωσι τῆς περὶ αὐτὸν
εὐνομίας καὶ δίκης καὶ ἀληθείας καὶ πρᾳότητος·
ὧν θειότερον οὐ πῦρ ἐστιν οὐ φῶς οὐχ ἡλίου δρόμος
οὐκ ἀνατολαὶ καὶ δύσεις ἄστρων οὐ τὸ ἀΐδιον καὶ
ἀθάνατον. οὐ γὰρ χρόνῳ ζωῆς ὁ θεὸς εὐδαίμων
ἀλλὰ τῆς ἀρετῆς τῷ ἄρχοντι· τοῦτο γὰρ θεῖόν ἐστι,
καλὸν δ' αὐτῆς καὶ τὸ ἀρχόμενον.

4. Ἀνάξαρχος μὲν οὖν ἐπὶ τῷ Κλείτου φόνῳ
δεινοπαθοῦντα παραμυθούμενος Ἀλέξανδρον ἔφη
B καὶ τῷ Διὶ τὴν Δίκην εἶναι καὶ τὴν Θέμιν[1] παρ-
έδρους, ἵνα πᾶν πραττόμενον ὑπὸ βασιλέως θεμιτὸν
δοκῇ καὶ δίκαιον, οὐκ ὀρθῶς οὐδ' ὠφελίμως τὴν
ἐφ' οἷς ἥμαρτε μετάνοιαν αὐτοῦ τῷ πρὸς τὰ ὅμοια
θαρρύνειν ἰώμενος. εἰ δὲ δεῖ ταῦτ' εἰκάζειν, ὁ μὲν
Ζεὺς οὐκ ἔχει τὴν Δίκην πάρεδρον, ἀλλ' αὐτὸς
Δίκη καὶ Θέμις ἐστὶ καὶ νόμων ὁ πρεσβύτατος
καὶ τελειότατος. οἱ δὲ παλαιοὶ οὕτω λέγουσι καὶ
γράφουσι καὶ διδάσκουσιν, ὡς ἄνευ Δίκης ἄρχειν
μηδὲ τοῦ Διὸς καλῶς δυναμένου· "ἡ δέ γε[2] παρ-
C θένος ἐστὶ" καθ' Ἡσίοδον ἀδιάφθορος, αἰδοῦς

___

¹ καὶ τῷ Διὶ ... τὴν Θέμιν Wyttenbach : κλείτω δὴ ... τὴν
τῶν θεῶν. ² γε] τε Hesiod.

___

ᵃ Just as at Athens the archons had their *paredroi* who
aided them in the performance of some of their functions,
so here Justice and Right are called the *paredroi* of Zeus.
ᵇ Hesiod, *Works and Days*, 256-257 ἡ δέ τε παρθένος ἐστι
Δίκη, Διὸς ἐκγεγαυῖα κυδρή τ' αἰδοίη τε θεῶν, οἳ Ὄλυμπον ἔχουσιν.
" And there is Virgin Justice, the daughter of Zeus, who is

in sculpture and painting, thus causing their folly to arouse hostile feelings, because they claim what they cannot attain. For God visits his wrath upon those who imitate his thunders, lightnings, and sunbeams, but with those who emulate his virtue and make themselves like unto his goodness and mercy he is well pleased and therefore causes them to prosper and gives them a share of his own equity, justice, truth, and gentleness, than which nothing is more divine,—nor fire, nor light, nor the course of the sun, nor the risings and settings of the stars, nor eternity and immortality. For God enjoys felicity, not through the length of his life, but through the ruling quality of his virtue; for this is divine; and excellent also is that part of virtue which submits to rule.

4. Now it is true that Anaxarchus, trying to console Alexander in his agony of mind over his killing of Cleitus, said that the reason why Justice and Right are seated by the side *a* of Zeus is that men may consider every act of a king as righteous and just; but neither correct nor helpful were the means he took in endeavouring to heal the king's remorse for his sin, by encouraging him to further acts of the same sort. But if a guess about this matter is proper, I should say that Zeus does not have Justice to sit beside him, but is himself Justice and Right and the oldest and most perfect of laws; but the ancients state it in that way in their writings and teachings, to imply that without Justice not even Zeus can rule well. " She is a virgin," according to Hesiod,*b* uncorrupted, dwelling

honoured and reverenced among the gods who dwell on Olympus " (tr. H. G. Evelyn White in L.C.L.).

(781) καὶ σωφροσύνης καὶ ὠφελείας¹ σύνοικος²· ὅθεν
'' αἰδοίους '' προσαγορεύουσι τοὺς βασιλεῖς· μάλιστα γὰρ αἰδεῖσθαι προσήκει τοῖς ἥκιστα φοβου-
μένοις. φοβεῖσθαι δὲ δεῖ τὸν ἄρχοντα τοῦ παθεῖν
κακῶς μᾶλλον τὸ ποιῆσαι· τοῦτο γὰρ αἴτιόν ἐστιν
ἐκείνου καὶ οὗτός ἐστιν ὁ φόβος τοῦ ἄρχοντος
φιλάνθρωπος καὶ οὐκ ἀγεννής, ὑπὲρ τῶν ἀρχομένων
δεδιέναι μὴ λάθωσι βλαβέντες,

    ὡς δὲ κύνες περὶ μῆλα δυσωρήσονται ἐν αὐλῇ,
    θηρὸς ἀκούσαντες κρατερόφρονος,

οὐχ ὑπὲρ αὑτῶν ἀλλ' ὑπὲρ τῶν φυλαττομένων. ὁ
δ' Ἐπαμεινώνδας, εἰς ἑορτήν τινα καὶ πότον ἀνει-
D μένων τῶν Θηβαίων ῥυέντων, μόνος ἐφώδευε τὰ
ὅπλα καὶ τὰ τείχη, νήφειν λέγων καὶ ἀγρυπνεῖν
ὡς ἂν ἐξῇ τοῖς ἄλλοις μεθύειν καὶ καθεύδειν. καὶ
Κάτων ἐν Ἰτύκῃ τοὺς ἄλλους ἅπαντας ἀπὸ τῆς
ἥττης ἐκήρυττε πέμπειν ἐπὶ θάλατταν· καὶ ἐμβι-
βάσας, εὔπλοιαν εὐξάμενος ὑπὲρ αὐτῶν, εἰς οἶκον
ἐπανελθὼν ἑαυτὸν ἀπέσφαξε· διδάξας ὑπὲρ τίνων
δεῖ τὸν ἄρχοντα τῷ φόβῳ χρῆσθαι καὶ τίνων δεῖ
τὸν ἄρχοντα καταφρονεῖν. Κλέαρχος δ' ὁ Ποντικὸς
τύραννος εἰς κιβωτὸν ἐνδυόμενος ὥσπερ ὄφις
E ἐκάθευδε. καὶ Ἀριστόδημος³ ὁ Ἀργεῖος εἰς
ὑπερῷον οἴκημα θύραν ἔχον ἐπιρρακτήν, ἧς
ἐπάνω τιθεὶς τὸ κλινίδιον ἐκάθευδε μετὰ τῆς
ἑταίρας· ἡ δὲ μήτηρ ἐκείνης ὑφεῖλκε κάτωθεν τὸ
κλιμάκιον, εἶθ' ἡμέρας πάλιν προσετίθει φέρουσα.

---

¹ ὠφελείας] ἀληθείας some mss.: ἀφ . . ίας codex Xylandri.
² σύνοικος Reiske : ἔνοικος.
³ Ἀριστόδημος] Ἀρίστιππος, *Life of Aratus*, chap. xxv.

with reverence, self-restraint, and helpfulness; and therefore kings are called "reverend,"[a] for it is fitting that those be most revered who have least to fear. But the ruler should have more fear of doing than of suffering evil; for the former is the cause of the latter; and that kind of fear on the part of the ruler is humane and not ignoble to be afraid on behalf of his subjects lest they may without his knowledge suffer harm,

> Just as the dogs keep their watch, toiling hard for the
>   flocks in the sheepfold,
> When they have heard a ferocious wild beast,[b]

not for their own sake but for the sake of those whom they are guarding. Epameinondas, when all the Thebans crowded to a certain festival and gave themselves up utterly to drink, went alone and patrolled the armouries and the walls, saying that he was keeping sober and awake that the others might be free to be drunk and asleep. And Cato at Utica issued a proclamation to send all the other survivors of the defeat to the seashore; he saw them aboard ship, prayed that they might have a good voyage, then returned home and killed himself; thereby teaching us in whose behalf the ruler ought to feel fear and what the ruler ought to despise. But Clearchus, tyrant of Pontus, used to crawl into a chest like a snake and sleep there, and Aristodemus of Argos would mount to an upper room entered by a trap-door, then put his bed on the door and sleep in it with his mistress; and the girl's mother would take the ladder away from below and set it up again in the morning. How do you

---

[a] *e.g.* Homer, *Il.* iv. 402.
[b] Homer, *Il.* x. 183-184.

πῶς οὗτος, οἴεσθε, τὸ θέατρον ἐπεφρίκει καὶ τὸ
ἀρχεῖον, τὸ βουλευτήριον, τὸ συμπόσιον, ὁ τὸν
θάλαμον ἑαυτῷ δεσμωτήριον πεποιηκώς; τῷ γὰρ
ὄντι δεδίασιν οἱ βασιλεῖς ὑπὲρ τῶν ἀρχομένων, οἱ
δὲ τύραννοι τοὺς ἀρχομένους· διὸ τῇ δυνάμει τὸ
δέος συναύξουσι· πλειόνων γὰρ ἄρχοντες πλείονας
φοβοῦνται.

F   5. Οὐ γὰρ εἰκὸς οὐδὲ πρέπον, ὥσπερ ἔνιοι φιλόσοφοι λέγουσι, τὸν θεὸν ἐν ὕλῃ πάντα πασχούσῃ
καὶ πράγμασι μυρίας δεχομένοις ἀνάγκας καὶ
τύχας καὶ μεταβολὰς ὑπάρχειν ἀναμεμιγμένον·
ἀλλ' ὁ μὲν[1] ἄνω που περὶ τὴν ἀεὶ κατὰ ταὐτὰ
ὡσαύτως[2] φύσιν ἔχουσαν ἱδρυμένος ἐν βάθροις
ἁγίοις ᾗ φησι Πλάτων, εὐθείᾳ[3] περαίνει κατὰ
φύσιν περιπορευόμενος· οἷον δ' ἥλιος ἐν οὐρανῷ
μίμημα τὸ περικαλλὲς αὑτοῦ δι' ἐσόπτρου εἴδωλον
ἀναφαίνεται τοῖς ἐκεῖνον ἐνορᾶν δι' αὐτοῦ δυνατοῖς,
οὕτω τὸ ἐν πόλεσι φέγγος εὐδικίας καὶ λόγου τοῦ
782   περὶ αὐτὸν[4] ὥσπερ εἰκόνα κατέστησεν, ἣν οἱ μακάριοι καὶ σώφρονες ἐκ φιλοσοφίας ἀπογράφονται
πρὸς τὸ κάλλιστον τῶν πραγμάτων πλάττοντες
ἑαυτούς. ταύτην δ' οὐδὲν ἐμποιεῖ τὴν διάθεσιν
ἢ λόγος ἐκ φιλοσοφίας παραγενόμενος· ἵνα μὴ
πάσχωμεν τὸ τοῦ Ἀλεξάνδρου, ὃς ἐν Κορίνθῳ
Διογένην θεασάμενος καὶ δι' εὐφυΐαν ἀγαπήσας
καὶ θαυμάσας τὸ φρόνημα καὶ τὸ μέγεθος τοῦ
ἀνδρὸς εἶπεν '' εἰ μὴ Ἀλέξανδρος ἤμην, Διογένης

---

[1] ὁ μὲν Wyttenbach : ἡμῖν.
[2] ὡσαύτως Reiske : οὕτως.
[3] εὐθείᾳ Reiske ; cf. Moralia, 601 B : εὐθέα.
[4] αὐτὸν Abresch : αὐτὴν or αὐτόν.

64

imagine he must have shuddered at the theatre, the city hall, the senate-chamber, the convivial feast, he who had made his bedchamber a prison cell? For in reality kings fear for their subjects, but tyrants fear their subjects; and therefore they increase their fear as they increase their power, for when they have more subjects they have more men to fear.

5. For it is neither probable nor fitting that god is, as some philosophers say, mingled with matter, which is altogether passive, and with things, which are subject to countless necessities, chances, and changes. On the contrary, somewhere up above in contact with that nature which, in accordance with the same principles, remains always as it is, established, as Plato *a* says, upon pedestals of holiness, proceeding in accordance with nature in his straight course, he reaches his goal.*b* And as the sun, his most beautiful image, appears in the heavens as his mirrored likeness to those who are able to see him in it, just so he has established in states the light of justice and of knowledge of himself as an image which the blessed and the wise copy with the help of philosophy, modelling themselves after the most beautiful of all things. But nothing implants this disposition in men except the teachings of philosophy, to keep us from having the same experience as Alexander, who, seeing Diogenes at Corinth, admiring him for his natural gifts, and being astonished by his spirit and greatness, said: "If I were not Alexander, I should be Diogenes," by

---

a *Phaedrus*, 254 B.
b *Cf.* Plato, *Laws*, 716 A.

782) ἂν ἤμην''· ὀλίγου δέων¹ εἰπεῖν, τὴν περὶ αὐτὸν²
εὐτυχίαν καὶ λαμπρότητα καὶ δύναμιν ὡς κώλυσιν
B ἀρετῆς καὶ ἀσχολίαν βαρυνόμενος καὶ ζηλοτυπῶν
τὸν τρίβωνα καὶ τὴν πήραν, ὅτι τούτοις ἦν ἀνίκη-
τος καὶ ἀνάλωτος Διογένης, οὐχ ὡς ἐκεῖνος ὅπλοις
καὶ ἵπποις καὶ σαρίσσαις. ἐξῆν οὖν φιλοσοφοῦντα
καὶ τῇ διαθέσει γίγνεσθαι Διογένην καὶ τῇ τύχῃ
μένειν Ἀλέξανδρον, καὶ διὰ τοῦτο γενέσθαι Διογένην μᾶλλον, ὅτι ἦν Ἀλέξανδρος, ὡς πρὸς
τύχην μεγάλην πολὺ πνεῦμα καὶ σάλον ἔχουσαν
ἕρματος πολλοῦ καὶ κυβερνήτου μεγάλου δεόμενον.
   6. Ἐν μὲν γὰρ τοῖς ἀσθενέσι καὶ ταπεινοῖς καὶ
ἰδιώταις τῷ ἀδυνάτῳ μιγνύμενον³ τὸ ἀνόητον εἰς
τὸ ἀναμάρτητον⁴ τελευτᾷ,⁵ ὥσπερ ἐν⁶ ὀνείρασι
φαύλοις τις ἀνία⁷ τὴν ψυχὴν διαταράττει συν-
C εξαναστῆναι ταῖς ἐπιθυμίαις μὴ δυναμένην· ἡ δ'
ἐξουσία παραλαβοῦσα τὴν κακίαν νεῦρα τοῖς⁸
πάθεσι προστίθησι· καὶ τὸ τοῦ Διονυσίου ἀληθές
ἐστιν· ἔφη γὰρ ἀπολαύειν μάλιστα τῆς ἀρχῆς,
ὅταν ταχέως ἃ βούλεται ποιῇ. μέγας οὖν ὁ
κίνδυνος βούλεσθαι ἃ μὴ δεῖ τὸν ἃ βούλεται ποιεῖν
δυνάμενον·
   αὐτίκ' ἔπειτά γε μῦθος ἔην, τετέλεστο δὲ ἔργον.
ὀξὺν ἡ κακία διὰ τῆς ἐξουσίας δρόμον ἔχουσα πᾶν
πάθος ἐξωθεῖ, ποιοῦσα τὴν ὀργὴν φόνον τὸν ἔρωτα
μοιχείαν τὴν πλεονεξίαν δήμευσιν.

   ¹ δέων] δέω Madvig; δεῖν Coraes; δέον Frerichs.
   ² αὐτὸν Duebner: αὐτὸν.
   ³ μιγνύμενον] δεδεμένον Stobaeus, xlvi. 100 (102).
   ⁴ ἀναμάρτητον] ἁμαρτάνειν Stobaeus.
   ⁵ τελευτᾷ omitted by Stobaeus.   ⁶ ἐν Stobaeus.
   ⁷ ἀνία] ἄγεται καὶ μάτην Frerichs; some mss. have a gap
after ἀνι; ἀνία τοῖς πάθεσι Stobaeus.

which he almost said that he was weighed down by his good fortune, glory, and power which kept him from virtue and left him no leisure, and that he envied the cynic's cloak and wallet because Diogenes was invincible and secure against capture by means of these, not, as he was himself, by means of arms, horses, and pikes. So by being a philosopher he was able to become Diogenes in disposition and yet to remain Alexander in outward fortunes, and to become all the more Diogenes because he was Alexander, since for his great ship of fortune, tossed by high winds and surging sea, he needed heavy ballast and a great pilot.

6. For in weak and lowly private persons folly is combined with lack of power and, therefore, results in no wrongdoing, just as in bad dreams a feeling of distress disturbs the spirit, and it cannot rouse itself in accordance with its desires ; but power when wickedness is added to it brings increased vigour to the passions. For the saying of Dionysius is true ; he said, namely, that he enjoyed his power most when he did quickly what he wished. There is indeed great danger that he who can do what he wishes may wish what he ought not to do :

> Straightway then was the word, and the deed was forthwith accomplished.[a]

Wickedness, when by reason of power it possesses rapid speed, forces every passion to emerge, making of anger murder, of love adultery, of covetousness confiscation.

[a] Homer, *Il.* xix. 242.

---

[a] νεύρα τοῖς Stobaeus : ἀνιάτοις.

(782)   αὐτίκ᾽ ἔπειθ᾽ ἅμα μῦθος ἔην,

καὶ ἀπόλωλεν ὁ προσκρούσας· ὑπόνοια, καὶ τέθνη-
D κεν ὁ διαβληθείς. ἀλλ᾽ ὥσπερ οἱ φυσικοὶ λέγουσι
τὴν ἀστραπὴν τῆς βροντῆς ὑστέραν μὲν ἐκπίπτειν
ὡς αἷμα τραύματος, προτέραν δὲ φαίνεσθαι, τὸν
μὲν ψόφον ἐκδεχομένης τῆς ἀκοῆς τῷ δὲ φωτὶ τῆς
ὄψεως ἀπαντώσης· οὕτως ἐν ταῖς ἀρχαῖς φθάνουσιν
αἱ κολάσεις τὰς κατηγορίας καὶ προεκπίπτουσιν αἱ
καταδίκαι τῶν ἀποδείξεων.

εἴκει[1] γὰρ ἤδη θυμὸς οὐδ᾽[2] ἔτ᾽ ἀντέχει,
θινῶδες ὡς ἄγκιστρον ἀγκύρας σάλῳ,[3]

ἂν μὴ βάρος ἔχων ὁ λογισμὸς ἐπιθλίβῃ καὶ πιέζῃ
τὴν ἐξουσίαν, μιμουμένου τὸν ἥλιον τοῦ ἄρχοντος,
E ὃς ὅταν ὕψωμα λάβῃ μέγιστον, ἐξαρθεὶς ἐν τοῖς
βορείοις, ἐλάχιστα κινεῖται, τῷ σχολαιοτέρῳ τὸν
δρόμον εἰς ἀσφαλὲς καθιστάμενος.

7. Οὐδὲ γὰρ λαθεῖν οἷόν τε τὰς κακίας ἐν ταῖς
ἐξουσίαις· ἀλλὰ τοὺς μὲν ἐπιληπτικούς, ἂν ἐν ὕψει
τινὶ γένωνται καὶ περιενεχθῶσιν, ἴλιγγος ἴσχει καὶ
σάλος, ἐξελέγχων τὸ πάθος αὐτῶν, τοὺς δ᾽ ἀπαι-
δεύτους καὶ ἀμαθεῖς ἡ τύχη μικρὸν ἐκκουφίσασα
πλούτοις τισὶν ἢ δόξαις ἢ ἀρχαῖς μετεώρους γενομένους εὐθὺς ἐπιδείκνυσι πίπτοντας· μᾶλλον
δ᾽, ὥσπερ τῶν κενῶν ἀγγείων οὐκ ἂν διαγνοίης
τὸ ἀκέραιον καὶ πεπονηκός, ἀλλ᾽ ὅταν ἐγχέῃς,
F φαίνεται τὸ ῥέον· οὕτως αἱ σαθραὶ ψυχαὶ τὰς
ἐξουσίας μὴ στέγουσαι ῥέουσιν ἔξω ταῖς ἐπιθυμίαις,
ταῖς ὀργαῖς, ταῖς ἀλαζονείαις, ταῖς ἀπειροκαλίαις.

[1] εἴκει F. G. Schmidt; cf. Moralia, 446 A : ἐκεῖ.
[2] οὐδ᾽ Moralia, 446 A : οὐκ.
[3] σάλῳ ibid.: σάλον (σάλων V[2]).

> Straightway then was the word,

and the offender is done away with ; suspicion arises, the man who is slandered is put to death. But as the physicists say that the lightning breaks forth later than the thunder, as the flowing of blood is later than the wound, but is seen sooner, since the hearing waits for the sound, whereas the sight goes to meet the light ; so in governments punishments come before the accusations and convictions are pronounced before the proofs are given.

> For now the spirit yields and holds no longer firm,
> As yields the anchor's fluke in sand when waves are high,[a]

unless the weight of reason presses upon power and holds it down, and the ruler imitates the sun, which, when it mounts up in the northern sky and reaches its greatest altitude, has the least motion, thus by greater slowness ensuring the safety of its course.

7. Nor is it possible in positions of power for vices to be concealed. Epileptics, if they go up to a high place and move about, grow dizzy and reel, which makes their disease evident; and just so Fortune by such things as riches, reputations, or offices exalts uneducated and uncultured men a little and then, as soon as they have risen high, gives them a conspicuous fall ; or, to use a better simile, just as in a number of vessels you could not tell which is whole and which is defective, but when you pour liquid into them the leak appears, just so corrupt souls cannot contain power, but leak out in acts of desire, anger, imposture, and bad taste. But what is the use of

---

[a] From a work of an unknown tragic poet ; see Nauck, *Trag. Graec. Frag.* p. 911, no. 379 ; *cf. Moralia*, 446 A.

(782) καίτοι¹ τί δεῖ ταῦτα λέγειν, ὅπου καὶ τὰ σμικρότατα τῶν ἐλλειμμάτων περὶ τοὺς ἐπιφανεῖς καὶ ἐνδόξους συκοφαντεῖται; Κίμωνος ἦν ὁ οἶνος διαβολή, Σκιπίωνος ὁ ὕπνος, Λεύκολλος ἐπὶ τῷ δειπνεῖν πολυτελέστερον ἤκουε κακῶς * * *

¹ καίτοι Reiske: καὶ.

saying these things, when even the slightest short-comings in men of conspicuous reputation are made the subject of calumny ? Too much wine caused slander against Cimon, too much sleep against Scipio, Lucullus was ill spoken of because his dinners were too expensive . . .

WHETHER AN OLD MAN SHOULD ENGAGE IN PUBLIC AFFAIRS
(AN SENI RESPUBLICA GERENDA SIT)

INTRODUCTION

EUPHANES, to whom this essay is addressed, is known from no other source. That he and Plutarch were aged men when the essay was written appears from the opening sentences (see also Chapter 17, towards the end, 792 F). He was evidently a man of some distinction at Athens, where he held important offices (Chapter 20, 794 B). It is not unlikely that he may have asked Plutarch's advice about retiring from public life and that this essay is in reply to his appeal, but there is no definite statement to that effect. Cicero's *Cato Maior* or *De Senectute* differs from this in not being limited to the discussion of old age in its relation to public activities, but the two essays have much in common and may well be read in connexion with each other.

B   1. "Οτι μέν, ὦ Εὔφανες, ἐπαινέτης ὢν Πινδάρου
πολλάκις ἔχεις διὰ στόματος ὡς εἰρημένον εὖ καὶ
πιθανῶς ὑπ᾽ αὐτοῦ

> τιθεμένων ἀγώνων πρόφασις
> ἀρετὰν ἐς[1] αἰπὺν ἔβαλε σκότον,

οὐκ ἀγνοοῦμεν. ἐπειδὴ δὲ πλείστας αἱ πρὸς τοὺς
πολιτικοὺς ἀγῶνας ἀποκνήσεις καὶ μαλακίαι προ-
φάσεις ἔχουσαι τελευταίαν ὥσπερ τὴν " ἀφ᾽ ἱερᾶς "
ἐπάγουσιν ἡμῖν τὸ γῆρας, καὶ μάλιστα δὴ τούτῳ
τὸ φιλότιμον ἀμβλύνειν καὶ δυσωπεῖν δοκοῦσαι
πείθουσιν εἶναί τινα πρέπουσαν οὐκ ἀθλητικῆς
μόνον ἀλλὰ καὶ πολιτικῆς περιόδου κατάλυσιν·
C οἴομαι δεῖν ἃ πρὸς ἐμαυτὸν ἑκάστοτε λογίζομαι καὶ
πρὸς σὲ διελθεῖν περὶ τῆς πρεσβυτικῆς πολιτείας·
ὅπως μηδέτερος ἀπολείψει τὴν μακρὰν συνοδίαν
μέχρι δεῦρο κοινῇ προερχομένην μηδὲ τὸν πολιτικὸν βίον ὥσπερ ἡλικιώτην καὶ συνήθη φίλον

---

[1] ἐς Pindar: εἰς.

---

[a] Pindar, ed. Bergk-Schroeder, p. 475, no. 228 (252).
[b] In one form of the game of draughts the " pieces " or
" men " stood on lines, of which there were five for each of
the two players.   One of these, perhaps the middle one, was

WHETHER AN OLD MAN SHOULD ENGAGE IN PUBLIC AFFAIRS

1. WE are well aware, Euphanes, that you, who are an outspoken admirer of Pindar, often repeat, as well and convincingly expressed, these lines of his,

> When contests are before us, an excuse
> Casts down our manhood into abysmal gloom.[a]

But inasmuch as our shrinking from the contests of political life and our various infirmities furnish innumerable excuses and offer us finally, like " the move from the sacred line " [b] in draughts, old age ; and since it is more especially because of this last that these excuses seem to blunt and baffle our ambition and begin to convince us that there is a fitting limit of age, not only to the athlete's career, but to the statesman's as well, I therefore think it my duty to discuss with you the thoughts which I am continually going over in my own mind concerning the activity of old men in public affairs, that neither of us shall desert the long companionship in the journey which we have thus far made together, and neither shall renounce public life, which is, as it were, a familiar friend of our own

called the " sacred line." The expression as here used seems to be about equivalent to " playing the highest trump."

(783) ἀπορρίψας μεταβαλεῖται[1] πρὸς ἄλλον ἀσυνήθη καὶ
χρόνον οὐκ ἔχοντα συνήθη γενέσθαι καὶ οἰκεῖον,
ἀλλ' ἐμμενοῦμεν οἷς ἀπ' ἀρχῆς προειλόμεθα, ταὐτὸ
τοῦ ζῆν καὶ τοῦ καλῶς ζῆν ποιησάμενοι πέρας·
εἴ γε δὴ μὴ μέλλοιμεν ἐν βραχεῖ τῷ λειπομένῳ τὸν
πολὺν ἐλέγχειν χρόνον, ὡς ἐπ' οὐδενὶ καλῷ μάτην
ἀνηλωμένον.

D   Οὐ γὰρ ἡ τυραννίς, ὥς τις εἶπε Διονυσίῳ,
καλὸν ἐντάφιον· ἀλλ' ἐκείνῳ γε τὴν μοναρχίαν
μετὰ τῆς ἀδικίας τό γε μὴ παύσασθαι συμφορὰν
τελεωτέραν ἐποίησε. καὶ καλῶς[2] Διογένης ὕστερον
ἐν Κορίνθῳ τὸν υἱὸν αὐτοῦ θεασάμενος ἰδιώτην
ἐκ τυράννου γεγενημένον "ὡς ἀναξίως," ἔφη,
"Διονύσιε, σεαυτοῦ πράττεις· οὐ γὰρ ἐνταῦθά
σε μεθ' ἡμῶν ἔδει ζῆν ἐλευθέρως καὶ ἀδεῶς,
ἀλλ' ἐκεῖ τοῖς τυραννείοις ἐγκατῳκοδομημένον
ὥσπερ ὁ πατὴρ ἄχρι γήρως ἐγκαταβιῶσαι."
πολιτεία δὲ δημοκρατικὴ καὶ νόμιμος ἀνδρὸς
εἰθισμένου παρέχειν αὐτὸν οὐχ ἧττον ἀρχόμενον
E ὠφελίμως ἢ ἄρχοντα καλὸν ἐντάφιον ὡς ἀληθῶς
τὴν ἀπὸ τοῦ βίου δόξαν τῷ θανάτῳ προστίθησι·
τοῦτο γὰρ

ἔσχατον δύεται κατὰ γᾶς

ὥς φησι Σιμωνίδης, πλὴν ὧν προαποθνήσκει τὸ
φιλάνθρωπον καὶ φιλόκαλον καὶ προαπαυδᾷ τῆς
τῶν ἀναγκαίων ἐπιθυμίας ὁ τῶν καλῶν ζῆλος, ὡς
τὰ πρακτικὰ μέρη καὶ θεῖα τῆς ψυχῆς ἐξιτηλότερα
τῶν παθητικῶν καὶ σωματικῶν ἐχούσης· ὅπερ[3]

---

[1] μεταβαλεῖται Duebner: μεταβάληται.
[2] καλῶς Emperius: καθῶς.
[3] ὅπερ] διόπερ Wyttenbach.

years, only to change and adopt another which is unfamiliar and for becoming familiar with which and making it our own time does not suffice, but that we shall abide by the choice which we made in the beginning when we fixed the same end and aim for life as for honourable life—unless indeed we were in the short time remaining to us to prove that the long time we have lived was spent in vain and for no honourable purpose.

For the fact is that tyranny, as someone said to Dionysius, is not an honourable winding-sheet [a]; no, and in his case its continuance made his unjust monarchy a more complete misfortune. And at a later time, at Corinth, when Diogenes saw the son of Dionysius no longer a tyrant but a private citizen, he very aptly said, "How unworthy of yourself, Dionysius, your conduct is! For you ought not to be living here with us in freedom and without fear, but you should pass your life to old age over yonder walled up in the royal palace, as your father did." But a democratic and legal government, by a man who has accustomed himself to be ruled for the public good no less than to rule, gives to his death the fair fame won in life as in very truth an honourable winding-sheet; for this, as Simonides [b] says,

> last of all descends below the ground,

except in the case of those whose love of mankind and of honour dies first, and whose zeal for what is noble fails before their desire for material necessities, as if the active and divine qualities of the soul were less enduring than the passive and physical. And

---

[a] *Cf.* Isocrates, vi. 125.
[b] Bergk, *Poet. Lyr. Graec.* iii. p. 417, no. 63 (104).

οὐδὲ λέγειν καλὸν οὐδ' ἀποδέχεσθαι τῶν λεγόντων,
F ὡς κερδαίνοντες μόνον οὐ κοπιῶμεν· ἀλλὰ καὶ τὸ
τοῦ Θουκυδίδου παράγειν ἐπὶ τὸ βέλτιον, μὴ τὸ
φιλότιμον ἀγήρων[1] μόνον ἡγουμένους, ἀλλὰ μᾶλλον τὸ κοινωνικὸν καὶ πολιτικόν, ὃ καὶ μύρμηξιν
ἄχρι τέλους παραμένει καὶ μελίτταις· οὐδεὶς
γὰρ πώποτ'[2] εἶδεν[3] ὑπὸ γήρως κηφῆνα γενομένην
μέλιτταν, ὥσπερ ἔνιοι τοὺς πολιτικοὺς ἀξιοῦσιν,
ὅταν παρακμάσωσιν, οἴκοι σιτουμένους καθῆσθαι
καὶ ἀποκεῖσθαι, καθάπερ ἰῷ σίδηρον ὑπ' ἀργίας
τὴν πρακτικὴν ἀρετὴν σβεννυμένην περιορῶντας.
784 ὁ γὰρ Κάτων ἔλεγεν, ὅτι πολλὰς ἰδίας ἔχοντι τῷ
γήρᾳ κῆρας οὐ δεῖ τὴν ἀπὸ τῆς κακίας ἑκόντας
ἐπάγειν αἰσχύνην· πολλῶν δὲ κακιῶν οὐδεμιᾶς
ἧττον ἀπραξία καὶ δειλία καὶ μαλακία καταισχύ-
νουσιν ἄνδρα πρεσβύτην, ἐκ πολιτικῶν ἀρχείων
καταδυόμενον εἰς οἰκουρίαν γυναικῶν ἢ κατ'
ἀγρὸν ἐφορῶντα καλαμητρίδας[4] καὶ θεριστάς·

ὁ δ' Οἰδίπους ποῦ καὶ τὰ κλείν' αἰνίγματα;

Τὸ μὲν γὰρ ἐν γήρᾳ πολιτείας ἄρχεσθαι καὶ μὴ
πρότερον, ὥσπερ Ἐπιμενίδην λέγουσι κατακοιμη-
θέντα νεανίαν ἐξεγρέσθαι γέροντα μετὰ πεντήκοντα

---

[1] ἀγήρων Thucydides, ii. 44. 4: ἀγήρω.
[2] πώποτε from Stobaeus, xlv. 20.
[3] εἶδεν ibid.: οἶδεν.
[4] καλαμητρίδας Coraes: καλαμητρίας.

---

[a] Thucydides, ii. 44. 4. Pericles, in his great oration over
the Athenians who fell in war, says "The love of honour
alone never grows old, and in the useless time of old age

it is not right to say, or to accept when said by others, that the only time when we do not grow weary is when we are making money. On the contrary, we ought even to emend the saying of Thucydides [a] and believe, not only that "the love of honour never grows old," but that the same is even truer of the spirit of service to the community and the State, which persists to the end even in ants and bees. For no one ever saw a bee that had on account of age become a drone, as some people claim that public men, when they have passed their prime, should sit down in retirement at home and be fed, allowing their worth in action to be extinguished by idleness as iron is destroyed by rust. Cato,[b] for example, used to say that we ought not voluntarily to add to the many evils of its own which belong to old age the disgrace that comes from baseness. And of the many forms of baseness none disgraces an aged man more than idleness, cowardice, and slackness, when he retires from public offices to the domesticity befitting women or to the country where he oversees the harvesters and the women who work as gleaners.

> But Oedipus, where is he and his riddles famed?[c]

For as to beginning public life in old age and not before (as they say that Epimenides slept while a youth and awoke as an aged man after fifty years),

---

the greatest pleasure is not, as some say, in gaining money, but in being honoured."

[b] See *Life of Cato the Elder*, ix. 10.

[c] Euripides, *Phoen.* 1688. This line is spoken by Antigonê to her blind father Oedipus. Plutarch seems to imply that the old man who enters political life without experience is no better off than was Oedipus, in spite of his famous solution of the riddle of the sphinx, when exposed to the vicissitudes of exile.

B ἔτη· εἶτα τὴν[1] οὕτω μακρὰν καὶ συμβεβιωκυῖαν[2]
(784) ἡσυχίαν ἀποθέμενον ἐμβαλεῖν ἑαυτὸν εἰς ἀγῶνας
καὶ ἀσχολίας, ἀήθη καὶ ἀγύμναστον ὄντα καὶ μήτε
πράγμασιν ἐνωμιληκότα πολιτικοῖς μήτ' ἀνθρώποις, ἴσως ἂν αἰτιωμένῳ τινὶ παράσχοι τὸ τῆς
Πυθίας εἰπεῖν " ὄψ'[3] ἦλθες " ἀρχὴν καὶ δημαγωγίαν
διζήμενος, καὶ παρ' ὥραν στρατηγίου κόπτεις
θύραν, ὥσπερ τις ἀτεχνότερος ὢν νύκτωρ ἐπί-
κωμος ἀφιγμένος, ἢ ξένος οὐ τόπον οὐδὲ χώραν
ἀλλὰ βίον, οὗ μὴ πεπείρασαι, μεταλλάττων. τὸ γὰρ
" πόλις ἄνδρα διδάσκει " κατὰ Σιμωνίδην ἀληθές
ἐστιν ἐπὶ τῶν ἔτι χρόνον ἐχόντων μεταδιδαχθῆναι
καὶ μεταμαθεῖν μάθημα, διὰ πολλῶν ἀγώνων καὶ
C πραγμάτων μόλις ἐκπονούμενον, ἅπερ ἐν καιρῷ
φύσεως ἐπιλάβηται καὶ πόνον ἐνεγκεῖν καὶ δυσ-
ημερίαν εὐκόλως δυναμένης. ταῦτα δόξει τις μὴ
κακῶς λέγεσθαι πρὸς τὸν ἀρχόμενον ἐν γήρᾳ
πολιτείας.

2. Καίτοι τοὐναντίον ὁρῶμεν ὑπὸ τῶν νοῦν
ἐχόντων τὰ μειράκια καὶ τοὺς νέους ἀποτρεπο-
μένους τοῦ τὰ κοινὰ πράττειν· καὶ μαρτυροῦσιν
οἱ νόμοι διὰ τοῦ κήρυκος ἐν ταῖς ἐκκλησίαις οὐκ
Ἀλκιβιάδας οὐδὲ Πυθέας ἀνιστάντες ἐπὶ τὸ βῆμα
πρώτους, ἀλλὰ τοὺς ὑπὲρ πεντήκοντ' ἔτη γεγονό-
D τας, λέγειν καὶ συμβουλεύειν παρακαλοῦντες· οὐ
γὰρ τοιούτους[4] ἀήθεια τόλμης καὶ τριβῆς ἔνδεια

---

[1] εἶτα τὴν Bernardakis: οὔτ' ἂν.
[2] συμβεβιωκυῖαν Reiske: συμβεβηκυῖαν.
[3] ὄψ' Haupt: ὀψέ μ' (or ὄψιμ'?).

and then, after casting off such a long-familiar state
of repose, throwing oneself into strife and time-
absorbing affairs when one is unaccustomed to them
and without practice and is conversant neither with
public affairs nor with public men ; that might give
a fault-finder a chance to quote the Pythia and say,
"Too late you have come " seeking for office and
public leadership, and you are knocking unseasonably
at the door of the praetorium, like some ignorant
man who comes by night in festive condition or a
stranger exchanging, not your place of residence or
your country, but your mode of life for one in which you
have had no experience. For the saying of Simonides, " the State teaches a man," [a] is true for those
who still have time to unlearn what they have been
taught and to learn a new subject which can hardly
be acquired through many struggles and labours,
even if it encounters at the proper time a nature
capable of bearing toil and misery with ease. Such
are the remarks which one may believe are fittingly
addressed to a man who begins public life in his
old age.

2. And yet, on the other hand, we see that the mere
lads and young men are turned away from public
affairs by those who are wise ; and the laws which
are proclaimed by the heralds in the assemblies bear
witness to this, when they call up first to the platform, not the young men like Alcibiades and Pytheas,
but men over fifty years of age, and invite them to
speak and offer advice. For such men are not incited
by lack of the habit of daring or by want of practice

---

[a] Bergk, *Poet. Lyr. Graec.* iii. p. 418, no. 67 (109).

[4] τοιούτους (or τοιοῦτον) Babbitt : τοσοῦτον.

(784) καλεῖ[1] πρὸς τροπαῖον[2] κατ' ἀντιστασιωτῶν.[3] ὁ δὲ
Κάτων μετ' ὀγδοήκοντ' ἔτη δίκην ἀπολογούμενος
ἔφη χαλεπὸν εἶναι βεβιωκότα μετ' ἄλλων ἐν ἄλλοις
ἀπολογεῖσθαι. Καίσαρος δὲ τοῦ καταλύσαντος
Ἀντώνιον οὔτι μικρῷ βασιλικώτερα καὶ δημ-
ωφελέστερα γενέσθαι πολιτεύματα πρὸς τῇ τελευτῇ
πάντες ὁμολογοῦσιν· αὐτὸς δὲ τοὺς νέους ἔθεσι
καὶ νόμοις αὐστηρῶς σωφρονίζων, ὡς ἐθορύβησαν,
" ἀκούσατ'," εἶπε, " νέοι γέροντος οὗ νέου γέροντες
E ἤκουον." ἡ δὲ Περικλέους πολιτεία τὸ μέγιστον
ἐν γήρᾳ κράτος ἔσχεν, ὅτε καὶ τὸν πόλεμον ἄρασθαι
τοὺς Ἀθηναίους ἔπεισε· καὶ προθυμουμένων οὐ
κατὰ καιρὸν μάχεσθαι πρὸς ἑξακισμυρίους ὁπλίτας,
ἐνέστη καὶ διεκώλυσε, μονονοὺ τὰ ὅπλα τοῦ δήμου
καὶ τὰς κλεῖς τῶν πυλῶν ἀποσφραγισάμενος.
ἀλλὰ μὴν ἅ γε Ξενοφῶν περὶ Ἀγησιλάου γέγραφεν,
αὐτοῖς ὀνόμασιν ἄξιόν ἐστι παραθέσθαι· " ποίας
γάρ," φησί, " νεότητος οὐ κρεῖττον τὸ ἐκείνου
γῆρας ἐφάνη; τίς μὲν γὰρ τοῖς ἐχθροῖς ἀκμάζων
οὕτω φοβερὸς ἦν, ὡς Ἀγησίλαος τὸ μήκιστον τοῦ
αἰῶνος ἔχων; τίνος δ' ἐκποδὼν γενομένου μᾶλλον
ἤσθησαν οἱ πολέμιοι ἢ Ἀγησιλάου, καίπερ γηραιοῦ
F τελευτήσαντος; τίς δὲ συμμάχοις θάρσος παρέσχεν
ἢ Ἀγησίλαος, καίπερ ἤδη πρὸς τῷ τέρματι τοῦ
βίου ὤν; τίνα δὲ νέον οἱ φίλοι πλέον ἐπόθησαν
ἢ Ἀγησίλαον γηραιὸν ἀποθανόντα;"

3. Εἶτ' ἐκείνους μὲν τηλικαῦτα πράττειν ὁ
χρόνος οὐκ ἐκώλυεν, ἡμεῖς δ' οἱ νῦν τρυφῶντες ἐν

---

[1] καλεῖ Babbitt : καὶ.
[2] πρὸς τροπαῖον Babbitt : προτρόπαιον.
[3] κατ' ἀντιστασιωτῶν Capps ; κατ' ἀνταγωνιστῶν Babbitt :
ἑκάστῳ στρατιωτῶν.

to try to score a victory over their political opponents. And Cato, when after eighty years he was defendant in a law-suit, said it was difficult when he had lived with one generation to defend himself before another. In the case of the Caesar [a] who defeated Antony, all agree that his political acts towards the end of his life became much more kingly and more useful to the people. And he himself, when the young men made a disturbance as he was rebuking them severely for their manners and customs, said, " Listen, young men, to an old man to whom old men listened when he was young." And the government of Pericles gained its greatest power in his old age, which was the time when he persuaded the Athenians to engage in the war ; and when they were eager to fight at an unfavourable time against sixty thousand heavy-armed men, he interposed and prevented it ; indeed he almost sealed up the arms of the people and the keys of the gates. But what Xenophon has written about Agesilaüs [b] certainly deserves to be quoted word for word : " For what youth," he says, " did not his old age manifestly surpass ? For who in the prime of life was so terrible to his enemies as Agesilaüs at the extreme of old age ? At whose removal were the enemy more pleased than at that of Agesilaüs, although his end came when he was aged ? Who inspired more courage in his allies than Agesilaüs, although he was already near the limit of life ? And what young man was more missed by his friends than Agesilaüs, who was aged when he died ? "

3. Time, then, did not prevent those men from doing such great things ; and shall we of the present

---

[a] *i.e.* Augustus.   [b] Xenophon, *Agesilaüs*, 11. 15.

πολιτείαις, μὴ τυραννίδα μὴ πόλεμόν τινα μὴ
πολιορκίαν ἐχούσαις, ἀπολέμους δ᾽ ἁμίλλας καὶ
φιλοτιμίας νόμῳ τὰ πολλὰ καὶ λόγῳ μετὰ δίκης
785 περαινομένας ἀποδειλιῶμεν; οὐ μόνον στρατηγῶν
τῶν τότε καὶ δημαγωγῶν, ἀλλὰ καὶ ποιητῶν καὶ
σοφιστῶν καὶ ὑποκριτῶν ὁμολογοῦντες εἶναι κα-
κίους· εἴγε Σιμωνίδης μὲν ἐν γήρᾳ χοροῖς ἐνίκα,
ὡς[1] τοὐπίγραμμα δηλοῖ τοῖς τελευταίοις ἔπεσιν·

ἀμφὶ διδασκαλίῃ δὲ Σιμωνίδῃ ἕσπετο κῦδος
ὀγδωκονταέτει παιδὶ Λεωπρέπεος.

Σοφοκλῆς δὲ λέγεται μὲν ὑπὸ παίδων[2] παρανοίας
δίκην φεύγων ἀναγνῶναι τὴν ἐν Οἰδίποδι τῷ ἐπὶ
Κολωνῷ[3] πάροδον, ᾗ ἐστιν ἀρχὴ

εὐίππου, ξένε, τᾶσδε χώρας
ἵκου τὰ κράτιστα γᾶς ἔπαυλα,
τὸν ἀργῆτα Κολωνόν, ἔνθ᾽
ἅ[4] λίγεια μινύρεται
θαμίζουσα μάλιστ᾽ ἀηδὼν
χλωραῖς ὑπὸ βάσσαις.

B θαυμαστοῦ δὲ τοῦ μέλους φανέντος, ὥσπερ ἐκ
θεάτρου τοῦ δικαστηρίου προπεμφθῆναι μετὰ
κρότου καὶ βοῆς τῶν παρόντων. τουτὶ δ᾽ ὁμο-
λογουμένως Σοφοκλέους ἐστὶ τοὐπιγραμμάτιον

ᾠδὴν Ἡροδότῳ τεῦξεν Σοφοκλῆς ἐτέων ὢν
πέντ᾽ ἐπὶ πεντήκοντα.

---

[1] ὡς Bernardakis: καὶ.
[2] παίδων Xylander: πολλῶν.
[3] Κολωνῷ Coraes: Κολωνοῦ.
[4] ἔνθ᾽ ἅ: ἔνθα.

day, who live in luxury in states that are free from
tyranny or any war or siege, be such cowards as to
shirk unwarlike contests and rivalries which are for
the most part terminated justly by law and argument
in accordance with justice, confessing that we are
inferior, not only to the generals and public men of
those days, but to the poets, teachers, and actors as
well ? Yes, if Simonides in his old age won prizes
with his choruses, as the inscription in its last lines
declares :

> But for his skill with the chorus great glory Simonides
>   followed,
> Octogenarian child sprung from Leoprepes' seed.[a]

And it is said that Sophocles, when defending himself against the charge of dementia brought by his
sons,[b] read aloud the entrance song of the chorus in
the *Oedipus at Colonus*, which begins [c] :

> Of this region famed for horses
> Thou hast, stranger, reached the fairest
> Dwellings in the land,
> Bright Colonus. where the sweet-voiced
> Nightingale most loves to warble
> In the verdant groves ;

and the song aroused such admiration that he was
escorted from the court as if from the theatre, with
the applause and shouts of those present. And this
little epigram of Sophocles corroborates the tale :

> Song for Herodotus Sophocles made when the years of
>   his age were
> Five in addition to fifty.[d]

---

[a] Bergk, *Poet. Lyr. Graec.* iii. p. 496, no. 147 (203).
[b] This story, though repeated by several ancient writers,
deserves no credit.
[c] Sophocles, *Oed. Col.* 668-673.
[d] Bergk, *Poet. Lyr. Graec.* ii. p. 245, no. 5.

(785) Φιλήμονα δὲ τὸν κωμικὸν καὶ Ἄλεξιν ἐπὶ τῆς σκηνῆς ἀγωνιζομένους καὶ στεφανουμένους ὁ θάνατος κατέλαβε. Πῶλον δὲ τὸν τραγῳδὸν Ἐρατοσθένης καὶ Φιλόχορος ἱστοροῦσιν ἑβδομή-
C κοντ' ἔτη γεγενημένον ὀκτὼ τραγῳδίας[1] ἐν τέτταρσιν ἡμέραις διαγωνίσασθαι μικρὸν ἔμπροσθεν τῆς τελευτῆς.

4. Ἆρ' οὖν οὐκ αἰσχρόν ἐστι τῶν ἀπὸ σκηνῆς γερόντων τοὺς ἀπὸ τοῦ βήματος ἀγεννεστέρους ὁρᾶσθαι, καὶ τῶν ἱερῶν ὡς ἀληθῶς ἐξισταμένους ἀγώνων ἀποτίθεσθαι τὸ πολιτικὸν πρόσωπον, οὐκ οἶδ' ὁποῖον ἀντιμεταλαμβάνοντας; καὶ γὰρ τὸ τῆς γεωργίας ἐκ βασιλικοῦ ταπεινόν· ὅπου γὰρ ὁ Δημοσθένης φησὶν ἀνάξια πάσχειν τὴν Πάραλον, ἱερὰν οὖσαν τριήρη, ξύλα καὶ χάρακας καὶ βοσκή-ματα τῷ Μειδίᾳ παρακομίζουσαν, ἦ που πολιτικὸς ἀνὴρ ἀγωνοθεσίας καὶ βοιωταρχίας καὶ τὰς ἐν
D Ἀμφικτύοσι προεδρίας ἀπολιπών, εἶθ' ὁρώμενος ἐν ἀλφίτων καὶ στεμφύλων διαμετρήσει καὶ πόκοις προβάτων οὐ παντάπασι δόξει τοῦτο δὴ τὸ καλού-μενον " ἵππου γῆρας " ἐπάγεσθαι, μηδενὸς ἀναγ-κάζοντος; ἐργασίας γε μὴν βαναύσου καὶ ἀγο-ραίας ἅπτεσθαι μετὰ πολιτείαν[2] ὅμοιόν ἐστι τῷ γυναικὸς ἐλευθέρας καὶ σώφρονος ἔνδυμα περι-σπάσαντα καὶ περίζωμα δόντα συνέχειν ἐπὶ

---

[1] τραγῳδίας] τραγῳδίαις Hartman.
[2] πολιτείαν Madvig : πολιτείας.

---

[a] Philemon, the chief rival of Menander, was born in 361 and died in 262 B.C. Suidas (s.v. Φιλήμων) states that he died in his sleep at the age of 99 years, the pseudo-Lucian (Macrobioi, 25) that he died of excessive laughter when 97 years old.

[b] There is epigraphic as well as literary evidence for the

88

But Philemon[a] the comic dramatist and Alexis[b] were overtaken by death while they were on the stage acting and being crowned with garlands. And Polus the tragic actor, as Eratosthenes and Philochorus tell us, when he was seventy years old acted in eight tragedies in four days shortly before his death.[c]

4. Is it, then, not disgraceful that the old men of the public platform are found to be less noble than those of the stage, and that they withdraw from the truly sacred contests, put off the political rôle, and assume I do not know what in its stead? For surely after the rôle of a king that of a farmer is a mean one. For when Demosthenes says[d] that the Paralus, being the sacred galley, was unworthily treated when it was used to transport beams, stakes, and cattle for Meidias, will not a public man who gives up such offices as superintendent of public games, Boeotian magistrate, and president of the Amphictyonic council, and is thereafter seen busying himself with measuring flour and olive cakes and with tufts of sheep's wool—will not he be thought to be bringing upon himself "the old age of a horse," as the saying is, when nobody forces him to do so? Surely taking up menial work fit only for the market-place after holding public offices is like stripping a freeborn and modest woman of her gown, putting a cook's apron on her, and keeping her in a tavern; for just so

prolific productiveness and great age of Alexis, the foremost poet of the Middle Comedy, who lived *circa* 376-270 B.C. See Kaibel in Pauly-Wissowa, Suppl. Bd., and *Am. Jour. Phil.* xxi. (1900) pp. 59 ff.

[c] A long list of Greeks who lived to an advanced age is given by B. E. Richardson, *Old Age among the Ancient Greeks*, pp. 215-222.

[d] Demosthenes, xxi. (*Against Meidias*) 568.

καπηλείου· καὶ γὰρ τῆς πολιτικῆς ἀρετῆς οὕτως
ἀπόλλυται τὸ ἀξίωμα καὶ τὸ μέγεθος πρός τινας
E οἰκονομίας καὶ χρηματισμοὺς ἀγομένης. ἂν δ',
ὅπερ λοιπόν ἐστι, ῥᾳστώνας καὶ ἀπολαύσεις τὰς
ἡδυπαθείας καὶ τὰς τρυφὰς ὀνομάζοντες ἐν ταύταις
μαραινόμενον ἡσυχῇ παρακαλῶσι γηράσκειν τὸν
πολιτικόν, οὐκ οἶδα ποτέρᾳ δυεῖν εἰκόνων αἰσχρῶν
πρέπειν δόξει μᾶλλον ὁ βίος αὐτοῦ· πότερον
ἀφροδίσια ναύταις ἄγουσι πάντα τὸν λοιπὸν ἤδη
χρόνον οὐκ ἐν λιμένι τὴν ναῦν ἔχουσιν ἀλλ' ἔτι
πλέουσαν ἀπολείπουσιν· ἢ καθάπερ ἔνιοι τὸν
Ἡρακλέα παίζοντες οὐκ εὖ γράφουσιν ἐν Ὀμφάλης
κροκωτοφόρον ἐνδιδόντα Λυδαῖς θεραπαινίσι ῥιπί-
ζειν καὶ παραπλέκειν ἑαυτόν, οὕτω τὸν πολιτικὸν
F ἐκδύσαντες τὴν λεοντὴν καὶ κατακλίναντες εὐ-
ωχήσομεν ἀεὶ καταψαλλόμενον καὶ καταυλούμενον,
οὐδὲ τῇ τοῦ Πομπηΐου Μάγνου φωνῇ διατραπέντες
τῇ πρὸς Λεύκολλον[1] αὐτὸν μὲν εἰς λουτρὰ καὶ
δεῖπνα καὶ συνουσίας μεθημερινὰς καὶ πολὺν ἄλυν
καὶ κατασκευὰς οἰκοδομημάτων νεοπρεπεῖς μετὰ
τὰς στρατείας καὶ πολιτείας ἀφεικότα, τῷ δὲ
Πομπηΐῳ φιλαρχίαν ἐγκαλοῦντα καὶ φιλοτιμίαν
παρ' ἡλικίαν· ἔφη γὰρ ὁ Πομπήϊος ἀωρότερον
786 εἶναι γέροντι τὸ τρυφᾶν ἢ τὸ ἄρχειν· ἐπεὶ δὲ
νοσοῦντι συνέταξε κίχλην ὁ ἰατρός, ἣν δὲ δυσπόρι-
στον καὶ παρ' ὥραν, ἔφη δέ τις εἶναι παρὰ Λευκόλλῳ
πολλὰς τρεφομένας, οὐκ ἔπεμψεν οὐδ' ἔλαβεν
εἰπών, "οὐκοῦν, εἰ μὴ Λεύκολλος ἐτρύφα, Πομπήϊος
οὐκ ἂν ἔζησε;"

5. Καὶ γὰρ εἰ ζητεῖ πάντως ἡ φύσις τὸ ἡδὺ καὶ

---

[1] Λεύκολλον Duebner: λεύκολλον ἦν εἶπεν.

the dignity and greatness of high ability in public life is destroyed when it is turned to household affairs and money-making. But if—the only thing left—they give to self-indulgence and luxury the names of rest and recreation, and urge the statesman quietly to waste away and grow old in them, I do not know which of two disgraceful pictures his life will seem to resemble more closely, that of sailors who desert their ship, when they have not brought it into the harbour but it is still under sail, and devote themselves to sexual indulgence for all time to come, or that of Heracles, as some painters playfully, but with evil influence, represent him in Omphalê's palace wearing a yellow gown and giving himself up to her Lydian maids to be fanned and have his hair curled. Shall we in like manner strip the statesman of his lion's skin and make him constantly recline at banquets to the music of harps and flutes ? And shall we not be deterred by the words addressed by Pompey the Great to Lucullus ? For Lucullus gave himself up after his military activities to baths, banquets, sexual intercourse in the daytime, great listlessness, and the erection of new-fangled buildings ; and he reproached Pompey for his love of office and of honour as unsuited to his age. Then Pompey said that it was more untimely for an old man to indulge in luxury than to hold office. And once when he was ill and the physician prescribed a thrush (which was hard to get and out of season), and someone said that Lucullus had plenty of them in his breeding-place, Pompey refused to send and get one, saying, " Could Pompey, then, not live if Lucullus were not luxurious ? "

5. For granted that nature seeks in every way

(786) τὸ χαίρειν, τὸ μὲν σῶμα τῶν γερόντων ἀπείρηκε
πρὸς πάσας, πλὴν ὀλίγων τῶν ἀναγκαίων, τὰς
ἡδονάς, καὶ οὐχ

ἡ Ἀφροδίτη τοῖς γέρουσιν ἄχθεται

B μόνον, ὡς Εὐριπίδης φησίν, ἀλλὰ καὶ τὰς περὶ
πόσιν καὶ βρῶσιν ἐπιθυμίας ἀπημβλυμμένας[1] τὰ
πολλὰ καὶ νωδὰς κατέχοντες μόλις οἷον ἐπιθήγουσι
καὶ χαράττουσιν· ἐν δὲ τῇ ψυχῇ παρασκευαστέον
ἡδονὰς οὐκ ἀγεννεῖς οὐδ' ἀνελευθέρους, ὡς Σιμωνίδης ἔλεγε πρὸς τοὺς ἐγκαλοῦντας αὐτῷ φιλαργυρίαν, ὅτι τῶν ἄλλων ἀπεστερημένος διὰ τὸ γῆρας
ἡδονῶν ὑπὸ μιᾶς ἔτι γηροβοσκεῖται τῆς ἀπὸ τοῦ
κερδαίνειν. ἀλλ' ἡ πολιτεία καλλίστας μὲν ἡδονὰς
ἔχει καὶ μεγίστας, αἷς καὶ τοὺς θεοὺς εἰκός ἐστιν
ἢ μόναις ἢ μάλιστα χαίρειν· αὗται δ' εἰσίν, ἃς τὸ
εὖ ποιεῖν καὶ καλόν τι πράττειν ἀναδίδωσιν. εἰ
γὰρ Νικίας ὁ ζωγράφος οὕτως ἔχαιρε τοῖς τῆς
C τέχνης ἔργοις, ὥστε τοὺς οἰκέτας ἐρωτᾶν πολλάκις,
εἰ λέλουται καὶ ἠρίστηκεν· Ἀρχιμήδην δὲ τῇ σανίδι
προσκείμενον ἀποσπῶντες βίᾳ καὶ ἀποδύοντες
ἤλειφον οἱ θεράποντες, ὁ δ' ἐπὶ τοῦ σώματος
ἀληλιμμένου διέγραφε τὰ σχήματα· Κάνος[2] δ' ὁ
αὐλητής, ὃν καὶ σὺ γιγνώσκεις, ἔλεγεν ἀγνοεῖν
τοὺς ἀνθρώπους, ὅσῳ μᾶλλον αὐτὸν αὐλῶν ἢ

---

[1] ἀπημβλυμμένας Bernardakis: ἀπημβλυμένας.
[2] Κάνος Life of Galba, chap. xvi.: κανός.

pleasure and enjoyment, old men are physically in-
capacitated for all pleasures except a few necessary
ones, and not only

> Aphroditê with old men is wroth,[a]

as Euripides says, but their appetites also for food
and drink are for the most part blunted and tooth-
less, so that they can, if I may say so, hardly
whet and sharpen them. They ought to prepare
for themselves pleasures in the mind, not ignoble and
illiberal ones like that of Simonides, who said to
those who reproached him for his avarice that, since
old age had deprived him of all other pleasures, he
was comforting his declining years with the only one
left, the pleasure of gain. Public life, on the other
hand, possesses pleasures most noble and great,
those in fact from which the gods themselves, as we
may reasonably suppose, derive their only or their
chief enjoyment. These are the pleasures that
spring from good deeds and noble actions. For if
Nicias the painter took such delight in the labours of
his art that he often had to ask his servants whether
he had had his bath and his breakfast ; and if
Archimedes when intent upon his drawing-tablet had
to be dragged away by force, stripped and anointed
by his servants, and then drew diagrams upon his
anointed body ; and if Canus the flute-player, with
whom you also are acquainted, used to say that
people did not know how much greater pleasure he
gave to himself than to others when he played, for

---

[a] Euripides, *Aeolus*, Frag. 23, Nauck, *Trag. Graec. Frag.*
p. 369. Plutarch, *Moralia* 285 в, gives two lines :

ἀλλ' ἢ τὸ γῆρας τὴν Κύπριν χαίρειν ἐᾷ
ἥ τ' Ἀφροδίτη τοῖς γερούσιν ἄχθεται,

"But either eld to Cypris bids farewell
Or Aphroditê with old men is wroth."

(786) ἑτέρους εὐφραίνει· λαμβάνειν γὰρ ἂν μισθὸν οὐ
διδόναι τοὺς ἀκούειν ἐθέλοντας· ἆρ' οὐκ ἐπινοοῦμεν,
ἡλίκας ἡδονὰς αἱ ἀρεταὶ τοῖς χρωμένοις ἀπὸ τῶν
καλῶν πράξεων καὶ τῶν κοινωνικῶν ἔργων καὶ
φιλανθρώπων παρασκευάζουσιν, οὐ κνῶσαι οὐδὲ
θρύπτουσαι, ὥσπερ αἱ εἰς σάρκα λεῖαι καὶ προσηνεῖς
D γινόμεναι κινήσεις; ἀλλ' αὗται μὲν οἰστρῶδες
καὶ ἀβέβαιον καὶ μεμιγμένον σφυγμῷ τὸ γαργα-
λίζον ἔχουσιν, αἱ δ' ἐπὶ τοῖς καλοῖς ἔργοις, οἵων
δημιουργὸς ὁ πολιτευόμενος ὀρθῶς ἐστιν, οὐ ταῖς
Εὐριπίδου χρυσαῖς πτέρυξιν, ἀλλὰ τοῖς Πλατωνικοῖς
ἐκείνοις καὶ οὐρανίοις πτεροῖς ὅμοια τὴν ψυχὴν
μέγεθος καὶ φρόνημα μετὰ γήθους λαμβάνουσαν
ἀναφέρουσιν.

6. Ὑπομίμνησκε δὲ σεαυτὸν ὧν πολλάκις ἀκή-
κοας· ὁ μὲν γὰρ Ἐπαμεινώνδας ἐρωτηθεὶς τί
ἥδιστον αὐτῷ γέγονεν, ἀπεκρίνατο τὸ τοῦ πατρὸς
ἔτι ζῶντος καὶ τῆς μητρὸς νικῆσαι τὴν ἐν Λεύκτροις
μάχην. ὁ δὲ Σύλλας, ὅτε τῶν ἐμφυλίων πολέμων
E τὴν Ἰταλίαν καθήρας προσέμιξε τῇ Ῥώμῃ
πρῶτον, οὐδὲ μικρὸν ἐν τῇ νυκτὶ κατέδαρθεν, ὑπὸ
γήθους καὶ χαρᾶς μεγάλης ὥσπερ πνεύματος
ἀναφερόμενος τὴν ψυχήν· καὶ ταῦτα περὶ αὑτοῦ
γέγραφεν ἐν τοῖς ὑπομνήμασιν. ἄκουσμα μὲν γὰρ
ἔστω μηδὲν ἥδιον ἐπαίνου κατὰ τὸν Ξενοφῶντα,
θέαμα δὲ καὶ μνημόνευμα καὶ διανόημα τῶν ὄντων
οὐδὲν ἔστιν ὃ τοσαύτην φέρει χάριν, ὅσην πράξεων
ἰδίων ἐν ἀρχαῖς καὶ πολιτείαις ὥσπερ ἐν τόποις
λαμπροῖς καὶ δημοσίοις ἀναθεώρησις. οὐ μὴν

_____

ᵃ Nauck, _Trag. Graec. Frag._ p. 655, no. 911.

if they did, those who wished to hear him would receive pay instead of giving it. In view of these examples, do we not perceive how great are the pleasures the virtues provide, for those who practise them, as the result of the noble deeds they do and their works for the good of the community and of mankind ; and that too without tickling or enervating them as do the smooth and gentle motions made on the body ? Those have a frantic, unsteady titillation mixed with convulsive throbbing, but the pleasures given by noble works, such as those of which the man who rightly serves the State is the author, not like the golden wings of Euripides *a* but like those heavenly Platonic pinions,*b* bear the soul on high as it acquires greatness and lofty spirit mingled with joy.

6. And recall to your mind stories you have often heard. For Epameinondas, when asked what was the pleasantest thing that had happened to him, replied that it was winning the battle of Leuctra while his father and mother were still living. And Sulla, when he first entered Rome after freeing Italy of its civil wars, did not sleep at all that night, he was so borne aloft in spirit by great joy and gladness as by a blast of wind. This he has written about himself in his memoirs. For granted that, as Xenophon *c* says, there is no sound sweeter than praise, yet there is no sight, reminder, or perception in the world which brings such great pleasure as the contemplation of one's own acts in offices and positions of State in which one may be said to be in places flooded with light and in view of all the

b Plato, *Phaedrus*, 246 B–248 E, where the soul is likened to a chariot and charioteer with winged steeds.
c Xenophon, *Memorabilia*, ii. 1. 31.

F ἀλλὰ καὶ χάρις εὐμενὴς συμμαρτυροῦσα[1] τοῖς
ἔργοις καὶ συναμιλλώμενος ἔπαινος, εὐνοίας δικαίας
ἡγεμών, οἷόν τι φῶς καὶ γάνωμα τῷ χαίροντι τῆς
ἀρετῆς προστίθησι· καὶ δεῖ μὴ περιορᾶν ὥσπερ
ἀθλητικὸν στέφανον ἐν γήρᾳ ξηρὰν γενομένην τὴν
δόξαν, ἀλλὰ καινὸν ἀεί τι καὶ πρόσφατον ἐπιφέροντα
τὴν τῶν παλαιῶν χάριν ἐγείρειν καὶ ποιεῖν ἀμείνω
καὶ μόνιμον· ὥσπερ οἱ τεχνῖται, οἷς ἐπέκειτο
φροντίζειν σῶον εἶναι τὸ Δηλιακὸν πλοῖον, ἀντὶ
τῶν πονούντων ξύλων ἐμβάλλοντες ἄλλα καὶ συμ-
πηγνύντες ἀίδιον ἐκ τῶν τότε χρόνων καὶ ἄφθαρτον
787 ἐδόκουν διαφυλάττειν. ἔστι δὲ καὶ δόξης καὶ
φλογὸς οὐ χαλεπὴ σωτηρία καὶ τήρησις ἀλλὰ
μικρῶν ὑπεκκαυμάτων δεομένη, κατασβεσθὲν δὲ
καὶ ὑποψυχθὲν οὐδέτερον ἄν τις ἀπραγμόνως πάλιν
ἐξάψειεν. ὡς δὲ Λάμπις ὁ ναύκληρος[2] ἐρωτηθεὶς
πῶς ἐκτήσατο τὸν πλοῦτον " οὐ χαλεπῶς " ἔφη
" τὸν μέγαν, τὸν δὲ βραχὺν ἐπιπόνως καὶ βραδέως ".
οὕτω τῆς πολιτικῆς δόξης καὶ δυνάμεως ἐν ἀρχῇ
τυχεῖν οὐ ῥᾴδιόν ἐστι, τὸ δὲ συναυξῆσαι καὶ δια-
φυλάξαι μεγάλην γενομένην ἀπὸ τῶν τυχόντων
ἕτοιμον.[3] οὔτε γὰρ φίλος ὅταν γένηται πολλὰς
B λειτουργίας ἐπιζητεῖ καὶ μεγάλας, ἵνα μένῃ φίλος,
μικροῖς δὲ σημείοις τὸ ἐνδελεχὲς ἀεὶ διαφυλάττει
τὴν εὔνοιαν· ἥ τε δήμου φιλία καὶ πίστις οὐκ

---

[1] συμμαρτυροῦσα Bernardakis: ἡ μαρτυροῦσα.
[2] ναύκληρος Leonicus: ναυκληρικὸς.
[3] So Wyttenbach: ἀπὸ τῶν τυχόντων γενομένην.

---

[a] By " Delian ship " is meant the *Paralus* which was sent

people. Yes, and moreover kindly gratitude, bearing witness to the acts, and praise, competing with gratitude and ushering in deserved goodwill, add, as it were, a light and brilliance to the joy that comes from virtue. And it is a man's duty not to allow his reputation to become withered in his old age like an athlete's garland, but by adding constantly something new and fresh to arouse the sense of gratitude for his previous actions and make it better and lasting ; just as the artisans who were responsible for keeping the Delian ship [a] in good condition, by inserting and fastening in new timbers to take the place of those which were becoming weak, seemed to keep the vessel from those ancient times everlasting and indestructible. Now the preservation and maintenance of reputation, as of fire, is not difficult and demands little fuel, but no one can without trouble rekindle either of them when it has gone out and grown cold. And just as Lampis the sea captain, when asked how he acquired his wealth, said, " My great wealth easily, but the small beginnings of it slowly and with toil," so political reputation and power are not easy to attain at first, but when once they have grown great it is easy to augment them and keep them great by taking advantage of casual opportunities. For when a man has once become a friend, he does not require many and great services that he may remain a friend, but constancy shown by small tokens always preserves his goodwill, and so likewise the friendship and confidence of the people do

annually from Athens with delegates to the festival at Delos. Annual repairs were so long continued that none of the original timbers remained and the question arose whether it was the same ship or not.

(787) ἀεὶ δεομένη[1] χορηγοῦντος οὐδὲ προδικοῦντος[2] οὐδ'
ἄρχοντος αὐτῇ τῇ προθυμίᾳ συνέχεται καὶ τῷ μὴ
προαπολείποντι μηδ' ἀπαγορεύοντι τῆς ἐπιμελείας
καὶ φροντίδος. οὐδὲ γὰρ αἱ στρατεῖαι παρατάξεις
ἀεὶ καὶ μάχας καὶ πολιορκίας ἔχουσιν, ἀλλὰ καὶ
θυσίας ἔστιν ὅτε καὶ συνουσίας διὰ μέσου καὶ
σχολὴν ἄφθονον ἐν παιδιαῖς καὶ φλυαρίαις δέχονται.
πόθεν γε δὴ τὴν πολιτείαν φοβητέον, ὡς ἀπαρα-
μύθητον καὶ πολύπονον καὶ βαρεῖαν, ὅπου καὶ
θέατρα καὶ πομπαὶ καὶ νεμήσεις καὶ '' χοροὶ καὶ
C Μοῖσα[3] καὶ Ἀγλαΐα '' καὶ θεοῦ τινος ἀεὶ τιμὴ
τὰς ἀφρῦς λύουσα παντὸς ἀρχείου καὶ συνεδρίου
πολλαπλάσιον τὸ ἐπιτερπὲς καὶ κεχαρισμένον ἀπο-
δίδωσιν;

7. Ὁ τοίνυν μέγιστον κακὸν ἔχουσιν αἱ πολιτεῖαι, τὸν φθόνον, ἥκιστα διερείδεται πρὸς τὸ
γῆρας· '' κύνες γὰρ καὶ βαΰζουσιν ὃν ἂν μὴ γινώ-
σκωσι '' καθ' Ἡράκλειτον, καὶ πρὸς τὸν[4] ἀρχόμενον
ὥσπερ ἐν θύραις τοῦ βήματος μάχεται καὶ πάροδον
οὐ δίδωσι· τὴν δὲ σύντροφον καὶ συνήθη δόξαν οὐκ
ἀγρίως οὐδὲ χαλεπῶς ἀλλὰ πράως ἀνέχεται. διὸ
τὸν φθόνον ἔνιοι τῷ καπνῷ παρεικάζουσι· πολὺς
γὰρ ἐν τοῖς ἀρχομένοις διὰ τὸ φλέγεσθαι προεκ-
D πίπτων, ὅταν ἐκλάμψωσιν, ἀφανίζεται. καὶ ταῖς
μὲν ἄλλαις ὑπεροχαῖς προσμάχονται καὶ διαμφισ-
βητοῦσιν ἀρετῆς καὶ γένους καὶ φιλοτιμίας, ὡς

---

[1] δεομένη Jannot: δεχομένη.
[2] προδικοῦντος Jannot: προσδοκῶντος.
[3] Μοῖσα Boeckh: μοῦσα.
[4] τὸν H.N.F.: τὸ.

---

[a] Pindar, Bergk-Schroeder, p. 467, no. 199 (213).

not constantly demand that a man pay for choruses,
plead causes, or hold offices ; no, they are maintained
by his mere readiness to serve and by not failing or
growing weary in care and concern for the people.
For even wars do not consist entirely of pitched
battles, fighting, and sieges, but they admit of
occasional sacrifices, social gatherings in between,
and abundant leisure for games and foolishness.
Why, then, forsooth, is public life feared as inexorable, toilsome, and burdensome, when theatrical
exhibitions, festive processions, distributions of food,
" choruses and the Muse and Aglaïa," [a] and constantly the worship of some god, smooth the brows
of legislators in every senate and assembly and
repay its troubles many times over with pleasure
and enjoyment ?

7. Now the greatest evil attendant upon public life,
envy, is least likely to beset old age, " for dogs do
indeed bark at whom they do not know," according
to Heracleitus, and envy fights against a man as he
begins his public career, at the doorway, as it were,
of the orator's platform, and tries to refuse him
access, but familiar and accustomed reputation it
does not savagely and roughly resent, but puts up
with mildly. For this reason envy is sometimes
likened to smoke, for in the case of those who are
beginning their public career it pours out before
them in great volume because they are enkindled,
but when they burst into full flame it disappears.
And whereas men attack other kinds of eminence
and themselves lay claim to good character, good
birth, and honour, as though they were depriving

Aglaïa, one of the Graces, was especially connected with
festive merriment.

(787) ἀφαιροῦντες αὐτῶν ὅσον ἄλλοις ὑφίενται· τὸ δ'
ἀπὸ τοῦ χρόνου πρωτεῖον, ὃ καλεῖται κυρίως
πρεσβεῖον, ἀζηλοτύπητόν ἐστι καὶ παραχωρούμενον·
οὐδεμιᾷ γὰρ οὕτω τιμῇ συμβέβηκε τὸν τιμῶντα
μᾶλλον ἢ τὸν τιμώμενον κοσμεῖν, ὡς τῇ τῶν
γερόντων. ἔτι τὴν μὲν ἀπὸ τοῦ πλούτου δύναμιν
ἢ λόγου δεινότητος ἢ σοφίας οὐ πάντες αὐτοῖς
γενήσεσθαι προσδοκῶσιν, ἐφ' ἣν δὲ προάγει τὸ
γῆρας αἰδῶ καὶ δόξαν οὐδεὶς ἀπελπίζει τῶν
πολιτευομένων. οὐδὲν οὖν διαφέρει κυβερνήτου
πρὸς ἐναντίον κῦμα καὶ πνεῦμα πλεύσαντος ἐπι-
E σφαλῶς, εὐδίας δὲ καὶ εὐαερίας γενομένης ὁρμί-
σασθαι ζητοῦντος, ὁ τῷ φθόνῳ διαναυμαχήσας
πολὺν χρόνον, εἶτα παυσαμένου καὶ στορεσθέντος,
ἀνακρουόμενος ἐκ τῆς πολιτείας καὶ προϊέμενος
ἅμα ταῖς πράξεσι τὰς κοινωνίας καὶ τὰς ἑταιρείας.
ὅσῳ γὰρ χρόνος γέγονε πλείων, καὶ φίλους πλείονας
καὶ συναγωνιστὰς πεποίηκεν, οὓς οὔτε συνεξάγειν
ἑαυτῷ πάντας ἐνδέχεται καθάπερ διδασκάλῳ χορὸν
F οὔτ' ἐγκαταλείπειν[1] δίκαιον· ἀλλ' ὥσπερ τὰ παλαιὰ
δένδρα τὴν μακρὰν πολιτείαν οὐ ῥάδιόν ἐστιν
ἀνασπάσαι πολύρριζον οὖσαν καὶ πράγμασιν ἐμ-
πεπλεγμένην, ἃ πλείονας παρέχει ταραχὰς καὶ
σπαραγμοὺς ἀπερχομένοις ἢ μένουσιν. εἰ δέ τι
καὶ περίεστι φθόνου λείψανον ἢ φιλονεικίας πρὸς
τοὺς γέροντας ἐκ τῶν πολιτικῶν ἀγώνων, κατα-
σβεστέον τοῦτο τῇ δυνάμει μᾶλλον ἢ δοτέον τὰ
νῶτα, γυμνοὺς καὶ ἀόπλους[2] ἀπιόντας· οὐ γὰρ

---

[1] ἐγκαταλείπειν Bernardakis : ἐγκαταλιπεῖν.
[2] ἀόπλους Bernardakis : ἀνόπλους.

themselves of so much of these as they grant to others ; yet the primacy which comes from time, for which there is the special word *presbeion* or " the prerogative due to seniority in age," arouses no jealousy and is freely conceded ; for of no honour is it so true that it adorns the giver more than the receiver as of that which is paid to old age. Moreover, not all men expect that the power derived from wealth, eloquence, or wisdom will accrue to them, but no one who takes part in public life is without hope of attaining the reverence and repute to which old age leads. So there is no difference between the pilot who has sailed in great danger against adverse winds and waves, and, after clear weather and fair winds have come, seeks his moorings, and the man who has struggled in the ship of State a long time against the billows of envy, and then, when they have ceased and become smooth, backs water and withdraws from public life, giving up his political affiliations and clubs along with his public activities. For the longer the time has been the greater the number of those whom he has made his friends and fellow-workers, and he cannot take them all out with him, as a trainer leads out his chorus, nor is it fair to leave them in the lurch. But a long public career is, like old trees, hard to pull up, for it has many roots and is interwoven with affairs which cause more troubles and torments to those who withdraw from them than to those who remain in them. And if any remnant of envy or jealousy does continue against old men from their political contests, they should rather extinguish this by power than turn their backs and go away naked and unarmed. For people

οὕτως ἀγωνιζομένοις φθονοῦντες ὡς ἀπειπαμένοις
καταφρονήσαντες ἐπιτίθενται.

788   8. Μαρτυρεῖ δὲ καὶ τὸ λεχθὲν ὑπ' Ἐπαμεινώνδα
τοῦ μεγάλου πρὸς τοὺς Θηβαίους, ὅτε χειμῶνος
ὄντος οἱ Ἀρκάδες παρεκάλουν αὐτοὺς ἐν ταῖς οἰκίαις
διαιτᾶσθαι παρελθόντας εἰς τὴν πόλιν· οὐ γὰρ
εἴασεν, ἀλλὰ "νῦν μέν," ἔφη, "θαυμάζουσιν ὑμᾶς
καὶ θεῶνται πρὸς τὰ ὅπλα γυμναζομένους καὶ
παλαίοντας· ἂν δὲ πρὸς τῷ πυρὶ καθημένους ὁρῶσι
τὸν κύαμον κάπτοντας,[1] οὐδὲν αὐτῶν ἡγήσονται
διαφέρειν." οὕτω δὴ σεμνόν ἐστι θέαμα πρεσβύτης
B λέγων τι καὶ πράττων καὶ τιμώμενος, ὁ δ' ἐν κλίνῃ
διημερεύων ἢ καθήμενος ἐν γωνίᾳ στοᾶς φλυαρῶν
καὶ ἀπομυττόμενος εὐκαταφρόνητος. τοῦτο δ'
ἀμέλει καὶ Ὅμηρος διδάσκει τοὺς ὀρθῶς ἀκούοντας·
ὁ μὲν γὰρ Νέστωρ στρατευόμενος ἐν Τροίᾳ σεμνὸς
ἦν καὶ πολυτίμητος, ὁ δὲ Πηλεὺς καὶ ὁ Λαέρτης
οἰκουροῦντες ἀπερρίφησαν καὶ κατεφρονήθησαν.
οὐδὲ γὰρ ἡ τοῦ φρονεῖν ἕξις ὁμοίως παραμένει τοῖς
μεθεῖσιν αὐτούς, ἀλλ' ὑπ' ἀργίας ἐξανιεμένη καὶ
ἀναλυομένη κατὰ μικρὸν ἀεί τινα ποθεῖ φροντίδος
μελέτην, τὸ λογιστικὸν καὶ πρακτικὸν ἐγειρούσης
καὶ διακαθαιρούσης·

λάμπει γὰρ ἐν χρείαισιν, ὥσπερ εὐπρεπὴς
χαλκός.

C οὐ γὰρ τόσον σώματος ἀσθένεια κακὸν πρόσεστι
ταῖς πολιτείαις τῶν παρ' ἡλικίαν ἐπὶ τὸ βῆμα καὶ
τὸ στρατήγιον βαδιζόντων, ὅσον ἔχουσιν ἀγαθὸν

---

[1] κάπτοντας Coraes : κόπτοντας.

do not attack them so much because of envy if they maintain the contest as because of contempt if they have given up.

8. Testimony to the point is what Epameinondas the Great said to the Thebans when in winter weather the Arcadians invited them to come into the city and be quartered in their houses. He forbade it, saying " Now they admire you and gaze at you as you do your military exercises and wrestle, but if they see you sitting by the fire and gobbling your bean porridge, they will think you are no better than they are." Just so an old man active in word and deed and held in honour is a sight to arouse reverence, but one who spends the day in bed or sits in the corner of the porch chattering and wiping his nose is an object of contempt. And undoubtedly Homer also teaches this to those who hear aright, for Nestor, who went to the war at Troy, was revered and highly honoured, but Peleus and Laërtes, who stayed at home, were put aside and despised. For the habit of prudence does not last so well in those who let themselves become slack, but, being gradually lost and dissipated by inactivity, it always calls for what may be called exercise of the thought, since thought rouses and purifies the power of reason and action ;

For when in use it gleams like beauteous bronze.[a]

For the evil caused by their physical weakness to the public activities of those who step into civil or military office when beyond the usual age is not so great as the advantage they possess in their caution and

---

[a] From an unknown drama of Sophocles ; Nauck, *Trag. Graec. Frag.* p. 314, no. 780 ; it is quoted in fuller form in *Moralia,* 792 A and 1129 c.

(788) τὴν εὐλάβειαν καὶ τὴν φρόνησιν, καὶ τὸ μὴ φερόμενον,[1] ἄλλοτε[2] μὲν δι᾽[3] ἐσφαλμένα ὅτε δ᾽[4] ὑπὸ δόξης
κενῆς, προσπίπτειν πρὸς τὰ κοινὰ καὶ συνεφέλκεσθαι
τὸν ὄχλον, ὥσπερ θάλατταν ὑπὸ πνευμάτων ἐκ-
ταραττόμενον, ἀλλὰ πράως τε χρῆσθαι[5] καὶ μετρίως
τοῖς ἐντυγχάνουσιν. ὅθεν αἱ πόλεις, ὅταν πταί-
σωσιν ἢ φοβηθῶσι, πρεσβυτέρων ποθοῦσιν ἀρχὴν
D ἀνθρώπων· καὶ πολλάκις ἐξ ἀγροῦ κατάγουσαι
γέροντα μὴ δεόμενον μηδὲ βουλόμενον ἠνάγκασαν
ὥσπερ οἰάκων ἐφαψάμενον εἰς ἀσφαλὲς καταστῆσαι
τὰ πράγματα, παρωσάμεναί τε στρατηγοὺς καὶ
δημαγωγοὺς βοᾶν μέγα καὶ λέγειν ἀπνευστὶ καὶ νὴ
Δία τοῖς πολεμίοις διαβάντας εὖ μάχεσθαι δυνα-
μένους· οἷον οἱ ῥήτορες Ἀθήνησι Τιμοθέῳ καὶ
Ἰφικράτει Χάρητα τὸν Θεοχάρους ἐπαποδύοντες
ἀκμάζοντα τῷ σώματι καὶ ῥωμαλέον ἠξίουν τοιοῦτον εἶναι τὸν τῶν Ἀθηναίων στρατηγόν, ὁ
E δὲ Τιμόθεος "οὐ μὰ τοὺς θεούς," εἶπεν, "ἀλλὰ
τοιοῦτον μὲν εἶναι τὸν μέλλοντα τῷ στρατηγῷ τὰ
στρώματα κομίζειν, τὸν δὲ στρατηγόν ' ἅμα πρόσω
καὶ ὀπίσω ' τῶν πραγμάτων ὁρῶντα καὶ μηδενὶ
πάθει τοὺς περὶ τῶν συμφερόντων λογισμοὺς ἐπι-
ταραττόμενον." ὁ γὰρ Σοφοκλῆς ἄσμενος ἔφη τὰ
ἀφροδίσια γεγηρακὼς ἀποπεφευγέναι καθάπερ ἄ-
γριον καὶ λυσσῶντα δεσπότην· ἐν δὲ ταῖς πολιτείαις

---

[1] καὶ τὸ μὴ φερόμενον Fowler: καὶ τὸ μὴ φαινόμενον.
Bernardakis suggests ἅτε μὴ φαινομένων (sc. τῶν παρ᾽ ἡλικίαν
ἐπὶ τὸ βῆμα βαδιζόντων) ἄλλοτε μὲν ἐσφαλμένως ὅτε δ᾽ ὑπὸ δόξης
κτέ. Reiske conjectured καὶ τὸ μὴ φαινόμενον (sc. τινα) ἅμα
τὰ μὲν ἐσφαλμένα τὰ δ᾽ ὑπὸ δόξης κτέ.
[2] ἄλλοτε Bernardakis: ἀλλὰ τά.
[3] δι᾽ added at Capps' suggestion by Fowler.
[4] ὅτε δ᾽ Bernardakis: τὰ δ᾽.

prudence and in the fact that they do not, borne along
sometimes because of past failures and sometimes
as the result of vain opinion, dash headlong upon
public affairs, dragging the mob along with them
in confusion like the storm-tossed sea, but manage
gently and moderately the matters which arise.
And that is why States when they are in difficulties
or in fear yearn for the rule of the elder men ; and
often they have brought from his field some aged
man, not by his request and even contrary to his
wish, and have forced him to take the helm, as it
were, and steer affairs into safety, and in so doing
they have pushed aside generals and politicians
who were able to shout loud and to speak without
pausing for breath and, by Zeus, even men who
were able, planting their feet firmly, to fight
bravely against the enemy.[a] So, for example, the
politicians at Athens grooming Chares, son of Theochares, a powerful man at the height of his physical strength, to be the opponent of Timotheüs
and Iphicrates, declared that the general of the
Athenians ought to be such as he, but Timotheüs
said, " No, by the gods, but such should be the
man who is to carry the general's bedding. The
general should be one who sees at the same time 'that
which is before and behind ' [b] and does not let anything that happens disturb his reasoning as to what
is for the best." Sophocles [c] indeed said that he was
glad to have escaped, now that he was old, from
sexual love, as from a cruel and raging tyrant ;

[a] A reminiscence of Tyrtaeus, 8. 31 ἀλλά τις εὖ διαβὰς
μενέτω, and Homer, *Il.* xii. 458.   [b] Homer, *Il.* i. 343.
[c] *Cf.* Plato, *Republic*, 329 c, with Shorey's note.

────────────────

[b] τε χρῆσθαι G. Papavassiliu : κεχρῆσθαι.

οὐχ ἕνα δεῖ δεσπότην, ἔρωτα παίδων ἢ γυναικῶν,
ἀποφεύγειν, ἀλλὰ πολλοὺς μανικωτέρους τούτου,
φιλονεικίαν, φιλοδοξίαν, τὴν τοῦ πρῶτον εἶναι καὶ
μέγιστον ἐπιθυμίαν, γονιμώτατον φθόνου νόσημα
F καὶ ζηλοτυπίας καὶ διχοστασίας· ὧν τὰ μὲν ἀνίησι
καὶ παραμβλύνει, τὰ δ' ὅλως ἀποσβέννυσι καὶ
καταψύχει τὸ γῆρας, οὐ τοσοῦτον τῆς πρακτικῆς
ὁρμῆς παραιρούμενον, ὅσον τῶν ἀκρατῶν καὶ δια-
πύρων ἀπερύκει παθῶν, ὥστε νήφοντα καὶ καθ-
εστηκότα τὸν λογισμὸν ἐπάγειν ταῖς φροντίσιν.

9. Οὐ μὴν ἀλλ' ἔστω καὶ δοκείτω διατρεπτικὸς
εἶναι λόγος πρὸς τὸν ἀρχόμενον ἐν πολιαῖς νεανι-
εύεσθαι λεγόμενος καὶ καθαπτόμενος ἐκ μακρᾶς
οἰκουρίας ὥσπερ νοσηλείας ἐξανισταμένου καὶ
κινουμένου γέροντος ἐπὶ στρατηγίαν ἢ πραγματείαν,

μέν', ὦ ταλαίπωρ', ἀτρέμα σοῖς ἐν δεμνίοις·

789 ὁ δὲ τὸν ἐμβεβιωκότα πολιτικαῖς πράξεσι καὶ δι-
ηγωνισμένον οὐκ ἐῶν ἐπὶ τὴν δᾷδα καὶ τὴν κορω-
νίδα τοῦ βίου προελθεῖν, ἀλλ' ἀνακαλούμενος καὶ
κελεύων ὥσπερ ἐξ ὁδοῦ μακρᾶς μεταβαλέσθαι,
παντάπασιν ἀγνώμων καὶ μηδὲν ἐκείνῳ προσ-
εοικώς ἐστιν. ὥσπερ γὰρ ὁ γαμεῖν παρασκευαζό-
μενον γέροντ' ἐστεφανωμένον καὶ μυριζόμενον
ἀποτρέπων καὶ λέγων τὰ πρὸς τὸν Φιλοκτήτην

τίς δ' ἂν σε νύμφη, τίς δὲ παρθένος νέα
δέξαιτ' ἄν; εὖ γοῦν[1] ὡς γαμεῖν ἔχεις τάλας

---

[1] γοῦν Musgrave : γ' οὖν.

[a] Euripides, *Orestes*, 258. These words are addressed to
the sick Orestes by his sister Electra.
[b] Kock, *Com. Att. Frag.* iii. p. 609, no. 1215, attributes

but in public life one must escape, not from one
tyrant, the love of boys or women, but from many
loves which are more insane than that : love of
contention, love of fame, the desire to be first and
greatest, which is a disease most prolific of envy,
jealousy, and discord. Some of these old age does
slacken and dull, but others it quenches and cools
entirely, not so much by withdrawing a man from
the impulse to action as by keeping him from excessive and fiery passions, so as to bring sober and
settled reasoning to bear upon his thoughts.

9. However, let us grant that the words

> Bide still, poor wretch, in thine own bedding wrapped [a]

are and appear to be deterrent when addressed to a
man who begins to act young when his hair is grey
and that they rebuke the old man who gets up from
long continued home-keeping, as from a long illness,
and sets out towards the office of general or of civil
administrator ; but the words which forbid a man
who has spent his life in public affairs and contests
to go on to the funeral torch and the end of his
life, and which call him back and tell him, as it were,
to leave the road he has travelled so long and take
a new one,—those words are altogether unkind and
not at all like those we have quoted. For just as he
is perfectly reasonable who tries to dissuade an old
man who is garlanded and perfumed in preparation
for his wedding, and says to him what was said to
Philoctetes,

> What bride, what virgin in her youth, you wretch,
> Would take you ? You're a pretty one to wed ! " [b]

these lines to Strattis, a poet of the Middle Comedy ; Nauck,
Trag. Graec. Frag. p. 841, no. 10, to an unknown tragic
poet.

B οὐκ ἄτοπός ἐστι· καὶ γὰρ αὐτοὶ πολλὰ τοιαῦτα
(789) παίζουσιν εἰς ἑαυτούς·

γαμῶ γέρων, εὖ οἶδα, καὶ τοῖς γείτοσιν·

ὁ δὲ τὸν πάλαι συνοικοῦντα καὶ συμβιοῦντα πολὺν
χρόνον ἀμέμπτως οἰόμενος δεῖν ἀφεῖναι διὰ τὸ
γῆρας τὴν γυναῖκα καὶ ζῆν καθ᾽ ἑαυτὸν ἢ παλλα-
κίδιον ἀντὶ τῆς γαμετῆς ἐπισπάσασθαι, σκαιότητος
ὑπερβολὴν οὐκ ἀπολέλοιπεν· οὕτως ἔχει τινὰ λόγον
τὸ προσιόντα δήμῳ πρεσβύτην, ἢ Χλίδωνα τὸν
γεωργὸν ἢ Λάμπωνα τὸν ναύκληρον ἤ τινα τῶν ἐκ
τοῦ κήπου φιλοσόφων, νουθετῆσαι καὶ κατασχεῖν
C ἐπὶ τῆς συνήθους ἀπραγμοσύνης· ὁ δὲ Φωκίωνος
ἢ Κάτωνος ἢ Περικλέους ἐπιλαβόμενος καὶ λέγων
" ὦ ξέν᾽ Ἀθηναῖε ἢ Ῥωμαῖε,

ἀζαλέῳ γήρᾳ κρᾶτ᾽ ἀνθίζων κήδει,"[1]

γραψάμενος ἀπόλειψιν[2] τῇ πολιτείᾳ καὶ τὰς περὶ
τὸ βῆμα καὶ τὸ στρατήγιον ἀφεὶς διατριβὰς καὶ
τὰς φροντίδας εἰς ἀγρὸν ἐπείγου σὺν ἀμφιπόλῳ
τῇ γεωργίᾳ συνεσόμενος ἢ πρὸς οἰκονομίᾳ τινὶ καὶ
λογισμοῖς διαθησόμενος τὸν λοιπὸν χρόνον," ἄδικα
πείθει καὶ ἀχάριστα πράττειν τὸν πολιτικόν.

10. Τί οὖν; φήσαι τις ἄν, οὐκ ἀκούομεν ἐν
κωμῳδίᾳ στρατιώτου λέγοντος

λευκή με θρὶξ ἀπόμισθον ἐντεῦθεν ποιεῖ;

---

[1] κρᾶτ᾽ ἀνθίζων κήδει Fowler; κατανθίζων κάρα, ἤδη Madvig;
κρᾶτ᾽ ἀνθίζων ἤδη Bernardakis: κατανθιδῶν.
[2] ἀπόλειψιν Junius: ἀπολείψειν.

for old men themselves crack many such jokes on themselves, saying

> I'm marrying old, I know—and for my neighbours, too ; [a]

so he who thinks that a man who has for a long time shared his life and his home blamelessly with his wife ought on account of his age to dismiss her and live alone or take on a paramour in place of his wedded spouse has reached the height of perversity. There is some sense in admonishing in that way and confining to his accustomed inactivity an old man such as Chlidon the farmer or Lampon the ship-captain or one of the philosophers of the Garden,[b] if he comes forward for popular favour ; but anyone who buttonholes a Phocion or a Cato or a Pericles and says, " My Athenian (or Roman) friend,

> With withered age bedecked for funeral rites,[c]

bring action for divorce from public life, give up your haunting the speakers' platform and the generals' office and your cares of State, and hurry away to the country to dwell with agriculture as your hand-maid or to devote the rest of your time to some sort of domestic management and keeping accounts," is urging the statesman to do what is wrong and unseemly.

10. " What then ? " someone may say ; " do we not hear a soldier say in a comedy

> My white hair grants me henceforth full discharge ? " [d]

[a] From a comedy of unknown authorship; Kock, *Com. Att. Frag.* iii. p. 451, no. 225.

[b] *i.e.* the Epicureans.

[c] Evidently a line from some tragedy or comedy.

[d] Kock, *Com. Att. Frag.* iii. p. 451, no. 226. Poet and play are unknown.

(789) πάνυ μὲν οὖν, ὦ ἑταῖρε· τοὺς γὰρ Ἄρεος θεράποντας ἡβᾶν πρέπει καὶ ἀκμάζειν, οἷα δή

πόλεμον πολέμοιό τε μέρμερα ἔργα

D διέποντας, ἐν οἷς τοῦ γέροντος κἂν τὸ κράνος
ἀποκρύψῃ τὰς πολιάς,

ἀλλά τε λάθρη γυῖα βαρύνεται

καὶ προαπολείπει τῆς προθυμίας ἡ δύναμις· τοὺς
δὲ τοῦ Βουλαίου καὶ Ἀγοραίου καὶ Πολιέως Διὸς
ὑπηρέτας οὐ ποδῶν ἔργα καὶ χειρῶν ἀπαιτοῦμεν,
ἀλλὰ βουλῆς καὶ προνοίας καὶ λόγου, μὴ ῥαχίαν
ποιοῦντος ἐν δήμῳ καὶ ψόφον ἀλλὰ νοῦν ἔχοντος
καὶ φροντίδα πεπνυμένην καὶ ἀσφάλειαν· οἷς
ἡ γελωμένη πολιὰ καὶ ῥυτὶς ἐμπειρίας μάρτυς
ἐπιφαίνεται, καὶ πειθοῦς συνεργὸν αὐτῷ καὶ δόξαν
E ἤθους προστίθησι. πειθαρχικὸν γὰρ ἡ νεότης
ἡγεμονικὸν δὲ τὸ γῆρας, καὶ μάλιστα σῴζεται πόλις

ἔνθα βουλαὶ γερόντων, καὶ νέων ἀνδρῶν ἀριστεύοισιν[1] αἰχμαί·

καὶ τὸ

βουλὴν δὲ πρῶτον μεγαθύμων ἷζε γερόντων
Νεστορέῃ παρὰ νηὶ

θαυμαστῶς ἐπαινεῖται. διὸ τὴν μὲν ἐν Λακεδαίμονι παραζευχθεῖσαν ἀριστοκρατίαν τοῖς βασιλεῦσιν ὁ Πύθιος '' πρεσβυγενέας '' ὁ δὲ Λυκοῦργος
ἄντικρυς '' γέροντας '' ὠνόμασεν, ἡ δὲ Ῥωμαίων

---

[1] ἀριστεύοισιν Boeckh : ἀριστεύουσιν.

[a] Homer, *Il.* viii. 453.
[b] Homer, *Il.* xix. 165.

Certainly, my friend, for the servants of Ares should properly be young and in their prime, as practising

> war and war's practices baneful,[a]

in which even if an old man's hoary hair is covered by a helmet,

> Yet are his limbs by unseen weight oppressed,[b]

and though the spirit is willing, the flesh is weak; but from the servants of Zeus, god of the Council, the Market-place, and the State, we do not demand deeds of hands and feet, but of counsel, foresight, and speech—not such speech as makes a roar and a clamour among the people, but that which contains good sense, prudent thought, and conservatism; and in these the hoary hair and the wrinkles that people make fun of appear as witnesses to a man's experience and strengthen him by the aid of persuasiveness and the reputation for character. For youth is meant to obey and old age to rule, and that State is most secure

> Where old men's counsels and the young men's spears
> Hold highest rank[c];

and the lines

> First he established a council of old men lofty in spirit
> Hard by the vessel of Nestor[d]

meet with wonderful approval. And therefore the Pythian Apollo named the aristocracy which was coupled with the kingship at Lacedaemon " Ancients " (*Presbygeneas*), and Lycurgus named it " Elders " (*Gerontes*), and the council at Rome is

---

[c] Pindar, Bergk-Schroeder, p. 467, no. 199 (213).
[d] Homer, *Il.* ii. 53.

111

σύγκλητος ἄχρι νῦν '' γερουσία '' καλεῖται. καὶ
καθάπερ ὁ νόμος τὸ διάδημα καὶ τὸν στέφανον,
οὕτω τὴν πολιὰν ἡ φύσις ἔντιμον ἡγεμονικοῦ σύμ-
F βολον ἀξιώματος ἐπιτίθησι· καὶ τὸ '' γέρας '' οἶμαι
καὶ τὸ '' γεραίρειν '' ὄνομα σεμνὸν ἀπὸ τῶν γερόντων γενόμενον διαμένει, οὐχ ὅτι θερμολουτοῦσι καὶ
καθεύδουσι μαλακώτερον, ἀλλ' ὡς βασιλικὴν ἐχόντων τάξιν ἐν ταῖς πόλεσι κατὰ τὴν φρόνησιν, ἧς
καθάπερ ὀψικάρπου φυτοῦ τὸ οἰκεῖον ἀγαθὸν καὶ
τέλειον ἐν γήρᾳ μόλις ἡ φύσις ἀποδίδωσι. τὸν
γοῦν βασιλέα τῶν βασιλέων εὐχόμενον τοῖς θεοῖς

> τοιοῦτοι δέκα μοι συμφράδμονες εἶεν Ἀχαιῶν,

790 οἷος ἦν ὁ Νέστωρ, οὐδεὶς ἐμέμψατο τῶν '' ἀρηίων ''
καὶ '' μένεα πνεόντων Ἀχαιῶν,'' ἀλλὰ συνεχώρουν
ἅπαντες οὐκ ἐν πολιτείᾳ μόνον ἀλλὰ καὶ ἐν πολέμῳ
μεγάλην ἔχειν ῥοπὴν τὸ γῆρας·

> σοφὸν γὰρ ἓν βούλευμα τὰς πολλὰς χέρας
> νικᾷ

καὶ μία γνώμη λόγον ἔχουσα καὶ πειθὼ τὰ κάλλιστα
καὶ μέγιστα διαπράττεται τῶν κοινῶν.

11. Ἀλλὰ μὴν ἥ γε[1] βασιλεία, τελεωτάτη πασῶν
οὖσα καὶ μεγίστη τῶν πολιτειῶν, πλείστας φροντίδας ἔχει καὶ πόνους καὶ ἀσχολίας· τὸν γοῦν Σέλευκον ἑκάστοτε λέγειν ἔφασαν, εἰ γνοῖεν οἱ πολλοὶ
τὸ γράφειν μόνον ἐπιστολὰς τοσαύτας καὶ ἀναγινώ-
B σκειν ὡς ἐργῶδές ἐστιν, ἐρριμμένον οὐκ ἂν ἀνελέσθαι[2] διάδημα· τὸν δὲ Φίλιππον ἐν καλῷ χωρίῳ

---

[1] γε Coraes: τε.   [2] ἂν ἀνελέσθαι Reiske: ἂν ἑλέσθαι.

[a] Homer, Il. ii. 372.   Agamemnon is the speaker.

still called the Senate (" body of elders "). And just as the law places diadem and crown upon the head, so nature puts grey hair upon it as an honourable symbol of the high dignity of leadership. And the words *geras* (" honour," also " reward ") and *gerairein* (" venerate ") retain, I believe, a meaning of veneration derived from old men (*gerontes*), not because they bathe in warm water or sleep in softer beds than other men, but because they hold royal rank in the States in accordance with their wisdom, the proper and perfect fruit of which, as of a late-bearing plant, nature produces after long effort in old age. At any rate when the king of kings prayed to the gods :

Would that I had ten such advisers among the Achaeans [a]

as Nestor was, not one of the " martial " and " might-breathing Achaeans " found fault with him, but all conceded that, not in civil affairs alone, but in war as well, old age has great weight ;

> For one wise counsel over many hands
> Is victor,[b]

and one sensible and persuasive expression of opinion accomplishes the greatest and most excellent public measures.

11. Certainly the office of king, the most perfect and the greatest of all political offices, has the most cares, labours, and occupations. At any rate Seleucus, they used to tell us, constantly repeated that if people in general knew what a task it was merely to read and write so many letters, they would not even pick up a crown that had been thrown away. And Philip, we are told, when he heard, as he was on the

[b] Euripides, *Antiopê*, Nauck, *Trag. Graec. Frag.* p. 419, no. 200.

(790) μέλλοντα καταστρατοπεδεύειν, ὡς ἤκουσεν ὅτι
χόρτος οὐκ ἔστι τοῖς ὑποζυγίοις " ὦ Ἡράκλεις,"
εἰπεῖν¹, "οἷος ἡμῶν ὁ βίος, εἰ καὶ πρὸς τὸν τῶν
ὄνων καιρὸν ὀφείλομεν ζῆν." ὥρα τοίνυν καὶ
βασιλεῖ παραινεῖν πρεσβύτῃ γεγενημένῳ τὸ μὲν
διάδημα καταθέσθαι καὶ τὴν πορφύραν, ἱμάτιον δ'
ἀναλαβόντα καὶ καμπύλην ἐν ἀγρῷ διατρίβειν, μὴ
δοκῇ περίεργα καὶ ἄωρα πράττειν ἐν πολιαῖς
βασιλεύων. εἰ δ' οὐκ ἄξιον ταῦτα λέγειν περὶ
C Ἀγησιλάου καὶ Νομᾶ² καὶ Δαρείου, μηδὲ τῆς ἐξ
Ἀρείου πάγου βουλῆς Σόλωνα μηδὲ τῆς συγκλήτου
Κάτωνα διὰ τὸ γῆρας ἐξάγωμεν, οὐκοῦν³ μηδὲ
Περικλεῖ συμβουλεύωμεν ἐγκαταλιπεῖν τὴν δημο-
κρατίαν· οὐδὲ γὰρ ἄλλως λόγον ἔχει νέον ὄντα
κατασκιρτῆσαι τοῦ βήματος, εἶτ' ἐκχέαντα τὰς
μανικὰς ἐκείνας φιλοτιμίας καὶ ὁρμὰς εἰς τὸ δημόσιον, ὅταν ἡ τὸ φρονεῖν ἐπιφέρουσα δι' ἐμπειρίαν
ἡλικία παραγένηται, προέσθαι καὶ καταλιπεῖν ὥσπερ γυναῖκα τὴν πολιτείαν καταχρησάμενον.

12. Ἡ μὲν γὰρ Αἰσώπειος ἀλώπηξ τὸν ἐχῖνον
οὐκ εἴα τοὺς κρότωνας αὐτῆς ἀφαιρεῖν βουλόμενον·
D " ἂν γὰρ τούτους," ἔφη, " μεστοὺς ἀπαλλάξῃς,
ἕτεροι προσίασι πεινῶντες"· τὴν δὲ πολιτείαν ἀεὶ
τοὺς γέροντας ἀποβάλλουσαν ἀναπίμπλασθαι νέων
ἀνάγκη διψώντων δόξης καὶ δυνάμεως, νοῦν δὲ
πολιτικὸν οὐκ ἐχόντων· πόθεν γάρ, εἰ μηδενὸς
ἔσονται μαθηταὶ μηδὲ θεαταὶ πολιτευομένου γέροντος; ἢ πλοίων μὲν ἄρχοντας οὐ ποιεῖ γράμματα
κυβερνητικά, μὴ πολλάκις γενομένους ἐν πρύμνῃ

---

¹ εἰπεῖν Reiske : εἶπεν.
² Νομᾶ Bernardakis : νουμᾶ.
³ οὐκοῦν Bernardakis : οὔκουν.

point of encamping in a suitable place, that there
was no fodder for the beasts of draught, exclaimed :
" O Heracles, what a life is mine, if I must needs live
to suit the convenience even of my asses ! " There is,
then, a time to advise even a king when he has become
an old man to lay aside the crown and the purple, to
assume a cloak and a crook, and to live in the country,
lest it be thought, if he continues to rule when his
hair is grey, that he is busying himself with super-
fluous and unseasonable occupations. But if it is not
fitting to say this about an Agesilaüs or a Numa or
a Dareius, let us neither remove a Solon from the
Council of the Areopagus nor a Cato from the Senate
on account of old age, and let us not advise a Pericles
to leave the democracy in the lurch. For anyhow
it is absurd that a man when he is young should
prance about upon the platform and then, after
having poured out upon the public all those insane
ambitions and impulses, when the age arrives which
brings wisdom through experience, should give up
public life and desert it like a woman of whom he
has had all the use.

12. Aesop's fox, we recall, would not let the hedge-
hog, although he offered to do so, remove the ticks
from her : " For if you remove these," she said, " which
are full, other hungry ones will come on " ; and the
State which always discards the old men must necessarily be filled up with young men who are thirsty
for reputation and power, but do not possess a statesmanlike mind. And where should they acquire it, if
they are not to be pupils or even spectators of any
old man active in public life ? Treatises on naviga-
tion do not make ship-captains of men who have
not often stood upon the stern and been spectators

θεατὰς τῶν πρὸς κῦμα καὶ πνεῦμα καὶ νύκτα
χειμέριον¹ ἀγώνων,

ὅτε Τυνδαριδᾶν ἀδελφῶν ἅλιον ναύταν πόθος
βάλλει,

πόλιν δὲ μεταχειρίσασθαι καὶ πεῖσαι δῆμον ἢ
E βουλὴν δύναιτ' ἂν ὀρθῶς νέος ἀναγνοὺς βίβλον
ἢ σχολὴν περὶ πολιτείας ἐν Λυκείῳ γραψάμενος,
ἂν μὴ παρ' ἡνίαν καὶ παρ' οἴακα πολλάκις στὰς
δημαγωγῶν καὶ στρατηγῶν ἀγωνιζομένων ἐμπει-
ρίαις ἅμα καὶ τύχαις συναποκλίνων ἐπ' ἀμφότερα,
μετὰ κινδύνων καὶ πραγμάτων λάβῃ τὴν μάθησιν;
οὐκ ἔστιν εἰπεῖν· ἀλλ' εἰ διὰ μηδὲν ἄλλο τῷ γέροντι
παιδείας ἕνεκα τῶν νέων καὶ διδασκαλίας πολιτευ-
τέον ἐστίν. ὡς γὰρ οἱ γράμματα καὶ μουσικὴν
διδάσκοντες, αὐτοὶ προανακρούονται καὶ προανα-
F γινώσκουσιν ὑφηγούμενοι τοῖς μανθάνουσιν, οὕτως
ὁ πολιτικὸς οὐ λέγων μόνον οὐδ' ὑπαγορεύων
ἔξωθεν ἀλλὰ πράττων τὰ κοινὰ καὶ διοικῶν ἐπ-
ευθύνει τὸν νέον, ἔργοις ἅμα καὶ λόγοις πλαττό-
μενον ἐμψύχως καὶ κατασχηματιζόμενον. ὁ γὰρ
τοῦτον ἀσκηθεὶς τὸν τρόπον οὐκ ἐν παλαίστραις
καὶ κηρώμασιν ἀκινδύνοις εὐρύθμων σοφιστῶν,
ἀλλ' ὡς ἀληθῶς ἐν Ὀλυμπιακοῖς καὶ Πυθικοῖς
ἀγῶσιν

ἄθλος ἵππῳ πῶλος ὡς ἅμα τρέχει

κατὰ Σιμωνίδην, ὡς Ἀριστείδης Κλεισθένει καὶ
791 Κίμων Ἀριστείδῃ καὶ Φωκίων Χαβρίᾳ καὶ Κάτων

---

¹ χειμέριον Reiske: χειμερίων.

ᵃ Castor and Pollux, who were supposed to aid sailors.
ᵇ Bergk, *Poet. Lyr. Graec.* iii. p. 719, no. 91.

116

of the struggles against wind and wave and wintry night,

> When yearning for the twin Tyndaridae [a]
> Doth strike the sailor driven o'er the sea ; [b]

and can a youngster manage a State rightly and persuade an assembly or a senate after reading a book or writing in the Lyceum a school exercise about political science, if he has not stood many a time by the driver's rein or the pilot's steering-oar,[c] leaning this way and that with the politicians and generals as they contend with the aid of their experiences and their fortunes, thus amid dangers and troubles acquiring the knowledge they need ? No one can assert that. But if for no other reason, old men should engage in affairs of State for the education and instruction of the young. For just as the teachers of letters or of music themselves first play the notes or read to their pupils and thus show them the way, so the statesman, not only by speech or by making suggestions from outside, but by action in administering the affairs of the community, directs the young man, whose character is moulded and formed by the old man's actions and words alike. For he who is trained in this way—not in the wrestling-schools or training-rings of masters of the arts of graceful speech where no danger is, but, we may say, in truly Olympic and Pythian games,—

> Keeps pace as foal just weaned runs with the mare,[d]

to quote Simonides. So Aristeides ran in the footsteps of Cleisthenes and Cimon in those of Aristeides, Phocion followed Chabrias, Cato had Fabius Maximus

---

[c] Aristophanes, *Knights* 542, uses the metaphor of the pilot, though with a different application.

[d] Bergk, *Poet. Lyr. Graec.* ii. p. 445, no. 5 (6).

(791) Μαξίμῳ Φαβίῳ καὶ Σύλλᾳ Πομπήιος καὶ Φιλοποίμενι Πολύβιος· νέοι γὰρ ὄντες πρεσβυτέροις
ἐπιβάλλοντες, εἶθ᾽ οἷον παραβλαστάνοντες καὶ συν-
εξανιστάμενοι ταῖς ἐκείνων πολιτείαις καὶ πράξεσιν, ἐμπειρίαν καὶ συνήθειαν ἐκτῶντο πρὸς τὰ
κοινὰ μετὰ δόξης καὶ δυνάμεως.

13. Ὁ μὲν οὖν Ἀκαδημαϊκὸς Αἰσχίνης, σοφιστῶν τινων λεγόντων ὅτι προσποιεῖται γεγονέναι
Καρνεάδου μὴ γεγονὼς μαθητής, " ἀλλὰ τότε γ᾽,"
εἶπεν, " ἐγὼ Καρνεάδου διήκουον, ὅτε τὴν ῥαχίαν
B καὶ τὸν ψόφον ἀφεικὼς ὁ λόγος αὐτοῦ διὰ τὸ γῆρας
εἰς τὸ χρήσιμον συνῆκτο καὶ κοινωνικόν "· τῆς δὲ
πρεσβυτικῆς πολιτείας οὐ τῷ λόγῳ μόνον ἀλλὰ καὶ
ταῖς πράξεσιν ἀπηλλαγμένης πανηγυρισμοῦ καὶ
δοξοκοπίας, ὥσπερ τὴν ἶριν[1] λέγουσιν ὅταν παλαιὰ
γενομένη τὸ βρομῶδες ἀποπνεύσῃ καὶ θολερὸν
εὐωδέστερον τὸ ἀρωματικὸν ἴσχειν, οὕτως οὐδέν
ἐστι δόγμα γεροντικὸν οὐδὲ βούλευμα τεταραγ-
μένον ἀλλ᾽ ἐμβριθῆ πάντα καὶ καθεστῶτα. διὸ καὶ
τῶν νέων ἕνεκα δεῖ, καθάπερ εἴρηται, πολιτεύεσθαι
τὸν πρεσβύτην, ἵνα, ὃν τρόπον φησὶ Πλάτων ἐπὶ
τοῦ μιγνυμένου πρὸς ὕδωρ ἀκράτου, μαινόμενον
C θεὸν ἑτέρῳ θεῷ νήφοντι σωφρονίζεσθαι κολαζό-
μενον, οὕτως εὐλάβεια γεροντικὴ κεραννυμένη
πρὸς ζέουσαν ἐν δήμῳ νεότητα, βακχεύουσαν ὑπὸ
δόξης καὶ φιλοτιμίας, ἀφαιρῇ τὸ μανικὸν καὶ
λίαν ἄκρατον.

14. Ἄνευ δὲ τούτων ἁμαρτάνουσιν οἱ οἷον[2] τὸ

---

[1] ἶριν Coraes : ἴβιν.
[2] οἱ οἷον Jannot, Junius, Reiske : οἱ.

as his guide, Pompey had Sulla, and Polybius had
Philopoemen ; for these men, coming when young in
contact with older men and then, as it were, sprouting up beside them and growing up with their policies
and actions, gained experience and familiarity with
public affairs and at the same time reputation and
power.

13. Aeschines the Academic philosopher, when
some sophists declared that he pretended to have
been a pupil of Carneades although he had not been
so, replied, "Oh, but I did listen to Carneades at the
time when his speech had given up noisy declamation on account of his old age and had reduced itself
to what is useful and of common interest." But the
public activity of old men is not only in speech but
also in actions, free from ostentation and desire for
popularity, and, therefore, just as they say that the
iris, when it has grown old and has blown off its fetid
and foul smell, acquires a more fragrant odour, so no
opinion or counsel of old men is turbulent, but they
are all weighty and composed. Therefore it is also
for the sake of the young, as has been said above,
that old men ought to engage in affairs of State, in
order that, as Plato said [a] in reference to pure wine
mixed with water, that an insane god was made
reasonable when chastised by another who was sober,
so the discretion of old age, when mixed in the people
with boiling youth drunk with reputation and ambition, may remove that which is insane and too violent.

14. But apart from all this, they are mistaken who

---

[a] Plato, *Laws*, 773 D. He refers to Dionysus (wine) and
Poseidon (water).

(791) πλεῦσαι καὶ τὸ στρατεύσασθαι, τοιοῦτον ἡγούμενοι
καὶ τὸ πολιτεύσασθαι πρὸς ἄλλο τι¹ πραττόμενον,
εἶτα καταλῆγον ἐν τῷ τυχεῖν ἐκείνου· λειτουργία
γὰρ οὐκ ἔστιν ἡ πολιτεία τὴν χρείαν ἔχουσα πέρας,
ἀλλὰ βίος ἡμέρου καὶ πολιτικοῦ καὶ κοινωνικοῦ
ζῴου καὶ πεφυκότος ὅσον χρὴ χρόνον πολιτικῶς καὶ
φιλοκάλως καὶ φιλανθρώπως ζῆν. διὸ πολιτεύεσθαι καθῆκόν ἐστιν οὐ πεπολιτεῦσθαι, καθάπερ
ἀληθεύειν οὐκ ἀληθεῦσαι καὶ δικαιοπραγεῖν οὐ
δικαιοπραγῆσαι καὶ φιλεῖν οὐ φιλῆσαι τὴν πατρίδα
D καὶ τοὺς πολίτας ἐπὶ ταῦτα γὰρ ἡ φύσις ἄγει, καὶ
ταύτας ὑπαγορεύει τὰς φωνὰς τοῖς μὴ διεφθορόσι
τελείως ὑπ' ἀργίας καὶ μαλακίας·

> πολλοῦ σε θνητοῖς ἄξιον τίκτει πατὴρ

καὶ

> μή τι² παυσώμεσθα δρῶντες εὖ βροτούς.

15. Οἱ δὲ τὰς ἀρρωστίας προβαλλόμενοι καὶ τὰς
ἀδυναμίας νόσου καὶ πηρώσεως μᾶλλον ἢ γήρως
κατηγοροῦσι· καὶ γὰρ νέοι πολλοὶ νοσώδεις καὶ
ῥωμαλέοι γέροντες· ὥστε δεῖ μὴ τοὺς γέροντας
ἀλλὰ τοὺς ἀδυνάτους ἀποτρέπειν, μηδὲ τοὺς νέους
E παρακαλεῖν ἀλλὰ τοὺς δυναμένους. καὶ γὰρ καὶ
Ἀριδαῖος ἦν νέος γέρων δ' Ἀντίγονος, ἀλλ' ὁ μὲν
ἅπασαν ὀλίγου δεῖν κατεκτήσατο τὴν Ἀσίαν, ὁ δ'
ὥσπερ ἐπὶ σκηνῆς δορυφόρημα κωφὸν ἦν ὄνομα

---

¹ ἄλλο τι Reiske : ἄλλα.
² μή τι Meziriacus : μήτε.

ᵃ Cf. Aristotle, Politics, i. 2, where man is called a social
(πολιτικόν) animal.

think that engaging in public affairs is, like going to sea or to a war, something undertaken for an object distinct from itself and ceasing when that object is attained ; for engaging in public affairs is not a special service which is ended when the need ends, but is a way of life of a tamed social animal [a] living in an organized society, intended by nature to live throughout its allotted time the life of a citizen and in a manner devoted to honour and the welfare of mankind. Therefore it is fitting that men should be engaged, not merely have ceased to be engaged, in affairs of State, just as it is fitting that they should be, not have ceased to be, truthful, that they should do, not have ceased to do, right, and that they should love, not have ceased to love, their native land and their fellow-citizens. For to these things nature leads, and these words she suggests to those who are not entirely ruined by idleness and effeminacy :

> Your sire begets you of great worth to men [b]

and

> Let us ne'er cease from doing mortals good.[b]

15. But those who adduce weakness and disability are accusing disease and infirmity rather than old age. For there are many sickly young men and vigorous old men, so that the proper course is to dissuade, not the aged, but the disabled, and to summon into service, not the young, but those who are competent to serve. Aridaeus, for example, was young and Antigonus an old man, but the latter gained possession of almost all Asia, whereas the former, like a mute guardsman on the stage, was

---

[b] Nauck, *Trag. Graec. Frag.* p. 917, adespota no. 410 quoted also *Moralia*, 1099 A.

βασιλέως καὶ πρόσωπον ὑπὸ τῶν ἀεὶ κρατούντων
παροινούμενον. ὥσπερ οὖν ὁ Πρόδικον τὸν σο-
φιστὴν ἢ Φιλήταν τὸν ποιητὴν ἀξιῶν πολιτεύεσθαι,
νέους μὲν ἰσχνοὺς δὲ καὶ νοσώδεις καὶ τὰ πολλὰ
κλινοπετεῖς δι' ἀρρωστίαν ὄντας, ἀβέλτερός ἐστιν·
οὕτως ὁ κωλύων ἄρχειν καὶ στρατηγεῖν τοιούτους
γέροντας, οἷος ἦν Φωκίων οἷος ἦν Μασανάσσης ὁ
Λίβυς οἷος Κάτων ὁ Ῥωμαῖος. ὁ μὲν γὰρ Φωκίων,
ὡρμημένων πολεμεῖν ἀκαίρως τῶν Ἀθηναίων,
F παρήγγειλε τοὺς ἄχρι ἑξήκοντ' ἐτῶν ἀκολουθεῖν
ὅπλα λαβόντας· ὡς δ' ἠγανάκτουν, ''οὐδέν,'' ἔφη,
'' δεινόν· ἐγὼ γὰρ ἔσομαι μεθ' ὑμῶν ὁ στρατηγὸς
ὑπὲρ ὀγδοήκοντ' ἔτη γεγονώς.'' Μασανάσσην δ'
ἱστορεῖ Πολύβιος ἐνενήκοντα μὲν ἐτῶν ἀποθανεῖν,
τετράετες καταλιπόντα παιδάριον ἐξ αὐτοῦ γεγενημένον,[1] ὀλίγῳ δ' ἔμπροσθεν τῆς τελευτῆς μάχῃ
792 νικήσαντα μεγάλῃ Καρχηδονίους ὀφθῆναι τῇ ὑστεραίᾳ πρὸ τῆς σκηνῆς ῥυπαρὸν ἄρτον ἐσθίοντα, καὶ
πρὸς τοὺς θαυμάζοντας εἰπεῖν, ὅτι τοῦτο ποιεῖ[2]

λάμπει γὰρ ἐν χρείαισιν ὥσπερ εὐπρεπὴς
χαλκός· χρόνῳ δ' ἀργῆσαν ἤμυσε στέγος,

ὥς φησι Σοφοκλῆς· ὡς δ' ἡμεῖς φαμεν, ἐκεῖνο τῆς
ψυχῆς τὸ γάνωμα καὶ τὸ φέγγος, ᾧ λογιζόμεθα καὶ
μνημονεύομεν καὶ φρονοῦμεν.

16. Διὸ καὶ τοὺς βασιλεῖς φασι γίγνεσθαι βελ-
τίονας ἐν τοῖς πολέμοις καὶ ταῖς στρατείαις ἢ

---

[1] γεγενημένον Bernardakis : γεγεννημένον.
[2] ποιεῖ] Reiske marks a gap here. Bernardakis supplies
διὰ τὴν ἕξιν (or διὰ τὸ πονεῖν) ἀεί, referring to Cicero, Cato
Major, chap. x.

the mere name and figure of a king, exposed to the
wanton insults of those who happened to have the
real power. As, therefore, he is a fool who would
demand that a person like Prodicus the sophist or
a person like Philetas the poet should take part
in the affairs of State,—they who were young, to
be sure, but thin, sickly, and for the most part bed-
ridden on account of sickness,—so he is foolish who
would hinder from being rulers or generals such old
men as were Phocion, the Libyan Masinissa, and the
Roman Cato. For Phocion, when the Athenians were
rushing into war at an unfavourable time, gave orders
that all citizens up to sixty years of age should take
their weapons and follow him ; and when they were
indignant he said : " There is nothing terrible about
it, for I shall be with you as general, and I am eighty
years old." And Polybius tells us that Masinissa
died at the age of ninety years, leaving a child of
his own but four years old, and that a little before
his end, on the day after defeating the Carthaginians
in a great battle, he was seen in front of his tent
eating a dirty piece of bread, and that when some
expressed surprise at this he said that he did it
[to keep in practice],

> For when in use it gleams like beauteous bronze ;
> An unused house through time in ruin falls,[a]

as Sophocles says ; but we say that this is true of
that brilliance and light of the soul, by means of
which we reason, remember, and think.

16. For that reason kings are said to grow better
among wars and campaigns than when they live at

---

[a] Nauck, *Trag. Graec. Frag.* p. 314, no. 780 ; *cf. Moralia*,
792 A, 1129 C.

(792) σχολὴν ἄγοντας. Ἄτταλον γοῦν τὸν Εὐμένους[1]
B ἀδελφόν, ὑπ' ἀργίας μακρᾶς καὶ εἰρήνης ἐκλυθέντα
κομιδῇ, Φιλοποίμην εἷς τῶν ἑταίρων ἐποίμαινεν
ἀτεχνῶς πιαινόμενον· ὥστε καὶ τοὺς Ῥωμαίους
παίζοντας ἑκάστοτε διαπυνθάνεσθαι παρὰ τῶν ἐξ
Ἀσίας πλεόντων, εἰ δύναται παρὰ τῷ Φιλοποίμενι
βασιλεύς. Λευκόλλου δὲ Ῥωμαίων οὐ πολλοὺς ἄν
τις εὕροι δεινοτέρους στρατηγούς, ὅτε τῷ πράττειν
τὸ φρονεῖν συνεῖχεν· ἐπεὶ δὲ μεθῆκεν ἑαυτὸν εἰς
βίον ἄπρακτον καὶ δίαιταν οἰκουρὸν καὶ ἄφροντιν,
ὥσπερ οἱ σπόγγοι ταῖς γαλήναις ἐννεκρωθεὶς καὶ
καταμαρανθείς, εἶτα Καλλισθένει τινὶ τῶν ἀπελευ-
C θόρων βόσκειν καὶ τιθασεύειν παρέχων τὸ γῆρας,
ἐδόκει καταφαρμακεύεσθαι φίλτροις ὑπ' αὐτοῦ καὶ
γοητεύμασιν, ἄχρι οὗ Μάρκος ὁ ἀδελφὸς ἀπελάσας
τὸν ἄνθρωπον αὐτὸς ᾠκονόμει καὶ ἐπαιδαγώγει τὸν
λοιπὸν αὐτοῦ βίον, οὐ πολὺν γενόμενον. ἀλλὰ Δαρεῖος ὁ Ξέρξου πατὴρ ἔλεγεν αὐτὸς αὑτοῦ παρὰ τὰ
δεινὰ γίγνεσθαι φρονιμώτερος, ὁ δὲ Σκύθης Ἀτέας
μηδὲν οἴεσθαι τῶν ἱπποκόμων διαφέρειν ἑαυτόν,
ὅτε σχολάζοι· Διονύσιος δ' ὁ πρεσβύτερος πρὸς τὸν
πυθόμενον εἰ σχολάζοι[2] "μηδέποτ'," εἶπεν, "ἐμοὶ
τοῦτο συμβαίη." τόξον μὲν γάρ, ὥς φασιν, ἐπι-
D τεινόμενον ῥήγνυται, ψυχὴ δ' ἀνιεμένη. καὶ γὰρ
ἁρμονικοὶ τὸ κατακούειν ἡρμοσμένου καὶ γεωμέτραι
τὸ ἀναλύειν καὶ ἀριθμητικοὶ τὴν ἐν τῷ λογίζεσθαι
συνέχειαν ἐκλιπόντες ἅμα ταῖς ἐνεργείαις ἀμαυροῦσι
ταῖς ἡλικίαις τὰς ἕξεις, καίπερ οὐ πρακτικὰς ἀλλὰ
θεωρητικὰς τέχνας ἔχοντες· ἡ δὲ τῶν πολιτικῶν

---

[1] Εὐμένους Coraes: εὐμενοῦς.
[2] σχολάζοι Moralia, 176 A: σχολάζει.

leisure. Attalus certainly, the brother of Eumenes, because he was completely enfeebled by long inactivity and peace, was actually kept and fattened like a sheep by Philopoemen, one of his courtiers; so that even the Romans used in jest to ask those who came from Asia if the king had any influence with Philopoemen. And it would be impossible to find many abler generals among the Romans than Lucullus, when he combined thought with action; but when he gave himself up to a life of inactivity and to a home-keeping and thought-free existence, he became a wasted skeleton, like sponges in calm seas, and then when he committed his old age to the care and nursing of one of his freedmen named Callisthenes, it seemed as if he were being drugged by him with potions and quackeries, until his brother Marcus drove the fellow away and himself managed and tended him like a child the rest of his life, which was not long. Dareius the father of Xerxes used to say that when dangers threatened he excelled himself in wisdom,[a] and Ateas the Scythian said that he considered himself no better than his grooms when he was idle; and Dionysius the Elder, when someone asked if he was at leisure, replied: " May that never happen to me ! " For a bow, they say, breaks when too tightly stretched, but a soul when too much relaxed. In fact musicians, if they give up listening to music, and geometricians if they give up solving problems, and arithmeticians if they give up the practice of calculating, impair, as they advance in age, their habits of mind as well as their activities, although the studies which they pursue are not concerned with action but with contemplation; but the

---

[a] *Cf. Moralia,* 172 F.

125

(792) ἕξις, εὐβουλία καὶ φρόνησις καὶ δικαιοσύνη, πρὸς δὲ
τούτοις ἐμπειρία στοχαστικὴ καιρῶν καὶ λόγων,
πειθοῦς δημιουργὸς δύναμις οὖσα, τῷ λέγειν ἀεί τι
καὶ πράττειν καὶ λογίζεσθαι καὶ δικάζειν συνέχεται·
καὶ δεινόν, εἰ τούτων ἀποδρᾶσα περιόψεται τηλι-
καύτας ἀρετὰς καὶ τοσαύτας ἐκρυείσας τῆς ψυχῆς·
E καὶ γὰρ τὸ φιλάνθρωπον εἰκός ἐστιν ἀπομαραίνε-
σθαι καὶ τὸ κοινωνικὸν καὶ τὸ εὐχάριστον, ὧν
οὐδεμίαν εἶναι δεῖ τελευτὴν οὐδὲ πέρας.

17. Εἰ γοῦν πατέρα τὸν Τιθωνὸν εἶχες, ἀθάνατον
μὲν ὄντα χρείαν δ' ἔχοντα διὰ γῆρας ἀεὶ πολλῆς
ἐπιμελείας, οὐκ ἂν οἶμαί σε φυγεῖν οὐδ' ἀπείπασθαι
τὸ θεραπεύειν καὶ προσαγορεύειν καὶ βοηθεῖν ὡς
λελειτουργηκότα πολὺν χρόνον· ἡ δὲ πατρὶς καὶ
μητρὶς ὡς Κρῆτες καλοῦσι, πρεσβύτερα καὶ μείζονα
F δίκαια γονέων ἔχουσα, πολυχρόνιος μέν ἐστιν οὐ
μὴν ἀγήρως οὐδ' αὐτάρκης, ἀλλ' ἀεὶ πολυωρίας
δεομένη καὶ βοηθείας καὶ φροντίδος ἐπισπᾶται καὶ
κατέχει τὸν πολιτικὸν

εἰανοῦ ἁπτομένη καί τ' ἐσσύμενον κατερύκει.

Καὶ μὴν οἶσθά με τῷ Πυθίῳ λειτουργοῦντα πολλὰς
Πυθιάδας· ἀλλ' οὐκ ἂν εἴποις " ἱκανά σοι, ὦ Πλού-
ταρχε, τέθυται καὶ πεπόμπευται καὶ κεχόρευται,
νῦν δ' ὥρα πρεσβύτερον ὄντα τὸν στέφανον ἀποθέσθαι καὶ τὸ χρηστήριον ἀπολιπεῖν διὰ τὸ γῆρας."
οὔκουν μηδὲ σεαυτὸν οἴου δεῖν, τῶν πολιτικῶν
ἱερῶν ἔξαρχον ὄντα καὶ προφήτην, ἀφεῖναι τὰς τοῦ

---

[a] Homer, *Il.* xvi. 9.
[b] Periods of four years marked by the quadrennial celebration of the Pythian games in honour of Apollo at Delphi.

mental habit of public men—deliberation, wisdom, and justice, and, besides these, experience, which hits upon the proper moments and words and is the power that creates persuasion—is maintained by constantly speaking, acting, reasoning, and judging; and it would be a crime if, by deserting these activities, it should allow such great and so many virtues to leak out from the soul; for it is reasonable to suppose that love of humanity, public spirit, and graciousness would waste away, none of which ought to have any end or limit.

17. Certainly if you had Tithonus as your father, who was immortal but always needed much care on account of old age, I do not believe you would avoid or grow weary of attending to him, speaking to him, and helping him on the ground that you had performed those duties for a long time; and your fatherland or, as the Cretans call it, your mother country, which has earlier and greater rights than your parents, is long lived, to be sure, but by no means ageless or self-sufficient; on the contrary, since it always needs much consideration and assistance and anxious thought, it draws the statesman to itself and holds him,

> Grasping him fast by the cloak, and restrains him though hastening onward.[a]

Now surely you know that I have been serving the Pythian Apollo for many Pythiads,[b] but you would not say: " Plutarch, you have done enough sacrificing, marching in processions, and dancing in choruses, and now that you are older it is time to put off the garland and to desert the oracle on account of your age." And so do not imagine that you yourself, being a leader and interpreter of the sacred rites of

Πολιέως καὶ Ἀγοραίου τιμᾶς Διός, ἔκπαλαι κατωργιασμένον αὐταῖς.

793   18. Ἀλλ' ἀφέντες, εἰ βούλει, τὸν ἀποσπῶντα τῆς πολιτείας λόγον ἐκεῖνο σκοπῶμεν ἤδη καὶ φιλοσοφῶμεν, ὅπως μηδὲν ἀπρεπὲς μηδὲ βαρὺ τῷ γήρᾳ προσάξωμεν ἀγώνισμα, πολλὰ μέρη τῆς πολιτείας ἐχούσης ἁρμόδια καὶ πρόσφορα τοῖς τηλικούτοις. ὥσπερ γάρ, εἰ καθῆκον ἦν ᾄδοντας διατελεῖν, ἔδει, πολλῶν τόνων καὶ τρόπων ὑποκειμένων φωνῆς, οὓς ἁρμονίας οἱ μουσικοὶ καλοῦσι, μὴ τὸν ὀξὺν ἅμα καὶ σύντονον διώκειν γέροντας γενομένους, ἀλλ' ἐν ᾧ τὸ ῥάδιον ἔπεστι μετὰ τοῦ πρέποντος ἤθους·

B οὕτως, ἐπεὶ τὸ πράττειν καὶ λέγειν μᾶλλον ἀνθρώποις ἢ κύκνοις τὸ ᾄδειν ἄχρι τελευτῆς κατὰ φύσιν ἔστιν, οὐκ ἀφετέον τὴν πρᾶξιν ὥσπερ τινὰ λύραν σύντονον, ἀλλ' ἀνετέον ἐπὶ τὰ κοῦφα καὶ μέτρια καὶ προσῳδὰ πρεσβύταις πολιτεύματα μεθαρμοττομένους. οὐδὲ γὰρ τὰ σώματα παντελῶς ἀκίνητα καὶ ἀγύμναστα περιορῶμεν, ὅτε μὴ δυνάμεθα σκαφείοις μηδ' ἁλτῆρσι χρῆσθαι μηδὲ δισκεύειν μηδ' ὁπλομαχεῖν ὡς καὶ πρότερον, ἀλλ' αἰώραις καὶ περιπάτοις, ἔνιοι δὲ καὶ σφαίρᾳ προσπαλαίοντες ἐλαφρῶς καὶ διαλεγόμενοι κινοῦσι τὸ πνεῦμα καὶ

C τὸ θερμὸν ἀναρριπίζουσι· μήτε δὴ τελέως ἐκπαγέντας ἑαυτοὺς καὶ καταψυχθέντας ἀπραξίᾳ περιίδωμεν[1] μήτ' αὖ πάλιν πᾶσαν ἀρχὴν ἐπαιρόμενοι καὶ παντὸς ἐπιδραττόμενοι πολιτεύματος ἀναγκάζωμεν

―――――――――
[1] περιίδωμεν Coraes : περιίδοιμεν.

civic life, ought to give up the worship of Zeus of the State and of the Forum, rites to which you have for a long time been consecrated.

18. But let us now, if you please, leave the argument which tries to withdraw the aged man from civic activities and turn to the examination and discussion of the question how we may assign to old age only what is appropriate without imposing upon it any burdensome struggle, since political activity has many parts fitting and suitable for men of such years. For just as, if it were fitting for us to continue singing to the end, we ought, since there are many underlying tones and modes of the voice, which musical people call harmonies, we ought, I say, when we have grown old, not to attempt that which is at once high pitched and intense, but that which is easy and also possesses the fitting ethical quality ; just so, since it is more natural for human beings to act and speak to the end than for swans to sing, we must not give up activity as if it were a lyre too tightly strung, but we should relax the activity and adapt it to those public services which are light and moderate and attuned to old men. For we do not let our bodies be entirely without motion and exercise when we are unable to wield the mattock or use jumping-weights or throw the discus or fight in armour as we used to do, but by swinging and walking, and in some instances by light ball-playing and by conversation, old men accelerate their breathing and revive the body's heat. Let us, then, neither allow ourselves to be entirely frozen and chilled by inaction nor, on the other hand, by again burdening ourselves with every office and engaging in every kind of public

793) τὸ γῆρας ἐξελεγχόμενον ἐπὶ τοιαύτας φωνὰς
καταφέρεσθαι

ὦ δεξιὰ χείρ, ὡς ποθεῖς λαβεῖν δόρυ·
ἐν δ' ἀσθενείᾳ τὸν πόθον διώλεσας.

οὐδὲ γὰρ ἀκμάζων καὶ δυνάμενος ἀνὴρ ἐπαινεῖται,
πάντα συλλήβδην ἀνατιθεὶς ἑαυτῷ τὰ κοινὰ πράγ-
D ματα καὶ μηδὲν ἑτέρῳ παριέναι βουλόμενος, ὥσπερ
οἱ Στωικοὶ τὸν Δία λέγουσιν, εἰς πάντα παρενείρων
καὶ πᾶσι καταμιγνὺς ἑαυτὸν ἀπληστίᾳ δόξης ἢ
φθόνῳ τῶν μεταλαμβανόντων ἁμωσγέπως τιμῆς
τινος ἐν τῇ πόλει καὶ δυνάμεως· πρεσβύτῃ δὲ
κομιδῇ, κἂν τὸ ἄδοξον ἀφέλῃς, ἐπίπονος καὶ ταλαί-
πωρος ἡ πρὸς πᾶν μὲν ἀεὶ κληρωτήριον ἀπαν-
τῶσα φιλαρχία, παντὶ δ' ἐφεδρεύουσα δικαστηρίου
καιρῷ καὶ συνεδρίου πολυπραγμοσύνη, πᾶσαν δὲ
E πρεσβείαν καὶ προδικίαν ὑφαρπάζουσα φιλοτιμία.
καὶ γὰρ ταῦτα πράττειν καὶ μετ' εὐνοίας βαρὺ παρ'
ἡλικίαν, συμβαίνει δέ γε τἀναντία· μισοῦνται μὲν
γὰρ ὑπὸ τῶν νέων, ὡς οὐ προϊέμενοι πράξεων
αὐτοῖς ἀφορμὰς μηδ' εἰς μέσον ἐῶντες προελθεῖν,
ἀδοξεῖ δὲ παρὰ τοῖς ἄλλοις τὸ φιλόπρωτον αὐτῶν
καὶ φίλαρχον οὐχ ἧττον ἢ τὸ φιλόπλουτον ἑτέρων
γερόντων καὶ φιλήδονον.

19. Ὥσπερ οὖν τὸν Βουκέφαλον ὁ Ἀλέξανδρος
πρεσβύτερον ὄντα μὴ βουλόμενος πιέζειν ἑτέροις
ἐπωχεῖτο πρὸ τῆς μάχης ἵπποις, ἐφοδεύων τὴν

ᵃ Euripides, *Herc. Fur.* 269.
ᵇ The Stoic doctrine of the infinite variety of Zeus and his
activities is beautifully expressed in the hymn to Zeus by

activity, force our old age, convicted of its weakness,
to descend to words like these:

> O my right hand, thou yearn'st to seize the spear,
> But weakness brings thy yearning all to naught.[a]

For even a man at the height of his powers is not
commended if he takes upon himself, in a word, all
public activities at once and is unwilling to leave, as
the Stoics say of Zeus,[b] anything to anyone else,
intruding and mixing himself in everything through
insatiable desire for reputation or through envy of
those who obtain any share whatsoever of honour
and power in the State. But for a very aged man
that love of office which invariably offers itself as a
candidate at every election, that busy restlessness
which lies in wait for every opportunity offered by
court of justice or council of State, and that ambition
which snatches at every ambassadorship and at
every precedence in legal matters, are, even if you
eliminate the discredit attached to them, toilsome
and miserable. For to do these things even with the
goodwill of others is too burdensome for advanced
age, but, in fact, the result is the very opposite;
for such old men are hated by the young, who feel
that they do not allow them opportunities for public
activity and do not permit them to come before the
public, and by people in general their love of precedence and of office is held in no less disrepute than
is other old men's love of wealth and pleasure.

19. And just as Alexander, wishing not to work
Bucephalus too hard when he was old, used to ride
other horses before the battle in reviewing the

Cleanthes, Stobaeus, *Ecl.* i. 1. 12, p. 25 ed. Wachsmuth;
A. C. Pearson, *The Fragments of Zeno and Cleanthes*, p. 274;
cf. Diogenes Laertius, vii. 147.

φάλαγγα καὶ καθιστὰς εἰς τὴν τάξιν, εἶτα δοὺς τὸ
F σύνθημα καὶ μεταβὰς ἐπ' ἐκεῖνον εὐθὺς ἐπῆγε τοῖς
πολεμίοις καὶ διεκινδύνευεν· οὕτως ὁ πολιτικός, ἂν
ἔχῃ νοῦν, αὐτὸς αὑτὸν ἡνιοχῶν πρεσβύτην γενόμενον ἀφέξεται τῶν οὐκ ἀναγκαίων καὶ παρήσει
τοῖς ἀκμάζουσι χρῆσθαι πρὸς τὰ μικρότερα τὴν
πόλιν, ἐν δὲ τοῖς μεγάλοις αὐτὸς ἀγωνιεῖται προθύμως. οἱ μὲν γὰρ ἀθληταὶ τὰ σώματα τῶν ἀναγκαίων πόνων ἄθικτα τηροῦσι καὶ ἀκέραια πρὸς τοὺς
ἀχρήστους· ἡμεῖς δὲ τοὐναντίον, ἐῶντες τὰ μικρὰ
καὶ φαῦλα, τοῖς ἀξίοις σπουδῆς φυλάξομεν ἑαυτούς.
" νέῳ " μὲν γὰρ ἴσως " ἐπέοικε " καθ' Ὅμηρον
" πάντα," καὶ δέχονται[1] καὶ ἀγαπῶσι τὸν μὲν
μικρὰ καὶ πολλὰ πράττοντα δημοτικὸν καὶ φιλό-
794 πονον τὸν δὲ[2] λαμπρὰ καὶ σεμνὰ γενναῖον καὶ
μεγαλόφρονα καλοῦντες· ἔστι δ' ὅπου καὶ τὸ φιλόνεικον καὶ παράβολον ὥραν ἔχει τινὰ καὶ χάριν
ἐπιπρέπουσαν τοῖς τηλικούτοις. ὁ πρεσβύτης δ'
ἀνὴρ ἐν πολιτείᾳ διακονικὰς λειτουργίας ὑπομένων,
οἷα τελῶν πράσεις καὶ λιμένων ἐπιμελείας καὶ
ἀγορᾶς, ἔτι δὲ πρεσβείας καὶ ἀποδημίας πρὸς
ἡγεμόνας καὶ δυνάστας ὑποτρέχων, ἐν αἷς ἀναγκαῖον
οὐδὲν οὐδὲ σεμνὸν ἔνεστιν ἀλλὰ θεραπεία καὶ τὸ
πρὸς χάριν, ἐμοὶ μὲν οἰκτρόν, ὦ φίλε, φαίνεται καὶ
ἄζηλον, ἑτέροις δ' ἴσως καὶ ἐπαχθὲς[3] φαίνεται καὶ
φορτικόν.

20. Οὐδὲ γὰρ ἐν ἀρχαῖς τὸν τηλικοῦτον ὥρα
B φέρεσθαι, πλὴν ὅσαι γε μέγεθός τι κέκτηνται καὶ

---

[1] δέχονται Wyttenbach: ἔχονται.
[2] τὸν μὲν . . . τὸν δὲ Wyttenbach: τὰ μὲν . . . τὰ δὲ.
[3] ἐπαχθὲς] ἀπαχθὲς, "detestable," Capps.

phalanx and drawing it up in line, and then, after giving the watchword and mounting him, immediately charged the enemy, and fought the battle to its end ; so the statesman, if he is sensible, will curb himself when he has grown old, will keep away from unnecessary activities and allow the State to employ men in their prime for lesser matters, but in important affairs will himself take part vigorously. For athletes keep their bodies untouched by necessary tasks and in full force for useless toils, but we, on the contrary, letting petty and worthless matters go, will save ourselves for things that are seriously worth while. For perhaps, as Homer says,[a] " to a young man everything is becoming," and people accept and love him, calling the one who does many little things a friend of the common folk and hard-working, and the one who does brilliant and splendid things noble and high-minded ; and under some conditions even contentiousness and rashness have a certain timeliness and grace becoming to men of that age. But the old man in public life who undertakes subordinate services, such as the farming of taxes and the supervision of harbours and of the market-place, and who moreover works his way into diplomatic missions and trips abroad to visit commanders and potentates, in which there is nothing indispensable or dignified, but which are merely flattery to curry favour, seems to me, my friend, a pitiable and unenviable object, and to some people, perhaps, a burdensome and vulgar one.

20. For it is not seasonable for an aged man even to be occupied in public offices, except in those which possess some grandeur and dignity, such as that

<hr />

[a] Homer, *Il.* xxii. 71.

(794) ἀξίωμα· καθάπερ ἦν σὺ νῦν Ἀθήνησι μεταχειρίζῃ
τῆς ἐξ Ἀρείου πάγου βουλῆς ἐπιστασίαν καὶ νὴ Δία
τὸ πρόσχημα τῆς Ἀμφικτυονίας, ἥν σοι διὰ τοῦ
βίου παντὸς ἡ πατρὶς ἀνατέθεικε " πόνον ἡδὺν κά-
ματόν τ' εὐκάματον " ἔχουσαν. δεῖ δὲ καὶ ταύτας
μὴ διώκειν τὰς τιμὰς ἀλλὰ φεύγοντας ἄρχειν, μηδ'
αἰτουμένους ἀλλὰ παραιτουμένους, μηδ' ὡς αὐτοῖς
τὸ ἄρχειν λαμβάνοντας ἀλλ' ὡς αὑτοὺς τῷ ἄρχειν
ἐπιδιδόντας. οὐ γάρ, ὡς Τιβέριος ὁ Καῖσαρ ἔλεγε,
C τὸ τὴν χεῖρα τῷ ἰατρῷ προτείνειν ὑπὲρ ἑξήκοντ'
ἔτη γεγονότας αἰσχρόν ἐστιν, ἀλλὰ μᾶλλον τὸ τὴν
χεῖρα τῷ δήμῳ προτείνειν ψῆφον αἰτοῦντας ἢ
φωνὴν ἀρχαιρεσιάζουσαν· ἀγεννὲς γὰρ τοῦτο καὶ
ταπεινόν· ὡς τοὐναντίον ἔχει τινὰ σεμνότητα καὶ
κόσμον, αἱρουμένης τῆς πατρίδος καὶ καλούσης
καὶ περιμενούσης, κατιόντα μετὰ τιμῆς καὶ φιλοφροσύνης γεραρὸν ὡς ἀληθῶς καὶ περίβλεπτον
ἀσπάσασθαι καὶ δεξιώσασθαι τὸ γέρας.

21. Οὕτω δέ πως καὶ λόγῳ χρηστέον ἐν ἐκκλησίᾳ πρεσβύτην γενόμενον, μὴ ἐπιπηδῶντα
συνεχῶς τῷ βήματι μηδ' ἀεὶ δίκην ἀλεκτρυόνος
ἀντᾴδοντα τοῖς φθεγγομένοις, μηδὲ τῷ συμπλέκε-
σθαι καὶ διερεθίζειν ἀποχαλινοῦντα τὴν πρὸς αὑτὸν
D αἰδῶ τῶν νέων μηδὲ μελέτην ἐμποιοῦντα καὶ
συνήθειαν ἀπειθείας καὶ δυσηκοΐας, ἀλλὰ καὶ παρ-
ιέντα ποτὲ καὶ διδόντα πρὸς δόξαν ἀναχαιτίσαι
καὶ θρασύνασθαι,[1] μηδὲ παρόντα μηδὲ πολυπραγ-
μονοῦντα, ὅπου μὴ μέγα τὸ κινδυνευόμενόν ἐστι

---

[1] θρασύνασθαι Coraes : θρασύνεσθαι.

---

[a] Cf. Euripides, Bacch. 66.
[b] i.e. for medical assistance.

which you are now administering at Athens, the
presidency of the Senate of the Areopagus, and, by
Zeus, the honour of membership in the Amphictyonic
Council, which your native State bestowed upon you
for life and which entails " a pleasant labour and un-
toilsome toil." [a] But even these offices aged men
ought not to seek ; they should exercise them
though trying to avoid them, not asking for them but
asking to be excused from them, as men who do not
take office to themselves, but give themselves to
office. For it is not, as the Emperor Tiberius said,
a disgrace for a man over sixty years of age to hold
out his hand to the physician [b] ; but rather is it a disgrace to hold out the hand to the people asking for
a ballot or a *viva voce* vote ; for this is ignoble and
mean, whereas the contrary possesses a certain
dignity and honour, when an aged man's country
chooses him, calls him, and waits for him, and he
comes down amid honour and friendly applause to
welcome and accept a distinction which is truly
revered and respected.

21. And in somewhat the same way a man who
has grown old ought to treat speech-making in the
assembly ; he should not be constantly jumping
up on the platform, nor always, like a cock, crowing
in opposition to what is said ; nor should he, by
getting involved in controversy, loose the curb of
reverence for him in the young men's minds and
instil into them the practice and custom of dis-
obedience and unwillingness to listen to him ; but
he should sometimes both slacken the reins and
allow them to throw up their heads boldly to oppose
his opinion and to show their spirit, without even
being present or interfering except when the matter

135

πρὸς σωτηρίαν κοινὴν ἢ τὸ καλὸν καὶ πρέπον. ἐκεῖ
δὲ χρὴ καὶ μηδενὸς καλοῦντος ὠθεῖσθαι δρόμῳ παρὰ
δύναμιν, ἀναθέντα χειραγωγοῖς αὑτὸν ἢ φοράδην
κομιζόμενον, ὥσπερ ἱστοροῦσιν ἐν Ῥώμῃ Κλαύδιον
Ἄππιον· ἡττημένων γὰρ ὑπὸ Πύρρου μάχῃ μεγάλῃ,
E πυθόμενος τὴν σύγκλητον ἐνδέχεσθαι λόγους περὶ
σπονδῶν καὶ εἰρήνης οὐκ ἀνασχετὸν ἐποιήσατο,
καίπερ ἀμφοτέρας ἀποβεβληκὼς τὰς ὄψεις, ἀλλ'
ἧκε δι' ἀγορᾶς φερόμενος πρὸς τὸ βουλευτήριον·
εἰσελθὼν δὲ καὶ καταστὰς εἰς μέσον ἔφη πρότερον
μὲν ἄχθεσθαι τῷ τῶν ὀμμάτων στέρεσθαι, νῦν δ' ἂν
εὔξασθαι μηδ' ἀκούειν οὕτως αἰσχρὰ καὶ ἀγεννῆ
βουλευομένους καὶ πράττοντας ἐκείνους. ἐκ δὲ
τούτου τὰ μὲν καθαψάμενος αὐτῶν τὰ δὲ διδάξας
F καὶ παρορμήσας, ἔπεισεν εὐθὺς ἐπὶ τὰ ὅπλα χωρεῖν
καὶ διαγωνίζεσθαι περὶ τῆς Ἰταλίας πρὸς τὸν
Πύρρον. ὁ δὲ Σόλων, τῆς Πεισιστράτου δημα-
γωγίας, ὅτι τυραννίδος ἦν μηχάνημα, φανερᾶς
γενομένης, μηδενὸς ἀμύνεσθαι μηδὲ κωλύειν τολ-
μῶντος, αὐτὸς ἐξενεγκάμενος τὰ ὅπλα καὶ πρὸ τῆς
οἰκίας θέμενος ἠξίου βοηθεῖν τοὺς πολίτας· πέμ-
ψαντος δὲ τοῦ Πεισιστράτου πρὸς αὐτὸν καὶ πυνθανο-
μένου τίνι πεποιθὼς ταῦτα πράττει, " τῷ γήρᾳ,"
εἶπεν.

22. Ἀλλὰ τὰ μὲν οὕτως ἀναγκαῖα καὶ τοὺς ἀπ-
εσβηκότας κομιδῇ γέροντας, ἂν μόνον ἐμπνέωσιν,
ἐξάπτει καὶ διανίστησιν· ἐν δὲ τοῖς ἄλλοις ποτὲ
μέν, ὥσπερ εἴρηται, παραιτούμενος ἐμμελὴς ἔσται
795 τὰ γλίσχρα καὶ διακονικὰ καὶ μείζονας ἔχοντα τοῖς

---

^a Cf. Aristotle, *Constitution of Athens*, 14. 2, and
Sandys' note.

at stake is important for the common safety or
for honour and decorum. But in such cases he
ought, even when no one calls him, to run at a speed
beyond his strength, letting himself be led by attendants who support him or having himself carried in a
litter, as we are told that Appius Claudius did in
Rome ; for after the Romans had been defeated
by Pyrrhus in a great battle, when he heard that
the senate was admitting proposals for a truce and
peace, he found that intolerable, and although he
had lost the sight of both his eyes, had himself
carried through the Forum to the Senate-house. He
went in, took his stand in the midst of the senate,
and said that hitherto he had been grieved by the
loss of his eyes, but now he could pray not even to
have ears to hear them discussing and doing things
so disgraceful and ignoble. And thereupon, partly
by rebuking them, partly by instructing and in-
citing them, he persuaded them to rush to arms
forthwith and fight it out with Pyrrhus for the rule
of Italy. And Solon, when it became clear that the
popular leadership of Peisistratus was a contrivance
to make him tyrant, since no one dared to oppose
or prevent it, brought out his own arms, stacked
them in front of his house, and called upon the citizens
to come to the aid of their country ; then, when
Peisistratus sent and asked him what gave him
confidence to do this, he replied, " My age." [a]

22. However, matters of such urgent necessity do
kindle and arouse aged men whose fire is quite
extinct, provided they merely have breath ; yet
in other matters the aged man will sometimes, as
has been said, act fittingly by declining mean and
petty offices which bring more trouble to those who

(795) πράττουσιν ἀσχολίας ἢ δι' οὓς πράττεται χρείας
καὶ ὠφελείας· ἔστι δ' ὅπου περιμένων καλέσαι καὶ
ποθῆσαι καὶ μετελθεῖν οἴκοθεν τοὺς πολίτας ἀξιο-
πιστότερος δεομένοις κάτεισι. τὰ δὲ πλεῖστα καὶ
παρὼν σιωπῇ τοῖς νεωτέροις λέγειν παρίησιν, οἷον
βραβεύων φιλοτιμίας πολιτικῆς ἅμιλλαν· ἐὰν δ'
ὑπερβάλλῃ τὸ μέτριον, καθαπτόμενος ἠπίως καὶ
μετ' εὐμενείας ἀφαιρῶν φιλονεικίας καὶ βλασφημίας
καὶ ὀργάς, ἐν δὲ ταῖς γνώμαις τὸν ἁμαρτάνοντα
παραμυθούμενος ἄνευ ψόγου καὶ διδάσκων, ἐπαινῶν
δ' ἀφόβως[1] τὸν κατορθοῦντα καὶ νικώμενος ἑκου-
B σίως καὶ προϊέμενος τὸ πεῖσαι καὶ περιγενέσθαι
πολλάκις ὅπως αὐξάνωνται καὶ θαρσῶσιν, ἐνίοις δὲ
καὶ συναναπληρῶν μετ' εὐφημίας τὸ ἐλλεῖπον, ὡς
ὁ Νέστωρ

οὔτις τοι τὸν μῦθον ὀνόσσεται ὅσσοι Ἀχαιοί,
οὐδὲ πάλιν ἐρέει· ἀτὰρ οὐ τέλος ἵκεο μύθων.
ἦ μὴν καὶ νέος ἐσσί, ἐμὸς δέ κε καὶ πάις εἴης.

23. Τούτου δὲ πολιτικώτερον, μὴ μόνον ἐμ-
φανῶς μηδὲ δημοσίᾳ ὀνειδίζων[2] ἄνευ δηγμοῦ
σφόδρα κολούοντος καὶ ταπεινοῦντος, ἀλλὰ μᾶλλον
ἰδίᾳ τοῖς εὖ πεφυκόσι πρὸς πολιτείαν ὑποτιθέμενος
C καὶ συνεισηγούμενος εὐμενῶς λόγους τε χρηστοὺς
καὶ πολιτεύματα, συνεξορμῶν πρὸς τὰ καλὰ καὶ
συνεπιλαμπρύνων τὸ φρόνημα καὶ παρέχων, ὥσπερ οἱ διδάσκοντες ἱππεύειν, ἐν ἀρχῇ χειρόηθη

---

[1] ἀφόβως] ἀφθόνως Reiske.
[2] ὀνειδίζων Madvig : ὀνειδίζειν.

---

[a] Homer, *Il.* ix. 55 ff.   Nestor speaks to Diomedes.

administer them than profit and advantage to those for whom they are administered ; and sometimes by waiting for the citizens to call for him, long for him, and send for him at his house, he will, when he comes, be received with greater confidence by those who begged for his presence. And for the most part he will, even when present, be silent and let younger men speak, acting as a kind of umpire at the contest of political ambition ; and if the contest passes the bounds of moderation, by administering a mild and kindly rebuke, he will endeavour to do away with contention, opprobrious language, and anger, will correct and instruct without fault-finding him who errs in his opinions, but will fearlessly praise him who is right ; and he will voluntarily suffer defeat and will often give up success in persuading the people to his will in order that the young may grow in power and courage, and for some of them he will supply what is lacking with kindly words, as Nestor said,

No one of all the Achaeans will blame the words thou hast spoken,
Nor will oppose them in speech ; and yet thou hast reached no conclusion.
Truly thou art a young man, and thou mightest e'en be my own offspring.[a]

23. But more statesmanlike than this it is, not merely to avoid, when rebuking them openly and in public, any biting speech which violently re-presses and humiliates them, but rather in kindly spirit to suggest and inculcate in private to those who have natural ability for public affairs advantage-ous words and policies, urging them on towards that which is noble, adding brilliancy to their minds, and, after the manner of riding-teachers,

(795) καὶ πρᾶον ἐπιβῆναι τὸν δῆμον· εἰ δέ τι σφαλείη,
μὴ περιορῶν ἐξαθυμοῦντα τὸν νέον, ἀλλ᾽ ἀνιστὰς
καὶ παραμυθούμενος, ὡς Ἀριστείδης Κίμωνα καὶ
Μνησίφιλος Θεμιστοκλέα, δυσχεραινομένους καὶ
κακῶς ἀκούοντας ἐν τῇ πόλει τὸ πρῶτον ὡς
ἰταμοὺς καὶ ἀκολάστους, ἐπῆραν καὶ ἀνεθάρρυναν.
λέγεται δὲ καὶ Δημοσθένους ἐκπεσόντος ἐν τῷ
D δήμῳ καὶ βαρέως φέροντος ἅψασθαι παλαιόν τινα
γέροντα τῶν ἀκηκοότων Περικλέους καὶ εἰπεῖν,
ὡς ἐκείνῳ τἀνδρὶ προσεοικὼς τὴν φύσιν οὐ δικαίως
αὑτοῦ κατέγνωκεν. οὕτω δὲ καὶ Τιμόθεον Εὐριπίδης συριττόμενον ἐπὶ τῇ καινοτομίᾳ καὶ παρα-
νομεῖν εἰς τὴν μουσικὴν δοκοῦντα θαρρεῖν ἐκέλευσεν,
ὡς ὀλίγου χρόνου τῶν θεάτρων ὑπ᾽ αὐτῷ γενησο-
μένων.

24. Καθόλου δ᾽ ὥσπερ ἐν Ῥώμῃ ταῖς Ἑστιάσι
παρθένοις τοῦ χρόνου διώρισται τὸ μὲν μανθάνειν
τὸ δὲ δρᾶν τὰ νενομισμένα τὸ δὲ τρίτον ἤδη διδάσκειν, καὶ τῶν ἐν Ἐφέσῳ περὶ τὴν Ἄρτεμιν
E ὁμοίως ἑκάστην[1] Μελλιέρην τὸ πρῶτον εἶθ᾽ Ἱέρην
τὸ δὲ τρίτον Παριέρην καλοῦσιν· οὕτως ὁ τελέως
πολιτικὸς ἀνὴρ τὰ μὲν πρῶτα μανθάνων ἔτι πολιτεύεται[2] καὶ μυούμενος τὰ δ᾽ ἔσχατα διδάσκων
καὶ μυσταγωγῶν· τὸν μὲν γὰρ ἐπιστάτην[3] ἀθλοῦσιν
ἑτέροις οὐκ ἔστιν αὐτὸν ἀθλεῖν, ὁ δὲ παιδοτριβῶν
νέον ἐν πράγμασι κοινοῖς καὶ δημοσίοις ἀγῶσι καὶ
παρασκευάζων τῇ πατρίδι

μύθων τε ῥητῆρ᾽ ἔμεναι πρηκτῆρά τε ἔργων

---

[1] ἑκάστην Xylander : ἑκάστου.
[2] πολιτεύεται Wyttenbach : πολιτεύεσθαι.
[3] τὸν . . . ἐπιστάτην Capps : τὸ . . . ἐπιστατεῖν.

enabling them at first to mount the populace when it is tractable and gentle ; then, if the young man fails in any way, not letting him be discouraged, but setting him on his feet and encouraging him, as Aristeides raised up and encouraged Cimon and Mnesiphilus did the like for Themistocles when they were at first disliked and decried in the city as being rash and unrestrained. And there is also a story that when Demosthenes had met with a reverse in the assembly and was disheartened thereby, an aged man who had formerly heard Pericles speak touched him with his hand and told him that he resembled that great man in natural ability and, therefore, had been unjust in condemning himself. And so also when Timotheüs was hissed for being new-fangled and was said to be committing sacrilege upon music, Euripides told him to be of good courage, for in a little while the theatres would be at his feet.

24. And in general, just as at Rome the Vestal Virgins have a definite time allotted them, first for learning, then for performing the traditional rites, and thirdly and lastly for teaching them, and as at Ephesus they call each one of the servants of Artemis first a novice, then a priestess, and thirdly an ex-priestess, so the perfect statesman engages in public affairs, first while still a learner and a neophyte and finally as a teacher and initiator. For although it is impossible for the overseer of other athletes to engage in contests himself, yet he who trains a young man in affairs of the community and political struggles and prepares him for the service of his country

Speaker of speeches to be and also a doer of actions,[a]

a Homer, *Il.* ix. 443.

ἐν οὐ μικρῷ μέρει πολιτείας οὐδὲ φαύλῳ χρήσιμός
ἐστιν, ἀλλ' εἰς ὃ μάλιστα καὶ πρῶτον ὁ Λυκοῦργος
F ἐντείνας ἑαυτὸν εἴθισε τοὺς νέους παντὶ πρεσβύτῃ
καθάπερ νομοθέτῃ πειθομένους διατελεῖν. ἐπεὶ
πρὸς τί βλέψας ὁ Λύσανδρος εἶπεν, ὡς ἐν Λακεδαίμονι κάλλιστα γηρῶσιν; ἆρ' ὅτι γ' ἀργεῖν[1]
ἔξεστι μάλιστα τοῖς πρεσβυτέροις ἐκεῖ καὶ δανείζειν
ἢ κυβεύειν συγκαθεζομένους ἢ πίνειν ἐν ὥρᾳ
συνάγοντας; οὐκ ἂν εἴποις· ἀλλ' ὅτι τρόπον τινὰ
πάντες οἱ τηλικοῦτοι τάξιν ἀρχόντων ἤ τινων
πατρονόμων ἢ παιδαγωγῶν ἔχοντες οὐ τὰ κοινὰ
796 μόνον ἐπισκοποῦσιν, ἀλλὰ καὶ τῶν νέων ἕκαστ'
ἀεὶ περί τε τὰ γυμνάσια καὶ παιδιὰς[2] καὶ διαίτας
καταμανθάνουσιν οὐ παρέργως, φοβεροὶ μὲν ὄντες
τοῖς ἁμαρτάνουσιν αἰδεστοὶ δὲ τοῖς ἀγαθοῖς καὶ
ποθεινοί· θεραπεύουσι γὰρ ἀεὶ καὶ διώκουσιν
αὐτοὺς οἱ νέοι, τὸ κόσμιον καὶ τὸ γενναῖον αὔξοντας
καὶ συνεπιγαυροῦντας ἄνευ φθόνου.

25. Τοῦτο γὰρ τὸ πάθος οὐδενὶ χρόνῳ πρέπον
ἡλικίας, ὅμως ἐν νέοις εὐπορεῖ χρηστῶν ὀνομάτων,
ἅμιλλα καὶ ζῆλος καὶ φιλοτιμία προσαγορευόμενον,
ἐν δὲ πρεσβύταις παντελῶς ἄωρόν ἐστι καὶ ἄγριον
καὶ ἀγεννές. διὸ δεῖ πορρωτάτω τοῦ φθονεῖν ὄντα
τὸν πολιτικὸν γέροντα μὴ καθάπερ τὰ βάσκανα
B γεράνδρυα τῶν παραβλαστανόντων καὶ ὑποφυο-
μένων σαφῶς ἀφαιρεῖσθαι καὶ κολούειν τὴν βλάστην
καὶ τὴν αὔξησιν, ἀλλ' εὐμενῶς προσδέχεσθαι καὶ
παρέχειν τοῖς ἀντιλαμβανομένοις καὶ προσπλεκο-

---

[1] γ' ἀργεῖν Faehse : γεωργεῖν.
[2] παιδιὰς Amyot : παιδείας.

is useful to the State in no small or mean degree, but helps towards that for which Lycurgus first and especially exerted himself when he accustomed the young always to obey every old man as if he were a lawgiver. For what had Lysander in mind when he said that men grow old most nobly in Lacedaemon ? Was it because there the older men are more than elsewhere allowed to live in idleness and to lend money or sit together and throw dice or get together betimes for drinking-parties *a* ? You could not say that. No, it was because all men of advanced age hold more or less the position of magistrates, fatherly counsellors, or instructors, and not only oversee public affairs, but also make it their business to learn all details about the gymnasia, the sports, and the daily lives of the young men, and, therefore, they are feared by those who do wrong but revered and desired by the good ; for the young men always cultivate and follow them, since they enhance and encourage the decorum and innate nobility of the young without arousing their envy.

25. For the emotion of envy is not fitting for any time of life, but nevertheless it has among young people plenty of fine names, being called " competition," " zeal," and " ambition " ; but in old men it is totally unseasonable, uncultured, and ignoble. Therefore the aged statesman, being far beyond the feeling of envy, should not, as envious old tree trunks clearly do, try to destroy and prevent the sprouting growth of the plants which spring up beside them and grow under them, but he should receive kindly those who claim his attention and attach themselves to him ; he should offer himself to

a Cf. Athenaeus 279 E and 365 c.

(796) μένοις ἑαυτὸν ὀρθοῦντα καὶ χειραγωγοῦντα καὶ
τρέφοντα μὴ μόνον ὑφηγήσεσι καὶ συμβουλίαις
ἀγαθαῖς, ἀλλὰ καὶ παραχωρήσεσι πολιτευμάτων
τιμὴν ἐχόντων καὶ δόξαν ἤ τινας ὑπουργίας ἀβλαβεῖς
μὲν ἡδείας δὲ τοῖς πολλοῖς καὶ πρὸς χάριν ἐσομένας·
ὅσα δ' ἐστὶν ἀντίτυπα καὶ προσάντη καὶ καθάπερ
τὰ φάρμακα δάκνει παραχρῆμα καὶ λυπεῖ τὸ δὲ
C καλὸν καὶ λυσιτελὲς ὕστερον ἀποδίδωσι, μὴ τοὺς
νέους ἐπὶ ταῦτα προσάγοντα μηδ' ὑποβάλλοντα
θορύβοις, ὄχλων ἀγνωμονούντων ἀήθεις ὄντας, ἀλλ'
αὐτὸν ἐκδεχόμενον τὰς ὑπὲρ τῶν συμφερόντων
ἀπεχθείας· τούτῳ γὰρ εὐνουστέρους τε ποιήσει
τοὺς νέους καὶ προθυμοτέρους ἐν ταῖς ἄλλαις
ὑπηρεσίαις.

26. Παρὰ πάντα δὲ ταῦτα χρὴ μνημονεύειν, ὡς
οὐκ ἔστι πολιτεύεσθαι μόνον τὸ ἄρχειν καὶ πρεσ-
βεύειν καὶ μέγα βοᾶν ἐν ἐκκλησίᾳ καὶ περὶ τὸ
βῆμα βακχεύειν λέγοντας ἢ γράφοντας, ἃ οἱ πολλοὶ
τοῦ[1] πολιτεύεσθαι νομίζουσιν, ὥσπερ ἀμέλει καὶ
D φιλοσοφεῖν τοὺς ἀπὸ τοῦ δίφρου διαλεγομένους
καὶ σχολὰς ἐπὶ βιβλίοις περαίνοντας· ἡ δὲ συνεχὴς
ἐν ἔργοις καὶ πράξεσιν ὁρωμένη καθ' ἡμέραν
ὁμαλῶς[2] πολιτεία καὶ φιλοσοφία λέληθεν αὐτούς.
καὶ γὰρ τοὺς ἐν ταῖς στοαῖς ἀνακάμπτοντας περι-
πατεῖν φασιν, ὡς ἔλεγε Δικαίαρχος, οὐκέτι δὲ τοὺς
εἰς ἀγρὸν ἢ πρὸς φίλον βαδίζοντας. ὅμοιον δ'
ἐστὶ τῷ φιλοσοφεῖν τὸ πολιτεύεσθαι. Σωκράτης

---

[1] τοῦ] τὸ Coraes; τοῦ omitted by Reiske.
[2] ὁμαλῶς Coraes: οὐδαμῶς.

direct, guide, and support them, not only with good
instructions and advice, but also by giving up to
them public offices which bring honour and reputation, or certain public services which will do no harm
to the people, but will be pleasing to it, and will make
them popular. But as for such things as arouse
opposition and are difficult and, like certain medi-
cines, smart and hurt at first but produce an excellent and profitable result afterwards, he should
not force young men into these and subject them to
popular outcries while they are still unaccustomed
to the inconsiderate mob ; but he should himself
assume the unpopularity arising from advantageous
measures, for in this way he will make the young
more well-disposed towards him and more eager in
performing other services.

26. But above all things we must remind them that
statesmanship consists, not only in holding office,
being ambassador, vociferating in the assembly,
and ranting round the speakers' platform proposing
laws and making motions. Most people think all
this is part of statesmanship, just as they think of
course that those are philosophers who sit in a chair
and converse and prepare their lectures over their
books ; but the continuous practice of statesmanship
and philosophy, which is every day alike seen in acts
and deeds, they fail to perceive. For, as Dicaearchus
used to remark, those who circulate in the porticoes
are said to be " promenading," [a] but those who walk
into the country or to see a friend are not. Now
being a statesman is like being a philosopher. Socrates
at any rate was a philosopher, although he did not

[a] This is a play on the name of the Peripatetic school of
philosophy. *Cf.* Müller, *Frag. Hist. Graec.* ii. p. 226.

γοῦν οὔτε βάθρα θεὶς οὔτ᾽ εἰς θρόνον καθίσας
οὔθ᾽ ὥραν διατριβῆς ἢ περιπάτου τοῖς γνωρίμοις
τεταγμένην φυλάττων, ἀλλὰ καὶ συμπαίζων,[1] ὅτε
τύχοι, καὶ συμπίνων καὶ συστρατευόμενος ἐνίοις
καὶ συναγοράζων, τέλος δὲ καὶ δεδεμένος[2] καὶ
E πίνων τὸ φάρμακον, ἐφιλοσόφει· πρῶτος ἀποδείξας
τὸν βίον ἅπαντι χρόνῳ καὶ μέρει καὶ πάθεσι καὶ
πράγμασιν ἁπλῶς ἅπασι φιλοσοφίαν δεχόμενον.
οὕτω δὴ διανοητέον καὶ περὶ πολιτείας, ὡς τοὺς
μὲν ἀνοήτους, οὐδ᾽ ὅταν στρατηγῶσιν ἢ γραμ-
ματεύωσιν ἢ δημηγορῶσι, πολιτευομένους ἀλλ᾽
ὀχλοκοποῦντας ἢ πανηγυρίζοντας ἢ στασιάζοντας
ἢ λειτουργοῦντας ἀναγκαίως· τὸν δὲ κοινωνικὸν
καὶ φιλάνθρωπον καὶ φιλόπολιν καὶ κηδεμονικὸν
καὶ πολιτικὸν ἀληθῶς, κἂν μηδέποτε τὴν χλαμύδα
περίθηται, πολιτευόμενον ἀεὶ τῷ παρορμᾶν τοὺς
F δυναμένους, ὑφηγεῖσθαι τοῖς δεομένοις, συμπαρεῖναι
τοῖς βουλευομένοις, διατρέπειν τοὺς κακοπραγμο-
νοῦντας, ἐπιρρωννύναι τοὺς εὐγνώμονας, φανερὸν
εἶναι μὴ παρέργως προσέχοντα τοῖς κοινοῖς μηδ᾽
ὅπου σπουδή τις ἢ παράκλησις διὰ τὸ πρωτεῖον[3]
εἰς τὸ θέατρον βαδίζοντα καὶ τὸ βουλευτήριον,
ἄλλως δὲ διαγωγῆς χάριν ὡς ἐπὶ θέαν ἢ ἀκρόασιν,
797 ὅταν ἐπέλθῃ, παραγινόμενον, ἀλλά, κἂν μὴ παραγένηται τῷ σώματι, παρόντα τῇ γνώμῃ καὶ τῷ
πυνθάνεσθαι τὰ μὲν ἀποδεχόμενον τοῖς δὲ δυσ-
κολαίνοντα τῶν πραττομένων.

27. Οὐδὲ γὰρ Ἀθηναίων Ἀριστείδης οὐδὲ Ῥω-

---

[1] συμπαίζων Reiske: παίζων.
[2] δεδεμένος Wyttenbach: συνδεδεμένος.
[3] πρωτεῖον Xylander's version: πρῶτον.

set out benches or seat himself in an armchair or
observe a fixed hour for conversing or promenading
with his pupils, but jested with them, when it so
happened, and drank with them, served in the army
or lounged in the market-place with some of them,
and finally was imprisoned and drank the poison.
He was the first to show that life at all times and in
all parts, in all experiences and activities, universally
admits philosophy. So this is what we must understand concerning statesmanship also : that foolish
men, even when they are generals or secretaries or
public orators, do not act as statesmen, but court the
mob, deliver harangues, arouse factions, or under compulsion perform public services ; but that the man
who is really public-spirited and who loves mankind
and the State and is careful of the public welfare
and truly statesmanlike, that man, although he never
put on a uniform, is always acting as a statesman by
urging those on who have power, guiding those who
need guidance, assisting those who are deliberating,
reforming those who act wrongly, encouraging those
who are right-minded, making it plain that he is not
just casually interested in public affairs and that he
goes to the assembly or the council, not for the sake
of getting the first seat when there is something
serious in prospect or he is summoned, but that
when he goes there he goes not merely for amusement as if to see or hear a performance, and that
even when he is not there in person he is present
in thought and through inquiry, thus approving of
some of the proceedings and disapproving of others.

27. For not even Aristeides was often ruler of the

(797) μαίων Κάτων ἦρξε πολλάκις, ἀλλὰ πάντα τὸν
αὑτῶν βίον ἐνεργὸν ἀεὶ ταῖς πατρίσι παρέσχον.
Ἐπαμεινώνδας δὲ πολλὰ μὲν καὶ μεγάλα κατ-
ώρθωσε στρατηγῶν, οὐκ ἔλαττον δ' αὑτοῦ μνημο-
νεύεται μηδὲ στρατηγοῦντος μηδ' ἄρχοντος ἔργον
περὶ Θετταλίαν, ὅτε τῶν στρατηγῶν εἰς τόπους
χαλεποὺς ἐμβαλόντων τὴν φάλαγγα καὶ θορυβου-
B μένων (ἐπέκειντο γὰρ οἱ πολέμιοι βάλλοντες),
ἀνακληθεὶς ἐκ τῶν ὁπλιτῶν πρῶτον μὲν ἔπαυσε
θαρρύνας τὸν τοῦ στρατεύματος τάραχον καὶ φόβον,
ἔπειτα διατάξας καὶ διαρμοσάμενος τὴν φάλαγγα
συγκεχυμένην ἐξήγαγε ῥᾳδίως καὶ κατέστησεν
ἐναντίαν τοῖς πολεμίοις, ὥστ' ἀπελθεῖν ἐκείνους
μεταβαλομένους. Ἆγιδος δὲ τοῦ βασιλέως ἐν
Ἀρκαδίᾳ τοῖς πολεμίοις ἐπάγοντος ἤδη τὸ στρά-
τευμα συντεταγμένον εἰς μάχην, τῶν πρεσβυτέρων
τις Σπαρτιατῶν ἐπεβόησεν, ὅτι διανοεῖται κακὸν
κακῷ ἰᾶσθαι, δηλῶν τῆς ἐξ Ἄργους ἐπαιτίου[1]
C ἀναχωρήσεως τὴν παροῦσαν ἄκαιρον προθυμίαν
ἀνάληψιν βουλόμενην[2] εἶναι, ὡς ὁ Θουκυδίδης φησίν·
ὁ δ' Ἆγις ἀκούσας ἐπείσθη καὶ ἀνεχώρησε. Μενεκράτει δὲ[3] καὶ δίφρος ἔκειτο καθ' ἡμέραν παρὰ ταῖς
θύραις τοῦ ἀρχείου, καὶ πολλάκις ἀνιστάμενοι πρὸς
αὐτὸν οἱ Ἔφοροι διεπυνθάνοντο καὶ συνεβουλεύοντο
περὶ τῶν μεγίστων. ἐδόκει γὰρ ἔμφρων ἀνὴρ εἶναι
καὶ συνετὸς ἱστορεῖσθαι· διὸ καὶ παντάπασιν ἤδη
τὴν τοῦ σώματος ἐξημαυρωμένος δύναμιν καὶ τὰ
πολλὰ κλινήρης διημερεύων, μεταπεμπομένων εἰς
ἀγορὰν τῶν Ἐφόρων, ὥρμησε μὲν ἐξαναστὰς

---

[1] ἰᾶσθαι... ἐπαιτίου Thucydides, v. 65 : ἰάσασθαι... ἐπετείου.
[2] βουλομένην Thucydides : βουλόμενον.
[3] Μενεκράτει δὲ Jannot : μέν, ἐκράτει δέ.

Athenians, nor Cato of the Romans, but they spent their whole lives in active service to their native States. And Epameinondas as general gained many great successes, but one deed of his equal to any of them is recorded, which he performed in Thessaly when he was neither general nor magistrate. The generals had led the phalanx into difficult ground and were in confusion (for the enemy were pressing them hard with missile weapons), when he was called out from his place among the infantry ; and first by encouraging the army he put an end to confusion and fear, then, after arranging the broken phalanx and putting it in order, he easily led it out and drew it up to face the enemy, so that they changed front and withdrew. And when King Agis, in Arcadia, was already leading against the enemy his army drawn up for battle, one of the elder Spartiates called out to him that he was planning to cure evil with evil, pointing out that his present unseasonable eagerness was an attempt to atone for his culpable retreat from Argos, as Thucydides says.[a] And when Agis heard this, he took the advice and retreated. For Menecrates a chair was placed every day by the door of the house of government, and often the ephors rose up from their session and went to him for information and advice on the most important matters ; for he was considered to be a wise man and an intelligent one to be consulted. And therefore, after his physical strength had become utterly exhausted and he had to spend most of the day in bed, when the ephors sent for him to come to the market-place, he got up and set out to walk,

[a] Thucydides, v. 65. 2.

(797) βαδίζειν, μόλις δὲ καὶ χαλεπῶς προερχόμενος, εἶτα
D παιδαρίοις ἐντυχὼν καθ᾽ ὁδόν, ἠρώτησεν, εἴ τι
γινώσκουσιν ἀναγκαιότερον ὂν τοῦ πείθεσθαι δε-
σπότῃ· τῶν δὲ φησάντων " τὸ μὴ δύνασθαι," τοῦτο
τῆς ὑπουργίας λογισάμενος πέρας ἀνέστρεψεν
οἴκαδε. δεῖ γὰρ μὴ προαπολείπειν¹ τὴν προθυμίαν
τῆς δυνάμεως, ἐγκαταλειφθεῖσαν δὲ μὴ βιάζεσθαι.
καὶ μὴν Γαΐῳ Λαιλίῳ Σκιπίων ἐχρῆτο συμβούλῳ
στρατηγῶν ἀεὶ καὶ πολιτευόμενος, ὥστε καὶ λέγειν
ἐνίους ὑποκριτὴν τῶν πράξεων Σκιπίωνα ποιητὴν
δὲ τὸν Γάιον εἶναι. Κικέρων δ᾽ αὐτὸς ὁμολογεῖ τὰ
κάλλιστα καὶ μέγιστα τῶν συμβουλευμάτων, οἷς
ὤρθωσεν ὑπατεύων τὴν πατρίδα, μετὰ Ποπλίου
Νιγιδίου τοῦ φιλοσόφου συνθεῖναι.

E   28. Οὕτω διὰ πολλῶν τρόπων τῆς πολιτείας
οὐδὲν ἀποκωλύει τοὺς γέροντας ὠφελεῖν τὸ κοινὸν
ἀπὸ τῶν βελτίστων, λόγου καὶ γνώμης καὶ παρρησίας καὶ φροντίδος πινυτῆς, ὡς δὴ ποιηταὶ λέγουσιν. οὐ γὰρ αἱ χεῖρες ἡμῶν οὐδ᾽ οἱ πόδες, οὐδ᾽
ἡ τοῦ σώματος ῥώμη κτῆμα καὶ μέρος ἐστὶ τῆς
πόλεως μόνον, ἀλλὰ πρῶτον ἡ ψυχὴ καὶ τὰ τῆς
ψυχῆς κάλλη, δικαιοσύνη καὶ σωφροσύνη καὶ
φρόνησις· ὧν ὀψὲ καὶ βραδέως τὸ οἰκεῖον ἀπολαμ-
βανόντων, ἄτοπόν ἐστι τὴν μὲν οἰκίαν καὶ τὸν ἀγρὸν
F ἀπολαύειν καὶ τὰ λοιπὰ χρήματα καὶ κτήματα,
κοινῇ δὲ τῇ πατρίδι καὶ τοῖς πολίταις μηκέτι
χρησίμους εἶναι διὰ τὸν χρόνον, οὐ τοσοῦτον τῶν
ὑπηρετικῶν παραιρούμενον δυνάμεων, ὅσον ταῖς

¹ προαπολείπειν Coraes: προαπολιπεῖν.

150

but proceeded slowly and with difficulty ; then, meeting some boys on the way, he asked them if they knew of anything stronger than the necessity of obeying one's master, and they replied, "Not being able to." Accounting this as the limit of his service, he turned round and went home. For a man's zeal ought not to fail before his strength, but when it is deserted by strength, it should not be forced. Certainly Scipio, both as general and as statesman, always made use of Gaius Laelius as his adviser, so that some people even said that Scipio was the actor, but Gaius the author, of his deeds. And Cicero himself confesses that the noblest and greatest of the plans through which as consul he restored his country to safety were devised with the help of the philosopher Publius Nigidius.

28. There are, then, many kinds of political activity by which old men may readily benefit the commonwealth by giving of their best, namely reason, judgement, frankness, and "sapience profound," as poets say [a] ; for not only do our hands or our feet or the strength of our body constitute a possession and a part of the State, but first of all our soul and the beauties of the soul—justice, moderation, and wisdom. And since these acquire their proper quality late and slowly, it is absurd that house, farm, and other property or possessions should derive all the benefit from aged men but that they should be no longer of use to their country in general and their fellow-citizens by reason of their age, for age does not so much diminish our power to perform

---

[a] Plutarch seems to have no particular poet in mind, but merely indicates that he is using poetic diction.

(797) ἡγεμονικαῖς καὶ πολιτικαῖς προστίθησι. διὸ καὶ
τῶν Ἑρμῶν τοὺς πρεσβυτέρους ἄχειρας καὶ ἄποδας
ἐντεταμένους δὲ τοῖς μορίοις δημιουργοῦσιν, αἰνιτ-
τόμενοι τῶν γερόντων ἐλάχιστα δεῖσθαι διὰ τοῦ
σώματος ἐνεργούντων, ἐὰν τὸν λόγον ἐνεργόν, ὡς
προσήκει, καὶ γόνιμον ἔχωσιν.

ᵃ Plutarch seems to be in error; at any rate the extant
Hermae which represent elderly men do not differ in the

inferior services as it increases our power for leading and governing. And that is the reason why they make the older Hermae without hands or feet, but with their private parts stiff,[a] indicating figuratively that there is no need whatsoever of old men who are active by their body's use, if they keep their mind, as it should be, active and fertile.

particular mentioned from those which represent younger men.

PRECEPTS OF STATECRAFT
(PRAECEPTA GERENDAE REIPUBLICAE)

INTRODUCTION

THIS essay is addressed to Menemachus, a young man who has asked Plutarch for advice concerning public life. Nothing further is known of the young man, except that Pardalas of Sardis is mentioned as his fellow-citizen (813 F; 825 D); but some of those to whom Plutarch's various essays are addressed are known to be real persons, and it is, therefore, probable that Menemachus also actually existed. Plutarch held at different times various public offices, and moreover he was highly regarded by his fellow-citizens and many others as a guide, philosopher, and friend; it is, therefore, not unnatural that a young man who was thinking of entering upon a political career should appeal to him for advice and counsel, though it is also possible that Plutarch wrote the essay without being asked to do so and addressed it to Menemachus merely as a matter of form.

There is nothing profoundly philosophical and very little purely theoretical to be found here. Greece, like most of the known world, was a part of the Roman Empire, and the exercise of statecraft on a large scale was virtually limited to Romans. The ancient Greek city-states retained, however, their local self-government, subject to the supervision of the proconsul; they could enter into agreements with each other, and could send envoys to Rome if occasion arose. A man could, therefore, find useful and honourable occupation in public life, as Plutarch himself did. Although he frequently uses the great men of the great days of Greece as examples, Plutarch gives the sort of advice which would be useful to one engaged in such political activity as was open to a Greek in his time. Some of his advice is applicable only to his own times and its conditions, but the politician or statesman of any age may recognize many of his precepts as common sense, the application of which is limited to no time or place. The essay is, then, of interest, not only because it throws a sidelight upon the conditions in Greece in Plutarch's time, but also on account of its own inherent value.

The reference to troubles which took place " recently under Domitian " (815 D, Chapter 19) may indicate that the essay was written not long after A.D. 96, the date of Domitian's death.

ΠΟΛΙΤΙΚΑ ΠΑΡΑΓΓΕΛΜΑΤΑ

798   1. Εἰ πρὸς ἄλλο τι χρήσασθαι καλῶς ἐστιν ἔχον,
ὦ Μενέμαχε, τῷ

οὔτις τοι τὸν μῦθον ὀνόσσεται ὅσσοι Ἀχαιοί,
οὐδὲ πάλιν ἐρέει· ἀτὰρ οὐ τέλος ἵκεο μύθων,

B καὶ πρὸς τοὺς προτρεπομένους τῶν φιλοσόφων
διδάσκοντας δὲ μηδὲν μηδ' ὑποτιθεμένους· ὅμοιοι
γάρ εἰσι τοῖς τοὺς λύχνους προμύττουσιν ἔλαιον δὲ
μὴ ἐγχέουσιν. ὁρῶν οὖν σε παρωρμημένον ἀξίως
τῆς εὐγενείας ἐν τῇ πατρίδι

μύθων τε ῥητῆρ' ἔμεναι πρηκτῆρά τε ἔργων,

ἐπειδὴ χρόνον οὐκ ἔχεις ἀνδρὸς φιλοσόφου βίον
ὕπαιθρον ἐν πράξεσι πολιτικαῖς καὶ δημοσίοις
ἀγῶσι κατανοῆσαι καὶ γενέσθαι παραδειγμάτων
C ἔργῳ μὴ λόγῳ περαινομένων θεατής, ἀξιοῖς δὲ
παραγγέλματα λαβεῖν πολιτικά, τὴν μὲν ἄρνησιν
οὐδαμῶς ἐμαυτῷ προσήκουσαν εἶναι νομίζω, τὸ
δ' ἔργον εὔχομαι καὶ τῆς σῆς ἄξιον σπουδῆς καὶ
τῆς ἐμῆς προθυμίας γενέσθαι· τοῖς δὲ παραδείγμασι
ποικιλωτέροις, ὥσπερ ἠξίωσας, ἐχρησάμην.
   2. Πρῶτον μὲν οὖν ὑποκείσθω πολιτείᾳ καθάπερ
158

PRECEPTS OF STATECRAFT

1. If, Menemachus, it is suitable to apply to anything at all the saying

> No one of all the Achaeans finds fault with the words thou
> hast uttered,
> Nor will oppose them in speech ; and yet thou hast reached
> no conclusion,[a]

it may be applied to those philosophers who urge
people to take lessons from them, but give no real
instruction or advice ; for they are like those who
trim the lamps, but fail to pour in oil. Therefore,
seeing that the desire has been aroused in you a

> Speaker of speeches to be, and also a doer of actions [b]

in your native State, as befits your noble birth, since
you have not time to gain an understanding of a
philosopher's life in the open among affairs of State
and public conflicts or to be a spectator of examples
worked out in deed, not merely in word, and since
you ask for some precepts of statecraft, I think it is
not at all fitting that I should refuse, and I pray that
the result may be worthy of your zeal and of my goodwill ; and, as you requested, I have made use of a
rather large variety of examples.

2. First, then, at the base of political activity there

[a] Homer, *Il.* ix. 55 ; *cf. Moralia*, 795 B.
[b] Homer, *Il.* ix. 443 ; *cf. Moralia*, 795 E.

(798) ἔδαφος βέβαιον καὶ ἰσχυρὸν ἡ προαίρεσις ἀρχὴν
ἔχουσα κρίσιν καὶ λόγον, ἀλλὰ μὴ πτοίαν ὑπὸ
δόξης κενῆς ἢ φιλονεικίας τινὸς ἢ πράξεων ἑτέρων
ἀπορίας. ὥσπερ γὰρ οἷς οὐδὲν ἔστιν οἴκοι χρηστόν,
ἐν ἀγορᾷ διατρίβουσι, κἂν μὴ δέωνται, τὸν πλεῖστον
D χρόνον, οὕτως ἔνιοι τῷ μηδὲν ἔχειν ἴδιον ἄλλο
πράττειν ἄξιον σπουδῆς ἐμβάλλουσιν ἑαυτοὺς εἰς
δημόσια πράγματα, τῇ πολιτείᾳ διαγωγῇ χρώμενοι.
πολλοὶ δ' ἀπὸ τύχης ἀψάμενοι τῶν κοινῶν καὶ
ἀναπλησθέντες οὐκέτι ῥᾳδίως ἀπελθεῖν δύνανται,
ταὐτὸ τοῖς ἐμβᾶσιν εἰς πλοῖον αἰώρας χάριν εἶτ'
ἀποσπασθεῖσιν εἰς πέλαγος πεπονθότες· ἔξω βλέ-
πουσι ναυτιῶντες καὶ ταραττόμενοι, μένειν δὲ καὶ
χρῆσθαι τοῖς παροῦσιν ἀνάγκην ἔχοντες·

> λευκᾶς καθύπερθε γαλάνας
> εὐπρόσωποι σφᾶς παρήισαν ἔρωτες ναΐας
> κλαΐδος[1] χαραξιπόντου[2] δαιμονίαν ἐς ὕβριν.

οὗτοι καὶ μάλιστα διαβάλλουσι τὸ πρᾶγμα τῷ
E μετανοεῖν καὶ ἀσχάλλειν, ὅταν ἢ δόξαν ἐλπίσαντες
ἀδοξίᾳ περιπέσωσιν, ἢ φοβεροὶ προσδοκήσαντες
ἑτέροις ἔσεσθαι διὰ δύναμιν εἰς πράγματα κινδύνους ἔχοντα καὶ ταραχὰς ἄγωνται. ὁ δ' ὡς μάλιστα
προσῆκον ἑαυτῷ καὶ κάλλιστον ἔργον ἀπὸ γνώμης
καὶ[3] λογισμῷ τὰ κοινὰ πράσσειν ἀρξάμενος ὑπ'
οὐδενὸς ἐκπλήττεται τούτων οὐδ' ἀναστρέφεται τὴν
γνώμην. οὔτε[4] γὰρ ἐπ' ἐργασίᾳ καὶ χρηματισμῷ
προσιτέον τοῖς κοινοῖς, ὡς οἱ περὶ Στρατοκλέα

---

[1] κλαΐδος Hermann : κληΐδος.
[2] χαραξιπόντου Xylander : χαράξει πόντου.
[3] καὶ added by Reiske.
[4] οὔτε Coraes : οὐδέ.

must be, as a firm and strong foundation, a choice of
policy arising from judgement and reason, not from
mere impulse due to empty opinion or contentiousness or lack of other activities. For just as those who
have no useful occupation at home spend most of
their time in the market-place, even if there is nothing
they need there, just so some men, because they have
no business of their own that is worth serious attention, throw themselves into public affairs, treating
political activity as a pastime, and many who have
become engaged in public affairs by chance and have
had enough of them are no longer able to retire from
them without difficulty ; they are in the same pre-
dicament as persons who have gone aboard a vessel
to be rocked a bit and then have been driven out into
the open sea ; they turn their gaze outside, seasick
and much disturbed, but obliged to stay where they
are and endure their present plight.

> Over the bright calm sea
> The fair-faced loves went past them to the mad
> Outrage of the ship's oars that plough the deep.[a]

These men cast the greatest discredit upon public
life by regretting their course and being unhappy
when, after hoping for glory, they have fallen into
disgrace or, after expecting to be feared by others on
account of their power, they are drawn into affairs
which involve dangers and popular disorders. But the
man who has entered upon public life from conviction
and reasoning, as the activity most befitting him and
most honourable, is not frightened by any of these
things, nor is his conviction changed. For neither is
it right to enter upon public life as a gainful trade, as

---

[a] Bergk, *Poet. Lyr. Graec.* iii. p. 396, ascribed to
Simonides.

καὶ Δρομοκλείδην ἐπὶ τὸ χρυσοῦν θέρος,[1] τὸ βῆμα
F μετὰ παιδιᾶς οὕτως ὀνομάζοντες, ἀλλήλους παρ-
εκάλουν· οὔθ' οἷον ἐπιλήπτους ὑπὸ πάθους ἄφνω
γενομένους, ὡς Γάιος Γράκχος ἐπὶ θερμοῖς τοῖς
περὶ τὸν ἀδελφὸν ἀτυχήμασιν ἀπωτάτω τῶν κοινῶν
τὸν βίον θέμενος, εἶθ' ὕβρει τινῶν καὶ λοιδορίᾳ πρὸς
αὐτὸν ἀναφλεχθεὶς ὑπ' ὀργῆς, ἐνέπεσε τοῖς κοινοῖς·
καὶ ταχὺ μὲν ἐπλήσθη πραγμάτων καὶ δόξης, ζητῶν
δὲ παύσασθαι καὶ δεόμενος μεταβολῆς καὶ ἡσυχίας
799 οὐχ εὗρε καταθέσθαι τὴν δύναμιν αὐτοῦ διὰ μέγεθος
ἀλλὰ προαπώλετο· τούς τε πρὸς ἅμιλλαν ἢ δόξαν
ὥσπερ ὑποκριτὰς εἰς θέατρον ἀναπλάττοντας ἑαυτοὺς ἀνάγκη μετανοεῖν, ἢ δουλεύοντας ὧν ἄρχειν
ἀξιοῦσιν ἢ προσκρούοντας οἷς ἀρέσκειν ἐθέλουσιν.
ἀλλ' ὥσπερ εἰς φρέαρ οἶμαι τὴν πολιτείαν τοὺς
μὲν ἐμπίπτοντας αὐτομάτως καὶ παραλόγως ταράτ-
τεσθαι καὶ μετανοεῖν, τοὺς δὲ καταβαίνοντας ἐκ
παρασκευῆς καὶ λογισμοῦ καθ' ἡσυχίαν χρῆσθαί τε
τοῖς πράγμασι μετρίως καὶ πρὸς μηδὲν δυσκολαί-
νειν, ἅτε δὴ τὸ καλὸν αὐτὸ καὶ μηδὲν ἄλλο τῶν
πράξεων ἔχοντας τέλος.

B 3. Οὕτω δὴ τὴν προαίρεσιν ἀπερείσαντας ἐν
ἑαυτοῖς καὶ ποιήσαντας ἄτρεπτον καὶ δυσμετά-
θετον, τρέπεσθαι χρὴ πρὸς κατανόησιν τοῦ ἤθους
τῶν πολιτῶν, ὃ μάλιστα συγκραθὲν ἐκ πάντων
ἐπιφαίνεται καὶ ἰσχύει. τὸ μὲν γὰρ εὐθὺς αὐτὸν

---

[1] θέρος] δέρος Salmasius.

Stratocles and Dromocleides and their set used to invite each other to come to the golden harvest (for so they called the orators' platform in jest); nor ought we to enter upon it as if we were suddenly seized by an onset of strong emotion, as Gaius Gracchus did, who, when his brother's misfortunes were still fresh, withdrew so far as possible from public affairs and then, inflamed by anger because certain persons insulted and reviled him, rushed into public life. And although he was quickly satiated with public affairs and fame, yet when he tried to stop and wished for a change and a quiet life, he found that his power was too great to be laid down but before he could lay it down he perished. And those who make themselves up for political competition or the race for glory, as actors do for the stage, must necessarily regret their action, since they must either serve those whom they think they should rule or offend those whom they wish to please. On the contrary, I believe that those who, like men who fall into a well, stumble into public life by mere chance and unexpectedly must be cast into confusion and regret their course, whereas those who enter into it quietly, as the result of preparation and reflection, will be moderate in their conduct of affairs and will not be discomposed by anything, inasmuch as they have honour itself and nothing else as the purpose of their actions.

3. So, after thus determining their choice in their own minds and making it invariable and unchangeable, statesmen must apply themselves to the understanding of the character of the citizens, which shows itself as in the highest degree a compound of all their individual characters and is powerful. For any attempt

(799) ἐπιχειρεῖν ἠθοποιεῖν καὶ μεθαρμόττειν τοῦ δήμου
τὴν φύσιν οὐ ῥᾴδιον οὐδ᾽ ἀσφαλές, ἀλλὰ καὶ
χρόνου δεόμενον πολλοῦ καὶ μεγάλης δυνάμεως.
δεῖ δ᾽, ὥσπερ οἶνος ἐν ἀρχῇ μὲν ὑπὸ τῶν ἠθῶν
κρατεῖται τοῦ πίνοντος ἡσυχῇ δὲ διαθάλπων καὶ
C κατακεραννύμενος αὐτὸς ἠθοποιεῖ τὸν πίνοντα καὶ
μεθίστησιν, οὕτω τὸν πολιτικόν, ἕως ἂν ἰσχὺν
ἀγωγὸν ἐκ δόξης καὶ πίστεως κατασκευάσηται,
τοῖς ὑποκειμένοις ἤθεσιν εὐάρμοστον εἶναι καὶ
στοχάζεσθαι τούτων, ἐπιστάμενον οἷς χαίρειν ὁ
δῆμος καὶ ὑφ᾽ ὧν ἄγεσθαι πέφυκεν· οἷον ὁ ᾽Αθηναίων
εὐκίνητός ἐστι πρὸς ὀργήν, εὐμετάθετος πρὸς ἔλεον,
μᾶλλον ὀξέως ὑπονοεῖν ἢ διδάσκεσθαι καθ᾽ ἡσυχίαν
βουλόμενος· ὥσπερ τῶν ἀνδρῶν τοῖς ἀδόξοις καὶ
ταπεινοῖς βοηθεῖν προθυμότερος,[1] οὕτω τῶν λόγων
τοὺς παιγνιώδεις καὶ γελοίους ἀσπάζεται καὶ προ-
τιμᾷ· τοῖς μὲν ἐπαινοῦσιν αὐτὸν μάλιστα χαίρει, τοῖς
δὲ σκώπτουσιν ἥκιστα δυσχεραίνει· φοβερός ἐστιν
D ἄχρι τῶν ἀρχόντων, εἶτα φιλάνθρωπος ἄχρι τῶν
πολεμίων. ἕτερον ἦθος τοῦ Καρχηδονίων δήμου,
πικρόν, σκυθρωπόν, ὑπήκοον τοῖς ἄρχουσι, βαρὺ
τοῖς ὑπηκόοις, ἀγεννέστατον ἐν φόβοις, ἀγριώ-
τατον ἐν ὀργαῖς, ἐπίμονον τοῖς γνωσθεῖσι, πρὸς
παιδιὰν καὶ χάριν ἀνήδυντον καὶ σκληρόν· οὐκ
ἂν οὗτοι, Κλέωνος ἀξιοῦντος αὐτούς, ἐπεὶ τέθυκε
καὶ ξένους ἑστιᾶν μέλλει, τὴν ἐκκλησίαν ὑπερ-
θέσθαι, γελάσαντες ἂν καὶ κροτήσαντες ἀνέστησαν·
οὐδ᾽ ᾽Αλκιβιάδην ὄρτυγος ἐν τῷ λέγειν διαφυγόντος

---

[1] προθυμότερος] προθυμότατος Reiske.

---

[a] The story of the adjournment of the assembly is told by
Plutarch in the *Life of Nicias*, chap. vii. p. 527.

on the part of the statesman to produce by himself at the very outset a change of character and nature in the people will not easily succeed, nor is it safe, but it is a matter that requires a long space of time and great power. But just as wine is at first controlled by the character of the drinker but gradually, as it warms his whole body and becomes mingled therewith, itself forms the drinker's character and changes him, just so the statesman, until he has by his reputation and by public confidence in him built up his leadership, must accommodate himself to the people's character as he finds it and make that the object of his efforts, knowing by what things the people is naturally pleased and led. For example, the Athenian populace is easily moved to anger, easily turned to pity, more willing to suspect quickly than to be informed at leisure ; as they are readier to help humble persons of no reputation, so they welcome and especially esteem facetious and amusing speeches; while they take most delight in those who praise them, they are least inclined to be angry with those who make fun of them; they are terrible even to their chief magistrates, then kindly even to their enemies. Quite different is the character of the Carthaginian people ; it is bitter, sullen, subservient to their magistrates, harsh to their subjects, most abject when afraid, most savage when enraged, stubborn in adhering to its decisions, disagreeable and hard in its attitude towards playfulness and urbanity. Never would these people, if a Cleon had asked them to postpone the meeting of the assembly on the ground that he had made sacrifice and had guests to entertain,[a] have adjourned the meeting amid laughter and the clapping of hands ; nor would they, when a quail escaped from Alcibiades'

ἐκ τοῦ ἱματίου, φιλοτίμως συνθηρεύσαντες ἀπ-
Ε έδωκαν ἄν¹· ἀλλὰ καὶ ἀπέκτειναν ἄν, ὡς ὑβρίζοντας
καὶ τρυφῶντας· ὅπου καὶ Ἄννωνα λέοντι χρώμενον
σκευοφόρῳ παρὰ τὰς στρατείας αἰτιασάμενοι τυ-
ραννικὰ φρονεῖν ἐξήλασαν. οἶμαι δ' ἂν ἔγωγε
μηδὲ Θηβαίους ἀποσχέσθαι γραμμάτων πολεμίων
κυρίους γενομένους, ὡς Ἀθηναῖοι Φιλίππου γραμ-
ματοφόρους λαβόντες ἐπιστολὴν ἐπιγεγραμμένην
Ὀλυμπιάδι κομίζοντας οὐκ ἔλυσαν οὐδ' ἀπεκάλυψαν
ἀπόρρητον ἀνδρὸς ἀποδήμου πρὸς γυναῖκα φιλο-
φροσύνην· οὐδέ γ' αὖ πάλιν Ἀθηναίους, Ἐπαμεινώνδου πρὸς τὴν κατηγορίαν ἀπολογεῖσθαι μὴ
F θέλοντος ἀλλ' ἀναστάντος ἐκ τοῦ θεάτρου καὶ διὰ
τῆς ἐκκλησίας εἰς τὸ γυμνάσιον ἀπιόντος, εὐκόλως
ἐνεγκεῖν τὴν ὑπεροψίαν καὶ τὸ φρόνημα τοῦ ἀνδρός·
πολλοῦ δ' ἂν ἔτι καὶ Σπαρτιάτας δεῆσαι τὴν
Στρατοκλέους ὕβριν ὑπομεῖναι καὶ βωμολοχίαν,
πείσαντος μὲν αὐτοὺς εὐαγγέλια θύειν ὡς νενικη-
κότας, ἐπεὶ δέ, τῆς ἥττης ἀληθῶς ἀπαγγελθείσης,
800 ἠγανάκτουν, ἐρωτῶντος τὸν δῆμον τί ἠδίκηται,
τρεῖς ἡμέρας δι' αὐτὸν ἡδέως γεγονώς. οἱ μὲν
οὖν αὐλικοὶ κόλακες ὥσπερ ὀρνιθοθῆραι μιμούμενοι
τῇ φωνῇ καὶ συνεξομοιοῦντες ἑαυτοὺς ὑποδύονται
μάλιστα καὶ προσάγουσι δι' ἀπάτης τοῖς βασιλεῦσι·
τῷ δὲ πολιτικῷ μιμεῖσθαι μὲν οὐ προσήκει τοῦ
δήμου τὸν τρόπον, ἐπίστασθαι δὲ καὶ χρῆσθαι πρὸς

¹ ἀπέδωκαν ἄν Reiske : ἀπέδωκαν.

ᵃ See *Life of Alcibiades*, chap. x. p. 195.
ᵇ Cf. *Life of Demetrius*, chap. xi.

cloak while he was speaking, have joined eagerly
in hunting it down and then have given it back to
him [a]; no, they would have put them both to death
for their insolence and their flippancy, seeing that
they banished Hanno on the charge of aspiring to be
tyrant, because he used a lion on his campaigns to
carry his luggage! And I do not believe that the
Thebans either, if they had obtained control of their
enemies' letters, would have refrained from reading
them, as the Athenians, when they captured Philip's
mail-carriers with a letter addressed to Olympias,
refrained from breaking the seal and making
known an affectionate private message of an absent
husband to his wife. Nor, on the other hand,
do I believe that the Athenians would have borne
with good temper the contemptuous pride of Epameinondas, when he refused to reply to the accusation
against him but rose from his seat and went out from
the theatre through the assembly to the gymnasium.
And I think, too, that the Spartans would have been
far from enduring the insolence and buffoonery of
Stratocles, who persuaded the Athenians to make
sacrifices on the ground that they had won a
victory, and then, after a true report of their
defeat had been received, when they were angry
with him, asked the people what wrong he had
done them seeing that, thanks to him, they had
been happy for three days.[b] Now court flatterers,
like bird-catchers, by imitating the voices of kings
and assimilating themselves to them, insinuate themselves deeply into their good graces and decoy them
by deceit; but for the statesman it is fitting, not to
imitate the character of his people, but to understand
it and to employ for each type those means by

(800) ἕκαστον, οἷς ἁλώσιμός ἐστιν· ἡ γὰρ ἄγνοια τῶν
ἠθῶν ἀστοχίας φέρει καὶ διαπτώσεις οὐχ ἥττονας
ἐν ταῖς πολιτείαις ἢ ταῖς φιλίαις τῶν βασιλέων.

4. Τὸ μὲν οὖν τῶν πολιτῶν ἦθος ἰσχύοντα δεῖ
καὶ πιστευόμενον ἤδη πειρᾶσθαι ῥυθμίζειν ἀτρέμα

B πρὸς τὸ βέλτιον ὑπάγοντα καὶ πράως μεταχειρι-
ζόμενον· ἐργώδης γὰρ ἡ μετάθεσις τῶν πολλῶν.
αὐτὸς δ' ὥσπερ ἐν θεάτρῳ τὸ λοιπὸν ἀναπεπταμένῳ
βιωσόμενος, ἐξάσκει καὶ κατακόσμει τὸν τρόπον·
εἰ δὲ μὴ ῥάδιον ἀπαλλάξαι παντάπασι τῆς ψυχῆς
τὴν κακίαν, ὅσα γοῦν ἐπανθεῖ μάλιστα καὶ προπίπτει[1] τῶν ἁμαρτημάτων ἀφαιρῶν καὶ κολούων.
ἀκούεις γάρ, ὅτι καὶ Θεμιστοκλῆς ἅπτεσθαι τῆς
πολιτείας διανοούμενος ἀπέστησε τῶν πότων καὶ
τῶν κώμων ἑαυτόν, ἀγρυπνῶν δὲ καὶ νήφων καὶ
πεφροντικὼς ἔλεγε πρὸς τοὺς συνήθεις, ὡς οὐκ
ἐᾷ καθεύδειν αὐτὸν τὸ Μιλτιάδου τρόπαιον·

C Περικλῆς δὲ καὶ περὶ τὸ σῶμα καὶ τὴν δίαιταν
ἐξήλλαξεν αὐτὸν ἠρέμα βαδίζειν καὶ πράως διαλέγεσθαι καὶ τὸ πρόσωπον ἀεὶ συνεστηκὸς ἐπι-
δείκνυσθαι καὶ τὴν χεῖρα συνέχειν ἐντὸς τῆς
περιβολῆς καὶ μίαν ὁδὸν πορεύεσθαι τὴν ἐπὶ τὸ
βῆμα καὶ τὸ βουλευτήριον. οὐ γὰρ εὐμεταχείριστον
οὐδὲ ῥάδιον ἁλῶναι τὴν σωτήριον ἅλωσιν ὑπὸ τοῦ
τυχόντος ὄχλος,[2] ἀλλ' ἀγαπητόν, εἰ μήτ' ὄψει μήτε
φωνῇ πτυρόμενος ὥσπερ θηρίον ὕποπτον καὶ
ποικίλον ἐνδέχοιτο τὴν ἐπιστασίαν. ᾧ τοίνυν οὐδὲ

D τούτων ἐπιμελητέον ἐστὶ παρέργως, ἦπου τῶν περὶ
τὸν βίον καὶ τὸ ἦθος ἀμελητέον ὅπως ᾖ ψόγου

---

[1] προπίπτει Coraes : προσπίπτει.
[2] ὄχλος Bernardakis (ὁ ὄχλος Cobet): ὄχλον or ὄχλου.

which it can be brought under his control. For ignorance of their characters leads to no less serious mistakes and failures in free States than in the friendships of kings.

4. So, then, the statesman who already has attained to power and has won the people's confidence should try to train the character of the citizens, leading them gently towards that which is better and treating them with mildness; for it is a difficult task to change the multitude. But do you yourself, since you are henceforth to live as on an open stage, educate your character and put it in order; and if it is not easy wholly to banish evil from the soul, at any rate remove and repress those faults which are most flourishing and conspicuous. For you know the story that Themistocles, when he was thinking of entering upon public life, withdrew from drinking-parties and carousals; he was wakeful at night, was sober and deeply thoughtful, explaining to his friends that Miltiades' trophy [a] would not let him sleep. And Pericles also changed his personal habits of life, so that he walked slowly, spoke gently, always showed a composed countenance, kept his hand under his cloak, and trod only one path—that which led to the assembly and the senate. For a populace is not a simple and easy thing for any chance person to subject to that control which is salutary; but one must be satisfied if the multitude accept authority without shying, like a suspicious and capricious beast, at face or voice. Since, then, the statesman must not treat even these matters carelessly, ought he to neglect the things which affect his life and character,

[a] Miltiades was the victorious general at Marathon, 490 B.C.

169

(800) καθαρὰ καὶ διαβολῆς ἁπάσης; οὐ γὰρ ὧν λέγουσιν
ἐν κοινῷ καὶ πράττουσιν οἱ πολιτευόμενοι μόνον
εὐθύνας διδόασιν, ἀλλὰ καὶ δεῖπνον αὐτῶν πολυ-
πραγμονεῖται καὶ κοίτη καὶ γάμος καὶ παιδιὰ καὶ
σπουδὴ πᾶσα. τί γὰρ δεῖ λέγειν 'Αλκιβιάδην,
ὃν περὶ τὰ κοινὰ πάντων ἐνεργότατον ὄντα καὶ
στρατηγὸν ἀήττητον ἀπώλεσεν ἡ περὶ τὴν δίαιταν
ἀναγωγία καὶ θρασύτης, καὶ τῶν ἄλλων ἀγαθῶν
αὐτοῦ τὴν πόλιν ἀνόνητον ἐποίησε διὰ τὴν πολυτέλειαν καὶ τὴν ἀκολασίαν; ὅπου καὶ Κίμωνος οὗτοι
E τὸν οἶνον, καὶ 'Ρωμαῖοι Σκιπίωνος οὐδὲν ἄλλο
ἔχοντες λέγειν τὸν ὕπνον ᾐτιῶντο· Πομπήιον δὲ
Μάγνον ἐλοιδόρουν οἱ ἐχθροί, παραφυλάξαντες ἑνὶ
δακτύλῳ τὴν κεφαλὴν κνώμενον. ὡς γὰρ ἐν
προσώπῳ φακὸς καὶ ἀκροχορδὼν δυσχεραίνεται
μᾶλλον ἢ στίγματα καὶ κολοβότητες καὶ οὐλαὶ τοῦ
λοιποῦ σώματος, οὕτω τὰ μικρὰ φαίνεται μεγάλα
τῶν ἁμαρτημάτων ἐν ἡγεμονικοῖς καὶ πολιτικοῖς
ὁρώμενα βίοις διὰ δόξαν, ἣν οἱ πολλοὶ περὶ ἀρχῆς
καὶ πολιτείας ἔχουσιν, ὡς πράγματος μεγάλου
καὶ καθαρεύειν ἀξίου πάσης ἀτοπίας καὶ πλημ-
F μελείας. εἰκότως οὖν Λιούιος[1] Δροῦσος ὁ δημαγωγὸς εὐδοκίμησεν ὅτι, τῆς οἰκίας αὐτοῦ πολλὰ
μέρη κάτοπτα τοῖς γειτνιῶσιν ἐχούσης καὶ τῶν
τεχνιτῶν τινος ὑπισχνουμένου ταῦτ' ἀποστρέψειν
καὶ μεταθήσειν ἀπὸ πέντε μόνων ταλάντων,
" δέκα," ἔφη, " λαβὼν ὅλην μου ποίησον κατα-
φανῆ τὴν οἰκίαν, ἵνα πάντες ὁρῶσιν οἱ πολῖται
πῶς διαιτῶμαι "· καὶ γὰρ ἦν ἀνὴρ σώφρων καὶ

---

[1] Λιούιος Xylander : λεούιος or ἰούλιος.

[a] Cf. Moralia, 972 f.
[b] Cf. Moralia, 89 e, with note a in Babbitt's translation

that they may be clear of blame and ill report of
every kind ? For not only are men in public life
held responsible for their public words and actions,
but people busy themselves with all their concerns :
dinner, love affair, marriage, amusement, and every
serious interest. What need is there, for instance,
to speak of Alcibiades, who, though he was most
active of all the citizens in public affairs and was
undefeated as general, was ruined by his audacious
and dissolute habits in private life, and, because
of his extravagance and lack of restraint, deprived
the State of the benefit of his other good qualities ?
Why, the Athenians blamed Cimon for wine-drinking,
and the Romans, having nothing else to say, blamed
Scipio [a] for sleeping ; and the enemies of Pompey the
Great, observing that he scratched his head with
one finger, reviled him for it.[b] For, just as a mole
or a wart on the face is more unpleasant than brand-
marks, mutilations, or scars on other parts of the
body, so small faults appear great when observed in
the lives of leaders and statesmen on account of the
opinion which the majority has of governing and
public office, regarding it as a great thing which
ought to be clean of all eccentricities and errors.
With good reason, therefore, did Livius Drusus the
tribune gain in reputation because, when many parts of
his house were exposed to the view of his neighbours
and an artisan promised to turn them the other way
and change their position for only five talents,
Drusus replied, " Take ten and make the whole
house open to view, that all the citizens may see
how I live." For he was a man of temperate and

(L.C.L.), where the habit is spoken of as a mark of effeminacy and licentiousness.

κόσμιος. ἴσως δὲ ταύτης οὐδὲν ἔδει τῆς κατα-
φανείας αὐτῷ· διορῶσι γὰρ οἱ πολλοὶ καὶ τὰ πάνυ
βαθέως περιαμπέχεσθαι δοκοῦντα τῶν πολιτευο-
801 μένων ἤθη καὶ βουλεύματα καὶ πράξεις καὶ βίους,
οὐχ ἧττον ἀπὸ τῶν ἰδίων ἢ τῶν δημοσίων ἐπι-
τηδευμάτων τὸν μὲν φιλοῦντες καὶ θαυμάζοντες
τὸν δὲ δυσχεραίνοντες καὶ καταφρονοῦντες.

Τί οὖν δή; οὐχὶ καὶ τοῖς ἀσελγῶς καὶ τεθρυμμένως
ζῶσιν αἱ πόλεις χρῶνται; καὶ γὰρ αἱ κιττῶσαι
λίθους καὶ οἱ ναυτιῶντες ἁλμυρίδας καὶ τὰ τοιαῦτα
βρώματα διώκουσι πολλάκις, εἶτ' ὀλίγον ὕστερον
ἐξέπτυσαν καὶ ἀπεστράφησαν· οὕτω καὶ οἱ δῆμοι
διὰ τρυφὴν καὶ ὕβριν ἢ βελτιόνων ἀπορίᾳ δημα-
B γωγῶν χρῶνται τοῖς ἐπιτυχοῦσι βδελυττόμενοι καὶ
καταφρονοῦντες, εἶτα χαίρουσι τοιούτων εἰς αὑτοὺς
λεγομένων, οἷα Πλάτων ὁ κωμικὸς τὸν Δῆμον
αὐτὸν λέγοντα ποιεῖ·

> λαβοῦ, λαβοῦ τῆς χειρὸς ὡς τάχιστά μου,
> μέλλω στρατηγὸν χειροτονεῖν Ἀγύρριον·

καὶ πάλιν αἰτοῦντα λεκάνην καὶ πτερόν, ὅπως
ἐμέσῃ, λέγοντα

> προσίσταταί μου πρὸς τὸ βῆμα Μαντίας

καὶ

> βόσκει δυσώδη Κέφαλον, ἐχθίστην νόσον.

ὁ δὲ Ῥωμαίων δῆμος, ὑπισχνουμένου τι Κάρβωνος
καὶ προστιθέντος ὅρκον δή τινα καὶ ἀράν, ἀντ-
ώμοσεν ὁμοῦ μὴ πιστεύειν. ἐν δὲ Λακεδαίμονι

ᵃ Kock, *Com. Att. Frag.* i. p. 652, no. 185 ; on Agyrrhius
cf. Aristophanes, *Plutus*, 176.

well-ordered life. And perhaps he had no need of that exposure to the public view; for the people see through the characters, counsels, acts, and lives of public men, even those that seem to be very thickly cloaked; they love and admire one man and dislike and despise another quite as much for his private as for his public practices.

"But," you say, "do not States put in office men who live licentiously and wantonly?" They do, and pregnant women often long for stones, and seasick persons for salt pickles and the like, which then a little later they spew out and detest. So the people of democracies, because of the luxury of their own lives or through sheer perversity, or for lack of better leaders, make use of those who happen to turn up, though they loathe and despise them, then take pleasure in hearing such things said about them as the comic poet Plato puts into the mouth of the People itself:

> Take, take my hand as quickly as you can;
> I'm going to choose Agyrrhius general [a];

and again, when he makes the People ask for a basin and a feather in order to vomit and then say,

> Beside my platform Mantias takes his stand,[b]

and

> It feeds foul Cephalus, most hateful pest.[b]

And the Roman people, when Carbo promised something and confirmed his promise with an oath and a curse, unanimously took a counter-oath that it did not trust him. And at Lacedaemon, when a

---

[b] From the same play as the preceding.

C τινὸς Δημοσθένους[1] ἀνδρὸς ἀκολάστου γνώμην
(801) εἰπόντος ἁρμόζουσαν, ἀπέρριψεν ὁ δῆμος, οἱ δ᾽
Ἔφοροι κληρώσαντες ἕνα τῶν γερόντων ἐκέλευσαν
εἰπεῖν τὸν αὐτὸν λόγον ἐκεῖνον, ὥσπερ εἰς καθαρὸν
ἀγγεῖον ἐκ ῥυπαροῦ μετεράσαντες,[2] ὅπως εὐπρόσ-
δεκτος γένηται τοῖς πολλοῖς. οὕτω μεγάλην ἔχει
ῥοπὴν ἐν πολιτείᾳ πίστις ἤθους καὶ τοὐναντίον.

5. Οὐ μὴν ἀμελητέον γε διὰ τοῦτο τῆς περὶ τὸν
λόγον χάριτος καὶ δυνάμεως ἐν ἀρετῇ θεμένους τὸ
σύμπαν, ἀλλὰ τὴν ῥητορικὴν νομίσαντας[3] μὴ δη-
μιουργὸν ἀλλά τοι συνεργὸν εἶναι πειθοῦς, ἐπανορθωτέον τὸ τοῦ Μενάνδρου

τρόπος ἔσθ᾽ ὁ πείθων τοῦ λέγοντος, οὐ λόγος·

καὶ γὰρ ὁ τρόπος καὶ ὁ λόγος· εἰ μὴ νὴ Δία φήσει
τις, ὡς τὸν κυβερνήτην ἄγειν τὸ πλοῖον οὐ τὸ πη-
D δάλιον, καὶ τὸν ἱππέα στρέφειν τὸν ἵππον οὐ τὸν
χαλινόν, οὕτω πόλιν πείθειν οὐ λόγῳ, ἀλλὰ τρόπῳ
χρωμένην ὥσπερ οἴακι καὶ χαλινῷ τὴν πολιτικὴν
ἀρετήν, ᾗπερ[4] εὐστροφώτατον ζῷον, ὥς φησι Πλάτων, οἷον ἐκ πρύμνης ἁπτομένην καὶ κατευθύνουσαν.
ὅπου γὰρ οἱ μεγάλοι βασιλεῖς ἐκεῖνοι καὶ διογενεῖς,
ὡς Ὅμηρός φησιν, ἁλουργίσι καὶ σκήπτροις καὶ
δορυφόροις καὶ θεῶν χρησμοῖς ἐξογκοῦσιν ἑαυτούς,
καὶ δουλούμενοι τῇ σεμνότητι τοὺς πολλοὺς ὡς

---

[1] Δημοσθένους] Τιμοσθένους Madvig.
[2] μετεράσαντες Dübner: μετακεράσαντες.
[3] νομίσαντας Madvig: νομίσαντες εἶναι.
[4] ᾗπερ Capps (cf. Plato's ᾗ): ὅπερ.

---

[a] Kock, Com. Att. Frag. iii. p. 135, no. 472.

dissolute man named Demosthenes made a desirable motion, the people rejected it, but the ephors chose by lot one of the elders and told him to make that same motion, in order that it might be made acceptable to the people, thus pouring, as it were, from a dirty vessel into a clean one. So great is the importance, in a free State, of confidence or lack of confidence in a man's character.

5. However, we should not on this account neglect the charm and power of eloquence and ascribe everything to virtue, but, considering oratory to be, not the creator of persuasion but certainly its coworker, we should correct Menander's line,

> The speaker's nature, not his speech, persuades,[a]

for both his nature and his speech do so ; unless, indeed, one is to affirm that just as the helmsman, not the tiller, steers the ship, and the rider, not the rein, turns the horse, so political virtue, employing, not speech, but the speaker's character as tiller or rein, sways a State, laying hold of it and directing it, as it were, from the stern, which is, in fact, as Plato says,[b] the easiest way of turning an animal about. For those great and, as Homer calls them, " Zeus-descended " kings pad themselves out with purple robes and sceptres and guards and divine oracles, and although they enslaved the multitude by their grandeur, as if they were superior beings, they

---

[b] *Critias*, 109 c " only it was not our bodies that they [the gods] constrained by bodily force, like shepherds guiding ther flocks by stroke of staff, but they directed from the stern, where the living creature is easiest to turn about (ᾗ μάλιστα εὔστροφον ζῷον), laying hold on the soul by persuasion, as by a rudder, according to their own disposition " (trans. R. G. Bury in L.C.L.).

κρείττονες, ὅμως ἐβούλοντο " μύθων ῥητῆρες "
εἶναι καὶ οὐκ ἠμέλουν τῆς τοῦ λέγειν χάριτος,

οὐδ' ἀγορέων, ἵνα τ' ἄνδρες ἀριπρεπέες τελέθουσιν,

E οὐδὲ Διὸς Βουλαίου μόνον[1] ἔχρῃζον οὐδ' Ἄρεος
Ἐνναλίου καὶ Στρατίας Ἀθηνᾶς, ἀλλὰ καὶ τὴν
Καλλιόπην παρεκάλουν

ἣ δὴ[2] βασιλεῦσιν ἄμ' αἰδοίοισιν ὀπηδεῖ,

πραΰνουσα πειθοῖ καὶ κατάδουσα[3] τῶν δήμων τὸ
αὔθαδες καὶ βίαιον· ἦ που δυνατὸν ἄνθρωπον ἰδιώτην ἐξ ἱματίου καὶ σχήματος δημοτικοῦ πόλιν ἄγειν
βουλόμενον ἐξισχῦσαι καὶ κρατῆσαι τῶν πολλῶν,
εἰ μὴ λόγον ἔχοι συμπείθοντα καὶ προσαγόμενον;
F οἱ μὲν οὖν τὰ πλοῖα κυβερνῶντες ἑτέροις χρῶνται
κελευσταῖς, ὁ δὲ πολιτικὸς ἐν ἑαυτῷ μὲν ὀφείλει
τὸν κυβερνῶντα νοῦν ἔχειν ἐν ἑαυτῷ δὲ τὸν ἐγκε-
λευόμενον λόγον, ὅπως μὴ δέηται φωνῆς ἀλλοτρίας
μηδ' ὥσπερ Ἰφικράτης ὑπὸ τῶν περὶ Ἀριστο-
φῶντα καταρρητορευόμενος λέγῃ " βελτίων μὲν
ὁ τῶν ἀντιδίκων ὑποκριτὴς δρᾶμα δὲ τοὐμὸν
ἄμεινον," μηδὲ πολλάκις δέηται τῶν Εὐριπιδείων
ἐκείνων

εἶθ' ἦν ἄφωνον σπέρμα δυστήνων βροτῶν·
802 καὶ

φεῦ φεῦ, τὸ μὴ τὰ πράγματ' ἀνθρώποις ἔχειν
φωνήν, ἵν' ἦσαν μηδὲν οἱ δεινοὶ λέγειν.

---

[1] μόνον Benseler: μόνον.
[2] δὴ] γὰρ καὶ Hesiod.
[3] κατάδουσα, suggested by Wyttenbach (also καταδέουσα,
καταιδοῦσα Bernardakis): καταδοῦσα.

wished nevertheless to be "speakers of words" and they did not neglect the charm of speech,

Nor the assemblies in which men make themselves greatly distinguished,[a]

and they worshipped not only Zeus of the Council, Ares Enyalius, and Athena of War, but they invoked also Calliopê,

who accompanies reverend monarchs,[b]

softening by persuasion and overcoming by charms the fierce and violent spirit of the people. How, then, is it possible that a private person of ordinary costume and mien who wishes to lead a State may gain power and rule the multitude unless he possesses persuasion and attractive speech? Now the pilots of ships employ others to give orders to the rowers, but the statesman needs to have in himself the mind that steers and also in himself the speech that gives orders, that he may not require some other man's voice and be obliged to say, as Iphicrates did when defeated through the eloquence of Aristophon's orators, "My opponents' actor is better, but superior my play," and may not often need those lines of Euripides,

Oh that the seed of wretched men were mute,[c]

and

Ah, would that deeds of men possessed a voice,
That clever speakers might become as naught[d];

---

[a] Homer, *Il.* ix. 441.
[b] Hesiod, *Theog.* 80.
[c] Nauck, *Trag. Graec. Frag.* p. 678, no. 987.
[d] Nauck, *Trag. Graec. Frag.* p. 494, no. 439, from the first *Hippolytus*.

(802) ταῦτα μὲν γὰρ ἴσως 'Αλκαμένει καὶ Νησιώτῃ καὶ
'Ικτίνῳ καὶ πᾶσι τοῖς βαναύσοις καὶ χειρώναξι τὸ
δύνασθαι λέγειν ἀπομνυμένοις δοτέον ἀποδιδρά-
σκειν· ὥσπερ 'Αθήνησιν ἀρχιτεκτόνων ποτὲ δυεῖν
ἐξεταζομένων πρὸς δημόσιον ἔργον ὁ μὲν αἱμύλος
καὶ κομψὸς εἰπεῖν λόγον τινὰ διελθὼν περὶ τῆς
κατασκευῆς μεμελετημένον ἐκίνησε τὸν δῆμον, ὁ
B δὲ βελτίων τῇ τέχνῃ λέγειν δ' ἀδύνατος, παρελθὼν
εἰς μέσον εἶπεν " ἄνδρες 'Αθηναῖοι, ὡς οὗτος
εἴρηκεν, ἐγὼ ποιήσω." τὴν γὰρ 'Εργάνην οὗτοι
μόνον θεραπεύουσιν, ὡς φησι Σοφοκλῆς, οἱ " παρ'
ἄκμονι τυπάδι βαρείᾳ " καὶ πληγαῖς ὑπακούουσαν
ὕλην ἄψυχον δημιουργοῦντες· ὁ δὲ τῆς Πολιάδος
'Αθηνᾶς καὶ τῆς Βουλαίας Θέμιδος,

ἥ τ' ἀνδρῶν ἀγορὰς ἠμὲν λύει ἠδὲ καθίζει,

προφήτης, ἑνὶ χρώμενος ὀργάνῳ τῷ λόγῳ τὰ μὲν
πλάττων καὶ συναρμόττων, τὰ δ' ἀντιστατοῦντα
πρὸς τὸ ἔργον ὥσπερ ὄζους τινὰς ἐν ξύλῳ καὶ
διπλόας ἐν σιδήρῳ μαλάσσων καὶ καταλεαίνων,
C κοσμεῖ τὴν πόλιν. διὰ τοῦτ' ἦν[1] ἡ κατὰ Περικλέα
πολιτεία " λόγῳ μέν," ὥς φησι Θουκυδίδης,
" δημοκρατία, ἔργῳ δ' ὑπὸ τοῦ πρώτου ἀνδρὸς
ἀρχὴ " διὰ τὴν τοῦ λόγου δύναμιν. ἐπεὶ καὶ
Κίμων ἀγαθὸς ἦν καὶ 'Εφιάλτης καὶ Θουκυδίδης,
ἀλλ' ἐρωτηθεὶς οὗτος ὑπ' 'Αρχιδάμου τοῦ[2] βασιλέως
τῶν Σπαρτιατῶν πότερον αὐτὸς ἢ Περικλῆς

[1] ἦν added by Bernardakis.
[2] τοῦ added by Bernardakis.

---

[a] Alcamenes and Nesiotes were sculptors of the fifth
century B.C. Ictinus was architect of the Parthenon.

for these sayings ought perhaps to be granted as a refuge to Alcamenes, Nesiotes, Ictinus,[a] and all artisans and craftsmen if they take an oath that they are no speakers ; as once at Athens, when two architects were being questioned with a view to a public work, one of them, a wheedling and elegant speaker, moved the people by declaiming a prepared speech about the construction of it, but the other, who was a better architect but lacked the power of speech, came forward and said : " Men of Athens, what he has said, I will do." For, as Sophocles says,[b] only those are servants of the goddess of artistry who " on the anvil with a heavy hammer " and with blows work the yielding and inanimate material of their art. But the spokesman for Athena of the City and Themis of Counsel,

> She who dismisses assemblies of men and who also convenes them,[c]

employing speech as his only instrument, moulding and adapting some things and softening and smoothing off those which are hindrances to his work, such as would be knots in wood or flaws in iron,[d] is an ornament to the city. For this reason the government in Pericles' time was " in name," as Thucydides says,[e] " a democracy, but in fact the rule of the foremost man," because of his power of speech. For Cimon also was a good man, as were Ephialtes and Thucydides, but when the last named was asked by Archidamus King of the Spartans whether he

[b] Nauck, *Trag. Graec. Frag.* p. 309, no. 760, perhaps from the satyr drama *Pandora*.

[c] Homer, *Od.* ii. 69.

[d] *Cf.* Plato, *Sophist*, 267 E.

[e] Thucydides, ii. 65. 8.

179

(802) παλαίει βέλτιον " οὐκ ἂν εἰδείη τις " εἶπεν· " ὅταν
γὰρ ἐγὼ καταβάλω παλαίων, ἐκεῖνος λέγων μὴ
πεπτωκέναι νικᾷ καὶ πείθει τοὺς θεωμένους."
τοῦτο δ' οὐκ αὐτῷ μόνον[1] ἐκείνῳ δόξαν ἀλλὰ καὶ
τῇ πόλει σωτηρίαν ἔφερε· πειθομένη γὰρ αὐτῷ
τὴν ὑπάρχουσαν εὐδαιμονίαν ἔσῳζε, τῶν δ' ἐκτὸς
D ἀπείχετο. Νικίας δὲ τὴν αὐτὴν προαίρεσιν ἔχων,
πειθοῦς δὲ τοιαύτης ἐνδεὴς ὢν καὶ καθάπερ ἀμβλεῖ
χαλινῷ τῷ λόγῳ πειρώμενος ἀποστρέφειν τὸν
δῆμον, οὐ κατέσχεν οὐδ' ἐκράτησεν, ἀλλ' ᾤχετο
βίᾳ φερόμενος εἰς Σικελίαν καὶ συνεκτραχηλι-
ζόμενος. τὸν μὲν οὖν λύκον οὔ φασι τῶν ὤτων
κρατεῖν, δῆμον δὲ καὶ πόλιν ἐκ τῶν ὤτων ἄγειν
δεῖ μάλιστα, μή, καθάπερ ἔνιοι τῶν ἀγυμνάστων
περὶ λόγον λαβὰς ἀμούσους καὶ ἀτέχνους ζητοῦντες
ἐν τοῖς πολλοῖς τῆς γαστρὸς ἕλκουσιν εὐωχοῦντες
ἢ τοῦ βαλλαντίου διδόντες, ἢ πυρρίχας τινὰς ἢ
μονομάχων θεάματα παρασκευάζοντες ἀεὶ δημ-
E αγωγοῦσι, μᾶλλον δὲ δημοκοποῦσι. δημαγωγία
γὰρ ἡ διὰ λόγου πειθομένων ἐστίν, αἱ δὲ τοιαῦται
τιθασεύσεις τῶν ὄχλων οὐδὲν ἀλόγων ζῴων ἄγρας
καὶ βουκολήσεως διαφέρουσιν.

6. Ὁ μέντοι λόγος ἔστω τοῦ πολιτικοῦ μήτε
νεαρὸς καὶ θεατρικός, ὥσπερ πανηγυρίζοντος καὶ
στεφανηπλοκοῦντος ἐξ ἀπαλῶν καὶ ἀνθηρῶν ὀνο-
μάτων· μήτ' αὖ πάλιν, ὡς ὁ Πυθέας τὸν Δημοσθένους ἔλεγεν, ἐλλυχνίων ὄζων[2] καὶ σοφιστικῆς
F περιεργίας ἐνθυμήμασι πικροῖς καὶ περιόδοις πρὸς
κανόνα καὶ διαβήτην ἀπηκριβωμέναις· ἀλλ' ὥσπερ
οἱ μουσικοὶ τὴν θίξιν ἀξιοῦσι τῶν χορδῶν ἠθικὴν

---

[1] μόνον Benseler: μόνῳ.   [2] ὄζων Meziriacus: ὄζειν.

or Pericles was the better wrestler, he replied, "Nobody can tell; for whenever I throw him in wrestling, he says he was not thrown and wins by persuading the onlookers." And this brought not only reputation to Pericles but safety to the State; for while it was swayed by him it preserved its existing prosperity and refrained from foreign entanglements. But Nicias, whose policy was the same, but who lacked such power of persuasion and tried to rein in the people with speech as easy as a snaffle, could not restrain or master it, but against his will went off to Sicily on its back and together with it came a cropper. The wolf, they say, cannot be held by the ears; but one must lead a people or a State chiefly by the ears, not, as some do who have no practice in speaking and seek uncultured and inartistic holds upon the people, pulling them by the belly by means of banquets or gifts of money or arranging ballet-dances or gladiatorial shows, by which they lead the common people or rather curry favour with them. For leadership of a people is leadership of those who are persuaded by speech; but enticing the mob by such means as have just been mentioned is exactly like catching and herding irrational beasts.

6. The speech of the statesman, however, must not be juvenile and theatrical, as if he were making a speech for show and weaving a garland of delicate and flowery words; on the other hand it must not, as Pytheas said of the speech of Demosthenes, smell of the lamp and elaborate literary labour, with sharp arguments and with periods precisely measured by rule and compass. No, just as musicians demand that the touch upon the strings exhibit feel-

181

καταφαίνεσθαι μὴ κρουστικήν, οὕτω τῷ λόγῳ τοῦ
πολιτευομένου καὶ συμβουλεύοντος καὶ ἄρχοντος
ἐπιφαινέσθω μὴ δεινότης μηδὲ πανουργία, μηδ' εἰς
ἔπαινον αὐτοῦ τιθέσθω τὸ ἑκτικῶς ἢ τεχνικῶς ἢ
διαιρετικῶς, ἀλλ' ἤθους ἀπλάστου καὶ φρονήματος
ἀληθινοῦ καὶ παρρησίας πατρικῆς καὶ προνοίας καὶ
803 συνέσεως κηδομένης ὁ λόγος ἔστω μεστός, ἐπὶ τῷ
καλῷ τὸ κεχαρισμένον ἔχων καὶ ἀγωγὸν ἔκ τε
σεμνῶν ὀνομάτων καὶ νοημάτων ἰδίων καὶ πιθανῶν.
δέχεται δ' ὁ πολιτικὸς λόγος δικανικοῦ μᾶλλον καὶ
γνωμολογίας καὶ ἱστορίας καὶ μύθους καὶ μετα-
φοράς, αἷς μάλιστα κινοῦσιν οἱ χρώμενοι μετρίως
καὶ κατὰ καιρόν· ὡς ὁ εἰπὼν " μὴ ποιήσητε ἑτερό-
φθαλμον τὴν Ἑλλάδα," καὶ Δημάδης τὰ ναυάγια
λέγων πολιτεύεσθαι τῆς πόλεως, καὶ Ἀρχίλοχος

μηδ' ὁ Ταντάλου λίθος
τῆσδ' ὑπὲρ νήσου κρεμάσθω·

καὶ Περικλῆς τὴν λήμην τοῦ Πειραιῶς ἀφελεῖν
κελεύων· καὶ Φωκίων ἐπὶ τῆς Λεωσθένους νίκης
B καλὸν τὸ στάδιον εἶναι, δεδιέναι δὲ τοῦ πολέμου
τὸν δόλιχον. καθόλου δ' ὁ μὲν ὄγκος καὶ τὸ μέγεθος τῷ πολιτικῷ μᾶλλον ἁρμόττει, παράδειγμα
δ' οἵ τε Φιλιππικοὶ καὶ τῶν Θουκυδίδου δημη-
γοριῶν ἡ Σθενελαΐδα τοῦ Ἐφόρου καὶ Ἀρχιδάμου

---

[a] These seem to be somewhat technical words employed
by the rhetoricians.
[b] Cf. Aristotle, *Rhetoric*, iii. 1017, p. 1411 A ; said by the
Athenian orator Leptines, in opposing the destruction of
Sparta, one of the " eyes of Greece."
[c] Cf. *Life of Phocion*, chap. i.
[d] Bergk, *Poet. Lyr. Graec.* ii. p. 396.
[e] Cf. *Life of Pericles*, chap. viii.   The reference is

ing, not mere technique, so the speech of the statesman, counsellor, and ruler must not exhibit shrewd-
ness or subtlety, and it must not be to his credit to
speak fluently or artistically or distributively,[a] but
his speech must be full of unaffected character,
true high-mindedness, a father's frankness, foresight, and thoughtful concern for others. His
speech must also have, in a good cause, a charm
that pleases and a winning persuasiveness; in addition to nobility of purpose it must possess grace
arising from stately diction and appropriate and
persuasive thoughts. And political oratory, much
more than that used in a court of law, admits
maxims, historical and mythical tales, and metaphors,
by means of which those who employ them sparingly
and at the proper moment move their audiences
exceedingly; as did he who said " Do not make
Hellas one-eyed," [b] and Demades when he said he
was "governing the wreck of the State,"[c] and
Archilochus saying

> Nor let the stone of Tantalus
> Hang o'er the head of this our isle,[d]

and Pericles when he bade the Athenians to remove
"the eyesore of the Peiraeus,"[e] and Phocion when
he said with reference to the victory of Leosthenes
that the furlong race of the war was good, but he
was fearful about the long-distance race.[f] And, in
general, loftiness and grandeur of style are more
fitting for political speech; examples are the
Philippics and among the speeches in Thucydides
that of the ephor Sthenelaïdas, that of King Archi-

to Aegina, whose thriving commerce threatened the prosperity of the Peiraeus.
  [f] *Cf. Life of Phocion*, chap. xxiii.

(803) τοῦ βασιλέως ἐν Πλαταιαῖς καὶ Περικλέους ἡ μετὰ
τὸν λοιμόν· ἐπὶ δὲ τῶν Ἐφόρου καὶ Θεοπόμπου
καὶ Ἀναξιμένους ῥητορειῶν καὶ περιόδων, ἃς
περαίνουσιν ἐξοπλίσαντες τὰ στρατεύματα καὶ
παρατάξαντες, ἔστιν εἰπεῖν

οὐδεὶς σιδήρου ταῦτα μωραίνει πέλας.

7. Οὐ μὴν ἀλλὰ καὶ σκῶμμα καὶ γελοῖον ἔστιν
ὅτε γίγνεται πολιτικοῦ λόγου μέρος, εἰ μὴ πρὸς
C ὕβριν ἢ βωμολοχίαν, ἀλλὰ χρησίμως ἐπιπλήττοντος
ἢ διασύροντος λέγοιτο. μάλιστα δ' εὐδοκιμεῖ τὰ
τοιαῦτα περὶ τὰς ἀμείψεις καὶ τὰς ἀπαντήσεις·
τὸ γὰρ ἐκ παρασκευῆς καὶ κατάρχοντα γελωτο-
ποιοῦντος ἐστι καὶ δόξα κακοηθείας πρόσεστιν, ὡς
προσῆν τοῖς Κικέρωνος σκώμμασι καὶ τοῖς Κάτωνος
τοῦ πρεσβυτέρου καὶ Εὐξιθέου τοῦ Ἀριστοτέλους
συνήθους· οὗτοι γὰρ ἔσκωπτον ἀρχόμενοι πολλάκις.
ἀμυνομένῳ δὲ συγγνώμην ἅμα καὶ χάριν ὁ καιρὸς
δίδωσι, καθάπερ Δημοσθένει πρὸς τὸν αἰτίαν ἔχοντα
D κλέπτειν χλευάζοντα δ' αὐτοῦ τὰς νυκτογραφίας,
" οἶδ' ὅτι σε λυπῶ λύχνον καίων"· καὶ πρὸς
Δημάδην βοῶντα Δημοσθένης ἐμὲ βούλεται δι-
ορθοῦν " ἡ ὗς τὴν Ἀθηνᾶν," " αὕτη μέντοι πέρυσιν
ἡ Ἀθηνᾶ μοιχεύουσα ἐλήφθη." χάριεν δὲ καὶ τὸ
Ξεναινέτου πρὸς τοὺς πολίτας λοιδοροῦντας αὐτὸν
ὅτι στρατηγὸς ὢν πέφευγε, " μεθ' ὑμῶν γ', ὦ

---

[a] Thucydides, i. 86 ; ii. 72 ; ii. 60.
[b] Nauck, *Trag. Graec. Frag.* p. 441, l. 22 ; from the
Autolycus of Euripides.
[c] These two retorts are recorded by Plutarch, *Life of
Demosthenes*, chap. xi. p. 851. The second obviously refers
to misconduct on the part of Demades. " The sow (teaches
184

damus at Plataea, and that of Pericles after the
pestilence.[a] But as for the rhetorical efforts and
grand periods of Ephorus, Theopompus, and Anaximenes, which they deliver after they have armed
and drawn up the armies, it can be said of them,

> None talks so foolishly when near the steel.[b]

7. It is true, however, that derision and ridicule
are sometimes proper parts of the statesman's
speech if employed, not as insults or buffoonery,
but for needful reproof and disparagement. That
sort of thing is most laudable in rejoinders and
replies ; for when employed of set purpose and
without provocation, it makes the speaker appear
to be a clown and carries with it a suspicion of malice,
such as was attached to the ridicule in the speeches
of Cicero, Cato the Elder, and Aristotle's pupil
Euxitheüs, all of whom frequently employed ridicule
without previous provocation. But for one who
employs it in self-defence the occasion makes it
pardonable and at the same time pleasing, as when
Demosthenes, in reply to a man who was suspected
of being a thief and who mocked him for writing at
night, said, " I am aware that I offend you by keeping a light burning," and to Demades who shouted,
" Demosthenes would correct *me*—' the sow correcting Athena,' " he replied, " Yes, your Athena
was caught in adultery last year ! " [c] Witty too was
Xenaenetus's rejoinder to the citizens who reviled
him for running away when he was general, " Yes,

or contends with) Athena " was a proverbial expression; *cf.*
Theocritus, *Idyl,* v. 23. As *sus* (*docet*) *Minervam* the proverb was current in Latin ; *cf.* Festus, p. 310 Müller, p. 408
Lindsay ; Cicero, *Ad Familiares,* ix. 18. 3 ; *Academica,* i. 4.
18 ; *De Oratore,* ii. 57. 233.

φίλαι κεφαλαί." τὸ δ' ἄγαν φυλακτέον ἐν τῷ
γελοίῳ καὶ τὸ λυποῦν ἀκαίρως τοὺς ἀκούοντας ἢ
τὸν λέγοντα ποιοῦν ἀγεννῆ καὶ ταπεινόν, ὥσπερ τὰ
Δημοκράτους· ἀναβαίνων μὲν γὰρ εἰς τὴν ἐκκλησίαν
ἔφη, καθάπερ ἡ πόλις, μικρὸν ἰσχύειν καὶ μέγα
φυσᾶν· ἐν δὲ τοῖς Χαιρωνικοῖς παρελθὼν εἰς τὸν
E δῆμον, " οὐκ ἂν ἐβουλόμην κακῶς οὕτω πεπραγέναι[1] τὴν πόλιν, ὥστε κἀμοῦ συμβουλεύοντος ὑμᾶς
ἀκούειν "· καὶ γὰρ καὶ τοῦτο μικροῦ κἀκεῖνο μανι-
κοῦ, πολιτικῷ δ' οὐδέτερον ἁρμόττον. Φωκίωνος
δὲ καὶ τὴν βραχυλογίαν ἐθαύμαζον· ὁ γοῦν Πολύ-
ευκτος ἀπεφαίνετο ῥήτορα μέγιστον εἶναι Δημοσθένην, δεινότατον δ' εἰπεῖν Φωκίωνα· πλεῖστον γὰρ
αὐτοῦ τὸν λόγον ἐν λέξει βραχυτάτῃ νοῦν περιέχειν.
καὶ ὁ Δημοσθένης τῶν ἄλλων καταφρονῶν εἰώθει
λέγειν, ἀνισταμένου Φωκίωνος, " ἡ τῶν ἐμῶν
λόγων κοπὶς ἀνίσταται."

F   8. Μάλιστα μὲν οὖν ἐσκεμμένῳ πειρῶ καὶ μὴ
διακένῳ τῷ λόγῳ χρῆσθαι πρὸς τοὺς πολλοὺς μετ'
ἀσφαλείας, εἰδὼς ὅτι καὶ Περικλῆς ἐκεῖνος εὔχετο[2]
πρὸ τοῦ δημηγορεῖν μηδὲ ῥῆμα μηδὲν ἀλλότριον
τῶν πραγμάτων ἐπελθεῖν αὐτῷ. δεῖ δ' ὅμως καὶ
πρὸς τὰς ἀπαντήσεις τὸν λόγον εὔστροφον ἔχειν
804 καὶ γεγυμνασμένον· ὀξεῖς γὰρ οἱ καιροὶ καὶ πολλὰ
φέροντες ἐν ταῖς πολιτείαις αἰφνίδια. διὸ καὶ
Δημοσθένης ἠλαττοῦτο πολλῶν, ὥς φασι, παρὰ τὸν
καιρὸν ἀναδυόμενος καὶ κατοκνῶν· Ἀλκιβιάδην δ'
ὁ Θεόφραστος ἱστορεῖ, μὴ μόνον ἃ δεῖ λέγειν ἀλλὰ

---

[1] πεπραγέναι Herwerden : πεπραχέναι.
[2] εὔχετο Bernardakis : ηὔχετο.

a Cf. *Life of Alcibiades*, chap. x.

the right thing, but to say it in the right way, often while actually speaking would search for words and arrange them into sentences, thereby causing hesitation and failure. But the man who is so moved by the events which take place and the opportunities which offer themselves that he springs to his feet is the one who most thrills the crowd, attracts it, and carries it with him. So it was, for example, with Leo [a] of Byzantium ; he once came to address the Athenians when they were in political discord, and when they laughed at him because he was a little man, he said, " What if you should see my wife, who hardly comes up to my knee ? " Then when they laughed louder, " And yet," he said, " little as we are, when we quarrel with each other, the city of Byzantium is not big enough to hold us." So also when Pytheas the orator was speaking in opposition to the granting of honours to Alexander and someone said to him, " Do you, at your age, dare to speak on such important matters ? " he replied : " And yet Alexander is younger than I, and you are voting to make him a god."

9. And the statesman must bring to the struggle of statecraft—a struggle which is not unimportant, but calls for all one's fighting power—speech which is severely trained in firmness of voice and strength of lungs, that he may not be frequently so weary and burnt out as to be defeated by some

Rapacious bawler with a torrent's voice.[b]

Cato, when he had no hope of winning his cause by persuasion because the popular assembly or the senate was gained over beforehand by favours and interests, used to get up and speak the whole day,

(804) καιρὸν οὕτως ἐξέκρουε. περὶ μὲν οὖν τῆς τοῦ λόγου παρασκευῆς καὶ χρείας ἱκανὰ ταῦτα τῷ δυναμένῳ τὸ ἀκόλουθον προσεξευρίσκειν.

10. Εἰσβολαὶ δὲ καὶ ὁδοὶ δύο τῆς πολιτείας εἰσίν, ἡ μὲν ταχεῖα καὶ λαμπρὰ πρὸς δόξαν οὐ D μὴν ἀκίνδυνος, ἡ δὲ πεζοτέρα καὶ βραδυτέρα τὸ δ' ἀσφαλὲς ἔχουσα μᾶλλον. οἱ μὲν γὰρ εὐθὺς ὥσπερ ἐξ ἄκρας πελαγίου πράξεως ἐπιφανοῦς καὶ μεγάλης ἐχούσης δὲ τόλμαν ἄραντες ἀφῆκαν ἐπὶ τὴν πολιτείαν, ἡγούμενοι λέγειν ὀρθῶς τὸν Πίνδαρον ὡς

ἀρχομένου δ' ἔργου πρόσωπον
χρὴ θέμεν τηλαυγές·

καὶ γὰρ δέχονται προθυμότερον οἱ πολλοὶ κόρῳ τινὶ καὶ πλησμονῇ τῶν συνήθων τὸν ἀρχόμενον, ὥσπερ ἀγωνιστὴν θεαταί, καὶ τὸν φθόνον ἐκπλήτ-τουσιν αἱ λαμπρὰν ἔχουσαι καὶ ταχεῖαν αὔξησιν E ἀρχαὶ καὶ δυνάμεις. οὔτε γὰρ πῦρ φησιν ὁ Ἀρί-στων καπνὸν ποιεῖν οὔτε δόξαν φθόνον, ἢν εὐθὺς ἐκλάμψῃ καὶ ταχέως, ἀλλὰ τῶν κατὰ μικρὸν αὐξα-νομένων καὶ σχολαίως ἄλλον ἀλλαχόθεν ἐπιλαμβά-νεσθαι· διὸ πολλοὶ πρὶν ἀνθῆσαι περὶ τὸ βῆμα κατεμαράνθησαν. ὅπου δ', ὥσπερ ἐπὶ τοῦ Λάδα λέγουσιν,

ὁ ψόφος ἦν ὕσπληγος ἐν οὔασιν,

ᵃ *Ol.* vi. 4. The translation is adapted from that of Sir John Sandys (L.C.L.).
ᵇ Paton's translation (in L.C.L.) of the phrase in *Anth.*

thus destroying his opponents' opportunity. On the subject, then, of the preparation of one's speech and the way to use it these remarks are enough for one who has the ability to go on and discover the conclusions to be drawn from them.

10. There are two entrances to public life and two paths leading to it : one the quick and brilliant road to reputation, by no means without risk, the other more prosaic and slower, but safer. For some men launch out at once into political life with some conspicuous, great, and daring action, like men who launch a vessel from a promontory that juts out into the sea ; they think Pindar is right in saying

> To a work's beginning we needs must set
> A front that shines afar,[a]

for the masses are more ready to accept the beginner because they are so palled and surfeited with those to whom they are accustomed, just as spectators at a show are glad to accept a new performer ; and authority and power that has a brilliant and rapid growth takes envy's breath away. For, as Ariston says, fire does not cause smoke, nor reputation envy, if it blazes up quickly at the start, but those who grow great gradually and slowly are attacked one from one side, another from another ; hence many men before coming to full bloom as public speakers have withered away. But if, as is said of Ladas,

> The noise o' the barrier's fall was in his ears [b]

Pal. xi. 86 on Pericles, quoted from the earlier epigram on Ladas, a famous runner of Sparta. The sudden cutting or loosening of the taut rope stretched across the starting-line was accompanied by an audible sound. See E. N. Gardiner, *Jour. Hell. Studies* xxiii. p. 262.

ἔνθα κἀστεφανοῦτο¹ πρεσβεύων ἢ θριαμβεύων ἢ
στρατηγῶν ἐπιφανῶς, οὔθ' οἱ φθονοῦντες οὔθ' οἱ
καταφρονοῦντες ὁμοίως ἐπὶ τοιούτων ἰσχύουσιν.
οὕτω παρῆλθεν εἰς δόξαν Ἄρατος, ἀρχὴν ποιη-
F σάμενος πολιτείας τὴν Νικοκλέους τοῦ τυράννου
κατάλυσιν· οὕτως Ἀλκιβιάδης, τὰ Μαντινικὰ
συστήσας ἐπὶ Λακεδαιμονίους. Πομπήιος δὲ καὶ
θριαμβεύειν ἠξίου μήπω παριὼν εἰς σύγκλητον· οὐκ
ἐῶντος δὲ Σύλλα, " πλείονες " ἔφη " τὸν ἥλιον
ἀνατέλλοντα προσκυνοῦσιν ἢ δυόμενον "· καὶ Σύλλας
ὑπεῖξε τοῦτ' ἀκούσας. καὶ Σκιπίωνα δὲ Κορνήλιον
οὐκ ἀφ' ἧς ἔτυχεν ἀρχῆς ὁ Ῥωμαίων δῆμος ἀγο-
ρανομίαν μετερχόμενον ἐξαίφνης ὕπατον ἀπέδειξε
805 παρὰ τὸν νόμον, ἀλλὰ θαυμάσας αὐτοῦ μειρακίου
μὲν ὄντος τὴν ἐν Ἰβηρίᾳ μονομαχίαν καὶ νίκην,
μικρὸν δ' ὕστερον τὰ πρὸς Καρχηδόνι χιλιαρχοῦντος
ἔργα, περὶ ὧν καὶ Κάτων ὁ πρεσβύτερος ἀν-
εφώνησεν

οἷος πέπνυται, τοὶ δὲ σκιαὶ ἀΐσσουσιν.

νῦν οὖν ὅτε τὰ πράγματα τῶν πόλεων οὐκ ἔχει
πολέμων ἡγεμονίας οὐδὲ τυραννίδων καταλύσεις
οὐδὲ συμμαχικὰς πράξεις, τίν' ἄν τις ἀρχὴν ἐπιφανοῦς λάβοι καὶ λαμπρᾶς πολιτείας; αἱ δίκαι τε
λείπονται αἱ² δημόσιαι καὶ πρεσβεῖαι πρὸς αὐτο-
B κράτορα ἀνδρὸς διαπύρου καὶ θάρσος ἅμα καὶ νοῦν
ἔχοντος δεόμεναι. πολλὰ δ' ἔστι καὶ τῶν παρει-

¹ κἀστεφανοῦτο Coraes, followed by Bernardakis: καὶ
στεφανοῦτο.
² As Bernardakis says, either αἱ should (so Reiske) be
omitted or (preferably) another αἱ should be inserted before
πρεσβεῖαι.

even when he has been crowned for his brilliant success on an embassy, for a notable triumph, or for achievement as a general, in such instances neither those who envy a man nor those who despise him have so much power as before. In this way Aratus arrived at fame, beginning his public life with the destruction of the tyrant Nicocles; so Alcibiades, by making the Mantinean alliance against the Lacedaemonians. Pompey demanded a triumph although he had not yet been admitted to the senate, and when Sulla voted against it, he said, " More worship the rising than the setting sun "; and Sulla, when he heard this, withdrew his opposition. And take the case of Cornelius Scipio; it was not because of any chance beginning that the Roman people suddenly and contrary to law appointed him consul when he was a candidate for the aedileship, but rather because they admired his victorious single combat in Iberia when he was a mere youth, and his deeds a little later at Carthage as military tribune, about which Cato the Elder exclaimed

> He and he only has sense, the rest are mere flickering shadows.[a]

Nowadays, then, when the affairs of the cities no longer include leadership in wars, nor the overthrowing of tyrannies, nor acts of alliances, what opening for a conspicuous and brilliant public career could a young man find? There remain the public lawsuits and embassies to the Emperor, which demand a man of ardent temperament and one who possesses both courage and intellect. But there are many excellent lines of endeavour that are neglected

---

[a] Homer, *Od.* xi. 495 (slightly changed).

(805) μένων ἐν ταῖς πόλεσι καλῶν ἀναλαμβάνοντα καὶ
τῶν ἐξ ἔθους φαύλου παραδυομένων ἐπ' αἰσχύνῃ
τινὶ τῆς πόλεως ἢ βλάβῃ μεθιστάντα πρὸς αὐτὸν
ἐπιστρέφειν. ἤδη δὲ καὶ δίκη μεγάλη καλῶς δικα-
σθεῖσα καὶ πίστις ἐν συνηγορίᾳ πρὸς ἀντίδικον
ἰσχυρὸν ὑπὲρ ἀσθενοῦς καὶ παρρησία πρὸς ἡγεμόνα
μοχθηρὸν ὑπὲρ τοῦ δικαίου κατέστησεν ἐνίους εἰς
ἀρχὴν πολιτείας ἔνδοξον. οὐκ ὀλίγοι δὲ καὶ δι'
ἔχθρας ηὐξήθησαν, ἐπιχειρήσαντες ἀνθρώποις ἐπίφθονον ἔχουσιν ἀξίωμα καὶ φοβερόν· εὐθὺς γὰρ ἡ
C τοῦ καταλυθέντος ἰσχὺς τῷ κρατήσαντι μετὰ βελ-
τίονος δόξης ὑπάρχει. τὸ μὲν γὰρ ἀνδρὶ χρηστῷ
καὶ δι' ἀρετὴν πρωτεύοντι προσμάχεσθαι κατὰ
φθόνον, ὡς Περικλεῖ Σιμμίας, Ἀλκμέων[1] δὲ
Θεμιστοκλεῖ, Πομπηίῳ δὲ Κλώδιος, Ἐπαμεινώνδᾳ
δὲ Μενεκλείδης ὁ ῥήτωρ, οὔτε πρὸς δόξαν καλὸν
οὔτ' ἄλλως συμφέρον· ὅταν γὰρ ἐξαμαρτόντες οἱ
πολλοὶ πρὸς ἄνδρα χρηστόν, εἶθ' ὃ γίγνεται ταχέως
ἐπ' ὀργῇ μετανοήσωσι, πρὸς τοῦτο τὴν ῥᾴστην
ἀπολογίαν δικαιοτάτην νομίζουσιν, ἐπιτρῖψαι τὸν
ἀναπείσαντα καὶ καταρξάμενον. τὸ μέντοι φαῦλον
ἄνθρωπον, ἀπονοίᾳ δὲ καὶ δεινότητι πεποιημένον
D ὑφ' αὑτῷ τὴν πόλιν, οἷος ἦν Κλέων Ἀθήνησι καὶ
Κλεοφῶν, ἐπαναστάντα καθελεῖν καὶ ταπεινῶσαι
λαμπρὰν ποιεῖται τὴν πάροδον ὥσπερ δράματος τῆς
πολιτείας. οὐκ ἀγνοῶ δ' ὅτι καὶ βουλήν τινες
ἐπαχθῆ καὶ ὀλιγαρχικὴν κολούσαντες, ὥσπερ

[1] Ἀλκμέων Bernardakis: ἀλκμαίων.

in our cities which a man may take up, and also
many practices resulting from evil custom, that have
insinuated themselves to the shame or injury of the
city, which a man may remove, and thus turn them
to account for himself. Indeed in past times a just
verdict gained in a great suit, or good faith in acting
as advocate for a weak client against a powerful
opponent, or boldness of speech in behalf of the right
against a wicked ruler, has opened to some men a
glorious entrance into public life. And not a few
also have grown great through the enemies they have
made by attacking men whose position made them
enviable or caused them to be feared ; for when
such a man is overthrown his power passes at once,
and with better reputation, to the man who overcame him. For attacking, through motives of envy,
a good man who, on account of his virtue, is leader
of the state, as Pericles was attacked by Simmias,
Themistocles by Alcmeon, Pompey by Claudius, and
Epameinondas by Menecleides the orator, is neither
conducive to a good reputation nor advantageous in
any other way ; for when the people have committed
a wrong against a good man and then (which happens
quickly) repent of their anger, they think the easiest
way to excuse themselves for this offence is the most
just, namely, to destroy the man who was the
author of it and persuaded them to commit it. On
the other hand, to revolt against a bad man who by
shameless audacity and cunning has made the city
subject to himself, such as Cleon and Cleophon were
at Athens, and to pull him down and humble him
provides a glorious entrance upon the stage of public
life. And I am not ignorant of the fact that some
men by curtailing the power of an oppressive and

(805) Ἐφιάλτης Ἀθήνησι καὶ Φορμίων παρ' Ἠλείοις,
δύναμιν ἅμα καὶ δόξαν ἔσχον· ἀλλὰ μέγας ἀρχομένῳ
πολιτείας οὗτος ὁ κίνδυνός ἐστι. διὸ καὶ βελτίονα
Σόλων ἔλαβεν ἀρχήν, διεστώσης ἐς τρία μέρη τῆς
E πόλεως, τὸ τῶν Διακρίων λεγομένων καὶ τὸ τῶν
Πεδιέων καὶ τὸ τῶν Παραλίων· οὐδενὶ γὰρ ἐμμίξας
ἑαυτόν, ἀλλὰ κοινὸς ὢν πᾶσι καὶ πάντα λέγων καὶ
πράττων πρὸς ὁμόνοιαν ᾑρέθη νομοθέτης ἐπὶ τὰς
διαλύσεις καὶ κατέστησεν οὕτω τὴν ἀρχήν. ἡ
μὲν οὖν ἐπιφανεστέρα πάροδος εἰς τὴν πολιτείαν
τοσαύτας ἔχει καὶ τοιαύτας ἀρχάς.

11. Τὴν δ' ἀσφαλῆ καὶ σχολαίαν εἵλοντο πολλοὶ
τῶν ἐνδόξων, Ἀριστείδης, Φωκίων, Παμμένης ὁ
Θηβαῖος, Λεύκολλος ἐν Ῥώμῃ, Κάτων, Ἀγησίλαος
ὁ Λακεδαιμόνιος· τούτων γὰρ ἕκαστος, ὥσπερ οἱ
κιττοὶ τοῖς ἰσχύουσι τῶν δένδρων περιπλεκόμενοι
F συνεξανίστανται, προσδραμὼν ἀνδρὶ πρεσβυτέρῳ
νέος ἔτι[1] καὶ ἄδοξος ἐνδόξῳ, κατὰ μικρὸν αἰρόμενος
ὑπὸ τῆς περὶ ἐκεῖνον δυνάμεως καὶ συναυξανόμενος
ἤρεισε καὶ κατερρίζωσεν ἑαυτὸν εἰς τὴν πολιτείαν.
Ἀριστείδην μὲν γὰρ ηὔξησε Κλεισθένης καὶ Φωκίωνα Χαβρίας, Λεύκολλον[2] δὲ Σύλλας, Κάτωνα δὲ
Μάξιμος, Ἐπαμεινώνδας δὲ Παμμένη,[3] καὶ Λύσανδρος Ἀγησίλαον· ἀλλ' οὗτος μὲν ὑπὸ[4] φιλοτιμίας
ἀκαίρου καὶ ζηλοτυπίας διὰ δόξαν[5] ὑβρίσας ἀπ-
έρριψε ταχὺ τὸν καθηγεμόνα τῶν πράξεων[6]· οἱ δ'
ἄλλοι καλῶς καὶ πολιτικῶς καὶ ἄχρι τέλους ἐθερά-

---

[1] νέος ἔτι Benseler : ἔτι νέος.
[2] Λεύκολλον] Πομπήιον Kaltwasser.
[3] Ἐπαμεινώνδας δὲ Παμμένη Kaltwasser : ἐπαμεινώνδαν δὲ
παμμένης.   [4] ὑπὸ added by Meziriacus.
[5] διὰ δόξαν Schaefer : δόξαν.
[6] πράξεων Emperius : πρακτέων.

oligarchical senate, as Ephialtes did at Athens and Phormio at Elis, have gained at the same time both power and glory; but to one who is just entering upon public life there is a great risk in this. Therefore Solon made a better beginning, when the State was divided into three factions called the Diacrians ("hill-folk"), the Pedieans ("plainsfolk"), and the Paralians ("coastfolk"); for he entangled himself with none of them, but acted for all in common and said and did everything to bring about concord among them, so that he was chosen lawgiver to reconcile their differences and in this way established his rule.[a] So many, then, and of such kinds are the more conspicuous ways of entering upon a public career.

11. But the safe and leisurely way has been chosen by many famous men—Aristeides, Phocion, Pammenes the Theban, Lucullus at Rome, Cato, the Lacedaemonian Agesilaüs. For just as ivy rises by twining itself about a strong tree, so each of these men, by attaching himself while still young to an older man and while still obscure to a man of reputation, being gradually raised up under the shelter of his power and growing great with him, fixed himself firmly and rooted himself in the affairs of State. For Aristeides was made great by Cleisthenes, Phocion by Chabrias, Lucullus by Sulla, Cato by Maximus, Epameinondas aided Pammenes, and Lysander Agesilaüs. But Agesilaüs through untimely ambition and jealousy of Lysander's reputation insulted and quickly cast aside the guide of his actions; but the others in noble and statesmanlike fashion cherished their teachers until

---

[a] *Cf.* Aristotle, *Constitution of Athens*, chap. v.

197

806 πευσαν καὶ συνεπεκόσμησαν, ὥσπερ τὰ πρὸς ἥλιον
ὑφιστάμενα σώματα, τὸ λαμπρῦνον αὐτοὺς πάλιν
ἀφ' ἑαυτῶν αὔξοντες καὶ συνεκφωτίζοντες. οἱ γοῦν
Σκιπίωνι βασκαίνοντες ὑποκριτὴν αὐτὸν ἀπεφαί-
νοντο τῶν πράξεων ποιητὴν δὲ Λαίλιον τὸν ἑταῖρον,
ὁ δὲ Λαίλιος ὑπ' οὐδενὸς ἐπήρθη τούτων ἀλλ' ἀεὶ
διετέλεσε τῇ Σκιπίωνος ἀρετῇ καὶ δόξῃ συμφιλοτι-
μούμενος. Ἀφράνιος δὲ Πομπηίου φίλος, εἰ καὶ
πάνυ ταπεινὸς ἦν, ὅμως ἐπίδοξος ὢν ὕπατος αἱρε-
B θήσεσθαι, Πομπηίου σπουδάζοντος ἑτέροις, ἀπέστη
τῆς φιλοτιμίας εἰπὼν οὐκ ἂν οὕτω λαμπρὸν αὑτῷ
γενέσθαι τὸ τυχεῖν ὑπατείας, ὡς ἀνιαρὸν ἅμα καὶ
δυσχερές, εἰ Πομπηίου μὴ θέλοντος μηδὲ συμπράτ-
τοντος· ἐνιαυτὸν οὖν ἀνασχόμενος μόνον οὔτε τῆς
ἀρχῆς ἀπέτυχε καὶ τὴν φιλίαν διετήρησε. τοῖς δ'
οὕτω χειραγωγουμένοις ὑφ' ἑτέρων ἐπὶ δόξαν ἅμα
συμβαίνει χαρίζεσθαί τε πολλοῖς, κἄν τι συμβαίνῃ
δύσκολον, ἧττον ἀπεχθάνεσθαι· διὸ καὶ Φίλιππος
Ἀλεξάνδρῳ παρῄνει κτᾶσθαι φίλους, ἕως ἔξεστι,
βασιλεύοντος ἑτέρου πρὸς χάριν ὁμιλοῦντα καὶ
φιλοφρονούμενον.

12. Αἱρεῖσθαι δὲ δεῖ τὸν ἀρχόμενον πολιτείας
C ἡγεμόνα μὴ ἁπλῶς τὸν ἔνδοξον καὶ δυνατόν, ἀλλὰ
καὶ τὸν δι' ἀρετὴν τοιοῦτον. ὡς γὰρ οὐ πᾶν δέν-
δρον ἐθέλει προσίεσθαι καὶ φέρειν περιπλεκομένην
τὴν ἄμπελον ἀλλ' ἔνια καταπνίγει καὶ διαφθείρει
τὴν αὔξησιν αὐτῆς, οὕτως ἐν ταῖς πόλεσιν οἱ μὴ
φιλόκαλοι, φιλότιμοι δὲ καὶ φίλαρχοι μόνον, οὐ
προΐενται τοῖς νέοις πράξεων ἀφορμάς, ἀλλ' ὥσπερ

---

^a *Cf. Life of Pompey*, chap. xliv., where another story con-
cerning the friendship of Pompey for Afranius is told.

the end and joined in honouring them, enhancing in turn with their own radiance, and illuminating, like the heavenly bodies that face the sun, that which caused themselves to shine. Certainly Scipio's detractors said that he was the actor, but his friend Laelius the real author of his deeds; Laelius, however, was not puffed up by any of those sayings but continued always eagerly to exalt Scipio's virtue and renown. And Pompey's friend Afranius, even though he was of humble station, nevertheless expected to be elected consul, but when Pompey favoured other candidates, he relinquished his ambition, saying that gaining the consulship would be to him not so much glorious as painful and troublesome, if it were against Pompey's will and without his co-operation ; and so after waiting only one year he both gained the office and retained the friendship.[a] Those who are thus led to renown by the hand of others gain favour with many, and at the same time, if anything unpleasant happens, are disliked ; and that is why Philip advised Alexander to gain friends as long as he could while another man was king by having pleasant intercourse with others and maintaining friendly relations with them.

12. But anyone who is entering upon a public career should choose as his leader a man who is not merely of established reputation and powerful, but one who is all this on account of real worth. For just as not every tree will accept and support the grape-vine which entwines itself about it, but some trees stifle and ruin its growth, so in States, the men who are not lovers of what is noble, but merely lovers of honours and of office, do not afford young men opportunities for public activities, but through

(806) τροφὴν ἑαυτῶν τὴν δόξαν ἀφαιρουμένους πιέζουσιν
ὑπὸ φθόνου καὶ καταμαραίνουσιν· ὡς Μάριος ἐν
Λιβύῃ καὶ πάλιν ἐν Γαλατίᾳ πολλὰ διὰ Σύλλα
κατορθώσας ἐπαύσατο χρώμενος, ἀχθεσθεὶς μὲν
D αὐτοῦ τῇ αὐξήσει, πρόφασιν δὲ τὴν σφραγῖδα
ποιησάμενος ἀπέρριψεν· ὁ γὰρ Σύλλας, ὅτε τῷ
Μαρίῳ στρατηγοῦντι συνῆν ταμιεύων ἐν Λιβύῃ,
πεμφθεὶς ὑπ' αὐτοῦ πρὸς Βῶκχον ἤγαγεν Ἰογόρθαν
αἰχμάλωτον· οἷα δὲ νέος φιλότιμος, ἄρτι δόξης
γεγευμένος, οὐκ ἤνεγκε μετρίως τὸ εὐτύχημα,
γλυψάμενος δ' εἰκόνα τῆς πράξεως ἐν σφραγῖδι
τὸν Ἰογόρθαν αὐτῷ παραδιδόμενον ἐφόρει· καὶ
τοῦτ' ἐγκαλῶν ὁ Μάριος ἀπέρριψεν αὐτόν· ὁ δὲ
πρὸς Κάτουλον[1] καὶ Μέτελλον ἄνδρας ἀγαθοὺς
καὶ Μαρίῳ διαφόρους μεταστὰς ταχὺ τὸν Μάριον
ἐξήλασε καὶ κατέλυσε τῷ ἐμφυλίῳ πολέμῳ μικροῦ
E δεήσαντα τὴν Ῥώμην ἀνατρέψαι. Σύλλας μέντοι
καὶ Πομπήιον ἐκ νέου μὲν ἦρεν ὑπεξανιστάμενος
αὐτῷ καὶ τὴν κεφαλὴν ἀποκαλυπτόμενος ἐπιόντι,
καὶ τοῖς ἄλλοις νέοις πράξεων ἡγεμονικῶν μεταδιδοὺς ἀφορμάς, ἐνίους δὲ καὶ παροξύνων ἄκοντας,
ἐνέπλησε φιλοτιμίας καὶ ζήλου τὰ στρατεύματα· καὶ
πάντων ἐκράτησε βουλόμενος εἶναι μὴ μόνος ἀλλὰ
πρῶτος καὶ μέγιστος ἐν πολλοῖς καὶ μεγάλοις.
τούτων οὖν ἔχεσθαι δεῖ τῶν ἀνδρῶν καὶ τούτοις
ἐμφύεσθαι, μή, καθάπερ ὁ Αἰσώπου βασιλίσκος
F ἐπὶ τῶν ὤμων τοῦ ἀετοῦ κομισθεὶς αἰφνίδιον ἐξ-

---

[1] Κάτουλον Bernardakis after the Basle ms. (Wyttenbach
reads Κάτλον): κάτουλλον.

ᵃ Equivalent here to adjutant.

envy repress them and, to speak figuratively, wither them up by depriving them of glory, their natural nourishment. So Marius, after having achieved many successes in Libya and again in Gaul with the help of Sulla, ceased to employ him and cast him off, being angered by his growth in power, but using the incident of the seal as a pretext. For Sulla, when Marius was general and he was quaestor [a] in Libya, was sent by Marius to Bocchus and took Jugurtha prisoner; and being a young man who had just had his first taste of glory, he did not bear his good fortune with moderation, but had a seal engraved with a representation of his deed—Jugurtha surrendering to him—and wore it.[b] Marius threw this up against him and cast him off. And Sulla, transferring his allegiance to Catulus and Metellus, worthy men and opposed to Marius, quickly drove Marius out and broke his power in the civil war after he had almost overthrown Rome. Sulla, however, exalted Pompey from the time of his youth, rising up and uncovering his head when he came near; and also by giving the other young men opportunities for acts of leadership and even by urging some on against their will, he filled his armies with ambition and eagerness; and he gained power over them all by wishing to be, not the only great man, but first and greatest among many great ones. Such, then, are the men to whom young statesmen should attach themselves and cling closely, not snatching glory away from them, like Aesop's wren who was carried up on the eagle's shoulders, then suddenly flew out and got ahead of him, but

[b] Cf. *Life of Marius*, chap. x., and *Life of Sulla*, chap. iii.

ἕπτη καὶ προέφθασεν, οὕτω τὴν ἐκείνων δόξαν ὑφ-
αρπάζοντας αὐτοὺς ἀλλὰ παρ' ἐκείνων ἅμα μετ'
εὐνοίας καὶ φιλίας λαμβάνοντας, ὡς οὐδ' ἄρξαι
καλῶς τοὺς μὴ πρότερον ὀρθῶς δουλεύσαντας, ᾗ
φησιν ὁ Πλάτων, δυναμένους.

13. Ἕπεται δὲ τούτοις ἡ περὶ φίλων κρίσις,
μήτε τὴν Θεμιστοκλέους ἐπαινοῦσα μήτε τὴν
Κλέωνος διάνοιαν. ὁ μὲν γὰρ Κλέων, ὅτε πρῶτον
ἔγνω τῆς πολιτείας ἅπτεσθαι, τοὺς φίλους συν-
αγαγὼν εἰς ταὐτὸ διελύσατο τὴν φιλίαν πρὸς αὐτούς,
ὡς πολλὰ τῆς ὀρθῆς καὶ δικαίας προαιρέσεως
μαλάσσουσαν ἐν τῇ πολιτείᾳ καὶ παράγουσαν·
ἄμεινον δ' ἂν ἐποίησε τὴν φιλοπλουτίαν ἐκβαλὼν
807 τῆς ψυχῆς καὶ τὴν φιλονεικίαν καὶ φθόνου καὶ
κακοηθείας καθήρας αὑτόν· οὐ γὰρ ἀφίλων αἱ
πόλεις ἀνδρῶν καὶ ἀνεταίρων ἀλλὰ χρηστῶν καὶ
σωφρόνων δέονται· νυνὶ δὲ τοὺς μὲν φίλους
ἀπήλασεν,

ἑκατὸν δὲ κύκλῳ κεφαλαὶ κολάκων οἰμωξομένων[1] ἐλιχμῶντο

περὶ αὐτόν, ὡς οἱ κωμικοὶ λέγουσι· καὶ τραχὺς
ὢν πρὸς τοὺς ἐπιεικεῖς καὶ βαρὺς αὖθις ὑπέβαλλε
τοῖς πολλοῖς πρὸς χάριν ἑαυτόν,

γερονταγωγῶν κἀναμισθαρνεῖν[2] διδούς,

καὶ τὸ φαυλότατον καὶ τὸ νοσοῦν μάλιστα τοῦ
δήμου προσεταιριζόμενος ἐπὶ τοὺς ἀρίστους. ὁ
δὲ Θεμιστοκλῆς πάλιν πρὸς τὸν ἀποφηνάμενον,
ὡς ἄρξει καλῶς ἴσον ἅπασι παρέχων ἑαυτόν,

---

[1] οἰμωξομένων Coraes : οἰμωζομένων.
[2] κἀναμισθαρνεῖν Coraes : καὶ ἀναμισθαρνεῖν, cf. Kock, Com.
Att. Frag. iii. p. 400.

receiving it from them in goodwill and friendship, knowing that no one can ever command well who has not first learned rightly to obey, as Plato says.[a]

13. Next after this comes the decision to be made concerning friends, and here we approve neither the idea of Themistocles nor that of Cleon. For Cleon, when he first decided to take up political life, brought his friends together and renounced his friendship with them as something which often weakens and perverts the right and just choice of policy in political life. But he would have done better if he had cast out from his soul avarice and love of strife and had cleansed himself of envy and malice; for the State needs, not men who have no friends or comrades, but good and self-controlled men. As it was, he drove away his friends,

But a hundred heads of cursed flatterers circling fawned [b]

about him, as the comic poets say; and being rough and harsh to the better classes he in turn subjected himself to the multitude in order to win its favour,

Its old age tending, dosing it with pay,[c]

and making the basest and most unsound element of the people his associates against the best. But Themistocles on the other hand, when someone said that he would govern well if he showed himself equally impartial to all, replied: " May I never

[a] *Laws*, 762 E.
[b] Aristophanes, *Peace*, 756. The poet refers to Cleon.
[c] Quoted by Plutarch, *Life of Nicias*, chap. ii. p. 524. A parody by an unknown comic poet (unless it be by Aristophanes) of a line from the *Peleus* of Sophocles, Nauck, *Trag. Graec. Frag.* 447, p. 239. See Kock, *Com. Att. Frag.* iii. p. 400.

B " μηδέποτ'," εἶπεν, " εἰς τοιοῦτον ἐγὼ καθίσαιμι
(807) θρόνον, ἐν ᾧ πλέον οὐχ ἕξουσιν οἱ φίλοι παρ'
ἐμοῦ[1] τῶν μὴ φίλων," οὐδ' οὗτος ὀρθῶς τῇ φιλίᾳ
κατεπαγγελλόμενος τὴν πολιτείαν καὶ τὰ κοινὰ
καὶ δημόσια ταῖς ἰδίαις χάρισι καὶ σπουδαῖς
ὑφιέμενος. καίτοι πρός γε Σιμωνίδην ἀξιοῦντά τι
τῶν μὴ δικαίων " οὔτε ποιητής," ἔφη, " σπουδαῖός
ἐστιν ᾄδων παρὰ μέλος οὔτ' ἄρχων ἐπιεικὴς παρὰ
τὸν νόμον χαριζόμενος." δεινὸν γὰρ ὡς ἀληθῶς
καὶ σχέτλιον, εἰ ναύτας μὲν ἐκλέγεται κυβερνήτης
καὶ κυβερνήτην ναύκληρος

C   εὖ μὲν ἐνὶ πρύμνῃ οἰήιον, εὖ δὲ κεραίην
    εἰδότας ἐντείνασθαι ἐπορνυμένου ἀνέμοιο·

καί τις ἀρχιτέκτων ὑπουργοὺς καὶ χειροτέχνας, οἳ
μὴ διαφθεροῦσιν αὐτοῦ τοὔργον ἀλλ' ἄριστα συν-
εκπονήσουσιν· ὁ δὲ πολιτικός, ἀριστοτέχνας τις
ὢν κατὰ Πίνδαρον καὶ δημιουργὸς εὐνομίας καὶ
δίκης, οὐκ εὐθὺς αἱρήσεται φίλους ὁμοιοπαθεῖς
καὶ ὑπηρέτας καὶ συνενθουσιῶντας αὐτῷ πρὸς
τὸ καλόν, ἀλλ' ἄλλους[2] πρὸς ἄλλην ἀεὶ χρείαν
D κάμπτοντας[3] αὐτὸν ἀδίκως καὶ βιαίως· οὐδέν τ'
ὀφθήσεται διαφέρων οἰκοδόμου τινὸς ἢ τέκτονος
ἀπειρίᾳ καὶ πλημμελείᾳ γωνίαις χρωμένου καὶ
κανόσι καὶ στάθμαις, ὑφ' ὧν διαστρέφεσθαι
τοὔργον ἔμελλεν· ὄργανα γὰρ οἱ φίλοι ζῶντα καὶ
φρονοῦντα τῶν πολιτικῶν ἀνδρῶν εἰσι, καὶ οὐ δεῖ
συνολισθάνειν αὐτοῖς παραβαίνουσιν, ἀλλὰ προσ-

---

[1] παρ' ἐμοῦ Anton Melissa : παρ' ἐμοί.
[2] ἀλλ' ἄλλους Wyttenbach : ἄλλον ἄλλου.
[3] κάμπτοντας Wyttenbach : κάμπτοντος.

take my seat on such a throne that my friends shall not have more from me than those who are not my friends ! " He also was wrong; for he put the government under pledge to his friendship, subordinating the affairs of the community and the public to private favours and interests. And yet when Simonides asked for something that was not just, he said to him : " Neither is he a good poet who sings contrary to metre, nor is he an equitable ruler who grants favours contrary to law." For truly it is an outrageous and abominable thing if a pilot selects sailors and a ship-captain selects a pilot

Well knowing how at the stern to hold steady the tiller and also
How to stretch taut the yard ropes when rises the onrushing tempest,[a]

and an architect chooses subordinates and handicraftsmen who will not spoil his work but will co-operate to perfect it, whereas the statesman, who is, as Pindar says,[b] the best of craftsmen and the maker of lawfulness and justice, does not immediately choose friends whose convictions are like his own, who will aid him and share his enthusiasm for what is noble, but rather those who are always wrongfully and by violent means trying to divert him to various other uses. Such a statesman will be found to be no better than a builder or a carpenter who through ignorance and error makes use of such squares and rulers and levels as are sure to make his work crooked. For friends are the living and thinking tools of the statesman, and he ought not to slip with them when they go wrong, but he must be on the watch that

---

[a] *Cf.* Callimachus, Frag. 382, p. 787, ed. Schneider.
[b] Pindar, Frag. 57, p. 403 Schroeder.

ἔχειν ὅπως μηδ᾽ ἀγνοούντων αὐτῶν ἐξαμαρτάνωσι.
τοῦτο γὰρ καὶ Σόλωνα κατῄσχυνε καὶ διέβαλε
πρὸς τοὺς πολίτας· ἐπεὶ γὰρ ἐν νῷ λαβὼν τὰ
E ὀφλήματα κουφίσαι καὶ τὴν σεισάχθειαν (τοῦτο
δ᾽ ἦν ὑποκόρισμα χρεῶν ἀποκοπῆς) εἰσενεγκεῖν
ἐκοινώσατο τοῖς φίλοις· οἱ δ᾽ ἔργον ἀδικώτατον
ἔπραξαν· ἐδανείσαντο γὰρ ὑποφθάσαντες ἀργύριον
πολὺ καὶ μετ᾽ ὀλίγον χρόνον εἰς φῶς τοῦ νόμου
προαχθέντος οἱ μὲν ἐφάνησαν οἰκίας τε λαμπρὰς
καὶ γῆν συνεωνημένοι πολλὴν ἐξ ὧν ἐδανείσαντο
χρημάτων, ὁ δὲ Σόλων αἰτίαν ἔσχε συναδικεῖν
ἠδικημένος. Ἀγησίλαος δὲ περὶ τὰς τῶν φίλων
σπουδὰς αὐτὸς αὑτοῦ γιγνόμενος ἀσθενέστατος
καὶ ταπεινότατος ὥσπερ ὁ Εὐριπίδου Πήγασος

ἔπτηξ᾽ ὑπείκων μᾶλλον εἰ μᾶλλον θέλοι,

καὶ ταῖς ἀτυχίαις προθυμότερον βοηθῶν τοῦ δέοντος
F ἐδόκει συνεξομοιοῦσθαι ταῖς ἀδικίαις· καὶ γάρ τοι
Φοιβίδαν κρινόμενον ἔσωσεν ἐπὶ τῷ τὴν Καδμείαν
καταλαβεῖν ἄνευ προστάγματος, φήσας τὰ τοιαῦτα
δεῖν αὐτοματίζειν· καὶ Σφοδρίαν ἐπ᾽ ἔργῳ παρα-
νόμῳ καὶ δεινῷ φεύγοντα δίκην (ἐνέβαλε γὰρ εἰς τὴν
Ἀττικὴν φίλων ὄντων καὶ συμμάχων) ἀφεθῆναι
διεπράξατο, δεήσεσιν ἐρωτικαῖς τοῦ παιδὸς μαλα-
χθείς· καὶ πρός τινα δυνάστην ἐπιστόλιον αὐτοῦ
808 τοιοῦτον φέρεται "Νικίαν, εἰ μὲν οὐκ ἀδικεῖ, ἄφες·
εἰ δ᾽ ἀδικεῖ, ἐμοὶ ἄφες· πάντως δ᾽ ἄφες." ἀλλὰ

ᵃ The cancellation of debts was one of the chief features
of Solon's reorganization of the government of Athens in
the sixth century B.C. The popular term means "shaking
off burdens." This incident is discussed by Aristotle, *Constitution of Athens*, chap. vi., where Solon's innocence of
wrongdoing is maintained.

favour in fact, have avoided harshness and bitterness of speech, by producing the impression that the offensive quality of his action was not due to his own will, but was forced upon him by law and justice. There are also in public life ways which are not dishonourable of helping friends who need money to acquire it ; as, for example, when after the battle Themistocles saw a corpse wearing a golden bracelet and necklace, he himself passed it by, but turned to his friend and said, " Take these things, for you are not, as I am, Themistocles." For the administration of affairs frequently gives the man in public life this sort of chance to help his friends ; for not every man is a Menemachus.[a] Hand over to one friend a case at law which will bring in a good fee as advocate in a just cause, to another introduce a rich man who needs legal oversight and protection, and help another to get some profitable contract or lease. Epameinondas even told a friend to go to a certain rich man and ask for a talent, saying that it was he who bade him give it; and when the man who had been asked for it came and asked him the reason, he replied : " Because this man is a good man and poor, but you are rich since you have appropriated much of the State's wealth." And Xenophon[b] says that Agesilaüs delighted in enriching his friends, he being himself above money.

14. But since, to quote Simonides,[c] " all larks must grow a crest," and every public career bears its crop of enmities and disagreements, the public man must give especial consideration to these matters. So most people commend Themistocles and Aristeides who, whenever they went on an embassy or in com-

[c] Bergk, *Poet. Lyr. Graec.* iii. p. 418, no. 68.

(809) τὴν ἔχθραν ἀποτιθεμένους, ὁσάκις ἐπὶ πρεσβείαν
ἢ στρατηγίαν ἐξίοιεν, εἶτα πάλιν ἀναλαμβάνοντας.
ἐνίοις δὲ καὶ τὸ Κρητίνου τοῦ Μάγνητος ὑπερφυῶς
C ἀρέσκει· Ἑρμείᾳ γὰρ ἀντιπολιτευόμενος ἀνδρὶ οὐ
δυνατῷ μὲν¹ φιλοτίμῳ δὲ καὶ λαμπρῷ τὴν ψυχήν,
ἐπεὶ κατέσχεν ὁ Μιθριδατικὸς πόλεμος, τὴν πόλιν
ὁρῶν κινδυνεύουσαν ἐκέλευσε τὸν Ἑρμείαν τὴν
ἀρχὴν παραλαβόντα χρῆσθαι τοῖς πράγμασιν, αὐτοῦ
μεταστάντος· εἰ δὲ βούλεται στρατηγεῖν ἐκεῖνον,
αὐτὸν ἐκποδὼν ἀπελθεῖν, ὡς μὴ φιλοτιμούμενοι
πρὸς ἀλλήλους ἀπολέσειαν τὴν πόλιν. ἤρεσεν ἡ
πρόκλησις τῷ Ἑρμείᾳ, καὶ φήσας ἑαυτοῦ πολε-
μικώτερον εἶναι τὸν Κρητίναν ὑπεξῆλθε μετὰ
παίδων καὶ γυναικός. ὁ δὲ Κρητίνας ἐκεῖνόν
τε προύπεμψε, τῶν ἰδίων χρημάτων ἐπιδοὺς ὅσα
D φεύγουσιν ἦν ἢ πολιορκουμένοις χρησιμώτερα, καὶ
τὴν πόλιν ἄριστα στρατηγήσας παρ' οὐδὲν ἐλ-
θοῦσαν ἀπολέσθαι περιεποίησεν ἀνελπίστως. εἰ γὰρ
εὐγενὲς καὶ φρονήματος μεγάλου τὸ ἀναφωνῆσαι

φιλῶ τέκν', ἀλλὰ πατρίδ' ἐμὴν μᾶλλον φιλῶ,

πῶς οὐκ ἐκείνοις γε προχειρότερον εἰπεῖν ἑκάστῳ
" μισῶ τὸν δεῖνα καὶ βούλομαι ποιῆσαι κακῶς,
ἀλλὰ πατρίδ' ἐμὴν μᾶλλον φιλῶ"; τὸ γὰρ μὴ
θέλειν διαλυθῆναι πρὸς ἐχθρόν, ὧν ἕνεκα δεῖ καὶ²
φίλον προέσθαι, δεινῶς ἄγριον καὶ θηριῶδες. οὐ
μὴν ἀλλὰ βέλτιον οἱ περὶ Φωκίωνα καὶ Κάτωνα,
μηδ' ὅλως ἔχθραν τινὰ πρὸς πολιτικὰς τιθέμενοι

¹ μὲν added by Benseler, but placed by him after ἀνδρί.
² καὶ added by Coraes.

ᵃ Nauck, Trag. Graec. Frag. p. 918, no. 411. Probably

mand of an army, laid down their private enmity at the frontier, then took it up again later. And some people also are immensely pleased by the conduct of Cretinas of Magnesia. He was a political opponent of Hermeias, a man who was not powerful but was of ambitious spirit and brilliant mind, and when the Mithridatic war broke out, seeing that the State was in danger, he told Hermeias to take over the command and manage affairs, while he himself withdrew; or, if Hermeias wished him to be general, then Hermeias should remove himself, that they might not by ambitious strife with one another destroy the State. The challenge pleased Hermeias, and saying that Cretinas was more versed in war than himself, he went away with his wife and children. And as he was departing Cretinas escorted him, first giving him out of his own means such things as were more useful to exiles than to people besieged in a city, after which by his excellent military leadership he saved the State unexpectedly when it was on the brink of destruction. For if it is a noble thing and the mark of an exalted spirit to exclaim

I love my children, but I love my country more,[a]

would it not have been easier for each of them to say, " I hate so-and-so and wish to do him harm, but I love my country more "? For to be unwilling to make peace with a personal enemy for the sake of those things for which we ought even to give up a friend is shockingly uncivilized and as low as the beasts. Certainly Phocion and Cato and their like acted much better, for they would allow no personal enmity to have any bearing whatsoever upon political

from the *Erechtheus* of Euripides and spoken by Praxithea, wife of Erechtheus.

215

E διαφοράς, ἀλλὰ δεινοὶ καὶ ἀπαραίτητοι μόνον ἐν
τοῖς δημοσίοις ἀγῶσιν ὄντες μὴ προέσθαι τὸ συμ-
φέρον, ἐν δὲ τοῖς ἰδίοις ἀμηνίτως καὶ φιλανθρώπως
χρώμενοι τοῖς ἐκεῖ διαφερομένοις. δεῖ γὰρ ἐχθρὸν
μηδένα πολίτην νομίζειν, ἂν μή τις, οἷος Ἀριστίων
ἢ Νάβις ἢ Κατιλίνας, νόσημα καὶ ἀπόστημα
πόλεως ἐγγένηται· τοὺς δ' ἄλλως ἀπᾴδοντας ὥσπερ
ἁρμονικὸν ἐπιτείνοντα καὶ χαλῶντα πράως εἰς τὸ
ἐμμελὲς ἄγειν, μὴ τοῖς ἁμαρτάνουσι σὺν ὀργῇ καὶ
πρὸς ὕβριν ἐπιφυόμενον, ἀλλ' ὡς Ὅμηρος ἠθικώ-
τερον·

F   ὦ πέπον, ἦ τ' ἐφάμην σε περὶ φρένας ἔμμεναι
     ἄλλων

καὶ

   οἶσθα καὶ ἄλλον μῦθον ἀμείνονα τοῦδε νοῆσαι.

ἄν τέ τι χρηστὸν εἴπωσιν ἢ πράξωσι, μὴ τιμαῖς
ἀχθόμενον αὐτῶν μηδὲ λόγων εὐφήμων ἐπὶ καλοῖς
ἔργοις[1] φειδόμενον· οὕτω γὰρ ὅ τε ψόγος ὅπου δεῖ
πίστιν ἕξει, καὶ πρὸς τὴν κακίαν διαβαλοῦμεν
αὐτοὺς αὔξοντες τὴν ἀρετὴν καὶ ταῦτα παραβάλ-
λοντες ἐκείνοις ὡς ἄξια καὶ πρέποντα μᾶλλον.
810 ἐγὼ δὲ καὶ μαρτυρεῖν ἀξιῶ τὰ δίκαια καὶ τοῖς
διαφόροις τὸν πολιτικὸν ἄνδρα καὶ βοηθεῖν κρινομένοις πρὸς τοὺς συκοφάντας καὶ ταῖς διαβολαῖς
ἀπιστεῖν, ἂν ὦσιν ἀλλότριαι τῆς προαιρέσεως
αὐτῶν· ὥσπερ ὁ Νέρων ἐκεῖνος ὀλίγον ἔμπροσθεν
ἢ κτεῖναι τὸν Θρασέαν μάλιστα μισῶν καὶ φοβού-

---

[1] καλοῖς ἔργοις Reiske : καλοῖς.

[a] Homer, Il. xvii. 171.
[b] Homer, Il. vii. 358.

differences, but were stern and inexorable only in public contests against sacrificing what was for the common good ; yet in private matters they treated kindly and without anger their political opponents. For the statesman should not regard any fellow-citizen as an enemy, unless some man, such as Aristion, Nabis, or Catiline, should appear who is a pest and a running sore to the State. Those who are in other ways out of harmony he should, like a skilful musician, bring into unison by gently tightening or relaxing the strings of his control, not attacking angrily and insultingly those who err, but making an appeal designed rather to make a moral impression, as Homer does :

> Truly, my friend, I did think you surpassed other men in your wisdom [a] ;

and

> Knowledge thou hast to devise other speech that is better than this was.[b]

But if they say or do anything good, he should not be vexed by their honours, nor should he be sparing of complimentary words for their good actions ; for if we act in this way our blame, where it is needed, will be thought justified, and we shall make them dislike evil by exalting virtue and showing through comparison that good actions are more worthy and fitting than the other kind. And I think also that the statesman should give testimony in just causes even for his opponents, should aid them in court against the blackmailers, and should discredit calumnies about them if such accusations are alien to the principles they profess ; just as the infamous Nero, a little before he put Thraseas to death, whom he hated and feared intensely, nevertheless

217

810) μενος, ὅμως ἐγκαλοῦντός τινος ὡς κακῶς κεκρι-
μένου καὶ ἀδίκως, " ἐβουλόμην ἄν," ἔφη, " Θρασέαν
οὕτως ἐμὲ φιλεῖν, ὡς δικαστὴς ἄριστός ἐστιν."

Οὐ χεῖρον δὲ καὶ πρὸς ἐπίπληξιν ἑτέρων φύσει
πονηρῶν καὶ[1] μᾶλλον ἁμαρτανόντων ἐχθροῦ μνη-
σθέντα κομψοτέρου τὸ ἦθος εἰπεῖν " ἀλλ' ἐκεῖνος
B οὐκ ἂν τοῦτ' εἶπεν οὐδ' ἐποίησεν." ὑπομνηστέον
δὲ καὶ πατέρων ἀγαθῶν ἐνίους, ὅταν ἐξαμαρ-
τάνωσιν· οἷον[2] Ὅμηρος

ἢ ὀλίγον οἷ παῖδα ἐοικότα γείνατο Τυδεύς·

καὶ πρὸς Σκιπίωνα τὸν Ἀφρικανὸν Ἄππιος ἐν
ἀρχαιρεσίαις διαγωνιζόμενος " ἡλίκον ἄν," εἶπεν,
" ὦ Παῦλε, στενάξειας ὑπὸ γῆς, αἰσθόμενος ὅτι
σου τὸν υἱὸν ἐπὶ τιμητικὴν ἀρχὴν καταβαίνοντα
Φιλόνικος[3] ὁ τελώνης δορυφορεῖ." τὰ γὰρ τοιαῦτα
νουθετεῖ τοὺς ἁμαρτάνοντας ἅμα καὶ κοσμεῖ τοὺς
νουθετοῦντας. πολιτικῶς δὲ καὶ ὁ Νέστωρ ὁ τοῦ
Σοφοκλέους ἀποκρίνεται λοιδορούμενος ὑπὸ τοῦ
Αἴαντος

C οὐ μέμφομαί σε· δρῶν γὰρ εὖ κακῶς λέγεις.

καὶ Κάτων διενεχθεὶς πρὸς τὸν Πομπήιον ἐν οἷς
ἐβιάζετο τὴν πόλιν μετὰ Καίσαρος, ἐπεὶ κατ-
έστησαν εἰς πόλεμον, ἐκέλευσε Πομπηίῳ παραδοῦναι τὴν ἡγεμονίαν, ἐπειπὼν ὅτι τῶν αὐτῶν ἐστι
καὶ ποιεῖν τὰ μεγάλα κακὰ καὶ παύειν. ὁ γὰρ
μεμιγμένος ἐπαίνῳ ψόγος οὐκ ἔχων ὕβριν ἀλλὰ

---

[1] καὶ added by H.N.F.
[2] οἷον added by Bernardakis.
[3] Φιλόνικος Reiske: φιλόνεικος.

218

when someone accused him of a bad and unjust decision in court, said : " I wish Thraseas were as good a friend to me as he is a most excellent judge."

And it is not a bad method for confounding persons of a different kind, men who are naturally vicious and prone to evil conduct, to mention to them some enemy of theirs who is of finer character and to say : " He would not have said that or done that." And some men, too, when they do wrong, should be reminded of their excellent fathers, as Homer says :

> Truly not much like his sire is the son who was gotten by Tydeus [a];

And Appius, when competing with Scipio Africanus [b] in the elections, said : " O Paulus, how you would groan in the lower world if you saw that when your son was standing for the censorship Philonicus the publican acted as his bodyguard !" Such sayings serve at once to rebuke wrongdoers and to add lustre to those who administer the rebuke. And the Nestor of Sophocles, too, made a statesmanlike reply when reviled by Ajax :

> I blame thee not ; for good thy acts, though ill thy speech. [c]

And Cato, although he had opposed Pompey in the violent measures which he and Caesar applied to the State, when war broke out between them advised handing over the leadership to Pompey, saying : " The men who can bring about great evils can also end them." For blame which is mingled with praise and contains nothing insulting but merely frankness

[a] Homer, *Il.* v. 800, referring to Diomedes.
[b] Scipio Africanus the younger (185–129 B.C.) was the son of Lucius Aemilius Paulus.
[c] Nauck, *Trag. Graec. Frag.* p. 312, no. 771.

219

(810) παρρησίαν, οὐδὲ θυμὸν ἀλλὰ δηγμὸν ἐμποιῶν καὶ
μετάνοιαν, εὐμενὴς φαίνεται καὶ θεραπευτικός· αἱ
δὲ λοιδορίαι τοῖς πολιτικοῖς ἥκιστα πρέπουσιν.
ὅρα δὲ τὰ πρὸς Αἰσχίνην ὑπὸ Δημοσθένους εἰρημένα καὶ τὰ πρὸς τοῦτον ὑπ᾽ Αἰσχίνου, καὶ πάλιν
ἃ πρὸς Δημάδην γέγραφεν Ὑπερείδης, εἰ Σόλων
D ἂν εἶπεν ἢ Περικλῆς ἢ Λυκοῦργος ὁ Λακεδαιμόνιος
ἢ Πιττακὸς ὁ Λέσβιος. καίτοι γε καὶ Δημοσθένης
ἐν τῷ δικανικῷ τὸ λοίδορον ἔχει μόνον, οἱ δὲ Φιλιππικοὶ καθαρεύουσι καὶ σκώμματος καὶ βωμολοχίας
ἁπάσης· τὰ γὰρ τοιαῦτα τῶν ἀκουόντων μᾶλλον
αἰσχύνει τοὺς λέγοντας, ἔτι δὲ[1] καὶ σύγχυσιν
ἀπεργάζεται τῶν πραγμάτων καὶ διαταράττει τὰ
βουλευτήρια καὶ τὰς ἐκκλησίας. ὅθεν ἄρισθ᾽ ὁ
Φωκίων ὑπεκστὰς τῷ λοιδοροῦντι καὶ παυσάμενος
τοῦ λέγειν, ἐπεὶ μόλις ἐσιώπησεν ὁ ἄνθρωπος, αὖθις
παρελθὼν "οὐκοῦν," ἔφη, "περὶ μὲν τῶν ἱππέων
καὶ τῶν ὁπλιτῶν ἀκηκόατε, λείπεται δέ μοι περὶ
E τῶν ψιλῶν καὶ πελταστῶν διελθεῖν." ἀλλ᾽ ἐπεὶ
πολλοῖς γε δυσκάθεκτόν ἐστι τὸ πρᾶγμα καὶ
πολλάκις οὐκ ἀχρήστως οἱ λοιδοροῦντες ἐπιστομί-
ζονται ταῖς ἀπαντήσεσιν, ἔστω βραχεῖα τῇ λέξει
καὶ μὴ θυμὸν ἐμφαίνουσα μηδ᾽ ἀκραχολίαν, ἀλλὰ
πρᾳότητα μετὰ παιδιᾶς καὶ χάριτος ἀμωσγέπως
δάκνουσαν· αἱ δ᾽ ἀντεπιστρέφουσαι μάλιστα τοιαῦται. καθάπερ γὰρ τῶν βελῶν ὅσα πρὸς τὸν
βαλόντα φέρεται πάλιν ῥώμῃ τινὶ δοκεῖ καὶ στερεό-
F τητι τοῦ πληγέντος ἀνακρουόμενα τοῦτο πάσχειν·

[1] ἔτι δὲ Wyttenbach : ἔτι (ὅτι Coraes).

of speech, and arouses not anger but a pricking of
the conscience and repentance, appears both kindly
and healing ; but abusive speech is not at all fitting
for statesmen. Observe the things that were said
by Demosthenes against Aeschines and by Aeschines
against him and again those which Hypereides
wrote against Demades, and ask yourself if a Solon
or a Pericles or Lycurgus the Lacedaemonian or
Pittacus the Lesbian would have said them. And
yet even Demosthenes employs abuse only in his
speeches before a court of law ; the Philippics are
free from all jeering and scurrility. For such things
bring disgrace upon the speakers rather than upon
those spoken of, and moreover they bring confusion
into the conduct of affairs and they disturb councils
and assemblies. Therefore Phocion did well when
he stopped speaking and yielded the floor to a man
who was reviling him, and then, when the fellow had
at last become silent, came forward again saying :
" Well, then, about the cavalry and the heavy
infantry you have heard already ; it remains for me
to discuss the light infantry and the targeteers."
But since many men find it hard to endure that sort
of thing quietly, and abusive speakers are often,
and not without general benefit, made to shut their
mouths by the retorts they evoke, let the reply
be brief in wording, showing no temper and no
extreme rancour, but urbanity mingled with playfulness and grace which somehow or other has a sting
in it. Retorts which turn his own words back upon
the speaker are especially good in this way. For
just as things which are thrown and return to the
thrower seem to do this because they are driven
back by some force and firmness of that against

οὕτω τὸ λεχθὲν ὑπὸ ῥώμης καὶ συνέσεως τοῦ
λοιδορηθέντος ἐπὶ τοὺς λοιδορήσαντας ἀναστρέφειν
ἔοικεν· ὡς τὸ Ἐπαμεινώνδου πρὸς Καλλίστρατον,
ὀνειδίζοντα Θηβαίοις καὶ Ἀργείοις τὴν Οἰδίποδος
πατροκτονίαν καὶ τὴν Ὀρέστου μητροκτονίαν,
ὅτι "τοὺς ταῦτα ποιήσαντας ἡμῶν ἐκβαλόντων
ὑμεῖς ἐδέξασθε"· καὶ τὸ Ἀνταλκίδου τοῦ Σπαρ-
τιάτου πρὸς τὸν Ἀθηναῖον τὸν φήσαντα "πολλάκις
ὑμᾶς ἀπὸ τοῦ Κηφισοῦ ἐδιώξαμεν," "ἀλλ' ἡμεῖς
811 γ' ὑμᾶς ἀπὸ τοῦ Εὐρώτα οὐδέποτε." χαριέντως
δὲ καὶ ὁ Φωκίων, τοῦ Δημάδου κεκραγότος
"Ἀθηναῖοί σε ἀποκτενοῦσιν"· "ἄν γε μανῶσιν,"
ἔφη, "σὲ δέ, ἂν σωφρονῶσι." καὶ Κράσσος ὁ
ῥήτωρ, Δομιτίου πρὸς αὐτὸν εἰπόντος "οὐ σὺ
μυραίνης ἐν κολυμβήθρᾳ σοι τρεφομένης εἶτ'
ἀποθανούσης ἔκλαυσας;" ἀντηρώτησεν "οὐ σὺ
τρεῖς γυναῖκας ἔθαψας καὶ οὐκ ἐδάκρυσας;"
ταῦτα μὲν οὖν ἔχει τινὰ χρείαν καὶ πρὸς τὸν ἄλλον
βίον.

15. Πολιτείας δ' οἱ μὲν εἰς ἅπαν ἐνδύονται
μέρος, ὥσπερ ὁ Κάτων, οὐδεμιᾶς ἀξιοῦντες εἰς
B δύναμιν ἀπολείπεσθαι φροντίδος οὐδ' ἐπιμελείας
τὸν ἀγαθὸν πολίτην· καὶ τὸν Ἐπαμεινώνδαν ἐπαινοῦσιν, ὅτι φθόνῳ καὶ πρὸς ὕβριν ἀποδειχθεὶς
τέλμαρχος[1] ὑπὸ τῶν Θηβαίων οὐκ ἠμέλησεν,
ἀλλ' εἰπὼν ὡς οὐ μόνον ἀρχὴ ἄνδρα δείκνυσιν ἀλλὰ

---

[1] τέλμαρχος Winckelmann and van Herwerden: τελέαρχος.

[a] No such official as *telearchos* is mentioned elsewhere,
and the word itself describes no function. On the other
hand, *telmarchos* or *telmatarchos*, conjectured independently

which they are thrown, so that which is spoken seems through the force and intellect of him who has been abused to turn back upon those who uttered the abuse. For example, the retort of Epameinondas to Callistratus, who reproached the Thebans and the Argives because Oedipus killed his father and Orestes killed his mother : " When we had driven out the doers of those deeds, you took them in," and that of Antalcidas the Spartan to the Athenian who said "We have often chased you away from the Cephissus," "Yes, but we have never had to chase you from the Eurotas." And Phocion also made a witty retort, when, after Demades had screamed "The Athenians will put you to death," he replied, " Yes, if they are crazy ; but you are the one whom they will execute, if they are sane." And Crassus the orator, when Domitius said to him, " It was you, was it not, who wept when a lamprey died that you kept in a tank ? " retorted with the question, " It was you, was it not, who buried three wives without shedding a tear ? " Apt replies of this sort, however, are of some use also in life in general.

15. There are men who enter upon every kind of public service, as Cato did, claiming that the good citizen ought, so far as in him lies, to omit no trouble or diligence ; and they commend Epameinondas because, when through envy and as an insult he had been appointed *telmarch* [a] by the Thebans, he did not neglect his duties, but saying that not only does the office distinguish the man, but also the man the

by Winckelmann and van Herwerden, although not found elsewhere, gives a meaning which accords with Plutarch's description, " official of stagnant pools," or a special kind of collector of refuse and other nuisances from the streets, very like the *koprologoi* of Athens.

(811) καὶ ἀρχὴν ἀνήρ, εἰς μέγα καὶ σεμνὸν ἀξίωμα προ-
ήγαγε τὴν τελμαρχίαν,[1] οὐδὲν οὖσαν πρότερον ἀλλ'
ἢ περὶ τοὺς στενωποὺς ἐκβολῆς κοπρίων καὶ ῥευ-
μάτων ἀποτροπῆς ἐπιμέλειάν τινα. κἀγὼ δ' ἀμέλει
παρέχω γέλωτα τοῖς παρεπιδημοῦσιν, ὁρώμενος ἐν
δημοσίῳ περὶ τὰ τοιαῦτα πολλάκις· ἀλλὰ βοηθεῖ
μοι τὸ τοῦ Ἀντισθένους μνημονευόμενον· θαυμά-
C σαντος γάρ τινος, εἰ δι' ἀγορᾶς αὐτὸς φέρει τάριχος,
" ἐμαυτῷ γ'," εἶπεν· ἐγὼ δ' ἀνάπαλιν πρὸς τοὺς
ἐγκαλοῦντας, εἰ κεράμῳ παρέστηκα διαμετρουμένῳ
καὶ φυράμασι καὶ λίθοις παρακομιζομένοις, οὐκ
ἐμαυτῷ γέ φημι ταῦτ' οἰκονομεῖν[2] ἀλλὰ τῇ πατρίδι.
καὶ γὰρ εἰς ἄλλα πολλὰ μικρὸς ἄν τις εἴη καὶ
γλίσχρος αὑτῷ διοικῶν καὶ δι' αὑτὸν πραγμα-
τευόμενος· εἰ δὲ δημοσίᾳ καὶ διὰ τὴν πόλιν, οὐκ
ἀγεννής, ἀλλὰ μεῖζον τὸ μέχρι μικρῶν ἐπιμελὲς
καὶ πρόθυμον. ἕτεροι δὲ σεμνότερον οἴονται καὶ
μεγαλοπρεπέστερον εἶναι τὸ τοῦ Περικλέους· ὧν
καὶ Κριτόλαός ἐστιν ὁ Περιπατητικὸς ἀξιῶν, ὥσπερ
D ἡ Σαλαμινία ναῦς Ἀθήνησι καὶ ἡ Πάραλος οὐκ ἐπὶ
πᾶν ἔργον ἀλλ' ἐπὶ τὰς ἀναγκαίας καὶ μεγάλας κατ-
εσπῶντο πράξεις, οὕτως ἑαυτῷ πρὸς τὰ κυριώτατα
καὶ μέγιστα χρῆσθαι, ὡς ὁ τοῦ κόσμου βασιλεύς,

τῶν ἄγαν γὰρ ἅπτεται
θεός, τὰ μικρὰ δ' εἰς τύχην ἀνεὶς[3] ἐᾷ

κατὰ τὸν Εὐριπίδην.

---

[1] τελμαρχίαν Winckelmann and van Herwerden : τελεαρχίαν.
[2] οἰκονομεῖν Xylander : οἰκοδομῶν.
[3] ἀνεὶς] ἀφεὶς *Moralia*, 464 A.

---

[a] Nauck, *Trag. Graec. Frag.* p. 675, no. 974. From an
unknown play, quoted also *Moralia*, 464 A.

office, he advanced the *telmarchy* to a position of great consideration and dignity, though previously it had been nothing but a sort of supervision of the alleys for the removal of dung and the draining off of water in the streets. And no doubt I myself seem ridiculous to visitors in our town when I am seen in public, as I often am, engaged in such matters. But I am helped by the remark of Antisthenes which has been handed down to memory ; for when some-one expressed surprise that he himself carried a dried fish through the market-place, he said, "Yes, but it's for myself" ; but I, on the other hand, say to those who criticize me for standing and watching tiles being measured or concrete or stones being delivered, that I attend to these things, not for myself, but for my native place. Yes, for there are many other things in regard to which a man would be petty and sordid who managed them for himself and attended to them for his own sake, but if he does it for the public and for the State's sake, he is not ignoble, on the contrary his attention to duty and his zeal are all the greater when applied to little things. But there are others who think the conduct of Pericles was more dignified and splendid, one of whom is Critolaüs the Peripatetic, who claims that just as the Salaminia and the Paralus, ships at Athens, were not sent out to sea for every service, but only for necessary and important missions, so the statesman should employ himself for the most momentous and important matters, as does the King of the Universe,

> For God great things doth take in hand,
> But small things passing by he leaves to chance,[a]

according to Euripides.

(811)   Οὐδὲ γὰρ τοῦ Θεαγένους τὸ φιλότιμον ἄγαν καὶ
φιλόνεικον ἐπαινοῦμεν, ὃς οὐ μόνον τὴν περίοδον
νενικηκὼς ἀλλὰ καὶ πολλοὺς ἀγῶνας, οὐ παγκρατίῳ
μόνον ἀλλὰ καὶ πυγμῇ καὶ δολίχῳ,[1] τέλος ἥρωα
δειπνῶν ἐπιταφίου τινός, ὥσπερ εἰώθει, προτεθείσης
E ἅπασι τῆς μερίδος, ἀναπηδήσας διεπαγκρατίασεν,
ὡς οὐδένα νικᾶν δέον αὐτοῦ παρόντος· ὅθεν ἤθροισε
χιλίους καὶ διακοσίους στεφάνους, ὧν συρφετὸν ἄν
τις ἡγήσαιτο τοὺς πλείστους. οὐδὲν οὖν τούτου
διαφέρουσιν οἱ πρὸς πᾶσαν ἀποδυόμενοι πολιτικὴν
πρᾶξιν, ἀλλὰ μεμπτούς τε ταχὺ ποιοῦσιν ἑαυτοὺς
τοῖς πολλοῖς, ἐπαχθεῖς τε γίγνονται καὶ κατ-
ορθοῦντες ἐπίφθονοι, κἂν σφαλῶσιν, ἐπίχαρτοι,
καὶ τὸ θαυμαζόμενον αὐτῶν ἐν ἀρχῇ τῆς ἐπιμελείας
εἰς χλευασμὸν ὑπονοστεῖ καὶ γέλωτα.   τοιοῦτον τὸ[2]

F Μητίοχος μὲν γὰρ στρατηγεῖ, Μητίοχος δὲ τὰς
ὁδούς,
Μητίοχος δ' ἄρτους ἐπωπᾷ,[3] Μητίοχος δὲ
τἄλφιτα,
Μητίοχος δὲ πάντ' ἀκεῖται,[4] Μητίοχος δ' οἰ-
μώξεται.

τῶν Περικλέους οὗτος εἷς ἦν ἑταίρων, τῇ δι' ἐκεῖνον, ὡς ἔοικε, δυνάμει χρώμενος ἐπιφθόνως καὶ
κατακόρως. δεῖ δέ, ὥς φασιν, ἐρῶντι τῷ δήμῳ
τὸν πολιτικὸν προσφέρεσθαι καὶ μὴ παρόντος

---

[1] δολίχῳ Bernardakis : δολιχῷ.
[2] τοιοῦτον τὸ Duebner : τοιοῦτον.
[3] ἐπωπᾷ Dindorf : ἐπώπτα or ἐποπτᾷ.
[4] πάντ' ἀκεῖται Abresch and Bernardakis : πάντα κεῖται.

---

^a Refers to the four great festivals : the Olympic, the
Pythian, the Isthmian, and the Nemean games.

Neither do we commend the ambition and contentiousness of Theagenes who, after being victorious, not only in the circuit of festivals,[a] but in many other contests besides, not only in the pancratium, but also in boxing and long-distance running,[b] at last, when at certain commemorative funeral ceremonies he was partaking of the feast to honour the deceased as a hero, and all present had, as was the custom, their several portions already set before them, sprang up and performed a whole pancratium, as if it were wrong for anyone else to be a victor when he was present; for he had collected by such means twelve hundred head-bands, most of which might be regarded as rubbish. Now there is no difference between him and those who strip for every political activity; they soon cause themselves to be criticized by the multitude; they become unpopular and arouse envy when they are successful, but joy when they meet with failure; and that which was admired in them when they began to hold office results at last in mockery and ridicule. Such are the lines:

Metiochus, you see, is general, Metiochus inspects the roads,
Metiochus inspects the bread, and Metiochus inspects the
  flour,
Metiochus takes care of all things, Metiochus will come to
  grief.[c]

He was one of Pericles' followers and seems to have used the power gained through him in such a way as to arouse odium and disgust. For the statesman ought, as they say, to find the people fond of him when he comes to them and to leave a longing for

[b] The length was twenty stadia, slightly more than two and a quarter miles.

[c] From a poet of the Old Comedy, Kock, *Com. Att. Frag.* iii. p. 629, no. 1325.

ἑαυτοῦ πόθον ἐναπολείπειν· ὃ καὶ Σκιπίων ὁ
812 Ἀφρικανὸς ἐποίει πολὺν χρόνον ἐν ἀγρῷ διαιτώ-
μενος, ἅμα καὶ τοῦ φθόνου τὸ βάρος ἀφαιρῶν καὶ
διδοὺς ἀναπνοὴν τοῖς πιέζεσθαι δοκοῦσιν ὑπὸ τῆς
ἐκείνου δόξης. Τιμησίας δ᾽ ὁ Κλαζομένιος τὰ μὲν
ἄλλα ἦν περὶ τὴν πόλιν ἀνὴρ ἀγαθός, τῷ δὲ πάντα
πράσσειν δι᾽ ἑαυτοῦ φθονούμενος ἠγνόει καὶ μισού-
μενος, ἕως αὐτῷ συνέβη τι τοιοῦτον· ἔτυχον ἐν ὁδῷ
παῖδες ἐκ λάκκου τινὸς ἀστράγαλον ἐκκόπτοντες,
ἐκείνου παριόντος· ὧν οἱ μὲν ἔφασκον μένειν, ὁ δὲ
πατάξας " οὕτως," εἶπεν, " ἐκκόψαιμι Τιμησίου
τὸν ἐγκέφαλον, ὡς οὗτος ἐκκέκοπται." τοῦθ᾽ ὁ
Τιμησίας ἀκούσας καὶ συνεὶς τὸν διήκοντα διὰ
B πάντων αὐτοῦ[1] φθόνον, ἀναστρέψας ἔφρασε τὸ
πρᾶγμα τῇ γυναικί, καὶ κελεύσας ἕπεσθαι συν-
εσκευασμένην εὐθὺς ἀπὸ τῶν θυρῶν ᾤχετ᾽ ἀπιὼν
ἐκ τῆς πόλεως. ἔοικε δὲ καὶ Θεμιστοκλῆς, τοιού-
του τινὸς ἀπαντῶντος αὐτῷ παρὰ τῶν Ἀθηναίων,
εἰπεῖν " τί, ὦ μακάριοι, κοπιᾶτε πολλάκις εὖ
πάσχοντες; "

Τῶν δὲ τοιούτων τὰ μὲν ὀρθῶς τὰ δ᾽ οὐκ εὖ
λέλεκται. τῇ μὲν γὰρ εὐνοίᾳ καὶ κηδεμονίᾳ δεῖ
μηδενὸς ἀφεστάναι τῶν κοινῶν, ἀλλὰ πᾶσι προσ-
έχειν καὶ γιγνώσκειν ἕκαστα, μηδ᾽ ὥσπερ ἐν
C πλοίῳ σκεῦος ἱερὸν ἀποκεῖσθαι τὰς ἐσχάτας περι-
μένοντα χρείας τῆς πόλεως καὶ τύχας· ἀλλ᾽ ὡς οἱ
κυβερνῆται τὰ μὲν ταῖς χερσὶ δι᾽ αὐτῶν πράττουσι,
τὰ δ᾽ ὀργάνοις ἑτέροις δι᾽ ἑτέρων ἄπωθεν καθ-

---

[1] αὐτοῦ Bernardakis : αὑτοῦ.

[a] Meaning the largest anchor, held in reserve and used
only in a crisis; cf. below, 815 D and Lucian, Iuppiter
Tragoedus, chap. li. and scholium.

228

him when he is not there ; which Scipio Africanus
accomplished by spending much of his time in the
country, thereby at one and the same time removing
the weight of envy and giving a breathing-space to
those who thought they were oppressed by his glory.
But Timesias of Clazomenae was in other respects
a good man in his service to the State, but by doing
everything himself he had aroused rancour and
hatred ; but of this he was unaware until the following incident took place :—Some boys were knocking
a knuckle-bone out of a hole when he was passing by ;
and some of them said it was still in the hole, but
the boy who had struck at it said : " I'd like to knock
the brains out of Timesias as truly as this has been
knocked out of the hole." Timesias, hearing this
and understanding that dislike of him had permeated
all the people, returned home and told his wife what
had happened ; and directing her to pack up and follow
him, he went immediately away from his house and
out from the city. And it appears that Themistocles,
when he met with some such treatment from the
Athenians, said, " Why, my dear people, are you
tired of receiving repeated benefits ? '

Now of such sayings some are well said, others are
not. For so far as goodwill and solicitude for the
common weal are concerned, a statesman should not
hold aloof from any part of public affairs, but should
pay attention to them all and inform himself about
all details ; nor should he, as the ship's gear called
sacred [a] is stowed apart, hold himself aloof, waiting
for the extreme necessities and fortunes of the State ;
but just as pilots do some things with their own hands
but perform other duties by means of different
instruments operated by different agents, thus giving

229

(802) ἥμενοι περιάγουσι καὶ στρέφουσι, χρῶνται δὲ καὶ
ναύταις καὶ πρωρεῦσι καὶ κελευσταῖς, καὶ τούτων
ἐνίους ἀνακαλούμενοι πολλάκις εἰς πρύμναν ἐγχει-
ρίζουσι τὸ πηδάλιον· οὕτω τῷ πολιτικῷ προσήκει
παραχωρεῖν μὲν ἑτέροις ἄρχειν καὶ προσκαλεῖσθαι
πρὸς τὸ βῆμα μετ᾽ εὐμενείας καὶ φιλανθρωπίας,
κινεῖν δὲ μὴ πάντα τὰ τῆς πόλεως τοῖς αὑτοῦ
λόγοις καὶ ψηφίσμασιν ἢ πράξεσιν, ἀλλ᾽ ἔχοντα
πιστοὺς καὶ ἀγαθοὺς ἄνδρας ἕκαστον ἑκάστῃ χρείᾳ
κατὰ τὸ οἰκεῖον προσαρμόττειν· ὡς Περικλῆς
D Μενίππῳ μὲν ἐχρῆτο πρὸς τὰς στρατηγίας, δι᾽
Ἐφιάλτου δὲ τὴν ἐξ Ἀρείου πάγου βουλὴν ἐταπεί-
νωσε, διὰ δὲ Χαρίνου τὸ κατὰ Μεγαρέων ἐκύρωσε
ψήφισμα, Λάμπωνα δὲ Θουρίων οἰκιστὴν ἐξέπεμψεν. οὐ γὰρ μόνον, τῆς δυνάμεως εἰς πολλοὺς
διανέμεσθαι δοκούσης, ἧττον ἐνοχλεῖ τῶν φθόνων
τὸ μέγεθος, ἀλλὰ καὶ τὰ τῶν χρειῶν ἐπιτελεῖται
μᾶλλον. ὡς γὰρ ὁ τῆς χειρὸς εἰς τοὺς δακτύλους
μερισμὸς οὐκ ἀσθενῆ πεποίηκεν ἀλλὰ τεχνικὴν καὶ
ὀργανικὴν αὐτῆς τὴν χρῆσιν, οὕτως ὁ πραγμάτων
E ἑτέροις ἐν πολιτείᾳ μεταδιδοὺς ἐνεργοτέραν ποιεῖ
τῇ κοινωνίᾳ τὴν πρᾶξιν· ὁ δ᾽ ἀπληστίᾳ δόξης ἢ
δυνάμεως πᾶσαν αὑτῷ τὴν πόλιν ἀνατιθεὶς καὶ πρὸς
ὃ μὴ πέφυκε μηδ᾽ ἤσκηται προσάγων αὐτόν, ὡς
Κλέων πρὸς τὸ στρατηγεῖν, Φιλοποίμην δὲ πρὸς
τὸ ναυαρχεῖν, Ἀννίβας δὲ πρὸς τὸ δημηγορεῖν, οὐκ
ἔχει παραίτησιν ἁμαρτάνων ἀλλὰ προσακούει τὸ
τοῦ Εὐριπίδου

τέκτων γὰρ ὢν ἔπρασσες οὐ ξυλουργικά

---

[a] Passed in 432 B.C. excluding Megara from commerce
with Athens and her allies.

[b] Nauck, *Trag. Graec. Frag.* p. 678, no. 988.

a turn or a twist to the instruments while they sit apart, and they make use of sailors, look-out men, and boatswains, some of whom they often call to the stern and entrust with the tiller, just so it is fitting that the statesman should yield office to others and should invite them to the orators' platform in a gracious and kindly manner, and he should not try to administer all the affairs of the State by his own speeches, decrees, and actions, but should have good, trustworthy men and employ each of them for each particular service according to his fitness. So Pericles made use of Menippus for the position of general, humbled the Council of the Areopagus by means of Ephialtes, passed the decree against the Megarians [a] by means of Charinus, and sent Lampon out as founder of Thurii. For, when power seems to be distributed among many, not only does the weight of hatreds and enmities become less troublesome, but there is also greater efficiency in the conduct of affairs. For just as the division of the hand into fingers does not make it weak, but renders it a more skillful instrument for use, so the statesman who gives to others a share in the government makes action more effective by co-operation. But he who through insatiable greed of fame or power puts the whole burden of the State upon himself and sets himself even to tasks for which he is not fitted by nature or by training (as Cleon set himself to leading armies, Philopoemen to commanding ships, and Hannibal to haranguing the people)—such a man has no excuse when he makes mistakes, but will have to hear Euripides quoted to boot,

> A joiner thou, yet didst a task essay
> That was no carpentry.[b]

λέγειν ἀπίθανος ὢν ἐπρέσβευες ἢ ῥᾴθυμος ὢν ὠκο-
νόμεις, ψήφων ἄπειρος ἐταμίευες ἢ γέρων καὶ
F ἀσθενὴς ἐστρατήγεις. Περικλῆς δὲ καὶ πρὸς Κίμωνα διενείματο τὴν δύναμιν, αὐτὸς μὲν ἄρχειν
ἐν ἄστει, τὸν δὲ πληρώσαντα τὰς ναῦς τοῖς βαρβάροις πολεμεῖν· ἦν γὰρ ὁ μὲν πρὸς πολιτείαν ὁ δὲ
πρὸς πόλεμον εὐφυέστερος. ἐπαινοῦσι δὲ καὶ τὸν
Ἀναφλύστιον Εὔβουλον, ὅτι πίστιν ἔχων ἐν τοῖς
μάλιστα καὶ δύναμιν οὐδὲν τῶν Ἑλληνικῶν ἔπραξεν
οὐδ' ἐπὶ στρατηγίαν ἦλθεν, ἀλλ' ἐπὶ τὰ χρήματα
τάξας ἑαυτὸν ηὔξησε τὰς κοινὰς προσόδους καὶ μεγάλα τὴν πόλιν ἀπὸ τούτων ὠφέλησεν. Ἰφικράτης
δὲ καὶ μελέτας λόγων ποιούμενος ἐν οἴκῳ πολλῶν
813 παρόντων, ἐχλευάζετο· καὶ γὰρ εἰ λογεὺς ἀγαθὸς
ἀλλὰ μὴ φαῦλος ἦν, ἔδει τὴν ἐν τοῖς ὅπλοις δόξαν
ἀγαπῶντα τῆς σχολῆς ἐξίστασθαι τοῖς σοφισταῖς.

16. Ἐπεὶ δὲ παντὶ δήμῳ τὸ κακόηθες καὶ φιλ-
αίτιον ἔνεστι πρὸς τοὺς πολιτευομένους καὶ πολλὰ
τῶν χρησίμων, ἂν μὴ στάσιν ἔχῃ μηδ' ἀντιλογίαν,
ὑπονοοῦσι πράττεσθαι συνωμοτικῶς, καὶ τοῦτο δια-
βάλλει μάλιστα τὰς ἑταιρείας καὶ φιλίας, ἀληθινὴν
μὲν ἔχθραν ἢ διαφορὰν οὐδεμίαν ἑαυτοῖς ὑπο-
λειπτέον, ὡς ὁ τῶν Χίων δημαγωγὸς Ὀνομάδημος
οὐκ εἴα τῇ στάσει κρατήσας πάντας ἐκβάλλειν τοὺς
B ὑπεναντίους " ὅπως " ἔφη " μὴ πρὸς τοὺς φίλους
ἀρξώμεθα διαφέρεσθαι, τῶν ἐχθρῶν παντάπασιν
ἀπαλλαγέντες." τοῦτο μὲν γὰρ εὔηθες· ἀλλ' ὅταν

---

a Negotiations with other Greek states.

232

So, being no persuasive speaker, you went on an embassy, or being easy-going you undertook administration, being ignorant of accounting you were treasurer, or when old and feeble you took command of an army. But Pericles divided the power with Cimon so that he should himself be ruler in the city and Cimon should man the ships and wage war against the barbarians ; for one of them was more gifted for civic government, the other for war. And Eubulus the Anaphlystian also is commended because, although few men enjoyed so much confidence and power as he, yet he administered none of the Hellenic affairs [a] and did not take the post of general, but applied himself to the finances, increased the revenues, and did the State much good thereby. But Iphicrates was jeered at when he did exercises in speaking at his home in the presence of many hearers ; for even if he had been a good speaker, and not, as he was, a poor one, he ought to have been contented with glory in arms and to have left the school to the sophists.

16. But since there is in every democracy a spirit of malice and fault-finding directed against men in public life, and they suspect that many desirable measures, if there is no party opposition and no expression of dissent, are done by conspiracy, and this subjects a man's associations and friends to calumny, statesmen ought not to let any real enmity or disagreement against themselves subsist, as Onomademus the popular leader of the Chians did when, after his victory in the factional strife, he refused to have all his opponents banished from the city, " that we may not," he said " begin to quarrel with our friends when we have altogether got rid of our enemies." Now that was silly ; but when the popu-

(813) ὑπόπτως ἔχωσιν οἱ πολλοὶ πρός τι πρᾶγμα καὶ μέγα
καὶ σωτήριον, οὐ δεῖ πάντας ὥσπερ ἀπὸ συντάξεως
ἥκοντας τὴν αὐτὴν λέγειν γνώμην, ἀλλὰ καὶ δύο
καὶ τρεῖς διαστάντας ἀντιλέγειν ἠρέμα τῶν φίλων,
εἶθ᾽ ὥσπερ ἐξελεγχομένους μετατίθεσθαι· συνεφ-
έλκονται γὰρ οὕτω τὸν δῆμον, ὑπὸ τοῦ συμφέροντος
ἄγεσθαι δόξαντες. ἐν μέντοι τοῖς ἐλάττοσι καὶ
C πρὸς μέγα μηδὲν διήκουσιν οὐ χεῖρόν ἐστι καὶ
ἀληθῶς ἐὰν διαφέρεσθαι τοὺς φίλους, ἕκαστον ἰδίῳ
λογισμῷ χρώμενον, ὅπως περὶ τὰ κυριώτατα καὶ
μέγιστα φαίνωνται πρὸς τὸ βέλτιστον οὐκ ἐκ παρασκευῆς ὁμοφρονοῦντες.

17. Φύσει μὲν οὖν ἄρχων ἀεὶ πόλεως ὁ πολιτικὸς ὥσπερ ἡγεμὼν ἐν μελίτταις, καὶ τοῦτο χρὴ
διανοούμενον ἔχειν τὰ δημόσια διὰ χειρός· ἃς δ᾽
ὀνομάζουσιν ἐξουσίας καὶ χειροτονοῦσιν ἀρχὰς μήτ᾽
ἄγαν διώκειν καὶ πολλάκις, οὐ γὰρ σεμνὸν οὐδὲ
δημοτικὸν ἡ φιλαρχία· μήτ᾽ ἀπωθεῖσθαι, τοῦ δήμου
κατὰ νόμον διδόντος καὶ καλοῦντος· ἀλλὰ κἂν
ταπεινότεραι τῆς δόξης ὦσι, δέχεσθαι καὶ συμ-
D φιλοτιμεῖσθαι· δίκαιον γὰρ ὑπὸ τῶν μειζόνων
κοσμουμένους ἀρχῶν ἀντικοσμεῖν τὰς ἐλάττονας,
καὶ τῶν μὲν βαρυτέρων οἷον στρατηγίας Ἀθήνησι
καὶ πρυτανείας ἐν Ῥόδῳ καὶ βοιωταρχίας παρ᾽
ἡμῖν, ὑφίεσθαί τι καὶ παρενδιδόναι μετριάζοντα ταῖς
δὲ μικροτέραις ἀξίωμα προστιθέναι καὶ ὄγκον,
ὅπως μήτε περὶ ταύτας εὐκαταφρόνητοι μήτ᾽ ἐπίφθονοι περὶ ἐκείνας ὦμεν. εἰσιόντα δ᾽ εἰς ἅπασαν

---

[a] The Greeks did not know that the most important bee
in the hive was female—the queen bee.

lace are suspicious about some important and salutary measure, the statesmen when they come to the assembly ought not all to express the same opinion, as if by previous agreement, but two or three of the friends should dissent and quietly speak on the other side, then change their position as if they had been convinced ; for in this way they draw the people along with them, since they appear to be influenced only by the public advantage. In small matters, however, which do not amount to much, it is not a bad thing to let one's friends really disagree, each following his own reasoning, that in matters of the highest importance their agreement upon the best policy may not seem to be prearranged.

17. Now the statesman is always by nature ruler of the State, like the leader [a] bee in the hive, and bearing this in mind he ought to keep public matters in his own hands ; but offices which are called " authorities " and are elective he ought not to seek too eagerly or often, for love of office is neither dignified nor popular ; nor should he refuse them, if the people offer them and call him to them in accordance with the law, but even if they be too small for a man of his reputation, he should accept them and exercise them with zeal ; for it is right that men who are adorned with the highest offices should in turn adorn the lesser, and that statesmen should show moderation, giving up and yielding some part of the weightier offices, such as the generalship at Athens, the prytany at Rhodes, and the Boeotarchy here, and should add to the minor offices dignity and grandeur, that we may not be despised in connexion with the latter, nor envied on account of the former. And when entering upon any office whatsoever, you

ἀρχὴν οὐ μόνον ἐκείνους δεῖ προχειρίζεσθαι τοὺς
λογισμούς, οὓς ὁ Περικλῆς αὐτὸν ὑπεμίμνησκεν
E ἀναλαμβάνων τὴν χλαμύδα, " πρόσεχε, Περίκλεις·
ἐλευθέρων ἄρχεις, Ἑλλήνων ἄρχεις, πολιτῶν 'Αθη-
ναίων ''· ἀλλὰ κἀκεῖνο λέγειν πρὸς ἑαυτόν, " ἀρχό-
μενος ἄρχεις, ὑποτεταγμένης πόλεως ἀνθυπάτοις,
ἐπιτρόποις Καίσαρος· ' οὐ ταῦτα λόγχη πεδιάς,'[1]
οὐδ' αἱ παλαιαὶ Σάρδεις οὐδ' ἡ Λυδῶν ἐκείνη δύναμις ''· εὐσταλεστέραν δεῖ τὴν χλαμύδα ποιεῖν, καὶ
βλέπειν ἀπὸ τοῦ στρατηγίου πρὸς τὸ βῆμα,[2] καὶ τῷ
στεφάνῳ μὴ πολὺ φρονεῖν μηδὲ[3] πιστεύειν, ὁρῶντα
τοὺς καλτίους ἐπάνω τῆς κεφαλῆς· ἀλλὰ μιμεῖσθαι
F τοὺς ὑποκριτάς, πάθος μὲν ἴδιον καὶ ἦθος καὶ
ἀξίωμα τῷ ἀγῶνι προστιθέντας,[4] τοῦ δ' ὑποβολέως
ἀκούοντας καὶ μὴ παρεκβαίνοντας τοὺς ῥυθμοὺς
καὶ τὰ μέτρα τῆς διδομένης ἐξουσίας ὑπὸ τῶν κρατούντων. ἡ γὰρ ἔκπτωσις οὐ φέρει συριγμὸν οὐδὲ
χλευασμὸν οὐδὲ κλωγμόν, ἀλλὰ πολλοῖς μὲν ἐπέβη

δεινὸς κολαστὴς πέλεκυς αὐχένος τομεύς,[a]

ὡς τοῖς περὶ Παρδάλαν τὸν ὑμέτερον ἐκλαθομένοις
τῶν ὅρων· ὁ δέ τις ἐκριφεὶς εἰς νῆσον γέγονε κατὰ
τὸν Σόλωνα

Φολεγάνδριος ἢ Σικινήτης,[5]
814   ἀντί γ' 'Αθηναίου πατρίδ' ἀμειψάμενος.

---

[1] λόγχη πεδιάς Duebner (from Sophocles, Trach. 1058):
λόγχης πεδία.
[2] ἀπὸ τοῦ στρατηγίου πρὸς τὸ βῆμα] ἀπὸ τοῦ βήματος πρὸς τὸ
στρατήγιον Kaltwasser.   [3] φρονεῖν μηδὲ Coraes: φρόνημα.
[4] προστιθέντας] μὴ προστιθέντας (?) Capps; cf. Life of
Demosthenes, chap. xxii. 856 A.
[5] Σικινήτης Bergk: σικινίτης.

[a] Sophocles, Trachiniae, 1058.

must not only call to mind those considerations of which Pericles reminded himself when he assumed the cloak of a general : "Take care, Pericles ; you are ruling free men, you are ruling Greeks, Athenian citizens," but you must also say to yourself : "You who rule are a subject, ruling a State controlled by proconsuls, the agents of Caesar ; ' these are not the spearmen of the plain,'[a] nor is this ancient Sardis, nor the famed Lydian power. "You should arrange your cloak more carefully and from the office of the generals keep your eyes upon the orators' platform, and not have great pride or confidence in your crown, since you see the boots of Roman soldiers just above your head. No, you should imitate the actors, who, while putting into the performance their own passion, character, and reputation, yet listen to the prompter and do not go beyond the degree of liberty in rhythms and metres permitted by those in authority over them.[b] For to fail in one's part in public life brings not mere hissing or catcalls or stamping of feet, but many have experienced

The dread chastiser, axe that cleaves the neck,[c]

as did your countryman Pardalas and his followers when they forgot their proper limitations. And many another, banished to an island, has become, as Solon says,[d]

Pholegandrian or Sicinete,
No more Athenian, having changed his home.

[b] In Greece of Plutarch's time "those in authority" in political matters were the Romans.

[c] Nauck, *Trag. Graec. Frag.* p. 918, no. 412; from an unknown play. [d] Bergk, *Poet. Lyr. Graec.* ii. p. 34.

(814) Τὰ μὲν γὰρ μικρὰ παιδία τῶν πατέρων ὁρῶντες
ἐπιχειροῦντα τὰς κρηπῖδας ὑποδεῖσθαι καὶ τοὺς στεφάνους περιτίθεσθαι μετὰ παιδιᾶς γελῶμεν, οἱ δ᾽
ἄρχοντες ἐν ταῖς πόλεσιν ἀνοήτως τὰ τῶν προγόνων
ἔργα καὶ φρονήματα καὶ πράξεις ἀσυμμέτρους τοῖς
παροῦσι καιροῖς καὶ πράγμασιν οὔσας μιμεῖσθαι κε-
λεύοντες ἐξαίρουσι τὰ πλήθη, γέλωτά τε ποιοῦντες[1]
οὐκέτι γέλωτος ἄξια πάσχουσιν, ἂν μὴ πάνυ κατα-
φρονηθῶσι. πολλὰ γὰρ ἔστιν ἄλλα τῶν πρότερον
B Ἑλλήνων διεξιόντα τοῖς νῦν ἠθοποιεῖν καὶ σωφρο-
νίζειν, ὡς Ἀθήνησιν ὑπομιμνήσκοντα μὴ τῶν
πολεμικῶν, ἀλλ᾽ οἷόν ἐστι τὸ ψήφισμα τὸ τῆς
ἀμνηστίας ἐπὶ τοῖς τριάκοντα· καὶ τὸ ζημιῶσαι
Φρύνιχον τραγῳδίᾳ διδάξαντα τὴν Μιλήτου ἅλωσιν·
καὶ ὅτι, Θήβας Κασάνδρου κτίζοντος, ἐστεφανη-
φόρησαν· τὸν δ᾽ ἐν Ἄργει πυθόμενοι σκυταλισμόν,
ἐν ᾧ πεντακοσίους καὶ χιλίους ἀνῃρήκεσαν ἐξ
αὑτῶν[2] οἱ Ἀργεῖοι, περιενεγκεῖν καθάρσιον περὶ
τὴν ἐκκλησίαν ἐκέλευσαν· ἐν δὲ τοῖς Ἁρπαλείοις
τὰς οἰκίας ἐρευνῶντες μόνην τὴν τοῦ γεγαμηκότος
νεωστὶ παρῆλθον. ταῦτα γὰρ καὶ νῦν ἔξεστι ζη-
C λοῦντας ἐξομοιοῦσθαι τοῖς προγόνοις· τὸν δὲ Μα-
ραθῶνα καὶ τὸν Εὐρυμέδοντα καὶ τὰς Πλαταιάς,
καὶ ὅσα τῶν παραδειγμάτων οἰδεῖν ποιεῖ καὶ φρυάτ-

---

[1] γέλωτά τε ποιοῦντες Bernardakis: γελωτοποιοῦντες or
γελοῖά τε ποιοῦντες.

[2] αὑτῶν Bernardakis: αὐτῶν.

---

[a] The Thirty Tyrants at Athens were overthrown in 403
B.C.; Phrynichus presented the tragedy shortly after Miletus
was captured by the Persians in 494 B.C.; Cassander

Furthermore when we see little children trying playfully to bind their fathers' shoes on their feet or fit their crowns upon their heads, we only laugh, but the officials in the cities, when they foolishly urge the people to imitate the deeds, ideals, and actions of their ancestors, however unsuitable they may be to the present times and conditions, stir up the common folk and, though what they do is laughable, what is done to them is no laughing matter, unless they are merely treated with utter contempt. Indeed there are many acts of the Greeks of former times by recounting which the statesman can mould and correct the characters of our contemporaries, for example, at Athens by calling to mind, not deeds in war, but such things as the decree of amnesty after the downfall of the Thirty Tyrants, the fining of Phrynichus for presenting in a tragedy the capture of Miletus, their decking their heads with garlands when Cassander refounded Thebes ; how, when they heard of the clubbing at Argos, in which the Argives killed fifteen hundred of their own citizens, they decreed that an expiatory sacrifice be carried about in the assembly ; and how, when they were searching the houses at the time of Harpalus's frauds,[a] they passed by only one, that of a newly married man. By emulating acts like these it is even now possible to resemble our ancestors, but Marathon, the Eurymedon, Plataea, and all the other examples which make the common folk vainly to swell with

refounded Thebes in 316–315 B.C., ten years after its destruction by Alexander ; the clubbing of aristocrats at Argos by the mob took place in 370 B.C. ; Harpalus, Alexander's treasurer, brought to Athens in 329 B.C. funds stolen from Alexander and was supposed to have bribed many prominent Athenians, one of whom was Demosthenes.

(814) τεσθαι διακενῆς τοὺς πολλούς, ἀπολιπόντας ἐν ταῖς σχολαῖς τῶν σοφιστῶν.

18. Οὐ μόνον δὲ δεῖ παρέχειν αὐτόν τε καὶ τὴν πατρίδα πρὸς τοὺς ἡγεμόνας ἀναίτιον, ἀλλὰ καὶ φίλον ἔχειν ἀεί τινα τῶν ἄνω δυνατωτάτων,[1] ὥσπερ ἕρμα τῆς πολιτείας βέβαιον· αὐτοὶ γάρ εἰσι ῾Ρωμαῖοι πρὸς τὰς πολιτικὰς σπουδὰς προθυμότατοι τοῖς φίλοις· καὶ καρπὸν ἐκ φιλίας ἡγεμονικῆς λαμβάνοντας,[2] οἷον ἔλαβε Πολύβιος καὶ Παναίτιος τῇ D Σκιπίωνος εὐνοίᾳ πρὸς αὐτοὺς[3] μεγάλα τὰς πατρίδας ὠφελήσαντες, εἰς εὐδαιμονίαν δημοσίαν[4] ἐξενέγκασθαι καλόν. ῎Αρειόν τε Καῖσαρ, ὅτε τὴν ᾿Αλεξάνδρειαν εἷλε, διὰ χειρὸς ἔχων καὶ μόνῳ προσομιλῶν τῶν συνήθων συνεισήλασεν, εἶτα τοῖς ᾿Αλεξανδρεῦσι τὰ ἔσχατα προσδοκῶσι καὶ δεομένοις ἔφη διαλλάττεσθαι διά τε τὸ μέγεθος τῆς πόλεως καὶ διὰ τὸν οἰκιστὴν ᾿Αλέξανδρον, '' καὶ τρίτον,'' ἔφη, '' τῷ φίλῳ μου τούτῳ χαριζόμενος.'' ἆρά γ' ἄξιον τῇ χάριτι ταύτῃ παραβαλεῖν τὰς πολυταλάντους ἐπιτροπὰς καὶ διοικήσεις τῶν ἐπαρχιῶν, ἃς διώκοντες οἱ πολλοὶ γηράσκουσι πρὸς ἀλλοτρίαις θύραις, τὰ οἴκοι προλιπόντες· ἢ

---

[1] τῶν ἄνω δυνατωτάτων] Bernardakis remarks that we should read either τῶν ἄνω (preferably) or τῶν δυνατωτάτων and that in the Palatine codex ἄνω is written above the line by the first hand.

[2] λαμβάνοντας Xylander: λαμβάνοντες.

[3] αὐτούς] αὑτούς Bernardakis.

[4] εὐδαιμονίαν δημοσίαν Bernardakis (δημοσίαν εὐδαιμονίαν Wyttenbach): εὐδαιμονίαν.

pride and kick up their heels, should be left to the schools of the sophists.

18. And not only should the statesman show himself and his native State blameless towards our rulers,[a] but he should also have always a friend among the men of high station who have the greatest power as a firm bulwark, so to speak, of his administration; for the Romans themselves are most eager to promote the political interests of their friends; and it is a fine thing also, when we gain advantage from the friendship of great men, to turn it to the welfare of our community, as Polybius and Panaetius, through Scipio's goodwill towards them, conferred great benefits upon their native States.[b] And Caesar,[c] when he took Alexandria, drove into the city holding Areius by the hand and conversing with him only of all his friends, then said to the Alexandrians, who were expecting the most extreme measures and were begging for mercy, that he pardoned them on account of the greatness of their city and for the sake of its founder Alexander, " and thirdly," said he, " as a favour to my friend here." Is there any comparison between such a favour and the procuratorships and governorships of provinces from which many talents may be gained and in pursuit of which most public men grow old haunting the doors of other men's houses [d] and leaving their own affairs uncared for?

---

[a] *i.e.* the Romans.

[b] Arcadia and Rhodes respectively. Polybius was a statesman and historian, Panaetius a Stoic philosopher.

[c] Augustus Caesar is meant. For a further account of his treatment of Areius see *Life of Antony*, chap. lxxx.

[d] This refers to the Roman custom of greeting at the front door.

E τὸν Εὐριπίδην ἐπανορθωτέον ᾄδοντα καὶ λέγοντα,
ὡς εἴπερ ἀγρυπνεῖν χρὴ καὶ φοιτᾶν ἐπ᾽ αὔλειον[1]
ἑτέρου καὶ ὑποβάλλειν ἑαυτὸν ἡγεμονικῇ συνηθείᾳ,
πατρίδος πέρι κάλλιστον ἐπὶ ταῦτα χωρεῖν, τὰ δ᾽
ἄλλα τὰς ἐπὶ τοῖς ἴσοις καὶ δικαίοις φιλίας ἀσπάζεσθαι καὶ φυλάττειν;

19. Ποιοῦντα μέντοι καὶ παρέχοντα τοῖς κρα-
τοῦσιν εὐπειθῆ τὴν πατρίδα δεῖ μὴ προσεκταπει-
F νοῦν, μηδὲ τοῦ σκέλους δεδεμένου προσυποβάλλειν
καὶ τὸν τράχηλον, ὥσπερ ἔνιοι, καὶ μικρὰ καὶ
μείζω φέροντες ἐπὶ τοὺς ἡγεμόνας ἐξονειδίζουσι
τὴν δουλείαν, μᾶλλον δ᾽ ὅλως τὴν πολιτείαν ἀν-
αιροῦσι, καταπλῆγα καὶ περιδεᾶ καὶ πάντων ἄ-
κυρον ποιοῦντες. ὥσπερ γὰρ οἱ χωρὶς ἰατροῦ μήτε
δειπνεῖν μήτε λούεσθαι συνεθισθέντες οὐδ᾽ ὅσον ἡ
φύσις δίδωσι χρῶνται τῷ ὑγιαίνειν, οὕτως οἱ παντὶ
δόγματι καὶ συνεδρίῳ καὶ χάριτι καὶ διοικήσει
προσάγοντες ἡγεμονικὴν κρίσιν ἀναγκάζουσιν ἑαυ-
815 τῶν μᾶλλον ἢ βούλονται δεσπότας εἶναι τοὺς
ἡγουμένους. αἰτία δὲ τούτου μάλιστα πλεονεξία καὶ
φιλονεικία τῶν πρώτων· ἢ γὰρ ἐν οἷς βλάπτουσι
τοὺς ἐλάττονας ἐκβιάζονται φεύγειν τὴν πόλιν ἢ
περὶ ὧν διαφέρονται πρὸς ἀλλήλους οὐκ ἀξιοῦντες

---

[1] αὔλειον Hartman: αὔλιον.

[a] Euripides in *Phoenissae* 524 f. represents Eteocles as
saying—

εἴπερ γὰρ ἀδικεῖν χρή, τυραννίδος πέρι
κάλλιστον ἀδικεῖν.

If wrong be ever right, for the throne's sake
Were wrong most right. (Way's translation.)

If Plutarch quotes this passage, correcting it to suit his pur-

Or should we correct Euripides[a] when he chants
the sentiment that if a man must spend sleepless
nights and haunt another man's court and subject
himself to an intimacy with a great man, it is best to
do so for the sake of his native land, but otherwise
it is best to welcome and hold fast friendships based
on equality and justice ?

19. However, the statesman, while making his
native State readily obedient to its sovereigns, must
not further humble it ; nor, when the leg has been
fettered, go on and subject the neck to the yoke, as
some do who, by referring everything, great or small,
to the sovereigns, bring the reproach of slavery upon
their country, or rather wholly destroy its constitu-
tional government, making it dazed, timid, and power-
less in everything.   For just as those who have become accustomed neither to dine nor to bathe except
by the physician's orders do not even enjoy that
degree of health which nature grants them, so those
who invite the sovereign's decision on every decree,
meeting of a council, granting of a privilege,[b] or
administrative measure, force their sovereign to be
their master more than he desires. And the cause of
this is chiefly the greed and contentiousness of the
foremost citizens ; for either, in cases in which they
are injuring their inferiors, they force them into
exile from the State, or, in matters concerning which
they differ among themselves, since they are un-

pose, he simply substitutes ἀγρυπνεῖν for ἀδικεῖν and πατρίδος
for τυραννίδος. And the sentiment about equality, as the
basis of true friendship, seems to be an echo of 535 f. of the
same play. This method of dealing with passages from the
poets is not infrequently employed by Plutarch.

[b] This doubtless refers to honorary citizenship, crowns,
statues, and the like.

243

(815) ἐν τοῖς πολίταις ἔχειν ἔλαττον ἐπάγονται τοὺς
κρείττονας· ἐκ τούτου δὲ καὶ βουλὴ καὶ δῆμος καὶ
δικαστήρια καὶ ἀρχὴ πᾶσα τὴν ἐξουσίαν ἀπόλλυσι.
δεῖ δὲ τοὺς μὲν ἰδιώτας ἰσότητι, τοὺς δὲ δυνατοὺς
ἀνθυπείξει πραΰνοντα κατέχειν ἐν τῇ πολιτείᾳ καὶ
διαλύειν τὰ πράγματα, πολιτικήν τινα ποιούμενον
B αὐτῶν ὥσπερ νοσημάτων ἀπόρρητον ἰατρείαν,
αὐτόν τε μᾶλλον ἡττᾶσθαι βουλόμενον ἐν τοῖς
πολίταις ἢ νικᾶν ὕβρει καὶ καταλύσει τῶν οἴκοι
δικαίων, τῶν τ' ἄλλων ἑκάστου δεόμενον καὶ διδάσκοντα τὴν φιλονεικίαν ὅσον ἐστὶ κακόν· νῦν δ'
ὅπως μὴ πολίταις καὶ φυλέταις οἴκοι καὶ γείτοσι
καὶ συνάρχουσιν ἀνθυπείξωσι μετὰ τιμῆς καὶ
χάριτος, ἐπὶ ῥητόρων θύρας καὶ πραγματικῶν
χεῖρας ἐκφέρουσι σὺν πολλῇ βλάβῃ καὶ αἰσχύνῃ
τὰς διαφοράς. οἱ μὲν γὰρ ἰατροὶ τῶν νοσημάτων
ὅσα μὴ δύνανται παντάπασιν ἀνελεῖν ἔξω τρέπουσιν
εἰς τὴν ἐπιφάνειαν τοῦ σώματος· ὁ δὲ πολιτικός, ἂν
μὴ δύνηται τὴν πόλιν ἀπράγμονα παντελῶς διαφυλάττειν, ἐν αὐτῇ γε πειράσεται τὸ ταρασσόμενον
αὐτῆς καὶ στασιάζον ἀποκρύπτων ἰᾶσθαι καὶ
διοικεῖν, ὡς ἂν ἥκιστα τῶν ἐκτὸς ἰατρῶν καὶ
φαρμάκων δέοιτο. ἡ μὲν γὰρ προαίρεσις ἔστω
C τοῦ πολιτικοῦ τῆς ἀσφαλείας ἐχομένη καὶ φεύ-
γουσα τὸ ταρακτικὸν τῆς κενῆς δόξης καὶ μανικόν,
ὡς εἴρηται· τῇ μέντοι διαθέσει φρόνημα καὶ

ᵃ The citizens of most ancient states were divided into
tribes or clans.

willing to occupy an inferior position among their
fellow-citizens, they call in those who are mightier;
and as a result senate, popular assembly, courts, and
the entire local government lose their authority. But
the statesman should soothe the ordinary citizens by
granting them equality and the powerful by concessions in return, thus keeping them within the
bounds of the local government and solving their
difficulties as if they were diseases, making for
them, as it were, a sort of secret political medicine; he will prefer to be himself defeated among
his fellow-citizens rather than to be successful by
outraging and destroying the principles of justice
in his own city and he will beg everyone else to do
likewise, and will teach them how great an evil is
contentiousness. But as it is, not only do they not
make honourable and gracious compromises with their
fellow-citizens and tribesmen [a] at home and with their
neighbours and colleagues in office, but they carry
their dissensions outside to the doors of professional
orators and put them in the hands of lawyers, to their
own great injury and disgrace. For when physicians
cannot entirely eradicate diseases, they turn them
outwards to the surface of the body; but the statesman, if he cannot keep the State entirely free from
troubles, will at any rate try to cure and control whatever disturbs it and causes sedition, keeping it mean-
while hidden within the State, so that it may have
as little need as possible of physicians and medicine
drawn from outside. For the policy of the statesman should be that which holds fast to security and
avoids the tumultuous and mad impulse of empty
opinion, as has been said. In his disposition, however, high spirit and

(815)   μένος πολυθαρσὲς ἐνέστω
ἄτρομον, οἷόν τ᾽ ἄνδρας ἐσέρχεται,[1] οἱ περὶ
πάτρης
ἀνδράσι δυσμενέεσσι

καὶ πράγμασι δυσκόλοις καὶ καιροῖς ἀντερείδουσι
καὶ διαμάχονται. δεῖ γὰρ οὐ ποιεῖν χειμῶνας
αὐτὸν ἀλλὰ μὴ προλείπειν ἐπιπεσόντων, οὐδὲ
D κινεῖν τὴν πόλιν ἐπισφαλῶς, σφαλλομένη δὲ καὶ
κινδυνευούσῃ βοηθεῖν, ὥσπερ ἄγκυραν ἱερὰν ἀρά-
μενον ἐξ αὐτοῦ τὴν παρρησίαν ἐπὶ τοῖς μεγίστοις·
οἷα Περγαμηνοὺς ἐπὶ Νέρωνος κατέλαβε πράγματα,
καὶ Ῥοδίους ἔναγχος ἐπὶ Δομετιανοῦ, καὶ Θεσ-
σαλοὺς πρότερον ἐπὶ τοῦ Σεβαστοῦ Πετραῖον
ζῶντα κατακαύσαντας.

         ἔνθ᾽ οὐκ ἂν βρίζοντα ἴδοις

οὐδὲ καταπτώσσοντα τὸν ἀληθῶς πολιτικὸν οὐδ᾽
αἰτιώμενον ἑτέρους αὐτὸν δὲ τῶν δεινῶν ἔξω
τιθέμενον, ἀλλὰ καὶ πρεσβεύοντα καὶ πλέοντα καὶ
λέγοντα πρῶτον οὐ μόνον

    ἥκομεν οἱ κτείναντες, ἀπότρεπε λοιγόν, Ἄπολ-
    λον,

ἀλλά, κἂν τῆς ἁμαρτίας μὴ μετάσχῃ τοῖς πολλοῖς,
E τοὺς κινδύνους ὑπὲρ αὐτῶν ἀναδεχόμενον. καὶ γὰρ
καλὸν τοῦτο καὶ πρὸς τῷ καλῷ πολλάκις ἑνὸς
ἀνδρὸς ἀρετὴ καὶ φρόνημα θαυμασθὲν ἠμαύρωσε

---

[1] ἐσέρχεται Homer : ἐπέρχεται.

^a Homer, Il. xvii. 156 ff.

> courage must be, full of daring,
> Dauntless, and such as inspires all men who for weal of
> their country
> 'Gainst men of hostile intent [a]

and against difficult conditions and times stand
firm in resistance and struggle to the end. For
he must not create storms himself, and yet he
must not desert the State when storms fall upon
it; he must not stir up the State and make it reel
perilously, but when it is reeling and in danger, he
must come to its assistance and employ his frankness of speech as a sacred anchor [b] heaved over in
the greatest perils. Such were the troubles which
overtook the Pergamenes under Nero and the
Rhodians recently under Domitian and the Thessalians earlier under Augustus, when they burned
Petraeus alive.

> Then slumb'ring thou never wouldst see him, [c]

nor cowering in fear, the man who is really a statesman, nor would you see him throwing blame upon
others and putting himself out of danger, but you
will see him serving on embassies, sailing the seas and
saying first not only

> Here we have come, the slayers; avert thou the plague, O
> Apollo, [d]

but, even though he had no part in the wrongdoing
of the people, taking dangers upon himself in their
behalf. For this is noble; and besides being noble,
one man's excellence and wisdom by arousing admiration has often mitigated anger which has been

---

[b] See note on 812 B above.
[c] Homer, *Il*. iv. 223. Spoken of Agamemnon.
[d] Callimachus, p. 787 ed. Schneider.

τὴν πρὸς πάντας ὀργὴν καὶ διεσκέδασε τὸ φοβερὸν
καὶ πικρὸν τῆς ἀπειλῆς· οἷα καὶ πρὸς Βούλιν ἔοικε
καὶ Σπέρχιν τοὺς Σπαρτιάτας παθεῖν ὁ Πέρσης,
καὶ πρὸς Σθέννωνα Πομπήιος ἔπαθεν, ὅτε, Μαμερ-
τίνους μέλλοντος αὐτοῦ κολάζειν διὰ τὴν ἀπόστασιν,
F οὐκ ἔφη δίκαια πράξειν αὐτὸν ὁ Σθέννων, εἰ
πολλοὺς ἀναιτίους ἀπολεῖ δι' ἕνα τὸν αἴτιον· ὁ γὰρ
ἀποστήσας τὴν πόλιν αὐτὸς εἶναι τοὺς μὲν φίλους
πείσας τοὺς δ' ἐχθροὺς βιασάμενος. οὕτω ταῦτα
διέθηκε τὸν Πομπήιον, ὥστε καὶ τὴν πόλιν ἀφεῖναι καὶ τῷ Σθέννωνι χρήσασθαι φιλανθρώπως.
ὁ δὲ Σύλλα ξένος ὁμοίᾳ μὲν ἀρετῇ πρὸς οὐχ ὁμοίαν
816 δὲ χρησάμενος εὐγενῶς ἐτελεύτησεν· ἐπεὶ γὰρ
ἑλὼν Πραίνεστον ὁ Σύλλας ἔμελλε τοὺς ἄλλους
ἅπαντας ἀποσφάττειν ἕνα δ' ἐκεῖνον ἠφίει διὰ τὴν
ξενίαν, εἰπὼν ὡς οὐ βούλεται σωτηρίας χάριν
εἰδέναι τῷ φονεῖ τῆς πατρίδος, ἀνέμιξεν ἑαυτὸν
καὶ συγκατεκόπη τοῖς πολίταις. τοιούτους μὲν
οὖν καιροὺς ἀπεύχεσθαι δεῖ καὶ τὰ βελτίονα
προσδοκᾶν.

20. Ἱερὸν δὲ χρῆμα καὶ μέγα πᾶσαν ἀρχὴν
οὖσαν καὶ ἄρχοντα δεῖ μάλιστα τιμᾶν, τιμὴ δ' ἀρχῆς
ὁμοφροσύνη καὶ φιλία πρὸς συνάρχοντας πολὺ
μᾶλλον ἢ στέφανοι καὶ χλαμὺς περιπόρφυρος. οἱ
B δὲ τὸ συστρατεύσασθαι καὶ συνεφηβεῦσαι φιλίας

ᵃ The story of these two is told in *Moralia*, 235 ꜰ, 236.

ᵇ See *Moralia*, 203 ᴅ, where the name is Sthennius, and
Life of Pompey, chap. x.

ᶜ Athenian youths from eighteen to twenty years of age
were called *ephebi*. For one year they were trained chiefly
in gymnastics and military drill, then for a year they served

aroused against the whole people and has dissipated the threatened terror and bitterness. Something of that sort seems to have happened to the Persian king in the case of Boulis and Sperchis [a] the Spartans, and happened to Pompey in the case of Sthenno,[b] when, as he was going to punish the Mamertines for revolting, Sthenno told him that he would be doing wrong if he should destroy many innocent men for the fault of one ; for, he said, it was he himself who had caused the city to revolt by persuading his friends and compelling his enemies. This so affected Pompey that he let the city go unpunished and also treated Sthenno kindly. But Sulla's guest-friend, practising virtue of the same sort but not having to do with the same sort of man, met with a noble end. For when Sulla, after the capture of Praenestê, was going to slaughter all the rest of the citizens but was letting that one man go on account of his guest-friendship, he declared that he would not be indebted for his life to the slayer of his fatherland, and then mingled with his fellow-citizens and was cut down with them. However, we must pray to be spared such crises and must hope for better things.

20. And deeming every public office to be something great and sacred, we must also pay the highest honour to one who holds an office ; but the honour of an office resides in concord and friendship with one's colleagues much more than in crowns and a purple-bordered robe. But those who consider that serving together in a campaign or in the school for young citizens [c] is the beginning

as guards on the frontier. *Cf.* Aristotle, *Constitution of Athens*, chap. xlii.

(816) ἀρχὴν τιθέμενοι, τὸ δὲ συστρατηγεῖν καὶ συνάρχειν
ἔχθρας αἰτίαν λαμβάνοντες, ἓν τῶν τριῶν κακῶν
οὐ διαπεφεύγασιν· ἢ γὰρ ἴσους ἡγούμενοι τοὺς
συνάρχοντας αὐτοὶ στασιάζουσιν ἢ κρείττονας φθο-
νοῦσιν ἢ ταπεινοτέρους καταφρονοῦσι. δεῖ δὲ καὶ
θεραπεύειν τὸν κρείττονα καὶ κοσμεῖν τὸν ἥττονα
καὶ τιμᾶν τὸν ὅμοιον, ἀσπάζεσθαι δὲ καὶ φιλεῖν
ἅπαντας, ὡς

οὐ διὰ τραπέζης

οὐδὲ κώθωνος,

οὐδ' ἐφ' ἑστίας,

ἀλλὰ κοινῇ καὶ δημοσίᾳ ψήφῳ φίλους γεγονότας
καὶ τρόπον τινὰ πατρῴαν τὴν ἀπὸ τῆς πατρίδος
C εὔνοιαν ἔχοντας. ὁ γοῦν Σκιπίων ἤκουσεν ἐν
Ῥώμῃ κακῶς, ὅτι φίλους ἑστιῶν ἐπὶ τῇ καθ-
ιερώσει τοῦ Ἡρακλείου τὸν συνάρχοντα Μόμμιον
οὐ παρέλαβε· καὶ γάρ, εἰ τἆλλα μὴ φίλους ἐνόμιζον
ἑαυτούς, ἐν τοῖς γε τοιούτοις ἠξίουν τιμᾶν καὶ
φιλοφρονεῖσθαι διὰ τὴν ἀρχήν. ὅπου τοίνυν ἀνδρὶ
τἆλλα θαυμασίῳ τῷ Σκιπίωνι μικρὸν οὕτω φιλ-
ανθρώπευμα παραλειφθὲν ὑπεροψίας ἤνεγκε δόξαν,
ἦπου κολούων ἄν τις ἀξίωμα συνάρχοντος ἢ πράξεσιν ἐχούσαις φιλοτιμίαν ἐπηρεάζων ἢ πάντα συλλήβδην ἀνατιθεὶς ἅμα καὶ περιάγων ὑπ' αὐθαδείας
D εἰς ἑαυτὸν ἐκείνου δ' ἀφαιρούμενος, ἐπιεικὴς ἂν
φανείη καὶ μέτριος; μέμνημαι νέον ἐμαυτὸν ἔτι
πρεσβευτὴν μεθ' ἑτέρου πεμφθέντα πρὸς ἀνθύπατον,
250

of friendship, but regard joint service in the generalship or other office as the cause of enmity, have
failed to avoid one of the three evils ; for either
they regard their colleagues as their equals and
are themselves factious, or they envy them as their
superiors, or despise them as their inferiors. But
a man ought to conciliate his superior, add prestige
to his inferior, honour his equal, and be affable and
friendly to all, considering that they have been made

> Friends, not of festive board,

nor of tankard,

> nor of fireside's cheer,[a]

but all alike by vote of the people, and that they
bear goodwill toward one another as a heritage, so to
speak, from their fatherland. At any rate Scipio was
criticized in Rome because, when he entertained his
friends at the dedication of the temple of Hercules, he
did not include his colleague Mummius ; for even if
in general the two men did not consider themselves
friends, on such occasions they usually thought it
proper to show honour and friendliness to each other
on account of their office. Inasmuch, therefore, as
the omission of so slight an act of courtesy brought a
reputation for haughtiness to Scipio, a man in other
respects admirable, how can anyone be considered
honourable and fair-minded who detracts from the
dignity of a colleague in office, or maliciously flouts
him by actions which reveal ambitious rivalry, or
is so self-willed that he arrogates and annexes to
himself everything, in short, at the expense of his
colleague ? I recollect that when I was still a
young man I was sent with another as envoy to

[a] Apparently a quotation from a comedy. See Kock,
Com. Att. Frag. iii. p. 495.

(816) ἀπολειφθέντος δέ πως ἐκείνου, μόνον ἐντυχόντα
καὶ διαπραξάμενον· ὡς οὖν ἔμελλον ἐπανελθὼν
ἀποπρεσβεύειν, ἀναστὰς[1] ὁ πατὴρ κατ᾽ ἰδίαν ἐκέλευσε μὴ λέγειν " ᾠχόμην " ἀλλ᾽ " ᾠχόμεθα," μηδ᾽
" εἶπον " ἀλλ᾽ " εἴπομεν," καὶ τἆλλα συνεφαπτό-
μενον οὕτω καὶ κοινούμενον ἀπαγγέλλειν. οὐ γὰρ
E μόνον ἐπιεικὲς τὸ τοιοῦτον καὶ φιλάνθρωπόν ἐστιν,
ἀλλὰ καὶ τὸ λυποῦν τὸν φθόνον ἀφαιρεῖ τῆς δόξης.
ὅθεν οἱ μεγάλοι καὶ δαίμονα καὶ τύχην τοῖς κατ-
ορθώμασι συνεπιγράφουσιν, ὡς Τιμολέων ὁ τὰς
ἐν Σικελίᾳ καταλύσας τυραννίδας Αὐτοματίας ἱερὸν
ἱδρύσατο· καὶ Πύθων ἐπὶ τῷ Κότυν ἀποκτεῖναι
θαυμαζόμενος καὶ τιμώμενος ὑπὸ τῶν Ἀθηναίων
" ὁ θεός," ἔφη, " ταῦτ᾽ ἔπραξε, τὴν χεῖρα παρ᾽ ἐμοῦ
χρησάμενος." Θεόπομπος δ᾽ ὁ βασιλεὺς τῶν Λακεδαιμονίων πρὸς τὸν εἰπόντα σῴζεσθαι τὴν Σπάρτην
διὰ τοὺς βασιλεῖς ἀρχικοὺς ὄντας " μᾶλλον," ἔφη,
" διὰ τοὺς πολλοὺς πειθαρχικοὺς ὄντας."

F 21. Γίγνεται μὲν οὖν δι᾽ ἀλλήλων ἀμφότερα
ταῦτα. λέγουσι δ᾽ οἱ πλεῖστοι καὶ νομίζουσι πολιτικῆς παιδείας ἔργον εἶναι τὸ καλῶς ἀρχομένους
παρασχεῖν· καὶ γὰρ πλέον ἐστὶ τοῦ ἄρχοντος ἐν
ἑκάστῃ πόλει τὸ ἀρχόμενον· καὶ χρόνον ἕκαστος
ἄρχει βραχύν, ἄρχεται δὲ τὸν ἅπαντα χρόνον ἐν
δημοκρατίᾳ πολιτευόμενος· ὥστε κάλλιστον εἶναι
μάθημα καὶ χρησιμώτατον τὸ πειθαρχεῖν τοῖς
ἡγουμένοις, κἂν ὑποδεέστεροι δυνάμει καὶ δόξῃ
τυγχάνωσιν ὄντες. ἄτοπον γάρ ἐστι τὸν μὲν ἐν τρα-

[1] ἀναστὰς] Bernardakis suggests παραστὰς.

the proconsul; the other man was somehow left behind; I alone met the proconsul and accomplished the business. Now when I came back and was to make the report of our mission, my father left his seat and told me in private not to say " I went," but " we went," not " I said," but " we said," and in all other ways to associate my colleague in a joint report. For that sort of thing is not only honourable and kind, but it also takes the sting out of any envy of our reputation. And therefore great men ascribe to God and to Fortune a share in their successes, as Timoleon, who put down the tyrannies in Sicily, founded a sanctuary of Automatia (Chance); and Python, when he was admired and honoured by the Athenians for slaying Cotys, said " God did this, borrowing from me the hand that did the deed." And Theopompus, King of the Lacedaemonians, replied to the man who said that Sparta was preserved because the kings were fitted to rule, " No, it is rather because the people are fitted to obey."

21. Now both of these arise from each other. Most people say and believe that it is the business of political teaching to cause men to be good subjects; for, they say, the subject class is in every State larger than the ruling class; and each official rules but a short time, whereas he is ruled all the time, if he is a citizen of a democracy; so that it is a most excellent and useful thing to learn to obey those in authority, even if they happen to be deficient in power and reputation. For it is absurd that in a tragedy the chief actor, even though he is

γῳδίᾳ πρωταγωνιστήν, Θεόδωρον ἢ Πῶλον ὄντα
μισθωτῷ[1] τὰ τρίτα λέγοντι πολλάκις ἔπεσθαι καὶ
προσδιαλέγεσθαι ταπεινῶς, ἂν ἐκεῖνος ἔχῃ τὸ διά-
817 δημα καὶ τὸ σκῆπτρον· ἐν δὲ πράξεσιν ἀληθιναῖς
καὶ πολιτείᾳ τὸν πλούσιον καὶ ἔνδοξον ὀλιγωρεῖν
καὶ καταφρονεῖν ἄρχοντος ἰδιώτου καὶ πένητος,
ἐνυβρίζοντα καὶ καθαιροῦντα[2] τῷ περὶ αὑτὸν[3] ἀξιώ-
ματι τὸ τῆς πόλεως, ἀλλὰ μὴ μᾶλλον αὔξοντα καὶ
προστιθέντα τὴν ἀφ' αὑτοῦ[4] δόξαν καὶ δύναμιν τῇ
ἀρχῇ. καθάπερ ἐν Σπάρτῃ τοῖς ἐθόροις οἵ τε
βασιλεῖς ὑπεξανίσταντο, καὶ τῶν ἄλλων ὁ κληθεὶς
οὐ βάδην ὑπήκουεν ἀλλὰ δρόμῳ καὶ σπουδῇ δι'
ἀγορᾶς θέοντες ἐπεδείκνυντο τὴν εὐπείθειαν τοῖς
πολίταις, ἀγαλλόμενοι τῷ τιμᾶν τοὺς ἄρχοντας·
B οὐχ ὥσπερ ἔνιοι τῶν ἀπειροκάλων καὶ σολοίκων,
οἷον ἰσχύος ἑαυτῶν καλλωπιζόμενοι περιουσίᾳ, βρα-
βευτὰς ἐν ἀγῶσι προπηλακίζουσι καὶ χορηγοὺς ἐν
Διονυσίοις λοιδοροῦσι καὶ στρατηγῶν καὶ γυμνασιάρχων[5] καταγελῶσιν, οὐκ εἰδότες οὐδὲ μαν-
θάνοντες ὅτι τοῦ τιμᾶσθαι τὸ τιμᾶν πολλάκις ἐστὶν
ἐνδοξότερον. ἀνδρὶ γὰρ ἐν πόλει δυναμένῳ μέγα
μείζονα φέρει κόσμον ἄρχων δορυφορούμενος ὑπ'
αὐτοῦ καὶ προπεμπόμενος ἢ δορυφορῶν καὶ προ-
πέμπων· μᾶλλον δὲ τοῦτο μὲν ἀηδίαν καὶ φθόνον,

---

[1] Madvig erroneously proposed to read μισθωτὸν τῷ for the
μισθωτῷ of the mss.

[2] καθαιροῦντα] συγκαθαιροῦντα Reiske.

[3] αὑτὸν Bernardakis: αὐτόν.

[4] ἀφ' αὑτοῦ Bernardakis: ἀπ' αὐτοῦ.

[5] γυμνασιάρχων Bernardakis: γυμνασιαρχῶν.

---

[a] Theodorus and Polus were famous actors at Athens in
the fourth century B.C. See J. B. O'Connor, *Chapters in the*

a Theodorus or a Polus,[a] often makes his entrance
after a hireling who takes third-class parts and addresses him in humble fashion, just because the
latter wears the diadem and sceptre, but that in real
affairs and in government the rich and famous man
belittles and despises the official who is plebeian and
poor, thereby using his own high standing to insult
and destroy that of the State, instead of enhancing
it rather and adding to the office the esteem and
power derived from himself. So at Sparta the kings
gave precedence to the ephors, and if any other
Spartan was summoned, he did not walk slowly in
obeying the summons, but by running eagerly at
full speed through the market-place they exhibited
to their fellow-citizens their spirit of obedience,
rejoicing in paying honour to their rulers. They
did not behave like some uncultured and unmannerly
persons who, as if swaggering in the excess of their
own power, abuse the umpires at the games, revile
the choregi at the Dionysiac festival, and jeer at
generals and gymnasiarchs, not knowing and not
understanding that it is often more glorious to pay
honour than to receive it. For to a man who has
great power in the State greater distinction accrues
through serving in the bodyguard and the escort of
an official than through being so served and escorted
by him, or rather the latter brings him dislike and

History of Actors and Acting in Ancient Greece, pp. 100,
128. The terms τραγῳδός and κωμῳδός were used for actors
who had been assigned to the highest rank and were privi-
leged to bring out old plays at the festivals, and they
stand in sharp contrast to the "hireling" actors, usually referred to after Demosthenes' time as "tritagonists," to whom
were often given the "third-class" roles of kings; see *ibid.*
chap. i.

(817) ἐκεῖνο δὲ τὴν ἀληθινὴν φέρει, τὴν ἀπ' εὐνοίας,
C δόξαν· ὀφθεὶς δ' ἐπὶ θύραις ποτὲ καὶ πρότερος
ἀσπασάμενος καὶ λαβὼν ἐν περιπάτῳ μέσον, οὐδὲν
ἀφαιρούμενος ἑαυτοῦ, τῇ πόλει κόσμον περιτίθησι.

22. Δημοτικὸν δὲ καὶ βλασφημίαν ἐνεγκεῖν καὶ
ὀργὴν ἄρχοντος ἢ τὸ τοῦ Διομόδους ὑπειπόντα

τούτῳ μὲν γὰρ κῦδος ἅμ' ἕψεται

ἢ τὸ τοῦ Δημοσθένους, ὅτι νῦν οὐκ ἔστι Δημοσθένης
μόνον ἀλλὰ καὶ θεσμοθέτης ἢ χορηγὸς ἢ στεφανη-
φόρος. ἀναθετέον οὖν τὴν ἄμυναν εἰς τὸν χρόνον[1]· ἢ
γὰρ ἐπέξιμεν ἀπαλλαγέντι τῆς ἀρχῆς ἢ κερδανοῦμεν
ἐν τῷ περιμένειν τὸ παύσασθαι τῆς ὀργῆς.

D 23. Σπουδῇ μέντοι καὶ προνοίᾳ περὶ τὰ κοινὰ
καὶ φροντίδι πρὸς ἅπασαν ἀρχὴν ἀεὶ διαμιλλητέον,
ἂν μὲν ὦσι χαρίεντες, αὐτὸν ὑφηγούμενον ἃ δεῖ καὶ
φράζοντα καὶ διδόντα χρῆσθαι τοῖς βεβουλευμένοις
ὀρθῶς καὶ τὸ κοινὸν εὐδοκιμεῖν ὠφελοῦντας[2]· ἐὰν δ'
ἐνῇ τις ἐκείνοις ὄκνος ἢ μέλλησις ἢ κακοήθεια πρὸς
τὴν πρᾶξιν, οὕτω χρὴ παρεῖναι καὶ λέγειν αὐτὸν εἰς
τοὺς πολλοὺς καὶ μὴ παραμελεῖν μηδ' ὑφίεσθαι τῶν
κοινῶν, ὡς οὐ προσῆκον, ἄρχοντος ἑτέρου, πολυ-

---

[1] Before χρόνον Reiske adds οἰκεῖον.
[2] ὠφελοῦντας Mittelhaus: ὠφελοῦντα.

---

[a] Cf. *Life of Cicero*, chap. ii., "Cicero placed in their
midst, as a mark of honour," Perrin's translation, L.C.L.

[b] Homer, *Il.* iv. 415.

[c] Demosthenes, xxi. (*Against Meidias*) 524. Meidias had
insulted Demosthenes in public when Demosthenes was
choregus, officially appointed to bear the expense of a chorus.

[d] The thesmothetae were the six junior archons at Athens.
Their chief duty was supervision of the courts of law.

envy, but the former brings true reputation, that
which comes from goodwill; and by being seen
sometimes at the official's door, by greeting him
first, and by putting him in the middle place[a] in
walking a man adds lustre to the State without
taking anything from himself.

22. And it is also a service to the people sometimes to endure the evil speech and anger of a man
in office, repeating to oneself either the words of
Diomedes:

> For unto him will accrue mighty glory,[b]

or the saying of Demosthenes,[c] that now he is not
only Demosthenes, but also one of the thesmothetae,[d]
or a choregus, or the wearer of a crown.[e] We should,
therefore, put off our requital to the right time;
for then either we shall attack him after his term of
office is ended or in the delay our gain will be the
cessation of anger.

23. One should, however, always vie with every
official in zeal, forethought for the common good,
and wisdom; if they are worthy men, by voluntarily
suggesting and pointing out the things to be done
and allowing them to make use of well-considered
ideas and to be held in high esteem because they
are benefactors of the community. But if there is
in them any reluctance, delay, or ill-will as to putting
such suggestions into effect, then a man ought to
come forward of himself and address the people, and
he should not neglect or slight the public interests
on the ground that because someone else is in office

---

[e] The stephanephori were officials whose duties varied in
different cities. At Athens they were concerned with public
festivals.

πραγμονεῖν καὶ παραδιοικεῖν. ὁ γὰρ νόμος ἀεὶ τῷ
Ε τὰ δίκαια πράσσοντι καὶ γιγνώσκοντι τὰ συμ-
φέροντα τὴν πρώτην τάξιν ἐν τῇ πολιτείᾳ δίδωσιν.
" ἦν δέ τις," φησίν, " ἐν τῷ στρατεύματι Ξενοφῶν,[a]
οὔτε στρατηγὸς οὔτε λοχαγός," ἀλλὰ τῷ φρονεῖν τὰ
δέοντα καὶ τολμᾶν αὐτὸν εἰς τὸ ἄρχειν καταστήσας
διέσωσε τοὺς Ἕλληνας. καὶ τῶν Φιλοποίμενος
ἔργων ἐπιφανέστατόν ἐστι τό, τοῦ Νάβιδος[1] Μεσσήνην καταλαβόντος οὐκ ἐθέλοντος δὲ τοῦ στρατηγοῦ τῶν Ἀχαιῶν βοηθεῖν ἀλλ' ἀποδειλιῶντος,
αὐτὸν ὁρμήσαντα μετὰ τῶν προθυμοτάτων ἄνευ
δόγματος ἐξελέσθαι τὴν πόλιν. οὐ μὴν διὰ μικρὰ
F δεῖ καὶ τὰ τυχόντα καινοτομεῖν, ἀλλ' ἐπὶ τοῖς
ἀναγκαίοις ὡς ὁ Φιλοποίμην, ἢ τοῖς καλοῖς ὡς
Ἐπαμεινώνδας, ἐπιβαλὼν τέτταρας μῆνας τῇ βοιωτ-
αρχίᾳ[c] παρὰ τὸν νόμον, ἐν οἷς εἰς τὴν Λακωνικὴν
ἐνέβαλε καὶ τὰ περὶ Μεσσήνην ἔπραξεν· ὅπως, κἂν
ἅπαντά τις ἐπὶ τούτῳ κατηγορία καὶ μέμψις, ἀπολογίαν τῆς αἰτίας τὴν ἀνάγκην ἔχωμεν ἢ παρα-
μυθίαν τοῦ κινδύνου τὸ μέγεθος τῆς πράξεως καὶ
τὸ κάλλος.

24. Ἰάσονος τοῦ Θεσσαλῶν μονάρχου γνώμην
ἀπομνημονεύουσιν, ἐφ' οἷς ἐβιάζετο καὶ παρ-
818 ηνώχλει τινάς, ἀεὶ λεγομένην, ὡς ἀναγκαῖον ἀδικεῖν
τὰ μικρὰ τοὺς βουλομένους τὰ μεγάλα δικαιοπραγεῖν. τοῦτον μὲν οὖν ἄν τις εὐθὺς καταμάθοι
τὸν λόγον ὡς ἔστι δυναστευτικός· ἐκεῖνο δὲ πολιτι-

---

[1] τοῦ Νάβιδος Meziriacus : ἄγιδος τοῦ αὔιδος or ἄγιδος.

[a] The author of the *Anabasis*. But Plutarch may have
written φησὶν αὐτός.　　[b] Xenophon, *Anab*. iii. 1. 4.
[c] The Boeotarchy was the chief office of the Boeotian confederacy. Its term was one year.

it is not proper for him to meddle and mix in the administration of affairs. For the law always gives the first rank in the government to him who does what is right and recognizes what is advantageous. "Now there was," says he,[a] "in the army a man named Xenophon, neither a general nor a captain,"[b] but by perceiving what was needed and daring to do it he put himself in command and saved the Greeks. And of Philopoemen's deeds the most brilliant is this, that when Nabis had taken Messenê, and the general of the Achaeans was so cowardly that he would not go to the assistance of the place, he himself with the most eager patriots set out and took the city without any decree of the council. Certainly it is well to make innovations, not for the sake of small or casual matters, but in cases of necessity, as Philopoemen did, or for glorious causes, as Epameinondas did when contrary to the law he added four months to the Boeotarchy,[c] in which time he invaded Laconia and carried out his measures at Messenê[d]; so that if any accusation or blame be brought against us on this account we may have necessity as our defence against the charge, or the greatness and glory of the action as a consolation for the risk.

24. A saying of Jason, monarch of the Thessalians, is recorded, which he always used to repeat whenever he was taking violent and annoying measures against individuals: "It is inevitable that those should act unjustly in small matters who wish to act justly in great matters." That is recognized at once as the saying of a despot; but this is a more

---

[d] These measures included the freeing of Messenia from Spartan domination and the founding of the city of Messenê.

(818) κώτερον παράγγελμα, τὸ τὰ μικρὰ τοῖς πολλοῖς
προΐεσθαι χαριζόμενον ἐπὶ τῷ τοῖς μείζοσιν ἐν-
ίστασθαι καὶ κωλύειν ἐξαμαρτάνοντας. ὁ γὰρ
αὖ περὶ πάντα λίαν ἀκριβὴς καὶ σφοδρός, οὐδὲν
ὑποχωρῶν οὐδ᾽ ὑπείκων ἀλλὰ τραχὺς ἀεὶ καὶ ἀ-
παραίτητος, ἀντιφιλονεικεῖν τὸν δῆμον αὐτῷ καὶ
προσδυσκολαίνειν ἐθίζει,

μικρὸν δὲ δεῖ¹ ποδὸς
χαλάσαι μεγάλῃ κύματος ἀλκῇ,

B τὰ μὲν αὐτὸν ἐνδιδόντα καὶ συμπαίζοντα κεχαρι-
σμένως οἷον ἐν θυσίαις καὶ ἀγῶσι καὶ θεάτροις,
τὰ δ᾽ ὥσπερ ἐν οἰκίᾳ νέων ἁμαρτήματα προσ-
ποιούμενον παρορᾶν καὶ παρακούειν, ὅπως ἡ τοῦ
νουθετεῖν καὶ παρρησιάζεσθαι δύναμις ὥσπερ φαρμάκου μὴ κατακεχρημένη μηδ᾽ ἕωλος ἀλλ᾽ ἀκμὴν
ἔχουσα καὶ πίστιν ἐν τοῖς μείζοσι μᾶλλον καθ-
άπτηται καὶ δάκνῃ τοὺς πολλούς. Ἀλέξανδρος μὲν
γὰρ ἀκούσας τὴν ἀδελφὴν ἐγνωκέναι τινὰ τῶν
C καλῶν καὶ νέων οὐκ ἠγανάκτησεν εἰπών, ὅτι
κἀκείνη τι δοτέον ἀπολαῦσαι τῆς βασιλείας· οὐκ
ὀρθῶς τὰ τοιαῦτα συγχωρῶν οὐδ᾽ ἀξίως ἑαυτοῦ·
δεῖ γὰρ ἀρχῆς τὴν κατάλυσιν καὶ ὕβριν ἀπόλαυσιν
μὴ νομίζειν. δήμῳ δ᾽ ὕβριν μὲν οὐδεμίαν εἰς
πολίτας οὐδὲ δήμευσιν ἀλλοτρίων οὐδὲ κοινῶν

---

¹ δὲ δεῖ Nauck ; δέον Bernardakis : δὲ.

ᵃ Nauck, *Trag. Graec. Frag.* p. 918, no. 413.

statesmanlike precept : " Win the favour of the
people by giving way in small things in order that
in greater matters you may oppose them stubbornly
and thus prevent them from committing errors."
For a man who is always very exact and strenuous
about everything, not giving way or yielding at all,
but always harsh and inexorable, gets the people
into the habit of opposing him and being out of
temper with him ;

> But he should let the sheet
> Run out a bit before the waves' great force,[a]

sometimes by giving way and playing graciously
with them himself, as at sacrifices, public games,
and spectacles in the theatre, and sometimes by pre-
tending not to see or hear their errors, just as we
treat the errors of the young people in a family,
in order that the force of his rebukes and outspoken
criticism—like that of a medicine—may not become
exhausted or stale, but may in matters of greater
importance, retaining its full strength and its credit,
take a stronger hold upon the people and sting
them into obedience.   Alexander, for example, when
he heard that his sister had had intercourse with a
handsome young man, did not burst into a rage,
but merely remarked that she also ought to be
allowed to get some enjoyment out of her royal
station.   In making such concessions he did not
act rightly or in a manner worthy of himself ; for
the weakening of a throne and outrageous conduct
should not be regarded as mere enjoyment.   But to
the people the statesman will, so far as is possible,
permit no outrageous conduct towards the citizens,
no confiscation of others' property, nor distribution

(818) διανέμησιν ὁ πολιτικὸς ἐφήσει κατὰ δύναμιν, ἀλλὰ
πείθων καὶ διδάσκων καὶ δεδιττόμενος διαμαχεῖται
ταῖς τοιαύταις ἐπιθυμίαις, οἵας οἱ περὶ Κλέωνα
βόσκοντες καὶ αὔξοντες πολύν, ὥς φησιν ὁ Πλάτων,
κηφῆνα τῇ πόλει κεκεντρωμένον ἐνεποίησαν. ἐὰν
δ᾽ ἑορτὴν πάτριον οἱ πολλοὶ καὶ θεοῦ τιμὴν πρόφασιν λαβόντες ὁρμήσωσι πρός τινα θέαν ἢ νέμησιν
ἐλαφρὰν ἢ χάριν τινὰ φιλάνθρωπον ἢ φιλοτιμίαν,
D ἔστω πρὸς τὰ τοιαῦτα ἡ τῆς ἐλευθερίας ἅμα καὶ
τῆς εὐπορίας ἀπόλαυσις αὐτοῖς. καὶ γὰρ τοῖς
Περικλέους πολιτεύμασι καὶ τοῖς Δημητρίου πολλὰ
τοιαῦτ᾽ ἔνεστι, καὶ Κίμων ἐκόσμησε τὴν ἀγορὰν
πλατάνων φυτείαις καὶ περιπάτοις· Κάτων δὲ τὸν
δῆμον ὑπὸ Καίσαρος ὁρῶν ἐν τοῖς περὶ Κατιλίναν
διαταρασσόμενον καὶ πρὸς μεταβολὴν τῆς πολιτείας ἐπισφαλῶς ἔχοντα συνέπεισε τὴν βουλὴν
ψηφίσασθαι νεμήσεις τοῖς πένησι, καὶ τοῦτο
δοθὲν ἔστησε τὸν θόρυβον καὶ κατέπαυσε τὴν ἐπ-
ανάστασιν. ὡς γὰρ ἰατρός, ἀφελὼν πολὺ τοῦ
E διεφθορότος αἵματος, ὀλίγον ἀβλαβοῦς τροφῆς
προσήνεγκεν, οὕτως ὁ πολιτικὸς ἀνήρ, μέγα τι
τῶν ἀδόξων ἢ βλαβερῶν παρελόμενος, ἐλαφρᾷ
πάλιν χάριτι καὶ φιλανθρώπῳ τὸ δυσκολαῖνον
καὶ μεμψιμοιροῦν παρηγόρησεν.

25. Οὐ χεῖρον δὲ καὶ μετάγειν ἐπ᾽ ἄλλα χρειώδη
τὸ σπουδαζόμενον, ὡς ἐποίησε Δημάδης, ὅτε τὰς
προσόδους εἶχεν ὑφ᾽ ἑαυτῷ τῆς πόλεως· ὡρμημένων
γὰρ ἐκπέμπειν τριήρεις βοηθοὺς τοῖς ἀφισταμένοις
Ἀλεξάνδρου καὶ χρήματα κελευόντων παρέχειν
ἐκεῖνον, " ἔστιν ὑμῖν," ἔφη, " χρήματα· παρ-

---

^a Plato, *Republic*, 552 c, d.

of public funds, but by persuasion, arguments, and threats he will oppose to the bitter end desires of that sort, by nourishing and increasing which Cleon and his partizans produced in the State, as Plato says,[a] a swarm of drones with stings. But if the people, taking an ancestral festival or the worship of some god as a pretext, are bent upon some public spectacle or a slight distribution of funds, or a gift for the general good or some lavish show prompted by private ambition, for such purposes let them reap the benefit both of their generosity and of their prosperity. Why, among the public acts of Pericles and of Demetrius are many of that sort, and Cimon beautified the market-place by planting plane-trees and laying out walks. And Cato, seeing that the people was being greatly stirred up by Caesar in the affair of Catiline and was dangerously inclined towards a revolution, persuaded the senate to vote a dole to the poor, and the giving of this halted the disturbance and ended the uprising. For just as a physician, after drawing off a great deal of infected blood, supplies a little harmless nourishment, so the statesman, after doing away with something big which was discreditable or harmful, appeases the spirit of discontent and fault-finding by some slight and kindly act of favour.

25. It is also expedient to divert the people's interest to other useful things, as Demades did when he had the revenues of the State in his charge ; for when the people were eager to send out triremes to aid those who were in revolt against Alexander,[b] and were urging him to furnish funds, " You have," he said, " funds available, for I have made preparations

[b] In 330 B.C. King Agis of Sparta headed the revolt.

ἐσκευασάμην γὰρ εἰς τοὺς χόας, ὥσθ' ἕκαστον
ὑμῶν λαβεῖν ἡμιμναῖον· εἰ δ' εἰς ταῦτα βούλεσθε
F μᾶλλον, αὐτοὶ καταχρῆσθε τοῖς ἰδίοις." καὶ τοῦτον τὸν τρόπον, ὅπως μὴ στεροῖντο τῆς διανομῆς,
ἀφέντων τὸν ἀπόστολον, ἔλυσε τὸ πρὸς Ἀλέξανδρον
ἔγκλημα τοῦ δήμου. πολλὰ γὰρ ἀπ' εὐθείας οὐκ
ἔστιν ἐξῶσαι τῶν ἀλυσιτελῶν, ἀλλὰ δεῖ τινος
ἀμωσγέπως καμπῆς καὶ περιαγωγῆς, οἵα καὶ
819 Φωκίων ἐχρῆτο κελευόμενος εἰς Βοιωτίαν ἐμβαλεῖν
παρὰ καιρόν· ἐκήρυξε γὰρ εὐθὺς ἀκολουθεῖν ἀφ'
ἥβης τοὺς μέχρι ἐτῶν ἑξήκοντα· καὶ θορύβου τῶν
πρεσβυτέρων γενομένου " τί δεινόν; " εἶπεν· " ἐγὼ
γὰρ ὁ στρατηγὸς ὀγδοήκοντα γεγονὼς ἔτη μεθ'
ὑμῶν ἔσομαι." τούτῳ δὴ τῷ τρόπῳ καὶ πρεσβείας
διακοπτέον ἀκαίρους, συγκαταλέγειν πολλοὺς τῶν
ἀνεπιτηδείως ἐχόντων, καὶ κατασκευὰς ἀχρήστους,
κελεύοντα συνεισφέρειν, καὶ δίκας καὶ ἀποδημίας[1]
ἀπρεπεῖς,[2] ἀξιοῦντα συμπαρεῖναι καὶ συναποδη-
μεῖν. πρώτους δὲ τοὺς γράφοντας τὰ τοιαῦτα
B καὶ παροξύνοντας ἕλκειν δεῖ καὶ παραλαμβάνειν·
ἢ γὰρ ἀναδυόμενοι τὴν πρᾶξιν αὐτοὶ διαλύειν
δόξουσιν ἢ μεθέξουσι τῶν δυσχερῶν παρόντες.
    26. Ὅπου μέντοι μέγα δεῖ τι[3] περανθῆναι καὶ
χρήσιμον ἀγῶνος δὲ πολλοῦ καὶ σπουδῆς δεόμενον,
ἐνταῦθα πειρῶ τῶν φίλων αἱρεῖσθαι τοὺς κρατί-

---

[1] δίκας καὶ ἀποδημίας Xylander's translation; ἀποδημίας
Coraes: δίκας.
[2] ἀπρεπεῖς] ἀτερπεῖς Coraes.
[3] δεῖ τι Bernardakis: δεῖ.

---

[a] The second day of the *Anthesteria*, a three-day festival
in worship of Dionysus, held in early spring at Athens.
[b] *Cf. Life of Phocion*, chap. xxiv.

for the Pitcher Festival ^{a} so that each of you is to receive a half-mina, but if you had rather apply the funds to this other purpose, use your own money for the festival." And in this way, since they gave up the expedition in order not to lose the distribution of money, he removed any ground of complaint on Alexander's part against the people of Athens. For there are many unprofitable measures which the statesman cannot avert by direct means, but he must use some sort of roundabout and circuitous methods, such as Phocion employed when ordered at an inopportune time to invade Boeotia. He immediately issued a proclamation ^{b} calling all those from the age of military service up to sixty years to join the ranks, and when the older men made a violent protest, he said : " What is there terrible about it ? For I, your general, who am eighty years old, shall be with you." So in this way we should prevent inopportune embassies by listing among the envoys many who are not qualified to go, and useless construction by calling for contributions, and improper lawsuits and missions abroad by ordering the parties to appear in court together and together to go abroad on the missions. And those who propose such measures and incite the people to adopt them should be the first to be haled into court and made to take the responsibility for putting them into effect ; for so they will either draw back and appear to be themselves nullifying the measure or they will stick to it and share its unpleasant features.

26. When, however, something important and useful but requiring much conflict and serious effort is to be accomplished, then try to select from among your friends those who are most powerful, or from

(819) στους ἢ τῶν κρατίστων τοὺς πραοτάτους· ἥκιστα
γὰρ ἀντιπράξουσιν οὗτοι καὶ μάλιστα συνεργήσουσι,
τὸ φρονεῖν ἄνευ τοῦ φιλονεικεῖν ἔχοντες. οὐ μὴν
ἀλλὰ καὶ τῆς ἑαυτοῦ φύσεως ἔμπειρον ὄντα δεῖ
πρὸς ὃ χείρων ἑτέρου πέφυκας αἱρεῖσθαι τοὺς
C μᾶλλον δυναμένους ἀντὶ τῶν ὁμοίων, ὡς ὁ Διομήδης
ἐπὶ τὴν κατασκοπὴν μεθ' ἑαυτοῦ τὸν φρόνιμον
εἵλετο, τοὺς ἀνδρείους παρελθών. καὶ γὰρ αἱ
πράξεις μᾶλλον ἰσορροποῦσι καὶ τὸ φιλόνεικον οὐκ
ἐγγίγνεται πρὸς ἀλλήλους τοῖς ἀφ' ἑτέρων ἀρετῶν
καὶ δυνάμεων φιλοτιμουμένοις. λάμβανε δὴ καὶ
δίκης συνεργὸν καὶ πρεσβείας κοινωνόν, ἂν λέγειν
μὴ δυνατὸς ᾖς, τὸν ῥητορικόν, ὡς Πελοπίδας
Ἐπαμεινώνδαν· κἂν ᾖς ἀπίθανος πρὸς ὁμιλίαν τῷ
πλήθει καὶ ὑψηλός, ὡς Καλλικρατίδας, τὸν εὔχαριν
καὶ θεραπευτικόν· κἂν ἀσθενὴς καὶ δύσεργος τὸ
σῶμα, τὸν φιλόπονον καὶ ῥωμαλέον, ὡς Νικίας
D Λάμαχον. οὕτω γὰρ ἂν[1] ἦν ὁ Γηρυόνης ζηλωτὸς
ἔχων σκέλη πολλὰ καὶ χεῖρας καὶ ὀφθαλμούς, εἰ
πάντα μιᾷ ψυχῇ διώκει. τοῖς δὲ πολιτικοῖς
ἔξεστι μὴ σώματα μηδὲ χρήματα μόνον, ἀλλὰ καὶ
τύχας καὶ δυνάμεις καὶ ἀρετάς, ἂν ὁμονοῶσιν, εἰς
μίαν χρείαν συντιθέντας εὐδοκιμεῖν μᾶλλον ἄλλου[2]
περὶ τὴν αὐτὴν πρᾶξιν· οὐχ ὥσπερ οἱ Ἀργοναῦται
τὸν Ἡρακλέα καταλιπόντες ἠναγκάζοντο διὰ τῆς
γυναικωνίτιδος καταδόμενοι καὶ φαρμακευόμενοι
σῴζειν ἑαυτοὺς καὶ κλέπτειν τὸ νᾶκος.

[1] γὰρ ἂν Wyttenbach : γὰρ.
[2] μᾶλλον ἄλλου] μᾶλλον ἀπ' ἄλλου Bernardakis; μᾶλλον ἢ
χωρὶς ἄλλου Capps; ἄλλον ἀπ' ἄλλου Kronenberg.

[3] Cf. Homer, Il. x. 243. He chose Odysseus.

among the most powerful those who are easiest to get along with ; for they are least likely to act against you and most likely to work with you, since they possess wisdom without contentiousness. And, moreover, you should know your own nature and choose for any purpose for which you are naturally less fitted than others, men who are more able rather than men like yourself, as Diomedes chose to go with him on the scouting expedition the man of prudence and passed over the men of courage.[a] For actions are thus more equally balanced, and contention does not arise among men whose ambitions proceed from different virtues and abilities. So, if you are not a good speaker, take an orator as your assistant in a lawsuit or your colleague in an embassy, as Pelopidas took Epameinondas ; and if, like Callicratidas, you are too lofty of speech and not persuasive in addressing the masses, choose a man who is winning in his speech and conciliatory ; and if you are physically weak and incapable of hard work, choose a man who is fond of labour and strong, as Nicias chose Lamachus. For on this principle Geryon would have been enviable for having many legs, arms, and eyes, if he had directed them all by one mind. But statesmen, by uniting for one purpose not only men's persons and funds, but also their fortunes, abilities, and virtues, if they are in agreement, can gain greater reputation in connexion with the same action than by other means, not behaving like the Argonauts, who left Heracles behind and then were forced to work through the women's quarters[b] and use magic and drugs to save themselves and steal the golden fleece.

[b] This refers to Jason's seduction of Medea.

E Χρυσὸν μὲν εἰς ἔνια τῶν ἱερῶν εἰσιόντες ἔξω
καταλείπουσι, σίδηρον δ᾽ ὡς ἁπλῶς εἰπεῖν εἰς
οὐδὲν συνεισφέρουσιν. ἐπεὶ δὲ κοινόν ἐστιν ἱερὸν
τὸ βῆμα Βουλαίου τε Διὸς καὶ Πολιέως καὶ
Θέμιδος καὶ Δίκης, αὐτόθεν μὲν ἤδη φιλοπλουτίαν
καὶ φιλοχρηματίαν, ὥσπερ σίδηρον μεστὸν ἰοῦ
καὶ νόσημα τῆς ψυχῆς, ἀποδυσάμενος εἰς ἀγορὰς
καπήλων ἢ δανειστῶν ἀπόρριψον,

αὐτὸς δ᾽ ἀπονόσφι τραπέσθαι

τὸν ἀπὸ δημοσίων χρηματιζόμενον ἡγούμενος ἀφ᾽
ἱερῶν κλέπτειν, ἀπὸ τάφων, ἀπὸ φίλων, ἐκ προδοσίας, ἀπὸ ψευδομαρτυρίας, σύμβουλον ἄπιστον
εἶναι, δικαστὴν ἐπίορκον, ἄρχοντα δωροδόκον, οὐδεμιᾶς ἁπλῶς καθαρὸν ἀδικίας. ὅθεν οὐ δεῖ πολλὰ
F περὶ τούτων λέγειν.

27. Ἡ δὲ φιλοτιμία, καίπερ οὖσα σοβαρωτέρα
τῆς φιλοκερδείας, οὐκ ἐλάττονας ἔχει κῆρας ἐν
πολιτείᾳ· καὶ γὰρ τὸ τολμᾶν αὐτῇ πρόσεστι μᾶλλον·
ἐμφύεται γὰρ οὐκ ἀργαῖς οὐδὲ ταπειναῖς ἀλλ᾽ ἐρρω-
μέναις μάλιστα καὶ νεανικαῖς προαιρέσεσι, καὶ τὸ
παρὰ τῶν ὄχλων ῥόθιον πολλάκις συνεξαῖρον αὐτὴν
820 καὶ συνεξωθοῦν τοῖς ἐπαίνοις ἀκατάσχετον ποιεῖ
καὶ δυσμεταχείριστον. ὥσπερ οὖν ὁ Πλάτων
ἀκουστέον εἶναι τοῖς νέοις ἔλεγεν ἐκ παίδων εὐθύς,
ὡς οὔτε περικεῖσθαι χρυσὸν αὐτοῖς ἔξωθεν οὔτε κε-
κτῆσθαι θέμις, οἰκεῖον ἐν τῇ ψυχῇ συμμεμιγμένον
ἔχοντας, αἰνιττόμενος οἶμαι τὴν ἐκ γένους δια-
τείνουσαν εἰς τὰς φύσεις αὐτῶν ἀρετήν· οὕτω παρα-

---

^a Cf. Plato, *Republic*, 609 A.
^b Homer, *Od.* v. 350.
^c Plato, *Republic*, 416 E.

When entering some sanctuaries men leave their
gold outside; but iron, one may say, they do not
at all carry into any sanctuary. And since the
orators' platform is a sanctuary common to Zeus the
Counsellor and the Protector of Cities, to Themis
and to Justice, do you strip off all love of wealth
and of money, as you would iron full of rust[a] and
a disease of the soul, cast them straightway at the
beginning into the market-place of hucksters and
money-lenders,

and turning your back depart from them,[b]

believing that a man who makes money out of public
funds is stealing from sanctuaries, from tombs, from
his friends, through treason and by false testimony,
that he is an untrustworthy adviser, a perjured judge,
a venal magistrate, in brief not free from any kind
of iniquity. And therefore there is no need of
saying much about these evils.

27. But ambition, although it is a more pre-
tentious word than "covetousness," is no less per-
nicious in the State; for there is more daring in it;
since it is innate, not in slothful and abject spirits,
but in the most vigorous and impetuous, and the
surge which comes from the masses, raising it on
the crest of the wave and sweeping it along by shouts
of praise, often makes it unrestrained and unmanage-
able. Therefore, just as Plato said[c] that young
people should be told from childhood that it is not
proper for them to wear gold on their persons or to
possess it, since they have a gold of their own
mingled in their souls,—a figurative reference, I
believe, to the virtue derived by descent, which
permeates their natures,—so let us moderate our

(820) μυθώμεθα τὴν φιλοτιμίαν, λέγοντες ἐν ἑαυτοῖς ἔχειν
χρυσὸν ἀδιάφθορον καὶ ἀκήρατον καὶ ἄχραντον ὑπὸ
φθόνου καὶ μώμου τιμήν, ἅμα¹ λογισμῷ καὶ παρα-
θεωρήσει τῶν πεπραγμένων ἡμῖν καὶ πεπολιτευμέ-
B νων αὐξανόμενον· διὸ μὴ δεῖσθαι γραφομένων τιμῶν
ἢ πλαττομένων ἢ χαλκοτυπουμένων, ἐν αἷς καὶ τὸ
εὐδοκιμοῦν ἀλλότριόν ἐστιν· ἐπαινεῖται γὰρ οὐχ ᾧ
γέγονεν ἀλλ' ὑφ' οὗ γέγονεν ὡς ὁ σαλπικτὴς² καὶ
ὁ δορυφόρος. ὁ δὲ Κάτων, ἤδη τότε τῆς Ῥώμης
καταπιμπλαμένης ἀνδριάντων, οὐκ ἐῶν αὑτοῦ γενέσθαι "μᾶλλον," ἔφη, "βούλομαι πυνθάνεσθαί τινας,
διὰ τί μου ἀνδριὰς οὐ κεῖται ἢ διὰ τί κεῖται." καὶ
γὰρ φθόνον ἔχει τὰ τοιαῦτα καὶ νομίζουσιν οἱ πολλοὶ
τοῖς μὴ λαβοῦσιν αὐτοὶ χάριν ὀφείλειν, τοὺς δὲ
λαβόντας αὑτοῖς³ καὶ βαρεῖς εἶναι, οἷον ἐπὶ μισθῷ
C τὰς χρείας ἀπαιτοῦντας. ὥσπερ οὖν ὁ παραπλεύ-
σας τὴν Σύρτιν εἶτ' ἀνατραπεὶς περὶ τὸν πορθμὸν
οὐδὲν μέγα πεποίηκεν οὐδὲ σεμνόν, οὕτως ὁ τὸ
ταμιεῖον φυλαξάμενος καὶ τὸ δημοσιώνιον ἁλοὺς δὲ
περὶ τὴν προεδρίαν ἢ τὸ πρυτανεῖον, ὑψηλῷ μὲν⁴
προσέπταικεν ἀκρωτηρίῳ βαπτίζεται δ' ὁμοίως.
ἄριστος μὲν οὖν ὁ μηδενὸς δεόμενος τῶν τοιούτων
ἀλλὰ φεύγων καὶ παραιτούμενος· ἂν δ' ᾖ μὴ ῥάδιον
D δήμου τινὰ χάριν ἀπώσασθαι καὶ φιλοφροσύνην
πρὸς τοῦτο ῥυέντος, ὥσπερ οὐκ ἀργυρίτην οὐδὲ δωρί-
την ἀγῶνα πολιτείας ἀγωνιζομένοις ἀλλ' ἱερὸν ὡς

---

¹ τιμήν, ἅμα] τίμημα Hartman.
² σαλπικτὴς Bernardakis: σαλπιγκτής.
³ αὑτοῖς Madvig: αὐτοῖς.
⁴ μὲν added by Reiske.

ambition, saying that we have in ourselves honour, a gold uncorrupted, undefiled, and unpolluted by envy and fault-finding, which increases along with reasoning and the contemplation of our acts and public measures. Therefore we have no need of honours painted, modelled, or cast in bronze, in which even that which is admired is really the work of another; for the person who receives praise is not the man for whom the "trumpeter" or the "doryphorus," [a] for example, was made, but the man by whom it was made. Cato, Rome being even then full of portrait statues, refused to let one be made of himself, saying, " I prefer to have people ask why there is not a statue of me rather than why there is one." Such honours do indeed arouse envy, and the people think that they are themselves under obligations to men who have not received them, but that those who have received them are oppressors of the people, as men who demand payment for their services. Therefore, just as a man who has sailed past the Syrtis and is then capsized at the channel has done nothing so very great or glorious, so the man who has watched over the treasury and the public revenue, but is then found wanting in the presidency or the prytany, is indeed dashed against a lofty promontory, but gets a ducking all the same. No, that man is the best who wants no such things and even avoids and refuses them when offered. But if it is not easy to reject some favour or some kindly sentiment of the people, when it is so inclined, for men engaged in a political struggle for which the prize is not money or gifts, but which is

[a] Two famous statues. The doryphorus (spear-bearer) was by Polycleitus.

271

0) ἀληθῶς καὶ στεφανίτην, ἐπιγραφή τις ἀρκεῖ καὶ πινάκιον καὶ ψήφισμα καὶ θαλλός, ὡς Ἐπιμενίδης ἔλαβεν ἐξ ἀκροπόλεως καθήρας τὴν πόλιν. Ἀναξαγόρας δὲ τὰς διδομένας ἀφεὶς τιμὰς ᾐτήσατο τὴν ἡμέραν ἐκείνην, καθ' ἣν ἂν τελευτήσῃ, τοὺς παῖδας ἀφιέναι παίζειν καὶ σχολάζειν ἀπὸ τῶν μαθημάτων. τοῖς δὲ τοὺς Μάγους ἀνελοῦσιν ἑπτὰ Πέρσαις ἔδωκαν αὐτοῖς καὶ τοῖς ἀπ' αὐτῶν γενομένοις εἰς τοὔμπροσθεν τῆς κεφαλῆς[1] τὴν τιάραν φορεῖν[2]· τοῦτο

E γὰρ ἐποιήσαντο σύμβολον, ὡς ἔοικε, χωροῦντες ἐπὶ τὴν πρᾶξιν. ἔχει δέ τι καὶ ἡ τοῦ Πιττακοῦ τιμὴ πολιτικόν· ἧς γὰρ ἐκτήσατο χώρας τοῖς πολίταις γῆν ὅσην ἐθέλοι λαβεῖν κελευσθεὶς ἔλαβε τοσαύτην, ὅσην ἐπῆλθε τὸ ἀκόντιον αὐτοῦ βαλόντος· ὁ δὲ Ῥωμαῖος Κόκλης,[3] ὅσην[4] ἡμέρᾳ μιᾷ χωλὸς ὢν περιήροσεν. οὐ γὰρ μισθὸν εἶναι δεῖ τῆς πράξεως ἀλλὰ σύμβολον τὴν τιμήν, ἵνα καὶ διαμένῃ πολὺν χρόνον, ὥσπερ ἐκεῖναι διέμειναν. τῶν δὲ Δημητρίου τοῦ Φαληρέως τριακοσίων ἀνδριάντων οὐδεὶς

F ἔσχεν ἰὸν οὐδὲ πίνον, ἀλλὰ πάντες ἔτι ζῶντος προανῃρέθησαν· τοὺς δὲ Δημάδου κατεχώνευσαν εἰς ἀμίδας· καὶ πολλαὶ τοιαῦτα τιμαὶ πεπόνθασιν οὐ μοχθηρίᾳ τοῦ λαβόντος μόνον ἀλλὰ καὶ μεγέθει τοῦ δοθέντος δυσχερανθεῖσαι. διὸ κάλλιστον καὶ βεβαιότατον εὐτέλεια τιμῆς φυλακτήριον, αἱ δὲ μεγά-

---

[1] τῆς κεφαλῆς] τὰ σκέλη συνάπτοντας τῇ κεφαλῇ Bernardakis with no indication of ms. authority.
[2] φορεῖν Wyttenbach and others: φέρειν.
[3] Κόκλης Codex Basileensis: πόπλιος.
[4] ὅσην Wyttenbach: ἢν.

---

[a] The prizes at the Olympic, Pythian, Isthmian, and Nemean games were crowns of wild olive, laurel, pine, and parsley respectively.

272

a truly sacred contest worthy of a crown,[a] a mere inscription suffices, a tablet, a decree, or a green branch such as Epimenides[b] received from the Acropolis after purifying the city. And Anaxagoras, giving up the honours which had been granted him, requested that on the day of his death the children be allowed to play and be free from their lessons. And to the seven Persians who killed the magi the privilege was granted that they and their descendants should wear their headdress tilted forward over the forehead ; for they made this, so it appears, their secret sign when they undertook their act. And there is something that indicates public spirit, too, about the honour received by Pittacus ; for, when he was told to take as much as he wished of the land which he had gained for the citizens, he took only as much as he could throw a javelin over. And the Roman Cocles received as much as he—and he was lame—could plough around in one day. For the honour should not be payment for the action, but a symbol, that it may last for a long time, as those just mentioned have lasted. But of all the three hundred statues of Demetrius of Phalerum not one acquired rust or dirt ; they were all destroyed while he was still living ; and those of Demades were melted down into chamber-pots. Things like that have happened to many honours, they having become offensive, not only because the recipient was worthless, but also because the gift bestowed was too great. And therefore the best and surest way to ensure the duration of honours is to reduce their

[b] Epimenides of Crete was called in by the Athenians, apparently not far from 500 B.C., to purify the city of a pestilence.

λαι καὶ ὑπέρογκοι καὶ βάρος ἔχουσαι παραπλησίως
τοῖς ἀσυμμέτροις ἀνδριᾶσι ταχὺ περιτρέπονται.

28. Ὀνομάζω δὲ νῦν τιμάς, ἃς οἱ πολλοὶ κατ'
Ἐμπεδοκλέα

ᾗ θέμις οὐ¹ καλέουσι, νόμῳ δ' ἐπίφημι καὶ αὐτός·

ἐπεὶ τήν γ' ἀληθινὴν τιμὴν καὶ χάριν ἱδρυμένην ἐν
εὐνοίᾳ καὶ διαθέσει τῶν μεμνημένων οὐχ ὑπερ-
821 όψεται πολιτικὸς ἀνήρ, οὐδέ γε δόξαν ἀτιμάσει
φεύγων τὸ "τοῖς πέλας ἀνδάνειν," ὡς ἠξίου Δημό-
κριτος. οὐδὲ γὰρ κυνῶν ἀσπασμὸς οὐδ' ἵππων
εὔνοια θηραταῖς καὶ ἱπποτρόφοις ἀπόβλητον, ἀλλὰ
καὶ χρήσιμον καὶ ἡδὺ συντρόφοις καὶ συνήθεσι ζῴοις
τοιαύτην ἐνεργάσασθαι διάθεσιν πρὸς αὑτόν, οἵαν ὁ
Λυσιμάχου κύων ἐπεδείκνυτο καὶ τῶν Ἀχιλλέως
ἵππων ὁ ποιητὴς διηγεῖται περὶ τὸν Πάτροκλον·
οἶμαι δ' ἂν καὶ τὰς μελίττας ἀπαλλάττειν βέλτιον,
B εἰ τοὺς τρέφοντας καὶ θεραπεύοντας ἀσπάζεσθαι καὶ
προσίεσθαι μᾶλλον ἢ κεντεῖν καὶ χαλεπαίνειν ἐβού-
λοντο· νυνὶ δὲ ταύτας μὲν καπνῷ κολάζουσιν,
ἵππους δ' ὑβριστὰς καὶ κύνας ἀποστάτας κλοιοῖς
καὶ χαλινοῖς ἄγουσιν ἠναγκασμένους· ἄνθρωπον δ'
ἀνθρώπῳ χειρόηθη καὶ πρᾶον ἑκουσίως οὐδὲν ἀλλ'
ἢ πίστις εὐνοίας καὶ καλοκαγαθίας δόξα καὶ δικαιοσύνης παρίστησιν. ᾗ καὶ Δημοσθένης ὀρθῶς
μέγιστον ἀποφαίνεται πρὸς τοὺς τυράννους φυλακτήριον ἀπιστίαν ταῖς πόλεσι· τοῦτο γὰρ μάλιστα
τῆς ψυχῆς τὸ μέρος, ᾧ πιστεύομεν, ἁλώσιμόν ἐστιν.

¹ ᾗ θέμις οὐ Meziriacus : ᾗ θέμις.

ᵃ Mullach, *Frag. Phil. Graec.* i. p. 3, 112.
ᵇ Quoted with slightly different wording by Plutarch,
Moralia, 1113 ʙ.

cost but those which are great and top-heavy and weighty are, like ill-proportioned statues, quickly overturned.

28. And I now give the name "honours" to those which the multitude, to quote Empedocles,[a]

Do not call as is right; and I, too, myself follow custom.[b]

For the statesman will not despise the true honour and favour founded upon the goodwill and disposition of those who remember his actions, nor will he disdain reputation and avoid "pleasing his neighbours," as Democritus[c] demanded. For not even the greeting of dogs nor the affection of horses is to be spurned by huntsmen and horse-trainers, but it is both advantageous and pleasant to instil into animals which are brought up with us and live with us such a disposition towards us as was exhibited by the dog of Lysimachus and as the poet tells us that Achilles' horses felt towards Patroclus.[d] And I believe even bees would come off better if they would only welcome and placate their keepers and attendants instead of stinging them and making them angry. But as it is, people punish bees with smoke and lead unruly horses and runaway dogs by force of bits and dog-collars; but nothing makes a man willingly tractable and gentle to another man except trust in his goodwill and belief in his nobility and justice. And therefore Demosthenes is right[e] in declaring that the greatest safeguard States possess against tyrants is distrust; for that part of the soul with which we trust is most easily taken captive. Therefore just as

---

[c] Mullach, *Frag. Phil. Graec.* i. p. 355.
[d] Homer, *Il.* xix. 404 ff.
[e] Demosthenes, vi. (second *Philippic*) 24.

(821) ὥσπερ οὖν τῆς Κασάνδρας ἀδοξούσης ἀνόνητος ἦν
ἡ μαντικὴ τοῖς πολίταις

"ἄκραντα γάρ με" φησίν "ἔθηκε θεσπίζειν
θεός,
C καὶ πρὸς παθόντων κἂν κακοῖσι κειμένων
σοφὴ κέκλημαι, πρὶν παθεῖν δέ 'μαίνομαι,'"

οὕτως ἡ πρὸς Ἀρχύταν πίστις καὶ πρὸς Βάττον εὔνοια τῶν πολιτῶν μεγάλα τοὺς χρωμένους αὐτοῖς
διὰ τὴν δόξαν ὠφέλησε. καὶ τοῦτο μὲν πρῶτον
καὶ μέγιστον ἔνεστι τῇ δόξῃ τῇ τῶν πολιτικῶν
ἀγαθόν, ἡ πάροδον ἐπὶ τὰς πράξεις διδοῦσα πίστις·
δεύτερον δ' ὅτι πρὸς τοὺς βασκάνους καὶ πονηροὺς
ὅπλον ἡ παρὰ τῶν πολλῶν εὔνοια τοῖς ἀγαθοῖς
ἐστιν

ὡς ὅτε μήτηρ
παιδὸς ἐέργει μυῖαν, ὅθ' ἡδέι λέξεται ὕπνῳ,

ἀπερύκουσα τὸν φθόνον καὶ πρὸς τὰς δυνάμεις
ἐπανισοῦσα τὸν ἀγεννῆ τοῖς εὐπατρίδαις καὶ τὸν
πένητα τοῖς πλουσίοις καὶ τὸν ἰδιώτην τοῖς ἄρχουσι·
D καὶ ὅλως, ὅταν ἀλήθεια καὶ ἀρετὴ προσγένηται,
φορόν ἐστι πνεῦμα καὶ βέβαιον ἐπὶ τὴν πολιτείαν.
σκόπει δὲ τὴν ἐναντίαν καταμανθάνων διάθεσιν ἐν
τοῖς παραδείγμασι. τοὺς μὲν γὰρ Διονυσίου παῖδας
καὶ τὴν γυναῖκα καταπορνεύσαντες οἱ περὶ τὴν
Ἰταλίαν ἀνεῖλον, εἶτα καύσαντες τὰ σώματα τὴν
τέφραν κατέσπειραν ἐκ πλοίου κατὰ τῆς θαλάττης.

---

[a] Nauck, *Trag. Graec. Frag.* p. 919, no. 414. From an
unknown play.
[b] Archytas of Tarentum was a statesman, Pythagorean
philosopher, and mathematician. He was seven times

Cassandra's prophetic power was useless to the citizens because she was held in no esteem, "For God," she says,

> "has made me prophesy in vain,
> And those who suffer or have suffered woes
> Have called me 'wise'; but ere they suffer, 'mad,'"[a]

so the trust which the citizens reposed in Archytas[b] and their goodwill towards Battus[c] was, on account of their reputation, of great advantage to those who made use of them. The first and most important advantage inherent in the reputation of statesmen is this : the trust in them which affords them an entrance into public affairs ; and the second is that the good-will of the multitude is a weapon of defence for the good against the slanderous and wicked,

> as when a mother
> Wards off a fly from her child when he lieth asleep in
> sweet slumber,[d]

keeping off envy and in the matter of power making the low-born equal to the nobles, the poor to the rich, and the private citizen to the office-holders ; and in short, when truth and virtue are added to it, such goodwill is a steady fair wind wafting a man into political office. Now consider the contrary disposition and learn of it by examples. For the men of Italy violated the daughters and the wife of Dionysius,[e] killed them, and then burned their bodies and scattered the ashes from a boat over the sea. But when

general and never defeated. He lived in the fourth century B.C. and was a friend of Plato.

[c] Probably Battus III. of Cyrene is meant, under whom the constitution of the city was reformed about the middle of the sixth century B.C.   [d] Homer, *Il.* iv. 130.

[e] Dionysius II. of Syracuse; *cf. Life of Timoleon*, chap. xiii., and Aelian, *Var. Hist.* vi. 12.

Μενάνδρου δέ τινος ἐν Βάκτροις ἐπιεικῶς βασι-
E λεύσαντος εἶτ᾽ ἀποθανόντος ἐπὶ στρατοπέδου, τὴν
μὲν ἄλλην ἐποιήσαντο κηδείαν κατὰ τὸ κοινὸν αἱ
πόλεις, περὶ δὲ τῶν λειψάνων αὐτοῦ καταστάντες
εἰς ἀγῶνα μόλις συνέβησαν, ὥστε νειμάμενοι μέρος
ἴσον τῆς τέφρας ἀπελθεῖν, καὶ γενέσθαι μνημεῖα
παρὰ πᾶσι τοῦ ἀνδρός. αὖθις δ᾽[1] Ἀκραγαντῖνοι μὲν
ἀπαλλαγέντες Φαλάριδος ἐψηφίσαντο μηδένα φορεῖν
ἱμάτιον γλαύκινον· οἱ γὰρ ὑπηρέται τοῦ τυράννου
γλαυκίνοις ἐχρῶντο περιζώμασι. Πέρσαι δ᾽, ὅτι
F γρυπὸς ἦν ὁ Κῦρος, ἔτι καὶ νῦν ἐρῶσι τῶν γρυπῶν
καὶ καλλίστους ὑπολαμβάνουσιν.

29. Οὕτως ἁπάντων ἐρώτων ἰσχυρότατος ἅμα
καὶ θειότατός ἐστιν ὁ πόλεσι καὶ δήμοις πρὸς ἕνα
δι᾽ ἀρετὴν ἐγγιγνόμενος· αἱ δ᾽ ἀπὸ θεάτρων ἢ νε-
μήσεων ἢ μονομάχων ψευδώνυμοι τιμαὶ καὶ ψευδο-
μάρτυρες ἑταιρικαῖς ἐοίκασι κολακείαις, ὄχλων
ἀεὶ τῷ διδόντι καὶ χαριζομένῳ προσμειδιώντων,
ἐφήμερόν τινα καὶ ἀβέβαιον δόξαν. εὖ μὲν οὖν ὁ
πρῶτος[2] εἰπὼν καταλυθῆναι δῆμον ὑπὸ τοῦ πρώτου
δεκάσαντος συνεῖδεν, ὅτι τὴν ἰσχὺν ἀποβάλλουσιν
822 οἱ πολλοὶ τοῦ λαμβάνειν ἥττονες γενόμενοι· δεῖ
δὲ καὶ τοὺς δεκάζοντας οἴεσθαι καταλύειν ἑαυτούς,
ὅταν ἀναλωμάτων μεγάλων ὠνούμενοι τὴν δόξαν
ἰσχυροὺς ποιῶσι καὶ θρασεῖς τοὺς πολλούς, ὡς
μέγα τι καὶ δοῦναι καὶ ἀφελέσθαι κυρίους ὄντας.

30. Οὐ μὴν διὰ τοῦτο μικρολογητέον ἐν τοῖς
νενομισμένοις φιλοτιμήμασι, τῶν πραγμάτων εὐ-

---

[1] αὖθις δ᾽ Bernardakis : αὖθις.
[2] πρῶτος] πρώτως Duebner.

a certain man named Menander, who had been a good king of the Bactrians, died in camp, the cities celebrated his funeral as usual in other respects, but in respect to his remains they put forth rival claims and only with difficulty came to terms, agreeing that they should divide the ashes equally and go away and should erect monuments to him in all their cities. But, on the other hand, the Agrigentines, when they had got rid of Phalaris, decreed that no one should wear a grey cloak ; for the tyrant's servants had worn grey garments. But the Persians, because Cyrus was hook-nosed, even to this day love hook-nosed men and consider them the most handsome.

29. So of all kinds of love that which is engendered in states and peoples for an individual because of his virtue is at once the strongest and the most divine ; but those falsely named and falsely attested honours which are derived from giving theatrical performances, making distributions of money, or offering gladiatorial shows, are like harlots' flatteries, since the masses always smile upon him who gives to them and does them favours, granting him an ephemeral and uncertain reputation. And so he who first said that the people was ruined by the first man who bought its favour was well aware that the multitude loses its strength when it succumbs to bribe-taking ; but those also who give such bribes should bear in mind that they are destroying themselves when they purchase reputation by great expenditures, thus making the multitude strong and bold in the thought that they have power to give and take away something important.

30. We ought not, however, on this account to be niggardly as to the customary public contributions,

(822) πορίαν παρεχόντων· ὡς μᾶλλον οἱ πολλοὶ μὴ
μεταδιδόντα τῶν ἰδίων πλούσιον ἢ πένητα τῶν
δημοσίων κλέπτοντα δι᾽ ἔχθους ἔχουσιν, ὑπεροψίαν
τοῦτο καὶ περιφρόνησιν αὐτῶν¹ ἐκεῖνο δ᾽ ἀνάγκην
B ἡγούμενοι. γιγνέσθωσαν οὖν αἱ μεταδόσεις πρῶτον
μὲν ἀντὶ μηδενός· οὕτω γὰρ ἐκπλήττουσι καὶ χει-
ροῦνται μᾶλλον τοὺς λαμβάνοντας· ἔπειτα σὺν καιρῷ
πρόφασιν ἀστείαν καὶ καλὴν ἔχοντι, μετὰ τιμῆς θεοῦ
πάντας ἀγούσης πρὸς εὐσέβειαν· ἐγγίγνεται γὰρ
ἅμα τοῖς πολλοῖς ἰσχυρὰ διάθεσις καὶ δόξα τοῦ τὸ
δαιμόνιον εἶναι μέγα καὶ σεμνόν, ὅταν, οὓς αὐτοὶ
τιμῶσι καὶ μεγάλους νομίζουσιν, οὕτως ἀφειδῶς
καὶ προθύμως περὶ τὸ θεῖον ὁρῶσι φιλοτιμου-
μένους. ὥσπερ οὖν ὁ Πλάτων ἀφεῖλε τῶν παι-
C δευομένων νέων τὴν ἁρμονίαν τὴν Λύδιον καὶ τὴν
ἰαστί, τὴν μὲν τὸ θρηνῶδες καὶ φιλοπενθὲς ἡμῶν
ἐγείρουσαν τῆς ψυχῆς, τὴν δὲ τὸ πρὸς ἡδονὰς ὀλι-
σθηρὸν καὶ ἀκόλαστον αὔξουσαν· οὕτω σὺ τῶν
φιλοτιμιῶν ὅσαι τὸ φονικὸν καὶ θηριῶδες ἢ τὸ
βωμολόχον καὶ ἀκόλαστον ἐρεθίζουσι καὶ τρέφουσι,
μάλιστα μὲν ἐξέλαυνε τῆς πόλεως, εἰ δὲ μή, φεῦγε
καὶ διαμάχου τοῖς πολλοῖς αἰτουμένοις τὰ τοιαῦτα
θεάματα· χρηστὰς δὲ καὶ σώφρονας ἀεὶ ποιοῦ τῶν
ἀναλωμάτων ὑποθέσεις, τὸ καλὸν ἢ τὸ ἀναγκαῖον
ἐχούσας τέλος ἢ τὸ γοῦν ἡδὺ καὶ κεχαρισμένον
ἄνευ βλάβης καὶ ὕβρεως προσούσης.

D 31. Ἂν δ᾽ ᾖ τὰ τῆς οὐσίας μέτρια καὶ κέντρῳ

_____

¹ αὐτῶν Bernardakis : αὑτῶν.

_____

ᵃ Plato, *Republic*, 398 E.

if we are in prosperous circumstances; since the masses are more hostile to a rich man who does not give them a share of his private possessions than to a poor man who steals from the public funds, for they think the former's conduct is due to arrogance and contempt of them, but the latter's to necessity. First, then, let the gifts be made without bargaining for anything; for so they surprise and overcome the recipients more completely; and secondly they should be given on some occasion which offers a good and excellent pretext, one which is connected with the worship of a god and leads the people to piety; for at the same time there springs up in the minds of the masses a strong disposition to believe that the deity is great and majestic, when they see the men whom they themselves honour and regard as great so liberally and zealously vying with each other in honouring the divinity. Therefore, just as Plato *a* withheld the Lydian and the Ionian musical modes from the education of the young, because the one arouses that part of the soul which is inclined towards mourning and grief and the other strengthens that part which readily slips into pleasures and grows wanton, so you must, if possible, remove from the State all those free exhibitions which excite and nourish the murderous and brutal or the scurrilous and licentious spirit, or if you cannot do that, avoid them and oppose the multitude when they demand them. But always make the objects of your expenditures useful and moderate, having as their purpose either what is good or what is necessary, or at any rate what is pleasant and agreeable without anything harmful or outrageous in it.

31. But if your property is moderate and in re-

(822) καὶ διαστήματι περιγραφόμενα πρὸς τὴν χρείαν,
οὔτ' ἀγεννὲς οὔτε ταπεινὸν οὐδέν ἐστι πενίαν ὁμο-
λογοῦντα ταῖς τῶν ἐχόντων ἐξίστασθαι φιλοτιμίαις,
καὶ μὴ δανειζόμενον οἰκτρὸν ἅμα καὶ καταγέλαστον
εἶναι περὶ τὰς λειτουργίας· οὐ γὰρ λανθάνουσιν
ἐξασθενοῦντες ἢ φίλοις ἐνοχλοῦντες ἢ θωπεύοντες
δανειστάς, ὥστε μὴ δόξαν αὐτοῖς μηδ' ἰσχὺν ἀλλὰ
μᾶλλον αἰσχύνην καὶ καταφρόνησιν ἀπὸ τῶν τοιού-
E των ἀναλωμάτων ὑπάρχειν. διὸ χρήσιμον ἀεὶ πρὸς
τὰ τοιαῦτα μεμνῆσθαι τοῦ Λαμάχου καὶ τοῦ Φω-
κίωνος· οὗτος μὲν γάρ, ἀξιούντων αὐτὸν ἐν θυσίᾳ
τῶν Ἀθηναίων ἐπιδοῦναι καὶ κροτούντων πολλάκις
" αἰσχυνοίμην ἄν " εἶπεν " ὑμῖν μὲν ἐπιδιδοὺς
Καλλικλεῖ δὲ τούτῳ μὴ ἀποδιδούς," δείξας τὸν
δανειστήν. Λάμαχος δ' ἐν τοῖς τῆς στρατηγίας ἀεὶ
προσέγραφεν ἀπολογισμοῖς ἀργύριον εἰς κρηπῖδας αὑτῷ καὶ ἱμάτιον· Ἕρμωνι δὲ Θεσσαλοὶ
φεύγοντι τὴν ἀρχὴν ὑπὸ πενίας ἐψηφίσαντο
λάγυνον οἴνου κατὰ μῆνα διδόναι καὶ μέδιμνον
ἀλφίτων ἀφ' ἑκάστης τετράδος. οὕτως οὔτ' ἀ-
F γεννές ἐστι πενίαν ὁμολογεῖν, οὔτε λείπονται πρὸς
δύναμιν ἐν πόλεσι τῶν ἑστιώντων καὶ χορηγούντων
οἱ πένητες, ἂν παρρησίαν ἀπ' ἀρετῆς καὶ πίστιν
ἔχωσι. δεῖ δὴ μάλιστα κρατεῖν ἑαυτῶν ἐν τοῖς
τοιούτοις καὶ μήτ' εἰς πεδία καταβαίνειν πεζὸν

---

[a] Lamachus was an Athenian general who was killed in
the battle at the Anopus near Syracuse in 414 B.C.

[b] Phocion was a famous Athenian general in the fourth
century B.C. He was elected general forty-five times. He
was virtual ruler of Athens when Antipater was in power,
but in 318 B.C. was tried and executed by the Athenians.

lation to your needs strictly circumscribed " as by centre and radius," it is neither ignoble nor humiliating at all to confess your poverty and to withdraw from among those who have the means for public expenditures, instead of borrowing money and making yourself at once a pitiful and a ridiculous object in the matter of your public contributions ; for men are plainly seen to lack resources when they keep annoying their friends or truckling to money-lenders ; so that it is not reputation or power, but rather shame and contempt, which they acquire by such expenditures. And therefore it is always desirable in connexion with such things to remember Lamachus [a] and Phocion [b] ; for the latter, when the Athenians at a sacrifice called upon him to contribute and repeatedly raised a clamour, said, " I should be ashamed if I gave you a contribution and did not pay Callicles here what I owe him," pointing to his money-lender. And Lamachus always, when he was general, entered in his accounts money for shoes and a cloak for himself. And when Hermon tried to avoid office on the plea of poverty, the Thessalians voted to give him a flask [c] of wine monthly and a measure [d] of meal every four days. So it is not ignoble to confess poverty, and poor men, if by reason of their virtue they enjoy freedom of speech and public confidence, have no less influence in their cities than those who give public entertainments and exhibitions. The statesman must, then, do his best to control himself in such matters and not go down

Soon after that a public burial and a statue were decreed for him. The story told here is found also in the *Moralia*, p. 533 A.

[c] About six pints.

[d] About a bushel and a half.

ἱππεῦσι μαχούμενον μήτ' ἐπὶ στάδια καὶ θυμέλας
καὶ τραπέζας πένητα πλουσίοις ὑπὲρ δόξης καὶ
δυναστείας διαγωνιζόμενον· ἀλλ' ἀπ' ἀρετῆς καὶ
φρονήματος ἀεὶ μετὰ λόγου πειρωμένοις ἄγειν τὴν
823 πόλιν, οἷς οὐ μόνον τὸ καλὸν καὶ τὸ σεμνὸν ἀλλὰ καὶ
τὸ κεχαρισμένον καὶ ἀγωγὸν ἔνεστι "Κροισείων
αἱρετώτερον στατήρων." οὐ γὰρ αὐθάδης οὐδ'
ἐπαχθὴς ὁ χρηστὸς οὐδ' αὐθέκαστός ἐστιν ὁ
σώφρων ἀνὴρ καὶ

στείχει πολίταις ὄμμ' ἔχων ἰδεῖν πικρόν,

ἀλλὰ πρῶτον μὲν εὐπροσήγορος καὶ κοινὸς ὢν
πελάσαι καὶ προσελθεῖν ἅπασιν, οἰκίαν τε παρέχων
ἄκλειστον ὡς λιμένα φύξιμον ἀεὶ τοῖς χρῄζουσι,
καὶ τὸ κηδεμονικὸν καὶ φιλάνθρωπον οὐ χρείαις
οὐδὲ πράξεσι μόνον ἀλλὰ καὶ τῷ συναλγεῖν πταίουσι
B καὶ κατορθοῦσι συγχαίρειν ἐπιδεικνύμενος· οὐδαμῇ
δὲ λυπηρὸς οὐδ' ἐνοχλῶν οἰκετῶν πλήθει περὶ λου-
τρὸν ἢ καταλήψεσι τόπων ἐν θεάτροις οὐδὲ τοῖς
εἰς τρυφὴν καὶ πολυτέλειαν ἐπιφθόνοις παράσημος¹·
ἀλλ' ἴσος καὶ ὁμαλὸς ἐσθῆτι καὶ διαίτῃ καὶ τροφαῖς
παίδων καὶ θεραπείᾳ γυναικός, οἷον ὁμοδημεῖν καὶ
συνανθρωπεῖν τοῖς πολλοῖς βουλόμενος. ἔπειτα
σύμβουλον εὔνουν καὶ συνήγορον ἄμισθον καὶ δι-
αλλακτὴν εὐμενῆ πρὸς γυναῖκας ἀνδρῶν καὶ φίλων
πρὸς ἀλλήλους παρέχων ἑαυτόν, οὐ μικρὸν ἡμέρας

---

¹ παράσημος] Reiske suggests παρασήμοις, Bernardakis
παρασήμων, Hartman ἐπίφθονος ἐπισήμοις.

ᵃ Cf. Pollux, iii. 87, ix. 84, but, as Bernardakis suggests,
Plutarch may have added the word for "more desirable,"
in which case there is here no real quotation.
284

into the plain on foot to fight with cavalry; if he is poor, he must not produce foot-races, theatrical shows, and banquets in competition with the rich for reputation and power, but he should vie with those who try always to lead the State on the strength of virtue and wisdom, combined with reason, for in such are found not only nobility and dignity but also the power to win and attract the people, a thing "more desirable than gold coins of Croesus." [a] For the good man is neither presumptuous nor offensive, and the prudent man is not over-blunt in speech, nor does he

> Walk with a mien his townsmen bitter find, [b]

but in the first place he is affable and generally accessible and approachable for all, keeping his house always unlocked as a harbour of refuge for those in need, and showing his solicitude and friendliness, not only by acts of service, but also by sharing the griefs of those who fail and the joys of those who succeed; and he is in no way disagreeable or offensive by reason of the number of the servants who attend him at the bath or by appropriating seats at the theatre, nor is he conspicuous for invidious exhibitions of luxury and extravagance; but he is on an equal level with others in his clothing and daily life, in the bringing up of his children and as regards the servants who wait upon his wife, as one who wishes to live like the masses and be friendly with them. And, moreover, he shows himself a kindly counsellor, an advocate who accepts no fee, and a kind-hearted conciliator when husbands are at variance with their wives or friends with one another. He spends no

---

[b] Nauck, *Trag. Graec. Frag.* p. 919, no. 415.

(823) μέρος ἐπὶ τοῦ βήματος ἢ τοῦ λογείου πολιτευόμενος, εἶτ᾽ ἤδη πάντα τὸν ἄλλον βίον

C   ἕλκων ἐφ᾽ αὑτὸν[1] ὥστε καικίας νέφη

τὰς χρείας καὶ τὰς οἰκονομίας πανταχόθεν· ἀλλὰ
δημοσιεύων ἀεὶ ταῖς φροντίσι, καὶ τὴν πολιτείαν
βίον καὶ πρᾶξιν οὐκ ἀσχολίαν ὥσπερ οἱ πολλοὶ καὶ
λειτουργίαν ἡγούμενος, πᾶσι τούτοις καὶ τοῖς
τοιούτοις ἐπιστρέφει καὶ προσάγεται τοὺς πολλούς,
νόθα καὶ κίβδηλα τὰ τῶν ἄλλων θωπεύματα καὶ
δελεάσματα πρὸς τὴν τούτου κηδεμονίαν καὶ
φρόνησιν ὁρῶντας. οἱ μὲν γὰρ Δημητρίου κόλακες
οὐκ ἠξίουν βασιλεῖς τοὺς ἄλλους προσαγορεύειν,
ἀλλὰ τὸν μὲν Σέλευκον ἐλεφαντάρχην τὸν δὲ Λυ-
D σίμαχον γαζοφύλακα τὸν δὲ Πτολεμαῖον ναύαρχον
ἐκάλουν, τὸν δ᾽ Ἀγαθοκλέα νησιάρχην· οἱ δὲ
πολλοί, κἂν ἐν ἀρχῇ τὸν ἀγαθὸν καὶ φρόνιμον
ἀπορρίψωσιν, ὕστερον καταμανθάνοντες τὴν ἀλή-
θειαν αὐτοῦ καὶ τὸ ἦθος τοῦτον ἡγοῦνται μόνον
πολιτικὸν καὶ δημοτικὸν καὶ ἄρχοντα, τῶν δ᾽ ἄλλων
τὸν μὲν χορηγὸν τὸν δ᾽ ἑστιάτορα τὸν δὲ γυμνασί-
αρχον καὶ νομίζουσι καὶ καλοῦσιν. εἶθ᾽ ὥσπερ ἐν
τοῖς συμποσίοις, Καλλίου δαπανῶντος ἢ Ἀλκι-
βιάδου, Σωκράτης ἀκούεται καὶ πρὸς Σωκράτην
E πάντες ἀποβλέπουσιν, οὕτως ἐν ταῖς ὑγιαινούσαις
πόλεσιν Ἰσμηνίας μὲν ἐπιδίδωσι καὶ δειπνίζει
Λίχας καὶ χορηγεῖ Νικήρατος, Ἐπαμεινώνδας δὲ
καὶ Ἀριστείδης καὶ Λύσανδρος καὶ ἄρχουσι καὶ

    [1] αὑτὸν Meziriacus : ἑαυτόν.

---

  [a] Nauck, *Trag. Graec. Frag.* p. 853, no. 75; Kock, *Com.
Att. Frag.* iii. p. 612, no. 1229. Plutarch, *Moralia*, 88 E.

small part of the day engaged in the public business
on the orators' platform of the senate or the assembly, and thenceforth all the rest of his life he

> Draws to himself as north-east wind draws clouds [a]

services and commissions from every quarter. But
since he is always devoting his thoughts to the public
weal and regards public office as his life and his
work, not, like most people, as an interruption to
leisure and a compulsory expense,—by all these and
similar qualities he turns and attracts the people
towards himself, for they see that the flatteries and
enticements of others are spurious and counterfeit
when compared with his care and forethought.
The flatterers of Demetrius would not address the
other monarchs as kings, but called Seleucus " Ruler
of Elephants " and Lysimachus " Guardian of the
Treasure " and Ptolemy " Admiral of the Fleet "
and Agathocles " Lord of the Isles " ; but the
multitude, even if at first they reject the good and
wise man, afterwards, when they have become acquainted with his truthfulness and his character,
consider him alone a statesmanlike, public-spirited
man and a ruler, whereas they consider and call the
others, one a provider of choruses, one a giver of
banquets, and one a director of athletics. Then,
just as at banquets, though Callias or Alcibiades
pay the bill, it is Socrates to whom they listen,
and Socrates on whom all eyes are turned, so in
States in which the conditions are sound Ismenias
makes contributions, Lichas gives dinners, and
Niceratus provides choruses, but it is Epameinondas,
Aristeides, and Lysander who are the rulers, public

uses the same simile, and this line is quoted as a proverb by
Aristotle, *Meteor.* 364 b 13.

πολιτεύονται καὶ στρατηγοῦσι. πρὸς ἃ χρὴ βλέποντα μὴ ταπεινοῦσθαι μηδ' ἐκπεπλῆχθαι τὴν ἐκ
θεάτρων καὶ ὀπτανείων καὶ πολυανδρίων προσ-
ισταμένην τοῖς ὄχλοις δόξαν, ὡς ὀλίγον χρόνον
ἐπιζῶσαν καὶ τοῖς μονομάχοις καὶ ταῖς σκηναῖς
ὁμοῦ συνδιαλυομένην, ἔντιμον δὲ μηδὲν μηδὲ
σεμνὸν ἔχουσαν.

F   32. Οἱ μὲν οὖν ἔμπειροι θεραπείας καὶ τροφῆς
μελιττῶν τὸν μάλιστα βομβοῦντα τῶν σίμβλων
καὶ θορύβου μεστὸν τοῦτον εὐθηνεῖν καὶ ὑγιαίνειν
νομίζουσιν· ᾧ δὲ τοῦ λογικοῦ καὶ πολιτικοῦ
σμήνους ἐπιμέλειαν ἔχειν ὁ θεὸς ἔδωκεν, ἡσυχίᾳ
μάλιστα καὶ πρᾳότητι δήμου τεκμαιρόμενος εὐδαιμονίαν τὰ μὲν ἄλλα τοῦ Σόλωνος ἀποδέξεται καὶ
μιμήσεται κατὰ δύναμιν, ἀπορήσει δὲ καὶ θαυμάσει
τί παθὼν ἐκεῖνος ὁ ἀνὴρ ἔγραψεν ἄτιμον εἶναι τὸν
824 ἐν στάσει πόλεως μηδετέροις προσθέμενον. οὔτε
γὰρ σώματι νοσοῦντι γίγνεται μεταβολῆς ἀρχὴ πρὸς
τὸ ὑγιαίνειν ἀπὸ τῶν συννοσούντων μερῶν, ἀλλ'
ὅταν ἡ παρὰ τοῖς ἐρρωμένοις ἰσχύσασα κρᾶσις
ἐκστήσῃ τὸ παρὰ φύσιν· ἔν τε δήμῳ στασιάσαντι
μὴ δεινὴν μηδ' ὀλέθριον στάσιν ἀλλὰ παυσομένην
ποτὲ δεῖ τὸ ἀπαθὲς καὶ τὸ ὑγιαῖνον ἐγκεκρᾶσθαι
πολὺ καὶ παραμένειν καὶ συνοικεῖν· ἐπιρρεῖ γὰρ
τούτῳ τὸ οἰκεῖον ἐκ τῶν σωφρονούντων καὶ δίεισι
διὰ τοῦ νενοσηκότος· αἱ δὲ δι' ὅλων ἀναταραχθεῖσαι
πόλεις κομιδῇ διεφθάρησαν, ἂν μή τινος ἀνάγκης
B ἔξωθεν τυχοῦσαι καὶ κολάσεως ὑπὸ κακῶν βίᾳ
σωφρονήσωσιν. οὐ μὴν ἀναίσθητον οὐδ' ἀνάλγητον

men, and generals. So, observing these things, we must not be humiliated or overwhelmed by the reputation with the masses gained from theatres, kitchens, and assembly-halls, remembering that it lasts but a short time and ends the minute the gladiatorial and dramatic shows are over, since there is nothing honourable or dignified in it.

32. Now those who are skilled in tending and keeping bees think that the hive which hums loudest and is most full of noise is thriving and in good condition ; but he to whom God has given the care of the rational and political swarm will judge of its happiness chiefly by the quietness and tranquillity of the people ; he will accept and imitate to the best of his ability the other precepts of Solon, but will wonder in great perplexity why that great man prescribed that in case of factional disorder whoever joined neither faction should be deprived of civic rights. For in a body afflicted with disease the beginning of a change to health does not come from the diseased parts, but it comes when the condition in the healthy parts gains strength and drives out that which is contrary to nature ; and in a people afflicted with faction, if it is not dangerous and destructive but is destined to cease sometime, there must be a strong, permanent, and permeating admixture of sanity and soundness ; for to this element there flows from the men of understanding that which is akin to it, and then it permeates the part which is diseased ; but States which have fallen into complete disorder are utterly ruined unless they meet with some external necessity and chastisement and are thus forcibly compelled by their misfortunes to be reasonable. Yet certainly it is not fitting in time

(824) ἐν στάσει καθῆσθαι προσήκει τὴν περὶ αὑτὸν
ἀταραξίαν ὑμνοῦντα καὶ τὸν ἀπράγμονα καὶ
μακάριον βίον, ἐν ἑτέροις ἐπιτερπόμενον ἀγνω
μονοῦσιν· ἀλλ' ἐνταῦθα δεῖ μάλιστα τὸν Θηρα
μένους κόθορνον ὑποδούμενον ἀμφοτέροις ὁμιλεῖν
καὶ μηδετέροις προστίθεσθαι· δόξεις γὰρ οὐχὶ τῷ
μὴ συναδικεῖν ἀλλότριος ἀλλὰ τῷ βοηθεῖν κοινὸς
εἶναι πάντων· καὶ τὸ μὴ συνατυχεῖν οὐχ ἕξει
φθόνον, ἂν πᾶσι φαίνῃ συναλγῶν ὁμοίως. κρά
C τιστον δὲ προνοεῖν ὅπως μηδέποτε στασιάζωσι,
καὶ τοῦτο τῆς πολιτικῆς ὥσπερ τέχνης μέγιστον
ἡγεῖσθαι καὶ κάλλιστον. ὅρα γὰρ ὅτι τῶν μεγί
στων ἀγαθῶν ταῖς πόλεσιν, εἰρήνης ἐλευθερίας
εὐετηρίας εὐανδρίας ὁμονοίας, πρὸς μὲν εἰρήνην
οὐδὲν οἱ δῆμοι τῶν πολιτικῶν ἔν γε τῷ παρόντι
χρόνῳ δέονται· πέφευγε γὰρ ἐξ ἡμῶν καὶ ἠφάνισται
πᾶς μὲν Ἕλλην πᾶς δὲ βάρβαρος πόλεμος· ἐλευ
θερίας δ' ὅσον οἱ κρατοῦντες νέμουσι τοῖς δήμοις
μέτεστι καὶ τὸ πλέον ἴσως οὐκ ἄμεινον· εὐφορίαν
δὲ γῆς ἄφθονον εὐμενῆ τε κρᾶσιν ὡρῶν καὶ τίκτειν
D γυναῖκας " ἐοικότα τέκνα γονεῦσι " καὶ[1] σωτηρίαν
τοῖς γεννωμένοις εὐχόμενος ὅ γε σώφρων αἰτήσεται
παρὰ θεῶν τοῖς ἑαυτοῦ πολίταις.

---

[1] καὶ added by Reiske.

---

[a] This refers to the doctrine held by the Epicurean and
Sceptic Schools of philosophy that the perfect state is that of
complete tranquillity.

[b] Theramenes was prominent in the oligarchy at Athens
in 411 b.c., but later turned against his former associates.
In 404 b.c. he was elected one of the " Thirty Tyrants," but

of disorder to sit without feeling or grief, singing the praises of your own impassiveness and of the inactive and blessed life,[a] and rejoicing in the follies of others ; on the contrary, at such times you should by all means put on the buskin of Theramenes,[b] conversing with both parties and joining neither ; for you will appear to be, not an outsider by not joining in wrongdoing, but a common partisan of all by coming to their aid ; and your not sharing in their misfortunes will not arouse envy, if it is plain that you sympathize with all alike. But the best thing is to see to it in advance that factional discord shall never arise among them and to regard this as the greatest and noblest function of what may be called the art of statesmanship. For observe that of the greatest blessings which States can enjoy,—peace, liberty, plenty, abundance of men, and concord,—so far as peace is concerned the peoples have no need of statesmanship at present ; for all war, both Greek and foreign,[c] has been banished from among us and has disappeared ; and of liberty the peoples have as great a share as our rulers grant them, and perhaps more would not be better for them ; but bounteous productiveness of the soil, kindly tempering of the seasons, that wives may bear " children like to their sires," [d] and that the offspring may live in safety—these things the wise man will ask the gods in his prayers to grant his fellow-citizens.

tried to restrain his colleagues and was put to death by them. He was nicknamed Cothurnus because the buskin could be worn on either foot, as he was a member of each party in turn (cf. " turncoat "). Aristotle, Constitution of Athens, 28. 5, praises him as a patriot.

  [c] For the phrase cf. Thucydides, ii. 364.
  [d] Hesiod, Works and Days, 233.

Λείπεται δὴ τῷ πολιτικῷ μόνον ἐκ τῶν ὑποκειμένων ἔργων,[1] ὃ μηδενὸς ἔλαττόν ἐστι τῶν
ἀγαθῶν, ὁμόνοιαν ἐμποιεῖν καὶ φιλίαν ἀεὶ τοῖς
συνοικοῦσιν, ἔριδας δὲ καὶ διχοφροσύνας καὶ
δυσμένειαν ἐξαιρεῖν ἅπασαν, ὥσπερ ἐν φίλων
διαφοραῖς, τὸ μᾶλλον οἰόμενον ἀδικεῖσθαι μέρος
ἐξομιλοῦντα πρότερον καὶ συναδικεῖσθαι δοκοῦντα
καὶ συναγανακτεῖν, εἶθ' οὕτως ἐπιχειροῦντα πραΰ-
νειν καὶ διδάσκειν ὅτι τῶν βιάζεσθαι καὶ νικᾶν
E ἐριζόντων οἱ παρέντες[2] οὐκ ἐπιεικείᾳ καὶ ἤθει
μόνον ἀλλὰ καὶ φρονήματι καὶ μεγέθει ψυχῆς
διαφέρουσι, καὶ μικρὸν ὑφιέμενοι νικῶσιν ἐν τοῖς
καλλίστοις καὶ μεγίστοις· ἔπειτα καὶ καθ' ἕνα καὶ
κοινῇ διδάσκοντα καὶ φράζοντα τὴν τῶν Ἑλληνικῶν
πραγμάτων ἀσθένειαν, ἧς ἐν ἀπολαῦσαι[3] ἄμεινόν[4]
ἐστι τοῖς εὖ φρονοῦσι, μεθ' ἡσυχίας καὶ ὁμονοίας
καταβιῶναι, μηδὲν ἐν μέσῳ τῆς τύχης ἆθλον
ὑπολελοιπυίας. τίς γὰρ ἡγεμονία, τίς δόξα τοῖς
περιγενομένοις; ποία δύναμις, ἣν μικρὸν ἀνθυπάτου
F διάταγμα κατέλυσεν ἢ μετέστησεν εἰς ἄλλον, οὐδὲν
οὐδ' ἂν παραμένῃ σπουδῆς ἄξιον ἔχουσαν; ἐπεὶ δέ,
ὥσπερ ἐμπρησμὸς οὐ πολλάκις ἐκ τόπων ἱερῶν
ἄρχεται καὶ δημοσίων, ἀλλὰ λύχνος τις ἐν οἰκίᾳ
παραμεληθεὶς ἢ συρφετὸς διακαεὶς ἀνῆκε φλόγα
πολλὴν καὶ δημοσίαν φθορὰν ἀπεργασαμένην, οὕτως
825 οὐκ ἀεὶ στάσιν πόλεως αἱ περὶ τὰ κοινὰ φιλονεικίαι
διακάουσιν, ἀλλὰ πολλάκις ἐκ πραγμάτων καὶ προσκρουμάτων ἰδίων εἰς δημόσιον αἱ διαφοραὶ προ-
ελθοῦσαι συνετάραξαν ἅπασαν τὴν πόλιν· οὐδενὸς

---

[1] ἔργων] ἔργον Coraes.
[2] παρέντες Xylander: παρόντες.   Bernardakis prefers
παριέντες.   [3] ἐν ἀπολαῦσαι Madvig: ἐναπολαῦσαι.
[4] ἄμεινόν] μόνον Kronenberg.

There remains, then, for the statesman, of those activities which fall within his province, only this— and it is the equal of any of the other blessings :— always to instil concord and friendship in those who dwell together with him and to remove strifes, discords, and all enmity. He will talk, as in the case of quarrels among friends, first with the persons who think they are the more aggrieved, and will appear to share their feeling of wrong and anger, then he will try in this way to mollify them and teach them that those who let wrongs go unheeded are superior to those who are quarrelsome and try to compel and overcome others, not only in reasonableness and character, but also in wisdom and greatness of spirit, and that by yielding in a small thing they gain their point in the best and most important matters. Then he will instruct his people both individually and collectively and will call attention to the weak condition of Greek affairs, in which it is best for wise men to accept one advantage—a life of harmony and quiet—since fortune has left us no prize open for competition. For what dominion, what glory is there for those who are victorious ? What sort of power is it which a small edict of a proconsul may annul or transfer to another man and which, even if it last, has nothing in it seriously worth while ? But just as a conflagration does not often begin in sacred or public places, but some lamp left neglected in a house or some burnt rubbish causes a great flame and works public destruction, so disorder in a State is not always kindled by contentions about public matters, but frequently differences arising from private affairs and offences pass thence into public life and throw the whole State into con-

(825) ἧττον τῷ πολιτικῷ προσήκει ταῦτ' ἰᾶσθαι καὶ
προκαταλαμβάνειν, ὅπως τὰ μὲν οὐδ' ὅλως ἔσται
τὰ δὲ παύσεται ταχέως, τὰ δ' οὐ λήψεται μέγεθος
οὐδ' ἅψεται τῶν δημοσίων, ἀλλ' ἐν αὑτοῖς μενεῖ
τοῖς διαφερομένοις, αὑτόν τε προσέχοντα καὶ
φράζοντα τοῖς ἄλλοις, ὡς ἴδια κοινῶν καὶ μικρὰ
μεγάλων αἴτια καθίσταται παροφθέντα καὶ μὴ
B τυχόντα θεραπείας ἐν ἀρχῇ μηδὲ παρηγορίας.

Οἷον ἐν Δελφοῖς ὁ μέγιστος λέγεται γενέσθαι
νεωτερισμὸς ὑπὸ Κράτητος, οὗ μέλλων θυγατέρα
γαμεῖν 'Ορσίλαος ὁ Φάλιδος, εἶτα, τοῦ κρατῆρος
αὐτομάτως ἐπὶ ταῖς σπονδαῖς μέσου ῥαγέντος, οἰω-
νισάμενος καὶ καταλιπὼν τὴν νύμφην ἀπῆλθε μετὰ
τοῦ πατρός· ὁ δὲ Κράτης ὀλίγον ὕστερον θύουσιν
αὐτοῖς ὑποβαλὼν χρυσίον τι τῶν ἱερῶν κατεκρή-
μνισε τὸν 'Ορσίλαον καὶ τὸν ἀδελφὸν ἀκρίτους, καὶ
πάλιν τῶν φίλων τινὰς καὶ οἰκείων ἱκετεύοντας ἐν
τῷ ἱερῷ τῆς Προναίας[1] ἀνεῖλε· πολλῶν δὲ τοιούτων
γενομένων, ἀποκτείναντες οἱ Δελφοὶ τὸν Κράτητα
C καὶ τοὺς συστασιάσαντας ἐκ τῶν χρημάτων ἐναγι-
κῶν προσαγορευθέντων τοὺς κάτω ναοὺς ἀνῳκο-
δόμησαν. ἐν δὲ Συρακούσαις δυεῖν νεανίσκων
συνήθων ὁ μὲν τὸν ἐρώμενον τοῦ ἑτέρου λαβὼν
φυλάσσειν διέφθειρεν ἀποδημοῦντος, ὁ δ' ἐκείνῳ
πάλιν ὥσπερ ἀνταποδιδοὺς ὕβριν ἐμοίχευσε τὴν
γυναῖκα· τῶν δὲ πρεσβυτέρων τις εἰς βουλὴν παρ-

[1] Προναίας Kaltwasser: προνοίας.

fusion. Therefore it behoves the statesman above all things to remedy or prevent these, that some of them may not arise at all and some may be quickly ended and others may not grow great and extend to public interests, but may remain merely among the persons who are at odds with one another. He should do this by noticing himself and pointing out to others that private troubles become the causes of public ones and small troubles of great ones, if they are overlooked and do not in the beginning receive treatment or soothing counsel.

For example, at Delphi the greatest insurrection is said to have been caused by Crates, whose daughter was to be married to Orsilaüs, the son of Phalis ; but then, when at the betrothal the mixing-bowl broke in the middle of its own accord, Orsilaüs regarded that as an omen, left his bride, and went away with his father. But Crates a little later, secretly putting a sacred object of gold into their possession while they were sacrificing, caused Orsilaüs and his brother to be hurled over the precipice without trial and later slew some of their friends and relatives when they were suppliants in the sanctuary of Athena-before-the-Temple. But after many such things had taken place the Delphians put Crates and his fellow-partisans to death, and with their property, which had been declared accursed, they built the lower temples. And at Syracuse there were two young men, intimate friends, one of whom, being entrusted with his friend's beloved for safe-keeping, seduced him while the other was away ; then the latter, as if to repay outrage with outrage, committed adultery with the offender's wife. Thereupon one of the elder men came forward in the senate and

(825) ἐλθὼν ἐκέλευσεν ἀμφοτέρους ἐλαύνειν, πρὶν ἀπολαῦσαι[1] καὶ ἀναπλησθῆναι τὴν πόλιν ἀπ' αὐτῶν τῆς
ἔχθρας· οὐ μὴν ἔπεισεν, ἀλλ' ἐκ τούτου στασιά-
D σαντες ἐπὶ συμφοραῖς μεγάλαις τὴν ἀρίστην
πολιτείαν ἀνέτρεψαν. ἔχεις δὲ δήπου καὶ αὐτὸς
οἰκεῖα παραδείγματα, τὴν Παρδάλα[2] πρὸς Τυρ-
ρηνὸν ἔχθραν, ὡς ὀλίγον[3] ἐδέησεν ἀνελεῖν τὰς Σάρδεις, ἐξ αἰτιῶν μικρῶν καὶ ἰδίων εἰς ἀπόστασιν
καὶ πόλεμον ἐμβαλοῦσα.

Διὸ χρὴ μὴ καταφρονεῖν τὸν πολιτικὸν ὥσπερ ἐν
σώματι προσκρουμάτων[4] διαδρομὰς ὀξείας ἐχόντων, ἀλλ' ἐπιλαμβάνεσθαι καὶ πιέζειν καὶ βοηθεῖν·
προσοχῇ γάρ, ὥς φησιν ὁ Κάτων, καὶ τὸ μέγα
γίγνεται μικρὸν καὶ τὸ μικρὸν εἰς τὸ μηδὲν ἄγεται.
μηχανὴ δ' ἐπὶ ταῦτα πειθοῦς οὐκ ἔστι μείζων ἢ τὸ
E παρέχειν ἑαυτὸν ἐν ταῖς ἰδίαις διαφοραῖς ἥμερον
διαλλακτήν, ἀμήνιτον, ἐπὶ τῶν πρώτων αἰτιῶν
μένοντα καὶ μηδενὶ προστιθέντα φιλονεικίαν μηδ'
ὀργὴν μηδ' ἄλλο πάθος ἐμποιοῦν τραχύτητα καὶ
πικρίαν τοῖς ἀναγκαίοις ἀμφισβητήμασι. τῶν μὲν
γὰρ ἐν ταῖς παλαίστραις διαμαχομένων ἐπισφαίροις
περιδέουσι τὰς χεῖρας, ὅπως εἰς ἀνήκεστον ἡ ἅμιλλα
μηδὲν ἐκπίπτῃ, μαλακὴν ἔχουσα τὴν πληγὴν καὶ
ἄλυπον· ἐν δὲ ταῖς κρίσεσι καὶ ταῖς δίκαις πρὸς
τοὺς πολίτας ἄμεινόν ἐστι καθαραῖς καὶ ψιλαῖς ταῖς
αἰτίαις χρώμενον ἀγωνίζεσθαι, καὶ μὴ καθάπερ
F βέλη τὰ πράγματα χαράσσοντα καὶ φαρμάσσοντα
ταῖς βλασφημίαις καὶ ταῖς κακοηθείαις καὶ ταῖς
ἀπειλαῖς ἀνήκεστα καὶ μεγάλα καὶ δημόσια ποιεῖν.

---

[1] ἀπολαῦσαι Coraes: ἀπολέσαι.
[2] Παρδάλα Bernardakis: παρδάλου or παρδάλαου.
[3] ὀλίγον Benseler: ὀλίγου.

moved that both be banished before the State reap the result and be infected with enmity through them. His motion, however, was not carried, and from this beginning disorder arose which caused great disasters and overthrew the most excellent government. And indeed you yourself also no doubt have excellent examples at home in the enmity of Pardalas and Tyrrhenus, which came near to destroying Sardis by involving the State in rebellion and war as the result of petty private matters.

Therefore the statesman should not despise such offences as may, like diseases in a person, spread quickly, but he should take hold of them, suppress them, and cure them. For by attention, as Cato says, the great is made small and the small is reduced to nothing. And for this there is no more persuasive device than for the statesman to show himself in his private differences mild and conciliatory, persisting without anger in his original reasons for disagreement, and treating no one with contentiousness, anger, or any other passion which injects harshness and bitterness into unavoidable disputes. For we put soft gloves on the hands of those who compete in the boxing-school, that the contest may not have a fatal result, its blows being soft and not painful ; and in law-suits against one's fellow-citizens it is better to treat the causes of disagreement pure and simple in one's pleading, and not, by sharpening and poisoning matters, as if they were darts or arrows, with bad words, malice, and threats, to make them incurable, great, and of public importance.

---

⁴ προσκρουμάτων Bernardakis : προσκρουσμάτων.

(825) ὁ γὰρ οὕτω προσφερόμενος τοῖς καθ᾽ αὑτὸν ὑπ-
ηκόους ἕξει καὶ τοὺς ἄλλους· αἱ δὲ περὶ τὰ δημόσια
φιλοτιμίαι, τῶν ἰδίων ὑφαιρουμένων ἀπεχθειῶν,
εὐτελεῖς γίγνονται καὶ δυσχερὲς οὐδὲν οὐδ᾽ ἀνήκεστον ἐπιφέρουσιν.

For a man who proceeds in this way towards those with whom he himself has to do will find that others also yield to him ; and rivalries affecting public interests, if private enmities are done away with, become of slight importance and do no serious or incurable harm.

ON MONARCHY, DEMOCRACY, AND OLIGARCHY

(DE UNIUS IN REPUBLICA DOMI-NATIONE, POPULARI STATU, ET PAUCORUM IMPERIO)

INTRODUCTION

This essay is evidently only a fragment, as Wyttenbach long ago pointed out. The opening words indicate that the author delivers it as an address before an audience to which he has spoken on the day before, but nothing further is known about the circumstances. Few scholars now believe that the author is Plutarch, though who the writer was is not known. The substance of the fragment is derived chiefly from the *Republic* of Plato.

ΠΕΡΙ ΜΟΝΑΡΧΙΑΣ ΚΑΙ ΔΗΜΟ-
ΚΡΑΤΙΑΣ ΚΑΙ ΟΛΙΓΑΡΧΙΑΣ

1. Εἰς[1] τοῦτο δὴ τὸ δικαστήριον καὶ αὐτὸς
B εἰσάγων τὴν γενομένην μοι πρὸς ὑμᾶς διάλεξιν
ἐχθές, ᾤμην τῆς πολιτικῆς ἀρετῆς ὕπαρ οὐκ[2] ὄναρ
ἀκοῦσαι λεγούσης

κεκρότηται χρυσέα κρηπὶς ἱεραῖσιν ἀοιδαῖς,

ὃ[3] προτρεπόμενος καὶ[4] διαίρων[5] ἐπὶ πολιτείαν βέ-
βληται λόγος· "εἶα τειχίζωμεν[6] ἤδη" τὴν ὀφειλο-
μένην ἐποικοδομοῦντες τῇ προτροπῇ διδασκαλίαν,
ὀφείλεται δὲ τῷ παραδεδεγμένῳ τὴν ἐπὶ τὸ πράττειν τὰ κοινὰ προτροπὴν καὶ ὁρμὴν ἑξῆς ἀκοῦσαι
καὶ λαβεῖν παραγγέλματα πολιτείας, οἷς χρώμενος,
C ὡς ἀνυστόν ἐστιν ἀνθρώπῳ, δημωφελὴς ἔσται, μετ'
ἀσφαλείας ἅμα καὶ τιμῆς δικαίας εὖ τιθέμενος τὸ
οἰκεῖον. ὃ δὲ προὔργου μέν ἐστιν εἰς τὰ μέλλοντα
τοῖς δὲ προλελεγμένοις ἕπεται, σκεπτέον ἥτις ἀρίστη
πολιτεία. καθάπερ γὰρ ἀνθρώπου βίοι πλείονες,[7]

---

[1] Wyttenbach assumes that the beginning is lost.
[2] οὐκ Xylander : ἦ.
[3] ὁ added by Wyttenbach.   [4] καὶ] δὲ καὶ codex E.
[5] διαίρων Salmasius : διαιρῶν.
[6] εἶα τειχίζωμεν H.N.F. from Pindar, Frag. 194 (206),
p. 465 ed. Schroeder ; ἐκτίνωμεν Wyttenbach : εἰ ἀττικῷ μὲν.
[7] πλείονες Bernardakis : πλέονες.

ON MONARCHY, DEMOCRACY, AND OLIGARCHY

1. Now as I was myself bringing before this company as a court of judgement the talk that I presented to you yesterday, I thought I heard, while wide awake, not in a dream,[a] Political Wisdom saying :

> Golden foundation is wrought for canticles sacred,[b]

so the speech, which exhorts and encourages you to enter political life has been laid as a basis. "Come, let us now build walls,"[c] building upon the exhortation the teaching which is due. And it is due to anyone who has received the exhortation and the impulse to engage in public affairs that he next hear and receive precepts of statecraft by the use of which he will, so far as is humanly possible, be of service to the people and at the same time manage his own affairs with safety and rightful honour. But as a step towards that which follows and a consequence of that which has been said, we must consider what is the best form of government. For just as there are numerous modes of life for a man, so the

---

[a] Cf. Homer, Od. xix. 547.
[b] Pindar, Frag. 194 (206), p. 465 ed. Schroeder.
[c] Pindar, ibid.

(826) ἔστι καὶ δήμου ἥ[1] πολιτεία βίος· ὥστε λαβεῖν τὴν
ἀρίστην ἀναγκαῖον· ἢ γὰρ ἐκ πασῶν αἱρήσεται
ταύτην ὁ πολιτικὸς ἢ τῶν λοιπῶν τὴν ὁμοιοτάτην,
εἰ ταύτην ἀδύνατον.

2. Λέγεται μὲν δὴ πολιτεία καὶ μετάληψις τῶν
ἐν πόλει δικαίων· ὥς φαμεν Ἀλεξάνδρῳ πολιτείαν
Μεγαρεῖς ψηφίσασθαι· τοῦ δ' εἰς γέλωτα θεμένου
τὴν σπουδὴν αὐτῶν, εἰπεῖν ἐκείνους ὅτι μόνῳ πρότερον τὴν πολιτείαν Ἡρακλεῖ καὶ μετ' ἐκεῖνον αὐτῷ
D ψηφίσαιντο· τὸν δὲ θαυμάσαντα δέξασθαι τὸ τίμιον
ἐν τῷ σπανίῳ τιθέμενον. λέγεται δὲ καὶ βίος
ἀνδρὸς πολιτικοῦ καὶ τὰ κοινὰ πράττοντος πολι-
τεία· καθὸ τὴν Περικλέους πολιτείαν ἐπαινοῦμεν
καὶ τὴν Βίαντος, ψέγομεν δὲ τὴν Ὑπερβόλου καὶ
Κλέωνος. ἔνιοι δὲ καὶ μίαν πρᾶξιν εὔστοχον εἰς τὰ
κοινὰ καὶ λαμπρὰν πολιτείαν προσαγορεύουσιν, οἷον
χρημάτων ἐπίδοσιν, διάλυσιν πολέμου, ψηφίσματος
εἰσήγησιν· καθὸ καὶ πολιτεύσασθαι τὸν δεῖνα σή-
μερον λέγομεν, εἰ τύχοι τι διαπραξάμενος ἐν κοινῷ
τῶν δεόντων.

3. Παρὰ πάντα ταῦτα λέγεται πολιτεία τάξις
E καὶ κατάστασις πόλεως διοικοῦσα τὰς πράξεις·
καθά φασι τρεῖς εἶναι πολιτείας, μοναρχίαν καὶ
ὀλιγαρχίαν καὶ δημοκρατίαν, ὧν καὶ Ἡρόδοτος ἐν
τῇ τρίτῃ σύγκρισιν πεποίηται· καὶ δοκοῦσι γενικώ-
ταται εἶναι. τὰς γὰρ ἄλλας, ὥσπερ ἐν τοῖς μου-
σικοῖς διαγράμμασι τῶν πρώτων τρόπων ἀνειμένων
ἢ ἐπιτεινομένων, συμβέβηκε παρακρούσεις καὶ

----

[1] ἥ added by Reiske.

 Herodotus, iii. 80-84.

government (*politeia*) is the life of a people, and therefore it is essential for us to take the best form of it ; for of all forms the statesman will choose the best or, if he cannot obtain that, then the one of all the rest which is most like it.

2. Now the word *politeia* (citizenship) is defined also as " having a share of the rights in a State," as we say the Megarians voted Alexander the *politeia* (citizenship) ; and when he made fun of their eagerness, they told him that up to that time they had conferred citizenship upon Heracles only and now upon himself. Then Alexander was astonished and accepted the gift, thinking that its rarity gave it value. But the life of a statesman, a man who is occupied in public affairs, is also called *politeia* (statecraft) ; as, for example, we commend the *politeia* (statecraft) of Pericles and of Bias, but condemn that of Hyperbolus and Cleon. And some people even call a single brilliant act for the public benefit a *politeia* (politic act), such, for example, as a gift of money, the ending of a war, the introduction of a bill in parliament ; and accordingly we say nowadays that so-and-so has performed a *politeia* if he happens to have put through some needed public measure.

3. Besides all these, *politeia* is defined as an order and constitution of a State, which directs its affairs ; and accordingly they say that there are three *politeiae* (forms of government), monarchy, oligarchy, and democracy, a comparison of which is given by Herodotus in his third book.[a] They appear to be the most typical forms ; for the others, as happens in musical scales when the strings of the primary notes are relaxed or tightened, turn out to be errors

F διαφθορὰς κατ' ἔλλειψιν καὶ ὑπερβολὴν εἶναι. ταύτας δὲ καὶ πλεῖστον καὶ μέγιστον ἐν ἡγεμονίαις δυνηθείσας τῶν ἐθνῶν ἀπεκληρώσαντο τὰς πολιτείας, Πέρσαι μὲν αὐτοκρατῆ βασιλείαν καὶ ἀνυπεύθυνον, Σπαρτιᾶται δ' ἀριστοκρατικὴν ὀλιγαρχίαν καὶ αὐθέκαστον, Ἀθηναῖοι δ' αὐτόνομον καὶ ἄκρατον δημοκρατίαν. ὧν ἁμαρτανομένων παρατροπαὶ καὶ ὑπερχύσεις εἰσὶν αἱ λεγόμεναι τυραννίδες καὶ δυναστεῖαι καὶ ὀχλοκρατίαι· ὅταν βασιλεία μὲν

827 ὕβριν ἐντέκῃ καὶ τὸ¹ ἀνυπεύθυνον· ὀλιγαρχία δ' ὑπερφροσύνην καὶ τὸ αὔθαδες· δημοκρατία δ' ἀναρχίαν, ἰσότης δ'² ἀμετρίαν, πᾶσαι δὲ τὸ ἀνόητον.

4. Ὥσπερ οὖν ὁ ἁρμονικὸς καὶ μουσικὸς ἀνὴρ παντὶ μὲν ὀργάνῳ χρήσεται προσῳδῷ τεχνικῶς ἁρμοσάμενος καὶ λόγῳ κρούων ἕκαστον, ὡς πέφυκεν ἐμμελὲς ὑπηχεῖν· ἤδη μέντοι συμβούλῳ Πλάτωνι χρησάμενος, πηκτίδας, σαμβύκας καὶ ψαλτήρια πολύφθογγα καὶ βαρβίτους καὶ τρίγωνα³ παραπέμψας,

B τὴν λύραν καὶ τὴν κιθάραν προτιμήσει· τὸν αὐτὸν τρόπον ὁ πολιτικὸς ἀνὴρ εὖ μὲν ὀλιγαρχίαν Λακωνικὴν καὶ Λυκούργειον μεταχειριεῖται, συναρμοσάμενος αὑτῷ τοὺς ἰσοκρατεῖς καὶ ὁμοτίμους ἄνδρας, ἡσυχῇ προσβιαζόμενος· εὖ δὲ πολυφθόγγῳ καὶ πολυχόρδῳ συνοίσεται δημοκρατίᾳ, τὰ μὲν ἀνιεὶς τὰ δ' ἐπιτείνων τῆς πολιτείας, χαλάσας τ' ἐν καιρῷ καὶ καρτερῶς αὖθις ἐμφύς, ἀντιβῆναι καὶ ἀντισχεῖν ἐπιστάμενος· εἰ δ' αἵρεσις αὐτῷ δοθείη, καθάπερ

---

¹ καὶ τὸ added by Patzig.   ² δ' added by Reiske.
³ τρίγωνα Xylander from Plato : τρίβωνα.

and corruptions through deficiency or excess. Of these forms of government, which have achieved the widest and greatest power in their periods of dominion, the Persians received as their lot royalty absolute and irresponsible, the Spartans oligarchy aristocratic and uncontrolled, the Athenians democracy self-governing and undiluted. When these forms are not hit exactly, their perversions and exaggerations are what are called (1) tyranny, (2) the predominance of great families,[a] (3) or mob-rule : that is, (1) when royalty breeds violence and irresponsible action ; (2) oligarchy, arrogance and presumptuousness ; (3) democracy breeds anarchy, equality, excess, and all of them folly.

4. So, just as a real musician will make use of every instrument harmoniously, adapting it skilfully and striking each one with regard to its natural tunefulness, and yet, following Plato's advice,[b] will give up guitars, banjoes, psalteries with their many sounds, harps and string triangles and prefer the lyre and the cithara ; in the same way the real statesman will manage successfully the oligarchy that Lycurgus established at Sparta, adapting to himself the colleagues who have equal power and honour and quietly forcing them to do his will ; he will also get on well in a democracy with its many sounds and strings by loosening the strings in some matters of government and tightening them in others, relaxing at the proper time and then again holding fast mightily, knowing how to resist the masses and to hold his ground against them. But if he were given the choice among governments,

---

[a] See Aristotle, *Politics*, iv. 4. 1 on δυναστεία.
[b] Plato, *Republic*, 399 c, d.

(827) ὀργάνων, τῶν πολιτειῶν, οὐκ ἂν ἄλλην ἕλοιτο πλὴν
τὴν μοναρχίαν, Πλάτωνι πειθόμενος, τὴν μόνην
δυναμένην τὸν ἐντελῆ καὶ ὄρθιον ἐκεῖνον ὡς ἀλη-
C θῶς τῆς ἀρετῆς τόνον ἀνασχέσθαι καὶ μήτε πρὸς
ἀνάγκην μήτε πρὸς χάριν ἁρμόσαι[1] τοῦ συμφέροντος.
αἱ μὲν γὰρ ἄλλαι πολιτεῖαι τρόπον τινὰ κρατούμεναι
κρατοῦσι καὶ φερόμεναι φέρουσι τὸν πολιτικόν, οὐκ
ἔχοντα τὴν ἰσχὺν βέβαιον ἐπὶ τούτους,[2] παρ᾽ ὧν
ἔχει τὸ ἰσχῦον, ἀλλὰ πολλάκις ἀναγκαζόμενον τὸ
Αἰσχύλειον ἀναφωνεῖν, ᾧ πρὸς τὴν τύχην ἐχρῆτο
Δημήτριος ὁ πολιορκητὴς ἀποβαλὼν τὴν ἡγεμονίαν

σύ τοί με φυσᾷς,[3] σύ με καταίθειν μοι[4] δοκεῖς.[5]

---

[1] ἁρμόσαι] ἁρμόσαι ἄνευ Wyttenbach; ἁρμόσαι τι Hutton;
ἁρμόσαι ἀπό?

[2] τούτους Meziriacus: τούτου.

[3] με φυσᾷς frequently changed to μ᾽ ἔφυσας, but needlessly.

[4] καταίθειν μοι Ziegler with some mss. in *Life of Demetrius*,
chap. xxxv.: καταίθειν.

like so many tools, he would follow Plato's advice
and choose no other than monarchy, the only one
which is able to sustain that top note of virtue,
high in the highest sense, and never let it be
tuned down under compulsion or expediency. For
the other forms of government in a certain sense,
although controlled by the statesman, control him,
and although carried along by him, carry him along,
since he has no firmly established strength to oppose
those from whom his strength is derived, but is often
compelled to exclaim in the words of Aeschylus [a]
which Demetrius the City-stormer employed against
Fortune after he had lost his hegemony,

Thou fanst my flame, methinks thou burnst me up.

[a] Nauck, *Trag. Graec. Frag.* p. 107, no. 359 ; *Life of
Demetrius*, chap. xxxv.

---

[5] Wyttenbach, followed by Dübner and others, indicates
a break at this point.

THAT WE OUGHT NOT TO BORROW
BORROW
(DE VITANDO AERE ALIENO)

INTRODUCTION

THIS brief essay consists of repeated warnings, enlivened by numerous examples and anecdotes, against running into debt. There is nothing to indicate that it was delivered as a lecture, but it would probably have been interesting to an audience of Plutarch's time, and may have been written with an audience in mind. It contains no profound or original doctrines, but is simply an agreeable presentation of somewhat commonplace thoughts—rather learned, rather literary, rather sensible, and, to the modern reader, rather amusing.

ΠΕΡΙ ΤΟΥ ΜΗ ΔΕΙΝ ΔΑΝΕΙΖΕΣΘΑΙ

1. Ὁ Πλάτων ἐν τοῖς Νόμοις οὐκ ἐᾷ μεταλαμβά-
E νειν ὕδατος ἀλλοτρίου τοὺς γείτονας, ἂν μὴ παρ'
αὑτοῖς ὀρύξαντες ἄχρι τῆς κεραμίτιδος καλουμένης
γῆς ἄγονον εὕρωσι νάματος τὸ χωρίον· ἡ γὰρ κερα-
μῖτις φύσιν ἔχουσα λιπαρὰν καὶ πυκνὴν στέγει
παραλαβοῦσα τὸ ὑγρὸν καὶ οὐ διίησι· δεῖν[1] δὲ μετα-
λαμβάνειν τἀλλοτρίου[2] τοὺς ἴδιον κτήσασθαι μὴ
δυναμένους· ἀπορίᾳ γὰρ βοηθεῖν τὸν νόμον. ἆρ' οὐ[3]
δὴ ἔδει καὶ[4] περὶ χρημάτων εἶναι νόμον, ὅπως μὴ
F δανείζωνται παρ' ἑτέρων μηδ' ἐπ' ἀλλοτρίας πηγὰς
βαδίζωσι, μὴ πρότερον οἴκοι τὰς αὑτῶν ἀφορμὰς
ἐξελέγξαντες καὶ συναγαγόντες ὥσπερ ἐκ λιβάδων
τὸ χρήσιμον καὶ ἀναγκαῖον αὑτοῖς; νυνὶ δ' ὑπὸ
τρυφῆς καὶ μαλακίας ἢ πολυτελείας οὐ χρῶνται τοῖς
ἑαυτῶν, ἔχοντες, ἀλλὰ λαμβάνουσιν ἐπὶ πολλῷ παρ'
ἑτέρων, μὴ δεόμενοι· τεκμήριον δὲ μέγα· τοῖς γὰρ
ἀπόροις οὐ δανείζουσιν, ἀλλὰ βουλομένοις εὐπορίαν
τιν' ἑαυτοῖς κτᾶσθαι· καὶ μάρτυρα δίδωσι καὶ βε-

---

[1] δεῖν Xylander: δεῖ.
[2] τἀλλοτρίου Bernardakis: τοῦ ἀλλοτρίου.
[3] ἆρ' οὐ Duebner: ἆρα or ἄρα.
[4] δὴ ἔδει καὶ Wyttenbach: δέδεικται.

THAT WE OUGHT NOT TO BORROW

1. Plato in the *Laws* [a] forbids people to take any
water from a neighbour's land unless they have dug
on their own land down to a layer of potter's clay,
as it is called, and found that the place will not produce a flow of water ; for the potter's clay, being
by nature oily and solid, holds back the water that
reaches it and does not let it through ; but, he says,
those shall have a share of others' water who cannot
get any of their own, for the law gives relief to those
in want. Ought there not, then, to be a law about
money also, that people shall not borrow from others
or resort to other people's springs who have not first
examined their resources at home and brought together, as from little trickles, what is useful and
necessary to themselves ? But now, because of
their luxury and effeminacy or their extravagance,
they make no use of what is their own, though they
possess it, but take from others at a high rate of
interest, though they have no need of doing so.
There is strong evidence of this : loans are not
made to people in need, but to those who wish to
acquire some superfluity for themselves. And a
man produces a witness and a surety to aver that,

[a] Plato, *Laws*, 844 B.

317

βαιωτὴν ἄξιον, ὅτι ἔχει, πιστεύεσθαι, δέον ἔχοντα
μὴ δανείζεσθαι.

2. Τί θεραπεύεις τὸν τραπεζίτην ἢ πραγματευ-
828 τήν; ἀπὸ τῆς ἰδίας δάνεισαι τραπέζης· ἐκπώματ'
ἔχεις, παροψίδας ἀργυρᾶς, λεκανίδας· ὑπόθου ταῦτα
τῇ χρείᾳ· τὴν δὲ τράπεζαν ἡ καλὴ Αὐλὶς ἢ Τένεδος
ἀντικοσμήσει τοῖς κεραμεοῖς, καθαρωτέροις οὖσι
τῶν ἀργυρῶν· οὐκ ὄζει τόκου βαρὺ καὶ δυσχερὲς
ὥσπερ ἰοῦ καθ' ἡμέραν ἐπιρρυπαίνοντος τὴν πολυτέλειαν, οὐδ' ἀναμνήσει τῶν καλανδῶν καὶ τῆς
νουμηνίας, ἣν ἱερωτάτην ἡμερῶν οὖσαν ἀποφράδα
ποιοῦσιν οἱ δανεισταὶ καὶ στύγιον. τοὺς μὲν γὰρ
ἀντὶ τοῦ πωλεῖν τιθέντας ἐνέχυρα τὰ αὑτῶν οὐδ'
B ἂν ὁ θεὸς σώσειεν ὁ Κτήσιος· αἰσχύνονται τιμὴν
λαμβάνοντες, οὐκ αἰσχύνονται τόκον τῶν ἰδίων
διδόντες. καίτοι ὅ γε Περικλῆς ἐκεῖνος τὸν τῆς
θεᾶς κόσμον, ἄγοντα τάλαντα τεσσαράκοντα χρυ-
σίου ἀπέφθου, περιαιρετὸν ἐποίησεν, ὅπως, ἔφη,
χρησάμενοι πρὸς τὸν πόλεμον αὖθις ἀποδῶμεν μὴ
ἔλαττον· οὐκοῦν καὶ ἡμεῖς ὥσπερ ἐν πολιορκίᾳ ταῖς
χρείαις μὴ παραδεχώμεθα φρουρὰν δανειστοῦ πολε-
μίου, μηδ' ὁρᾶν τὰ αὑτῶν ἐπὶ δουλείᾳ διδόμενα·
ἀλλὰ τῆς τραπέζης περιελόντες τὰ μὴ χρήσιμα, τῆς
κοίτης, τῶν ὀχημάτων, τῆς διαίτης, ἐλευθέρους δια-
φυλάττωμεν ἑαυτούς, ὡς ἀποδώσοντες αὖθις, ἐὰν
εὐτυχήσωμεν.

C 3. Αἱ μὲν οὖν Ῥωμαίων γυναῖκες εἰς ἀπαρχὴν
τῷ Πυθίῳ Ἀπόλλωνι τὸν κόσμον ἐπέδωκαν, ὅθεν

---

[a] The Greek word means *bank*, as well as *table*.
[b] That interest was due on the first of the month is amply
attested. *Cf.* Aristophanes, *Clouds*, 17, 1134, Horace,

318

since the man has property, he deserves credit, whereas, since he has it, he ought not to be borrowing.

2. Why do you pay court to the banker or broker ? Borrow of your own table *a* ; you have drinking-cups, silver dishes, *bonbonnières*. Pawn these for your needs. Beautiful Aulis or Tenedos will adorn your table in their stead with pottery that is cleaner than the silver ware ; it does not have the heavy, disagreeable smell of interest defiling every day like rust the surface of your extravagance, nor will it keep reminding you of the first of the month and the new moon,*b* which, though really the holiest day of the month, the money-lenders have made accursed and detested. For as to those who, instead of selling their belongings, give them as security, not even the God of Property could save them. They are ashamed to accept a price, but not ashamed to pay interest on what is their own. And yet the great Pericles made the ornaments of the Goddess, which weighed forty talents of refined gold,*c* so that they could be taken off, " in order," he said, " that we may use it for the expenses of the war, and then pay back an equal amount." And so let us likewise, when we are, as it were, besieged by our needs, refuse to admit the garrison of a money-lender, our enemy, or to allow our property to be sold into slavery. No, let us preserve our liberty by taking off what is useless from our table, our bed, our vehicles, and our daily expenses, intending to pay it back if we are fortunate.

3. Now the Roman women gave their ornaments as an offering to Pythian Apollo and from them made the

Satires, i. 3. 87 (*tristes kalendae*), for the detestation of the day.   *c* Thucydides, ii. 13.

(828) ὁ χρυσοῦς κρατὴρ εἰς Δελφοὺς ἐπέμφθη· αἱ δὲ
Καρχηδονίων γυναῖκες ἐκείραντο τὰς κεφαλὰς καὶ
ταῖς θριξὶν ἐντεῖναι τὰς μηχανὰς καὶ τὰ ὄργανα
παρέσχον ὑπὲρ τῆς πατρίδος· ἡμεῖς δὲ τὴν αὐτ-
άρκειαν αἰσχυνόμενοι καταδουλοῦμεν ἑαυτοὺς ὑπο-
θήκαις καὶ συμβολαίοις, δέον εἰς αὐτὰ τὰ χρήσιμα
συσταλέντας καὶ συσπειραθέντας ἐκ τῶν ἀχρήστων
καὶ περιττῶν κατακοπέντων ἢ πραθέντων ἐλευθερίας
αὐτοῖς ἱερὸν ἱδρύσασθαι καὶ τέκνοις καὶ γυναιξίν.

D ἡ μὲν γὰρ Ἄρτεμις ἡ ἐν Ἐφέσῳ τοῖς χρεώσταις,
ὅταν καταφύγωσιν εἰς τὸ ἱερὸν αὐτῆς, ἀσυλίαν
παρέχει καὶ ἄδειαν ἀπὸ τῶν δανείων[1]· τὸ δὲ τῆς
εὐτελείας καὶ ἄσυλον καὶ ἄβατον πανταχοῦ τοῖς
σώφροσιν ἀναπέπταται, πολλῆς σχολῆς εὐρυχωρίαν
παρέχον ἱλαρὰν καὶ ἐπίτιμον. ὡς γὰρ ἡ Πυθία τοῖς
Ἀθηναίοις περὶ τὰ Μηδικὰ τεῖχος ξύλινον διδόναι
τὸν θεὸν ἔφη, κἀκεῖνοι τὴν χώραν καὶ τὴν πόλιν
καὶ τὰ κτήματα καὶ τὰς οἰκίας ἀφέντες εἰς τὰς ναῦς
κατέφυγον ὑπὲρ τῆς ἐλευθερίας, οὕτως ἡμῖν ὁ θεὸς
δίδωσι ξυλίνην τράπεζαν καὶ κεραμεᾶν λεκάνην καὶ
τραχὺ ἱμάτιον, ἐὰν ἐλεύθεροι ζῆν ἐθέλωμεν.

E   μηδὲ σύ γ' ἱπποσύνας τε μένειν,
μηδ' ὀχήματα ζευκτὰ κερασφόρα[2] καὶ κατάργυρα, ἃ
τόκοι ταχεῖς καταλαμβάνουσι καὶ παρατρέχουσιν·
ἀλλ' ὄνῳ τινὶ τῷ τυχόντι καὶ καβάλλῃ χρώμενος
φεῦγε πολέμιον καὶ τύραννον δανειστήν, οὐ γῆν[3]

---

[1] δανείων] "a creditoribus," i.e. δανειστῶν, Xylander's version.

[2] κερασφόρα] κατάχρυσα or καταπόρφυρα Reiske.

[3] γῆν Xylander: πῦρ.

---

[a] Beginning with the fourth century B.C. the ancients
employed various machines to hurl projectiles. They are
commonly called catapults (καταπέλτης). Their power lay
in the elasticity of wooden beams which were bent by means

golden bowl which was sent to Delphi; and the
women of Carthage shore their heads and gave their
hair to make ropes for the tension of machines and
instruments [a] in defence of their native city. But
we, ashamed to be independent, enslave ourselves
by mortgages and notes, when we ought to limit and
restrict ourselves to actual necessities and from the
proceeds of the breaking up or the sale of useless
superfluities to found a sanctuary of Liberty for ourselves, our children, and our wives. The goddess
Artemis at Ephesus grants to debtors when they take
refuge in her sanctuary protection and safety from
their debts, but the protecting and inviolable sanctuary of Frugality is everywhere wide open to sensible
men, offering them a joyous and honourable expanse
of plentiful leisure. For just as the Pythian prophetess [b] in the time of the Persian wars told the Athenians
that the God offered them a wooden wall, and they,
giving up their land, their city, their possessions,
and their houses, took refuge in their ships for the
sake of liberty, so to us God offers a wooden table, a
pottery dish, and a coarse cloak if we wish to live as
free men.

Do not abide the attack of the horsemen, [b]

nor of yoked chariots adorned with horn or silver,
which rapid interest overtakes and outruns. No,
make use of any chance donkey or nag and flee from
your enemy and tyrant, the money-lender, who does

---

of ropes rendered taut by twisting, whence the Latin name
tormentum. The story is found in Appian, viii. 13. 93.

[b] Herodotus, vii. 141. The quotation is from the oracle
in hexameters delivered to the Athenians by the priestess at
Delphi when the Persians invaded Attica in 480 B.C. before
the battle of Salamis.

αἰτοῦντα καὶ ὕδωρ ὡς ὁ Μῆδος, ἀλλὰ τῆς ἐλευθερίας ἁπτόμενον καὶ προγράφοντα[1] τὴν ἐπιτιμίαν·
κἂν μὴ διδῷς, ἐνοχλοῦντα· κἂν ἔχῃς, μὴ λαμβά-
νοντα· κἂν πωλῇς, ἐπευωνίζοντα· κἂν μὴ πωλῇς,
ἀναγκάζοντα· κἂν δικάζῃς, ἐντυγχάνοντα· κἂν
F ὀμόσῃς, ἐπιτάττοντα· κἂν βαδίζῃς ἐπὶ θύρας,
ἀποκλείοντα· κἂν οἴκοι μένῃς, ἐπισταθμεύοντα
καὶ θυροκοποῦντα.

4. Τί γὰρ ὤνησε Σόλων 'Αθηναίους ἀπαλλάξας
τοῦ ἐπὶ τοῖς σώμασιν ὀφείλειν; δουλεύουσι γὰρ
ἅπασι τοῖς ἀφανισταῖς, μᾶλλον δ' οὐδ' αὐτοῖς·
τί γὰρ ἦν τὸ δεινόν; ἀλλὰ δούλοις ὑβρισταῖς καὶ
βαρβάροις καὶ ἀγρίοις, ὥσπερ οὓς ὁ Πλάτων φησὶ
καθ' 'Αιδου διαπύρους κολαστὰς καὶ δημοκοίνους
ἐφεστάναι τοῖς ἠσεβηκόσι. καὶ γὰρ οὗτοι τὴν ἀγορὰν
829 ἀσεβῶν χώραν ἀποδείξαντες τοῖς ἀθλίοις χρεώσταις
γυπῶν δίκην ἔσθουσι καὶ ὑποκείρουσιν αὐτοὺς
" δέρτρον ἔσω δύνοντες," τοὺς δ' ὥσπερ Ταντάλους
ἐφεστῶτες εἴργουσι γεύσασθαι τῶν ἰδίων τρυγώντας
καὶ συγκομίζοντας. ὡς δὲ Δαρεῖος ἐπὶ τὰς 'Αθήνας
ἔπεμψε Δᾶτιν καὶ 'Αρταφέρνην ἐν ταῖς χερσὶν
ἁλύσεις ἔχοντας καὶ δεσμὰ κατὰ τῶν αἰχμαλώτων,
παραπλησίως οὗτοι τῶν χειρογράφων καὶ συμ-
βολαίων ὥσπερ πεδῶν ἐπὶ τὴν Ἑλλάδα κομίζοντες
ἀγγεῖα μεστὰ τὰς πόλεις ἐπιπορεύονται καὶ διελαύ-
B νουσι, σπείροντες οὐχ ἥμερον καρπὸν ὡς ὁ Τρι-
πτόλεμος, ἀλλ' ὀφλημάτων ῥίζας πολυπόνους καὶ
πολυτόκους καὶ δυσεκλείπτους τιθέντες, αἳ κύκλῳ
νεμόμεναι καὶ περιβλαστάνουσαι κάμπτουσι καὶ

_____
[1] προγράφοντα Madvig : προσγράφοντα.

_____
[a] Plato, *Republic*, 615 E.
[b] Homer, *Od.* xi. 578.

not, like the Persian, demand earth and water, but attacks your liberty and brings suit against your honour. If you will not pay him, he duns you ; if you have funds, he won't accept payment ; if you sell, he beats down the price ; if you will not sell, he forces you to do so ; if you sue him, he meets you in court ; if you take your oath, he orders you to do so ; if you go to his door, he shuts it in your face ; if you stay at home, he installs himself there and keeps knocking at your door.

4. For what good did Solon do the Athenians when he put an end to giving one's person as security for debt ? For debtors are slaves to all the men who ruin them, or rather not to them either (for what would be so terrible in that ?), but to outrageous, barbarous, and savage slaves, like those who Plato says[a] stand in Hades as fiery avengers and executioners over those who have been impious in life. For these money-lenders make the market-place a place of the damned for the wretched debtors ; like vultures they devour and flay them, " entering into their entrails,"[b] or in other instances they stand over them and inflict on them the tortures of Tantalus by preventing them from tasting their own produce which they reap and harvest. And as Dareius sent Datis and Artaphernes against Athens with chains and fetters in their hands for their captives, in similar fashion these men, bringing against Greece jars full of signatures and notes as fetters, march against and through the cities, not, like Triptolemus, sowing beneficent grain, but planting roots of debts, roots productive of much toil and much interest and hard to escape from, which, as they sprout and shoot up round about, press down and strangle the

(829) ἄγχουσι τὰς πόλεις. τοὺς μὲν γὰρ λαγὼς λέγουσι
τίκτειν ἅμα καὶ τρέφειν ἕτερα καὶ ἐπικυΐσκεσθαι
πάλιν, τὰ δὲ τῶν μαστιγιῶν τούτων καὶ βαρβάρων
χρέα πρὶν ἢ συλλαβεῖν τίκτει· διδόντες γὰρ εὐθὺς
ἀπαιτοῦσι καὶ τιθέντες αἴρουσι καὶ δανείζουσιν ὃ
λαμβάνουσιν ὑπὲρ τοῦ δανεῖσαι.

5. Λέγεται μὲν παρὰ Μεσσηνίοις

C   ἔστι Πύλος πρὸ Πύλοιο, Πύλος γε μὲν ἔστι καὶ
     ἄλλος·

λεχθήσεται δὲ πρὸς τοὺς δανειστὰς

     ἔστι τόκος πρὸ τόκοιο, τόκος γε μὲν ἔστι καὶ
     ἄλλος.

εἶτα τῶν φυσικῶν δήπου καταγελῶσι, λεγόντων
μηδὲν ἐκ τοῦ μὴ ὄντος γενέσθαι· παρὰ τούτοις γὰρ
ἐκ τοῦ μηκέτ' ὄντος μηδ' ὑφεστῶτος γεννᾶται
τόκος· καὶ τὸ τελωνεῖν ὄνειδος ἡγοῦνται, τοῦ νόμου
διδόντος· αὐτοὶ γὰρ[1] παρανόμως δανείζουσι τελω-
νοῦντες, μᾶλλον δ', εἰ δεῖ τἀληθὲς εἰπεῖν, ἐν τῷ δανείζειν χρεωκοποῦντες· ὁ γὰρ οὗ[2] γράφει λαμβάνων
ἔλαττον χρεωκοπεῖται. καίτοι Πέρσαι γε τὸ ψεύδεσθαι δεύτερον ἡγοῦνται τῶν ἁμαρτημάτων, πρῶτον
δὲ τὸ ὀφείλειν· ὅτι καὶ τὸ ψεύδεσθαι τοῖς ὀφείλουσι
D συμβαίνει πολλάκις· ψεύδονται δὲ μᾶλλον οἱ δανεί-
ζοντες καὶ ῥᾳδιουργοῦσιν ἐν ταῖς ἑαυτῶν ἐφημερίσι,
γράφοντες ὅτι τῷ δεῖνι τοσοῦτον διδόασιν, ἔλαττον
διδόντες· καὶ τὸ ψεῦδος αἰτίαν ἔχει πλεονεξίαν, οὐκ
ἀνάγκην οὐδ' ἀπορίαν, ἀλλ' ἀπληστίαν, ἧς ἀναπό-

---

[1] αὐτοὶ γὰρ Bernardakis; αὐτοὶ δὲ Meziriacus: αὐτοὶ.
[2] οὗ Bongars: οὐ.

---

[a] There is here, and also above and below, a play on the

cities. They say that hares at one and the same time give birth to one litter, suckle another, and conceive again ; but the loans of these barbarous rascals give birth to interest before conception [a] ; for while they are giving they immediately demand payment, while they lay money down they take it up, and they lend what they receive for money lent.

5. There is a saying among the Messenians,

Pylos there is before Pylos, and Pylos, a third, there is also,[b]

but as to the money-lenders we may say

Int'rest there is before int'rest, and int'rest a third there is also.

And then they make a laughing-stock forsooth of the scientists, who say that nothing arises out of nothing ; for with these men interest arises out of that which has as yet no being or existence. And they think it is a disgrace to be a tax-collector, which the law allows ; for they themselves lend money contrary to law, collecting taxes from their debtors, or rather, if the truth is to be told, cheating them in the act of lending ; for he who receives less than the face value of his note is cheated. And yet the Persians regard lying as the second among wrong-doings and being in debt as the first [c] ; for lying is often practised by debtors ; but money-lenders lie more than debtors and cheat in their ledgers, when they write that they give so-and-so much to so-and-so, though they really give less ; and the cause of their lie is avarice, not necessity or want, but insatiable

word τόκος, which means " offspring " and also " interest," the offspring of debt.

[b] Strabo, viii. 7, p. 339 ; Aristophanes, *Knights*, 1059.

[c] Herodotus, i. 138, puts lying first and debt second.

λαυστόν ἐστιν αὐτοῖς τὸ τέλος καὶ ἀνωφελὲς ὀλέθριον δὲ τοῖς ἀδικουμένοις. οὔτε γὰρ ἀγροὺς οὓς
ἀφαιροῦνται τῶν χρεωστῶν γεωργοῦσιν, οὔτ' οἰκίας
αὐτῶν, ἐκβαλόντες ἐκείνους, οἰκοῦσιν, οὔτε τραπέζας παρατίθενται οὔτ' ἐσθῆτας ἐκείνων· ἀλλὰ
πρῶτός τις ἀπόλωλε, καὶ δεύτερος κυνηγετεῖται
E ὑπ' ἐκείνου δελεαζόμενος. νέμεται γὰρ ὡς πῦρ τὸ
ἄγριον αὐξόμενον ὀλέθρῳ καὶ φθορᾷ τῶν ἐμπεσόν-
των, ἄλλον ἐξ ἄλλου καταναλίσκον· ὁ δὲ τοῦτο
ῥιπίζων καὶ τρέφων ἐπὶ πολλοὺς δανειστὴς οὐδὲν
ἔχει πλέον ἢ διὰ χρόνου λαβὼν ἀναγνῶναι πόσους
πέπρακε καὶ πόσους ἐκβέβληκε καὶ πόθεν που κυ-
λινδόμενον καὶ σωρευόμενον διαβέβηκε τὸ ἀργύριον.

6. Καὶ ταῦτα μή μ' οἴεσθε λέγειν πόλεμον ἐξ-
ενηνοχότα πρὸς τοὺς δανειστάς·

οὐ γὰρ πώποτ' ἐμὰς βοῦς ἤλασαν οὐδὲ μὲν
   ἵππους·

F ἀλλ' ἐνδεικνύμενον τοῖς προχείρως δανειζομένοις,
ὅσην ἔχει τὸ πρᾶγμα αἰσχύνην καὶ ἀνελευθερίαν
καὶ ὅτι τὸ δανείζεσθαι τῆς ἐσχάτης ἀφροσύνης καὶ
μαλακίας ἐστίν. ἔχεις; μὴ δανείσῃ, οὐ γὰρ ἀ-
πορεῖς. οὐκ ἔχεις; μὴ δανείσῃ, οὐ γὰρ ἐκτίσεις.
κατ' ἰδίαν δ' οὕτως ἑκάτερα σκοπῶμεν. ὁ Κάτων
πρός τινα πρεσβύτην πονηρευόμενον " ὦ ἄνθρωπε,
τί τῷ γήρᾳ," ἔφη, " πολλὰ κακὰ ἔχοντι τὴν ἐκ τῆς
πονηρίας αἰσχύνην προστίθης; " οὐκοῦν καὶ σὺ
830 τῇ πενίᾳ, πολλῶν κακῶν προσόντων, μὴ ἐπισώρευε

---

greed, which in the end brings neither enjoyment
nor profit to them and ruin to those whom they
wrong. For they do not till the fields which they
take from their debtors, nor do they live in their
houses after evicting them, nor do they eat at their
tables or wear their clothes, but they ruin one man
first, then hunt a second, using the other as bait.
For the savage practice spreads like fire, growing
by the ruin and destruction of those who fall into
it, consuming one after another. And the money-
lender who fans and feeds this fire to the ruin of
many men gains nothing, except that from time to
time he can take his account-books and read how
many men he has sold out, how many he has driven
from their homes, and, in general, the sources from
which his hoard of money, rolling in and piling up,
has made such gains.

6. And do not think that I say this because I
have declared war against the money-lenders;

Ne'er have they harried my cattle, nor ever made off with
my horses [a];

but that I am pointing out to those who are too
ready to become borrowers how much disgrace and
servility there is in the practice and that borrowing
is an act of extreme folly and weakness. Have you
money? Do not borrow, for you are not in need.
Have you no money? Do not borrow, for you will
not be able to pay. Let us look at each of these
two alternatives separately. Cato once said to an
old man who was behaving wickedly : " Sir, when
old age has so many evils of its own, why do you add
to them the disgrace of wickedness ? " Therefore in
your own case do not heap up upon poverty, which
has many attendant evils, the perplexities which

(830) τὰς ἐκ τοῦ δανείζεσθαι καὶ ὀφείλειν ἀμηχανίας μηδ'
ἀφαιροῦ τῆς πενίας, ᾧ μόνῳ τοῦ πλούτου διαφέρει,
τὴν ἀμεριμνίαν. ἐπεὶ τὸ τῆς παροιμίας ἔσται
γελοῖον

οὐ δύναμαι τὴν αἶγα φέρειν, ἐπί μοι θέτε[1] τὸν
βοῦν.

πενίαν φέρειν μὴ δυνάμενος δανειστὴν ἐπιτίθης
σεαυτῷ, φορτίον καὶ πλουτοῦντι δύσοιστον. πῶς
οὖν διατραφῶ; τοῦτ' ἐρωτᾷς, ἔχων χεῖρας, ἔχων
πόδας, ἔχων φωνήν, ἄνθρωπος ὤν, ᾧ τὸ φιλεῖν
ἔστι καὶ φιλεῖσθαι καὶ τὸ χαρίζεσθαι καὶ τὸ εὐχα-
B ριστεῖν; γράμματα διδάσκων, καὶ παιδαγωγῶν, καὶ
θυρωρῶν, πλέων, παραπλέων· οὐδέν ἐστι τούτων
αἴσχιον οὐδὲ δυσχερέστερον τοῦ ἀκοῦσαι " ἀπόδος."
7. Ὁ Ῥουτίλιος ἐκεῖνος ἐν Ῥώμῃ τῷ Μουσωνίῳ
προσελθὼν " Μουσώνιε," εἶπεν, " ὁ Ζεὺς ὁ σωτήρ,
ὃν σὺ μιμῇ καὶ ζηλοῖς, οὐ δανείζεται." καὶ ὁ
Μουσώνιος μειδιάσας εἶπεν " οὐδὲ δανείζει." ὁ
γὰρ Ῥουτίλιος, δανείζων αὐτὸς ὠνείδιζεν ἐκείνῳ
δανειζομένῳ. Στωικὴ[2] τις αὕτη τυφομανία· τί γάρ
σε δεῖ τὸν Δία τὸν σωτῆρα κινεῖν, αὐτόθεν ὑπο-
μνῆσαι τοῖς φαινομένοις ἐνόν; οὐ δανείζονται
χελιδόνες, οὐ δανείζονται μύρμηκες, οἷς ἡ φύσις οὐ
C χεῖρας, οὐ λόγον, οὐ τέχνην δέδωκεν· ἄνθρωποι δὲ
περιουσίᾳ συνέσεως διὰ τὸ εὐμήχανον ἵππους παρα-
τρέφουσι, κύνας, πέρδικας, λαγωούς,[3] κολοιούς· τί
οὖν γε σεαυτοῦ κατέγνωκας, ἀπιθανώτερος ὢν

---

[1] ἐπί μοι θέτε Reiske : κἀπίθετε.
[2] Στωϊκή Wyttenbach : ὡς στωϊκή.
[3] πέρδικας λαγωοὺς Aldine edition : πέρδικας.

arise from borrowing and owing, and do not deprive poverty of the only advantage which it possesses over wealth, namely freedom from care ; since by so doing you will incur the derision of the proverb,

I am unable to carry the goat, put the ox then upon me.[a]

Being unable to carry the burden of poverty you put the money-lender upon your back, a burden difficult for even the rich to bear. "How, then, am I to live ?" Do you ask this, when you have hands and feet and a voice, when you are a man capable of loving and being loved, of doing favours and being grateful for them ? Live by teaching letters, by leading children to school, by being a door-keeper, by working as a sailor or a boatman ; none of these is so disgraceful or disagreeable as hearing the order "Pay up."

7. The well-known Roman Rutilius went up to Musonius and said, "Musonius, Zeus the Saviour, whom you imitate and emulate, is no borrower"; and Musonius answered with a smile, "He is no lender, either." For Rutilius, who was himself a lender, was finding fault with Musonius for borrowing. This is an example of the vanity of the Stoics ; for why should you bring in Zeus the Saviour, when you can use as examples things that are here before your eyes ? Swallows do not borrow, ants do not borrow, creatures upon which nature has bestowed neither hands, reason, nor art ; but men, with their superior intellect, support through their ingenuity horses, dogs, partridges, hares, and jackdaws in addition to themselves. Why, then, have you come to the poor opinion of yourself, that you are less

[a] *Paroemiographi Graeci*, ii. 592.

(830) κολοιοῦ καὶ ἀφωνότερος πέρδικος καὶ κυνὸς ἀγεν-
νέστερος, ὥστ᾽ ἀπ᾽ ἀνθρώπου μηδενὸς ὠφελεῖσθαι
περιέπων, ψυχαγωγῶν, φυλάττων, προμαχόμενος;
οὐχ ὁρᾷς, ὡς πολλὰ μὲν γῆ παρέχει πολλὰ δὲ
θάλαττα;

καὶ μὴν Μίκκυλον[1] εἰσεῖδον[2]

φησὶν ὁ Κράτης

τῶν ἐρίων ξαίνοντα, γυναῖκά τε συγξαίνουσαν,
τὸν λιμὸν φεύγοντας ἐν αἰνῇ δηιοτῆτι.

Κλεάνθη δ᾽ ὁ βασιλεὺς Ἀντίγονος ἠρώτα διὰ χρόνου
θεασάμενος ἐν ταῖς Ἀθήναις '' ἀλεῖς ἔτι, Κλέ-
D ανθες;'' '' ἀλῶ,'' φησίν, '' ὦ βασιλεῦ· ὃ ποιῶ
ἕνεκα τοῦ Ζήνωνος μὴ[3] ἀποστῆναι μηδὲ φιλοσοφίας.'' ὅσον τὸ φρόνημα τοῦ ἀνδρός, ἀπὸ τοῦ
μύλου καὶ τῆς μάκτρας πεττούσῃ χειρὶ καὶ ἀλούσῃ
γράφειν περὶ θεῶν καὶ σελήνης καὶ ἄστρων καὶ
ἡλίου. ἡμῖν δὲ δουλικὰ δοκεῖ ταῦτ᾽ ἔργα. τοιγαροῦν ἵν᾽ ἐλεύθεροι ὦμεν δανεισάμενοι, κολα-
κεύομεν οἰκοτριβέας[4] ἀνθρώπους καὶ δορυφοροῦμεν
καὶ δειπνίζομεν καὶ δῶρα καὶ φόρους ὑποτελοῦμεν,
οὐ διὰ τὴν πενίαν (οὐδεὶς γὰρ δανείζει πένητι),
ἀλλὰ διὰ τὴν πολυτέλειαν. εἰ γὰρ ἠρκούμεθα τοῖς

---

[1] Μίκκυλον Xylander: μίκυλλον or μίκυλον. Cobet supplies
κρατέρ᾽ ἄλγε᾽ ἔχοντα from Homer, Od. xi. 593; cf. Bergk,
Poet. Lyr. Graec. ii. p. 366.

[2] Cf. C. Wachsmuth, Sillograph. Graecorum Reliquiae,
p. 194.

[3] Ζήνωνος μὴ von Arnim, Stoicorum Veterum Fragmenta,
p. 134: ζῆν μόνος δ᾽. Diogenes Laertius, Life of Cleanthes, ii.,
gives a longer version of this story and adds καὶ γὰρ ὁ Ζήνων
αὐτὸν συνεγύμναζεν εἰς τοῦτο, "for Zeno trained him for this."
Capps suggests ὃ ποιῶ . . . τοῦ ζῆν μόνον, ὥς μ᾽ ἀποστῆναι

persuasive than a jackdaw, more dumb than a partridge, less well-born than a dog, so that you can obtain no help from any human being by waiting on him, entertaining him, guarding him, or fighting for him? Do you not see how many opportunities are offered on land and on the sea?

> Lo, even Miccylus I beheld,[a]

says Crates,

> Carding the wool, and his wife too carding the wool along with him,
> Striving in terrible conflict to 'scape from the onslaught of famine.

King Antigonus asked Cleanthes, when he met him in Athens after not seeing him for a while, "Are you still grinding corn, Cleanthes?" "Yes, Your Majesty," he replied; "and I do it on account of Zeno's precept not to desist from it, nor from philosophy either." What a great spirit the man had who came from the mill and the kneading-trough, and with the hand which ground the flour and baked the bread wrote about the gods, the moon, the stars, and the sun! But to us such labours seem slavish. And therefore, in order to be free, we contract debts and pay court to men who are ruiners of homes, we act as bodyguard to them, dine them, make them presents, and pay them tribute, not because of our poverty (for no one lends to poor men), but because of our extravagance. For if we were content with the necessaries of life,

[a] Crates, Frag. 6, Bergk, *Poet. Lyr. Graec.* ed. 4, ii. p. 366. The last three words occur also in Homer, *Od.* xii. 257.

μὴ δέῃ φιλοσοφίας, "merely to live, that I may not have to abandon philosophy."

[4] οἰκοτριβέας Capps: οἰκότριβας.

ἀναγκαίοις πρὸς τὸν βίον, οὐκ ἂν ἦν γένος δανειστῶν, ὥσπερ οὐδὲ Κενταύρων ἔστιν οὐδὲ Γοργόνων·
E ἀλλ' ἡ τρυφὴ δανειστὰς ἐποίησεν οὐχ ἧττον ἢ
χρυσοχόους καὶ ἀργυροκόπους καὶ μυρεψοὺς καὶ
ἀνθοβάφους. οὐ γὰρ ἄρτων οὐδ' οἴνου τιμὴν
ὀφείλομεν, ἀλλὰ χωρίων καὶ ἀνδραπόδων καὶ
ἡμιόνων καὶ τρικλίνων καὶ τραπεζῶν, καὶ χορη-
γοῦντες ἐκλελυμένως πόλεσι, φιλοτιμούμενοι φιλοτιμίας ἀκάρπους καὶ ἀχαρίστους. ὁ δ' ἅπαξ
ἐνειληθεὶς μένει χρεώστης διὰ παντός, ἄλλον ἐξ
ἄλλου μεταλαμβάνων ἀναβάτην, ὥσπερ ἵππος ἐγ-
F χαλινωθείς· ἀποφυγὴ δ' οὐκ ἔστιν ἐπὶ τὰς νομὰς
ἐκείνας καὶ τοὺς λειμῶνας, ἀλλὰ πλάζονται καθάπερ οἱ θεήλατοι καὶ οὐρανοπετεῖς ἐκεῖνοι τοῦ
Ἐμπεδοκλέους δαίμονες·

αἰθέριον μὲν γάρ σφε μένος πόντονδε διώκει,
πόντος δ' ἐς[1] χθονὸς οὖδας ἀπέπτυσε[2]· γαῖα δ' ἐς
αὐγὰς
ἠελίου ἀκάμαντος· ὁ δ' αἰθέρος ἔμβαλε δίναις·

831 " ἄλλος δ' ἐξ ἄλλου δέχεται " τοκιστὴς ἢ πραγ-
ματευτὴς Κορίνθιος, εἶτα Πατρεύς, εἶτ' Ἀθηναῖος,
ἄχρι ἂν ὑπὸ πάντων περικρουόμενος εἰς τόκους
διαλυθῇ καὶ κατακερματισθῇ. καθάπερ γὰρ ἀναστῆναι δεῖ τὸν πεπηλωμένον ἢ μένειν, ὁ δὲ στρεφό-
μενος καὶ κυλινδούμενος ὑγρῷ τῷ σώματι καὶ
διαβρόχῳ προσπεριβάλλεται πλείονα μολυσμόν·
οὕτως ἐν ταῖς μεταγραφαῖς καὶ μεταπτώσεσι τῶν
δανείων τοὺς τόκους προσαναλαμβάνοντες αὐτοῖς

---

[1] δ' ἐς Meziriacus: δὲ.
[2] ἀπέπτυσε Moralia, 361 c: ἀνέπτυσε.

the race of money-lenders would be as non-existent
as that of Centaurs and Gorgons ; but luxury produced money-lenders just as it did goldsmiths, silver-
smiths, perfumers, and dyers in gay colours ; for
our debts are incurred, not to pay for bread or wine,
but for country-seats, slaves, mules, banquet-halls,
and tables, and because we give shows to the cities
with unrestrained expenditure, contending in fruit-
less and thankless rivalries. But the man who is
once involved remains a debtor all his life, exchanging, like a horse that has once been bridled, one
rider for another. And there is no escape to those
former pastures and meadows, but they wander
like the spirits described by Empedocles, who have
been expelled by the gods and thrown out from
heaven :

> Into the waves of the sea they are driv'n by the might of the
>   ether ;
> Then on the floor of the earth the sea vomits them ; earth
>   then ejects them
> Into the untiring sun's rays ; and he hurls them to eddying
>   ether.[a]

And so " one after another takes over "[b] the borrower, first a usurer or broker of Corinth, then one
of Patrae, then an Athenian, until, attacked on all
sides by all of them, he is dissolved and chopped up
into the small change of interest payments. For
just as a man who has fallen into the mire must
either get up or stay where he is, but he who turns
and rolls over covers his wet and drenched person
with more dirt ; so in their transfers and changes
of loans, by assuming additional interest payments

---

[a] Mullach, *Frag. Phil. Graec.* i. p. 2, vss. 32 ff. ; quoted
also in *Moralia*, 361 c.

[b] Mullach, *ibid.* vs. 35.

Β καὶ προσπλάττοντες ἀεὶ βαρύτεροι γίγνονται καὶ
(831) τῶν χολερικῶν οὐδὲν διαφέρουσιν, οἳ θεραπείαν μὲν
οὐ προσδέχονται, τὸ δὲ προστεταγμένον ἐξερῶντες,[1]
εἶτα πλέον αὖθις συλλέγοντες ἀεὶ διατελοῦσι· καὶ
γὰρ οὗτοι καθαρθῆναι μὲν οὐ θέλουσιν, ἀεὶ δ', ὅσαι
τοῦ ἔτους ὧραι, μετ' ὀδύνης καὶ σπαραγμῶν τὸν
τόκον ἀναφέροντες, ἐπιρρέοντος εὐθὺς ἑτέρου καὶ
προσισταμένου, πάλιν ναυτιῶσι καὶ καρηβαροῦσι·
δέον ἀπαλλαγέντας εἰλικρινεῖς καὶ ἐλευθέρους
γίγνεσθαι.

8. Ἤδη γάρ μοι πρὸς τοὺς εὐπορωτέρους καὶ
μαλακωτέρους ὁ λόγος ἔστι, τοὺς λέγοντας " ἄδουλος οὖν γένωμαι καὶ ἀνέστιος καὶ ἄοικος; " ὥσπερ
C εἰ λέγοι πρὸς ἰατρὸν ἄρρωστος ὑδρωπιῶν καὶ
ᾠδηκὼς " ἰσχνὸς οὖν γένωμαι καὶ κενός; " τί δ'
οὐ μέλλεις, ἵν' ὑγιαίνῃς; καὶ σὺ γενοῦ ἄδουλος, ἵνα
μὴ δοῦλος ᾖς· καὶ ἀκτήμων, ἵνα μὴ κτῆμ' ᾖς ἄλλου.
καὶ τὸν τῶν γυπῶν λόγον ἄκουσον· ἐμοῦντος τοῦ
ἑτέρου καὶ λέγοντος τὰ σπλάγχν' ἐκβάλλειν, ἕτερος
παρὼν " καὶ τί δεινόν; " εἶπεν· " οὐ γὰρ τὰ
σεαυτοῦ σπλάγχν' ἐκβάλλεις, ἀλλὰ τὰ[2] τοῦ νεκροῦ
ὃν ἄρτι ἐσπαράττομεν." καὶ τῶν χρεωστῶν οὐ
πωλεῖ ἕκαστος τὸ ἑαυτοῦ χωρίον οὐδὲ τὴν ἰδίαν
οἰκίαν, ἀλλὰ τὴν τοῦ δανείσαντος ὃν τῷ νόμῳ
D κύριον αὐτῶν πεποίηκε. " νὴ Δία," φησίν, " ἀλλ'
ὁ πατήρ μου τὸν ἀγρὸν τοῦτον κατέλιπε." καὶ γὰρ
καὶ τὴν ἐλευθερίαν καὶ τὴν ἐπιτιμίαν ὁ πατὴρ

---

[1] ἐξερῶντες Reiske: ἐξαίροντες.
[2] τὰ added by Bernardakis.

[a] Evidently the man in debt is supposed to borrow from
one lender in order to pay another.

334

and plastering themselves with them,[a] they weigh
themselves down more and more ; and they are
much like persons ill with cholera, who do not accept
treatment, but vomit up the prescribed medicine
and then continue constantly to collect more disease.
Similarly these borrowers refuse to be purged, and
always, at every season of the year, when painfully
and with convulsions they cough up the interest
while another payment immediately accrues and
presses upon them, they suffer a fresh attack of
nausea and headache. What they ought to do is
to get rid of debts and become healthy and free
again.

8. From now on my words are addressed to those
who are more well-to-do and accustomed to a softer
way of living, those who say " Am I, then, to be
without slaves, without hearth and home ? ", as if a
sick man who is swollen up with dropsy should say
to his physician " Am I, then, to be made thin and
empty ? " Why not, to make you get well ? And
so you should do without slaves, that you may not
be a slave yourself, and without property, that you
may not be the property of another. Hear the tale
of the vultures : One of them had an attack of
vomiting and said he was spewing out bowels, but
the other, who was there, said " What harm is there
in that ? For you are not spewing out your own
bowels, but those of the corpse we tore to pieces
a little while ago." So any man in debt sells, not
his own plot of land, nor his own house, but those of
his creditor whom by law he has made their owner.
" Not so, by Zeus," he says ; " why my father left
me this field." Yes, and your father left you your
liberty and your good reputation, which you ought

(831) ἔδωκεν, ὧν σε δεῖ λόγον ἔχειν πλείονα. καὶ τὸν
πόδα καὶ τὴν χεῖρ᾽ ὁ γεννήσας ἐποίησεν, ἀλλ᾽ ὅταν
σαπῇ, μισθὸν δίδως τῷ ἀποκόπτοντι. τῷ δ᾽ Ὀδυσ-
σεῖ τὴν ἐσθῆτα ἡ Καλυψὼ περιέθηκεν '' εἵματ᾽
ἀμφιέσασα θυώδεα¹ '' χρωτὸς ἀθανάτου πνέοντα,
δῶρα καὶ μνημόσυνα τῆς φιλίας ὄντα τῆς ἐκείνης·
ἀλλ᾽ ἐπεὶ περιτραπεὶς καὶ βυθισθεὶς μόλις ἀνέσχε,
τῆς ἐσθῆτος γενομένης διαβρόχου καὶ βαρείας,
ἐκείνην μὲν ἔρριψεν ἀποδυσάμενος, κρηδέμνῳ δέ
τινι γυμνὸν ὑποζώσας τὸ στέρνον

E   νῆχε παρὲξ ἐς γαῖαν ὁρώμενος

καὶ διασωθεὶς οὔτ᾽ ἐσθῆτος οὔτε τροφῆς ἠπόρησε.
τί οὖν; οὐ γίγνεται χειμὼν περὶ τοὺς χρεώστας,
ὅταν ἐπιστῇ διὰ χρόνου δανειστὴς λέγων
'' ἀπόδος '';

ὣς εἰπὼν σύναγεν νεφέλας, ἐτάραξε δὲ πόντον·
σὺν δ᾽ εὖρός τε νότος τ᾽ ἔπεσε ζέφυρός τε δυσαὴς

τόκων τόκοις ἐπικυλισθέντων· ὁ δὲ συγκλυζόμενος
ἀντέχεται τῶν βαρυνόντων, ἀπονήξασθαι καὶ φυγεῖν
μὴ δυνάμενος· ἀλλ᾽ ὠθεῖται κατὰ βυθοῦ, μετὰ τῶν
ἐγγυησαμένων φίλων ἀφανιζόμενος. Κράτης δ᾽ ὁ
F Θηβαῖος ὑπ᾽ οὐδενὸς ἀπαιτούμενος οὐδ᾽ ὀφείλων,
αὐτὰς δὲ τὰς οἰκονομίας καὶ φροντίδας καὶ περι-
σπασμοὺς δυσχεραίνων, ἀφῆκεν οὐσίαν ὀκτὼ ταλάντων, καὶ τρίβωνα καὶ πήραν ἀναλαβὼν εἰς
φιλοσοφίαν καὶ πενίαν κατέφυγεν. Ἀναξαγόρας
δὲ τὴν χώραν κατέλιπε μηλόβοτον. καὶ τί δεῖ

---

¹ θυώδεα Xylander from Od. v. 264: εὐώδεα.

ᵃ Homer, Od. v. 264.   ᵇ Homer, Od. v. 439.

to value more. So, too, he who begat you made
your foot and your hand, but when it is mortified,
you pay a surgeon for cutting it off. Calypso clothed
Odysseus in her garment, " putting fragrant raiment
upon him " [a] that breathed of her divine person,
as a gift and a memento of her love ; but when he
was capsized and engulfed by the waves and could
hardly keep himself up since the garment had become soaked and heavy, he took it off and threw it
from him, then, binding a wimple about his naked
breast,

> Long-shore he swam looking landward, [b]

and when he reached safety he had no lack of garment or food. Well, then, is it not a tempest that
arises about debtors when the lender after a while
comes up to them saying " Pay " ?

> Thus having spoken he gathered the clouds and stirred up
> the great waters ;
> East wind and South wind and West with furious blasts
> raged together, [c]

as interest rolled up upon interest ; and the debtor,
overwhelmed, struggles against them as they weigh
him down, but cannot swim away and escape ;
no, he sinks down to the bottom and disappears
along with the friends who have endorsed his notes.
Crates the Theban, when he was not pressed for
payment and did not even owe anything, because
he disliked the mere administration of property,
its cares and distractions, abandoned an estate
valued at eight talents and, donning cloak and
wallet, took refuge in philosophy and poverty.
Anaxagoras also left his land to be grazed over by

[c] Homer, *Od.* v. 291, 292.

τούτους λέγειν, ὅπου Φιλόξενος ὁ μελοποιὸς ἐν
ἀποικίᾳ Σικελικῇ, κλήρου μετασχὼν καὶ βίου καὶ
οἴκου πολλὴν εὐπορίαν ἔχοντος, ὁρῶν δὲ τρυφὴν καὶ
ἡδυπάθειαν καὶ ἀμουσίαν ἐπιχωριάζουσαν " μὰ τοὺς
θεούς," εἶπεν, " ἐμὲ ταῦτα τἀγαθὰ " οὐκ ἀπολεῖ,
ἀλλ' ἐγὼ ταῦτα· καὶ καταλιπὼν ἑτέροις τὸν κλῆ-
832 ρον ἐξέπλευσεν. οἱ δ' ὀφείλοντες ἀπαιτούμενοι
δασμολογούμενοι δουλεύοντες ὑπαργυρεύοντες ἀν-
έχονται, καρτεροῦσιν, ὡς ὁ Φινεύς, Ἁρπυίας τινὰς
ὑποπτέρους βόσκοντες, αἳ φέρουσι τὴν τροφὴν καὶ
διαρπάζουσιν, οὐ καθ' ὥραν ἀλλὰ πρὶν θερισθῆναι
τὸν σῖτον ὠνούμενοι, καὶ πρὶν ἢ πεσεῖν τὴν ἐλαίαν
ἀγοράζοντες τοὔλαιον· καὶ " τὸν οἶνον ἔχω," φησί,
" τοσούτου " καὶ πρόσγραφον ἔδωκε τῆς τιμῆς· ὁ
δὲ βότρυς κρέμαται καὶ προσπέφυκεν ἔτι τὸν
ἀρκτοῦρον ἐκδεχόμενος.

---

[a] Cf. Himerius, Eclogues, iii. 18.

sheep.[a] But what need is there of mentioning these men, when Philoxenus the lyric poet, who shared in the allotment of lands in a colony in Sicily, which ensured him a livelihood and a household furnished with abundant resources, when he saw that luxury, indulgence in a life of pleasure, and lack of culture were prevalent there, said, " By the Gods, these good things shall not make me lose myself ; I will rather lose them," and leaving his allotment to others, he sailed away. But people in debt are content to be dunned, mulcted of tribute, enslaved, and cheated ; they endure, like Phineus, to feed winged harpies which carry off their food and devour it, buying their grain, not at the proper season, but before it is harvested, and purchasing the oil before the olives have been plucked. And " I have wine," says the borrower, " at such and such a price," and he gives his note for its value ; but the cluster still hangs clinging on the vine and waiting for the rising of Arcturus.

LIVES OF THE TEN ORATORS
(VITAE DECEM ORATORUM)

INTRODUCTION

AT some time in the second century before Christ
ten Attic orators were selected, probably by Apollodorus of Pergamum, as the orators whose speeches
were most worthy of preservation and study, and
this " Canon " of the Ten Attic Orators was generally
accepted. The *Lives* of these orators which are
contained in manuscripts of Plutarch's *Moralia* were
certainly not written by Plutarch. They are altogether lacking in the charm which characterizes
Plutarch's careful and elaborate style. Facts are
stated one after another with little variety and with
little or no distinction between mere anecdotes and
matters of real importance ; but the *Lives* are of
interest on account of their subject matter.

The " decrees " appended to the *Lives* are, except
in some details, fairly accurate copies of official
documents (see F. Ladek, *Wiener Studien*, xiii., 1891,
pp. 111 ff.). The two which are concerned with
Demosthenes and his family are not really decrees,
but petitions addressed to the Senate, copies of
which were undoubtedly kept among the official
records at Athens, whereas the third—that in honour
of Lycurgus—is a decree of the people. A large part
of the inscription recording this decree has been
found and is published in the *Inscriptiones Graecae*, ii.
No. 240 (editio minor, ii. No. 457), Dittenberger,

LIVES OF THE TEN ORATORS

Sylloge Inscriptionum Graecarum, third edition, No. 326. The text which has been handed down in the manuscripts of Plutarch varies somewhat from that of the inscription, but hardly more than is to be expected. It may well be that whoever appended the "decrees" to the *Lives* of the orators derived them, not directly from inscriptions or other official documents, but (as suggested by B. Keil in *Hermes*, xxx. pp. 210 ff.) from the work of Heliodorus *On Monuments*.

The *Lives*, with the "decrees," are published by Anton Westermann in his *Biographi Graeci* (1833 and 1845).

Α΄. ΑΝΤΙΦΩΝ

C

D

E

Ἀντιφῶν Σοφίλου μὲν ἦν πατρὸς τῶν δὲ δήμων Ῥαμνούσιος· μαθητεύσας δὲ τῷ πατρὶ (ἦν γὰρ σοφιστής, ᾧ καὶ Ἀλκιβιάδην φασὶν ἔτι παῖδα ὄντα φοιτῆσαι) καὶ δύναμιν λόγων κτησάμενος, ὥς τινες νομίζουσιν, ἀπ᾽ οἰκείας φύσεως, ὥρμησε μὲν πολιτεύεσθαι· διατριβὴν δὲ συνέστησε καὶ Σωκράτει τῷ φιλοσόφῳ διεφέρετο τὴν ὑπὲρ τῶν λόγων διαφορὰν οὐ φιλονείκως ἀλλ᾽ ἐλεγκτικῶς, ὡς Ξενοφῶν ἱστόρηκεν ἐν τοῖς Ἀπομνημονεύμασι. καί τινας λόγους τοῖς δεομένοις τῶν πολιτῶν συνέγραφεν εἰς τοὺς ἐν τοῖς δικαστηρίοις ἀγῶνας πρῶτος[1] ἐπὶ τοῦτο τραπείς, ὥσπερ τινές φασι· τῶν γοῦν πρὸ αὐτοῦ γενομένων οὐδενὸς φέρεται δικανικὸς λόγος, ἀλλ᾽ οὐδὲ τῶν κατ᾽ αὐτόν, διὰ τὸ μηδέπω ἐν ἔθει τοῦ συγγράφειν εἶναι, οὐ Θεμιστοκλέους οὐκ Ἀριστείδου οὐ Περικλέους, καίτοι πολλὰς ἀφορμὰς καὶ ἀνάγκας παρασχόντων αὐτοῖς τῶν καιρῶν· καὶ γὰρ οὐ δι᾽ ἀσθένειαν ἀπελείποντο τοῦ συγγράφειν, ὡς δῆλον ἐκ τῶν εἰρημένων παρὰ τοῖς συγγραφεῦσι περὶ ἑνὸς ἑκάστου τῶν προειρημένων ἀνδρῶν. ὅσους μέντοι ἔχομεν ἐπὶ τὸ παλαιότατον ἀναφέροντες ἀπομνημονεῦσαι τὴν ἰδέαν τῶν λόγων ταύτην μεταχειρισαμένους, τούτους εὕροι τις ἂν ἐπιβεβληκότας

---

[1] πρῶτος Meziriacus : πρῶτον.

I. ANTIPHON

ANTIPHON was the son of Sophilus, and his deme was Rhamnus. He was a pupil of his father (for his father was a sophist, and it is said that Alcibiades as a boy attended his school), and having acquired power in speaking—as some think, through his own natural ability—he entered upon a public career. And he set up a school and had his disagreement with Socrates on the subject of words, not in a contentious spirit, but for the sake of argument, as Xenophon has narrated in his *Memoirs*.[a] And he wrote some speeches for citizens who wanted them for their suits in the law-courts, being the first who practised this profession, as some say. At any rate no legal oration is extant of any of those who lived before his time, nor of his contemporaries either, because the custom of speech-writing had not yet arisen; there is none by Themistocles, Aristeides, or Pericles, although the times afforded them many opportunities and also occasions when such speeches were needed. And it was not for lack of ability that they refrained from such speech-writing, as is evident from what is said by the historians about each of the above-mentioned orators. Yet all those whom we are able to record as having practised this kind of speeches, going back to the earliest occurrence, will be found

---

[a] Xenophon, *Memorabilia*, i. 6.

(832) Ἀντιφῶντι, πρεσβύτῃ ἤδη ὄντι, οἷον Ἀλκιβιάδην,
Κριτίαν, Λυσίαν, Ἀρχῖνον.[1] πρῶτος δὲ καὶ ῥη-
τορικὰς τέχνας ἐξήνεγκε, γενόμενος ἀγχίνους· διὸ
καὶ Νέστωρ ἐπεκαλεῖτο.

Καικίλιος δ' ἐν τῷ περὶ αὐτοῦ συντάγματι
Θουκυδίδου τοῦ συγγραφέως καθηγητὴν[2] τεκμαί-
ρεται γεγονέναι ἐξ ὧν ἐπαινεῖται παρ' αὐτῷ ὁ
Ἀντιφῶν. ἔστι δ' ἐν τοῖς λόγοις ἀκριβὴς καὶ
πιθανὸς καὶ δεινὸς περὶ τὴν εὕρεσιν καὶ ἐν τοῖς
ἀπόροις τεχνικὸς καὶ ἐπιχειρῶν ἐξ ἀδήλου καὶ ἐπὶ
τοὺς νόμους καὶ τὰ πάθη τρέπων τοὺς λόγους τοῦ
F εὐπρεποῦς μάλιστα στοχαζόμενος. γέγονε δὲ κατὰ
τὰ Περσικὰ καὶ Γοργίαν τὸν σοφιστήν, ὀλίγῳ
νεώτερος αὐτοῦ· καὶ παρατέτακεν ἕως καταλύσεως
τῆς δημοκρατίας ὑπὸ τῶν τετρακοσίων γενομένης,
ἣν αὐτὸς δοκεῖ συγκατασκευάσαι, ὁτὲ μὲν δυσὶ
τριηραρχῶν ναυσὶν ὁτὲ δὲ στρατηγῶν, καὶ πολλαῖς
μάχαις νικῶν, καὶ συμμαχίας μεγάλας αὐτοῖς
προσαγόμενος, καὶ τοὺς ἀκμάζοντας ὁπλίζων, καὶ

---

[1] Ἀρχῖνον Taylor : ἀρχίνοον.
[2] καθηγητὴν Wyttenbach : μαθητὴν.

---

[a] Cf. Thucydides, viii. 68 ἀνὴρ Ἀθηναίων τῶν καθ' ἑαυτὸν
ἀρετῇ τε οὐδενὸς δεύτερος καὶ κράτιστος ἐνθυμηθῆναι γενόμενος
καὶ ἃ γνοίη εἰπεῖν, "a man inferior to none of the Athenians
of his own day in force of character, and one who had proved
himself most able both to formulate a plan and to set forth
his conclusions in speech " (Smith's translation, L.C.L.).

[b] In 411 B.C. when for some four months an oligarchy
ruled Athens.

[c] The duty of fitting out ships for the navy devolved upon
wealthy citizens, who were then called trierarchs.

[d] Antiphon was a common name at Athens in the fifth
century. Blass, Die attische Beredsamkeit, 2nd ed. i.
346

to have followed Antiphon when he was already old ;
I mean such as Alcibiades, Critias, Lysias, and
Archinus. He was also the first to publish rules of
the art of oratory, being of sharp intellect, and for
this reason he was nicknamed Nestor.

And Caecilius, in the treatise he compiled about
him, conjectures from the terms in which Antiphon
is praised in the work of the historian Thucydides
that he was the latter's teacher.[a] In his speeches
he is accurate and persuasive, clever in invention,
ingenious in handling perplexing cases ; he attacks
unexpectedly, and he addresses his arguments to
both the laws and the emotions, aiming especially at
propriety. He was born at the time of the Persian
wars and of the sophist Gorgias, who was somewhat
older than he ; and his life extended until the destruction of the democracy by the Four Hundred,[b]
in causing which he seems himself to have had a
part, at one time by being trierarch[c] of two ships, at
another by being general[d] and gaining many victories
in battle and winning important alliances for the
Four Hundred, by arming the men of military age,

pp. 93 ff., distinguishes, in addition to the orator: (1) a
patriotic and worthy citizen (Xenophon, *Hell.* ii. 3. 40) in
defence of whose daughter Lysias wrote a speech, and to
whom the military activities belong which are here ascribed
to the orator; (2) the tragic poet who was put to death by
Dionysius of Syracuse (Aristotle, *Rhet.* ii. 6. p. 1385 a 9);
(3) Antiphon the sophist (Xenophon, *Mem.* i. 6. 5; Diog.
Laert. ii. 5. 25), who is probably the one who practised
mental healing at Corinth; (4) the son of Pyrilampus (Plato,
Parmenides, 127 A); (5) the son of Lysonides (*Moralia,*
833 A); and (6) an Antiphon derided by Aristophanes
(*Wasps,* 1270), as a starveling. The Pseudo-Plutarch has
evidently fused several of these personalities with that of
the orator.

τριήρεις πληρῶν ἑξήκοντα, καὶ πρεσβεύων δ' ἑκάστοτε ὑπὲρ¹ αὐτῶν εἰς Λακεδαίμονα, ἡνίκα ἐτε-
833 τείχιστο Ἠετιώνεια.² μετὰ δὲ τὴν κατάλυσιν τῶν
τετρακοσίων εἰσαγγελθεὶς σὺν Ἀρχεπτολέμῳ, ἑνὶ
τῶν τετρακοσίων, ἑάλω, καὶ τοῖς περὶ τῶν προ-
δοτῶν ἐπιτιμίοις ὑπαχθεὶς ἄταφος ἐρρίφη καὶ σὺν
τοῖς ἐκγόνοις ἄτιμος ἀνεγράφη.³ οἱ δ' ὑπὸ τῶν
τριάκοντα⁴ ἀνῃρῆσθαι αὐτὸν ἱστοροῦσιν, ὥσπερ
Λυσίας ἐν τῷ ὑπὲρ τῆς Ἀντιφῶντος θυγατρὸς λόγῳ·
ἐγένετο γὰρ αὐτῷ θυγάτριον, οὗ Κάλλαισχρος
ἐπεδικάσατο. ὅτι δ' ὑπὸ τῶν τριάκοντα ἀπέθανεν,
ἱστορεῖ καὶ Θεόπομπος ἐν τῇ πεντεκαιδεκάτῃ τῶν
B Φιλιππικῶν· ἀλλ' οὗτός γ'⁵ ἂν εἴη ἕτερος,⁶ Λυσι-
δωνίδου πατρός, οὗ⁷ καὶ Κρατῖνος ἐν Πυτίνῃ ὡς
πονηροῦ μνημονεύει· πῶς γὰρ ἂν ὁ προτεθνεὼς καὶ
ἀναιρεθεὶς ὑπὸ τῶν τετρακοσίων πάλιν ἐπὶ τῶν
τριάκοντα εἴη; ἔστι δὲ καὶ ἄλλος λόγος περὶ τῆς
τελευτῆς αὐτοῦ. πρεσβευτὴν γὰρ ὄντα αὐτὸν εἰς
Συρακούσας πλεῦσαι, ἡνίκα ἤκμαζεν ἡ τοῦ προτέρου Διονυσίου τυραννίς· γενομένης δὲ παρὰ πότον
ζητήσεως, τίς ἄριστός ἐστι χαλκός, καὶ τῶν πολλῶν
διαφερομένων, αὐτὸν εἰπεῖν ἄριστον εἶναι ἐξ οὗ
Ἁρμόδιος καὶ Ἀριστογείτων πεποίηνται· τοῦτο
δ' ἀκούσαντα τὸν Διονύσιον καὶ ὑπονοήσαντα προ-

---

¹ ὑπὲρ Reiske: ὑπ'.
² Ἠετιώνεια Blass: ἡ ἐτεωνία (Ἠετιωνεία Xylander).
³ ἀνεγράφη Westermann: ἐνεγράφη.
⁴ τριάκοντα] ν' (i.e. τετρακοσίων) Photius.
⁵ οὗτός γ' Taylor: οὗτος τὲ.
⁶ ἂν εἴη ἕτερος Taylor: ἂν ἡμέτερος.
⁷ οὗ added by Sauppe.

ᵃ Eëtioneia, the mole which formed the northern side of

by manning sixty triremes, and by being on every
occasion their envoy to Lacedaemon at the time
when Eëtioneia had been fortified.[a] And after the
overthrow of the Four Hundred he was indicted along
with Archeptolemus, one of the Four Hundred, was
found guilty, subjected to the punishments prescribed for traitors, thrown out unburied, and inscribed along with his descendants in the list of the
disfranchised. But some tell us that he was put to
death by the Thirty,[b] as Lysias says in his speech
in defence of Antiphon's daughter ; for he had a
daughter whom Callaeschrus claimed in marriage by
legal process. And that he was put to death by the
Thirty is told also by Theopompus in the fifteenth
book of his *Philippics*[c] ; but that must have been
another Antiphon, the son of Lysidonides, whom
Cratinus also, in his play *The Flask*, mentions as a
rascal ; for how could a man who had died previously
and had been put to death by the Four Hundred be
living again in the time of the Thirty ? But there is
also another story of his death : that he sailed as
envoy to Syracuse when the tyranny of Dionysius
the First was at its height, and at a convivial gather-
ing the question arose what bronze was the best ;
then when most of the guests disagreed, he said
that bronze was the best from which the statues of
Harmodius and Aristogeiton were made ; and when
Dionysius heard this, suspecting that the remark

the great Harbour of Peiraeus, was fortified by the Four
Hundred in order to command the entrance.
   [b] In 404 B.C., when Athens was occupied by the Lacedaemonians, a body of Thirty men was appointed to revise the
constitution. They seized all power and ruled ruthlessly
until overthrown in May 403 B.C.
   [c] Müller, *Frag. Hist. Graec.* i. p. 300.

(833) τροπὴν εἰς ἐπίθεσιν εἶναι τὸ ῥηθὲν προστάξαι
C ἀναιρεθῆναι αὐτόν· οἱ δέ, ὅτι τὰς τραγῳδίας αὐτοῦ
διέσυρε χαλεπήναντα.

Φέρονται δὲ τοῦ ῥήτορος λόγοι ἑξήκοντα, ὧν
κατεψευσμένους φησὶ Καικίλιος εἶναι τοὺς εἴκοσι-
πέντε. κεκωμῴδηται δ᾽ εἰς φιλαργυρίαν ὑπὸ
Πλάτωνος ἐν[1] Πεισάνδρῳ. λέγεται δὲ τραγῳδίας
συνθεῖναι καὶ ἰδίᾳ καὶ σὺν Διονυσίῳ τῷ τυράννῳ.
ἔτι δ᾽ ὧν πρὸς τῇ ποιήσει τέχνην ἀλυπίας συνεστήσατο, ὥσπερ τοῖς νοσοῦσιν ἡ παρὰ τῶν ἰατρῶν
θεραπεία ὑπάρχει· ἐν Κορίνθῳ τε κατεσκευασμένος
οἴκημά τι παρὰ τὴν ἀγορὰν προέγραψεν, ὅτι δύναται
D τοὺς λυπουμένους διὰ λόγων θεραπεύειν· καὶ πυν-
θανόμενος τὰς αἰτίας παρεμυθεῖτο τοὺς κάμνοντας.
νομίζων δὲ τὴν τέχνην ἐλάττω ἢ καθ᾽ αὑτὸν εἶναι
ἐπὶ ῥητορικὴν ἀπετράπη. εἰσὶ δ᾽ οἳ καὶ τὸ Γλαύκου
τοῦ Ῥηγίνου περὶ ποιητῶν βιβλίον εἰς Ἀντιφῶντα
ἀναφέρουσιν. ἐπαινεῖται δ᾽ αὐτοῦ μάλιστα ὁ περὶ
Ἡρώδου,[2] καὶ ὁ[3] πρὸς Ἐρασίστρατον περὶ τῶν
ταῶν,[4] καὶ ὁ περὶ τῆς εἰσαγγελίας,[5] ὃν ὑπὲρ ἑαυτοῦ
γέγραφε, καὶ ὁ πρὸς Δημοσθένη τὸν στρατηγὸν
παρανόμων. ἔγραψε δὲ καὶ κατὰ Ἱπποκράτους τοῦ
στρατηγοῦ[6] λόγον καὶ εἷλεν αὐτὸν ἐξ ἐρήμου.

Ψήφισμα ἐπὶ Θεοπόμπου ἄρχοντος, ἐφ᾽ οὗ οἱ

---

[1] ἐν Casaubon from Photius: σύν.
[2] Ἡρώδου Palmer: Ἡροδότου.
[3] καὶ ὁ Duebner: καὶ.   [4] ταῶν Ruhnken: ἰδεῶν.
[5] εἰσαγγελίας Xylander: ἀγγελίας.
[6] στρατηγοῦ Westermann: ἰατροῦ στρατηγοῦ (ἰατροῦ Photius).

was intended to encourage an attack upon himself, he ordered that Antiphon be put to death. But others say that he was angry because Antiphon made fun of his tragedies.

There are current sixty orations ascribed to this orator, twenty-five of which Caecilius says are spurious. He is ridiculed as a lover of money by Plato in his *Peisander*.[a] And he is said to have written tragedies both by himself and in collaboration with the tyrant Dionysius. But while he was still busy with poetry he invented a method of curing distress, just as physicians have a treatment for those who are ill ; and at Corinth, fitting up a room near the market-place, he wrote on the door that he could cure by words those who were in distress ; and by asking questions and finding out the causes of their condition he consoled those in trouble. But thinking this art was unworthy of him he turned to oratory. There are some who ascribe also to Antiphon the book *On Poets* by Glaucus of Rhegium.[b] His most admired orations are the one concerning Herodes, that against Erasistratus about the peacocks, that on the Indictment, which he wrote in his own defence, and that against the general Demosthenes for moving an illegal measure. He wrote also a speech against the general Hippocrates and caused him to be convicted by default.

Caecilius has appended a decree passed in the archonship of Theopompus,[c] the year in which the

---

[a] Kock, *Com. Att. Frag.* i. p. 629, no. 103.

[b] *Cf.* Müller, *Frag. Hist. Graec.* ii. p. 23.

[c] 411–410 B.C. Caecilius derived his text of the decree from Craterus's collection of decrees. See Harpocration, *s.v.* Ἄνδρων and Blass, *Die attische Beredsamkeit*, 2nd ed., i. p. 99.

E τετρακόσιοι κατελύθησαν, καθ' δ¹ ἔδοξεν Ἀντιφῶντα κριθῆναι, ὃ Καικίλιος παρατέθειται·

Ἔδοξε² τῇ βουλῇ μιᾷ καὶ εἰκοστῇ τῆς πρυτανείας· Δημόνικος Ἀλωπεκῆθεν ἐγραμμάτευε, Φιλόστρατος Παλληνεὺς³ ἐπεστάτει· Ἀνδρῶν εἶπε περὶ τῶν ἀνδρῶν, οὓς ἀποφαίνουσι οἱ στρατηγοὶ πρεσβευομένους εἰς Λακεδαίμονα ἐπὶ κακῷ τῆς πόλεως τῆς Ἀθηναίων, καὶ ἐκ τοῦ στρατοπέδου πλεῖν ἐπὶ πολεμίας νεὼς καὶ πεζεῦσαι F διὰ Δεκελείας, Ἀρχεπτόλεμον καὶ Ὀνομακλέα καὶ Ἀντιφῶντα συλλαβεῖν καὶ ἀποδοῦναι εἰς τὸ δικαστήριον, ὅπως δῶσι δίκην· παρασχόντων δ' αὐτοὺς οἱ στρατηγοί, καὶ ἐκ τῆς βουλῆς οὕστινας ἂν δοκῇ τοῖς στρατηγοῖς, προσελομένοις⁴ μέχρι δέκα, ὅπως ἂν περὶ παρόντων γένηται ἡ κρίσις. προσκαλεσάσθωσαν δ' αὐτοὺς οἱ θεσμοθέται ἐν τῇ αὔριον ἡμέρᾳ καὶ εἰσαγόντων, ἐπειδὰν αἱ κλήσεις ἐξήκωσιν εἰς τὸ δικαστήριον, περὶ προδοσίας κατηγορεῖν τοὺς ᾑρημένους⁵ συνηγόρους καὶ τοὺς στρατηγοὺς καὶ ἄλλους,⁶ ἄν τις βούληται· ὅτου δ' ἂν καταψηφίσηται τὸ δικαστήριον, περὶ αὐτοῦ ποιεῖν κατὰ τὸν νόμον, ὃς κεῖται περὶ τῶν προδόντων.

834   Τούτῳ⁷ ὑπογέγραπται τῷ δόγματι ἡ καταδίκη.

Προδοσίας ὦφλον⁸ Ἀρχεπτόλεμος Ἱπποδάμου Ἀγρύληθεν παρών, Ἀντιφῶν Σοφίλου Ῥαμνούσιος παρών· τούτοιν ἐτιμήθη τοῖς ἕνδεκα παραδοθῆναι καὶ τὰ χρήματα δημόσια εἶναι καὶ τῆς θεοῦ τὸ ἐπιδέκατον, καὶ τὼ οἰκία⁹ κατασκάψαι αὐτῶν καὶ ὅρους θεῖναι τοῖν οἰκοπέδοιν, ἐπιγράψαντας "Ἀρχεπτολέμου καὶ Ἀντιφῶντος τοῖν προδότοιν.¹⁰" τὼ δὲ δημάρχω¹¹ ἀποφῆναι τὴν οὐσίαν

¹ καθ' ὃ Dübner : ψήφισμα καθ' ὅ.
² ἔδοξε Reiske : ἔδοξαν.
³ Παλληνεὺς Taylor : πελληνεὺς.
⁴ προσελομένοις Reiske : προσελομένους (προσελόμενοι Emperius).   ⁵ ᾑρημένους Turnebus : εἰρημένους.

352

Four Hundred were overthrown, according to which the senate voted the trial of Antiphon :

Voted by the senate on the twenty-first day of the prytany. Demonicus of Alopecê was secretary, Philostratus of Pallenê was president. Andron moved in regard to the men whom the generals denounce for acting to the detriment of the State of the Athenians while serving as envoys to Lacedaemon and for sailing from the camp in a ship of the enemy and for having passed by land through Deceleia, namely Archeptolemus, Onomacles, and Antiphon, that they be arrested and brought before the court for trial. And the generals, with those members of the senate whom they shall co-opt to the number of ten, are directed to produce them in court, that they may be present at the trial. And the Thesmothetae[a] shall summon them to-morrow, and when the summonses have been returned to the court, they shall propose that the chosen prosecutors and the generals and others, if anyone so desire, shall accuse them of treason ; and whomsoever the court may convict, he shall be treated in accordance with the law which has been passed relating to traitors.

Under this enactment the judgement is written :

Archeptolemus, son of Hippodamus, of Agrylê, and Antiphon, son of Sophilus, of Rhamnus, both being present, were found guilty of treason. The sentence passed upon them was that they be handed over to the Eleven for execution, that their belongings be confiscated and ten per cent thereof be given to the Goddess, that their houses be torn down and boundary-stones be set up on their sites with the inscription "Land of Archeptolemus and Antiphon the two traitors"; and that the two demarchs make a declaration of their

---

[a] Six of the annually elected archons ; their duties were to administer the courts of justice.

---

⁶ ἄλλους Turnebus : ἄλλος or ἄλλο.
⁷ τούτῳ Turnebus : τοῦτο.   ⁸ ὦφλον Turnebus : ὦ φίλον.
⁹ τὼ οἰκία Franke : τῷ οἰκίᾳ.
¹⁰ προδόντοιν Dübner : προδόταιν.
¹¹ τὼ δὲ δημάρχω Meier : τῷ δὲ δημάρχῳ.

(834) αὑτοῖν[1] καὶ μὴ ἐξεῖναι θάψαι Ἀρχεπτόλεμον καὶ
Ἀντιφῶντα Ἀθήνησι, μηδ' ὅσης Ἀθηναῖοι κρατοῦσι·
καὶ ἄτιμον εἶναι Ἀρχεπτόλεμον καὶ Ἀντιφῶντα καὶ
γένος τὸ ἐκ τούτοιν, καὶ νόθους καὶ γνησίους· καὶ ἐάν
B τις[2] ποιήσηταί τινα τῶν ἐξ Ἀρχεπτολέμου καὶ Ἀντιφῶντος, ἄτιμος ἔστω ὁ ποιησάμενος. ταῦτα δὲ γράψαι
ἐν στήλῃ χαλκῇ· καὶ[3] ᾗπερ ἀνάκειται τὰ[4] ψηφίσματα
τὰ περὶ Φρυνίχου, καὶ τοῦτο[5] θέσθαι.

Β'. ΑΝΔΟΚΙΔΗΣ

Ἀνδοκίδης Λεωγόρου μὲν ἦν πατρὸς τοῦ
Ἀνδοκίδου[6] τοῦ θεμένου ποτὲ πρὸς Λακεδαιμονίους
εἰρήνην Ἀθηναίοις, τῶν δήμων δὲ Κυδαθήναιος ἢ
Θορεύς,[7] γένους εὐπατριδῶν, ὡς δ' Ἑλλάνικος καὶ
C ἀπὸ Ἑρμοῦ· καθήκει γὰρ εἰς αὐτὸν τὸ κηρύκων
γένος· διὸ καὶ προεχειρίσθη ποτὲ μετὰ Γλαύκωνος
σὺν ναυσὶν εἴκοσι Κερκυραίοις βοηθήσων, διαφερομένοις πρὸς Κορινθίους. μετὰ δὲ ταῦτα αἰτιαθεὶς
ἀσεβεῖν ὡς καὶ αὐτὸς τοὺς Ἑρμᾶς περικόψας καὶ
D εἰς τὰ τῆς Δήμητρος ἁμαρτὼν μυστήρια,[8] [διὰ τὸ

---

[1] ἀποφῆναι τὴν οὐσίαν αὐτοῖν Westermann: ἀποφῆναί τε
οἰκίαν ἐς (or εἰς) τόν.
[2] τις added by Blass.   [3] καὶ added by Westermann.
[4] ἀνάκειται τὰ Reiske: ἂν καὶ τὰ.   [5] τοῦτο Reiske: τούτου.
[6] τοῦ Ἀνδοκίδου added by Ruhnken.
[7] Taylor: θουρεὺς (Θούριος Bergk).
[8] The passage in brackets, διὰ .... μυστήρια, was seen
by Dübner and Westermann to be a gloss on the preceding
words ἁμαρτὼν μυστήρια.

---

[a] The Thirty Years' Peace, by the terms of which Athens
gave up Megara and its ports in 446–445 B.C.
[b] See note d below for the source of this error

property; and that it be forbidden to bury Archeptolemus and Antiphon at Athens or in any place ruled by the Athenians; and that Archeptolemus and Antiphon be attainted, and also their descendants legitimate and illegitimate; and that if anyone shall adopt any descendant of Archeptolemus or Antiphon, he who so adopts shall be attainted; and that this be inscribed on a bronze tablet, which shall be set up where the decrees relating to Phrynichus are placed.

II. ANDOCIDES

Andocides was the son of Leogoras, son of that Andocides who once made peace between the Lacedaemonians and the Athenians [a]; he was as regards his deme a Cydathenian or a Thorian [b] and was descended from nobles, and even, according to Hellanicus,[c] from Hermes; for the race of heralds traces its origin to him. On this account, too, he was once chosen along with Glaucon to go with twenty ships to aid the Corcyraeans who were embroiled with the Corinthians.[d] And after this he was accused of impiety as being one of those who mutilated the Hermae [e] and as profaning the mysteries of Demeter [because at an earlier time he was

---

[c] Cf. Müller, *Frag. Hist. Graec.* i. p. 55, no. 78.

[d] Cf. Thucydides, i. 51, who seems to have been the source of this error. The colleague of Glaucon on this expedition was Dracontides, son of Leogoras of Thurae, and not Andocides, who at the time, 433 B.C., was too young. See *I.G.* i. 295 (ed. min.), and Kirchner, *Prosopographia Attica*, 828 and 4551.

[e] The Hermae, square pillars surmounted by the head of the god Hermes, stood before the doors of Athenian houses. In 415 B.C., just as the great expedition against Sicily was about to sail, these Hermae were systematically mutilated in the night by unknown persons.

(834) πρότερον ἀκόλαστον ὄντα, νύκτωρ κωμάσαντα,
θραῦσαί τι τῶν ἀγαλμάτων τοῦ θεοῦ καὶ εἰσ-
αγγελθέντα, ἐπειδὴ οὐκ ἠβουλήθη ὃν ἐζήτουν[1] οἱ
κατήγοροι δοῦλον ἐκδοῦναι, διαβληθῆναι καὶ πρὸς
τὴν αἰτίαν τῆς δευτέρας γραφῆς ὕποπτον γενέσθαι·
Κορινθίων εἰσπεμψάντων[2] Λεοντίνους τε καὶ Αἰγε-
σταίους ἄνδρας, ἰδίᾳ μελλόντων βοηθεῖν αὐτοῖς τῶν
Ἀθηναίων, νύκτωρ τοὺς περὶ τὴν ἀγορὰν Ἑρμᾶς
περιέκοψαν, ὡς Κράτιππός φησι, προσαμαρτὼν
μυστήρια] κριθεὶς ἐπὶ τούτοις ἀπέφυγεν ἐπὶ τῷ
μηνύσειν τοὺς ἀδικοῦντας· σπουδὴν δὲ πᾶσαν εἰσ-
E ἐνεγκάμενος[3] ἐξεῦρε τοὺς περὶ τὰ ἱερὰ ἁμαρτόντας,
ἐν οἷς καὶ τὸν αὐτοῦ πατέρα ἐμήνυσε. καὶ τοὺς μὲν
ἄλλους πάντας ἐλέγξας ἐποίησεν ἀπολέσθαι, τὸν δὲ
πατέρα ἐρρύσατο, καίτοι δεδεμένον ἤδη, ὑποσχό-
μενος πολλὰ λυσιτελήσειν αὐτὸν τῇ πόλει. καὶ οὐκ
ἐψεύσατο· ἤλεγξε γὰρ ὁ Λεωγόρας πολλοὺς δημόσια
χρήματα σφετεριζομένους καὶ ἄλλα τινὰ ἀδικοῦντας.
καὶ διὰ μὲν ταῦτα ἀφείθη τῆς αἰτίας.

Οὐκ[4] εὐδοκιμῶν δ' ὁ Ἀνδοκίδης ἐπὶ τοῖς πολι-
τευομένοις ἐπέθετο ναυκληρίᾳ, καὶ τοῖς τε Κυπρίων
βασιλεῦσι καὶ πολλοῖς ἄλλοις δοκίμοις ἐπεξενώθη·
ὅτε καὶ μίαν τῶν πολιτίδων, Ἀριστείδου θυγατέρα,
ἀνεψιὰν οὖσαν αὐτῷ, λάθρα τῶν οἰκείων ἐξαγαγὼν

[1] ἐζήτουν] ἐξήτουν Emperius.
[2] Here Westermann marks a lacuna, which he supplies
from the *Life of Alcibiades*, chap. xviii., and the *Lexicon* of
Photius, *s.v.* Ἑρμοκοπίδαι, about as follows: τοὺς δράσοντας
διὰ τοὺς Συρακουσίους ἀποίκους ὄντας. οὗτοι οὖν τῶν ἐν Σικελίᾳ
Ἑλλήνων ὑπὸ τῶν Συρακουσίων κακῶς διατεθέντων περὶ
βοηθείας δὲ πεμψάντων Λεοντίνων τε καὶ Αἰγεσταίων ἄνδρας,
"the Corinthians having sent in] the men who were to do it
on account of the Syracusans, who were colonists of Corinth.
These men, then, since the Greeks in Sicily were being

dissipated and in a nocturnal revel had broken one
of the images of the god, and when he was indicted
refused to surrender the slave whom his accusers
were looking for, so that he gained a bad name and
was suspected and accused in the second suit also,
which was brought shortly after the expedition went
to Sicily, when the Corinthians sent in men from
Leontini and Egesta and, as the Athenians hesitated
about aiding them privately, they mutilated the
Hermae about the market-place, as Cratippus says,
and profaned the mysteries besides]. At his trial
on these charges he was acquitted on condition that
he should inform against the wrongdoers. He
exerted himself greatly and discovered those who
were guilty of the sacrilege, among whom he informed against his own father. And he brought
about the conviction and death of all the others, but
saved his father, although he had already been put
in prison, by promising that he would be of great
service to the city. And he kept his promise ; for
Leogoras caused the conviction of many men who
were embezzling public funds and committing other
misdeeds. And for these reasons he was acquitted
of the charge.

But Andocides, since his reputation in public life
was not good, took to merchandising and became a
friend of the Cypriote kings and many other men of
note, at which time he abducted a girl of Athenian
birth, daughter of Aristeides and his own niece,
without the knowledge of her family, and sent her as

---

oppressed by the Syracusans, and the Leontines and
Egestaeans, had sent men to ask for assistance, [as the
Athenians . . .''

[3] εἰσενεγκάμενος Reiske from Photius : ἐνεγκάμενος.
[4] οὐκ added by Emperius.

F ἔπεμψε δῶρον τῷ Κυπρίων βασιλεῖ. μέλλων δ'
ἐπὶ τούτοις εἰς δικαστήριον εἰσάγεσθαι πάλιν αὐτὴν
ἐξέκλεψεν ἀπὸ τῆς Κύπρου, καὶ ληφθεὶς ὑπὸ τοῦ
βασιλέως ἐδέθη· διαδρὰς δ' ἧκεν εἰς τὴν πόλιν, καθ'
ὃν χρόνον οἱ τετρακόσιοι διεῖπον τὰ πράγματα·
δεθεὶς δ' ὑπὸ τούτων καὶ διαφυγών, αὖθις ὁπότε
κατελύθη ἡ ὀλιγαρχία,[1] . . . ἐξέπεσε τῆς πόλεως,
τῶν τριάκοντα τὴν ἀρχὴν παραλαβόντων. οἰκήσας
835 δὲ τὸν τῆς φυγῆς χρόνον ἐν Ἤλιδι, κατελθόντων
τῶν περὶ Θρασύβουλον, καὶ αὐτὸς ἧκεν εἰς τὴν
πόλιν. πεμφθεὶς δὲ περὶ τῆς εἰρήνης εἰς Λακεδαίμονα καὶ δόξας ἀδικεῖν ἔφυγε. δηλοῖ δὲ περὶ
πάντων ἐν τοῖς λόγοις οἷς συγγέγραφεν· οἱ μὲν γὰρ
ἀπολογουμένου περὶ τῶν μυστηρίων εἰσίν, οἱ δὲ
καθόδου δεομένου. σῴζεται δ' αὐτοῦ καὶ ὁ περὶ
τῆς Ἐνδείξεως λόγος καὶ Ἀπολογία πρὸς Φαίακα
καὶ περὶ τῆς Εἰρήνης. καὶ ἤκμακε μὲν κατὰ τοῦτον
τὸν χρόνον ἅμα Σωκράτει τῷ φιλοσόφῳ· ἀρχὴ[2]
δ' αὐτῷ τῆς γενέσεως ὀλυμπιὰς μὲν ἑβδομηκοστὴ
ὀγδόη, ἄρχων δ' Ἀθήνησι Θεογενίδης· ὥστ' εἶναι
πρεσβύτερον αὐτὸν Λυσίου ἔτεσί που δέκα.[3]

---

[1] Dübner, followed by Bernardakis, marks a gap here.
[2] ἀρχὴ Photius: ἄρχει; but cf. Thuc. v. 19. 1.
[3] δέκα Westermann; ὀκτὼ Taylor: ἑκατόν.

---

[a] In the summer of 404 B.C. thirty men had been appointed to draw up laws and manage the state temporarily.
They seized all power and ruled like tyrants. Thrasybulus
seized the hill-fortress of Phylê in December and maintained
his position against two attacks by the Thirty. In May
403 Thrasybulus and his followers seized Peiraeus. In

a gift to the King of Cyprus. Then, when he was to be brought to trial for this, he stole her back again from Cyprus and was caught and put in prison by the king; but he ran away and came back to Athens at the time when the Four Hundred were in control of affairs. He was put in prison by them, but escaped, and again, when the oligarchy was overthrown, he . . . was banished from the city after the Thirty had taken over the government. He spent the period of his exile in Elis, but when Thrasybulus and his band returned,[a] he also returned to the city. He was sent to Lacedaemon to negotiate a peace, but was suspected of wrongdoing[b] and banished. He gives information about all this in the speeches which he wrote; for some of them he composed in his defence in the matter of the mysteries, and others when he was asking to be allowed to return home. There is also extant his speech *On the Indictment*, also the Defence against Phaeax and the speech *On the Peace*. He flourished at the same time as Socrates the philosopher; the date of his birth was the seventy-eighth Olympiad, when Theogenides was archon[c] at Athens, so that he was about ten years older than Lysias. The Hermes called the

September the Thirty were overthrown and the democracy re-established.

[b] The nature of the accusation cannot be determined. See Blass, *Die attische Beredsamkeit*, 2nd ed., pp. 293 ff. The oration *On the Peace*, delivered between 393 and 390 B.C., deals with the terms proposed by the mission in which Andocides participated.

[c] 468-467 B.C. This date, however, is based upon a false reckoning, and from the orator's own statements he could not have been born much before 440. See Blass, *ibid.* i. p. 283, and Kirchner, *Prosop. Att.* 828.

(835) τούτου δ' ἐπώνυμός ἐστι καὶ Ἑρμῆς ὁ Ἀνδοκίδου
B καλούμενος, ἀνάθημα μὲν ὧν φυλῆς Αἰγηῖδος, ἐπι-
κληθεὶς δ' Ἀνδοκίδου διὰ τὸ πλησίον παροικῆσαι
τὸν Ἀνδοκίδην. καὶ αὐτὸς δ' ἐχορήγησε κυκλίῳ
χορῷ τῇ αὑτοῦ[1] φυλῇ ἀγωνιζομένη διθυράμβῳ, καὶ
νικήσας ἀνέθηκε τρίποδα ἐφ' ὑψηλοῦ[2] ἀντικρὺ[3] τοῦ
πωρίνου Σειληνοῦ. ἔστι δ' ἁπλοῦς καὶ ἀκατά-
σκευος ἐν τοῖς λόγοις, ἀφελής τε καὶ ἀσχημάτιστος.

Γ′. ΛΥΣΙΑΣ

C Λυσίας υἱὸς ἦν Κεφάλου τοῦ Λυσανίου τοῦ
Κεφάλου, Συρακουσίου μὲν γένος μεταναστάντος δ'
εἰς Ἀθήνας ἐπιθυμίᾳ τε τῆς πόλεως καὶ Περικλέους
τοῦ Ξανθίππου πείσαντος αὐτόν, φίλον ὄντα καὶ
ξένον, πλούτῳ διαφέροντα[4]· ὡς δέ τινες, ἐκπεσόντα
τῶν Συρακουσῶν, ἡνίκα ὑπὸ Γέλωνος ἐτυραν-
νοῦντο. γενόμενος δ'[5] Ἀθήνησιν ἐπὶ Φιλοκλέους
ἄρχοντος τοῦ μετὰ Φρασικλῆ κατὰ τὸ δεύτερον ἔτος
τῆς ὀγδοηκοστῆς ὀλυμπιάδος,[6] τὸ μὲν πρῶτον συν-
επαιδεύετο τοῖς ἐπιφανεστάτοις Ἀθηναίων· ἐπεὶ
D δὲ τὴν εἰς Σύβαριν ἀποικίαν τὴν ὕστερον Θουρίους
μετονομασθεῖσαν ἔστελλεν ἡ πόλις, ᾤχετο σὺν τῷ
πρεσβυτάτῳ ἀδελφῶν Πολεμάρχῳ (ἦσαν γὰρ αὐτῷ

---

[1] αὑτοῦ Westermann : αὐτοῦ.
[2] ὑψηλοῦ] ὑψηλοῦ βάθρου Reiske.
[3] ἀντικρὺ Bernardakis : ἀντικρυς.
[4] διαφέροντα Meziriacus : διαφέρων.
[5] δ' added by Westermann.
[6] ὀλυμπιάδος Meursius : καὶ δευτέρας ὀλυμπιάδος.

---

^a A decree of the tribe Pandionis in which the orator

Hermes of Andocides is named after him. It is a dedication of the tribe Aegeïs and is called Hermes of Andocides because Andocides lived near it. He himself supplied the chorus for his tribe [a] when it was competing in a dithyrambic contest, and he gained the victory, for which he set up a tripod on a high spot opposite the limestone Silenus. He is simple and free from artifice in his orations, plain and employing no figures of speech.

III. LYSIAS

Lysias was the son of Cephalus, grandson of Lysanias, and great-grandson of Cephalus. His father was by birth a Syracusan but moved to Athens because he wished to live in that city and also because Pericles, son of Xanthippus, persuaded him to do so, as he was a personal friend of Pericles and they were connected by ties of hospitality, and he was a man of great wealth. But some say that he moved because he was banished from Syracuse when Gelo was tyrant. Lysias was born at Athens in the archonship of the Philocles [b] who succeeded Phrasicles, [c] in the second year of the eightieth Olympiad, and at first he was a schoolmate of the most prominent Athenians; but when the city sent the colony to Sybaris, which was afterwards renamed Thurii, he went out with his eldest brother Polemarchus (for he had two others,

is named among the victorious choregi is extant, *I.G.* ii. 1138 (ed. min.); it was with a chorus of boys at the Dionysia.

[b] 459–458 B.C.

[c] The archon in 460–459 B.C. was Phrasicleides, not Phrasicles.

(835) καὶ ἄλλοι δύο, Εὐθύδημος[1] καὶ Βράχυλλος[2]), τοῦ
πατρὸς ἤδη τετελευτηκότος, ὡς κοινωνήσων τοῦ
κλήρου, ἔτη γεγονὼς πεντεκαίδεκα,[3] ἐπὶ Πραξιτέλους ἄρχοντος, κἀκεῖ διέμεινε παιδευόμενος παρὰ
Τεισίᾳ καὶ Νικίᾳ[4] τοῖς Συρακουσίοις, κτησάμενός
τ' οἰκίαν καὶ κλήρου τυχὼν[5] ἐπολιτεύσατο ἕως
Κλεοκρίτου[6] τοῦ Ἀθήνησιν ἄρχοντος ἔτη ἑξήκοντα[7]
τρία. τῷ δ' ἑξῆς Καλλίᾳ[8] ὀλυμπιάδι ἐνενηκοστῇ
E δευτέρᾳ τῶν κατὰ Σικελίαν συμβάντων Ἀθηναίοις
καὶ κινήσεως γενομένης τῶν τ' ἄλλων συμμάχων
καὶ μάλιστα τῶν τὴν Ἰταλίαν οἰκούντων, αἰτιαθεὶς
ἀττικίζειν ἐξέπεσε μετ' ἄλλων τριακοσίων.[9] παρα-
γενόμενος δ' Ἀθήνησιν ἐπὶ Καλλίου τοῦ μετὰ
Κλεόκριτον ἄρχοντος, ἤδη τῶν τετρακοσίων κατ-

---

[1] Εὐθύδημος Taylor from Plato, *Republic*, 328 B : εὐδιδος.
[2] Βράχυλλος Xylander : βράχιλλος.
[3] πεντεκαίδεκα] ἑξκαιδέκατον Photius.
[4] Νικίᾳ] Spengel suspects a corruption arising from Τισίᾳ.
[5] κλήρου τυχὼν Taylor from Photius : κλήρῳ λαχών.
[6] Κλεοκρίτου Taylor : Κλεάρχου.
[7] ἑξήκοντα] τριάκοντα Taylor.
[8] ἑξῆς Καλλίᾳ] Xylander puts a gap after ἑξῆς ; ἐπὶ Καλλίου
Meziriacus ; ἑξῆς ἐνιαυτῷ Photius, omitting the words to
οἰκούντων inclusive. Westermann doubts if the name Καλλίᾳ
is correct. Bernardakis suggests as giving the proper sense
τῷ δ' ἑξῆς ἐνιαυτῷ ἐπ' ἄρχοντος Καλλίου.
[9] τριακοσίων Xylander : τριων.

---

[a] The scene of Plato's *Republic* is laid at the house of
Cephalus. The dialogue is not historical, and its imagined
date cannot be fixed, but it seems to show that Plato knew
Cephalus and his sons, see Blass, *Die attische Beredsamkeit*,
2nd ed., i. p. 341.

[b] 444–443 B.C.   [c] 413–412 B.C.

Euthydemus and Brachyllus), their father being already dead, to share in the allotment of land.[a] This was in the archonship of Praxiteles,[b] and he was then fifteen years old.[c] He remained there, was instructed by the Syracusans Teisias and Nicias, acquired a house, had a share of the allotment, and was a citizen for thirty-three years, until Cleocritus was archon at Athens.[d] But in the next year, when Callias was archon,[e] in the ninety-second Olympiad, when the misfortunes in Sicily [f] had happened to the Athenians and unrest had arisen among the allies in general and especially those who dwelt in Italy, he was accused of favouring Athens and, with three hundred others, was banished. Arriving at Athens in the archonship of the Callias [g] who succeeded Cleocritus, when the Four Hundred already had possession of the city,[h] he re-

[d] 412–411 b.c. The ninety-second Olympiad is the date of the archonship of another Callias, 406–405 b.c.

[e] The dates given by our author for events in the life of Lysias are consistent (see also 835 a above, and 836 f below, *cf.* also Dion. Hal. *Isocrates*, i.), on the assumption that he went to Thurii when the colony was founded, in 444 b.c. But if that is correct, his activity as a writer of speeches to be delivered in the Athenian courts would not begin until his fifty-seventh year. Blass, *Die attische Beredsamkeit*, 2nd ed., i. p. 345, after stating the evidence, comes to the conclusion that Lysias was born at Athens probably about 446 b.c., the only certain date being his age (fifteen years), when he went to Thurii, and his return to Athens in 413–412 b.c. or the year following. It is quite possible that he did not go to Thurii until some years after the foundation of the colony. The latest of his extant speeches may be dated about 380 b.c., so that we may believe that he died not long after that date.

[f] The great expedition which the Athenians had sent out in 415 b.c. expecting to conquer Sicily was utterly annihilated in the autumn of 413 b.c.

[g] 411–410 b.c.   [h] Summer of 411 b.c.

εχόντων τὴν πόλιν, διέτριβεν αὐτόθι. τῆς δ' ἐν
Αἰγὸς ποταμοῖς ναυμαχίας γενομένης καὶ τῶν
τριάκοντα παραλαβόντων τὴν πόλιν, ἐξέπεσεν ἑπτὰ
ἔτη μείνας, ἀφαιρεθεὶς τὴν οὐσίαν καὶ τὸν ἀδελφὸν
F Πολέμαρχον· αὐτὸς δὲ διαδρὰς ἐκ τῆς οἰκίας ἀμφι-
θύρου οὔσης, ἐν ᾗ ἐφυλάσσετο ὡς ἀπολούμενος,
διῆγεν ἐν Μεγάροις. ἐπιθεμένων δὲ τῶν ἀπὸ
Φυλῆς τῇ καθόδῳ, ἐπεὶ[1] χρησιμώτατος ἁπάντων
ὤφθη, χρήματά τε παρασχὼν δραχμὰς δισχιλίας
καὶ ἀσπίδας διακοσίας πεμφθεὶς τε σὺν Ἑρμᾶνι[2]
ἐπικούρους ἐμισθώσατο τριακοσίους, δύο τ' ἔπεισε
τάλαντα δοῦναι Θρασυδαῖον[3] τὸν Ἠλεῖον, ξένον
αὐτῷ γεγονότα. ἐφ' οἷς γράψαντος αὐτῷ Θρασυ-
βούλου πολιτείαν μετὰ τὴν κάθοδον ἐπ' ἀναρχίας
τῆς πρὸ Εὐκλείδου, ὁ μὲν δῆμος ἐκύρωσε τὴν
δωρεάν, ἀπενεγκαμένου δ' Ἀρχίνου γραφὴν παρα-
836 νόμων διὰ τὸ ἀπροβούλευτον εἰσαχθῆναι, ἑάλω τὸ
ψήφισμα· καὶ οὕτως ἀπελαθεὶς τῆς πολιτείας τὸν
λοιπὸν ᾤκησε χρόνον ἰσοτελὴς ὤν, καὶ ἐτελεύτησεν
αὐτόθι ὀγδοήκοντα τρία ἔτη βιούς, ἢ ὥς τινες ἓξ
καὶ ἑβδομήκοντα, ἢ ὥς τινες ὑπὲρ ὀγδοήκοντα,

---

[1] ἐπεὶ] ἔπειτα Franke; ἐκεῖ Westermann; Bernardakis
would omit ἐπεί.
[2] Ἑρμᾶνι] Ἕρμωνι Westermann. *Cf. Life of Alcibiades*,
chap. xxv., Thuc. viii. 92.
[3] Θρασυδαῖον Photius: θρασύλαιον.

---

[a] 405 b.c. The Athenian fleet was destroyed by the
Lacedaemonians, which virtually ended the Peloponnesian
War. [b] 404 b.c.
[c] See Lysias, xii. (*Against Eratosthenes*) 15.

mained there. But when the battle of Aegospotami [a] had taken place and the Thirty had taken possession of the city, [b] he was banished after having been there seven years. He was deprived of his property and lost his brother Polemarchus, but he himself escaped from the house in which he was kept to be executed (for it had two doors) [c] and lived at Megara. But when the men at Phylê [d] set about their return to Athens, he was seen to be more helpful than anyone else, since he supplied two thousand drachmas and two hundred shields and, when sent with Hermas, hired three hundred mercenaries and persuaded Thrasydaeus of Elis, who had become his guest-friend, to give two talents. For these services Thrasybulus, after the restoration of the exiles to the city and in the period of anarchy [e] before Eucleides, proposed a grant of citizenship for him, and the popular assembly ratified the grant, but when Archinus had him up for illegality because it had not been previously voted by the senate, [f] the enactment was declared void. And after losing his citizenship in this way, he lived the rest of his life at Athens with all the rights of citizenship except the vote and eligibility to office, and died there at the age of eighty-three years or, as some say, seventy-six or, as others

[d] Thrasybulus and his followers, May 303 B.C. After these exiles seized Peiraeus, there was a period of confusion until the democracy was re-established and Eucleides made archon for the year 403-402 B.C.

[e] The Athenians termed any period an "anarchy" in which no archon could be elected because of party strife.

[f] The Senate or Council of Five Hundred prepared the business for the Popular Assembly, which could not legally vote upon any measure not previously adopted by the Senate.

(836) ἰδὼν Δημοσθένη μειράκιον ὄντα. γεννηθῆναι δέ
φασιν ἐπὶ Φιλοκλέους ἄρχοντος.

Φέρονται δ' αὐτοῦ λόγοι τετρακόσιοι εἰκοσιπέντε·
τούτων γνησίους φασὶν οἱ περὶ Διονύσιον καὶ
Καικίλιον εἶναι διακοσίους τριάκοντα καὶ τρεῖς,[1] ἐν
οἷς δὶς μόνον ἡττῆσθαι λέγεται. ἔστι δ' αὐτοῦ
καὶ ὁ[2] ὑπὲρ τοῦ ψηφίσματος ὁ[3] ἐγράψατο Ἀρχῖνος,
B τὴν πολιτείαν αὐτοῦ[4] περιελών,[5] καὶ κατὰ τῶν
τριάκοντα ἕτερος. ἐγένετο δὲ πιθανώτατος καὶ
βραχύτατος, τοῖς ἰδιώταις τοὺς πολλοὺς λόγους
ἐκδούς. εἰσὶ δ' αὐτῷ καὶ Τέχναι ῥητορικαὶ πεποιημέναι καὶ Δημηγορίαι, Ἐπιστολαί τε καὶ Ἐγκώμια,
καὶ Ἐπιτάφιοι καὶ Ἐρωτικοὶ καὶ Σωκράτους
Ἀπολογία ἐστοχασμένη τῶν δικαστῶν. δοκεῖ δὲ
κατὰ τὴν λέξιν εὔκολος εἶναι, δυσμίμητος ὤν.
Δημοσθένης δ' ἐν τῷ κατὰ Νεαίρας λόγῳ ἐραστὴν
αὐτόν φησι γεγονέναι Μετανείρας, ὁμοδούλου τῇ
Νεαίρᾳ· ὕστερον δ' ἔγημε Βραχύλλου τοῦ ἀδελφοῦ
θυγατέρα. μνημονεύει δ' αὐτοῦ καὶ Πλάτων ἐν
C τῷ Φαίδρῳ ὡς δεινοτάτου εἰπεῖν καὶ Ἰσοκράτους
πρεσβυτέρου. ἐποίησε δὲ καὶ εἰς αὐτὸν ἐπίγραμμα
Φιλίσκος ὁ Ἰσοκράτους μὲν γνώριμος ἑταῖρος δὲ

---

[1] καὶ τρεῖς Dübner from Photius: τρία ἔτη codex F;
lacking in the others.
[2] ὁ Taylor: ὄν.   [3] ὁ added by Taylor.
[4] αὐτοῦ Taylor: αὐτῷ.
[5] περιελὼν Taylor: περιέχων.

---

[a] Cicero, *De Oratore*, i. 231, and Diogenes Laertius,
ii. 20, 40, say that Lysias composed an oration in defence
of Socrates, and offered it to him, but Socrates refused it.
A speech in defence of Socrates (ὑπὲρ Σωκράτους πρὸς Πολυ-
κράτην) is mentioned several times by the scholiast on
Aristeides. It was composed probably some years after

say, over eighty ; and he lived to see Demosthenes as a youth. They say he was born in the archonship of Philocles.

Four hundred and twenty-five orations attributed to him are current. Of these Dionysius and Caecilius and their school say that two hundred and thirty-three are genuine, and he is said to have lost his case with only two of them. There is also his speech in support of the enactment against which Archinus brought suit and deprived him of citizenship, and another against the Thirty. He was very persuasive and concise and produced most of his speeches for private clients. There are also Textbooks of Rhetoric prepared by him, and Public Addresses, Letters and Eulogies, Funeral Speeches, Love Speeches, and a Defence of Socrates addressed to the judges.[a] In the matter of his diction he appears to be easy, although in fact he is hard to imitate.[b] Demosthenes in his speech against Neaera[c] says that he was in love with Metaneira, a fellow-slave with Neaera ; but later he married the daughter of his brother Brachyllus. Plato also mentions him in the *Phaedrus*[d] as an able speaker and older than Isocrates. Moreover Philiscus, a pupil of Isocrates and comrade of

the death of Socrates, as an epideictic oration in reply to a similar speech against Socrates by the sophist Polycrates. This is doubtless the speech which Cicero and Diogenes wrongly believed to have been composed for use in the actual trial of Socrates. See Blass, *Die attische Beredsamkeit*, 2nd ed., i. p. 351.

[b] *Cf.* Dionysius of Halicarnassus, 'Αρχαίων κρίσις, v. 1 ὡς ἀναγιγνωσκόμενον μὲν εὔκολον νομίζεσθαι χαλεπὸν δὲ εὑρίσκεσθαι ζηλοῦν πειρωμένοις, " when read he is considered easy, but is found to be difficult by any who try to imitate him."

[c] Demosthenes, Or. lix. 21.

[d] Plato, *Phaedrus*, 279 A.

(836) Λυσίου, δι' οὗ φανερὸν ὡς προέλαβε τοῖς ἔτεσιν, ὃ
καὶ ἐκ τῶν ὑπὸ Πλάτωνος εἰρημένων ἀποδείκνυται·
ἔχει δ' οὕτως·

> νῦν ὦ[1] Καλλιόπης[2] θύγατερ, πολυηγόρε Φρόντι,
> δείξεις εἴ τι φρονεῖς καί τι περισσὸν ἔχεις·
> τὸν γὰρ ἐς ἄλλο σχῆμα μεθαρμοσθέντα καὶ ἄλλοις
> ἐν κόσμοισι βίου σῶμα λαβόνθ' ἕτερον,
> δεῖ σ' ἀρετῆς κήρυκα τεκεῖν τινα Λύσιδα ὑμνεῖν,[3]
> δύντα[4] κατὰ φθιμένων καὶ ζόφου[5] ἀθάνατον·
> ὃς τό τ'[6] ἐμῆς ψυχῆς δείξει[7] φιλέταιρον ἅπασι,
> καὶ τὴν τοῦ φθιμένου πᾶσι βροτοῖς ἀρετήν.

D

συνέγραψε δὲ λόγω[8] καὶ Ἰφικράτει, τὸν μὲν πρὸς
Ἁρμόδιον, τὸν δὲ προδοσίας κρίνοντι Τιμόθεον·
καὶ ἀμφοτέροις[9] ἐνίκα· ἀναδεξαμένου δ' Ἰφικράτους
τὰς τοῦ Τιμοθέου πράξεις, ταῖς εὐθύναις ἀναλαβὼν
τὴν τῆς προδοσίας αἰτίαν ἀπολογεῖται διὰ τοῦ
Λυσίου λόγου· καὶ αὐτὸς μὲν ἀπελύθη, ὁ δὲ Τιμόθεος ἐζημιώθη πλείστοις χρήμασιν. ἀνέγνω δὲ
καὶ ἐν τῇ Ὀλυμπιακῇ πανηγύρει λόγον μέγιστον,
διαλλαγέντας τοὺς Ἕλληνας καταλῦσαι Διονύσιον.

---

[1] νῦν ὦ Jacobs : ὦ.
[2] Καλλιόπης and Φρόντι Wyttenbach : καλλίππης and φρόντιδι.
[3] Λύσιδα ὑμνεῖν Bernardakis ; Λύσιδι ὕμνον Wyttenbach : λυσιδαΐμνον.   [4] δύντα Jacobs : δόντα.
[5] ζόφου Bernardakis : σοφῷ.   [6] τό τ' Wyttenbach : τότ'.
[7] δείξει Brunck : δείξαι.   [8] λόγω Meier : λόγον.
[9] ἀμφοτέροις Reiske : ἀμφοτέρους.

---

[a] Lysis, because the word Lysias is inadmissible in the
Greek metre. Wyttenbach suggests that the verses were
really written in honour of Lysis the Pythagorean.
[b] Bergk, Poet. Lyr. Graec. ii. p. 640. Bergk rightly says
that this is only part of a longer poem. The fragment does
not indicate that Lysias was older than Isocrates, but some

Lysias, composed an elegiac poem to him, from which it is plain that he was earlier in years, which is indicated also by what Plato said. The verses are as follows :

> Now, O Calliopê's daughter endowed with great eloquence,
> Phrontis,
>   Show if thy wisdom is aught, if thou hast anything new.
> Him who is altered and changed to another form, him who
> in other
>   Orders and manners of life hath a new body assumed,
> Thou must bring forth some herald of virtue to celebrate:
> Lysis [a]
>   Gone to the dead and the gloom, there an immortal to
>   dwell :
> One who will show unto all the love of my soul for my
> comrade,
>   Show, too, the worth of the dead unto the whole of
>   mankind. [b]

He also wrote two speeches for Iphicrates, one against Harmodius, the other for use in accusing Timotheüs of treason, with both of which he won his case ; but when Iphicrates accepted the responsibility for the actions of Timotheüs,[c] assuming at the rendering of accounts the accusation for treason, he defended himself with the speech by Lysias ; and he himself was acquitted, but Timotheüs was very heavily fined. And at the Olympic festival also he read a very great oration urging that the Greeks make peace with one another and overthrow Dionysius.[d]

such statement may have been contained in a later part of the poem.
   [c] In 355 B.C. Iphicrates and Timotheüs, Athenian generals who had been unsuccessful, were accused by their colleague, Chares, of treason. Although Iphicrates accepted full responsibility, he was acquitted, but Timotheüs was fined one hundred talents, which he could not pay. He left Athens and soon died.
   [d] Only a fragment (Or. xxxiii.) of this is extant.

E

Δ΄. ΙΣΟΚΡΑΤΗΣ

Ἰσοκράτης Θεοδώρου μὲν ἦν παῖς τοῦ Ἐρ-
χιέως¹ τῶν μετρίων πολιτῶν, θεράποντας αὐλο-
ποιοὺς κεκτημένου καὶ εὐπορήσαντος ἀπὸ τούτων,
ὡς καὶ χορηγῆσαι καὶ παιδεῦσαι τοὺς υἱούς· ἦσαν
γὰρ αὐτῷ καὶ ἄλλοι, Τελέσιππος καὶ Διόμνηστος·
ἦν δὲ καὶ θυγάτριον· ὅθεν εἰς τοὺς αὐλοὺς κεκωμῴ-
F δηται ὑπ' Ἀριστοφάνους καὶ Στράττιδος. γενόμενος δὲ κατὰ τὴν ὀγδοηκοστὴν ἕκτην ὀλυμπιάδα
Λυσιμάχου Μυρρινουσίου ἄρχοντος, νεώτερος μὲν
Λυσίου² δυσὶ καὶ εἴκοσιν ἔτεσι, πρεσβύτερος δὲ
Πλάτωνος ἑπτά, παῖς μὲν ὢν ἐπαιδεύετο οὐδενὸς
ἧττον Ἀθηναίων, ἀκροώμενος Προδίκου τε τοῦ
Κείου³ καὶ Γοργίου τοῦ Λεοντίνου καὶ Τεισίου τοῦ
Συρακουσίου καὶ Θηραμένους τοῦ ῥήτορος· οὗ καὶ
συλλαμβανομένου ὑπὸ τῶν τριάκοντα καὶ φυγόντος
ἐπὶ τὴν Βουλαίαν Ἑστίαν, ἁπάντων καταπεπληγ-
μένων, μόνος ἀνέστη βοηθήσων καὶ πολὺν χρόνον
837 ἐσίγησε κατ' ἀρχάς, ἔπειτα ὑπ' αὐτοῦ παρῃτήθη,
εἰπόντος ὀδυνηρότερον αὐτῷ συμβήσεσθαι, εἴ τις
τῶν φίλων ἀπολαύσει τῆς συμφορᾶς· καὶ ἐκείνου
τινὰς οὔσας τέχνας αὐτῷ φασι συμπραγματεύσα-

---

¹ Ἐρχιέως Reiske from Photius : ἀρχιερέως.
² Λυσιμάχου Μυρρινουσίου ἄρχοντος νεώτερος μὲν Λυσίου
Bernardakis adapting an emendation by Wolf : λυσιμάχου
μυρρινουσίου.
³ Κείου Turnebus : κίου.

ᵃ Wealthy Athenians performed in turn special services
to the state called " liturgies." The most expensive of these
was the choregy, which involved the payment, training, and
equipment of a chorus for a lyrical or dramatic performance.

IV. ISOCRATES

Isocrates was the son of Theodorus of Erchia, a citizen of the middle class, an owner of slaves who made flutes, through whom he gained a competence, so that he paid for a public chorus[a] and gave his children an education[b] (for he had other sons, Telesippus and Diomnestus, and also a daughter), and hence he is ridiculed on account of the flutes by Aristophanes and Strattis. Isocrates was born in the eighty-sixth Olympiad, in the archonship of Lysimachus[c] of Myrrhinus, being twenty-two years younger than Lysias and seven years older than Plato.[d] In his boyhood he was as well educated as any Athenian, for he attended the lectures of Prodicus of Ceos, Gorgias of Leontini, Teisias of Syracuse, and the orator Theramenes ; and when the last-named was in danger of being arrested by the Thirty and had fled for safety to the altar of Hestia Boulaea,[e] everyone else was terrified, but Isocrates alone arose to speak in his aid; and at first he was silent for a long time, then afterwards he was urged to be silent by Theramenes himself, who said that his misfortune would be more painful if any of his friends should share it. And it is said that certain rhetorical teachings of Theramenes—those which go under the name of Boton—were of use to Isocrates when he was

[b] See Isocrates, *On the Exchange of Property* (Or. xv.), 161.

[c] 436–435 B.C.

[d] Plato was born in 428–427 B.C. Lysias, according to this statement, in 459–458. But see note on 835 D above.

[e] The sanctuary of this Goddess of the Senate's Hearth was in or near the Prytaneum, which was somewhere on the northern slope of the Acropolis.

(837) σθαι ἡνίκα ἐν τοῖς δικαστηρίοις ἐσυκοφαντεῖτο, αἵ
εἰσιν ἐπιγεγραμμέναι Βότωνος. ἐπεὶ δ' ἠνδρώθη,
τῶν μὲν πολιτικῶν πραγμάτων ἀπέσχετο ἰσχνό-
φωνός τ' ὢν καὶ εὐλαβὴς τὸν τρόπον καὶ τὰ πατρῷα
ἀποβεβληκὼς ἐν τῷ πρὸς Λακεδαιμονίους πολέμῳ·
ἄλλοις δὲ μεμελετηκὼς[1] φαίνεται, ἕνα δὲ μόνον
εἰπὼν λόγον, τὸν περὶ τῆς Ἀντιδόσεως. διατριβὴν
B δὲ συστησάμενος, ἐπὶ τὸ φιλοσοφεῖν καὶ γράφειν
ἃ διανοηθείη[2] ἐτράπετο, καὶ τόν τε Πανηγυρικὸν
λόγον καὶ τινας ἄλλους τῶν συμβουλευτικῶν, οὓς
μὲν αὐτὸς γράφων ἀνεγίνωσκεν οὓς δ' ἑτέροις
παρεσκεύαζεν, ἡγούμενος οὕτως ἐπὶ τὸ τὰ δέοντα
φρονεῖν τοὺς Ἕλληνας προτρέψεσθαι.[3] διαμαρτάνων
δὲ τῆς προαιρέσεως, τούτων μὲν ἀπέστη σχολῆς δ'
ἡγεῖτο, ὥς τινές φασι, πρῶτον ἐπὶ Χίου, μαθητὰς
ἔχων ἐννέα· ὅτε καὶ ἰδὼν τὸν μισθὸν ἀριθμούμενον
εἶπε δακρύσας ὡς " ἐπέγνων ἐμαυτὸν νῦν τούτοις
πεπραμένον." ὡμίλει δὲ τοῖς βουλομένοις, χωρίσας
πρῶτος τοὺς ἐριστικοὺς λόγους τῶν πολιτικῶν, περὶ
C οὓς ἐσπούδασε. καὶ ἀρχὰς δὲ καὶ περὶ τὴν Χίον
κατέστησε καὶ τὴν αὐτὴν τῇ πατρίδι πολιτείαν·
ἀργύριόν τε ὅσον οὐδεὶς σοφιστῶν εὐπόρησεν, ὡς
καὶ τριηραρχῆσαι.

Ἀκροαταὶ δ' αὐτοῦ ἐγένοντο εἰς ἑκατόν, ἄλλοι
τε[4] πολλοὶ καὶ Τιμόθεος ὁ Κόνωνος, σὺν ᾧ καὶ

---

[1] μεμελετηκὼς Wolf: μεμαρτυρηκὼς.
[2] ἃ διανοηθείη Wolf from Dionysius: διανοηθείς.
[3] προτρέψεσθαι Coraes: προτρέψασθαι.
[4] τε Franke from Photius: δὲ.

falsely accused in the courts. But when he became
a man he kept away from political affairs, since he had
a weak voice and a timid disposition[a] and had lost his
inherited property in the war against the Lacedaemonians. It is evident that he composed speeches
for others, but he delivered only one, that on the
Exchange of Property. He set up a school and turned
to philosophy and to writing out the results of his
thinking, and he composed his Festival Oration[b] and
some others of an advisory nature, some of which he
delivered himself and some of which he prepared for
others to deliver, hoping that in this way he might
lead the Greeks to think as they ought. But when
he failed of his purpose he gave up that sort of thing
and became the head of a school, at first, as some say,
at Chios, where he had nine pupils. That was the
time when, as he saw the tuition fees counted out,
he burst into tears and said, "Now I recognize that I
have sold myself to these people." He would carry
on conversation with all who desired it and was the
first to make a distinction between contentious
speeches and those of a political character, to which
latter he devoted himself. And he also instituted at
Chios public offices and the same constitution which
existed in his native city. He made more money
than any other sophist, so that he was even a trierarch.[c]

His pupils numbered about one hundred, including
among many others Timotheüs, son of Conon, with

[a] See Isocrates, *Philip* (Or. v.), 81; *Panathenaic* (Or.
xii.), 9.
[b] *i.e.* the *Panegyric*, delivered at Olympia.
[c] The trierarchy was one of the "liturgies" which wealthy
citizens were obliged to perform. Being trierarch thus
showed wealth.

(837) πολλὰς πόλεις ἐπῆλθε, συντιθεὶς τὰς πρὸς Ἀθη
ναίους ὑπὸ Τιμοθέου πεμπομένας ἐπιστολάς· ὅθεν
ἐδωρήσατο αὐτῷ τάλαντον τῶν ἀπὸ Σάμου περι
γενομένων. ἐμαθήτευσε δ' αὐτῷ καὶ[1] Θεόπομπος
ὁ Χῖος, καὶ Ἔφορος ὁ Κυμαῖος καὶ Ἀσκληπιάδης
ὁ τὰ τραγῳδούμενα συγγράψας καὶ Θεοδέκτας[2] ὁ
Φασηλίτης ὁ τὰς τραγῳδίας ὕστερον γράψας, οὗ
ἐστι τὸ μνῆμα ἐπὶ τὴν Κυαμῖτιν πορευομένοις κατὰ
D τὴν ἱερὰν ὁδὸν τὴν ἐπ' Ἐλευσῖνα, τὰ νῦν κατ
ερηρειμμένον· ἔνθα καὶ τοὺς ἐνδόξους τῶν ποιη
τῶν ἀνέστησαν[3] σὺν αὐτῷ, ὧν Ὅμηρος ὁ ποιητὴς
σῴζεται μόνος· Λεωδάμας[4] τ' Ἀθηναῖος καὶ Λά
κριτος ὁ νομοθέτης Ἀθηναίοις, ὡς δέ τινές φασι
καὶ Ὑπερείδης καὶ Ἰσαῖος. καὶ Δημοσθένη[5] δ' ἔτι
ῥητορεύοντί φασι μετὰ σπουδῆς προσελθεῖν αὐτῷ,
καὶ χιλίας μὲν ἃς[6] εἰσεπράττετο οὐκ ἔχειν φάναι
παρασχεῖν, διακοσίας δὲ δώσειν, ἐφ' ᾧ τε τὸ
πέμπτον μέρος ἐκμαθεῖν[7]· τὸν δ' ἀποκρίνασθαι ὡς
E " οὐ τεμαχίζομεν, ὦ Δημόσθενες, τὴν πραγματείαν·
ὥσπερ δὲ τοὺς καλοὺς ἰχθῦς ὅλους πωλοῦμεν, οὕτω
κἀγώ σοι, εἰ βούλοιο μαθητεύειν, ὁλόκληρον ἀπο
δώσομαι τὴν τέχνην."

Ἐτελεύτα δ' ἐπὶ Χαιρώνδου[8] ἄρχοντος, ἀπαγγελ
θέντων τῶν περὶ Χαιρώνειαν ἐν τῇ Ἱπποκράτους

---

[1] καὶ] Ξενοφῶν ὁ Γρύλλου καὶ Photius.
[2] Θεοδέκτας Capps, cf. I.G. ii.² 2325 b: Θεοδέκτης.
[3] ἀνέστησαν Westermann: ἀνέστησε.
[4] Λεωδάμας Westermann and inscriptions; cf. Kirchner,
Prosop. Att.; Λαοδάμας Photius: Λεώδαμος.
[5] Dübner: Δημοσθένην or Δημοσθένης.
[6] μὲν ἃς Coraes: μὲν ἃς μόνας.
[7] ἐκμαθεῖν Photius: ἐκμάθῃ.
[8] Χαιρώνδου Meursius: χερωνίδου.

whom he visited many cities ; and he composed the
letters which Timotheüs sent to the Athenians, on
account of which Timotheüs presented him with a
talent out of the sum remaining after the relief
of Samos.[a]   Pupils of his were also Theopompus [b] of
Chios, Ephorus of Cumae, Asclepiades who compiled the arguments of tragedies, and Theodectas of
Phaselis, who afterwards wrote tragedies and whose
monument stood as you go to the Bean-market along
the Sacred Way which leads to Eleusis ; it is now in
ruins.   There, too, were set up statues of the famous
poets along with his ; of these only the poet Homer
exists now.   And Leodamas the Athenian and
Lacritus the Athenian law-maker and, as some say,
Hypereides and Isaeus were his pupils.   And they
say that while he was still teaching oratory Demosthenes came to him eager to learn and said that he
could not pay the thousand drachmas which he asked
as tuition fee, but would give two hundred for one
fifth of the instruction ; whereupon Isocrates replied :
" We do not cut our instruction into bits, Demosthenes, but just as people sell fine fish whole, so, if
you wish to be my pupil, I will sell you my course
whole."

He died in the archonship of Chaerondas [c] after
hearing in the palaestra of Hippocrates the news of

[a] 365 B.C.
[b] The text of Photius reads Xenophon the son of Gryllus
and Theopompus.
[c] 338–337 B.C.

παλαίστρᾳ πυθόμενος, ἐξαγαγὼν αὑτὸν τοῦ βίου
τέτταρσιν[1] ἡμέραις διὰ τοῦ σιτίων ἀποσχέσθαι,
προειπὼν τρεῖς ἀρχὰς δραμάτων Εὐριπίδου

Δαναὸς ὁ πεντήκοντα θυγατέρων πατήρ·

Πέλοψ ὁ Ταντάλειος εἰς Πῖσαν μολών·

Σιδώνιόν ποτ᾽ ἄστυ Κάδμος ἐκλιπών·

F ὀκτὼ καὶ ἐνενήκοντα ἔτη βιοὺς ἢ ὥς τινες ἑκατόν,
οὐχ ὑπομείνας τετράκις ἰδεῖν τὴν Ἑλλάδα καταδου-
λουμένην· πρὸ ἐνιαυτοῦ ἢ ὥς τινες πρὸ τεσσάρων
ἐτῶν[2] τῆς τελευτῆς συγγράψας τὸν Παναθηναϊκόν.
τὸν δὲ Πανηγυρικὸν ἔτεσι δέκα συνέθηκεν, οἱ δὲ
δεκαπέντε λέγουσιν, ὃν μετενηνοχέναι ἐκ τῶν[3] Γοργίου τοῦ Λεοντίνου καὶ Λυσίου· τὸν δὲ περὶ τῆς
Ἀντιδόσεως δύο καὶ ὀγδοήκοντα ἔτη γεγονώς· τοὺς
δὲ πρὸς Φίλιππον ὀλίγῳ πρότερον τοῦ θανάτου.
838 ἐγένετο δ᾽ αὐτῷ καὶ παῖς Ἀφαρεὺς πρεσβύτῃ ὄντι

---

[1] τέτταρσιν Bernardakis : τέτρασιν.
[2] ἐτῶν Turnebus : τῶν.   [3] ἐκ τῶν Reiske : ἐκ τοῦ.

---

[a] This popular story of Isocrates' death is given also by
Lucian (?), *Macrobioi* 23, Pausanias, i. 18. 8, and Plutarch,
838 below. It is made famous by Milton in his tenth sonnet:

> . . . as that dishonest victory
> At Chaeronea, fatal to liberty,
> Killed by report that old man eloquent.

But Isocrates himself, at the end of his third letter, writes
to Philip: "But I am grateful to old age for this thing only,
that it has continued my life to this point, so that of the
things which I meditated in my youth and undertook to
write in my *Panegyric Oration* and in that which I sent to
you, I now see some being accomplished through your deeds
and hope that others will be accomplished." Apparently he
was well pleased with Philip's success. See Blass, *Die
attische Beredsamkeit*, 2nd ed., ii. p. 97.

the battle of Chaeroneia ; [a] and he removed himself
from life by abstaining from food for four days. Just
before the end he declaimed the opening lines of
three dramas of Euripides :

> Danaüs of fifty daughters fair the sire, [b]
> Pelops the Tantalid to Pisa came, [c]
> Once Sidon's city Cadmus having left. [d]

He died at the age of ninety-eight or, as some say,
one hundred years, for he could not endure the sight
of Greece enslaved four times. [e] A year (or, as some
say, four years) before his end he wrote the Panathenaic Oration ; [f] and the Festival Oration he composed ten (but some say fifteen) years before his
death. This, they say, he derived from the speeches
of Gorgias of Leontini and Lysias. The speech on the
Exchange of Property [g] he wrote at the age of eighty-
two years, and those against Philip shortly before
his death. When he was an old man he adopted

---

[b] From the *Archelaüs* ; Nauck, *Trag. Graec. Frag.* p. 427,
no. 228.

[c] *Iphigeneia in Tauris*, 1.

[d] From the *Phrixus* ; Nauck, *Trag. Graec. Frag.* p. 627,
no. 819. Blass, *Die attische Beredsamkeit*, 2nd ed., ii. p. 97,
thinks these lines enumerate three intrusions of foreigners into
Greece. The fourth—not mentioned—would then be that
of the Macedonians under Philip.

[e] Under the Athenian empire in the fifth century, by the
Spartans after the Peloponnesian War, by the Thebans under
Epameinondas, and by the Macedonians. All these Isocrates
himself had seen. But see note *d* above.

[f] In L.C.L. Isocrates, vol. ii. pp. 368 ff.

[g] *Ibid.* pp. 181 ff. If anyone proposed that a certain man
be obliged to perform one of the " liturgies " which were
required of wealthy Athenians, the man of whom this was
required could challenge the proposer to an exchange of
properties, which might transfer the obligation.

(838) ἐκ Πλαθάνης τῆς Ἱππίου τοῦ ῥήτορος ποιητός, τῶν
δὲ τῆς γυναικὸς τριῶν παίδων ὁ νεώτατος. εὐπόρησε δ'¹ ἱκανῶς οὐ μόνον ἀργύριον εἰσπράττων
τοὺς γνωρίμους, ἀλλὰ καὶ παρὰ² Νικοκλέους τοῦ
Κυπρίων βασιλέως, ὃς ἦν υἱὸς Εὐαγόρου, εἴκοσι
τάλαντα λαβὼν ὑπὲρ τοῦ πρὸς αὐτὸν γραφέντος
λόγου· ἐφ' οἷς φθονηθεὶς τρὶς προεβλήθη τριηραρχεῖν,³ καὶ δὶς⁴ μὲν ἀσθένειαν σκηψάμενος διὰ
τοῦ παιδὸς παρῃτήσατο, τὸ δὲ τρίτον ὑποστὰς⁵ ἀν-
ήλωσεν οὐκ ὀλίγα. πρὸς δὲ τὸν εἰπόντα πατέρα ὡς
οὐδὲν ἀλλ' ἢ ἀνδράποδον συνέπεμψε τῷ παιδίῳ
"τοιγαροῦν" ἔφη "ἄπιθι· δύο γὰρ ἀνθ' ἑνὸς ἕξεις
B ἀνδράποδα." ἠγωνίσατο δὲ καὶ τὸν ἐπὶ Μαυσώλῳ
τεθέντα ὑπ' Ἀρτεμισίας ἀγῶνα· τὸ δ' ἐγκώμιον
οὐ σῴζεται. ἐποίησε δὲ καὶ εἰς Ἑλένην ἐγκώμιον
καὶ Ἀρεοπαγιτικόν. ἐξελθεῖν δὲ τοῦ βίου οἱ μὲν
ἐναταῖόν φασι σίτων ἀποσχόμενον, οἱ δὲ τεταρταῖον
ἅμα ταῖς ταφαῖς τῶν ἐν Χαιρωνείᾳ πεσόντων.
συνέγραψε δ' αὐτοῦ καὶ ὁ παῖς Ἀφαρεὺς λόγους.
ἐτάφη δὲ μετὰ τῆς συγγενείας πλησίον Κυνοσάρ-
γους ἐπὶ τοῦ λόφου ἐν⁶ ἀριστερᾷ αὐτός⁷ τε καὶ ὁ
πατὴρ αὐτοῦ Θεόδωρος καὶ ἡ μήτηρ αὐτοῦ· ταύτης
τ' ἀδελφὴ τηθὶς τοῦ ῥήτορος Ἀνακὼ καὶ ὁ ποιητὸς
C υἱὸς Ἀφαρεὺς καὶ ὁ ἀνεψιὸς αὐτοῦ Σωκράτης,

---

¹ εὐπόρησε δ' Coraes with Photius : εὐπόρησεν.
² παρὰ Coraes with Photius : τὰ παρά.
³ τριηραρχεῖν Photius ; τριήραρχος Turnebus : τριήρας.
⁴ καὶ δὶς Meziriacus with Photius : καὶ τὸ δίς.
⁵ ὑποστὰς Coraes : ἀναστάς.
⁶ ἐν added by Turnebus.
⁷ αὐτός Reiske : ὁ υἱός.

Aphareus, the youngest of the three sons of Plathanê, daughter of the orator Hippias. He acquired ample wealth, for he not only collected money from his pupils, but he also received from Nicocles, king of Cyprus, who was the son of Evagoras, twenty talents for the oration written in his honour. On account of his wealth he was envied and was proposed three times as trierarch. Twice he alleged illness and was exempted by petitions presented by his son, but the third time he undertook the duty and spent no small sum. To a father who said that he gave his son only a slave as companion he said, "Go your ways, then, for you will have two slaves instead of one." He took part also in the competition offered by Artemisia in honour of Maussolus,[a] but his Eulogy is not extant. He wrote also a Eulogy of Helen and a speech called the Areopagitic. He departed this life some say on the ninth day of his abstention from food, others on the fourth day at the time of the funeral of those who fell at Chaeroneia. His son Aphareus also wrote speeches. Isocrates was buried with his family near Cynosarges[b] on the left side of the hill—he himself, his father Theodorus, and his mother ; and her sister Anaco, the orator's aunt, and his adopted son Aphareus, and his cousin Socrates, son of Anaco

[a] Mausolus ruler of Halicarnassus, died in 353 B.C. His widow, Artemisia, caused eulogies to be written in competition by Greek orators and completed the magnificent tomb which he had, apparently, begun. This magnificent building —the Mausoleum—was designed by Greek architects and decorated by famous Greek sculptors. The remains of the sculpture include portrait statues of Maussolus and Artemisia and are among the most highly prized possessions of the British Museum.

[b] Cynosarges was a region in Athens in which was a great gymnasium.

(838) μητρὸς Ἰσοκράτους ἀδελφῆς Ἀνακοῦς υἱὸς[1] ὤν, ὅ
τ᾽ ἀδελφὸς αὐτοῦ ὁμώνυμος τοῦ πατρὸς Θεόδωρος
καὶ οἱ υἱωνοὶ αὐτοῦ, τοῦ ποιηθέντος αὐτῷ παιδὸς
Ἀφαρέως, Ἀφαρεὺς καὶ ὁ τούτου πατὴρ Θεόδωρος
ἥ τε γυνὴ Πλαθάνη, μήτηρ δὲ τοῦ ποιητοῦ Ἀφαρέως.[2] ἐπὶ μὲν οὖν τούτων τράπεζαι ἐπῆσαν ἕξ, αἱ
νῦν οὐ σῴζονται· αὐτῷ δ᾽ Ἰσοκράτει ἐπὶ τοῦ μνή-
ματος ἐπῆν κίων[3] τριάκοντα πηχῶν, ἐφ᾽ οὗ σειρὴν
πηχῶν ἑπτὰ συμβολικῶς, ὃς νῦν οὐ σῴζεται. ἦν δὲ
D καὶ αὐτοῦ τράπεζα πλησίον ἔχουσα ποιητάς τε
καὶ τοὺς διδασκάλους αὐτοῦ, ἐν οἷς καὶ Γοργίαν
εἰς σφαῖραν ἀστρολογικὴν βλέποντα αὐτόν τε τὸν
Ἰσοκράτην παρεστῶτα. ἀνάκειται δ᾽ αὐτοῦ καὶ ἐν
Ἐλευσῖνι εἰκὼν χαλκῆ ἔμπροσθεν τοῦ προστῴου
ὑπὸ Τιμοθέου τοῦ Κόνωνος, καὶ ἐπιγέγραπται

> Τιμόθεος φιλίας τε χάριν ξύνεσίν[4] τε προτιμῶν
> Ἰσοκράτους εἰκὼ τήνδ᾽ ἀνέθηκε θεαῖς·

Λεωχάρους ἔργον.

Φέρονται δ᾽ αὐτοῦ λόγοι ἑξήκοντα, ὧν εἰσι
γνήσιοι κατὰ μὲν Διονύσιον εἰκοσιπέντε κατὰ δὲ
Καικίλιον εἰκοσιοκτώ, οἱ δ᾽ ἄλλοι κατεψευσμένοι.
εἶχε δ᾽ ἀλλοτρίως πρὸς ἐπίδειξιν, ὡς ἀφικομένων
E ποτὲ πρὸς αὐτὸν τριῶν ἐπὶ τὴν ἀκρόασιν τοὺς μὲν
δύο κατασχεῖν τὸν δὲ τρίτον ἀπολῦσαι, φάμενος εἰς
τὴν ἐπιοῦσαν ἥξειν· νῦν γὰρ αὐτῷ τὸ θέατρον εἶναι
ἐν ἀκροατηρίῳ.[5] εἰώθει δὲ καὶ πρὸς τοὺς γνωρίμους
αὐτοῦ λέγειν, ὡς αὐτὸς μὲν δέκα μνῶν διδάσκοι,
τῷ δ᾽ αὐτὸν διδάξαντι τόλμαν καὶ εὐφωνίαν δώσειν

---

[1] Ἀνακοῦς υἱὸς Turnebus: ἀνακούσιος.
[2] Ἀφαρεὺς . . . τοῦ ποιητοῦ Ἀφαρέως bracketed by Dübner; Bernardakis marks a lacuna after Ἀφαρεὺς.

Isocrates' mother's sister, and his brother Theodorus who had the same name as his father, and his grandsons, the sons of his adopted son Aphareus, Aphareus and his father Theodorus, and the latter's wife Plathanê, mother of the adopted son Aphareus. And over them there were six tablets which do not now exist. On the monument of Isocrates himself was a column thirty cubits high, on which was a siren seven cubits high as a symbol; but this exists no longer. There was also a tablet near by with poets and his instructors on it, among whom was Gorgias gazing into an astrological sphere and Isocrates standing beside him. There is also a bronze statue of him, dedicated by Timotheüs, son of Conon, at Eleusis in front of the vestibule. It bears this inscription :

Here to the goddesses twain Timotheüs giveth this statue
Tribute to friend and to sage, image of Isocrates.

It is a work of Leochares.

Sixty orations are current under his name, of which twenty-five are genuine according to Dionysius, twenty-eight according to Caecilius, and the rest are spurious. He was averse to public declamation, so much so that once, when three persons came to hear him, he retained two but let the third go, telling him to come the next day, since now the lecture-room had a full audience. And he used to say to his pupils that he himself gave instruction for ten minas, but would give ten thousand to anyone who would teach him self-confidence and a pleasant voice. And when he

---

³ κίων Bernardakis : κριῶν (κιών Turnebus).
⁴ ξύνεσιν Dübner : ξενίην.
⁵ ἀκροατηρίῳ Wolf : ἀκρωτηρίῳ.

δεκακισχιλίας. καὶ πρὸς τὸν ἐρόμενον διὰ τί οὐκ
ὢν αὐτὸς ἱκανὸς ἄλλους ποιεῖ, εἶπεν ὅτι καὶ αἱ
ἀκόναι αὐταὶ μὲν τέμνειν[1] οὐ δύνανται τὸν δὲ
F σίδηρον τμητικὸν ποιοῦσιν. εἰσὶ δ' οἳ καὶ τέχνας
αὐτὸν λέγουσι συγγεγραφέναι, οἱ δ' οὐ μεθόδῳ ἀλλ'
ἀσκήσει χρήσασθαι. πολίτην δ' οὐδέποτ' εἰσέπραξε
μισθόν. προσέταττε δὲ τοῖς γνωρίμοις εἰς τὰς
ἐκκλησίας ἀπαντῶσιν ἀναφέρειν αὐτῷ τὰ εἰρημένα.
ἐλυπήθη δὲ καὶ οὐ μετρίως ἐπὶ τῷ Σωκράτους
θανάτῳ καὶ μελανειμονῶν τῇ ὑστεραίᾳ προῆλθε.
πάλιν δ' ἐρομένου τινὸς αὐτὸν τί ῥητορική, εἶπε
" τὰ μὲν μικρὰ μεγάλα τὰ δὲ μεγάλα μικρὰ
ποιεῖν." ἑστιώμενος δέ ποτε παρὰ Νικοκρέοντι
τῷ Κύπρου τυράννῳ, προτρεπομένων αὐτὸν τῶν
παρόντων διαλεχθῆναι, ἔφη " οἷς μὲν ἐγὼ δεινὸς
οὐχ ὁ νῦν καιρός, οἷς δ' ὁ νῦν καιρὸς οὐκ ἐγὼ
δεινός." Σοφοκλέα δὲ τὸν τραγικὸν θεασάμενος
ἑπόμενον ἐρωτικῶς παιδί, εἶπεν " οὐ μόνον δεῖ,
839 Σοφόκλεις, τὰς χεῖρας ἔχειν παρ' αὑτῷ, ἀλλὰ καὶ
τοὺς ὀφθαλμούς." τοῦ δὲ Κυμαίου Ἐφόρου ἀ-
πράκτου τῆς σχολῆς ἐξελθόντος καὶ πάλιν ὑπὸ τοῦ
πατρὸς Δημοφίλου πεμφθέντος ἐπὶ δευτέρῳ μισθῷ,
παίζων Δίφορον[2] αὐτὸν ἐκάλει· ἐσπούδασε μέντοι
ἱκανῶς περὶ τὸν ἄνδρα καὶ τὴν ὑπόθεσιν τῆς χρείας
αὐτὸς ὑπεθήκατο. ἐγένετο δὲ καὶ πρὸς τὰ ἀφροδίσια καταφερής, ὡς ὑποπάστῳ παρειλκυσμένῳ
ἐν τῇ κοίτῃ χρῆσθαι, κρόκῳ διάβροχον ἔχοντα τὸ

---

[1] Coraes from Photius : τεμεῖν.
[2] Δίφορον Amyot : δίφρον.

---

[a] Cf. Moralia, 613 A.
[b] Attributed to Pericles by Plutarch, Life of Pericles,
chap. viii., and Cicero, De Officiis, i. 40. 144.

was asked how he, not being a good speaker himself, could make others so, he replied that whetstones cannot themselves be cut, but make iron fit to do so. Some say that he also wrote textbooks of oratory, others that in his teaching he made use of practice, not of method. He never demanded a fee from a fellow-citizen. When his pupils went to meetings of the assembly, he told them to report to him what was said there. He was greatly grieved by the death of Socrates, and the next day he appeared in black clothing. And again, when someone asked him " What is oratory ? " he said, " the art of making small things great and great things small." And once when he was a guest at a banquet in the house of Nicocreon, despot of Cyprus, and some of those present urged him to discourse, he said, " for subjects in which I am competent this is not the time ; in the subjects for which this is the time I am not competent." [a] When he saw the tragic poet Sophocles amorously following a boy, he said, " Sophocles, we must not only keep our hands to ourselves, but our eyes as well." [b] And when Ephorus of Cumae had left his school without learning anything and had been sent back by his father with a second tuition-fee, he called him in fun Diphorus (Twice-bringer) ; he took, however, great pains with him and even suggested to him the subject of his work.[c] He showed himself also prone to sexual indulgence ; he used an additional mattress beside him on his bed and kept his

---

[c] The great work of Ephorus was a history of the world (primarily of Greece) from the return of the Heracleidae to the siege of Perinthus in 340 B.C. From this work Plutarch and others derived much of their information. Ephorus was born early in the fourth century and died about 320 B.C.

(839) προσκεφάλαιον. καὶ νέον μὲν ὄντα μὴ γῆμαι,

B γηράσαντα δ' ἑταίρᾳ συνεῖναι ᾗ ὄνομα ἦν Λαγίσκη,
ἐξ ἧς ἔσχε θυγάτριον ὃ γενόμενον ἐτῶν δώδεκα πρὸ
γάμων ἐτελεύτησεν. ἔπειτα Πλαθάνην τὴν Ἱππίου
τοῦ ῥήτορος γυναῖκα ἠγάγετο τρεῖς παῖδας ἔχουσαν,
ὧν τὸν Ἀφαρέα ὡς προείρηται ἐποιήσατο, ὃς καὶ
εἰκόνα αὐτοῦ χαλκῆν ἀνέθηκε πρὸς τῷ Ὀλυμπιείῳ[1]
ἐπὶ κίονος καὶ ἐπέγραψεν

> Ἰσοκράτους Ἀφαρεὺς πατρὸς εἰκόνα τήνδ'
>   ἀνέθηκε
> Ζηνί, θεούς τε σέβων καὶ γονέων ἀρετήν.

C λέγεται δὲ καὶ κελητίσαι[2] ἔτι παῖς ὤν· ἀνάκειται
γὰρ ἐν ἀκροπόλει χαλκοῦς ἐν τῇ σφαιρίστρᾳ τῶν
Ἀρρηφόρων κελητίζων[3] ἔτι παῖς ὤν, ὡς εἶπόν
τινες. δύο δ' ἐν ἅπαντι τῷ βίῳ συνέστησαν αὐτῷ
ἀγῶνες· πρότερος μὲν εἰς ἀντίδοσιν προκαλεσαμένου αὐτὸν Μεγακλείδου, πρὸς ὃν οὐκ ἀπήντησε
διὰ νόσον, τὸν δ' υἱὸν πέμψας Ἀφαρέα ἐνίκησε·
δεύτερος δὲ Λυσιμάχου αὐτὸν προκαλεσαμένου περὶ
τριηραρχίας εἰς ἀντίδοσιν· ἡττηθεὶς δὲ τὴν τριηρ-
αρχίαν ὑπέστη. ἦν δ' αὐτοῦ καὶ γραπτὴ εἰκὼν ἐν
τῷ Πομπείῳ. ὁ δ' Ἀφαρεὺς συνέγραψε μὲν λόγους
οὐ πολλοὺς δέ, δικανικούς τε καὶ συμβουλευτικούς·
ἐποίησε δὲ καὶ τραγῳδίας περὶ ἑπτὰ καὶ τριάκοντα,

---

[1] Ὀλυμπιείῳ Wyttenbach: ὀλυμπίῳ ὡς.
[2] κελητίσαι Turnebus: κερητίσαι.
[3] κελητίζων Turnebus: κερητίζων.

---

[a] Bergk, *Poet. Lyr. Graec.* ii. p. 329. The column and
statue existed in the time of Pausanias (Paus. i. 18. 8). A
bust in the Villa Albani in Rome may be a late copy of the
head of this statue or, more probably, since Leochares was a
famous sculptor, of the statue at Eleusis mentioned above.

pillow wet with saffron. And when he was young he did not marry, but in his old age he kept a mistress named Lagiscê, by whom he had a daughter who died unmarried at twelve years of age. Then he married the daughter of the orator Hippias, Plathanê, who had three sons, one of whom, Aphareus, as has been said above, he adopted. This Aphareus dedicated a bronze statue of him near the Olympieium on a column with the inscription :

> Aphareus set up this statue his father Isocrates' image,
> Sacred to Zeus, to exalt gods and his ancestors' worth.[a]

And it is said that he rode a horse in a race when he was still a boy ; for a bronze figure of him as a boy riding a horse is set up on the Acropolis in the ball-ground of the Arrhephoroi,[b] as some have said. In all his life but two lawsuits were brought against him : first when Megacleides challenged him to an exchange of property.[c] He did not appear in court in this suit, because he was ill, but sent his son Aphareus and won his case. The second suit was when Lysimachus challenged him to exchange property in connexion with the trierarchy ; and this case he lost and performed the trierarchy. There was also a painted portrait of him in the Pompeium.[d] Aphareus wrote speeches, both juridical and deliberative, but not many. He also composed about thirty-seven tragedies, but the authorship of two of them is contested.

---

[b] This seems to have been situated near the north-west wall of the Acropolis, west of the Erechtheum : cf. Judeich, Topographie von Athen², p. 283. Two maidens were chosen each year to carry the peplos at the Panathenaic festival and were called Arrephoroi.   [c] See note on 837 F.

[d] The Pompeium was just inside the Dipylon gate, at which point the processions began. It was the storehouse for objects used in processions.

D ὧν ἀντιλέγονται δύο. ἀρξάμενος δ᾽ ἀπὸ Λυσι-
(839) στράτου διδάσκειν ἄχρι Σωσιγένους ἐν ἔτεσιν
εἰκοσιοκτὼ διδασκαλίας ἀστικὰς καθῆκεν ἓξ καὶ
δὶς ἐνίκησε διὰ Διονυσίου, καθεὶς καὶ δι᾽ ἑτέρων
ἑτέρας δύο Ληναϊκάς. τῆς δὲ μητρὸς αὐτῶν
Ἰσοκράτους καὶ Θεοδώρου καὶ τῆς ταύτης ἀδελφῆς Ἀνακοῦς¹ εἰκόνες ἀνέκειντο ἐν ἀκροπόλει· ὧν
ἡ τῆς μητρὸς παρὰ τὴν Ὑγίειαν νῦν κεῖται μετεπι-
γεγραμμένη, ἡ δ᾽ Ἀνακοῦς¹ οὐ σῴζεται. ἔσχε
δὲ δύο υἱούς, Ἀλέξανδρον μὲν ἐκ Κοίνου² Σωσι-
κλέα³ δ᾽ ἐκ Λυσίου.

Ε΄. ΙΣΑΙΟΣ

E Ἰσαῖος Χαλκιδεὺς μὲν ἦν τὸ γένος, παραγενό-
μενος δ᾽ εἰς Ἀθήνας, καὶ σχολάσας⁴ . . . Λυσίᾳ
κατά τε τὴν τῶν ὀνομάτων ἁρμονίαν καὶ τὴν ἐν τοῖς
πράγμασι δεινότητα, ὥστ᾽ εἰ μή τις ἔμπειρος *πάνυ
τοῦ χαρακτῆρος τῶν ἀνδρῶν εἴη, οὐκ ἂν διαγνοίη

¹ Ἀνακοῦς Xylander: νακοῦς.
² Κοίνου Reiske: Κοινοῦς.
³ Σωσικλέα Turnebus: οὐσικλέα (Λυσικλέα Dübner).
⁴ σχολάσας] Bernardakis, following Westermann and
Dübner, marks a gap to be filled with the name of Isocrates
and other words, e.g. Ἰσοκράτει, φαίνεται ἀκολουθήσας Λυσίᾳ
(or ζηλήσας Λυσίαν).

---

^a 369-368 B.C.   ^b 342-341 B.C.
^c When a poet (διδάσκαλος) wished to avoid the labour of
presenting a play he could delegate the management to a
hypodidascalus, another poet experienced in such matters.
We have many instances of this practice in the didascalic
notices, notably in the case of Aristophanes.
^d The City or Greater Dionysia were celebrated in March,
the Rural or Lesser Dionysia in the various demes of Attica

Beginning in the archonship of Lysistratus [a] he presented in the twenty-eight years to the archonship of Sosigenes [b] six series of dramas at the City Dionysia and won the prize twice, Dionysius as his manager, [c] and, other poets managing, he presented two other series at the Lenaean festival. [d] There were statues of the mother of Isocrates and Theodorus and of her sister Anaco set up on the Acropolis ; of these the statue of the mother is now placed, with a changed inscription, [e] near that of Hygieia, but the statue of Anaco is gone. She had two sons, Alexander by Coenus, and Sosicles by Lysias.

V. ISAEUS

Isaeus was a Chalcidian by birth, but came to Athens and went to school [to Isocrates. He resembled] Lysias [f] in his melodious diction and in his skilful arrangement and treatment of the subject matter in his speeches, so that unless a person were thoroughly familiar with the characters of the two men, he could not easily tell to which of the orators

in December, and the Lenaean festival in December. At all of these dramas were performed, but new tragedies were not produced at the Rural Dionysia, and for a time the same was true of the Lenaean festival. A series of dramas comprised three tragedies and a satyr drama. The two prizes of Aphareus are recorded in an inscription, *I.G.* ii.[2] 2325 b (ed. min.).

[e] Statues erected to honour one person were not infrequently transferred to another by changing the inscriptions. Dio Chrysostom in his *Oration to the Rhodians* condemns this practice.

[f] *Cf.* Dion. Hal. *De Isaeo Iudicium*, 2 χαρακτῆρα δὲ Λυσίου κατὰ τὸ πλεῖστον ἐζήλωσε, " he emulated in the highest degree the character of Lysias."

πολλοὺς τῶν λόγων ῥᾳδίως ὁποτέρου τῶν ῥητόρων
εἰσίν. ἤκμασε δὲ μετὰ τὸν Πελοποννησιακὸν πόλεμον, ὡς ἔστι τεκμήρασθαι ἐκ λόγων αὐτοῦ, καὶ
F μέχρι τῆς Φιλίππου ἀρχῆς παρέτεινε. καθηγήσατο
δὲ Δημοσθένους, ἀποστὰς τῆς σχολῆς, ἐπὶ δραχμαῖς
μυρίαις· διὸ καὶ μάλιστα ἐπιφανὴς ἐγένετο. αὐτὸς
δὲ καὶ τοὺς ἐπιτροπικοὺς λόγους συνέταττε τῷ
Δημοσθένει, ὥς τινες εἶπον. καταλέλοιπε δὲ λόγους
ἑξήκοντα τέσσαρας, ὧν εἰσι γνήσιοι πεντήκοντα,
καὶ ἰδίας τέχνας. πρῶτος δὲ καὶ σχηματίζειν
ἤρξατο καὶ τρέπειν ἐπὶ τὸ πολιτικὸν τὴν διάνοιαν·
ὃ μάλιστα μεμίμηται Δημοσθένης. μνημονεύει δ᾽
αὐτοῦ Θεόπομπος ὁ κωμικὸς ἐν τῷ Θησεῖ.

840   Ϛ΄. ΑΙΣΧΙΝΗΣ

Αἰσχίνης Ἀτρομήτου, φυγόντος μὲν ἐπὶ τῶν
τριάκοντα συγκαταγαγόντος δὲ τὸν δῆμον, καὶ
Γλαυκοθέας· τῶν δὲ δήμων Κοθωκίδης, οὔτε κατὰ
γένος τῶν ἐπιφανῶν οὔτε κατὰ περιουσίαν χρημάτων. νέος δ᾽ ὢν καὶ ἐρρωμένος τῷ σώματι περὶ τὰ
γυμνάσια ἐπόνει· λαμπρόφωνος δ᾽ ὢν μετὰ ταῦτα
τραγῳδίαν ἤσκησεν· ὡς δὲ Δημοσθένης φησίν,
ὑπογραμματεύων καὶ τριταγωνιστῶν Ἀριστοδήμῳ

---

^a See below, Demosthenes, 844 B.
^b Blass, *Die attische Beredsamkeit*, 2nd ed., ii. p. 499,
interprets this as referring to figures of thought (construing
τὴν διάνοιαν with σχηματίζειν). *Cf.* 835 B *supra* ἀσχημάτιστος
of Andocides.
^c *Cf.* Kock, *Com. Att. Frag.* i. p. 737, no. 18.
^d A catalogue of the tribe Oeneis, *I.G.*² 2408, gives his
full name: Ἀτρόμητος Αἰσχίνου Κοθωκίδης. It gives also the
name of Aeschines' son Ἀτρόμητος.

many of the speeches belong. He was in his prime after the Peloponnesian War, as may be inferred from his speeches, and lived until the reign of Philip. He taught Demosthenes,[a] not at his school, but privately, for ten thousand drachmas, whereby he acquired great distinction. And he himself composed for Demosthenes the speeches against his guardians, as some said. He has left behind him sixty-four speeches, fifty of which are genuine, and some rules of rhetoric of his own. He was also the first to give artistic form to his speech [b] and to turn his attention to the urbane style of the orator ; in which Demosthenes has closely imitated him. Theopompus the comic playwright mentions him [c] in the *Theseus.*

VI. AESCHINES

Aeschines was the son of Atrometus,[d] who was exiled in the time of the Thirty and helped to restore the democracy, and of Glaucothea. He belonged to the deme of the Cothocidae and was not of distinguished family or great wealth. When he was young and physically strong he worked hard in the gymnasia ; and afterwards, since he had a clear voice, he practised tragedy ; and according to Demosthenes [e] he was for a long time under-secretary and regularly played as a third-rate actor with Aristodemus at the

---

[e] Demosthenes, xviii. 261 ; xix. 246. The festivals in question are those held in the small towns of Attica. Aristodemus was one of the most noted tragic actors of his time. Born at Metapontum, he was granted Athenian citizenship and was one of the envoys (among whom were Aeschines, Demosthenes, and Philocrates) who made the peace of Philocrates with Philip in 346 B.C.

(840) ἐν τοῖς Διονυσίοις διετέλει, ἀναλαμβάνων ἐπὶ σχολῆς
B τὰς παλαιὰς τραγῳδίας. καὶ ἔτι παῖς ὢν ἐδίδασκε
γράμματα σὺν τῷ πατρί, καὶ μειράκιον ὢν ἐστρα-
τεύετο ἐν τοῖς περιπόλοις.[1] ἀκροατὴς δὲ γενόμενος
ὡς μέν τινες λέγουσιν Ἰσοκράτους καὶ Πλάτωνος,
ὡς δὲ Καικίλιος Λεωδάμαντος, καὶ πολιτευόμενος
οὐκ ἀφανῶς ἐκ τῆς ἐναντίας μερίδος τοῖς περὶ
Δημοσθένη, ἐπρέσβευσεν ἄλλας τε πρεσβείας πολλὰς
καὶ πρὸς Φίλιππον ὑπὲρ τῆς εἰρήνης· ἐφ' ᾗ κατηγορήθη[2] ὑπὸ Δημοσθένους ὡς[3] ἀνῃρημένου τοῦ
Φωκέων ἔθνους, ἔτι δ' ὡς πόλεμον ἐξάψας, ἡνίκα
πυλαγόρας ᾑρέθη Ἀμφικτύοσι πρὸς Ἀμφισσεῖς
τοὺς τὸν λιμένα ἐργαζομένους·[4] ἐξ οὗ συνέβη τοὺς
C Ἀμφικτύονας Φιλίππῳ προσφυγεῖν, τὸν δ' ὑπὸ τοῦ
Αἰσχίνου συνεργούμενον ἐπιθέσθαι τοῖς πράγμασι
καὶ τὴν Φωκίδα λαβεῖν· ἀλλὰ συνειπόντος αὐτῷ
Εὐβούλου τοῦ Σπινθάρου Προβαλλουσίου[5] δημαγω-
γοῦντος, τριάκοντα ψήφοις ἀπέφυγεν. εἰσὶ δ' οἳ
φασι συγγράψαι μὲν τοὺς ῥήτορας τοὺς λόγους, ἐμ-

---

[1] περιπόλοις Hemsterhuis from Aeschines, *False Legation*,
§ 167 : πολλοῖς.
[2] κατηγορήθη Reiske from Photius : κατηγορηθείς.
[3] ὡς added by Dübner.
[4] τοὺς . . . ἐργαζομένους Wolf : καὶ (ὡς Emperius) τὸν λιμένα
ἐργαζομένοις.
[5] Προβαλλουσίου] Προβαλουσίου Photius ; Προβαλεισίου
Westermann ; *cf.* Demosthenes, lix. (*Against Neaera*) 48, 123.

---

[a] More accurately in Photius, the dramatic festivals held
in the small towns of Attica. For the ancient accounts of
Aeschines' career as an actor see O'Connor, *Actors and Acting in Ancient Greece*, pp. 74 ff. Kelly Rees, *The Rule of
Three Actors in the Classical Greek Drama*, pp. 31 ff., has
shown that the term "tritagonist" was invented by Demosthenes as an opprobrious epithet and it is applied in antiquity

Dionysiac festivals,[a] repeating the old tragedies [b] in his spare time. And while still a child he helped his father to teach letters, and as a young man he served in the patrol of the frontiers. After studying with Isocrates and Plato, as some say, but with Leodamas according to Caecilius,[c] he was prominent in public life in the party opposed to that of Demosthenes, and was sent on many embassies, among them the one to Philip concerning the peace.[d] For this he was accused by Demosthenes of having destroyed the Phocian nation and moreover of having stirred up war between the Amphissians, who were building the harbour when he was chosen as delegate to the Amphictyonic Council, and the Amphictyons; as a result of which the Amphictyons turned to Philip for protection, and he, assisted by Aeschines, took matters in hand and conquered Phocis. But through the aid of Eubulus, son of Spintharus, of the deme of Probalinthus, who spoke publicly in his behalf, he was acquitted by thirty votes; but some say that though the orators composed their speeches, yet

to no other actor than Aeschines; also that it meant, not "actor of third-rate rôles," but "third-rate actor"; *cf.* Bekker, *Anecdota*, p. 309. 31 ἀδοκιμώτατος τῶν ὑποκριτῶν, ἐν τῇ τρίτῃ τάξει καταριθμούμενος.

[b] "Old tragedies" are those which had been performed in Athens before.

[c] But see below, 840 ε, where the more probable statement is made that he had no teacher. *Cf.* the anonymous *Life of Aeschines*, 13, Quintilian, ii. 17. 12, and Blass, *Die attische Beredsamkeit*, 2nd ed., iii. p. 157.

[d] Aeschines was sent in 347 and 346 B.C. on two embassies to Philip concerning peace. The second is probably the one especially referred to here. In his orations *On the Peace* (346 B.C.) and *On the False Legation* (343 B.C.) Demosthenes attacks Aeschines and his colleagues.

(840) ποδῶν δὲ γενομένων τῶν περὶ Χαιρώνειαν, μηκέτι
τὴν δίκην εἰσελθεῖν. χρόνῳ δ' ὕστερον, Φιλίππου
μὲν τετελευτηκότος Ἀλεξάνδρου δὲ διαβαίνοντος
εἰς τὴν Ἀσίαν, ἐγράψατο Κτησιφῶντα παρανόμων
ἐπὶ ταῖς Δημοσθένους τιμαῖς· οὐ μεταλαβὼν δὲ τὸ
πέμπτον μέρος τῶν ψήφων ἔφυγεν εἰς τὴν Ῥόδον,
χιλίας δραχμὰς ὑπὲρ τῆς ἥττης οὐ βουληθεὶς
D καταθέσθαι. οἱ δ' ἀτιμίας αὐτῷ προστιμηθῆναι
λέγουσιν οὐ θέλοντι ἐξελθεῖν τῆς πόλεως, καὶ
ἐλθεῖν εἰς Ἔφεσον ὡς Ἀλέξανδρον. τοῦ δὲ τελευτήσαντος, ταραχῆς οὔσης, ἀπάρας εἰς τὴν Ῥόδον ἐνταῦθα σχολὴν καταστησάμενος ἐδίδασκεν. ἀνέγνω
τε τοῖς Ῥοδίοις τὸν κατὰ Κτησιφῶντος λόγον
ἐπιδεικνύμενος· θαυμαζόντων δὲ πάντων εἰ ταῦτ'
E εἰπὼν ἡττήθη " οὐκ ἄν," ἔφη, " ἐθαυμάζετε, Ῥό-
διοι, εἰ πρὸς ταῦτα Δημοσθένους λέγοντος ἠκού-
σατε." σχολήν τ' ἐκεῖ προσκατέλιπε, τὸ Ῥοδιακὸν
διδασκαλεῖον κληθέν. ἔπειτα πλεύσας εἰς Σάμον
καὶ διατρίβων ἐπὶ τῆς νήσου ὀλίγον ὕστερον ἐτελεύτησεν. ἐγένετο δ' εὔφωνος, ὡς δῆλον ἔκ τε ὧν
φησι Δημοσθένης καὶ ἐκ τοῦ Δημοχάρους λόγου.

Φέρονται δ' αὐτοῦ λόγοι τέσσαρες, ὅ τε κατὰ
Τιμάρχου καὶ ὁ τῆς Παραπρεσβείας καὶ ὁ κατὰ
Κτησιφῶντος, οἳ καὶ μόνοι εἰσὶ γνήσιοι. ὁ γὰρ
ἐπιγραφόμενος Δηλιακὸς οὐκ ἔστιν Αἰσχίνου· ἀπ-
εδείχθη μὲν γὰρ ἐπὶ τὴν κρίσιν τὴν περὶ[1] τοῦ ἱεροῦ

---

[1] τὴν περὶ Dübner: τοῦ περί.

---

[a] The author's extreme brevity reduces to two sentences
the events of about eight years. The acquittal of Aeschines
took place in 343 B.C.

[b] Anyone who brought a suit against another for proposing

392

the suit never came to trial because the battle of Chaeroneia intervened.[a] At a later time, when Philip was dead and Alexander was crossing over to Asia, he brought a suit against Ctesiphon for illegal conduct in proposing the honours for Demosthenes; and when he did not receive one-fifth of the votes cast, he went into exile at Rhodes, not being willing to pay a fine of a thousand drachmas for his defeat.[b] But some say that he was further punished by disfranchisement and did not leave the city of his own accord, and that he went to Alexander at Ephesus. During the confusion following Alexander's death he sailed to Rhodes, set up a school there, and taught. He read to the Rhodians his oration against Ctesiphon as an exhibition of his powers, and when they all wondered that after delivering that speech he had lost his case, "You would not wonder, Rhodians," he said, "if you had heard Demosthenes speak in reply to it." And he left a school behind him there, called the Rhodian school. Then he sailed to Samos and not long after, while lingering on that island, died. He had an excellent voice, as is clear from what Demosthenes says [c] and from the oration of Demochares.

Four orations are current under his name : that *Against Timarchus*, that *On the False Legation*,[d] and that *Against Ctesiphon*,[e] and these alone are genuine, since the one entitled the *Delian Oration* is not by Aeschines ; for he was, to be sure, appointed associate advocate in the trial relating to the sanctuary

a measure forbidden by law was subject to a fine and was debarred from bringing any similar suit if he received less than one-fifth of the votes cast by the dicasts.

[c] Demosthenes, xviii. (*On the Crown*) 259, 308.

[d] In L.C.L. Aeschines, pp. 15 ff.

[e] *Ibid.* pp. 303 ff.

τοῦ ἐν Δήλῳ συσταθεὶς συνήγορος· οὐ μὴν εἶπε τὸν
λόγον· ἐχειροτονήθη γὰρ Ὑπερείδης ἀντ᾽ αὐτοῦ, ὡς
F φησι Δημοσθένης. ἔσχε δὲ καὶ ἀδελφούς, ὥς φησιν
αὐτός, Ἀφόβητον¹ καὶ Φιλοχάρη.² ἀπήγγειλε δὲ
καὶ τὴν ἐν Ταμύναις νίκην πρῶτος Ἀθηναίοις, ἐφ᾽
ᾧ καὶ ἐστεφανώθη τὸ δεύτερον.³

Οἱ δ᾽ εἶπον μηδὲ μαθητεῦσαί τισι τὸν Αἰσχίνην,
ἀλλ᾽ ἐκ τῆς ὑπογραμματείας ἀρθῆναι ἐν τοῖς δικαστηρίοις τότε διάγοντα· πρῶτον δ᾽ εἰπεῖν ἐν
τῷ δήμῳ κατὰ Φιλίππου, εὐδοκιμήσαντά τε πρεσβευτὴν χειροτονηθῆναι πρὸς Ἀρκάδας· πρὸς οὓς
ἀφικόμενον συστῆσαι τοὺς μυρίους ἐπὶ Φίλιππον.
ἐγράψατο δὲ καὶ Τίμαρχον ἑταιρήσεως· ὁ δ᾽
841 ἐκλιπὼν τὸν ἀγῶνα αὐτὸν ἀνήρτησεν, ὥς πού
φησι Δημοσθένης. ἐχειροτονήθη δὲ⁴ πρεσβευτὴς
ὡς Φίλιππον μετὰ⁵ Κτησιφῶντος καὶ Δημοσθένους
περὶ τῆς εἰρήνης, ἐν ᾗ ἄμεινον τοῦ Δημοσθένους
ἠνέχθη· τὸ δὲ⁶ δεύτερον δέκατος ὤν, κυρώσας
ὅρκοις τὴν εἰρήνην, κριθεὶς ἀπέφυγεν, ὡς προείρηται.

Ζ΄. ΛΥΚΟΥΡΓΟΣ

Λυκοῦργος πατρὸς μὲν ἦν Λυκόφρονος τοῦ Λυ-
B κούργου, ὃν οἱ τριάκοντα τύραννοι ἀπέκτειναν,
αἰτίου αὐτῷ τῆς ἀναιρέσεως γενομένου Ἀριστο-

---

¹ Ἀφόβητον Westermann from Aeschines: ἄφοβον.
² Φιλοχάρη Wyttenbach from Aeschines: δημοχάρη.
³ τὸ δεύτερον placed here by Franke: in mss. is after
Ἀθηναίοις; cf. Aeschines, False Legation, § 169.
⁴ δὲ added by Westermann.
⁵ μετὰ Franke: κατὰ.   ⁶ δὲ added by Bernardakis.

at Delos, but he did not deliver the speech; for
Hypereides was elected in his place, as Demosthenes
says.[a] He had, as he himself says,[b] two brothers,
Aphobetus and Philochares. He was the first to
bring to the Athenians the news of the victory at
Tamynae, for which he was crowned a second time.

Some have said that Aeschines did not study under
any teachers, but rose from the under-clerkship in the
courts, which he held at that time. And they say
that his first speech before the people was against
Philip, by which he gained such reputation as to be
chosen envoy to the Arcadians; and when he came
to them he raised the ten thousand troops with which
to oppose Philip. He also prosecuted for unchastity
Timarchus, who gave up the defence and hanged
himself, as Demosthenes says somewhere.[c] He was
elected envoy to Philip with Ctesiphon and Demosthenes to treat for peace, on which occasion he was
more successful than Demosthenes; and the second
time, when he was one of ten,[d] he confirmed the peace
with oaths, was tried for it, and was acquitted, as has
been said above.

VII. LYCURGUS

Lycurgus was the son of Lycophron and grandson of the Lycurgus whom the Thirty Tyrants put to
death, his execution being brought about by Aristo-

---

[a] Demosthenes, xviii. (*On the Crown*) p. 271, 134.
[b] Demosthenes, xix. (*On the False Legation*) 149.
[c] *Ibid.* 2 and 285.
[d] Aeschines, *On the False Legation*, 178.

(841) δήμου Βατῆθεν, ὃς καὶ ἑλληνοταμίας γενόμενος
ἔφυγεν ἐν τῇ δημοκρατίᾳ· τῶν δήμων δὲ Βουτάδης,
γένους τοῦ τῶν Ἐτεοβουταδῶν. ἀκροατὴς δὲ
γενόμενος Πλάτωνος τοῦ φιλοσόφου, τὰ πρῶτα
ἐφιλοσόφησεν· εἶτα καὶ Ἰσοκράτους τοῦ ῥήτορος
γνώριμος γενόμενος ἐπολιτεύσατο ἐπιφανῶς, καὶ
λέγων καὶ πράττων καὶ δὴ πιστευσάμενος τὴν
διοίκησιν τῶν χρημάτων· ταμίας γὰρ ἐγένετο ἐπὶ
τρεῖς πενταετηρίδας ταλάντων μυρίων τετρακισχι-
λίων, ἢ ὥς τινες μυρίων ὀκτακισχιλίων ἑξακοσίων
πεντήκοντα, καὶ ὁ τὰς τιμὰς αὐτῷ ψηφιζόμενος
C Στρατοκλῆς ὁ ῥήτωρ, τὸ μὲν πρῶτον αἱρεθεὶς
αὐτός, ἔπειτα τῶν φίλων ἐπιγραψάμενός τινα,
αὐτὸς ἐποιεῖτο τὴν διοίκησιν διὰ τὸ φθάσαι νόμον
εἰσενεγκεῖν, μὴ πλείω πέντε ἐτῶν διέπειν τὸν
χειροτονηθέντα ἐπὶ τὰ δημόσια χρήματα, ἀεί τ'
ἐφεστὼς τοῖς ἔργοις διετέλεσε, καὶ θέρους καὶ
χειμῶνος. καὶ ἐπὶ τὴν τοῦ πολέμου παρασκευὴν
χειροτονηθεὶς πολλὰ τῆς πόλεως ἐπηνώρθωσε, καὶ
τριήρεις παρεσκεύασε τῷ δήμῳ τετρακοσίας, καὶ τὸ
D ἐν Λυκείῳ[1] γυμνάσιον ἐποίησε καὶ ἐφύτευσε καὶ τὴν
παλαίστραν ᾠκοδόμησε καὶ τὸ ἐν Διονύσου θέατρον
ἐπιστατῶν ἐπετέλεσε.[2] πιστευσάμενος δ' ἐν παρα-

---

[1] Λυκείῳ Xylander : λυκίῳ.

[2] ἐπετέλεσε the Turin editors from *Moralia*, 852 c : ἐτελεύτησε.

---

[a] The Hellenotamiae were a board of ten members who
collected and administered the tribute paid to Athens by the
members of the Delian Confederacy.

[b] 338–326 B.C. The title of his office is not known. No
regular office so extensive as this is mentioned in Aristotle's
Constitution of Athens. He may have been in charge of the
theoric fund or the military fund, or both, by virtue of a
special commission, which in the next generation became a

demus of Batê, who also, after having been one of the
Hellenotamiae,[a] was banished under the democracy.
Lycurgus was of the deme of the Butadae and the
family of the Eteobutadae. He attended the
lectures of Plato the philosopher and at first devoted
himself to philosophy ; then, after being a pupil of
the orator Isocrates, he had a notable public career
both as a speaker and as a man of action, and he was
also entrusted with the management of the finances
of the State ; for he was made treasurer for three
periods of four years [b] in charge of fourteen thousand
talents, or, as some say (and among them the man
who proposed the vote of honours for him,[c] Stratocles
the orator), eighteen thousand, six hundred and
fifty.[d] He was elected in his own person the first
time, but afterwards he entered the name of one of
his friends, though he himself administered the office,
because a law had previously been introduced forbidding anyone elected treasurer of the public funds
to hold the office more than four years ; and he was
always intent upon the public business summer and
winter. When he was elected to provide munitions
of war he restored many edifices in the city, he
provided four hundred triremes for the people, he con-
structed the gymnasium in the Lyceum and planted
trees in it, he built the palaestra and finished the
Dionysiac theatre when he was the commissioner
in charge of that work.[e] He took care of two hundred

regular office ; see Ferguson, *Hellenistic Athens*, p. 10, Tarn,
Cambridge Ancient History, vi. p. 441. The period meant
may be the quinquennium.   [c] See Decree III, below, 852.
    [d] Roughly equivalent to £3,026,000 or $15,130,000, or
more at present values.
    [e] Probably while he was in control of the finances. *Cf.*
Dörpfeld and Reisch, *Das griechische Theater*, pp. 39 f.

(841) καταθήκῃ παρὰ τῶν ἰδιωτῶν διακόσια πεντήκοντα
τάλαντα ἐφύλαξε, πομπεῖά τε χρυσᾶ καὶ ἀργυρᾶ τῇ
πόλει κατεσκεύασε καὶ νίκας χρυσᾶς. πολλὰ δ'
ἡμίεργα παραλαβὼν ἐξετέλεσε καὶ νεωσοίκους καὶ
τὴν σκευοθήκην· καὶ τῷ σταδίῳ τῷ Παναθηναϊκῷ
τὴν κρηπῖδα περιέθηκεν, ἐξεργασάμενος τοῦτό τε
καὶ τὴν χαράδραν ὁμαλὴν ποιήσας, Δεινίου[1] τινός,
ὃς ἐκέκτητο τοῦτο τὸ χωρίον, ἀνέντος τῇ πόλει,
προείπαντος[2] αὐτῷ[3] χαρίσασθαι Λυκούργου.[4]

E Ἔσχε δὲ καὶ τοῦ ἄστεος τὴν φυλακὴν καὶ τῶν
κακούργων τὴν σύλληψιν, οὓς ἐξήλασεν ἅπαντας,
ὡς καὶ τῶν σοφιστῶν ἐνίους λέγειν Λυκοῦργον οὐ
μέλανι ἀλλὰ θανάτῳ[5] χρίοντα τὸν κάλαμον κατὰ
τῶν πονηρῶν, οὕτω συγγράφειν. ὅθεν ἐξαιτηθέντα
αὐτὸν ὑπ' Ἀλεξάνδρου τοῦ βασιλέως ὁ δῆμος οὐ
προήκατο. καθ' ὃν δὲ χρόνον ἐπολέμει Φίλιππος
πρὸς Ἀθηναίους τὸν δεύτερον πόλεμον, ἐπρέσβευε
μετὰ Πολυεύκτου καὶ Δημοσθένους εἴς τε Πελο-
F πόννησον καί τινας ἑτέρας πόλεις. διετέλεσέ τε
τὸν ἅπαντα χρόνον εὐδοκιμῶν παρὰ τοῖς Ἀθηναίοις
καὶ δίκαιος εἶναι νομιζόμενος, ὥστε καὶ ἐν τοῖς
δικαστηρίοις τὸ φῆσαι Λυκοῦργον ἐδόκει βοήθημα
εἶναι τῷ συναγορευομένῳ.

Εἰσήνεγκε δὲ καὶ νόμους, τὸν μὲν περὶ τῶν
κωμῳδῶν, ἀγῶνα τοῖς Χύτροις ἐπιτελεῖν ἐφάμιλλον
ἐν τῷ θεάτρῳ καὶ τὸν νικήσαντα εἰς ἄστυ κατα-

---

[1] Δεινίου Coraes: δινίου.
[2] προείπαντος Emperius: περὶ παντός.
[3] αὐτῷ added by Bernardakis.
[4] Λυκούργου Bernardakis: λυκούργῳ.
[5] θανάτῳ] αἵματι Amyot from *Life of Solon*, chap. xvii.

and fifty talents entrusted to him on deposit by
private persons, he provided for the city objects of
gold and silver for use in processions and golden
Victories, and many buildings which came into his
hands half-finished he completed, among them the
ship-sheds and the arsenal. And he put the founda-
tion-walls round the Panathenaic stadium. This he
accomplished, and also the levelling of the ravine,
because a certain Deinias who owned this plot of
land gave it to the city when Lycurgus suggested to
him that he make the gift.

He was charged also with guarding the city and
arresting malefactors, whom he drove out entirely,
so that some of the sophists said that Lycurgus
signed warrants against evil-doers with a pen dipped,
not in ink, but in death. And therefore, when King
Alexander demanded his surrender, the people did
not give him up. When Philip was carrying on the
second war with the Athenians, Lycurgus went as
envoy with Polyeuctus and Demosthenes to the
Peloponnesus and to some other States. Throughout
his life he was always highly esteemed among the
Athenians and considered a just man, so that in the
courts of law the word of Lycurgus was regarded as
a help to anyone requiring an advocate.

He also introduced laws : the law relating to
comic actors, that a competitive performance be held
on the festival of Pots [a] and that the victor's name

---

[a] The third day of the Anthesteria, the thirteenth day of
the month Anthesterium.

λέγεσθαι πρότερον οὐκ ἐξόν, ἀναλαμβάνων τὸν
ἀγῶνα ἐκλελοιπότα· τὸν δέ, ὡς χαλκᾶς εἰκόνας
ἀναθεῖναι τῶν ποιητῶν, Αἰσχύλου Σοφοκλέους Εὐριπίδου, καὶ τὰς τραγῳδίας αὐτῶν ἐν κοινῷ γραψα-
μένους φυλάττειν καὶ τὸν τῆς πόλεως γραμματέα
παραναγινώσκειν τοῖς ὑποκρινομένοις· οὐκ ἐξεῖναι
γὰρ παρ᾽ αὐτὰς[1] ὑποκρίνεσθαι. καὶ τρίτον, μηδενὶ
842 ἐξεῖναι Ἀθηναίων μηδὲ τῶν οἰκούντων Ἀθήνησιν
ἐλεύθερον σῶμα πρίασθαι ἐπὶ δουλείᾳ ἐκ τῶν ἁλι-
σκομένων ἄνευ τῆς τοῦ προτέρου δεσπότου γνώμης. ἔτι δέ, ὡς τοῦ Ποσειδῶνος ἀγῶνα ποιεῖν ἐν
Πειραιεῖ, κυκλίων χορῶν οὐκ ἔλαττον τριῶν, καὶ[2]
δίδοσθαι μὲν τοῖς νικῶσιν οὐκ ἔλαττον δέκα μνᾶς,
τοῖς δὲ δευτέροις ὀκτώ, ἐξ δὲ τοῖς τρίτοις κριθεῖσιν.
ἔτι δ᾽[3] ἐπὶ ζεύγους μὴ ἀπιέναι[4] γυναῖκα Ἐλευσῖνάδε,
ὅπως μὴ ἐλαττῶνται αἱ δημοτικαὶ[5] ὑπὸ τῶν
πλουσίων· εἰ δέ τις φωραθείη, ἀποτίνειν δραχμὰς
ἑξακισχιλίας. τῆς δὲ γυναικὸς αὐτοῦ μὴ πει-
σθείσης, τῶν συκοφαντῶν φωρασάντων, τάλαντον
B αὐτοῖς ἔδωκε· κατηγορούμενος δ᾽ ἐν ὑστέρῳ ἐν τῷ

---

[1] γὰρ παρ᾽ αὐτὰς Bernardakis : γὰρ αὐτάς.
[2] καὶ added by Dübner.
[3] ἔτι δ᾽ added by Sauppe.
[4] ἀπιέναι Taylor : ἀπεῖναι.
[5] αἱ δημοτικαὶ added by Baiter from Photius.

---

[a] The τραγῳδοί and κωμῳδοί alone were eligible to be
chosen by lot as protagonists for the tragedies and comedies
to be presented at the City Dionysia, the subordinate rôles
being assigned to plain ὑποκριταί. Prior to the passage of
the law of Lycurgus those only were eligible who had
previously won a victory at the City Dionysia. The effect of
the law of Lycurgus was, therefore, to increase the number
of those from whom the archon could choose a κωμῳδός for
each of the five comedies to be presented. See Rohde,

be inscribed as eligible for the City Dionysia,[a] which had not been permitted before, and thus he revived a contest which had fallen out of use ; the law that bronze statues of the poets Aeschylus, Sophocles, and Euripides be erected, that their tragedies be written out and kept in a public depository, and that the clerk of the State read them to the actors who were to perform their plays for comparison of the texts and that it be unlawful to depart from the authorized text in acting ; a third law that no Athenian or foreign resident of Athens should be permitted to buy from among captives a person of free birth to be a slave without the consent of his former master[b] ; furthermore, that a festival of Poseidon should be held in Peiraeus, consisting of no fewer than three cyclic choruses, that not less than ten minas be given to the victors, eight to those ranked second by the judges, and six to those ranked third ; furthermore, that no woman should go to Eleusis[c] in a carriage, lest the women of the people appear inferior to the rich, and if any woman should be caught doing this, she should pay a fine of six thousand drachmas. His own wife disobeyed, the informers caught her in the act, and he gave them a talent ; and at a later time, when accused of this in the popular assembly,

---

Rheinisches Museum, xxxviii. p. 276, and J. B. O'Connor, *Chapters in the History of Actors and Acting*, pp. 57 ff.

[b] Prisoners of war were usually auctioned off into slavery regardless of their previous condition. If such a captive could prove his free birth through the testimony of the man who owned him when taken captive, he could not under this new law be purchased by any Athenian for slavery, *cf.* M. H. E. Meier, *Comment. de vita Lycurgi*, xxxix. ff.

[c] This refers to the great annual procession to Eleusis in the celebration of the mysteries of Demeter and Persephonê.

(842) δήμῳ, ἔφη " ἀλλ' οὖν ἐγὼ μὲν διδοὺς οὐ λαμβάνων
ἑώραμαι." τελώνου δέ ποτ' ἐπιβαλόντος Ξενο-
κράτει τῷ φιλοσόφῳ τὰς χεῖρας καὶ πρὸς τὸ
μετοίκιον αὐτὸν ἀπάγοντος,[1] ἀπαντήσας ῥάβδῳ τε
κατὰ τῆς κεφαλῆς τοῦ τελώνου κατήνεγκε, καὶ τὸν
μὲν Ξενοκράτην ἀπέλυσε, τὸν δ' ὡς οὐ τὰ πρέποντα
δράσαντα εἰς τὸ δεσμωτήριον κατέκλεισεν· ἐπαινου-
μένου δ' ἐπὶ τῇ πράξει, μεθ' ἡμέρας τινὰς συντυχὼν
ὁ Ξενοκράτης τοῖς παισὶ τοῦ Λυκούργου, ἔφη
" ταχέως γε τῷ πατρὶ ὑμῶν ἀπέδωκα, ὦ παῖδες,
C τὴν χάριν· ἐπαινεῖται γὰρ ὑπὸ πολλῶν ἐπὶ τῷ
βοηθῆσαί μοι."

Εἰσήνεγκε[2] δὲ καὶ ψηφίσματα Εὐκλείδῃ τινὶ
Ὀλυνθίῳ χρώμενος ἱκανωτάτῳ περὶ τὰ ψηφίσματα.
εὔπορος δ' ὢν ἱμάτιον ἓν καὶ ταὐτὸν[3] ἐφόρει τοῦ
χειμῶνος καὶ τοῦ θέρους καὶ ὑπεδέδετο ταῖς ἀναγ-
καίαις ἡμέραις. ἐμελέτα δὲ καὶ νυκτὸς καὶ ἡμέρας,
οὐκ εὖ πρὸς τὰ αὐτοσχέδια πεφυκώς, κλινιδίου δ'
αὐτῷ ὑποκειμένου, ἐφ' ᾧ μόνον ἦν κώδιον καὶ
προσκεφάλαιον, ὅπως ἐγείροιτο ῥᾳδίως καὶ με-
λετῴη. ἐγκαλοῦντος δ' αὐτῷ τινος ὅτι μισθοὺς
D σοφισταῖς δίδωσι περὶ λόγους διατρίβων, ἀλλ' εἴ τις
γ' ἐπαγγέλλοιτο, ἔφη, τοὺς υἱοὺς ἀμείνους αὐτῷ
ποιήσειν, οὐ χιλίας ἀλλὰ τὰ ἡμίση τῆς οὐσίας
προΐεσθαι. ἦν δὲ καὶ παρρησιαστὴς διὰ τὴν εὐ-
γένειαν· Ἀθηναίων γέ τοί ποτε οὐκ ἀνεχομένων

---

[1] ἀπάγοντος Coraes : ἀπαγαγόντος.
[2] μοι. εἰσήνεγκε Solanus : μόγις. ἤνεγκε.
[3] καὶ ταὐτὸν Bernardakis; καὶ ταὐτὸ Meziriacus : καθ' αὑτό.

---

[a] The story may well be apocryphal. The saying of
Lycurgus, repeated by Plutarch in his *Comp. of Nicias and*

he said, " At any rate I am found to have been the
giver, not the receiver." *a* And once when a tax-
collector laid hands on Xenocrates the philosopher
and Lycurgus met him as he was leading him away
to enforce payment of his tax as a resident alien,*b*
he brought his walking-stick down on the tax-
collector's head, set Xenocrates free, and shut the
other man up in prison for improper conduct. As he
was generally commended for his act, Xenocrates,
happening to meet Lycurgus's children some days
later, said " I have repaid your father quickly for the
favour he did me, boys ; for he is widely commended
for coming to my assistance."

He also proposed decrees,*c* making use of a certain
Olynthian named Eucleides, who was an expert in
decrees. And although he was well-to-do, he wore
one and the same cloak winter and summer and put
on sandals only on days when they were necessary.
He studied night and day, since he had no natural
gift for extemporaneous speaking, and he lay on a
cot with only a sheepskin and a pillow on it, so that
he might wake up easily and study. When someone
found fault with him for paying money to sophists
although he made words his profession, he replied
that if anyone would promise to make his sons better,
he would pay him, not thousands only, but half his
property. He was an outspoken speaker on account
of his good birth. Once, indeed, when the Athenians

Crassus, 3, is not there connected with the Eleusis incident ;
and Aelian, *Var. Hist.* xiii. 24, expressly states that the
statesman's wife paid a fine after legal condemnation, not a
bribe to the informer.

b The tax was twelve drachmas.

c Several decrees moved by him are extant, *e.g. I.G.*
ii.² 337, 338.

(842) αὐτοῦ δημηγοροῦντος, ἀνέκραγεν ἐκβαλλόμενος " ὦ
Κερκυραία μάστιξ, ὡς πολλῶν ταλάντων εἶ ἀξία."
πάλιν δὲ θεὸν ἀναγορευόντων Ἀλέξανδρον " καὶ
ποδαπὸς ἂν εἴη[1]," εἶπεν, " ὁ θεός, οὗ τὸ ἱερὸν
ἐξιόντας δεήσει περιρραίνεσθαι[2];" ἀποθανόντος

E δ' αὐτοῦ, παρέδωκαν τοὺς παῖδας τοῖς ἕνδεκα,
Μενεσαίχμου μὲν κατηγορήσαντος γραψαμένου δὲ
Θρασυκλέους· Δημοσθένους δὲ καθ' ὃν ἔφευγε[3]
χρόνον ἐπιστείλαντος τοῖς Ἀθηναίοις, ὡς κακῶς
ἀκούοιεν ἐπὶ τοῖς Λυκούργου παιδίοις, μετενόησαν
καὶ ἀφῆκαν αὐτούς, Δημοκλέους τοῦ Θεοφράστου
μαθητοῦ ὑπὲρ αὐτῶν ἀπολογησαμένου. ἐτάφη δ'
αὐτὸς καὶ τῶν ἐκγόνων τινὲς δημοσίᾳ· καὶ ἔστιν
αὐτῶν τὰ μνήματα ἀντικρὺ[4] τῆς Παιωνίας Ἀθηνᾶς
ἐν τῷ Μελανθίου τοῦ φιλοσόφου κήπῳ, τράπεζαι
πεποιημέναι, αὐτοῦ τε τοῦ Λυκούργου καὶ τῶν
παίδων αὐτοῦ ἐπιγεγραμμέναι καὶ εἰς ἡμᾶς ἔτι

F σωζόμεναι. τὸ μέγιστον, χίλια διακόσια τάλαντα
προσόδου τῇ πόλει κατέστησε, πρότερον ἑξήκοντα
προσιόντων. μέλλων δὲ τελευτήσειν εἰς τὸ
μητρῷον καὶ τὸ βουλευτήριον ἐκέλευσεν αὑτὸν
κομισθῆναι, βουλόμενος εὐθύνας δοῦναι τῶν πεπο-
λιτευμένων· οὐδενὸς δὲ κατηγορῆσαι τολμήσαντος
πλὴν Μενεσαίχμου, τὰς διαβολὰς ἀπολυσάμενος εἰς

---

[1] εἴη added by Coraes.
[2] περιρραίνεσθαι Dübner: περιρράνεσθαι.
[3] ἔφευγε Coraes: ἔφυγε.
[4] ἀντικρὺ Herwerden: ἀντικρυς.

---

[a] The Corcyraean whip was especially stinging, and the
orator's outbreak means : " I would give a great deal to use
a cat-o'-nine-tails on you people."
[b] *Cf.* Demosthenes, *Epistle* iii., and Aeschines, *Epistle* xii.
14.

were showing dissent as he was speaking, he burst
out with : " O Corcyraean whip, how ma ly talents
you are worth ! " [a]   And when they were proclaiming
Alexander a god, " What sort of god," he said, " is
he when those who *come out* of his temple have to
sprinkle themselves with holy water ? "   After his
death his sons were handed over to the eleven executioners on the accusation of Menesaechmus, the
indictment being written by Thrasycles ; but when
Demosthenes, who was at that time in exile, wrote
a letter to the Athenians [b] saying that their reputation was suffering because of Lycurgus's sons, they
changed their mind and released them, Democles,
a pupil of Theophrastus, speaking in their defence.
He himself and some of his descendants were buried
at public expense ; and their monuments are opposite
the Paeonian Athena in the garden of the philosopher
Melanthius [c] ; they are in the form of tables, and
those of Lycurgus and his children have inscriptions
and are still preserved in our day. His greatest
achievement was the raising of the State revenue to
twelve hundred talents when it had previously been
sixty. When he was at the point of death he gave
orders that he be carried to the temple of the Great
Mother and into the Bouleuterion,[d] as he wished
to give an accounting for his public acts ; and when
no one had the face to accuse him except Menesaechmus, he freed himself from his false accusations,

[c] Judeich, *Topogr. v. Athen*[2], p. 409, conjectures that the
garden of Melanthius was in the neighbourhood of the
Academy.

[d] The Bouleuterion was the meeting-place of the Boulê or
Senate ; the foundations of this and of the temple of the
Great Mother have recently been found on the west side of
the Agora. See T. L. Shear, *Hesperia*, iv. pp. 349 ff.

τὴν οἰκίαν ἀπεκομίσθη καὶ ἐτελεύτησεν, ἐπιεικὴς
νομισθεὶς παρὰ πάντα τὸν τοῦ βίου[1] χρόνον καὶ ἐν
λόγοις ἐπαινεθείς· καὶ μηδένα ἀγῶνα ἁλούς, καίτοι
πολλῶν κατηγορησάντων.

Ἔσχε δὲ τρεῖς παῖδας ἐκ Καλλιστοῦς τῆς
Ἄβρωνος μὲν θυγατρός, Καλλίου[2] δὲ τοῦ Ἄβρωνος
Βατῆθεν ἀδελφῆς, τοῦ ταμιεύσαντος στρατιωτικῶν
843 ἐπὶ Χαιρώνδου ἄρχοντος· περὶ δὲ τῆς κηδείας
ταύτης λέγει ὁ Δείναρχος ἐν τῷ κατὰ Πιστίου.[3]
κατέλιπε δὲ παῖδας Ἄβρωνα Λυκοῦργον Λυκό-
φρονα· ὧν ὁ Ἄβρων καὶ ὁ Λυκοῦργος ἄπαιδες
μετήλλαξαν· ἀλλ' ὅ γ' Ἄβρων καὶ πολιτευσάμενος
ἐπιφανῶς μετήλλαξε, Λυκόφρων δὲ γήμας Καλλι-
στομάχην Φιλίππου Αἰξωνέως[4] ἐγέννησε Καλλιστώ.
ταύτην δὲ γήμας Κλεόμβροτος Δεινοκράτους Ἀχαρ-
νεύς, ἐγέννησε Λυκόφρονα· τοῦτον δ' ὁ πάππος
εἰσεποιήσατο Λυκόφρων· οὗτος δ' ἐτελεύτησεν
ἄπαις· μετὰ δὲ τὴν Λυκόφρονος τελευτὴν ἔγημε τὴν
B Καλλιστὼ Σωκράτης καὶ ἔσχεν υἱὸν Σύμμαχον· τοῦ
δ' ἐγένετο Ἀριστώνυμος, τοῦ δὲ Χαρμίδης τοῦ δὲ
Φιλίππη· ταύτης δὲ καὶ Λυσάνδρου Μήδειος, ὁ
καὶ ἐξηγητὴς ἐξ Εὐμολπιδῶν γενόμενος· τούτου δὲ
καὶ Τιμοθέας τῆς Γλαύκου παῖδες Λαοδάμεια καὶ
Μήδειος, ὃς τὴν ἱερωσύνην Ποσειδῶνος Ἐρεχθέως
εἶχε, καὶ Φιλίππη, ἥτις ἱεράσατο τῆς Ἀθηνᾶς
ὕστερον· πρότερον δ' αὐτὴν γήμας Διοκλῆς ὁ
Μελιτεύς[5] ἐγέννησε Διοκλέα, τὸν ἐπὶ τοὺς ὁπλίτας
στρατηγήσαντα· γήμας δ' οὗτος Ἡδίστην Ἄβρωνος

---

[1] τοῦ βίου Coraes from Photius : βίου.
[2] Καλλίου Salmasius : καλαιοῦ.
[3] Πιστίου Meursius from Harpocration : παπτίου.
[4] Αἰξωνέως Xylander : ἀειξωνέος.
[5] Μελιτεὺς Coraes : Μελιττεύς.

was carried to his house, and died,[a] having been considered a honourable man throughout his whole life, and highly praised for his speeches. He never was convicted, though many brought accusations against him.

He had three children by Callisto, the daughter of Habron and sister of Callias the son of Habron of the deme Batê, the one who was treasurer of military funds in the archonship of Charondas.[b] Deinarchus, in his speech against Pistius, tells about this connexion by marriage. He left three sons, Habron, Lycurgus, and Lycophron, of whom Habron and Lycurgus died without issue. However, Habron at any rate had a distinguished public career before he died; but Lycophron married Callistomachê, daughter of Philippus of Aexonê, and had a daughter Callisto. She was married to Cleombrotus of Acharnae, son of Deinocrates, to whom she bore a son Lycophron, who was adopted by his grandfather Lycophron and died without issue. After Lycophron's death Socrates married Callisto and had a son Symmachus. Symmachus had a son Aristonymus, he a son Charmides, and Charmides a daughter Philippa. Her son by Lysander was Medeius, who became an expounder of rites,[c] being of the family of the Eumolpidae. He and Timothea, daughter of Glaucus, had three children, Laodameia and Medeius, who held the priestship of Poseidon-Erechtheus, and Philippa, who afterwards became priestess of Athena; but before that Diocles of Melitê married her, and their son was the Diocles who was general in command of the heavy-armed force. He married Hedistê, daughter

[a] His death occurred about 324 B.C.   [b] 338-337 B.C.
[c] At Eleusis in connexion with the Eleusinian Mysteries.

(843) Φιλιππίδην καὶ Νικοστράτην ἐγέννησε· γήμας δὲ
C τὴν Νικοστράτην Θεμιστοκλῆς ὁ Θεοφράστου ὁ
δαδοῦχος ἐγέννησε Θεόφραστον καὶ Διοκλέα· δι-
ετάξατο δὲ καὶ τὴν ἱερωσύνην τοῦ Ποσειδῶνος
Ἐρεχθέως.

Φέρονται δὲ τοῦ ῥήτορος λόγοι δεκαπέντε. ἐστεφανώθη δ' ὑπὸ τοῦ δήμου πολλάκις καὶ εἰκόνων
ἔτυχεν· ἀνάκειται δ' αὐτοῦ χαλκῆ εἰκὼν ἐν Κερα-
μεικῷ κατὰ ψήφισμα ἐπ' Ἀναξικράτους ἄρχοντος·
ἐφ' οὗ ἔλαβε καὶ σίτησιν ἐν πρυτανείῳ αὐτός τε ὅ[1]
Λυκοῦργος καὶ ὁ πρεσβύτατος αὐτοῦ τῶν ἐκγόνων
κατὰ τὸ αὐτὸ ψήφισμα· ἀποθανόντος τε Λυκούργου,
ὁ πρεσβύτατος τῶν παίδων Λυκόφρων ἠμφισβήτησε
D τῆς δωρεᾶς. εἶπε δὲ καὶ περὶ ἱερῶν πολλάκις,
γραψάμενος Αὐτόλυκον τὸν Ἀρεοπαγίτην καὶ
Λυσικλέα τὸν στρατηγὸν καὶ Δημάδην τὸν Δημέου[2]
καὶ Μενέσαιχμον ἄλλους τε πολλούς, καὶ πάντας
εἷλεν. ἔκρινε δὲ καὶ Δίφιλον, ἐκ τῶν ἀργυρείων[3]
μετάλλων τοὺς μεσοκρινεῖς,[4] οἳ ἐβάσταζον τὰ ὑπερ-
κείμενα βάρη, ὑφελόντα καὶ ἐξ αὐτῶν πεπλουτηκότα
παρὰ τοὺς νόμους· καὶ θανάτου ὄντος ἐπιτιμίου
ἁλῶναι ἐποίησε, καὶ πεντήκοντα δραχμὰς ἐκ τῆς
οὐσίας αὐτοῦ ἑκάστῳ τῶν πολιτῶν διένειμε, τῶν
E πάντων συναχθέντων ταλάντων ἑκατὸν ἑξήκοντα·
ἤ, ὥς τινες, μνῶν. ὁ δ' εὐθύνας Ἀριστογείτονα καὶ

---

[1] τε ὅ Wyttenbach : τε καὶ ὅ.
[2] Δημέου Westermann : δημίου.
[3] ἀργυρείων Baiter : ἀργυρίων.
[4] μεσοκρινεῖς Xylander from Pollux, vii. 98 : μεσοκρανεῖς.

of Habron, and had two children, Philippides and Nicostrata. Themistocles, the Torch-bearer,[a] son of Theophrastus, married Nicostrata and had two sons, Theophrastus and Diocles. He also organizéd the priesthood of Poseidon-Erechtheus.

Fifteen speeches of the orator are current.[b] He was crowned by the people many times and was honoured with statues. A bronze statue[c] of him stands in the Cerameicus, set up in accordance with a decree passed in the archonship of Anaxicrates,[d] in which year Lycurgus and his eldest descendant were granted maintenance in the Prytaneum by the same decree. After Lycurgus died his eldest son, Lycophron, brought a suit for the grant. Lycurgus spoke also many times on religious matters, bringing suit against Autolycus the Areopagite, Lysicles the general, Demades the son of Demeas, Menesaechmus, and many others, and he caused them all to be convicted. He also brought Diphilus to trial, who removed from the silver mines the rock props which supported the weight above and made himself rich from them contrary to the law; and though the penalty for this was death, Lycurgus brought about his conviction, and from the confiscated estate distributed fifty drachmas to every citizen, since the total sum collected was one hundred and sixty talents or, as some say, he distributed a mina to each

---

[a] The Torch-bearer was an important functionary in the Eleusinian Mysteries. The office was hereditary.

[b] Of these only the speech against Leocrates has come down to us.

[c] The inscription on the base of this statue is probably preserved in *I.G.* ii.² 3776. Another statue stood not far from the Prytaneium; *cf.* Pausanius, i. 8. 2.

[d] 307–306 B.C. See the Decree below, 851 ff.

(843) Λεωκράτην καὶ Αὐτόλυκον δειλίας.[1] ἐπεκαλεῖτο δ'
ὁ Λυκοῦργος ἶβις[2]

ἶβις Λυκούργῳ, Χαιρεφῶντι[3] νυκτερίς.

κατῆγον δὲ τὸ γένος ἀπωτάτω μὲν ἀπ'[4] Ἐρεχθέως
τοῦ Γῆς καὶ Ἡφαίστου· τὰ δ' ἐγγυτάτω ἀπὸ
Λυκομήδους καὶ Λυκούργου, οὓς ὁ δῆμος ταφαῖς
ἐτίμησε δημοσίᾳ· καὶ ἔστιν αὕτη ἡ καταγωγὴ τοῦ
γένους τῶν ἱερασαμένων τοῦ Ποσειδῶνος ἐν πίνακι
τελείῳ, ὃς ἀνάκειται ἐν Ἐρεχθείῳ, γεγραμμένος ὑπ'
Ἰσμηνίου τοῦ Χαλκιδέως· καὶ εἰκόνες ξύλιναι[5] τοῦ
τε Λυκούργου καὶ τῶν υἱῶν αὐτοῦ, Ἅβρωνος
F Λυκούργου Λυκόφρονος, ἃς εἰργάσαντο Τίμαρχος
καὶ Κηφισόδοτος, οἱ Πραξιτέλους υἱεῖς· τὸν δὲ
πίνακα ἀνέθηκεν Ἅβρων ὁ παῖς αὐτοῦ, λαχὼν ἐκ
τοῦ γένους τὴν ἱερωσύνην καὶ παραχωρήσας τῷ
ἀδελφῷ Λυκόφρονι· καὶ διὰ τοῦτο πεποίηται ὁ
Ἅβρων προσδιδοὺς αὐτῷ τὴν τρίαιναν. πάντων δ'
ὧν διῴκησεν ἀναγραφὴν ποιησάμενος ἀνέθηκεν ἐν
στήλῃ πρὸ τῆς ὑπ' αὐτοῦ κατασκευασθείσης παλαί-
στρας σκοπεῖν τοῖς βουλομένοις· οὐδεὶς μέντοι
ἐδυνήθη ἐλέγξαι τὸν ἄνδρα νοσφισμοῦ. ἔγραψε δὲ
καὶ Νεοπτόλεμον Ἀντικλέους στεφανῶσαι καὶ
εἰκόνα ἀναθεῖναι, ὅτι ἐπηγγείλατο χρυσώσειν τὸν

---

[1] δειλίας Valesius : δουλείας.
[2] Wyttenbach suggests that ὥς φησιν Ἀριστοφάνης be added.
[3] Χαιρεφῶντι Taylor : Ξενοφῶντι.
[4] ἀπωτάτω μὲν ἀπ' Turin editors; ἀπὸ Βούτου καὶ Sauppe;
ἀπὸ Βουταδῶν καὶ Bernardakis : ἀπὸ τούτων καὶ.
[5] ξύλιναι Sauppe : ξύλινοι.

citizen.[a] He it was who called Aristogeiton, Leocrates, and Autolycus to account for cowardice.
Lycurgus was nicknamed "Ibis,"

An ibis for Lycurgus, for Chaerephon a bat.[b]

His family was derived ultimately from Erechtheus,
the son of Gaea and Poseidon, but in the nearest
generations from Lycomedes and Lycurgus, whom the
people honoured with funerals at the public expense ;
and this succession from father to son of those of the
family who have been priests of Poseidon exists on a
complete tablet which has been set up in the Erechtheum, painted by Ismenias the Chalcidian ; and
there are wooden statues of Lycurgus and his sons
Habron, Lycurgus, and Lycophron, made by Timarchus and Cephisodotus, the sons of Praxiteles. But
the tablet was put up by his son Habron, who received the priesthood by inheritance and handed it
over to his brother Lycophron ; and that is why
Habron is represented as handing Lycophron the
trident. And Lycurgus had a record made of all his
acts as a public official and set it up on a tablet, for
all men to see who wished, in front of the palaestra
that he had built ; no one, however, could convict
him of embezzlement. He made the motion to crown
Neoptolemus the son of Anticles and to set up a
statue of him because he had promised to gild the

[a] The drachma was worth, in silver, about 9d. or 18 cents,
the mina 100 drachmas, the talent 60 minas. The sums
mentioned are therefore roughly equivalent to £1 : 16s. ($9),
£40,960 ($172,800), and £3 : 12s. ($18), but the fluctuations in
the value of modern currencies render such calculations very
inexact. See Decree III. below, 851 f-852 e.

[b] Aristophanes, *Birds*, 1296 and scholium. But it was
the grandfather of the orator and statesman to whom
Aristophanes referred.

411

844 βωμὸν τοῦ Ἀπόλλωνος ἐν ἀγορᾷ κατὰ τὴν μαντείαν
τοῦ θεοῦ. ἐψηφίσατο δὲ καὶ Διοτίμῳ[1] Διοπείθους
Εὐωνυμεῖ τιμὰς ἐπὶ Κτησικλέους ἄρχοντος.

Η΄. ΔΗΜΟΣΘΕΝΗΣ

Δημοσθένης Δημοσθένους καὶ Κλεοβούλης τῆς
Γύλωνος[2] θυγατρός, τῶν δὲ δήμων Παιανιεύς, κατα-
λειφθεὶς ὑπὸ τοῦ πατρὸς ἐτῶν ἑπτὰ μετ' ἀδελφῆς
B πενταέτιδος[3] τὸν μὲν τῆς ὀρφανίας χρόνον παρὰ τῇ
μητρὶ διῆγε, σχολάζων Ἰσοκράτει ὥς τινες ἔφασαν,
ὡς δ' οἱ πλεῖστοι Ἰσαίῳ τῷ Χαλκιδεῖ, ὃς ἦν Ἰσοκράτους μαθητής, διάγοντι ἐν Ἀθήναις, ζηλῶν
Θουκυδίδην καὶ Πλάτωνα τὸν φιλόσοφον, ᾧ τινες
εἶπον προηγουμένως αὐτὸν[4] σχολάσαι. ὡς δ' Ἡγη-
σίας ὁ Μάγνης φησίν, ἐδεήθη τοῦ παιδαγωγοῦ, ἵνα
Καλλιστράτου Ἐμπέδου[5] Ἀφιδναίου, ῥήτορος δο-
κίμου καὶ ἱππαρχήσαντος καὶ ἀναθέντος τὸν βωμὸν
τῷ Ἑρμῇ τῷ ἀγοραίῳ, μέλλοντος ἐν τῷ δήμῳ
λέγειν, ἀκούσῃ· ἀκούσας δ' ἐραστὴς ἐγένετο τῶν
C λόγων. καὶ τούτου μὲν ἐπ' ὀλίγον ἤκουσεν, ἕως
ἐπεδήμει. ἐπειδὴ δ' ὁ μὲν ἔφυγεν εἰς Θρᾴκην ὁ
δ' ἐγεγόνει ἐξ ἐφήβων, τηνικαῦτα παρέβαλεν[6]

---

[1] Διοτίμῳ Westermann : διοτίμου.
[2] Γύλωνος Xylander : γυναικὸς τῆς.
[3] πενταέτιδος Bernardakis : πενταετίδος.
[4] ᾧ τινες . . . αὐτὸν Xylander : ὅν (or οἱ) τινες . . . αὐτῷ.
[5] Ἐμπέδου Pausanias, vii. 16. 4 : ἐμπαίδου.
[6] παρέβαλεν Dübner : παρέβαλλεν.

---

[a] This altar may have stood in front of the temple of
Apollo Patroüs ; cf. Judeich, *Topographie von Athen*[2], p. 345,
n. 4.
[b] 334–333 B.C.

altar of Apollo [a] in the Market-place in accordance with the God's prophecy. He also moved a decree granting honours to Diotimus, son of Diopeithes, of the deme Euonymus, in the archonship of Ctesicles.[b]

VIII. DEMOSTHENES

Demosthenes, son of Demosthenes and Cleobulê daughter of Gylon, was of the deme Paeonia. He was left an orphan at the age of seven years [c] by his father, along with his five-year-old sister, and lived during his minority with his mother. Some say that he went to school to Isocrates, but most authorities say that he went to Isaeus of Chalcis, who was a pupil of Isocrates living in Athens. He imitated Thucydides and also the philosopher Plato, whose instruction, some say, he followed with especial zeal. But Hegesias of Magnesia says that he asked his attendant to let him hear Callistratus of Aphidna, son of Empedus, a noted orator who had been a commander of cavalry and had set up the altar to Hermes-of-the-Market [d] and was about to address the popular assembly ; and Demosthenes, when he had heard him speak, fell in love with oratory. Demosthenes heard him, it is true, for only a short time, as long as Callistratus remained in Athens ; but when he had been banished to Thrace and Demosthenes had finished his service as ephebe,[e] he went over to Iso-.

[c] He was born in 384 B.C.; cf. Orations xxx. 15 and xxi 154.

[d] The bronze Hermes Agoraios was ἐν μέσῃ τῇ ἀγορᾷ (schol. Aristoph. Eq. 297; cf. Paus. i. 15. 1) and παρὰ τὴν ποικίλην (Lucian, Iup. Trag. 33).

[e] i.e. at the age of twenty. This service, designed to be a training for citizenship, lasted two years.

413

(844) Ἰσοκράτει καὶ Πλάτωνι· εἶτα καὶ Ἰσαῖον ἀναλαβὼν
εἰς τὴν οἰκίαν τετραετῆ χρόνον αὐτὸν¹ διεπόνησε,
μιμούμενος αὐτοῦ τοὺς λόγους. ὡς δὲ Κτησίβιός
φησιν ἐν τῷ περὶ Φιλοσοφίας, διὰ Καλλίου τοῦ
Συρακουσίου πορίσας τοὺς² Ζήθου τοῦ Ἀμφι-
πολίτου λόγους, διὰ δὲ Χαρικλέους τοῦ Καρυ-
στίου τοὺς Ἀλκιδάμαντος, διέλαβεν³ αὐτούς.

Τελειωθεὶς δέ, ἐλάττω παρὰ τῶν ἐπιτρόπων
παραλαβών, ἔκρινεν αὐτοὺς ἐπιτροπῆς ἐπὶ Τιμοκράτους ἄρχοντος, τρεῖς ὄντας, Ἄφοβον Θηριπ-
D πίδην⁴ Δημοφῶντα ἢ Δημέαν· καὶ μάλιστα τούτου
κατηγόρησεν ἀδελφοῦ τῆς μητρὸς ὄντος, δέκα
τάλαντα τίμημα ἑκάστῃ τῶν δικῶν ἐπιγραψάμενος·
καὶ εἷλεν αὐτούς· τῆς δὲ καταδίκης οὐδὲν ἐπράξατο,
τοὺς μὲν ἀφεὶς⁵ ἀργυρίου τοὺς δὲ καὶ χάριτος.
Ἀριστοφῶντος δ' ἤδη τὴν προστασίαν διὰ γήρας
καταλιπόντος, καὶ χορηγὸς ἐγένετο. Μειδίαν δὲ
τὸν Ἀναγυράσιον πλήξαντα αὐτὸν ἐν τῷ θεάτρῳ
χορηγοῦντα εἰς κρίσιν καταστήσας, λαβὼν τρισ-
χιλίας ἀφῆκε τῆς δίκης. λέγουσι δ' αὐτὸν ἔτι νέον
ὄντα εἰς σπήλαιον ἀπιέναι κἀκεῖ φιλολογεῖν τὸ
ἥμισυ τῆς κεφαλῆς ξυράμενον, ἵνα μὴ προέρχοιτο·

¹ αὐτὸν Xylander: αὐτόν.
² τοὺς Lambinus: τοῦ.
³ διέλαβεν Dübner: ἀνέλαβεν.
⁴ Θηριππίδην Reiske: θηριπίδην.
⁵ ἀφεὶς added by Wolf from Photius.

ᵃ 364–363 B.C.
ᵇ This is incorrect. The author seems to have confused
Demophon and his father Demeas. Demosthenes accused
Aphobus chiefly, and Aphobus was his cousin, not his uncle.
Cf. Demosthenes, xxix. (*Against Aphobus for False Witness*)
59, also 6 and 20: xxviii. (*Against Aphobus* II.) 15; xxvii.
(*Against Aphobus* I.) 4.

crates and Plato ; then he took Isaeus into his house
and for four years exerted himself to imitate his
speeches. But Ctesibius says in his work *On Philosophy* that through Callias of Syracuse he obtained
the speeches of Zethus of Amphipolis and through
Charicles of Carystus those of Alcidamas and that he
studied them thoroughly.

When he attained his majority, because he received from his guardians less than was right, he
brought them to trial for their administration, in the
archonship of Timocrates.[a] There were three of
them : Aphobus, Therippides, and Demophon or
Demeas, and he accused the last-named especially,
since he was his mother's brother.[b] He fixed the
penalty in each suit at ten talents, and he obtained
conviction of all three defendants ; but he exacted no
part of the penalty, for he let them off, some for money
and some as an act of grace. When Aristophon[c] at
last on account of age resigned political leadership,
Demosthenes was even made choregus.[d] And when
Meidias of the deme of Anagyros struck him as he
was performing his duties in the theatre as choregus,
he sued him for the act, but on receipt of three
thousand drachmas he dropped the suit. They say
that when he was still a young man he withdrew into
a cave and studied there, shaving half of his head to
keep himself from going out ; also that he slept on a

---

[c] Aristophon, a second-rate but influential politician, was
especially active in the decade preceding the choregia of
Demosthenes, but no connexion can be perceived between
his retirement and Demosthenes' choregia. He lived to be
nearly 100 years old (ἤδη).
[d] An indication of Demosthenes' restored fortune. The
choregus was a wealthy man who equipped the chorus for
dramas and superintended its training.

E καὶ ἐπὶ στενῆς κλίνης κοιμᾶσθαι, ἵνα διὰ ταχέων
ἀνίστηται· τό τε ῥῶ μὴ δυνάμενον λέγειν ἐκπονῆσαι,
καὶ τὸν ὦμον ἐν τῷ μελετᾶν κινοῦντα ἀπρεπῶς
καταπαῦσαι, παραρτήσαντα ὀβελίσκον ἢ ὥς τινες
ξιφίδιον ἐκ τῆς ὀροφῆς, ἵνα φοβούμενος ἠρεμοίη.
προβαίνοντα δὲ[1] κατὰ τὴν τῶν λόγων ἰσχὺν ἔσοπ-
τρον ἰσομέγεθες αὑτῷ κατασκευάσαι καὶ πρὸς
τοῦτο ἀφορῶντα μελετᾶν, ἵν' ἐπανορθώσηται τὰ
F ἐλλείποντα· καὶ κατιόντα ἐπὶ τὸ Φαληρικὸν πρὸς
τὰς τῶν κυμάτων ἐμβολὰς τὰς σκέψεις ποιεῖσθαι,
ἵν', εἴ ποτε θορυβοίη ὁ δῆμος, μὴ ἐκσταίη· τοῦ δὲ
πνεύματος αὐτῷ ἐνδέοντος, Νεοπτολέμῳ τῷ ὑπο-
κριτῇ μυρίας δοῦναι, ἵν' ὅλας περιόδους ἀπνεύστως
λέγῃ.

Ἐπεὶ δὲ τῷ πολιτεύεσθαι προσῆλθεν, εἰς δύο
διῃρημένων τῶν ἐν τῇ πόλει, καὶ τῶν μὲν φιλιπ-
πιζόντων τῶν δ' ὑπὲρ τῆς ἐλευθερίας δημηγο-
ρούντων, τὴν τῶν ἀντιπολιτευομένων Φιλίππῳ
τάξιν εἵλετο· καὶ διὰ[2] παντὸς τοῦ χρόνου διετέλεσε συμβουλεύων τοῖς κινδυνεύουσιν ὑπὸ Φιλίππῳ
γενέσθαι βοηθεῖν, συμπολιτευόμενος Ὑπερείδῃ
845 Ναυσικλεῖ Πολυεύκτῳ Διοτίμῳ· διὸ καὶ συμμάχους
τοῖς Ἀθηναίοις ἐποίησε Θηβαίους Εὐβοεῖς Κερ-
κυραίους Κορινθίους Βοιωτούς, καὶ πολλοὺς ἄλλους
πρὸς τούτοις. ἐκπεσὼν δέ ποτ' ἐπὶ τῆς ἐκκλησίας
καὶ ἀθυμῶν ἐβάδιζεν οἴκοι· συντυχὼν δ' αὐτῷ
Εὔνομος ὁ Θριάσιος πρεσβύτης ἤδη ὢν προετρέψατο
τὸν Δημοσθένη, μάλιστα δ' ὁ[3] ὑποκριτὴς Ἀνδρό-

---

[1] δὲ Westermann : δὴ.
[2] διὰ added by Lambinus.
[3] δ' ὁ Westermann : δὲ.

narrow bed in order to get up quickly, and that since he could not pronounce the sound of R he learned to do so by hard work, and since in declaiming for practice he made an awkward movement with his shoulder, he put an end to the habit by fastening a spit or, as some say, a dagger from the ceiling to make him through fear keep his shoulder motionless. They say, too, that as he progressed in his ability to speak he had a mirror made as large as himself and kept his eyes on it while practising, that he might correct his faults ; and that he used to go down to the shore at Phalerum and address his remarks to the roar of the waves, that he might not be disconcerted if the people should ever make a disturbance ; and that because he was short of breath he paid Neoptolemus the actor ten thousand drachmas to teach him to speak whole paragraphs without taking breath.

And when he entered upon political life, finding that the public men of the city were divided into two parties, one favouring Philip and the other addressing the populace in defence of liberty, he enrolled himself among those opposed to Philip and always constantly advised the people to support the cause of those peoples which were in danger of being subjected by Philip, in which policy he was associated with Hypereides, Nausicles, Polyeuctus, and Diotimus ; and thus he also brought the Thebans, Euboeans, Corcyraeans, Corinthians, Boeotians, and many others into alliance with the Athenians. Once he was hissed out of the assembly and was walking home feeling discouraged ; but Eunomus of the deme Thria, who was already an old man, happened to meet him and encouraged him, and more than anyone else the actor

(845) νικος εἰπὼν ὡς οἱ μὲν λόγοι καλῶς ἔχοιεν λείποι δ'
B αὐτῷ τὰ τῆς ὑποκρίσεως, ἀπεμνημόνευσέ τε τῶν
ἐπὶ τῆς ἐκκλησίας ὑπ' αὐτοῦ λελεγμένων· καὶ δὴ
πιστεύσαντα τὸν Δημοσθένη παραδοῦναι αὐτὸν τῷ
Ἀνδρονίκῳ. ὅθεν ἐρομένου αὐτόν τινος[1] τί πρῶτον
ἐν ῥητορικῇ, εἶπεν " ὑπόκρισις"· καὶ τί δεύτερον
" ὑπόκρισις"· καὶ τί τρίτον " ὑπόκρισις." προ-
ελθὼν δὲ πάλιν εἰς τὰς ἐκκλησίας, νεωτερικῶς
τινα λέγων διεσύρετο, ὡς κωμῳδηθῆναι αὐτὸν
ὑπ' Ἀντιφάνους καὶ Τιμοκλέους

μὰ γῆν μὰ κρήνας μὰ ποταμοὺς μὰ νάματα·

ὁμόσας δὲ τοῦτον τὸν τρόπον ἐν τῷ δήμῳ θόρυβον
ἐκίνησεν. ὤμνυε δὲ καὶ τὸν Ἀσκληπιόν, προπαρ-
οξύνων Ἀσκλήπιον· καὶ παρεδείκνυεν αὐτὸν ὀρθῶς
λέγοντα· εἶναι γὰρ τὸν θεὸν ἤπιον· καὶ ἐπὶ τούτῳ
C πολλάκις ἐθορυβήθη. σχολάσας δ' Εὐβουλίδῃ τῷ
διαλεκτικῷ Μιλησίῳ ἐπηνωρθώσατο πάντα. γενόμενος δὲ καὶ ἐν τῇ Ὀλυμπιακῇ πανηγύρει καὶ
ἀκούσας Λαμάχου τοῦ Τερειναίου[2] Φιλίππου καὶ
Ἀλεξάνδρου ἐγκώμιον ἀναγινώσκοντος Θηβαίων δὲ
καὶ Ὀλυνθίων κατατρέχοντος, παραναστὰς ἀρχαίων
ποιητῶν μαρτυρίας προηνέγκατο περὶ τῶν Θηβαίοις
καὶ Ὀλυνθίοις καλῶς πραχθέντων, ὡς παύσασθαί

---

[1] τινος added by Meziriacus.
[2] Τερειναίου] Τεριναίου Lambinus; Μυριναίου Life of Demosthenes, chap. ix.

---

[a] A tragic actor of the first part of the fourth century B.C.
See O'Connor, Chapters in the History of Actors and Acting
in Ancient Greece, p. 78. Plutarch, Life of Demosthenes,

Andronicus,[a] by telling him that his words were excellent but that his delivery was deficient, and then Andronicus declaimed from memory the speech which Demosthenes had delivered in the assembly; whereupon Demosthenes was convinced and put himself in the hands of Andronicus. Therefore when someone asked him what was the first thing in oratory, he replied "Delivery," and what the second, "Delivery," and the third, "Delivery."[b] And when he spoke again in the assemblies he was hissed for some new-fangled expressions, so that Antiphanes and Timocles made fun of him in their comedies,

By earth, by founts, by rivers, and by floods,[c]

for it was by swearing in this way that he had caused an uproar in the assembly. He used also to swear by Asclépius, putting the accent on the third syllable from the end, though it is properly on the final syllable; and he offered a proof that he was right, for he said that the god was "mild" (ἤπιος). For this also he often provoked a clamour from the audience. But by going to school to Eubulides the Milesian philosopher he corrected all his faults. Once when he was at the Olympic festival and heard Lamachus of Tereina reading a eulogy of Philip and Alexander and decrying the Thebans and Olynthians, he stood up and quoted the words of the ancient poets testifying to the glorious deeds of the Thebans and Olyn-

chap. vii. assigns to Satyrus about the same relation to the orator's training as is here assigned to Andronicus.

[b] On the meaning, broader than that of our "delivery," in Greek rhetoric see Aristotle, *Rhetoric*, iii., *ad init.*

[c] Kock, *Com. Att. Frag.* ii. p. 128, no. 296. For Demosthenes' metrical oath here parodied see *Life of Demosthenes*, chap. vii.

(845) τε τὸ λοιπὸν τὸν Λάμαχον καὶ φυγεῖν ἐκ τῆς
D πανηγύρεως. Φίλιππον δὲ πρὸς τοὺς ἀναφέροντας
αὐτῷ τὰς κατ' αὐτοῦ δημηγορίας εἰπεῖν ὅτι '' καὶ
αὐτὸς ἂν ἀκούων λέγοντος Δημοσθένους ἐχειρο-
τόνησα τὸν ἄνδρα πρὸς τὸν κατ' ἐμοῦ πόλεμον.''
ἐκάλει δὲ τοὺς μὲν αὐτοῦ λόγους ὁμοίους τοῖς
στρατιώταις διὰ τὴν πολεμικὴν[1] δύναμιν, τοὺς δ'
Ἰσοκράτους τοῖς ἀθληταῖς· τέρψιν γὰρ παρέχειν
αὐτοὺς θεατρικήν.

Ἑπτὰ δὲ καὶ τριάκοντα ἔτη γεγονώς, λογιζο-
μένοις ἀπὸ Δεξιθέου εἰς Καλλίμαχον, ἐφ' οὗ πρὸς
Ὀλυνθίων ἧκε πρεσβεία περὶ τῆς βοηθείας, ἐπεὶ
E ἐπιέζοντο ὑπὸ Φιλίππου τῷ πολέμῳ, ἔπεισεν ἐκ-
πέμψαι τὴν βοήθειαν· τῷ δ' ἑξῆς, ἐφ' οὗ Πλάτων
ἐτελεύτησε, Φίλιππος Ὀλυνθίους κατεστρέψατο.
ἔγνω δ' αὐτὸν καὶ Ξενοφῶν ὁ Σωκρατικὸς ἢ
ἀρχόμενον ἢ ἀκμάζοντα· τῷ μὲν γὰρ τὰ Ἑλληνικὰ
ἐτελεῖτο τὰ περὶ τὴν ἐν Μαντινείᾳ μάχην, ἄρχοντα
δὲ Χαρικλείδην· ὁ δὲ[2] πρότερον ἐπὶ Τιμοκράτους
εἷλε τοὺς ἐπιτρόπους. φεύγοντος δ' Αἰσχίνου μετὰ
τὴν καταδίκην, ἵππῳ κατεδίωξεν αὐτόν· τοῦ δ'
οἰηθέντος αὐτὸν συλλαμβάνεσθαι καὶ προσπεσόντος
F καὶ συγκαλυψαμένου, ἀναστήσας αὐτὸν παρεμυ-
θήσατο καὶ τάλαντον ἔδωκεν ἀργυρίου. καὶ συνεβούλευσε δὲ τῷ δήμῳ ξενικὸν ἐν Θάσῳ τρέφειν,

---

[1] πολεμικὴν Xylander from Photius: πομπικὴν.
[2] δὲ] δ' ἤδη Capps.

---

[a] 385–384 B.C.   [b] 349–348 B.C.
[c] 348–347 B.C.   [d] 363–362 B.C.   [e] 324–323 B.C.
[f] Aeschines brought a suit on grounds of illegality against
Ctesiphon, who proposed in 336 B.C. that Demosthenes be

thians, with the result that Lamachus was silenced
and fled from the festival. And Philip said to those
who reported to him the public speeches of Demosthenes against him, " I myself, if I had heard
Demosthenes speak, would have elected the man
general to carry on the war against me." And Philip
used to say that Demosthenes' speeches were like
soldiers because of their warlike power, but those of
Isocrates were like athletes, because they afforded
pleasure like that of a show.

When he was thirty-seven years old, reckoning
from the archonship of Dexitheus [a] to that of Callimachus,[b] who was in office when an embassy came from
the Olynthians asking for help because they were
being hard pressed by Philip in the war, he persuaded
the Athenians to send the help ; but in the following
year, in which Plato died,[c] Philip overthrew the
Olynthians. Xenophon, the follower of Socrates,
knew him either in his youth or in his prime ; for
Xenophon's *Hellenica* ended with the battle of
Mantineia and the archonship of Charicles,[d] and
Demosthenes had already before that time, in the
archonship of Timocrates,[e] caused the conviction of
his guardians. When Aeschines fled after his condemnation,[f] he followed him on horseback, and
Aeschines, thinking he was arresting him, fell at his
feet and covered his head, but Demosthenes raised
him up, encouraged him, and gave him a talent of
silver. And he advised the people to support a force

honoured by the city with a golden crown. The case was
tried in 330 B.C., when Aeschines delivered his oration *Against
Ctesiphon* and Demosthenes his oration *On the Crown*.
Aeschines received less than one-fifth of the votes of the
dicasts, and was therefore condemned to pay a fine of 1000
drachmas and to forfeit the right to bring any similar suit.

καὶ ἐπὶ τούτῳ τριηράρχης ἐξέπλευσε. σιτώνης
δὲ γενόμενος καὶ κατηγορηθεὶς κλοπῆς ἀφείθη.
Φιλίππου δ' Ἐλάτειαν καταλαβομένου καὶ αὐτὸς
τοῖς ἐν Χαιρωνείᾳ μαχεσαμένοις συνεξῆλθεν· ὅτε[1]
καὶ δοκεῖ τὴν τάξιν λιπεῖν, φεύγοντος δ' αὐτοῦ
βάτον ἐπιλαβέσθαι τῆς χλαμύδος, τὸν δ' ἐπιστρα-
φέντα εἰπεῖν " ζώγρει." εἶχε δὲ καὶ ἐπίσημον ἐπὶ
τῆς ἀσπίδος " ἀγαθῇ τύχῃ." [2] εἶπε μέντοι τὸν
ἐπιτάφιον ἐπὶ τοῖς πεσοῦσι. μετὰ δὲ ταῦτα πρὸς
τὴν ἐπισκευὴν τῆς πόλεως τῇ ἐπιμελείᾳ προσελθὼν
καὶ τῶν τειχῶν ἐπιμελητὴς χειροτονηθεὶς ἀπὸ τῆς
846 ἰδίας οὐσίας εἰσήνεγκε τὸ ἀναλωθὲν ἀργύριον, μνᾶς
ἑκατόν· ἐπέδωκε δὲ καὶ θεωροῖς μυρίας· τριήρους τ'
ἐπιβὰς περιέπλευσε τοὺς συμμάχους ἀργυρολογῶν.
ἐφ' οἷς πολλάκις ἐστεφανώθη, πρότερον μὲν ὑπὸ
Δημομελοῦς Ἀριστονίκου[3] Ὑπερείδου χρυσῷ στεφάνῳ, τελευταῖον δ' ὑπὸ Κτησιφῶντος· καὶ γραφέντος τοῦ ψηφίσματος παρανόμων ὑπὸ Διοδότου
καὶ Αἰσχίνου, ἀπολογούμενος ἐνίκησεν, ὥστε τὸ
πέμπτον μέρος τῶν ψήφων τὸν διώκοντα μὴ
μεταλαβεῖν.

Ὕστερον δ' Ἀλεξάνδρου ἐπὶ τὴν Ἀσίαν στρα-
τευομένου καὶ φυγόντος Ἁρπάλου μετὰ χρημάτων

---

[1] ὅτε Wyttenbach : ὅθεν.
[2] ἀγαθῇ τύχῃ Dübner from *Life of Demosthenes*, chap. xx. :
ἀγαθὴν τύχην.
[3] Ἀριστονίκου Lambinus : ἀριστονείκου.

---

[a] In 338 b.c., when Philip destroyed the independence of
Greece.
[b] Apparently a jest in connexion with the story of his
cowardice.
[c] This indicates that he had not disgraced himself.

of mercenaries at Thasos, and sailed out as commander of a trireme on that occasion. After he had been in charge of the food supply he was accused of embezzlement but was acquitted. When Philip had taken Elateia Demosthenes himself went out with those who fought at Chaeroneia,[a] on which occasion it appears that he deserted his post, and that, as he was running away, a bramble-bush caught his cloak, whereupon he turned and said, "Take me alive." And he had as a device on his shield the words "With good fortune."[b] However, he delivered the funeral address for those who fell.[c] And after that, directing his efforts to the improvement of the city and being elected commissioner in charge of the fortifications, he contributed out of his own pocket the funds expended, amounting to one hundred minae ; he also presented ten thousand drachmas[d] for sacred envoys,[e] and he made a cruise in a trireme to the allied cities collecting money. For these activities he was crowned many times, on earlier occasions on motions offered by Demomeles, Aristonicus, and Hypereides with golden crowns, and the last time on the motion of Ctesiphon ; and when the decree granting this honour was attacked as illegal by Diodotus and Aeschines, he was so successful in his defence that the accuser did not receive one-fifth of the votes.

And at a later time, when Alexander was campaigning in Asia and Harpalus[f] came fleeing to Athens

[a] On these contributions cf. Aeschines, iii. (*Against Ctesiphon*) 17, and Demosthenes, xviii. (*On the Crown*) 118.

[e] Delegations sent to sacred places to attend festivals and the like.

[f] Harpalus, treasurer of Alexander, embezzled a large sum and fled first to Tarsus, then, in 324 B.C., to Greece.

PLUTARCH'S MORALIA

846) εἰς Ἀθήνας, τὸ μὲν πρῶτον ἐκώλυσεν αὐτὸν εἰσ-
δεχθῆναι· ἐπειδὴ δ' εἰσέπλευσε, λαβὼν δαρεικοὺς
B χιλίους μετετάξατο· βουλομένων τ' Ἀθηναίων
Ἀντιπάτρῳ παραδοῦναι τὸν ἄνθρωπον ἀντεῖπεν,
ἔγραψέ τ' ἀποθέσθαι τὰ χρήματα εἰς ἀκρόπολιν
μηδὲ[1] τῷ δήμῳ τὸν ἀριθμὸν εἰπόντα· φήσαντος δ'
Ἁρπάλου ἑπτακόσια συγκατακομίσαι τάλαντα, τὰ
ἀνενεχθέντα εἰς τὴν ἀκρόπολιν εὑρέθη[2] τριακόσια
καὶ πεντήκοντα[3] ἢ ὀλίγῳ πλείονα ὥς φησι Θιλό-
χορος· μετὰ δὲ ταῦτα φυγόντος Ἁρπάλου ἐκ τοῦ
δεσμωτηρίου, ἐν ᾧ ἐφυλάσσετο μέχρις ἂν ἀφίκηταί
τις παρ' Ἀλεξάνδρου, καὶ πορευθέντος εἰς τὴν
Κρήτην ἢ ὡς ἔνιοι ἐπὶ Ταίναρον τῆς Λακωνικῆς,
C αἰτίαν ἔσχεν ὁ Δημοσθένης δωροδοκίας, ὡς[4] διὰ
τοῦτο μήτε τὸν ἀριθμὸν τῶν ἀνακομισθέντων με-
μηνυκὼς μήτε τὴν τῶν φυλασσόντων ἀμέλειαν.
εἰσαχθεὶς δ' εἰς δικαστήριον ὑπὸ Ὑπερείδου Πυθέου
Μενεσαίχμου Ἱμεραίου Πατροκλέους,[5] οἳ ἐποίησαν
καταγνῶναι αὐτοῦ τὴν ἐξ Ἀρείου πάγου βουλήν,
καὶ ἁλοὺς ἔφυγε, πενταπλασίονα ἀποτῖσαι μὴ δυνάμενος (εἶχε δ' αἰτίαν τριάκοντα τάλαντα λαβεῖν), ἢ
ὡς ἔνιοι οὐχ ὑπομείνας τὴν κρίσιν. μετὰ δὲ τοῦτον
τὸν χρόνον τῶν Ἀθηναίων Πολύευκτον πεμψάντων
D πρεσβευτὴν πρὸς τὸ κοινὸν τῶν Ἀρκάδων, ὥστ'
ἀποστῆναι αὐτοὺς τῆς τῶν Μακεδόνων συμμαχίας,
καὶ τοῦ Πολυεύκτου πεῖσαι μὴ δυναμένου, ἐπι-
φανεὶς Δημοσθένης καὶ συνειπὼν ἔπεισεν. ἐφ' ᾧ
θαυμασθεὶς μετὰ χρόνον τινὰ κάθοδον εὕρατο, ψηφί-

[1] μηδὲ Photius: ἤδη.
[2] συγκατακομίσαι . . . εὑρέθη supplied from Photius.
[3] τριακόσια καὶ πεντήκοντα Dübner: ἢ πεντήκοντα mss.;
ὀκτὼ καὶ τριακόσια Photius.
[4] ὡς Westermann: καὶ.

424

with money, at first Demosthenes kept him from being admitted, but after he had entered the harbour, Demosthenes accepted one thousand darics and changed his attitude, and when the Athenians wished to surrender the man to Antipater, he spoke against it and made a motion that Harpalus deposit the money on the Acropolis without even stating the amount to the people ; and although Harpalus stated that he had brought with him seven hundred talents, that which was taken up to the Acropolis was found to amount to only three hundred and fifty or a little more, as Philochorus says. And after this, when Harpalus escaped from the prison in which he was being kept until a representative of Alexander should arrive, and had gone to Crete or, as some say, to Taenarum in Laconia, Demosthenes was accused of bribe-taking and of having this reason for not mentioning the amount of the money taken up or the carelessness of the guard. He was brought to trial by Hypereides, Pytheas, Menesaechmus, Himeraeus, and Patrocles, and they obtained his conviction by the Senate of the Areopagus ; and after his conviction he went into exile, not being able to pay back five times the amount (he was accused of having accepted thirty talents), or, as some say, he did not wait for the trial. After this time the Athenians sent Polyeuctus as envoy to the commonwealth of the Arcadians in order to detach them from their alliance with the Macedonians, and when Polyeuctus was unable to persuade them, Demosthenes appeared to help him and did persuade them. For this he was admired, and after some time he was permitted to return, a decree in his favour having been passed

---

⁵ Πατροκλέους Amyot (Vatic.): προκλέους.

(846) σματος γραφέντος καὶ τριήρους[1] ἀποσταλείσης. τῶν
δ' Ἀθηναίων ψηφισαμένων οἷς[2] ὤφειλε τριάκοντα
ταλάντοις κοσμῆσαι[3] αὐτὸν τὸν βωμὸν τοῦ σωτῆρος
Διὸς ἐν Πειραιεῖ καὶ ἀφεῖσθαι, τοῦτο γράψαντος
τὸ ψήφισμα Δήμωνος Παιανιέως, ὃς ἦν ἀνεψιὸς
αὐτῷ, πάλιν ἐπὶ[4] τούτοις ἦν πολιτευόμενος.

Ἀντιπάτρου δ' εἰς Λάμειαν ὑπὸ τῶν Ἑλλήνων
E συγκλεισθέντος, τῶν Ἀθηναίων εὐαγγέλια θυόντων,
πρός τινα τῶν ἑταίρων Ἀγησίστρατον ἔφη οὐ τὴν
αὐτὴν γνώμην ἔχειν τοῖς ἄλλοις περὶ τῶν πραγ-
μάτων· " ἐπίσταμαι γάρ " εἰπεῖν " τοὺς Ἕλληνας
στάδιον μὲν πολεμεῖν καὶ εἰδότας καὶ δυναμένους,
δόλιχον δ' οὐκέτι." Φάρσαλον δ' ἑλόντος Ἀντιπάτρου καὶ πολιορκήσειν ἀπειλοῦντος Ἀθηναίους,
εἰ μὴ τοὺς ῥήτορας ἐκδοῖησαν, καταλιπὼν ὁ Δημοσθένης τὴν πόλιν ἔφυγε πρῶτον μὲν εἰς Αἴγιναν
ἐπὶ τὸ Αἰάκειον[5] καθεδούμενος, φοβηθεὶς δ' εἰς
Καλαυρίαν μετέστη. ἐκδιδόναι δὲ τοὺς ῥήτορας
F τῶν Ἀθηναίων ψηφισαμένων κἀκεῖνον, καθέζετο
ἱκέτης ἐν τῷ τοῦ Ποσειδῶνος ἱερῷ· ἐλθόντος δ' ἐπ'
αὐτὸν Ἀρχίου τοῦ Φυγαδοθήρου ἐπικαλουμένου, ὃς
παρέβαλεν Ἀναξιμένει τῷ ῥήτορι καὶ πείθοντος
αὐτὸν ἀναστῆναι, ὡς φίλον Ἀντιπάτρῳ γενησό-
μενον, εἶπεν ὅτι " οὔτε, ὅτε ἐτραγῴδεις, ἔπειθές
με οὔτε νῦν πείσεις συμβουλεύων "· τοῦ δ' ἐπι-
χειροῦντος βιάζεσθαι, ἐκώλυσαν αὐτὸν οἱ κατὰ

---

[1] γραφέντος καὶ τριήρους Photius: γραφέντος τριήρους.
[2] οἷς Photius: εἰς ἃ.
[3] ταλάντοις κοσμῆσαι supplied by Bernardakis after Photius and Sintenis.
[4] ἐπὶ Dübner: ἐν.
[5] τὸ Αἰάκειον Xylander: τὸν ἀκραῖον.

---

[a] A stadium was about equal to a furlong and was the usual short-distance run. The *dolichos* was twenty stadia.

and a trireme dispatched to bring him. When the
Athenians passed a decree proposed by his cousin
Demon of Paeania that he should use the thirty
talents which he owed in adorning the altar of Zeus
the Saviour at Peiraeus and should then be absolved,
he returned on those conditions to public life.

When Antipater was shut up in Lamia by the
Greeks, and the Athenians were making thank-
offerings for the good news, he said to his friend
Agesistratus that he did not agree with the rest about
these matters, "for," he said, "I know that the
Greeks have both the knowledge and the strength
for a stadium dash ^{a} in warfare, but cannot hold out
for a long-distance run." When Antipater had taken
Pharsalus and threatened to besiege the Athenians
unless they surrendered the orators, Demosthenes
left the city and fled first to Aegina to sit as suppliant
in the sanctuary of Aeacus, but was frightened and
changed over to Calauria; and when the Athenians
voted to surrender the orators including himself, he
took his seat as a suppliant there in the temple of
Poseidon. And when Archias,^{b} nicknamed "Exile-
Hunter," who had been a pupil of the orator Anaximenes, came to fetch him and urged him to leave his
sanctuary, indicating that Antipater would receive
him as a friend, he said, "Your acting in tragedy was
not convincing to me, nor will your advice be convincing now"; and when Archias tried to use force,
the authorities of the city prevented him, and Demo-

^{b} This Archias was a tragic actor recorded as victor at the
Lenaea *circa* 330 B.C. in *I.G.* ii.^{2} 2325 n. Plutarch, *Life of
Demosthenes*, chap. xxviii. names several other prominent
Athenians "hunted down" by him, among them Hypereides.
Cf. p. 441 below. Another version of Demosthenes' retort
to Archias is given *ibid.* 29.

τὴν πόλιν· καὶ Δημοσθένης ἔφη " οὐ σωτηρίας δεόμενος κατέφυγον εἰς Καλαυρίαν, ἀλλ' ὡς ἐλέγξων
847 Μακεδόνας καὶ τὰ¹ τῶν θεῶν βιασομένους²"· αἰτή-
σας τε γραμματεῖον ἔγραψεν, ὡς μὲν Δημήτριος ὁ
Μάγνης φησί, τὸ ἐπὶ τῆς εἰκόνος αὐτοῦ ἐλεγεῖον
ἐπιγεγραμμένον ὑπὸ τῶν Ἀθηναίων ὕστερον

εἴπερ ἴσην ῥώμην γνώμῃ, Δημόσθενες, ἔσχες,
οὔποτ' ἂν Ἑλλήνων ἦρξεν Ἄρης Μακεδών.

κεῖται δ' ἡ³ εἰκὼν πλησίον τοῦ περισχοινίσματος
καὶ τοῦ βωμοῦ τῶν δώδεκα θεῶν, ὑπὸ Πολυεύκτου
πεποιημένη. ὡς δ' ἔνιοί φασι, τοῦτο εὑρέθη γε-
γραμμένον " Δημοσθένης Ἀντιπάτρῳ χαίρειν."
ἀποθανεῖν δ' αὐτὸν Φιλόχορος μέν φησι φάρμακον
πιόντα, Σάτυρος δ' ὁ συγγραφεὺς τὸν κάλαμον
B πεφαρμάχθαι, ᾧ γράφειν ἤρξατο τὴν ἐπιστολήν, οὗ
γευσάμενον ἀποθανεῖν· Ἐρατοσθένης δ' ἐκ πολλοῦ
δεδοικότα Μακεδόνας περὶ τῷ βραχίονι κρίκον περικεῖσθαι πεφαρμαγμένον. εἰσὶ δ' οἵ φασι συσχόντα
αὐτὸν τὸ πνεῦμα ἀποθανεῖν· οἱ δ' εἶπον τοῦ κατὰ
τὴν σφραγῖδα φαρμάκου γευσάμενον. ἐβίω δ' ὡς
μὲν οἱ τὰ πλείω λέγουσιν ἔτη ἑβδομήκοντα, ὡς δ'
οἱ τὰ ἐλάττω, ἑπτὰ καὶ ἑξήκοντα. ἐπολιτεύσατο⁴
δὲ δύο καὶ εἴκοσιν.

¹ καὶ τὰ Photius : καὶ κατά.
² βιασομένους Dübner : βιασαμένους.
³ ἡ added by Dübner.
⁴ ἐβίω . . . ἐπολιτεύσατο Salmasius from Photius : lacking
in the mss.

ᵃ See Bergk, *Poet. Lyr. Graec.* ii. p. 331.
ᵇ This was a large area in the Market Place which was
enclosed at ostracisms, and perhaps at other times, within a

sthenes said, " I took refuge in Calauria, not to save my life, but to convict the Macedonians of using force even against the sanctuaries of the gods," and asking for writing materials he wrote—so Demetrius of Magnesia says—the distich which was later inscribed by the Athenians upon his statue :

> Had you possessed but the strength, Demosthenes, like to your spirit,
> Never would Macedon's war Greece to submission have brought.[a]

The statue, a work of Polyeuctus, is placed near the Roped-off Enclosure [b] and the altar of the Twelve Gods. But according to some authorities he was found to have written " Demosthenes to Antipater, greeting." [c] Philochorus [d] says that he died by drinking poison, but Satyrus the historian says that the pen with which he began to write the letter was poisoned, and he died by sucking it ; and Eratosthenes says that for a long time he wore a poisoned bracelet on his arm through fear of the Macedonians. There are those who say that he died by holding his breath, but others assert that it was by sucking poison from his seal ring. He lived, according to those who give the higher number, seventy years, according to those who give the lower, sixty-seven. He was active in politics twenty-two years.

barrier of rope for the better control of the popular assembly. Since the contiguous altar of the Twelve Gods has recently (*vide* Shear in *Hesperia*, iv. pp. 355 ff.) been uncovered in the northern part of the Agora, this enclosure can no longer, with Judeich (*Topographie von Athen*[2], p. 250), be placed in the south-west area, on the slopes of the Areopagus.

    [c] These were the words usually employed at the beginning of letters.

    [d] Müller, *Frag. Hist. Graec.* i. p. 407.

(847) Ἡνίκα δὲ Φίλιππος ἐτεθνήκει, λαμπρὰν ἐσθῆτα
προῆλθεν ἔχων, καίτοι τῆς θυγατρὸς αὐτοῦ νεωστὶ
τετελευτηκυίας, ἐφηδόμενος τῷ τοῦ Μακεδόνος
C θανάτῳ. συνήργησε δὲ καὶ Θηβαίοις πρὸς Ἀλέξανδρον πολεμοῦσι καὶ τοὺς ἄλλους Ἕλληνας
ἐπέρρωσεν ἀεί· διόπερ Θήβας κατασκάψας ἐξῄτει[1]
παρ' Ἀθηναίων Ἀλέξανδρος αὐτόν, ἀπειλῶν, εἰ μὴ
δοίησαν. στρατευομένῳ δ' αὐτῷ ἐπὶ Πέρσας καὶ
αἰτοῦντι ναυτικὸν παρ' Ἀθηναίων ἀντεῖπεν, ἄδηλον
εἰπών, εἰ οὐ κατὰ τῶν παρασχόντων χρήσεται.

Κατέλιπε δὲ δύο παῖδας ἐκ μιᾶς γυναικὸς τῶν
εὐδοκίμων,[2] Ἡλιοδώρου τινὸς θυγατρός· θυγατέρα
δὲ[3] μίαν ἔσχεν, ἣ παῖς ἔτι οὖσα πρὸ γάμου ἐτε-
λεύτησεν· εἶχε δὲ καὶ ἀδελφήν, ἐξ ἧς καὶ Λάχου
Λευκονοέως[4] ἀδελφιδοῦς αὐτῷ Δημοχάρης ἐγένετο,
ἀνὴρ καὶ κατὰ πόλεμον ἀγαθὸς καὶ κατὰ τοὺς πο-
D λιτικοὺς λόγους οὐδενὸς χείρων. ἔστι δ' αὐτοῦ
εἰκὼν ἐν τῷ πρυτανείῳ εἰσιόντων πρὸς τὴν ἑστίαν
ἐν[5] δεξιᾷ ὁ πρῶτος περιεζωσμένος ἅμα τῷ ἱματίῳ
καὶ ξίφος· οὕτω γὰρ δημηγορῆσαι λέγεται, ἡνίκα
Ἀντίπατρος ἐξῄτει[6] τοὺς ῥήτορας. χρόνῳ δ'
ὕστερον Ἀθηναῖοι σίτησίν τ' ἐν πρυτανείῳ τοῖς
συγγενέσι τοῦ Δημοσθένους ἔδοσαν καὶ αὐτῷ τε-
τελευτηκότι τὴν εἰκόνα ἀνέθεσαν ἐν ἀγορᾷ ἐπὶ
Γοργίου ἄρχοντος, αἰτησαμένου αὐτῷ τὰς δωρεὰς

---

    [1] ἐξῄτει Sintenis: ἐζήτει.
    [2] εὐδοκίμων Meziriacus: εὐδοκίμου.
    [3] δὲ added by Dübner.
    [4] Λευκονοέως Westermann: λευκονέως.
    [5] ἐν added by Westermann.
    [6] ἐξῄτει Lambinus: ἐζήτει.

---

    [a] 336 B.C.
    [b] See *Life of Demosthenes*, chap. xxii.

When Philip died,[a] Demosthenes came out from
his house dressed in a white garment, in spite of the
fact that his daughter had lately died, thus showing his joy at the death of the Macedonian.[b] He
also assisted the Thebans when they were at war
with Alexander, and he always encouraged the rest
of the Greeks ; for which reason Alexander after
razing Thebes demanded him of the Athenians and
threatened them if they should refuse to surrender
him. And when Alexander was making war on the
Persians and called upon the Athenians for a naval
force, he spoke against it, saying that it was not clear
whether Alexander would not employ the force
against those who furnished it.

He left two sons by one wife of noble family,
daughter of a certain Heliodorus ; and he had one
daughter who died unmarried while still a child. He
had also a sister to whom and her husband Laches of
Leuconoë his nephew Demochares was born, a man
both brave in war and inferior to none in political
speeches. There is a statue of him in the Prytaneum,[c]
the first on the right as you go in towards the hearth,
wearing both a cloak and a sword ; for he is said to
have worn this costume in addressing the people when
Antipater was demanding the surrender of the
orators. At a later time the Athenians voted maintenance in the Prytaneum to the relatives of Demosthenes and erected to him after his death the statue
in the Market-place,[d] in the archonship of Gorgias.[e]
The grants to him were requested by his nephew

---

[c] The Prytaneum was the building in which the Prytanes
who formed the executive committee of the Senate held their
meetings. Maintenance in the Prytaneum was often voted
in recognition of service to the state.

[d] See above, 847 A.   [e] 280–279 B.C.

τοῦ ἀδελφιδοῦ Δημοχάρους· ᾧ καὶ αὐτῷ πάλιν ὁ
υἱὸς Λάχης Δημοχάρους Λευκονοεὺς[1] ᾐτήσατο δω-
E ρεὰς ἐπὶ Πυθαράτου ἄρχοντος, δεκάτῳ ὕστερον
ἔτει,[2] εἰς τὴν τῆς εἰκόνος στάσιν ἐν ἀγορᾷ καὶ
σίτησιν ἐν πρυτανείῳ αὐτῷ τε καὶ ἐκγόνων ἀεὶ τῷ
πρεσβυτάτῳ καὶ προεδρίαν ἐν ἅπασι τοῖς ἀγῶσι.
καὶ ἔστι τὰ ψηφίσματα ὑπὲρ ἀμφοτέρων ἀνα-
γεγραμμένα, ἡ δ᾽ εἰκὼν τοῦ Δημοχάρους εἰς τὸ
πρυτανεῖον μετεκομίσθη, περὶ ἧς προείρηται.

Φέρονται δ᾽ αὐτοῦ λόγοι γνήσιοι ἑξήκοντα πέντε.
φασὶ δέ τινες καὶ ἀσώτως αὐτὸν βιῶναι, γυναικείαις
τ᾽ ἐσθῆσι χρώμενον καὶ κωμάζοντα ἑκάστοτε, ὅθεν
Βάταλον ἐπικληθῆναι· οἱ δ᾽ ὑποκοριστικῶς ἀπὸ τοῦ
F ὀνόματος τῆς τροφοῦ λέγουσιν αὐτὸν οὕτω λελοι-
δορῆσθαι. Διογένης δ᾽ ὁ κύων θεασάμενος αὐτὸν
ποτ᾽ ἐν καπηλείῳ αἰσχυνόμενον καὶ ὑποχωροῦντα,
εἶπεν '' ὅσῳ μᾶλλον ὑποχωρεῖς, τοσούτῳ μᾶλλον ἐν
τῷ καπηλείῳ ἔσῃ.'' ἔλεγε δ᾽ αὐτὸν παρασκώπτων
ἐν μὲν τοῖς λόγοις Σκύθην εἶναι, ἐν δὲ ταῖς μάχαις
ἀστικόν. ἔλαβε δὲ[3] καὶ παρ᾽ Ἐφιάλτου χρυσίον
ἑνὸς τῶν δημαγωγῶν, ὃς πρεσβεύσας πρὸς βασιλέα
χρήματα φέρων ἧκε λάθρα, ὅπως διανείμας τοῖς
δημαγωγοῖς τὸν πρὸς Φίλιππον ἐξάψῃ πόλεμον·
848 καὶ ἰδίᾳ αὐτὸν δωροδοκῆσαι παρὰ βασιλέως φασὶ
δαρεικοὺς τρισχιλίους. Ἀναξίλαν[4] δέ τινα Ὠρείτην,
ξένον αὐτοῦ γεγονότα, συλλαβὼν ἐβασάνιζεν ὡς
κατάσκοπον, οὐδὲν δ᾽ ἐξειπόντα ἐψηφίσατο τοῖς

---

[1] Λευκονοεὺς Westermann : λευκονεύς.
[2] ἔτει added by Xylander.
[3] δὲ added by Bernardakis.
[4] Ἀναξίλαν] Ἀνάξινον Demosthenes, xviii. (*On the Crown*),
137, Aeschines, iii. (*Against Ctesiphon*), 223.

Demochares, for whom in turn his son Laches, son of Demochares, of Leuconoë, asked in the archonship of Pytharatus,[a] the tenth year after, for grants extending to the erection of the statue in the Market-place, maintenance in the Prytaneum for Demochares and his eldest descendant in perpetuity, and front seats at all competitive spectacles. And the decrees in favour of both are inscribed, but the statue of Demochares mentioned above was transferred to the Prytaneum.

Sixty-five genuine speeches of Demosthenes are current. Some say that he lived a dissolute life, wearing women's clothes and indulging in revels on every occasion, on which account he was nicknamed Batalus[b]; but others say that this was a diminutive derived from the name of his nurse and was given to him in reproach. And Diogenes the Cynic, seeing him once in a tavern looking ashamed and trying to withdraw from sight, said, " The more you withdraw, the more you will be in the tavern." And he jeered at him, saying that in his speeches he was a Scythian, but in battle a city man. He received money from Ephialtes also, one of the politicians, who had been on an embassy to the King of Persia and came secretly bringing funds for distribution among the politicians for the purpose of stirring up the war against Philip ; and they say that he received a private bribe of three thousand darics from the King. He arrested a certain Anaxilas of Oreus, who had been a guest-friend of his, subjected him to torture as a spy, and when he confessed nothing proposed a decree

---

[a] 271–270 B.C.

[b] Cf. Aeschines, i. (Against Timarchus) 131. The nick-name is also said to refer to his stammering.

(848) ἔνδεκα παραδοῦναι. λέγειν δέ ποτε κωλυόμενος ὑπ'
Ἀθηναίων ἐν ἐκκλησίᾳ βραχὺ ἔφη βούλεσθαι πρὸς
αὐτοὺς εἰπεῖν, τῶν δὲ σιωπησάντων "νεανίας,"
εἶπε, "θέρους ὥρᾳ ἐμισθώσατο ἐξ ἄστεος ὄνον
Μέγαράδε· μεσούσης δὲ τῆς ἡμέρας καὶ σφοδρῶς
φλέγοντος τοῦ ἡλίου, ἑκάτερος αὐτῶν ἐβούλετο
ὑποδύεσθαι ὑπὸ τὴν σκιάν· εἶργον δ' ἀλλήλους, ὁ
B μὲν μεμισθωκέναι τὸν ὄνον οὐ τὴν σκιὰν λέγων, ὁ
δὲ μεμισθωμένος τὴν πᾶσαν ἔχειν ἐξουσίαν"· καὶ
ταῦτ' εἰπὼν ἀπῄει. τῶν δ' Ἀθηναίων ἐπισχόντων
καὶ δεομένων πέρας ἐπιθεῖναι τῷ λόγῳ, "εἶθ' ὑπὲρ
μὲν ὄνου σκιᾶς," ἔφη, "βούλεσθε ἀκούειν, λέγοντος
δὲ ὑπὲρ σπουδαίων πραγμάτων οὐ βούλεσθε."
Πώλου δέ ποτε τοῦ ὑποκριτοῦ πρὸς αὐτὸν εἰπόντος,
ὅτι δυσὶν ἡμέραις ἀγωνισάμενος τάλαντον λάβοι
μισθόν, "ἐγὼ δ'," εἶπε, "πέντε τάλαντα, μίαν
ἡμέραν σιωπήσας." παραφθαρεὶς δὲ τὴν φωνὴν ἐν
ἐκκλησίᾳ καὶ θορυβηθεὶς τοὺς ὑποκριτὰς ἔφη δεῖν
κρίνειν ἐκ τῆς φωνῆς τοὺς δὲ ῥήτορας ἐκ τῆς
C γνώμης. ὀνειδίσαντος δ' αὐτὸν Ἐπικλέους ὅτι ἀεὶ
σκέπτοιτο, "αἰσχυνοίμην γὰρ ἄν[1]," εἶπεν, "εἰ
τηλικούτῳ δήμῳ συμβουλεύων αὐτοσχεδιάζοιμι."
ἱστοροῦσι δ' ὡς οὐδὲ λύχνον ἔσβεσεν, ἄχρι πεντήκοντα ἐτῶν ἐγένετο, διακριβῶν[2] τοὺς λόγους. αὐτὸς
δέ φησιν ὑδροποσίᾳ χρήσασθαι. ἔγνω δ' αὐτὸν καὶ
Λυσίας ὁ ῥήτωρ καὶ Ἰσοκράτης εἶδε πολιτευόμενον
ἄχρι τῆς ἐν Χαιρωνείᾳ μάχης, καί τινες τῶν
Σωκρατικῶν φιλοσόφων. τοὺς δὲ πλείστους λόγους

---

[1] ἄν added by Dübner.
[2] διακριβῶν Lambinus: διακρίνων.

---

[a] "An ass's shadow" was proverbial for things utterly
trivial.

that he be handed over to the executioners. And once when he was being prevented by the Athenians from speaking in the assembly, he said that he only wished to speak briefly to them, and when they became silent he said, "A young man in the summer time hired an ass to go from the city to Megara. When noon came and the sun was blazing fiercely, both he and the owner of the ass wished to lie down in its shadow. Each tried to prevent the other from so doing, the owner maintaining that he had rented him the ass, not its shadow, and the one who had hired the ass that he had complete rights in him." When he had said this, he began to go away; and when the Athenians stopped him and asked him to tell the rest of the tale, he said, "You are willing to listen when I speak about the shadow of an ass,[a] but when I speak of serious matters, you refuse." Once when Polus the actor told him that he received a talent as pay for acting two days, he replied, "And I five talents for being silent one day." And when his voice failed in the assembly and the people jeered at him, he said "It is actors who should be judged by their voices, but statesmen by their opinions." And when Epicles rebuked him for always preparing his speeches, he said, "I should be ashamed to speak off-hand to such a great people." They say that he never put out his lamp until he was fifty years old—polishing his speeches. And he says himself that he was a water-drinker.[b] Lysias the orator was acquainted with him, and Isocrates saw him engaged in public affairs until the battle of Chaeroneia, as did some of the Socratic philosophers. He delivered most of his

[b] Demosthenes, vi. (*Second Philippic*) 30; xix. (*False Legation*) 46.

(848) εἶπεν αὐτοσχεδιάσας, εὖ πρὸς αὐτὸ[1] πεφυκώς.
D πρῶτος δ᾽ ἔγραψε στεφανωθῆναι αὐτὸν χρυσῷ
στεφάνῳ Ἀριστόνικος Νικοφάνους Ἀναγυράσιος,
ὑπωμόσατο δὲ Διώνδας.

Θ΄. ΥΠΕΡΕΙΔΗΣ

Ὑπερείδης[2] Γλαυκίππου μὲν ἦν πατρὸς τοῦ
Διονυσίου, τῶν δὲ δήμων[3] Κολλυτεύς. ἔσχε δ᾽
υἱὸν ὁμώνυμον τῷ πατρὶ Γλαύκιππον, ῥήτορα καὶ
λόγους συγγράψαντα· οὗ πάλιν Ἀλφίνους ἐγένετο.
ἀκροατὴς δὲ Πλάτωνος γενόμενος τοῦ φιλοσόφου
ἅμα Λυκούργῳ[4] καὶ Ἰσοκράτους τοῦ ῥήτορος
E ἐπολιτεύσατο Ἀθήνησι, καθ᾽ ὃν χρόνον Ἀλέξανδρος
τῶν Ἑλληνικῶν ἥπτετο πραγμάτων· καὶ περὶ τῶν
στρατηγῶν ὧν ᾔτει παρ᾽ Ἀθηναίων ἀντεῖπε, καὶ
περὶ τῶν τριήρων· συνεβούλευσε δὲ καὶ τὸ ἐπὶ
Ταινάρῳ ξενικὸν μὴ διαλῦσαι, οὗ Χάρης ἡγεῖτο,
εὐνόως πρὸς τὸν στρατηγὸν διακείμενος. τὸ δὲ
πρῶτον μισθοῦ δίκας ἔλεγε. δόξας δὲ κεκοινωνη-
κέναι τῶν Περσικῶν χρημάτων Ἐφιάλτῃ τριήρ-
αρχός τε αἱρεθείς, ὅτε Βυζάντιον ἐπολιόρκει
Φίλιππος, βοηθὸς Βυζαντίοις ἐκπεμφθείς, κατὰ τὸν
ἐνιαυτὸν τοῦτον ὑπέστη χορηγῆσαι, τῶν ἄλλων

---

[1] αὐτὸ Reiske: αὐτούς.
[2] Ὑπερείδης] usually ὑπερίδης in mss.
[3] τῶν δὲ δήμων Westermann: τὸν δὲ δῆμον.
[4] Λυκούργῳ Blum: λυκούργου.

---

[a] This does not agree with what has been said above about
his preparing all his speeches.
[b] In the Athenian courts of law the parties to a suit were
obliged to speak in person, therefore those who were not sure
of their own ability hired others to write their speeches, which
they learned by heart and delivered.

speeches extemporaneously, as he was well endowed for that by nature.[a] The first who moved that he be crowned with a crown of gold was Aristonicus of Anagyrus, son of Nicophanes, but Diondas prevented it by an affidavit.

IX. HYPEREIDES

Hypereides was the son of Glaucippus and grandson of Dionysius, of the deme of Collytê. He had a son, Glaucippus, named after his grandfather, who was an orator and writer of speeches.[b] He in turn had a son Alphinous. After being a pupil of the philosopher Plato, along with Lycurgus, and of the orator Isocrates, Hypereides entered upon public life at Athens at the time when Alexander was interfering in the affairs of Greece. And he spoke in opposition to him concerning the generals whose surrender he demanded of the Athenians and concerning the triremes. He also advised against disbanding the mercenary force at Taenarum under the command of Chares, since he was well disposed towards that general. At first he pleaded in suits at law in return for a fee. And since he was believed to have shared the Persian funds [c] with Ephialtes, and was elected trierarch when Philip was besieging Byzantium, he was sent out to aid the Byzantines; and in that year he bore the expense of a chorus,[d]

[c] The comic poets of the time were very free with such insinuations, e.g. Timocles in his Delos (Kock, Com. Att. Frag. ii. p. 432) mentions both Demosthenes and Hypereides.

[d] Such offices or " liturgies " were imposed upon wealthy men only, and the fact that he undertook one may have led to the belief that he partook of the Persian funds, or that belief may have led to the imposition of the offices.

F λειτουργίας πάσης ἀφειμένων. ἔγραψε δὲ καὶ
Δημοσθένει¹ τιμάς, καὶ τοῦ ψηφίσματος ὑπὸ Διώνδα
παρανόμων γραφέντος ἀπέφυγε. φίλος δ' ὢν τοῖς
περὶ Δημοσθένη καὶ Λυσικλέα καὶ Λυκοῦργον, οὐκ
ἐνέμεινε μέχρι τέλους· ἀλλ' ἐπεὶ Λυσικλῆς μὲν καὶ
Λυκοῦργος ἐτεθνήκεσαν, Δημοσθένης δ' ὡς παρ'
Ἁρπάλου δωροδοκήσας ἐκρίνετο, προχειρισθεὶς ἐξ
ἀπάντων (μόνος γὰρ ἔμεινεν ἀδωροδόκητος) κατηγόρησεν αὐτοῦ. κριθεὶς δ' ὑπὸ τοῦ Ἀριστογείτονος
849 παρανόμων ἐπὶ τῷ γράψαι μετὰ Χαιρώνειαν τοὺς
μετοίκους πολίτας ποιήσασθαι τοὺς δὲ δούλους
ἐλευθέρους, ἱερὰ δὲ καὶ παῖδας καὶ γυναῖκας εἰς τὸν
Πειραιᾶ ἀποθέσθαι, ἀπέφυγεν. αἰτιωμένων δέ
τινων αὐτὸν ὡς παριδόντα πολλοὺς νόμους ἐν τῷ
ψηφίσματι, " ἐπεσκότει," ἔφη, " μοι τὰ Μακεδόνων
ὅπλα " καὶ " οὐκ² ἐγὼ τὸ ψήφισμα ἔγραψα ἡ δ' ἐν
Χαιρωνείᾳ μάχη." μετὰ μέντοι τοῦτο νεκρῶν
ἔδωκεν ἀναίρεσιν ὁ Φίλιππος φοβηθείς, πρότερον
οὐ δοὺς τοῖς ἐλθοῦσιν ἐκ Λεβαδείας κήρυξιν.
ὕστερον δὲ μετὰ τὰ περὶ Κραννῶνα³ συμβάντα
ἐξαιτηθεὶς ὑπ' Ἀντιπάτρου καὶ μέλλων ἐκδίδοσθαι
B ὑπὸ τοῦ δήμου ἔφυγεν ἐκ τῆς πόλεως εἰς Αἴγιναν
ἅμα τοῖς κατεψηφισμένοις· καὶ συμβαλὼν Δημο-

---

¹ Δημοσθένει Reiske after Photius : Δημοσθένους.
² καὶ οὐκ Photius : οὐκ.
³ Κραννῶνα Blass : κράνωνα.

ᵃ The shadow of the shields made him fail to see the laws
(taking παριδόντα literally).

when others were released from all contributions to the
public service.   He also proposed honours for Demosthenes, and when suit was brought by Diondas on the
ground that the decree was contrary to law, he was
acquitted.   Although he was a friend of Demosthenes, Lysicles, Lycurgus, and their associates, he
did not remain so to the end ; but when Lysicles and
Lycurgus were dead and Demosthenes was being
tried for receiving bribes from Harpalus, he was
chosen from all the orators (for he alone was unbribed)
and brought the accusation against him.   And when
he was brought to trial by Aristogeiton for illegal
conduct in proposing a decree after the battle of
Chaeroneia to grant citizenship to the resident aliens,
to set the slaves free, and to put the sacred objects,
the children, and the women in Peiraeus for safe-
keeping, he was acquitted.   And when certain
persons blamed him for having disregarded many laws
in his decree, he said, " The shields of the Macedonians cast a shadow *a* over my eyes," and " It was
not I, but the battle of Chaeroneia, that proposed the
decree."   After this, however, Philip was frightened
and granted permission to remove the bodies of the
slain, though before that he had refused it to the
heralds who came from Lebadeia.   Later, however,
after the battle of Crannon,*b* when his surrender was
demanded by Antipater and the people was on the
point of surrendering him, he fled from the city to
Aegina along with those against whom decrees had
been passed.   Here he met Demosthenes and excused

b After the death of Alexander the Great the Greeks
revolted, but they lacked leadership, and when they were
defeated in an engagement at Crannon, Thessaly, in August
322 B.C., the Greek states came to terms separately with
Antipater.

849) σθένει καὶ περὶ τῆς διαφορᾶς ἀπολογησάμενος,
ἀπαλλαγεὶς ἐκεῖθεν, ὑπ᾽ Ἀρχίου τοῦ Φυγαδοθήρου
ἐπικληθέντος, Θουρίου μὲν τὸ γένος ὑποκριτοῦ δὲ
τὰ πρῶτα τότε δὲ τῷ Ἀντιπάτρῳ βοηθοῦντος,
ἐλήφθη πρὸς βίαν ἐν τῷ ἱερῷ τοῦ Ποσειδῶνος
ἐχόμενος τοῦ[1] ἀγάλματος· καὶ ἀχθεὶς πρὸς Ἀντίπατρον εἰς Κόρινθον, ἔπειτα βασανιζόμενος, δι-
έφαγε τὴν γλῶτταν, ὥστε μηδὲν ἐξειπεῖν τῶν
τῆς πόλεως ἀπορρήτων δυνηθῆναι· καὶ οὕτως
C ἐτελεύτησε, Πυανεψιῶνος ἐνάτῃ ἱσταμένου. Ἕρ-
μιππος δέ φησιν αὐτὸν γλωττοτομηθῆναι εἰς
Μακεδονίαν ἐλθόντα καὶ ῥιφῆναι ἄταφον, Ἀλφίνουν
δ᾽ ἀνεψιὸν ὄντα αὐτῷ ἤ, ὥς τινες, Γλαυκίππου τοῦ
υἱοῦ[2] τὸν υἱὸν διὰ Φιλοπείθους τινὸς ἰατροῦ λαβόντα
ἐξουσίαν τοῦ σώματος καῦσαι αὐτὸν καὶ τὰ ὀστᾶ
κομίσαι εἰς Ἀθήνας τοῖς προσήκουσι παρὰ τὰ
Ἀθηναίων καὶ Μακεδόνων δόγματα· οὐ μόνον γὰρ
κελεῦσαι αὐτοὺς φυγεῖν, ἀλλὰ μηδ᾽ ἐν τῇ οἰκείᾳ
ταφῆναι. οἱ δ᾽ ἐν Κλεωναῖς ἀποθανεῖν αὐτὸν λέγουσιν, ἀπαχθέντα μετὰ τῶν ἄλλων, ὅπου γλωττοτομηθῆναι καὶ διαφθαρῆναι ὃν προείρηται τρόπον·
τοὺς δ᾽ οἰκείους τὰ ὀστᾶ λαβόντας[3] θάψαι τε ἅμα
τοῖς γονεῦσι πρὸ τῶν Ἱππάδων πυλῶν, ὥς φησιν
D Ἡλιόδωρος[4] ἐν τῷ τρίτῳ περὶ Μνημάτων. νυνὶ δὲ
κατερήρειπται τὸ μνῆμα καὶ ἔστιν ἄδηλον.

Πάντων δὲ κατὰ τὴν δημηγορίαν διενεγκεῖν
λέγεται· τέτακται δὲ ὑπ᾽ ἐνίων πρὸ Δημοσθένους.
φέρονται δ᾽ αὐτοῦ λόγοι ἑβδομήκοντα ἑπτά, ὧν

---

[1] τοῦ added by Blass.
[2] τοῦ υἱοῦ Bernardakis: τινὸς or υἱοῦ.
[3] Blass, followed by Bernardakis, marks a gap here.
[4] Ἡλιόδωρος] Διόδωρος Ruhnken, cf. Müller, Frag. Hist.
Graec. ii. p. 354.

himself for his disagreement with him. After leaving
Aegina he was seized forcibly by Archias,[a] nicknamed
" The Exile-Hunter " (a Thurian by birth, at first an
actor, but at that time an assistant of Antipater), in
the temple of Poseidon [b] while clinging to the statue
of the god. He was brought to Antipater at Corinth,
and when put to the torture he bit off his tongue that
he might not be able to utter any secrets of his native
city. And in this way he died, on the ninth day of the
month of Pyanepsion. But Hermippus [c] says that he
went to Macedonia, where his tongue was cut out and
he was thrown out unburied, and that Alphinous, who
was his cousin (or, as some say, the son of his son
Glaucippus), obtained possession of the body by the
aid of a physician named Philopeithes, burned it and
brought the bones to Athens to his relatives contrary
to the decrees of the Athenians and the Macedonians ;
for they had ordered, not only that he be exiled, but
that he be not even buried in his own country. And
others say that he died at Cleonae after being brought
there with the rest, where his tongue was cut out and
he perished in the manner related above ; and that
his relatives obtained the bones and buried them with
his ancestors before the gates of the Hippades,[d] as
Heliodorus says in the third book of his work *On
Monuments*. But now the monument has fallen in
ruins and cannot be identified.

He is said to have excelled all in addressing the
people ; and by some critics he is ranked above
Demosthenes. Seventy-seven speeches are current

[a] See above, p. 427, note *b*.
[b] At Hermionê.
[c] Müller, *Frag. Hist. Graec.* i. p. 50.
[d] At Athens, probably south-east from the Acropolis.

(849) γνήσιοί εἰσι πεντήκοντα δύο. ἐγένετο δὲ καὶ πρὸς
τὰ ἀφροδίσια καταφερής, ὡς ἐκβαλεῖν μὲν τὸν
υἱὸν εἰσαγαγεῖν δὲ Μυρρίνην τὴν πολυτελεστάτην
ἑταίραν, ἐν Πειραιεῖ δ' ἔχειν Ἀρισταγόραν, ἐν
Ἐλευσῖνι δ' ἐν τοῖς ἰδίοις κτήμασι Φίλαν τὴν¹
E Θηβαίαν, εἴκοσι μνῶν λυτρωσάμενος. ἐποιεῖτο
τε τὸν περίπατον ἐν τῇ ἰχθυοπώλιδι ὁσημέραι.
ὡμιληκὼς δέ, ὡς εἰκός δή, καὶ² Φρύνῃ τῇ ἑταίρᾳ
ἀσεβεῖν κρινομένῃ συνεστάθη³· αὐτὸς γὰρ τοῦτο ἐν
ἀρχῇ τοῦ λόγου δηλοῖ· μελλούσης δ' αὐτῆς ἁλί-
σκεσθαι, παραγαγὼν εἰς μέσον καὶ περιρρήξας τὴν
ἐσθῆτα ἐπέδειξε τὰ στέρνα τῆς γυναικός· καὶ τῶν
δικαστῶν εἰς τὸ κάλλος ἀπιδόντων, ἀφείθη. συν-
ετίθει δ' ἡσυχῇ κατὰ τοῦ Δημοσθένους ἐγκλήματα,
ὡς καὶ φωραθῆναι· νοσοῦντος γὰρ τοῦ Ὑπερείδου,
F ἥκοντα εἰς τὴν οἰκίαν τὸν Δημοσθένη ὡς ἐπισκεψό-
μενον καταλαβεῖν κατέχοντα τὸ καθ' αὑτοῦ βιβλίον·
τούτου δ' ἀγανακτοῦντος, εἶπε " φίλον μὲν ὄντα
οὐδὲν⁴ λυπήσει, ἐχθρὸν δὲ γενόμενον κωλύσει τι κατ'

---

¹ Φίλαν τὴν Keil, from Athenaeus, p. 590 d : φίλτην.

² ὡμιληκὼς δὲ (Bücheler) ὡς εἰκός δή, καὶ Capps ; ὡμιληκὼς
δὲ καὶ Bücheler ; ἐωθινός. καὶ δίκη Blass ; ὡς εἰκὸς δὲ καὶ δίκη.
For καὶ δίκη Bernardakis prefers κἂν δίκη.

³ συνεστάθη conj. Capps ; cf. van Herwerden, Lex. Suppl.,
s.v. συνίστασθαι (" de advocatis ") : συνεξητάσθη.

⁴ οὐδὲν Reiske : οὐδένα.

ᵃ Only small fragments of these were preserved until, at
various times in the nineteenth century, six more or less
complete orations were discovered in Egyptian papyrus
manuscripts.

ᵇ Another comic gibe against a public man supposed to
be a gourmand. Athenaeus viii. 341 ff. quotes from the
Delos and Icarians of Timocles gossip of this kind against
Hypereides.

ᶜ The traditional text is certainly corrupt ; cf. critical

under his name, fifty-two of which are genuine.[a] He
was also very prone to sexual indulgence, so that he
turned his son out of the house and brought in
Myrrhina, the most expensive prostitute, kept Aristagora in Peiraeus, and at his own estate in Eleusis kept
the Theban girl Phila, whom he had ransomed for
twenty minas. He used to walk in the Fish-market
every day.[b] And, as it is indeed reasonable to
suppose, it was because he had been intimate also
with Phrynê[c] the courtesan that when she was on
trial for impiety he became her advocate ; for he
makes this plain himself at the beginning of his
speech.[d] And when she was likely to be found
guilty, he led the woman out into the middle of the
court and, tearing off her clothes, displayed her
breasts. When the judges saw her beauty, she was
acquitted.[e] He quietly compiled accusations against
Demosthenes and the fact became known ; for once,
when he was ill, Demosthenes came to his house to
visit him and found him with the document against
himself in his hand ; and when Demosthenes was
angry, Hypereides said, " It will do you no harm
while you are my friend, but if you become my
enemy, it will prevent your doing anything against

notes. The inference seems to have been drawn from the
orator's amatory record that his advocacy of Phrynê at her
famous trial was due to an intimacy with her. An advocate
was never " examined with " the defendant.

[d] Explained by Athenaeus xiii. 590 d ἐν τῷ ὑπὲρ Φρύνης
λόγῳ Ὑπερείδης ὁμολογῶν ἐρᾶν τῆς γυναικός. Hypereides'
speech was translated into Latin by Messala Corvinus
(Quintilian x. 5. 2).

[e] This version is found also in Athenaeus xiii. 590 e,
but the comic poet Poseidippus in his *Ephesian Lady* (*ibid.*
591 e; Kock, *Com. Att. Frag.* iii. p. 339) attributes Phrynê's
acquittal to her own arts.

ἐμοῦ πρᾶξαι." ἐψηφίσατο δὲ καὶ τιμὰς Ἰόλᾳ τῷ
δοκοῦντι¹ Ἀλεξάνδρῳ τὸ φάρμακον δοῦναι. ἐκοι-
νώνησε δὲ καὶ Λεωσθένει² τοῦ Λαμιακοῦ πολέμου,
καὶ ἐπὶ τοῖς πεσοῦσιν εἶπε τὸν ἐπιτάφιον θαυμασίως.
Φιλίππου δὲ πλεῖν ἐπ' Εὐβοίας παρεσκευασμένου
καὶ τῶν Ἀθηναίων εὐλαβῶς ἐχόντων, τεσσαράκοντα τριήρεις ἤθροισεν ἐξ ἐπιδόσεως καὶ πρῶτος
ὑπὲρ αὐτοῦ καὶ τοῦ παιδὸς ἐπέδωκε δύο τριήρεις.
850 συστάντος δὲ πρὸς Δηλίους ἀμφισβητήματος, ποτέ-
ρους δεῖ προΐστασθαι τοῦ ἱεροῦ, αἱρεθέντος Αἰσχίνου
συνειπεῖν, ἡ ἐξ Ἀρείου πάγου βουλὴ Ὑπερείδην
ἐχειροτόνησεν· καὶ ἔστιν ὁ λόγος Δηλιακὸς ἐπι-
γεγραμμένος. ἐπρέσβευσε δὲ καὶ πρὸς Ῥοδίους.
ἡκόντων δὲ καὶ παρ' Ἀντιπάτρου πρέσβεων,
ἐπαινούντων τὸν Ἀντίπατρον ὡς χρηστόν, ἀπαντήσας αὐτοῖς εἶπεν, "οἴδαμεν³ ὅτι χρηστὸς ὑπάρχει,
ἀλλ' ἡμεῖς γ' οὐ δεόμεθα χρηστοῦ δεσπότου."
λέγεται δ' ἄνευ ὑποκρίσεως δημηγορῆσαι καὶ μόνον
Β διηγεῖσθαι τὰ πραχθέντα καὶ τούτοις οὐκ ἐνοχλεῖν
τοὺς δικαστάς. ἐπέμφθη δὲ καὶ πρὸς Ἠλείους
ἀπολογησόμενος ὑπὲρ Καλλίππου τοῦ ἀθλητοῦ,
ἔχοντος αἰτίαν φθεῖραι τὸν ἀγῶνα, καὶ ἐνίκησε.
γραψάμενος δὲ καὶ τὴν Φωκίωνος δωρεάν, ἣν εἶπε
Μειδίας Μειδίου Ἀναγυράσιος ἐπὶ Ξενίου ἄρχοντος,
Γαμηλιῶνος ἑβδόμῃ φθίνοντος, ἡττήθη.

---

¹ δοκοῦντι Reiske : δόντι.
² Λεωσθένει Xylander : δημοσθένη.
³ οἴδαμεν Xylander from Photius : οἶδα μὲν; cf. Stobaeus,
Ecl. iii. 13. 51 (xiii. 31 Mein.).

ᵃ The belief that Alexander died of poison was apparently
unfounded.

ᵇ In 323–322 B.C. after Alexander's death, when the Greeks
under Leosthenes besieged the Macedonian Antipater in

me." He also proposed a decree conferring honours upon Iolas, who was supposed to have given Alexander the poison.[a] He took part with Leosthenes in the Lamian War [b] and delivered the funeral oration for the fallen in marvellous fashion. When Philip was preparing to sail against Euboea, and the Athenians were afraid, he assembled forty triremes by private contributions, and in his own name and his son's he gave two triremes, the first contribution made. And when a dispute arose with the Delians as to which people should have control of the sanctuary, although Aeschines was chosen Athenian advocate, the senate of the Areopagus elected Hypereides ; and his speech is the one entitled *The Delian*. He was also an envoy to the Rhodians. And when envoys came from Antipater and praised their sender as a good man, in replying to them he said, " We know that he is good, but we do not want a good master." It is said that in addressing the public he did not employ the actor's art, that he merely related the facts of the case and did not bore the jurors even with these. He was sent also to the Eleans to defend the athlete Callippus against the charge of having used corruption in the contest, and he won his case ; but when he brought a suit against the grant of a gift for Phocion, which Meidias, son of Meidias, of the deme Anagyros, proposed in the archonship of Xenias,[c] on the twenty-fourth day of Gamelion, he was defeated.

Lamia near Thermopylae. A large part of Hypereides' funeral oration is preserved.

[c] An archon Xenias is unknown. Euxenippus, suggested by Schäfer, was archon in 305-304 B.C., but Hypereides was then dead. Possibly the archon Archias, 346-345 B.C., is intended, in which case the gift for Phocion may have had some connexion with the battle of Tamynae.

Ι΄. ΔΕΙΝΑΡΧΟΣ

Δείναρχος Σωκράτους ἢ Σωστράτου, ὡς μέν
τινες ἐγχώριος, ὡς δέ τισι δοκεῖ Κορίνθιος, ἀφικό-
C μενος εἰς Ἀθήνας ἔτι νέος, καθ᾽ ὃν χρόνον Ἀλέξανδρος ἐπῄει[1] τὴν Ἀσίαν, κατοικήσας αὐτόθι ἀκροατὴς
μὲν ἐγένετο Θεοφράστου τοῦ διαδεξαμένου τὴν
Ἀριστοτέλους διατριβήν, ὡμίλησε δὲ καὶ Δημητρίῳ
τῷ Φαληρεῖ· μάλιστα δὲ προσῄει τῷ[2] πολιτεύεσθαι
μετὰ τὴν Ἀντιπάτρου τελευτήν, τῶν μὲν ἀνηρη-
μένων ῥητόρων τῶν δὲ πεφευγότων. φίλος δὲ
Κασάνδρῳ γενόμενος, ὡς ἐπὶ πλεῖστον προέκοψε
χρήματα τῶν λόγων εἰσπραττόμενος, οὓς τοῖς δεομένοις συνέγραφεν· ἀντετάξατο δὲ πρὸς τοὺς ἐπι-
φανεστάτους τῶν ῥητόρων, οὐκ εἰς δῆμον παριών·
οὐ γὰρ οἷός τ᾽ ἦν· ἀλλὰ τοῖς ἐναντιουμένοις λόγους
συγγράφων· καὶ ἐπεὶ Ἅρπαλος διέδρα, πλείους
D λόγους συνέγραψε[3] κατὰ τῶν αἰτίαν λαβόντων
δωροδοκῆσαι, καὶ τούτους τοῖς κατηγόροις ἐξ-
έδωκε. χρόνῳ δ᾽ ὕστερον αἰτιαθεὶς εἰς λόγους
παραγίνεσθαι Ἀντιπάτρῳ καὶ Κασάνδρῳ περὶ τὴν
κατάληψιν τῆς Μουνυχίας, ἡνίκα ὑπ᾽ Ἀντιγόνου
καὶ Δημητρίου ἐφρουρήθη ἐπ᾽ Ἀναξικράτους ἄρχοντος, ἐξαργυρισάμενος τὰ πλεῖστα τῆς οὐσίας
ἔφυγεν εἰς Χαλκίδα. διατρίψας δ᾽ ἐπὶ τῆς φυγῆς
ὡς πεντεκαίδεκα ἔτη, καὶ πολλὴν οὐσίαν κτησάμενος κατῆλθε, πραξάντων αὐτῷ τὴν κάθοδον τῶν

---

[1] ἐπῄει Xylander : ἐπί.
[2] δὲ προσῄει τῷ Wyttenbach : δὲ τῷ.
[3] συνέγραψε Blass : συνέγραφε.

---

[a] 334–323 b.c.
[b] The Lyceum, i.e. the Peripatetic School.

X. DEINARCHUS

Deinarchus, son of Socrates or Sostratus, an Athenian according to some, but, as others think, a Corinthian, came to Athens while still young at the time when Alexander was invading Asia,[a] settled there, and became a pupil of Theophrastus, who had succeeded Aristotle as head of his School[b]; but he also attended the lectures of Demetrius of Phalerum. He took part most actively in public affairs after the death of Antipater,[c] since some of the public men had been put to death and the rest were in exile. Since he became a friend of Cassander he prospered exceedingly through the fees he charged for the speeches which he wrote for those who requested his services; and he had as his opponents the most distinguished public men, although he did not speak before the popular assembly (for he was unable to do so[d]); but he merely wrote speeches for their opponents. And when Harpalus absconded he composed many speeches against those who were accused of having accepted bribes from him, and these he furnished to their accusers. But at a later time he was accused of having dealings with Antipater and Cassander in connexion with their occupation of Munichia when it was garrisoned by Antigonus and Demetrius in the archonship of Anaxicrates,[e] whereupon he turned most of his property into cash and went into exile at Chalcis. And after living in exile about fifteen years and amassing considerable wealth, he returned, his restoration, and at the same time

[c] 318 B.C.
[d] If he was a Corinthian by birth, he would be debarred from such speaking.   [e] 307–306 B.C.

447

PLUTARCH'S MORALIA

περὶ Θεόφραστον ἅμα τοῖς ἄλλοις φυγάσι. καταλύσας δὲ παρὰ Προξένῳ ἑταίρῳ αὐτοῦ καὶ τὸ
E χρυσίον ἀπολέσας, ἤδη γηραιὸς ὢν καὶ τὰς ὁράσεις
ἀσθενής, οὐ¹ βουλομένου τοῦ Προξένου ἀναζητεῖν,
λαγχάνει αὐτῷ δίκην καὶ τότε πρῶτον εἶπεν ἐν
δικαστηρίῳ.   σῴζεται δ᾽ αὐτοῦ καὶ ὁ λόγος.
φέρονται δ᾽ αὐτοῦ καὶ λόγοι γνήσιοι ἑξήκοντα
τέσσαρες· τούτων ἔνιοι παραλαμβάνονται ὡς
Ἀριστογείτονος. ζηλωτὴς δ᾽ ἐγένετο Ὑπερείδου ἢ
ὥς τινες διὰ τὸ παθητικὸν Δημοσθένους καὶ τὸ
σφοδρόν· τῶν σχημάτων δ᾽ αὐτοῦ μιμητὴς ὑπάρχει.

ΨΗΦΙΣΜΑΤΑ

Α΄

F   Δημοχάρης² Λάχητος Λευκονοεὺς³ αἰτεῖ Δημοσθένει
τῷ Δημοσθένους Παιανιεῖ δωρεὰν εἰκόνα χαλκῆν
ἐν ἀγορᾷ καὶ σίτησιν ἐν πρυτανείῳ καὶ προεδρίαν
αὐτῷ καὶ ἐκγόνων⁴ ἀεὶ τῷ πρεσβυτάτῳ, εὐεργέτῃ καὶ
συμβούλῳ γεγονότι πολλῶν καὶ καλῶν τῷ δήμῳ τῷ⁵
Ἀθηναίων καὶ τήν τε οὐσίαν εἰς τὸ κοινὸν καθεικότι
τὴν ἑαυτοῦ καὶ ἐπιδόντι τάλαντα ὀκτὼ καὶ τριήρη, ὅτε
ὁ δῆμος ἠλευθέρωσεν Εὔβοιαν, καὶ ἑτέραν, ὅτε εἰς
851 Ἑλλήσποντον Κηφισόδωρος ἐξέπλευσε· καὶ ἑτέραν, ὅτε
Χάρης καὶ Φωκίων στρατηγοὶ ἐξεπέμφθησαν εἰς Βυζάντιον ὑπὸ τοῦ δήμου· καὶ λυτρωσαμένῳ πολλοὺς τῶν

¹ οὐ added by Xylander.
² Δημοχάρης Basle ms.: Τιμοχάρης.
³ Λευκονοεὺς Westermann: λευκονθεύς.
⁴ ἐκγόνων Emperius: ἐγγόνων.
⁵ δήμῳ τῷ Ladeke: δήμῳ τῶν.

ᵃ Evidently Deinarchus suspected theft or fraud.

448

that of the other exiles, having been effected by Theophrastus and his friends. He lodged at the house of a friend of his named Proxenus and lost his money, when he was already an old man and his eyes were weak, and when Proxenus refused to investigate the matter [a] he brought a suit against him, and then for the first time he spoke in a court of law. His speech is extant, too.[b] There are sixty-four speeches of his extant which are regarded as genuine; of these some are handed down as by Aristogeiton. He was a zealous follower of Hypereides or, as some say on account of his emotional and vehement qualities, of Demosthenes. He certainly is an imitator of the latter's figures of speech.

DECREES [c]

I

Demochares [d] of Leuconoë, son of Laches, asks for Demosthenes of Paeania, son of Demosthenes, the grant of a bronze statue in the Market-place and maintenance in the Prytaneum and the privilege of front seats at the public spectacles for him and for the eldest of his descendants in perpetuity, because he has shown himself as a public benefactor and counsellor, and has brought about many benefits for the people of the Athenians, not only having relinquished his property for the common weal but also having contributed eight talents and a trireme when the people freed Euboea, and another trireme when Cephisodorus sailed to the Hellespont, and another when Chares and Phocion were sent as generals to Byzantium by the vote of the popular assembly, and having ransomed many of those who were taken prisoners

[b] Only quoted fragments of his writings are extant.

[c] On the following documents, called in the manuscripts "Decrees," see the Introduction to these *Lives*, p. 342 above.

[d] Apparently the son of the Laches, son of Demochares, mentioned above, 847 D, that is, the orator's nephew.

(851) ἁλόντων ἐν Πύδνῃ καὶ Μεθώνῃ καὶ Ὀλύνθῳ ὑπὸ
Φιλίππου· καὶ χορηγίαν ἀνδράσιν ἐπιδόντι, ὅτι ἐκ-
λιπόντων τῶν Πανδιονιδῶν τοῦ χορηγεῖν ἐπέδωκε, καὶ
καθώπλισε τοὺς πολίτας τῶν ἐλλειπόντων· καὶ εἰς τὴν
τειχοποιίαν ἀνάλωσε χειροτονηθεὶς ὑπὸ τοῦ δήμου,
ἐπιδόντος αὐτοῦ τρία τάλαντα καὶ ἃς ἐπέδωκε δύο
τάφρους περὶ τὸν Πειραιᾶ ταφρεύσας· καὶ μετὰ τὴν ἐν
B Χαιρωνείᾳ μάχην ἐπέδωκε τάλαντον, καὶ εἰς τὴν σιτω-
νίαν ἐπέδωκεν ἐν τῇ σιτοδείᾳ τάλαντον· καὶ ὅτι¹ εἰς
συμμαχίαν τῷ δήμῳ προσηγάγετο πείσας καὶ εὐεργέτης
γενόμενος καὶ σύμβουλος, δι' ὧν ἔπεισε Θηβαίους
Εὐβοεῖς Κορινθίους Μεγαρεῖς Ἀχαιοὺς Λοκροὺς Βυ-
ζαντίους Μεσσηνίους, καὶ δυνάμεις ἃς συνεστήσατο τῷ
δήμῳ καὶ τοῖς συμμάχοις, πεζοὺς μὲν μυρίους ἱππέας δὲ
χιλίους, καὶ σύνταξιν χρημάτων ἣν ἔπεισε πρεσβεύσας
διδόναι τοὺς μὲν συμμάχους εἰς τὸν πόλεμον πλείω
πεντακοσίων ταλάντων· καὶ ὅτι² ἐκώλυσε Πελοποννησίους
ἐπὶ Θήβας Ἀλεξάνδρῳ βοηθῆσαι, χρήματα δοὺς καὶ
C αὐτὸς πρεσβεύσας· καὶ ἄλλων πολλῶν καὶ καλῶν τῷ
δήμῳ συμβούλῳ γεγονότι καὶ πεπολιτευμένῳ τῶν καθ'
ἑαυτὸν πρὸς ἐλευθερίαν καὶ δημοκρατίαν ἄριστα· φυγόντι
δὲ δι' ὀλιγαρχίαν, καταλυθέντος τοῦ δήμου, καὶ τελευτήσαντος αὐτοῦ ἐν Καλαυρίᾳ διὰ τὴν πρὸς τὸν δῆμον
εὔνοιαν, πεμφθέντων στρατιωτῶν ἐπ' αὐτὸν ὑπὸ Ἀντιπάτρου, διαμείναντι ἐν τῇ πρὸς τὸ πλῆθος εὐνοίᾳ καὶ
οἰκειότητι, καὶ οὔτε ὑποχειρίῳ γενομένῳ τοῖς ἐχθροῖς
οὔτε τι³ ἀνάξιον ἐν τῷ κινδύνῳ πράξαντι τοῦ δήμου.

Β′

D Ἄρχων Πυθάρατος· Λάχης Δημοχάρους Λευκονοεὺς αἰτεῖ δωρεὰν τὴν βουλὴν καὶ τὸν δῆμον τὸν⁴

¹ ὅτι Westermann and Ladeke: ὅτε.

by Philip at Pydna, Methonê, and Olynthus,[a] and having contributed the expense of a chorus of men because when the members of the tribe of Pandionis failed to furnish this chorus, he contributed the money and, besides, furnished arms to the citizens who lacked them ; and when elected Commissioner of the Fortifications by the popular assembly he supplied the money for the work, himself contributing three talents in addition to the cost of two trenches about the Peiraeus, which he dug as his contribution. And after the battle of Chaeroneia he contributed a talent, and in the scarcity of food he contributed a talent for the food-supply. And because, through persuasion, benefactions, and the advice by which he moved them, he brought into alliance with the people the Thebans, Euboeans, Corinthians, Megarians, Achaeans, Locrians, Byzantines, and Messenians and gained troops for the people and its allies, namely ten thousand foot, one thousand horse, and a contribution of money which he as envoy persuaded the allies to give for the war—more than five hundred talents—and because he prevented the Peloponnesians from going to the aid of the Boeotians, giving money and going in person as envoy. And he advised the people to adopt many other excellent measures, and of all his contemporaries he performed the best public actions in the cause of liberty and democracy. And having been exiled by the oligarchy when the democracy had been destroyed, and having died at Calauria on account of his devotion to the democracy, when soldiers were sent against him by Antipater, persisting in his loyalty and devotion to the democracy and neither surrendering to its enemies nor doing anything in his time of danger that was unworthy of the democracy.

II

Archon Pytharatus.[b] Laches, son of Demochares, of Leuconoë, asks from the senate and people of the Athenians

---

[a] 356, 353, and 348 B.C.

[b] 271–270 B.C. See above, pp. 431 f., where the same facts are given.

---

[2] ὅτι Westermann : ὡς.

[3] οὔτε τι Meziriacus : οὔτε.   [4] τὸν Ladeke : τῶν.

(851) Ἀθηναίων Δημοχάρει Λάχητος Λευκονοεῖ εἰκόνα χαλκῆν
ἐν ἀγορᾷ καὶ σίτησιν ἐν πρυτανείῳ αὐτῷ[1] καὶ τῶν ἐκγόνων[2] ἀεὶ τῷ πρεσβυτάτῳ καὶ προεδρίαν ἐν πᾶσι τοῖς
ἀγῶσιν, εὐεργέτῃ καὶ συμβούλῳ γεγονότι ἀγαθῷ τῷ
δήμῳ τῷ[3] Ἀθηναίων καὶ εὐεργετηκότι τὸν δῆμον τάδε·
πρεσβεύοντι καὶ γράφοντι καὶ πολιτευομένῳ . . .[4] οἰκο-
δομὴν τειχῶν, καὶ παρασκευῇ ὅπλων καὶ βελῶν καὶ
μηχανημάτων, καὶ ὀχυρωσαμένῳ τὴν πόλιν ἐπὶ τοῦ τετραε-
E τοῦς πολέμους, καὶ εἰρήνην καὶ ἀνοχὰς καὶ συμμαχίαν
ποιησαμένῳ πρὸς Βοιωτούς· ἀνθ' ὧν ἐξέπεσεν ὑπὸ[5] τῶν
καταλυσάντων τὸν δῆμον· καὶ ὡς κατῆλθεν ἐπὶ Διοκλέους
ἄρχοντος ὑπὸ τοῦ δήμου, συστείλαντι τὴν διοίκησιν πρώτῳ
καὶ φεισαμένῳ τῶν ὑπαρχόντων καὶ πρεσβεύσαντι[6] πρὸς
Λυσίμαχον καὶ λαβόντι τῷ δήμῳ τριάκοντα τάλαντα
ἀργυρίου καὶ πάλιν ἕτερα ἑκατόν· καὶ γράψαντι πρεσβείαν
πρὸς Πτολεμαῖον εἰς Αἴγυπτον, καθ' ἣν ἐκπλεύσαντες
πεντήκοντα ἐκόμισαν τάλαντα ἀργυρίου τῷ δήμῳ· καὶ πρὸς
Ἀντίπατρον πρεσβεύσαντι καὶ λαβόντι εἴκοσι τάλαντα
F ἀργυρίου καὶ Ἐλευσῖνα[7] κομισαμένῳ τῷ δήμῳ· καὶ
ταῦτα πείσαντι ἑλέσθαι τὸν δῆμον καὶ πράξαντι, καὶ
φυγόντι μὲν ὑπὲρ[8] δημοκρατίας, μετεσχηκότι δὲ οὐδεμιᾶς
ὀλιγαρχίας οὐδὲ ἀρχὴν οὐδεμίαν ἠρχότι καταλελυκότος
τοῦ δήμου· καὶ μόνῳ Ἀθηναίων τῶν κατὰ τὴν αὐτὴν
ἡλικίαν πολιτευσαμένων μὴ μεμελετηκότι τὴν πατρίδα
κινεῖν ἑτέρῳ πολιτεύματι ἢ δημοκρατίᾳ· καὶ τὰς κρίσεις
καὶ τοὺς νόμους καὶ τὰ δικαστήρια καὶ τὰς οὐσίας πᾶσιν
Ἀθηναίοις ἐν ἀσφαλεῖ ποιήσαντι διὰ τῆς αὐτοῦ πολιτείας
καὶ μηδὲν ὑπεναντίον τῇ δημοκρατίᾳ πεπραχότι μήτε
λόγῳ μήτε ἔργῳ.

[1] αὐτῷ added by Westermann.
[2] ἐκγόνιον Emperius: ἐγγόνων.   [3] τῷ Ladeke: τῶν.
[4] Westermann indicates a gap here to be filled with such
words as ἀεὶ καλῶς καὶ καθαρῶς, καὶ κατεργασαμένῳ.

for Demochares, son of Laches, of Leuconoë, a grant of a
bronze statue in the Market-place, and maintenance in the
Prytaneum for him and the eldest of his descendants in
perpetuity, and the privilege of a front seat at all public
spectacles, because he proved himself a benefactor and a good
counsellor to the people of the Athenians and benefited the
people as follows: He was a good ambassador, proposer
of legislation, and statesman [. . . , and he superintended]
the building of the walls and the preparation of armour,
missiles, and engines of war, he fortified the city at the time
of the four years' war[a] and made peace, truce, and alliance
with the Boeotians, in return for which he was banished by
those who overthrew the democracy. When he was recalled
by the people in the archonship of Diocles,[b] he first reduced
the expenses of the administration and was sparing of the
public resources; he went as envoy to Lysimachus and
secured for the people thirty talents of silver and again one
hundred more; he proposed the sending of an embassy to
Ptolemy in Egypt, and those who took part in it brought
back for the people fifty talents of silver; he was envoy to
Antipater and secured twenty talents of silver which he
brought to Eleusis for the people. He won the assent of the
people to all these measures and accomplished them; he was
exiled for the sake of the democracy, he took no part in any
oligarchy, he held no office after the democracy had been
overthrown, and he was the only Athenian of those who were
engaged in public life in his time who never plotted to alter
the government of the country by changing it to a form other
than democracy; he made the decisions of the courts, the
laws, the courts, and property, safe for all Athenians by
the policy he pursued, and he never did anything adverse to
the democracy by word or deed.

[a] 294–290 B.C. The war ended with the surrender of
Athens to Demetrius Poliorcetes.
[b] 288–287 B.C.

---

[5] ὑπὸ Westermann: ἀπό.
[6] πρεσβεύσαντι Meziriacus: πρεσβευόντων or πρεσβευσάντων.
[7] Ἐλευσῖνα Niebuhr: ἐλευσίνια.
[8] ὑπὲρ Xylander: ὑπό.

Γ´

Λυκόφρων Λυκούργου Βουτάδης ἀπεγράψατο αὐτῷ
εἶναι σίτησιν ἐν πρυτανείῳ κατὰ τὴν δοθεῖσαν δωρεὰν
ὑπὸ τοῦ δήμου Λυκούργῳ Βουτάδῃ. ἐπὶ Ἀναξικράτους
852 ἄρχοντος, ἐπὶ τῆς Ἀντιοχίδος ἕκτης πρυτανείας,[1] Στρατοκλῆς Εὐθυδήμου Διομειεὺς[2] εἶπεν. ἐπειδὴ Λυκοῦργος
Λυκόφρονος Βουτάδης παραλαβὼν παρὰ τῶν ἑαυτοῦ
προγόνων οἰκείαν ἐκ παλαιοῦ τὴν πρὸς τὸν δῆμον
εὔνοιαν, καὶ οἱ πρόγονοι οἱ Λυκούργου, Λυκομήδης[3] τε
καὶ Λυκοῦργος, καὶ ζῶντες ἐτιμῶντο ὑπὸ τοῦ δήμου
καὶ τελευτήσασιν αὐτοῖς δι᾽ ἀνδραγαθίαν ἔδωκεν ὁ δῆμος
δημοσίας ταφὰς ἐν Κεραμεικῷ· καὶ Λυκοῦργος αὐτὸς
B πολιτευόμενος νόμους τε πολλοὺς καὶ καλοὺς ἔθηκε τῇ
πατρίδι, καὶ γενόμενος τῆς κοινῆς προσόδου ταμίας τῇ
πόλει ἐπὶ τρεῖς[4] πενταετηρίδας καὶ διανείμας ἐκ τῆς
κοινῆς προσόδου μύρια καὶ ὀκτακισχίλια καὶ ἐνακόσια
τάλαντα· πολλὰ δὲ τῶν ἰδιωτῶν διὰ πίστεως λαβὼν καὶ
προδανείσας καὶ εἰς τοὺς τῆς πόλεως καιροὺς καὶ τοῦ
δήμου τὰ πάντα ἑξακόσια[5] καὶ πεντήκοντα τάλαντα·
δόξας δὲ ἅπαντα ταῦτα δικαίως διῳκηκέναι πολλάκις
ἐστεφανώθη ὑπὸ τῆς πόλεως· ἔτι δὲ αἱρεθεὶς ὑπὸ τοῦ
δήμου χρήματα πολλὰ συνήγαγεν εἰς τὴν ἀκρόπολιν,
καὶ παρασκευάσας τῇ θεῷ κόσμον, νίκας τε ὁλοχρύσους
πομπεῖά τε χρυσᾶ καὶ ἀργυρᾶ[6] καὶ κόσμον χρυσοῦν εἰς
C ἑκατὸν κανηφόρους· χειροτονηθεὶς δὲ ἐπὶ τῆς τοῦ πολέμου
παρασκευῆς ὅπλα μὲν πολλὰ καὶ βελῶν μυριάδας πέντε
ἀνήνεγκεν εἰς τὴν ἀκρόπολιν, τετρακοσίας δὲ[7] τριήρεις
πλωίμους κατεσκεύασε, τὰς μὲν ἐπισκευάσας τὰς δὲ ἐξ ἀρχῆς

[1] ἕκτης πρυτανείας Schömann: ἐν τῇ πρυτανείᾳ.
[2] Διομειεὺς Xylander: διομηδεύς.
[3] Λυκομήδης Pinzger from *Moralia*, 843 ε: διομηδής.
[4] ἐπὶ τρεῖς Meziriacus from *Moralia*, 841 β.
[5] ἑξακόσια] διακόσια Sauppe from *Moralia*, 841 D.

III

Lycophron, son of Lycurgus, of the deme Butadae, presented in writing a claim for maintenance in the Prytaneum for himself in accordance with the gift presented by the people to Lycurgus of the deme Butadae. In the archonship of Anaxicrates,[a] in the sixth prytany, that of the tribe Antiochis, Stratocles, son of Euthydemus, of the deme Diomeia, made the following motion : Whereas Lycurgus, son of Lycophron, of the deme Butadae, having inherited from early times from his ancestors that loyalty to the democracy which has been peculiar to his family, and the progenitors of Lycurgus, Lycomedes and Lycurgus, were not only honoured by the people during their lives, but also after their death the people granted them for their courage and virtue public burials in the Cerameicus ; and whereas Lycurgus himself during his public career made many excellent laws for his country, and when he was treasurer of the public revenues of the city for three periods of four years distributed from the public revenue eighteen thousand nine hundred talents ; and having received in trust large funds from private citizens, from which he made loans previously agreed upon in order to meet the exigencies of the city and the people, in all six hundred and fifty talents ; and, because he was believed to have administered all these funds justly, was often crowned by the State ; and whereas when chosen by the people he brought together large sums of money upon the Acropolis, providing adornment for the Goddess, solid gold Victories, gold and silver vessels for the processions, and ornaments of gold for one hundred basket-carriers,[b] and when chosen to be in charge of the equipment for the war he brought to the Acropolis many pieces of armour and fifty thousand missiles and fitted out four hundred triremes ready to set sail, providing the equipment for some of them and causing some to be built from the beginning ;

---

[a] 307–306 B.C. Much of the substance of this document is contained in the *Life* of Lycurgus, see pp. 395 ff. above.

[b] Maidens of good birth who carried baskets of offerings in the processions.

---

⁶ ἀργυρᾶ Coraes: ἀργύρεα.   ⁷ δὲ added by Coraes.

(852) ναυπηγησάμενος· πρός τε τούτοις ἡμίεργα παραλαβὼν
τούς τε νεωσοίκους καὶ τὴν σκευοθήκην καὶ τὸ θέατρον τὸ
Διονυσιακὸν ἐξειργάσατο, καὶ ἐπετέλεσε τό τε στάδιον τὸ
Παναθηναϊκὸν καὶ τὸ γυμνάσιον τὸ κατὰ τὸ[1] Λύκειον
κατεσκεύασε, καὶ ἄλλαις πολλαῖς κατασκευαῖς ἐκόσμησε
τὴν πόλιν· Ἀλεξάνδρου τε τοῦ βασιλέως ἅπασαν μὲν
D τὴν Ἀσίαν κατεστραμμένου, κοινῇ δὲ πᾶσι τοῖς Ἕλλησιν
ἐπιτάττειν ἀξιοῦντος, ἐξαιτήσαντος[2] Λυκοῦργον ὡς
ἐναντία πράττοντα[3] αὐτῷ,[4] οὐκ ἐξέδωκεν ὁ δῆμος παρ᾽
Ἀλεξάνδρου φόβον· καὶ διδοὺς εὐθύνας πολλάκις τῶν
πεπολιτευμένων ἐν ἐλευθέρᾳ καὶ δημοκρατουμένῃ τῇ
πόλει διετέλεσεν ἀνεξέλεγκτος καὶ ἀδωροδόκητος τὸν
ἅπαντα χρόνον· ὅπως ἂν εἰδῶσι πάντες, διότι τοὺς προ-
αιρουμένους ὑπὲρ τῆς δημοκρατίας καὶ τῆς ἐλευθερίας
δικαίως πολιτεύεσθαι καὶ ζῶντας μὲν περὶ πλείστου[5]
ποιεῖται καὶ τελευτήσασι δὲ ἀποδίδωσι χάριτας ἀειμνή-
E στους· ἀγαθῇ τύχῃ δεδόχθαι τῷ δήμῳ ἐπαινέσαι μὲν
Λυκοῦργον Λυκόφρονος Βουτάδην ἀρετῆς ἕνεκα καὶ
δικαιοσύνης καὶ στῆσαι αὐτοῦ τὸν δῆμον χαλκῆν εἰκόνα
ἐν ἀγορᾷ, πλὴν εἴ που ὁ νόμος ἀπαγορεύει μὴ ἱστάναι,
δοῦναι δὲ σίτησιν ἐν πρυτανείῳ τῶν ἐκγόνων[6] ἀεὶ τῶν
Λυκούργου τῷ πρεσβυτάτῳ εἰς ἅπαντα τὸν χρόνον καὶ
εἶναι κύρια πάντα τὰ ψηφίσματα αὐτοῦ, ἀναθεῖναι δὲ τὸν
γραμματέα[7] τοῦ δήμου ἐν στήλαις λιθίναις καὶ στῆσαι
ἐν ἀκροπόλει πλησίον τῶν ἀναθημάτων· εἰς δὲ τὴν
ἀναγραφὴν τῶν στηλῶν δοῦναι τὸν ταμίαν τοῦ δήμου
πεντήκοντα δραχμὰς ἐκ τῶν εἰς τὰ ψηφίσματα ἀναλισκο-
μένων τῷ δήμῳ.

---

[1] τὸ κατὰ τὸ a sure reading in the inscription; τὸ κατὰ
Schömann: καὶ τὸ.

and besides all this he finished the ship-sheds and the arsenal, which were half done when they came into his hands, and completed the Panathenaic stadium and erected the gymnasium at the Lyceum, and adorned the city with many other edifices. And when King Alexander, after overthrowing all Asia, assumed to give orders to all the Greeks in common and demanded that Lycurgus be surrendered because he was acting in opposition to him, the city did not surrender him in spite of fear of Alexander. And although he had many times submitted his accounts while the city was free and had a democratic form of government, he never was convicted of wrongdoing or of taking bribes through all his career. Therefore, that all may know that those who choose to act justly in public life in behalf of democracy and freedom are held in the highest esteem while living and receive after death enduring gratitude : With good Fortune : Be it resolved by the people to commend Lycurgus, son of Lycophron, of the deme Butadae, for his virtue and justice, and to set up a bronze statue of him in the Market-place, only not in any place where the law forbids its erection, and to grant maintenance in the Prytaneum to the eldest descendant of Lycurgus for all time, and that all his decrees be valid, and that the secretary of the people inscribe them on stone tablets and place them on the Acropolis near the dedicatory offerings ; and that the treasurer of the people give for inscribing the tablets fifty drachmas from the funds expended by the people for decrees.

---

² ἐξαιτήσαντος Meziriacus, confirmed by the inscription : ἐξαιτήσας.

³ πράττοντα Meziriacus : πράττοντος.

⁴ αὐτῷ Blum : αὐτοῦ.

⁵ πλείστου Meziriacus : πλεῖστον.

⁶ ἐκγόνων Turin editors : ἐγγόνων.

⁷ καὶ εἶναι κύρια . . . γραμματέα] the words are in the order proposed by Dübner : ἀναθεῖναι δ᾽ αὐτοῦ καὶ εἶναι κύρια πάντα τὰ ψηφίσματα τὸν γραμματέα.

SUMMARY OF A COMPARISON BETWEEN ARISTOPHANES AND MENANDER

(COMPARATIONIS ARISTOPHANIS ET MENANDRI COMPENDIUM)

INTRODUCTION

THIS is at best a summary of one of Plutarch's lost essays, and it may well be that we have only part of the summary. Bernardakis believes that the beginning is wanting, and even for a summary the end, as we have it, appears somewhat abrupt.

The Old Comedy of the fifth century B.C., whose chief representative is, and always was, Aristophanes, with its brilliant wit, occasionally beautiful poetry, biting invective, unrestrained ribaldry, and unashamed indecency, was followed in the fourth century, after the brief vogue of the Middle Comedy, by the New Comedy, whose chief representative is Menander. The New Comedy abstained from politics, indulged in no personal invective, was indecent only by innuendo, and produced dramas in which the life of the times was reflected somewhat after the manner of modern " society plays." Plutarch not unnaturally preferred Menander's polished comedies of character to the boisterous wit and humour of Aristophanes, and he seems to have had no appreciation of the earlier dramatist's vigour or of his poetic imagination.

ΣΥΓΚΡΙΣΕΩΣ ΑΡΙΣΤΟΦΑΝΟΥΣ ΚΑΙ
ΜΕΝΑΝΔΡΟΥ ΕΠΙΤΟΜΗ

1. * * * Ὡς μὲν κοινῶς καὶ καθόλου εἰπεῖν πολλῷ
προκρίνει τὸν Μένανδρον, ὡς δ᾽ ἐπὶ μέρους καὶ
ταῦτα προστίθησι·

B   "Τὸ φορτικόν," φησίν, " ἐν λόγοις καὶ θυμελικὸν[1]
καὶ βάναυσον ὥς ἐστιν[2] Ἀριστοφάνει, Μενάνδρῳ δ᾽
οὐδαμῶς. καὶ γὰρ ὁ μὲν ἀπαίδευτος καὶ ἰδιώτης,
οἷς ἐκεῖνος λέγει, ἁλίσκεται· ὁ δὲ πεπαιδευμένος
δυσχερανεῖ· λέγω δὲ τὰ ἀντίθετα καὶ ὁμοιόπτωτα
καὶ παρωνυμίας. τούτοις γὰρ ὁ μὲν μετὰ τοῦ
προσήκοντος λόγου καὶ ὀλιγάκις χρῆται ἐπιμελείας
αὐτὰ ἀξιῶν, ὁ δὲ καὶ πολλάκις καὶ οὐκ εὐκαίρως
καὶ ψυχρῶς· ἐπαινεῖται γάρ," φησίν,

ὅτι τοὺς ταμίας ἐβάπτισεν,

οὐχὶ ταμίας ἀλλὰ Λαμίας

ὄντας. καὶ

---

[1] θυμελικὸν] Kronenberg suggests βωμολόχον; cf. Moralia
68 c τὸ γέλοιον καὶ βωμολόχον.
[2] ὥς ἐστιν] πρόσεστιν Bernardakis.

---

[a] "He" seems to mean Plutarch; the compiler of this
summary (or the editor who included it among Plutarch's
works) regarding Plutarch as the author of the statements
which are introduced in this first sentence.

SUMMARY OF A COMPARISON
BETWEEN ARISTOPHANES
AND MENANDER

1. . . . In general he[a] much prefers Menander, and
in particular he adds what follows :

"Coarseness," he says, "in words, vulgarity and
ribaldry are present in Aristophanes, but not at all
in Menander ; obviously, for the uneducated, ordinary
person is captivated by what the former says, but
the educated man will be displeased. I refer to
antitheses and similar endings and plays on words.
For of these Menander does make use with proper
consideration and rarely, believing that they should
be treated with care, but Aristophanes employs
them frequently, inopportunely, and frigidly ; for
his punning is applauded," he says, "in

> because he soused the bankers—
> Though they never were that but damn curs,[b]

and

[b] This quotation is not found in any collection of the
fragments of Aristophanes (Bernardakis). The play on
words in the Greek consists in the change of the initial letters
of the words *tamias* ("treasurers") and *Lamias*, fabulous
creatures such as the bugbears with which children are
frightened by their nurses.

463

(853)
C

οὗτος ἤτοι κακίας ἢ συκοφαντίας πνεῖ

καὶ

γάστριζε καὶ τοῖς ἐντέροις καὶ τοῖς κόλοις[1]

καὶ

ὑπὸ τοῦ[2] γέλωτος εἰς Γέλαν[3] ἀφίξομαι

καὶ

τί δῆτά[4] δράσω σ᾽,[5] κακόδαιμον, ἀμφορεὺς
ἐξοστρακισθείς;

καὶ

ἄγρια γὰρ ἡμᾶς, ὦ γυναῖκες, δρᾷ[6] κακά,
ἅτ᾽ ἐν ἀγρίοισι[7] τοῖς λαχάνοις αὐτὸς τραφείς

καὶ

ἀλλ᾽ ἢ τριχόβρωτες[8] τὸν λόφον μου κατέφαγον

καὶ

---

[1] γάστριζε and κόλοις Wyttenbach from Aristophanes:
γαστρὶ ζῇ and κώλοις.
[2] τοῦ added by Elmsley.
[3] Γέλαν Xylander: τὸ γελᾶν.
[4] δῆτα Meineke: δέ.
[5] δράσω σ᾽ Meineke; σὲ δράσω Reiske: σοι δράσω.
[6] δρᾷ Wyttenbach and Reiske from Aristophanes: ἄρα.
[7] ἀγρίοισι Bernardakis: ἀγρίοις.
[8] ἀλλ᾽ ἢ τριχόβρωτες Aristophanes: ἀλλ᾽ αἱ τριχοβόστρυχες.

---

[a] *Knights*, 437. In the Greek "north-east" and "calumny"
both have the same endings in -*ias*, characteristic of the
names of winds.
[b] *Knights*, 454. The play here consists in the use of
gastrize, usually meaning "stuff the belly" with food, as
464

This fellow blows an ill north-east or calumny,[a]

and

Give him a belly-punch in his bowels and guts,[b]

and

By laughter driven I soon shall be in Laughter-town,[c]

and

Whatever shall I do to you, you wretched pot,
When gone the way of pots?[d]

and

Since, women, what he does to us are evils wild,
For one who e'en himself in the wild-greens market grew,[e]

and

But look, the moths have eaten up my plumes entire,[f]

and

" punch in the belly." The language is intentionally coarse as being characteristic of the Sausage-dealer, Cleon's rival for political leadership.

[c] Kock, *Com. Att. Frag.* i. p. 546, no. 618. The play is on the word *gelōs* " laughter " and the city of Gela in Sicily.

[d] Kock, *ibid.* p. 543, no. 593. The speaker seems to be about to smash a pot in order to get some *ostraka* or potsherds on which to inscribe the name of the politician for whose " ostracism " he desires to vote.

[e] *Women Celebrating the Thesmophoria*, 455. One of the assembled women is arraigning Euripides for the wrongs he has done to the sex in his tragedies. The reference in the second line is to the then current story that the poet's mother earned her living by selling wild greens and vegetables.

[f] *Acharnians*, 1110. The speaker is the general Lamachus, who comes on the scene in his full officer's regalia. The word for moth in Greek is *trichobros* " haireater."

(853) φέρε δεῦρο γοργόνωτον ἀσπίδος κύκλον.
       κἀμοὶ πλακοῦντος τυρόνωτον[1] δὸς κύκλον

καὶ πολλὰ τοιαῦτα. ἔνεστι μὲν οὖν ἐν τῇ κατα-
σκευῇ τῶν ὀνομάτων αὐτῷ τὸ τραγικὸν τὸ κωμικὸν
τὸ σοβαρὸν τὸ πεζόν, ἀσάφεια, κοινότης, ὄγκος καὶ
δίαρμα, σπερμολογία καὶ φλυαρία ναυτιώδης. καὶ
D τοσαύτας διαφορὰς ἔχουσα καὶ ἀνομοιότητας ἡ
λέξις οὐδὲ τὸ πρέπον ἑκάστῃ καὶ οἰκεῖον ἀπο-
δίδωσιν· οἶον λέγω βασιλεῖ τὸν ὄγκον ῥήτορι τὴν
δεινότητα γυναικὶ τὸ ἁπλοῦν ἰδιώτῃ τὸ πεζὸν
ἀγοραίῳ τὸ φορτικόν· ἀλλ' ὥσπερ ἀπὸ κλήρου
ἀπονέμει τοῖς προσώποις τὰ προστυχόντα τῶν ὀνομάτων, καὶ οὐκ ἂν διαγνοίης εἴθ' υἱός ἐστιν εἴτε
πατὴρ εἴτ' ἄγροικος εἴτε θεὸς εἴτε γραῦς εἴθ' ἥρως
ὁ διαλεγόμενος.

    2. '' Ἡ δὲ Μενάνδρου φράσις οὕτω συνέξεσται
καὶ συμπέπνευκε κεκραμένη πρὸς ἑαυτήν, ὥστε διὰ
E πολλῶν ἀγομένη παθῶν καὶ ἠθῶν καὶ προσώποις
ἐφαρμόττουσα παντοδαποῖς μία τε φαίνεσθαι καὶ
τὴν ὁμοιότητα τηρεῖν ἐν τοῖς κοινοῖς καὶ συνήθεσι
καὶ ὑπὸ τὴν χρείαν ὀνόμασιν· ἐὰν δέ τινος ἄρα
τερατείας εἰς τὸ πρᾶγμα καὶ ψόφου δεήσῃ, καθάπερ
αὐλοῦ πάντρητον ἀνασπάσας ταχὺ πάλιν καὶ πιθανῶς ἐπέβαλε καὶ κατέστησε τὴν φωνὴν εἰς τὸ
οἰκεῖον. πολλῶν δὲ γεγονότων εὐδοκίμων τεχνιτῶν, οὔθ' ὑπόδημα δημιουργὸς οὔτε προσωπεῖον

───────────────
[1] τυρόνωτον Xylander from Aristophanes : γυρόνωτον.

───────────────
[a] The first line is spoken by Lamachus, who has been

Lam. I say, bring here my shield's round orb all Gorgon-
    faced.
Dic. I say, hand me a flat-cake's orb all faced with cheese,ᵃ

and many things of the same sort. Moreover, in his
diction there are tragic, comic, pompous, and prosaic
elements, obscurity, vagueness, dignity, and eleva-
tion, loquacity and sickening nonsense. And with
all these differences and dissimilarities his use of
words does not give to each kind its fitting and appropriate use ; I mean, for example, to a king his
dignity, to an orator his eloquence, to a woman her
artlessness, to an ordinary man his prosaic speech,
to a market-lounger his vulgarity ; but he assigns to
his characters as if by lot such words as happen to
turn up, and you could not tell whether the speaker
is son or father, a rustic or a god, or an old woman
or a hero.

2. " But Menander's diction is so polished and its
ingredients mingled into so consistent a whole that,
although it is employed in connexion with many
emotions and many types of character and adapts
itself to persons of every kind, it nevertheless appears
as one and preserves its uniformity in common and
familiar words in general use ; but if the action
should anywhere call for strange and deceptive
language and for bluster, he opens, as it were, all
the stops of his flute, but then quickly and plausibly
closes them and brings the sound back to its natural
quality. And although there have been many noted
artisans, no shoemaker ever made the same shoe, no

---

ordered to lead out his forces for the defence of the frontier in
blustery wintry weather. Everything he says is parodied by
the pacifist Dicaeopolis, the charcoal-burner, who for his part
is preparing for a grand banquet.

σκευοποιὸς οὔτε τις ἱμάτιον ἅμα ταὐτὸν ἀνδρὶ καὶ
γυναικὶ καὶ μειρακίῳ καὶ γέροντι καὶ οἰκοτρίβι
F πρέπον ἐποίησεν· ἀλλὰ Μένανδρος οὕτως ἔμιξε[1] τὴν
λέξιν, ὥστε πάσῃ καὶ φύσει καὶ διαθέσει καὶ ἡλικίᾳ
σύμμετρον εἶναι, καὶ ταῦτα νέος μὲν ἔτι τοῦ
πράγματος ἁψάμενος, ἐν ἀκμῇ δὲ τοῦ ποιεῖν καὶ
διδάσκειν τελευτήσας, ὅτε μάλιστα καὶ πλείστην
ἐπίδοσιν, ὡς Ἀριστοτέλης φησί, λαμβάνει τὰ περὶ
τὴν λέξιν τοῖς γράφουσιν. εἰ οὖν πρὸς τὰ πρῶτα
τῶν Μενάνδρου δραμάτων τὰ μέσα καὶ τὰ τελευ-
ταῖα παραβάλοι τις, ἐξ αὐτῶν ἐπιγνώσεται, ὅσα
ἔμελλεν, εἰ ἐπεβίω, καὶ τούτοις ἕτερα προσθήσειν.

854   3. " Ὅτι τῶν διδασκόντων οἱ μὲν πρὸς τὸν ὄχλον
καὶ τὸν δῆμον γράφουσιν οἱ δὲ τοῖς ὀλίγοις, τὸ δ'
ἐν ἀμφοῖν ἁρμόττον τοῖς γένεσιν οὐ ῥᾴδιον ὅτῳ
τῶν πάντων ὑπῆρξεν εἰπεῖν. Ἀριστοφάνης μὲν οὖν
οὔτε τοῖς πολλοῖς ἀρεστὸς οὔτε τοῖς φρονίμοις ἀν-
εκτός, ἀλλ' ὥσπερ ἑταίρας τῆς ποιήσεως παρηκμα-
κυίας, εἶτα μιμουμένης γαμετήν, οὔθ' οἱ πολλοὶ τὴν
αὐθάδειαν ὑπομένουσιν[2] οἵ τε σεμνοὶ βδελύττονται
τὸ ἀκόλαστον καὶ κακόηθες. ὁ δὲ Μένανδρος μετὰ
χαρίτων μάλιστα ἑαυτὸν αὐτάρκη παρέσχηκεν, ἐν
θεάτροις ἐν διατριβαῖς ἐν συμποσίοις, ἀνάγνωσμα
B καὶ μάθημα καὶ ἀγώνισμα κοινότατον ὧν ἡ Ἑλλὰς
ἐνήνοχε καλῶν παρέχων τὴν ποίησιν, δεικνὺς ὅ τι
δὴ καὶ ὁποῖον ἦν ἄρα δεξιότης λόγου, ἐπιὼν ἀπαν-
ταχόσε μετὰ πειθοῦς ἀφύκτου καὶ χειρούμενος ἅπα-

----

[1] ἔμιξε Herwerden : ἔδειξε.
[2] ὑπομένουσιν Reiske : περιμένουσιν.

----

[a] Menander was born in 342 B.C. and died in 292–291 B.C. at
the age of fifty-two. His first play, probably the *Heauton-
timoroumenos*, was brought out when he was somewhat

468

mask-maker the same mask, and no tailor the same cloak, that would be appropriate at the same time for man and woman and youth and old man and domestic slave ; but Menander so blended his diction that it comports with every nature, disposition, and age, and he did this although he entered upon his career while still a young man and died at the height of his powers as playwright and poet,[a] when, as Aristotle says, writers make the greatest progress in the matter of diction. If, therefore, we were to compare Menander's earliest dramas with those of his middle and final periods, we should perceive from them how many qualities he would, had he lived longer, have added to these.

3. " Some dramatists write for the common people, and others for the few, but it is not easy to say which of them all is capable of adapting his work to both classes. Now Aristophanes is neither pleasing to the many nor endurable to the thoughtful, but his poetry is like a harlot who has passed her prime and then takes up the rôle of a wife, whose presumption the many cannot endure and whose licentiousness and malice the dignified abominate. But Menander, along with his charm, shows himself above all satisfying. He has made his poetry, of all the beautiful works Greece has produced, the most generally accepted subject in theatres, in discussions, and at banquets, for readings, for instruction, and for dramatic competitions. For he shows, indeed, what the essence and nature of skill in the use of language really are, approaching all subjects with a persuasiveness from which there is no escape, and controlling

under twenty years of age. See Clark, *Class. Phil.* i. (1906) pp. 313 ff.

(854) σαν ἀκοὴν καὶ διάνοιαν Ἑλληνικῆς φωνῆς. τίνος
γὰρ ἄξιον ἀληθῶς εἰς θέατρον ἐλθεῖν ἄνδρα πε-
παιδευμένον ἢ Μενάνδρου ἕνεκα; πότε δὲ θέατρα
πίμπλαται ἀνδρῶν φιλολόγων, κωμικοῦ¹ προσώπου
δειχθέντος; ἐν δὲ συμποσίοις τίνι δικαιότερον ἡ
τράπεζα παραχωρεῖ καὶ τόπον ὁ Διόνυσος δίδωσι;
φιλοσόφοις δὲ καὶ φιλολόγοις,² ὥσπερ ὅταν οἱ
γραφεῖς ἐκπονηθῶσι τὰς ὄψεις, ἐπὶ τὰ ἀνθηρὰ
C καὶ ποώδη χρώματα τρέπουσιν, ἀνάπαυλα τῶν
ἀκράτων³ καὶ συντόνων ἐκείνων Μένανδρός ἐστιν,
οἷον εὐανθεῖ λειμῶνι καὶ σκιερῷ καὶ πνευμάτων
μεστῷ δεχόμενος τὴν διάνοιαν.

4. "Ὅτι κωμῳδίας ὑποκριτὰς⁴ τοῦ χρόνου τούτου
πολλοὺς καὶ ἀγαθοὺς τῆς πόλεως ἐνεγκούσης, * * *⁵
αἱ Μενάνδρου κωμῳδίαι ἀφθόνων ἁλῶν καὶ ἱλαρῶν⁶
μετέχουσιν, ὥσπερ ἐξ ἐκείνης γεγονότων τῆς θαλάττης, ἐξ ἧς⁷ Ἀφροδίτη γέγονεν. οἱ δ' Ἀριστοφάνους
ἅλες πικροὶ καὶ τραχεῖς ὄντες ἑλκωτικὴν δριμύτητα
καὶ δηκτικὴν ἔχουσι· καὶ οὐκ οἶδ' ἐν οἷς ἔστιν ἡ
θρυλουμένη δεξιότης ὑπ' αὐτοῦ, ἐν λόγοις ἢ προσ-
ώποις· ἀμέλει καὶ τὰ μεμιμημένα πρὸς τὸ χεῖρον
D μεμίμηται· τὸ γὰρ πανοῦργον οὐ πολιτικὸν ἀλλὰ
κακόηθες, καὶ τὸ ἄγροικον οὐκ ἀφελὲς⁸ ἀλλ' ἠλίθιον,
καὶ τὸ γελοῖον οὐ παιγνιῶδες ἀλλὰ καταγέλαστον,

---

¹ κωμικοῦ Wyttenbach: ἢ κωμικοῦ.
² φιλολόγοις Wyttenbach: φιλοπόνοις.
³ ἀκράτων Reiske: ἀκροατῶν.
⁴ ὑποκριτὰς] ποιητὰς Haupt.
⁵ A gap here was first suggested by Wyttenbach. Something is certainly wanting.
⁶ καὶ ἱλαρῶν Emperius; κἀπίκρων Bernardakis; καὶ πράων
Kronenberg, who suggests rendering ἀφθόνων by "sine in-
vidia," cf. Plato, Republic 500 A: καὶ ἱερῶν.
⁷ ἧς Haupt: ὦν.   ⁸ ἀφελὲς Bryan: ἀσφαλὲς.

every sound and meaning which the Greek language affords. For what reason, in fact, is it truly worth while for an educated man to go to the theatre, except to enjoy Menander? And when else are theatres filled with men of learning, if a comic character has been brought upon the stage ?[a] And at banquets for whom is it more proper for the festive board to yield its place and for Dionysus to waive his rights[b] ? And just as painters, when their eyes are tired, turn to the colours of flowers and grass, so to philosophers and men of learning Menander is a rest from their concentrated and intense studies, inviting the mind, as it were, to a meadow flowery, shady, and full of breezes.

4. " Although the city has supplied at the present time many excellent actors of comedy . . . Menander's comedies contain an abundance of salty wit and merriment, which seem like the salt[c] derived from that sea out of which Aphroditê was born. But the witticisms of Aristophanes are bitter and rough and possess a sharpness which wounds and bites. And I do not know wherein his vaunted cleverness resides, whether in his words or his characters. Certainly even whatever he imitates he makes worse ; for with him roguishness is not urbane but malicious, rusticity not simple but silly, facetiousness not playful but ridiculous, and love

  [a] *i.e.* when comedies are given only those of Menander draw the crowds of men of culture.

  [b] That scenes from Menander's plays may be recited or acted.

  [c] *Cf.* Cicero, *De Officiis* i. 37. 133 " sale vero et facetiis Caesar vicit omnes," where *facetiis* corresponds to Emperius's conjecture ἱλαρῶν.

καὶ τὸ ἐρωτικὸν οὐχ ἱλαρὸν ἀλλ' ἀκόλαστον. οὐδενὶ
γὰρ ὁ ἄνθρωπος ἔοικε μετρίῳ τὴν ποίησιν γεγρα-
φέναι, ἀλλὰ τὰ μὲν αἰσχρὰ καὶ ἀσελγῆ τοῖς ἀκο-
λάστοις, τὰ βλάσφημα δὲ καὶ πικρὰ τοῖς βασκάνοις
καὶ κακοήθεσιν.''

not joyous but licentious. For the fellow seems to
have written his poetry, not for any decent person,
but the indecent and wanton lines for the licentious,
the slanderous and bitter passages for the envious
and malicious."

INDEX

ACHAEANS, 113, 139, 159, 259, 451.

Acharnae, Attic deme, 407.

Achilles, 275.

Acropolis, 273, 385, 387, 425, 455, 457.

Actaeon, son of Melissus, 9, 11.

Aeacus, 427: son of Zeus and Aegina.

Aegeis, an Attic tribe, 361.

Aegina, 427, 439, 441.

Aegospotami, 365: on the Hellespont. The Athenian fleet was defeated here in 405 B.C. by Lysander.

Aemilius Paulus, L., 35: Roman consul 168 B.C., father of Scipio Africanus the Younger. Plutarch wrote his life.

Aeschines, Academic philosopher, 119.

Aeschines, Attic orator, 221, 389, 391, 393, 395, 421, 423, 445; 390–after 330 B.C.

Aeschylus, 311, 401: great tragic poet, 525–456 B.C.

Aeschylus quoted, 41, 311.

Aesop, 15, 201: supposed inventor of beast-fables.

Aexonê, Attic deme, 407.

Afranius, L., 199: friend of Pompey, consul 60 B.C., killed 46 B.C.

Agathocles, 287: son of Lysimachus, defeated Demetrius Poliorcetes 287 B.C., was murdered 284 B.C.

Agesilaüs, 85, 115, 197, 207, 213: king of Lacedaemon, circa 438–358. Plutarch wrote his life.

Agesistratus, 427: friend of Demosthenes.

Agis, 149: king of Sparta, died 398 B.C. Plutarch wrote his life.

Aglaïa, 43, 99: one of the Muses.

Agrigentines, 279.

Agrylê, Attic deme, 353.

Agyrrhius, 173.

Ajax, 219.

Alcamenes, 179: sculptor of the 5th century B.C.

Alcibiades, 83, 165, 171, 187, 193, 287, 345, 347: brilliant Athenian general. Plutarch wrote his life.

Alcidamas, 415: author of speeches.

Alcippus, 21: a Lacedaemonian.

Alcmeon, 195: attacked Themistocles.

Alexander, son of Anaco, 387.

Alexander, 61, 65, 67, 131, 189, 199, 241, 261, 263, 265, 307, 393, 399, 405, 419, 423, 425, 431, 437, 447, 457: king of Macedon, overthrew the Persian empire; is called the Great, 356–323 B.C. Plutarch wrote his life.

Alexandria, 241.

Alexis, 89: comic dramatist, circa 376–270 B.C.

Alopecê, Attic deme, 353.

Alphinous, grandson of Hypereides, 437; (or his cousin), 441.

Amphictyon, 17: son of Deucalion and Pyrrha, freed Thebes from the Chalcidians.

Amphictyonic Council, Amphictyons, 89, 135, 391.

Amphion, 45.

Amphipolis, 415.

Amphissians, 391.

Anaco, aunt of Isocrates, 379, 387.

Anagyros, Attic deme, 415, 437, 445.

Anaxagoras, 33, 273, 337: Ionic philosopher, 500–428 B.C.

475

INDEX

Anaxarchus, 61: philosopher, 4th century B.C., was teacher of Pyrrho who founded the school of the Skeptics.

Anaxicrates, Athenian archon, 307–306 B.C., 409, 447, 455.

Anaxilas, of Oreus, 433.

Anaximenes, 185, historian of Alexander; 427, orator of the 4th century B.C.

Ancients, 111.

Andocides, 355, 357, 359: Attic orator, *circa* 445–after 391 B.C.

Andocides, grandfather of the orator, 355.

Andron, an Athenian, 353.

Andronicus, an actor, 419.

Antalcidas, a Spartan, 223.

Anticles, father of Neoptolemus, 411.

Antigonus, 121, 331, 447: general under Alexander; afterwards ruler of Asia and king, 382–301 B.C.

Antiochis, Attic tribe, 455.

Antipater, 425, 427, 429, 431, 439, 441, 445, 447, 451, 453: general of Alexander, besieged in Lamia, defeated the Greeks at Crannon, demanded the death of Athenian orators, 388–318 B.C.

Antiphanes, 419: comic poet, 4th century B.C.

Antiphon, 345, 347, 349, 351, 353, 355: Attic orator, *circa* 480–411 B.C.; others named Antiphon, 347, note, 349.

Antisthenes, 41, 225: founder of the Cynic school of philosophy, 5th and 4th centuries B.C.

Antony, Mark (Marcus Antonius), 85: consul with Julius Caesar, 44 B.C., opposed Augustus, killed himself in Egypt, 30 B.C. Plutarch wrote his life.

Aphareus, adopted by Isocrates, 379, 381, 385.

Aphidna, Attic deme, 413.

Aphobetus, brother of Aeschines, 395.

Aphobus, guardian of Demosthenes, 415.

Aphrodite, 37, 39, 93, 471.

Apollo, 111, 319, 413.

Apollodorus, 45: tyrant of Cassandreia.

Appius Claudius, 137; Roman general, statesman, and writer, builder of a great road and an aqueduct; 4th century B.C.; 219, another, 2nd century B.C.

Aratus, 193, of Sicyon: general of the Achaean League in 245 and 243 B.C. Plutarch wrote his life.

Arcadia, 149.

Arcadians, 103, 395, 425.

Archeptolemus, an Athenian, son of Hippodamus, 353, 355.

Archias, a wealthy Corinthian, 9, 11; an actor nicknamed Exile-Hunter, 427, 441.

Archidamus, king of Sparta, 179, 183: invaded Attica 431 and 430 B.C.; besieged Plataea, 429 B.C.

Archilochus, 183: Iambic poet, 1st half of 7th century B.C.

Archimedes, 93, of Syracuse: engineer and mathematician, 287–212 B.C.

Archinus, 347, 365, 367: orator who brought suit against Lysias.

Archytas, 277: Pythagorean philosopher about 450 B.C.

Arcturus, 339: a bright star in the northern sky.

Areius, 241: Alexandrian philosopher, treated as a friend by Augustus.

Areopagus, 115, 135, 231, 425, 445: hill and senate at Athens.

Ares, 111, 177: god of war.

Arethusa, daughter of Archias, 11; a fountain, 31.

Argives, 223, 239.

Argo, 47: ship in which the Argonauts sailed for the golden fleece.

Argonauts, 267.

Argos, city in Peloponnesus, 7, 13, 63, 149, 239.

Aridaeus, 121: son of Philip of Macedon and a Thessalian woman, hence called Philip III.; put to death by Olympias 317 B.C.

Aristagora, a prostitute kept by Hypereides, 443.

Aristeides, 117, 141, 147, 197, 213, 287, 345: Athenian statesman, often called "the Just," fought

INDEX

at Marathon and Salamis; died 468 B.C. Plutarch wrote his life; another, 357.

Aristion, 217: Athenian sophist, tyrant of Athens, opposed Sulla, who had him killed, 86 B.C.

Aristocleia, 5: maiden of Haliartus.

Aristodemus, a Spartan, 15; of Argos, 63; an Athenian actor, 389; of Batê, banished, 397.

Aristogeiton, 349 (the tyrannicide); 411, 439, 449, Athenian accused by Lycurgus and accuser of Hypereides.

Ariston of Chios, 29, 191: Stoic philosopher, circa 275 B.C.

Aristonicus, 423, 437: moved to crown Demosthenes.

Aristonymus, son of Symmachus, 407.

Aristophanes, 371, 463, 469, 471: poet of the Old Comedy, circa 450-385 B.C.

Aristophanes quoted, 189, 203, 325, 463, 465, 467.

Aristophon, 177, 415: Athenian politician of the 4th century B.C.

Aristotle, 185, 447, 469: the philosopher, 384-322 B.C.

Arrhephoroi, at Athens, 385.

Artaphernes, 323: Persian general defeated, with his colleague Datis, at Marathon, 490 B.C.

Artemis, 141, 321.

Artemisia, widow of Maussolus, 379.

Asclepiades, 375: composed arguments of tragedies.

Asclepius, 419: god of medicine; mispronounced by Demosthenes.

Asia, 121, 125, 393, 423, 447, 457.

Ass, shadow of, 435.

Ateas, 125: a Scythian.

Athena, 185, 407; of the city, 179; Itonia, 19; of war, 177; before-the - Temple, 295; Paeonian, 405.

Athenians, 85, 105, 123, 149, 165, 167, 171, 183, 189, 207, 223, 229, 237, 253, 283, 309, 321, 323, 333, 353, 355, 357, 361, 363, 371, 375, 395, 399, 401, 403, 405, 417, 421, 425, 427, 429, 431, 435, 437, 441, 445, 447, 449, 451, 453.

Athenodorus of Tarsus, 33: Stoic philosopher, died in Cato's house in Rome, 70 B.C.

Athens, 105, 179, 195, 197, 225, 235, 239, 265, 323, 331, 359, 361, 363, 365, 387, 401, 413, 423, 437, 441, 447.

Atrometus, father of Aeschines, 389.

Attalus II., 125: king (159-138 B.C.) of Pergamum.

Attica, 207.

Augustus, 247 (C. Julius Caesar Octavianus): adopted by Julius Caesar, became Emperor, 63 B.C.-A.D. 14; see Caesar.

Aulis, 319: town on the coast of Boeotia, known for its pottery.

Autolycus, 41: a wrestler; 409, 411, the Areopagite.

Automatia, 253: goddess of chance.

Axones, 47: revolving wooden tablets on which Solon's laws were written.

BACCHIADAE, a noble family of Corinth, 11.

Bactrians, 279.

Batalus, nickname of Demosthenes, 433.

Batê, Attic deme, 397, 407.

Bato, 35: mentioned as a person in private station.

Battus, 277: probably Battus III. of Cyrene, circa 550 B.C.

Bean-market, 375.

Bees, 289.

Berecynthian land, 41.

Bias, 307: of Priene, one of the Seven Wise Men; about the middle of the 6th century B.C.

Bocchus, 201: king of Mauretania, latter part of the 3rd century B.C.

Boeotarchy, 235, 259.

Boeotia, 5, 7, 15, 19, 265.

Boeotian, 19, 21, 417, 451.

Boeotian magistrate, 89.

Boton, 371: name under which some teachings of Theramenes passed.

Bouleuterion, 405.

INDEX

Boulis, 249: a Spartan youth, who, with Sperchis, offered himself to be slain in expiation, but was sent home by Xerxes.

Brachyllus, brother of Lysias, 363, 367.

Bucephalus, Alexander's horse, 131.

Butadae, Attic deme, 397, 455, 457.

Byzantines, 437, 451.

Byzantium, 189, 437, 449.

CADMEIA, citadel of Thebes, 207.

Cadmus, 377: mythical founder of Thebes and inventor of the alphabet.

Caecilius, 347, 351, 367, 381, 391: of Calacté, writer on rhetoric and literature; about 20 B.C.

Caesar, Augustus (C. Julius Caesar Octavianus), 85, 241: adopted son of Julius Caesar, became Roman Emperor, 63 B.C.-A.D. 14; see Augustus.

Caesar, C. Julius, 219, 263: famous Roman general, statesman, and writer. Plutarch wrote his life.

Caesar, meaning emperor, 237.

Calauria, 427, 429, 451: small island off the coast of Peloponnesus where Demosthenes died.

Callaeschrus, 349: Athenian who claimed Antiphon's daughter in marriage.

Callias, 43, 287, 407: Athenians; archon, 411-410 B.C.; 363; a Syracusan, 415.

Callicles, 283: an Athenian money-lender, 4th century B.C.

Callicratidas, 267: noted for too lofty speech.

Callimachus, 421: Athenian archon 349-348 B.C.

Callimachus quoted, 205, 247: of Cyrené, poet and scholar, succeeded Zenodotus as librarian at Alexandria; circa 310-240 B.C.

Calliopé, 37, 177, 369: Muse of epic poetry.

Callippus, an athlete accused of using corruption, 445.

Callirrhoé, daughter of Phocus, 19.

Callisthenes, young man of Hali-

artus, 5, 7; freedman of Lucullus, 125.

Callisto, 407, wife of Lycurgus; 407, granddaughter of Lycurgus.

Callistomaché, wife of Lycophron, 407.

Callistratus, 223, 413: Athenian orator, 4th century B.C.

Calypso, 337: a sea nymph.

Canus, a flute-player, 93.

Carbo, 173: perhaps, Cn. Papirius Carbo, Roman consul, 83 B.C.

Carneades, 119: of Cyrene, founder of the New Academy, circa 215-129 B.C.

Carthage, 193, 321.

Carthaginians, 123, 165.

Carystus, 415: city on the island of Euboea.

Cassander, 239, 447: son of Antipater, became king of Macedonia, circa 354-297 B.C.

Cassandra, 277: daughter of Priam of Troy; a prophetess whose prophecies no one believed.

Catiline, L. Sergius Catilina, 217, 263: Roman patrician who led an attempted revolution and was killed in battle, 62 B.C.

Cato (M. Porcius Cato the Elder), 81, 85, 109, 115, 117, 123, 149, 185, 189, 193, 197: commonly called the Censor, 234 (?)-149 B.C. Plutarch wrote his life.

Cato, M. Porcius, 29, 33, 63, 211, 215, 219, 223, 263, 271, 297, 327: commonly called Cato Uticensis or Cato Minor, 95-46 B.C. Plutarch wrote his life.

Catulus (Q. Lutatius), 201, 211: consul with Aemilius Lepidus, 78 B.C.; opposed grants of power to Pompey.

Centaurs, 333.

Ceos, 371: an island in the Aegean Sea.

Cephalus, 173: an unknown person ridiculed by the comic poet Plato.

Cephalus, 361: father and great-grandfather of Lysias.

Cephisodorus, 449.

Cephissus, 223: river at Athens.

Cerameicus, 409, 455: Potters quarter at Athens.

478

INDEX

Chabrias, 117, 197: Athenian general, slain in a naval battle at Chios, 357 B.C.

Chaerephon, an Athenian, 411.

Chaerondas, Athenian archon, 338-337 B.C., 375.

Chaeroneia, 187, 377, 379, 393, 423, 435, 439, 451: town in Boeotia where Philip (338 B.C.) defeated the Boeotians and Athenians.

Chalcidian, 17, 387, 411.

Chalcis, 413, 447: city of Euboea.

Chalcodon, 17: king of Chalcis, son of Abas; killed in battle by Amphitryon.

Chares, 105, Athenian of physical strength; 487, 449, Athenian general, 4th century B.C.

Charicles, Athenian archon, 363-362 B.C., 209, 421; of Carystus, 415.

Charinus, 231: Athenian, aided Pericles.

Charmides, son of Aristonymus, 407.

Chians, 233.

Chios, 371, 375.

Chleidon, a farmer, 109.

Choregi, 255, 257.

Cicero, M. Tullius, 151, 185: Roman orator, statesman, and philosopher, 106–43 B.C. Plutarch wrote his life.

Cimon, 71, 117, 141, 171, 179, 233, 263: son of Miltiades; Athenian general and statesman, died while besieging Citium, 449 B.C. Plutarch wrote his life.

Cissoessa, a spring at Haliartus, 7.

City Dionysia, 387, 401.

Claudius, 195: see Appius.

Cleanthes, 331: Stoic philosopher, and successor of Zeno in the Stoic school; author of a hymn to Zeus, which has been preserved; circa 300–320 B.C.

Clearchus, 63: tyrant of Pontus, killed 353 B.C.

Cleisthenes, 117, 197: reformed the government of Athens about 510 B.C.

Cleitus, 61: killed by Alexander.

Cleobulê, mother of Demothenes, 413

Cleocritus, 363: Athenian archon, 412-411 B.C.

Cleombrotus, married Callisto, 407.

Cleon, 165, 195, 203, 231, 263, 307: Athenian demagogue, slain at Amphipolis, 422 B.C.

Cleophon, 195: Athenian demagogue in the later years of the 5th century B.C.

Clio, 37: Muse of history.

Cocles, Horatius, 273: saved Rome from destruction by guarding the bridge over the Tiber, 508 (?) B.C.

Coenus, father of Anaco's son Alexander, 387.

Collytê, Attic deme, 437.

Conon, father of Timotheüs, 373, 381: Athenian general and naval commander in the last years of the 5th and early part of the 4th centuries B.C.

Corcyraean whip, 405.

Corcyraeans, 355, 417.

Corinth, 9, 11, 65, 79, 209, 333, 351, 441.

Corinthians, 7, 9, 11, 355, 357, 417, 447, 451.

Coroneia, a town in Boeotia, 19, 21.

Cothocidae, Attic deme, 389.

Cotys, 253: cruel and drunken king of Thrace, murdered by Python, 358 B.C.

Crannon, 439: city of Thessaly where Antipater defeated the allied Greeks, 322 B.C.

Crassus, Lucius, 203: Roman orator, circa 140–91 B.C.

Crates, a Delphian, 295; a lyric poet, 331; Cynic philosopher of the 4th century B.C., 337.

Crates quoted, 331.

Cratinus, 349: produced comedies circa 450–423 B.C.

Cratippus, 357: a historian, contemporary of Thucydides.

Cretans, 127.

Crete, 425.

Cretinas, of Magnesia, 215.

Critias, 347: Athenian aristocrat; one of the Thirty Tyrants, 404 B.C.

Critolaüs, 225: Peripatetic philosopher; succeeded Ariston of

INDEX

Ceos as head of the school, *circa* 240-157 B.C.

Croesus, 285: king of Lydia in Asia Minor, 560-546 B.C., famous for his wealth, conquered by Cyrus the Great.

Crow's Rock, 31.

Ctesibius, 415: writer on philosophy.

Ctesicles, Athenian archon, 334-333 B.C., 413.

Ctesiphon, 393, 395, 423: proposed a crown for Demosthenes.

Cumae, 375, 383: city in Italy, birthplace of the historian Ephorus.

Cydathenian, 355: belonging to the Attic deme of Cydathenê, which was in the city of Athens.

Cynosarges, a region in Athens, 379.

Cypriote kings, 357.

Cyprus, 359, 379, 383.

Cyrenaeans, 53.

Cyrus, 279: probably Cyrus the Great, founder of the Persian empire, who was killed in 538 B.C.

DAMOCRITA, daughter of Alcippus, 21, 23.

Danaüs, 377: father of the fifty Danaïds, with whom he fled from Egypt to Greece.

Dareius, 115, 125, 323: third king of Persia (521-485 B.C.); conquered Thrace; sent army under Datis and Artaphernes, which was defeated at Marathon, 490 B.C.

Datis, 323: Persian general, defeated at Marathon, 490 B.C.

Deceleia, Attic deme, 353.

Deinarchus, 407, 447: Attic orator, before 343-after 292 B.C.

Deinias, 399: gave land for stadium.

Deinocrates, father of Cleombrotus, 407.

Delian ship, 97.

Delians, 445.

Delivery, 419.

Delos, 395.

Delphi, seat of the famous oracle, 13, 295, 321.

Delphians, 295.

Demades, 183, 221, 223, 263, 273, 409: Attic orator and demagogue opposed to Demosthenes; *circa* 385-318 B.C.

Demeas, father of Demades, 409; father of Demophon, 415.

Demeter, 355.

Demetrius, of Magnesia, 429.

Demetrius, of Phalerum, 263, 273, 447: orator and Peripatetic philosopher, 350 (?)-283 B.C.; put in charge of Athens by the Macedonians (317 B.C.), but forced to flee by Demetrius Poliorcetes, 308-307 B.C.

Demetrius Poliorcetes, 287, 311, 447: king of Macedonia and famous as a general (son of Antigonus). Plutarch wrote his life.

Demochares, 393, 431, 433, 451, 453: nephew of Demosthenes.

Democles, 405: spoke in defence of the sons of Lycurgus.

Democrates, 187: Athenian orator, 4th century B.C.

Democritus, 275: one of the founders of the Atomic school of philosophy; 460 (?)-360 B.C.

Demomeles, 423: proposed a crown for Demosthenes.

Demon, 427: cousin of Demosthenes.

Demonicus, 353: secretary of the senate which voted the trial of Antiphon, 411-410 B.C.

Demophon, 415: grandson of Demosthenes.

Demosthenes, 175: a Lacedaemonian.

Demosthenes, 351: Athenian general of the 5th century B.C.

Demosthenes, 89, 141, 181, 185, 187, 221, 257, 275, 365, 367, 375, 389, 391, 393, 395, 405, 413, 415, 419, 421, 423, 425, 427, 429, 431, 433, 439, 441, 443, 449: Athenian orator and statesman, 384-322 B.C. Plutarch wrote his life.

Demosthenes, 413, 449, father of the orator; 449, great-grand-nephew of the orator.

Dexander, 7, 9.

INDEX

Dexitheus, Athenian archon, 385–384 B.C., 421.

Diacrians, 197.

Dicaearchus, 145 : Peripatetic philosopher, geographer, and historian, 4th and 3rd centuries B.C.

Diocles, married Philippa, 407 ; his son, 407 ; his great-grandson, 409 ; Athenian archon, 288–287 B.C., 453.

Diodotus, 423 : attacked Ctesiphon's proposal of a crown for Demosthenes.

Diogenes, 65, 67, 79, 433 : of Sinopê, 420 (?)–323 B.C., famous Cynic philosopher.

Diomedes, 209, 257, 267.

Diomeia, Attic deme, 455.

Diomnestus, brother of Isocrates, 371.

Dion, 33 : of Syracuse ; friend and pupil of Plato, 408–353 B.C. Plutarch wrote his life.

Diondas, opposed granting a crown to Demosthenes, 347, 349.

Dionysiac festival, 255, 391.

Dionysiac theatre, 397.

Dionysius, grandfather of Hypereides, 437.

Dionysius, of Halicarnassus, 367, 381 : historian and rhetorician, about 20 B.C.

Dionysius, a schoolmaster, 29.

Dionysius, theatrical manager for Aphareus, 387.

Dionysius I., tyrant of Syracuse, 45, 125, 349, 351, 369 ; circa 430–367 B.C.

Dionysius II. of Syracuse, 47, 67, 79, 277 : succeeded his father, Dionysius the Elder, in 367 ; was removed in 343 B.C.

Dionysus, god of wine, 471.

Diopeithes, father of Diotimus, 413.

Diotimus, an Athenian, 413, 417 : associated with Demosthenes.

Diphilus, 409 : brought to trial by Lycurgus.

Diphorus, 383 : pun on the name of Ephorus.

Domitian, 157, 247 : Roman emperor, A.D. 81–96.

Domitius, 223 : a witty Roman.

Doryphorus, statue by Polycleitus, 271.

Dromocleides, 163 : a self-seeking politician.

Drusus, M. Livius, 171 : tribune of the people at Rome, 91 B.C.

Earthquake, at Sparta, 23.

Eëtioneia, 349 : mole at Peiraeus.

Egesta, 357 : town in Sicily.

Egypt, 453.

Elateia, 423 : taken by Philip, 338 B.C.

Elders, 111.

Eleans, 445.

Eleusis, 375, 381, 401, 443, 453.

Eleven, executioners at Athens, 353.

Elis, 197, 359, 365.

Empedocles, 275, 333 : poetic philosopher, circa 492–432 B.C.

Empedocles quoted, 37, 275, 333.

Empedus, father of Callistratus, 413.

Enyalius, epithet of Ares, 177.

Epameinondas, 17, 63, 95, 103, 149, 167, 195, 211, 213, 223, 259, 267, 287 : Boeotian statesman and general, overthrew the power of Sparta at Leuctra (371 B.C.), killed in the battle of Mantineia, 362 B.C. Plutarch wrote his life.

Ephesus, 141, 321, 393.

Ephialtes, 179, 197, 231 : Athenian statesman of the 5th century B.C. ; 433, 437 : politician of the 4th century B.C.

Ephors at Sparta, 13, 15, 21, 53, 149, 183.

Ephorus, 185, 375, 383 : author of a history of Greece from the return of the Heracleidae to 340 B.C. (?)–circa 320 B.C.

Epicles, 435, rebuked Demosthenes for preparing his speeches.

Epicurus, 43 : founder of the Epicurean school of philosophy, 342–270 B.C.

Epileptics, 69.

Epimenides, 81, 273 : religious poet and giver of oracles, circa 600 B.C.

INDEX

Erasistratus, 351 : Antiphon composed an oration against him.

Eratosthenes, 89, 429 : of Cyrene, writer on geography and chronography, succeeded Callimachus as head of the Alexandrian Library, *circa* 275-195 B.C.

Erchia, Attic deme, 371.

Erechtheum, 411 : temple in Athens.

Erechtheus, 411.

Eringium, a plant, 33.

Erinyes, 15.

Eteobutadae, 397 : a family at Athens.

Euboea, 445, 449.

Euboeans, 17, 417, 451.

Eubulides, Milesian philosopher, teacher of Demosthenes, 419.

Eubulus, the Anaphlystian, 233 : son of Spintharus, 391.

Eucleides, Athenian archon, 403-402 B.C., 365.

Eucleides, an Olynthian, 403.

Eumenes II., king (197-159) of Pergamum, 125.

Eumolpidae, family at Athens, 407.

Eunomus, encourages Demosthenes, 417.

Euonymus, Attic deme, 413.

Euphanes, 75, 77, 93 : an Athenian of some distinction, to whom Plutarch addressed the essay, "Whether an Old Man should engage in Public Affairs."

Euphrosynê, 43 ; one of the Graces.

Eupolis, 43 : poet of the Old Comedy, 446-411 B.C.

Euripides, 93, 95, 141, 177, 207, 225, 231, 241, 377, 401 : Athenian tragic poet, *circa* 485-406 B.C.

Euripides quoted, 39, 41, 59, 81, 93, 95, 103, 107, 113, 131, 177, 185, 207, 215, 225, 231, 377.

Eurotas, 223 : river at Sparta.

Eurymedon, 239 : river in Pamphylia, near which Cimon defeated the Persians, 464 B.C.

Euthydemus, brother of Lysias, 363 ; father of Stratocles, 455.

Euxippê, daughter of Scedasus, 11.

Euxitheus, 185 : a pupil of Aristotle.

Evagoras, father of Nicocles, 379.

Exile-Hunter, 427, 441 : nickname of Archias who arrested Demosthenes and Hypereides.

FABIUS MAXIMUS, Q., 117 : Roman general in the second Punic War, surnamed Cunctator ; died 203 B.C. Plutarch wrote his life.

Fortifications, Demosthenes Commissioner of, 451.

Fortune, 69.

Forum, 137

Four Hundred, 347, 349, 353, 359, 363 : ruled Athens four months, 411 B.C.

Four years' war, 453 : 294-290 B.C., ending with the surrender of Athens.

Frugality, 321.

GAEA, 411.

Gaius Gracchus, 163 : orator and reformer, 154-121 B.C.

Gaius Laelius, 151 : man of letters, friend of Scipio, *circa* 140 B.C.

Gamelion, Attic month, 445.

Garden, philosophers of, *i.e.* Epicureans, 109.

Gaul, 201.

Gelo, 361 : tyrant of Syracuse.

Geryon, 267 : a three-bodied giant.

Glaucippus, father of Hypereides, 437 ; son of Hypereides, 437, 441.

Glaucon, 355 : an Athenian.

Glaucothea, mother of Aeschines, 389.

Glaucus, of Rhegium, 351 ; father of Timothea, 407.

Glisas, a town in Boeotia, 19, 21.

Gorgias, of Leontini, 347, 371, 377, 381 : famous sophist, *circa* 485-380 B.C.

Gorgias, 431 : Athenian archon, 280-279 B.C.

Gorgons, 333.

Gracchus, Gaius, 163 : Roman orator and reformer, 154-121 B.C. Plutarch wrote his life.

Graces, 43.

Great Mother, temple of, 405.

Gylon, grandfather of Demosthenes, 413.

INDEX

HABRON, 9, friend of Pheidon and Dexander ; 407, father of Callisto ; 407, father of Callias ; 407, son of Lycurgus ; 409, 411, father of Hedistê.

Haliartus, 5 : a town in Boeotia.

Hannibal, 35, 231 : Carthaginian general, 247–183 B.C.

Hanno, 167 : Carthaginian general, political [opponent of Hannibal, circa 275–200 B.C.

Harmodius, 349 (the tyrannicide), 369 (another).

Harpalus, 209, 239, 423, 425, 439, 447 : treasurer of Alexander, brought stolen funds to Athens, 324 B.C.

Hedistê, wife of Diocles, 407.

Hegesias, of Magnesia, 413.

Helen, 379.

Helicon, 19, 21 : a mountain in Boeotia.

Heliodorus, father-in-law of Demosthenes, 431 ; author of work On Monuments, 441.

Hellanicus, 355 : historian (logographer), 5th century B.C.

Hellas, 47, 183.

Hellespont, 449.

Hera, 39.

Heracleidae, noble family at Corinth, 9.

Heracleitus, 99 : physical philosopher of Ephesus, sometimes called "the Obscure," circa 560–500 B.C.

Heracles, 31, 91, 115, 267, 307.

Herculis, 251.

Hercynê, a fountain at Lebadeia, 5.

Hermae, 153, 355, 357.

Hermas, 365 : fellow envoy with Lysias.

Hermeias, 215: opponent of Cretinas at Magnesia.

Hermes, 35, 37, 355, 359, 361 ; of the Market, 413.

Hermippus, 441 : historian and biographer, Peripatetic of the 3rd century B.C.

Hermon, 283 : a Thessalian who pleaded poverty to avoid public office.

Herodes, 351 : subject of an oration by Antiphon.

Herodotus, 87, 307: author of history of the Persian wars ; circa 484–425 B.C.

Herodotus quoted, 321.

Hesiod, 61 : epic and didactic poet, circa 750 B.C.

Hesiod quoted, 61, 177.

Hestia, Boulaea, altar of, 371.

Hestiaea, 13 : a city of Euboea.

Himeraeus, 425 : accused Demosthenes.

Hippaes, gate of, 441.

Hippias, orator, father of Plathanê, 379, 385.

Hippo, daughter of Scedasus, 11.

Hippocrates, 375 : gave land for stadium.

Hippodamas, 353, father of Archeptolemus.

Hippolytus, 39, son of Theseus.

Hippotae, a village in Boeotia, 19, 21.

Homer, 31, 103, 133, 175, 217, 219, 375 : author of the Iliad and the Odyssey.

Homer, the Iliad quoted, 63, 67, 111, 113, 127, 133, 139, 141, 159, 177, 211, 217, 219, 247, 257, 277, 327.

Homer, the Odyssey quoted, 31, 33, 47, 179, 193, 269, 337.

Hygieia, statue of, 387.

Hyperbolus, 307: Athenian demagogue, killed 411 B.C.

Hypereides, 221, 375, 395, 417, 423, 425, 437, 443, 445, 449: Athenian orator, 389–322 B.C.

IBERIA, 193: the south-western peninsula of Europe.

Ibis, nickname of Lycurgus, 411.

Ictinus, 179 ; architect of the Parthenon.

Iolas, supposed to have poisoned Alexander, 445.

Ionian mode in music, 281.

Iphicrates, 105, 177, 233, 369: Athenian general of the 1st half of the 4th century B.C.

Isaeus, 375, 387, 413, 415 : Attic orator, circa 410–350 (?) B.C.

Ismenias, a painter, 411.

Isocrates, 367, 371, 375, 377, 381, 385, 387, 391, 397, 413, 435, 437:

483

INDEX

Attic orator and philosopher,
436–338 B.C.
Isthmian festival, 11.
Italiote Greeks, 33.
Italy, 95, 363.
Ixion, 39 : tried to seduce Hera,
and was bound by Zeus upon a
fiery wheel.

JASON, Thessalian ruler, 259, probably Jason of Pherae, 4th century B.C.
Jugurtha, 201 : king of Numidia,
died in prison in Rome, 204 B.C.
Justice, 61, 269.

KINGS, at Sparta, 53, 55; of
Persians, 57, 249, 433 ; of Universe,
225.

LACEDAEMON, 13, 111, 143, 173, 349,
353, 359.
Lacedaemonians, 13, 15, 17, 21, 23,
45, 193, 197, 221, 253, 273.
Laches, 433, 449, 451 : son of
Demochares.
Laches, 431, 451 : brother-in-law of
Demosthenes.
Laconia, 259, 425.
Ladas, a famous runner, 191.
Laelius, Gaius, 151, 199 : man of
letters, friend of Scipio, *circa*
140 B.C.
Laërtes, 103 : father of Odysseus.
Lagiscê, mistress of Isocrates, 385.
Lamachus, 267, 283 : Athenian
general, 5th century B.C.; of
Tereina, 419, 421.
Lamia, 427 : town on the Malian
gulf, where Antipater was be-
sieged, 323–322 B.C.
Lamian War, 445.
Lampis, a sea captain, 97.
Lampon, a ship captain, 109.
Lampon, founder of Thurii, 231.
Laodameia, son of Medeius, 407.
Lebadeia, a town in Boeotia, 5, 439.
Lenaean festival, 387.
Leo of Byzantium, 189.
Leochares, sculptor of the 4th
century B.C., 381.
Leocrates, 411 : name applied to
Lycurgus.

Leodamas, 375, 391 : Athenian
orator, 4th century B.C.
Leogoras, father of Andocides, 355,
357.
Leontini, 357, 371, 377 : a town in
Sicily.
Leoprepes, 87 : father of the poet
Simonides.
Leosthenes, 183, 445 : general in
the Lamian War ; killed at Lamia,
322 B.C.
Leptines, Athenian orator, quoted,
183.
Lesbian, 221.
Leuconoê, Attic deme, 431, 433, 449,
451, 453.
Leuctra, 11, 13, 17, 95 : village in
Boeotia, where, in 371 B.C., the
Thebans broke the power of
Sparta.
Leuctrian war, 209.
Liberty, 321.
Libya, 201.
Lichas, 287 : perhaps the Spartan,
son of Arcesilaüs, who died *circa*
411 B.C.
Livius Drusus, M., Roman tribune,
91 B.C., 171.
Locrians, 451.
Lucullus (L. Licinius), 71, 91, 125,
197 : Roman general of the 1st
half of the 1st century B.C. In
his later years he gave himself up
to luxury. Plutarch wrote his
life.
Lyceum, 117, 397, 457 : gymnasium
at Athens where Aristotle taught.
Lycomedes, 411, 455 : progenitor of
the orator Lycurgus, 455.
Lycophron, father of the orator
Lycurgus, 395, 455; son of
Lycurgus, 407, 409, 411, 455,
457.
Lycurgus, early Spartan lawgiver,
111, 143, 221, 309. Plutarch wrote
his life.
Lycurgus, grandfather of the orator,
395, 411.
Lycurgus, Attic orator, *circa* 390–
324 B.C., 395, 397, 399, 403, 405,
409, 411, 437, 439, 455, 457.
Lycurgus, son of the orator, 407,
411.
Lydian maids, 91.

484

INDEX

Lydian mode in music, 281.

Lydian power, 237.

Lysander, married Philippa, 407.

Lysander, 143, 197, 287 : Lacedaemonian general, slain in battle at Haliartus, 395 B.C. Plutarch wrote his life.

Lysanias, 361 ; grandfather of Lysias.

Lysias, 347, 349, 361, 369, 371, 377 387, 435 : Attic orator, circa 450–circa 380 B.C.

Lysias, father of Anaco's son Sosicles, 387.

Lysicles, Athenian general, 409 ; friend of Demosthenes, 439.

Lysimachus, 275, 453 : archon at Athens, 436-435 B.C. ; challenged Isocrates to exchange property, 385.

Lysis, 369.

Lysistratus, 387, Athenian archon, 369-368 B.C.

Lysonides, 349 : father of an Antiphon, not of the orator.

Macedon, 429.

Macedonia, 441.

Macedonians, 425, 429, 431, 441.

Magnesia, 215, 413, 429.

Mamertines, 249 : mercenaries who occupied Messina.

Mantias, 173 : an Athenian ridiculed by the comic poet Plato.

Mantinean alliance, 193 (420 B.C.).

Mantineia, 421 : city in Arcadia.

Marathon, 283 : Attic deme in which the Persians were defeated, 490 B.C.

Marcus, brother of L. Licinius Lucullus, 125.

Marius, C., 201: Roman general, 155-86 B.C. Plutarch wrote his life.

Masinissa, 123 : Numidian king, 238-148 B.C.

Maussolus, of Halicarnassus, 379 : died 353 B.C., and his wife Artemisia erected for him a splendid tomb, the Mausoleum.

Maximus (Q. Fabius), 197: see Fabius.

Medeius, son of Lysander and Philippa, 407 ; his son, 407.

Megacleides, 385 : challenged Isocrates to exchange of property.

Megara, 365, 435 : city between Athens and Corinth.

Megarians, 231, 307, 451.

Meidias, 89, 415, 445 : a wealthy Athenian, 4th century B.C.

Melanthius, garden of, 405.

Meletê, Attic deme, 407.

Melissus, a village in Corinthian territory, 9.

Melissus, son of Habron, 9.

Menander, king of the Bactrians, 279.

Menander, 175, 463, 467, 469, 471 : greatest poet of the New Comedy, circa 344-292 B.C.

Menander quoted, 175.

Menecleides, 195 : an orator who attacked Epameinondas.

Menecrates, 149 : an aged Spartan.

Menemachus, 156, 159, 213 : the young man to whom the essay entitled "Precepts of Statecraft" is addressed.

Menesaechmus, 405, 409, 425 : Athenian of the 4th century B.C.

Menippus, 231 : a general employed by Pericles.

Messenê, 259 : city in Messenia, founded by Epameinondas.

Messenians, 325, 451.

Metaneira, 367 : slave girl with whom Lysias was said to be in love.

Metellus (Q. Caecilius Metellus Pius), 201 : Roman consul with Sulla, 80 B.C.

Methonê, 451 : Athenians defeated by Philip, 353 B.C.

Metiochus, 227 : Athenian politician of the 5th century B.C.

Miccylus, 331 : not mentioned elsewhere.

Miletia, daughter of Scedasus, 11.

Miletus, 239 : a city of Asia Minor.

Miltiades, 169 : commander of the Greeks at Marathon, 490 B.C. Plutarch wrote his life.

Minos, 31 : king of Cnossus in Crete ; judge in the lower world.

Mnesiphilus, 141 : Athenian who aided Themistocles.

INDEX

Mummius (L.), 251 : Roman consul, destroyed Corinth, 146 B.C.

Munychia, 447 : hill and fortification in Peiraeus.

Muse, 37, 99.

Musonius (C. Musonius Rufus), 329 : Stoic philosopher, teacher of Epictetus ; 1st century A.D.

Myron, 59 : sculptor of the 5th century B.C.

Myrrhina, a prostitute, 443.

Myrrhinus, Attic deme, 371.

NABIS, 217, 259 : tyrant (205–192 B.C.) of Sparta.

Nausicles, 417 : associated with Demosthenes in opposing Philip.

Neaera, 367 : slave girl at Athens against whom Demosthenes composed a speech.

Neoptolemus, an Athenian, 411 ; an actor, 417.

Nero, 217, 247 : Roman emperor (A.D. 54–68).

Nesiotes, 179 : a sculptor of the time of the Persian wars.

Nestor, 103, 111, 113, 139, 219, 347.

Niceratus, 287 : probably the wealthy Athenian, son of Nicias, who is one of the characters in Plato's *Symposium*.

Nicias, 181, 267 : Athenian general, (?)-413 B.C. Plutarch wrote his life. Syracusan rhetorician, 363 ; a painter, 93 ; another, 207.

Nicocles, 193, tyrant destroyed by Aratus ; 379, king of Cyprus.

Nicocreon, despot of Cyprus, 383.

Nicophanes, father of Aristonicus, 437.

Nicostrata, daughter of Phoedus, 21 ; daughter of Diocles, 409.

Nigidius, Publius, 151 : philosopher who aided Cicero, died in 45 B.C.

Numa Pompilius, 115 : second king of Rome (716 (?)-673 (?) B.C.). Plutarch wrote his life.

OARISTES, 31.

Odysseus, 337.

Oedipus, 81, 223.

Olympias, 167 : wife of Philip and mother of Alexander.

Olympic games, 117, 419.

Olympieium in Athens, 385.

Olynthian, 403, 419, 421.

Olynthus, 451 : town in Chalcidicê ; Athenians defeated by Philip in 348 B.C.

Omphalê, 91 : Lydian queen whom Heracles was forced to serve.

Onomacles, an Athenian, 353.

Onomademus, 233 : popular leader of the Chians.

Oracle, 11 : Pythian, at Delphi, 13, 19.

Orchomenians, 19.

Orchomenus, a town in Boeotia, 5, 19.

Orestes, 223 : son of Agamemnon.

Oreus, village in the territory of Hestiaea, 13, 15, 433.

Oromasdes, 57 : Greek form of Ahura Mazdah, Persian god.

Orsilaüs, 295 : son of Phalis, a Delphian.

Ortygia, daughter of Archias, 11.

PAEANIA, Attic deme, 413, 437, 449.

Pallenê, Attic deme, 353.

Pamboeotia, festival of the united Boeotians, celebrated at Coroneia, 19.

Pammenes, 197 : a Theban aided in his career by Epameinondas.

Panaetius, 33, 35, 241 : Stoic philosopher, *circa* 185–*circa* 110 B.C.

Panathenaic stadium, 399, 457.

Pandionis, Attic tribe, 451.

Paralians, 197 : the "coast folk" of Attica.

Paralus, 89, 225 : sacred ship at Athens.

Pardalas of Sardis, 237, 297.

Patrae, 333 : city in Achaea.

Patrocles, 425.

Patroclus, 275 : one of those who brought Demosthenes to trial.

Paulus (L. Aemilius), 219 : father of the younger Scipio Africans of consul 168 B.C., defeated King Perseus of Macedonia at Pydnau ;

Pedieans, 197 : the "plain folk". Attica.

486

INDEX

Pegasus, 207.

Peiraeus, 183, 401, 427, 443, 451: the port of Athens.

Peisistratus, 137: tyrant of Athens, 560–527 B.C.

Peleus, 103: father of Achilles.

Pelopidas, 17, 211, 267: Theban patriot and general; killed at Cynoscephalae, 364 B.C. Plutarch wrote his life.

Peloponnesian War, 389.

Peloponnesians, 7, 451.

Peloponnesus, 9, 399.

Pelops, 377.

Pergamenes, 247.

Pericles, 29, 33, 85, 109, 115, 141, 169, 179, 181, 183, 185, 187, 195, 209, 221, 225, 227, 231, 233, 237, 263, 307, 319, 345, 361: Athenian statesman (?)–429 B.C. Plutarch wrote his life.

Peripatetic, 225: school of philosophy founded by Aristotle.

Persia, 433.

Persian, 249, 273, 279, 309, 323, 325, 431; Persian wars, 321; 347; Persian funds, 437.

Petraeus, 247: burned alive by the Thessalians.

Phaeax, 359: Andocides defended himself against him.

Phaedrus of Plato, 367.

Phalaris, 45, 279: cruel tyrant of Acragas, probably between 571 and 549 B.C.

Phalerum, 273, 417, 447: deme and roadstead near Athens.

Phalis, 295: a Delphian, father of Orsilaüs.

Pharsalus, 427: city in Thessaly.

Pheidias, 59: great Athenian sculptor of the 5th century B.C.

Pheidon, 7, 9: tyrant of Argos, 7th century B.C.

Phila, a Theban girl kept by Hypereides, 443.

Philemon, 89: comic dramatist, 361–262 B.C.

Philetas, 123: elegiac poet, *circa* 340–285 B.C.

Philip II., of Macedon, 167, 199, 377, 389, 391, 393, 395, 399, 417, 419, 421, 423, 429, 433, 437, 439,

445, 451: founder of the Macedonian empire, father of Alexander, 382–336 B.C.

Philippa, daughter of Charmides, 407; her granddaughter, 407.

Philippics, of Demosthenes, 183, 221; of Theopompus, 349.

Philippides, son of Diocles, 409.

Philiscus, 367: composed a poem in honour of Lysias.

Philochorus, 89, 425, 429: soothsayer, writer on Attic history, *circa* 335–261 B.C.

Philochorus, brother of Aeschines, 395.

Philocles, 361, 367: Athenian archon, 459–458 B.C.

Philoctetes, 107: a Greek hero of the Trojan war.

Philonicus, 219: a Roman publican, 2nd century B.C.

Philopeithes, 441: a physician.

Philopoemen, 119, 231, 259: eight times general of the Achaean League, 252–182 B.C. Plutarch wrote his life.

Philopoemen, courtier of Attalus, 125.

Philostratus, an Athenian, 353.

Philoxenus, 339: a lyric poet.

Phineus, 339: put out his daughters eyes, was blinded by the gods, and plagued with harpies which snatched away his food.

Phocion, 391.

Phocion, 109, 117, 123, 183, 187, 197, 207, 215, 221, 223, 265, 283, 445, 449: Athenian statesman and general, *circa* 402–317 B.C. Plutarch wrote his life.

Phocis, 391.

Phocus, a Boeotian, 19, 21.

Phoebidas, 207, 209; Spartan general who seized Thebes, 382 B.C.

Phoedus, a Theban general, 21.

Pholegandrian, 237.

Phormio, 197: pupil of Plato, curtailed the power of the senate at Elis.

Phrasicles, 361: for Phrasicleides, Athenian archon, 460–459 B.C.

Phrontis, 369: "Thought," daughter of the Muse Calliopê.

INDEX

Phrynê, famous courtesan of the 4th century B.C., 443.

Phrynichus, 239, 355 : Athenian tragic poet, *circa* 540-476 B.C.

Phylê, 365 : mountain fortress occupied by Thrasybulus in 404 B.C.

Pindar, 31, 37, 57, 77, 191, 205 ; great lyric poet, 518-438 B.C.

Pindar quoted, 31, 37, 57, 77, 99, 111, 191, 305.

Pisa, 377 : place in Elis ; Olympia was in its territory.

Pistius, 407 : Athenian against whom a speech by Deinarchus was directed.

Pitcher Festival, 265.

Pittacus, 221, 273 : one of the Seven Wise Men, ruler of Mytilene for ten years ; *circa* 651-569 B.C.

Plataea, 185, 239 : small city in Boeotia.

Plathanê, mother of Aphareus, 379, 381.

Plato, 33, 47, 53, 65, 95, 119, 175, 203, 211, 263, 269, 281, 309, 317, 323, 367, 369, 371, 391, 397, 413, 415, 421, 437 : great philosopher, *circa* 427-347 B.C.

Plato, comic poet of the 5th and 4th centuries B.C., 173, 351.

Plutarch, 127 : philosopher, biographer, and essay-writer ; *circa* A.D. 50-125.

Polemarchus, brother of Lysias, 361, 365.

Polemo, 57 : succeeded Xenocrates as head of the Academic school of philosophy in 314 B.C.

Politeia defined, 307.

Political Wisdom, 305.

Polus, 89, 255, 435 : a famous actor in the 4th century B.C.

Polybius, 119, 123, 241 : historian of the growth of Roman power, friend of the younger Scipio Africanus, *circa* 210 - *circa* 120 B.C.

Polycleitus, 59 : famous sculptor of the 5th century B.C.

Polydeuces, 35 : mentioned as a person in private station.

Polyeuctus, 187, 399, 417, 425, 429 : a sculptor.

Pompeium, building in Athens, 385.

Pompey (Cn. Pompeius Magnus), 47, 91, 119, 171, 193, 195, 199, 201, 219, 249 : great Roman general ; friend, then rival and enemy of Julius Caesar, 106-48 B.C. Plutarch wrote his life.

Pontus, 63 : region on the southern shore of the Black Sea.

Poseidon, 11, 401, 411, 427, 441.

Poseidon-Erechtheus, 407, 409.

Poseidonius, 35 : Stoic philosopher and scholar, 130 ?-50 B.C. *circa*

Pots, festival of, 399.

Praenestê, city in Italy, 249.

Praxiteles, Athenian archon, 444-443 B.C.

Presbeion, 101.

Probalinthus, Attic deme, 391.

Prodicus, 123, 371 : of Ceos, sophist, *circa* 450 B.C.

Propoetus, 37 : a mythical character.

Proxenus, 449 : a friend of Deinarchus.

Prytaneum, 431, 433, 449, 453, 457.

Ptolemy, 287, 453 : first Macedonian king of Egypt.

Pyanepsion, Attic month in which Hypereides died, 441.

Pydna, 451 : Athenians were defeated here by Philip, 356 B.C.

Pylos, 325 : a town in Peloponnesus.

Pyrrhus, 137 : king of Epeirus ; called in by the Tarentines to break the Roman power ; was successful at first, but finally defeated, *circa* 318-272 B.C. Plutarch wrote his life.

Pythagoras, 33 : philosopher and mathematician, 2nd half of the 6th century B.C.

Pytharatus, 433, 451 : Athenian archon, 271-270 B.C.

Pytheas, 83, 181, 189, 425 : Athenian orator who entered into public life when young ; was one of those who brought Demosthenes to trial, 324 B.C.

Pythia, 83 : prophetess at Delphi.

Pythiad, 127 : period of four years between Pythian festivals.

INDEX

Pythian Apollo, 111, 127, 319.
Pythian games, 117.
Pythian prophetess, 321.
Python, 253 : Thracian who killed Cotys, 358 B.C.

RHAMNUS, a deme of Attica, 345, 353.
Rhodes, 235, 393.
Rhodians, 247, 393, 445.
Right personified, 61.
Roman women, 319.
Romans, 125, 149, 171, 173, 193, 237, 241.
Rome, 95, 111, 141, 197, 271.
Roped-off Enclosure, 429 : part of the agora at Athens.
Rutilius (P. Rutilius Lupus), 329 : a Roman, rhetorician, contemporary with Augustus or Tiberius.

SACRED ANCHOR, 247.
Sacred way leading to Eleusis, 375.
Salaminia, 225 : sacred ship at Athens.
Samos, 375, 393.
Sardis, 237, 297 : capital of Lydia.
Satyrus, historian, 429.
Scedasus, 11, 13, 15, 17 : a man of Leuctra.
Scipio, 33, 193 : P. Cornelius Scipio Africanus, consul 218 and 205 B.C. ; defeated Hannibal at Zama, 202 B.C. ; died 183 B.C.
Scipio (P. Cornelius) Africanus the younger, 35, 71, 151, 171, 199, 219, 229, 241, 251 : son of L. Aemilius Paulus, adopted by the eldest son of the elder Scipio Africanus, friend of Panaetius and Polybius, consul 148 B.C., died 129 B.C.
Scythians, 433.
Seisachtheia, 207 : Solon's measure for reducing the burden of debt.
Seleucus I. (Nicator), 113, 287 : one of Alexander's generals, afterwards ruler of the greater part of Alexander's empire, assassinated 280 B.C.
Senate, at Rome, 112, 115, 137.
Sicily, 11, 47, 181, 349, 357, 363.
Sicinete, 237.
Sidon, 377 : Phoenician city.

Silenus, of limestone, 361.
Simmias, 195 : Athenian who attacked Pericles.
Simo, 29 : a cobbler.
Simonides, of Ceos, 83, 87, 93, 117, 205, 213 : choral lyric poet, 556–478 B.C.
Simonides quoted, 117, 161.
Social animal, man a, 121.
Socrates, 29, 145, 287, 345, 359, 367, 383, 421 : famous Athenian philosopher, 469–399 B.C.
Socrates, perhaps father of Deinarchus, 447.
Socrates, cousin of Isocrates, 379.
Socrates, married Callisto, 407.
Socratic philosophers, 435.
Solon, 47, 115, 137, 197, 207, 221, 237, 323 : great Athenian lawgiver and poet, 640 (?) – 558 (?) B.C. Plutarch wrote his life.
Sophilus, father of the orator Antiphon, 345, 353.
Sophocles, 87, 105, 123, 179, 219, 401 : Athenian tragic poet, 497–405 B.C.
Sophocles quoted, 87, 123, 179, 219, 237.
Sorcanus, 27, 29 : unknown person evidently of some importance.
Sosicles, son of Anaco, 387.
Sosigenes, 387 : Athenian archon, 342–341 B.C.
Sostratus, perhaps father of Deinarchus, 447.
Sparta, 15, 21, 53, 209, 253, 255, 309.
Spartans, 167, 179, 223, 249, 307.
Spartiate, 149.
Sperchis, 249 : a Spartan youth who was honoured by Xerxes for his patriotism.
Sphodrias, 207, 209 : Spartan who invaded Attica in time of peace (circa 375 B.C.) and was killed at Leuctra, 371 B.C.
Spintharus, father of Eubulus, 391.
Stadium, Panathenaic, 399.
Sthenelaïdas, ephor at Sparta, 183.
Sthenelus, 17 : son of Perseus and Andromeda ; was killed by Hyllus, son of Heracles.
Sthenno, of Messina, 249 : kindly treated by Pompey.

489

INDEX

Stoics, 131, 329.

Strato, 5, 7: wooer of Aristocleia.

Stratocles, 163, 167, 397, 455: Athenian orator who proposed honours for Lycurgus; was opponent of Demosthenes.

Strattis, 371: poet of the Old Comedy, 5th century B.C.

Sulla, L. Cornelius, 95, 119, 193, 197, 201, 249: Roman general, victor in war with Mithradates and in civil war, 138-78 B.C. Plutarch wrote his life.

Swans, singing, 129.

Sybaris, 361: Greek city in Italy, afterwards named Thurii.

Symmachus, son of Socrates and Callisto, 407.

Syracusa, daughter of Archias, 11.

Syracusan, 361, 363.

Syracuse, city in Sicily, 11, 295, 361, 371.

Syrtis, 271: a dangerous shoal off the African coast.

TAENARUM, 425, 437: southern promontory of Peloponnesus.

Tamynae, 395: city of Euboea, near which Phocion defeated Callias of Chalcis, 350 B.C.

Tantalus, 323: punished in the lower world by thirst while standing in water, and hunger while grapes hung just beyond his reach.

Tegea, city in Arcadia, 17.

Teisias, Syracusan rhetorician, 363, 371, circa 460 B.C.

Telephus, 11: murderer of Archias.

Telesippus, brother of Isocrates, 371.

Telmarch, 223: minor official at Thebes.

Telmarchy, 225: minor office at Thebes.

Tenedos, 319; an island off the coast of Asia Minor, noted for pottery.

Thales, 45: mentioned, probably through an error, as a musician.

Thalia, 43: one of the Muses.

Thasos, 423: an island in the Aegean Sea.

Theagenes, 227: an athlete.

Theano, daughter of Scedasus, 11.

Theban, Thebans, 17, 19, 63, 103, 167, 197, 223, 417, 419, 431, 443, 451.

Thebes, 21, 45.

Themis, 179, 269: goddess of law.

Themistocles, 47, 141, 169, 195, 203, 213, 229, 345: Athenian statesman to whom the victory at Salamis, 480 B.C., is chiefly due. Plutarch wrote his life.

Themistocles, son of Theophrastus, 409.

Theochares, 105: an Athenian, father of Chares.

Theodectas, of Phaselis, 375.

Theodorus, brother of Isocrates, 381, 387.

Theodorus, father of Isocrates, 371, 379, 381.

Theodorus, an actor in the 4th century B.C., 255.

Theognides, 359: Athenian archon, 468-467 B.C.

Theognis, 35: elegiac poet, 6th century B.C.

Theophanes, 5, 7: father of Aristocleia.

Theophrastus, 187, 447, 449: Peripatetic philosopher, circa 372-287 B.C.

Theophrastus, married Nicostrata, 409; his son, 409.

Theopompus, 53, 55, 253: king of Sparta, 8th century B.C.

Theopompus, 185, 349, 375: historian, born circa 380 B.C.

Theopompus, Athenian archon, 411-410 B.C., 351.

Theopompus, comic playwright, 389.

Theramenes, 291: Athenian oligarch, one of the "Thirty Tyrants," 404 B.C.; orator, 371.

Therippides, guardian of Demosthenes, 415.

Thesmothetae, 257, 353: the six junior archons at Athens.

Thespians, 11.

Thessalians, 247, 259, 283.

Thessalians, 247, 259, 283.

Thirty Tyrants, 239, 349, 359, 365, 367, 371, 389, 395.

Thisbê, a town in Boeotia, 19, 21.

Thorian, 355.

Thrace, 413.

INDEX

Thraseas, 217, 219 : put to death by Nero.

Thrasybulus, 359, 365 : restored the democracy at Athens, 404–403 B.C.

Thrasydaeus of Elis, 365.

Thria, Attic deme, 417.

Thucydides, 179 : Athenian politician.

Thucydides, 81, 149, 179, 183, 347, 413 : historian of the Peloponnesian War, *circa* 465–400 B.C.

Thurian, 441.

Thurii, 361 : city in Italy.

Tiberius (Claudius Nero), 135 : '42 B.C.–A.D. 37, Roman Emperor, A.D. 14–37.

Timarchus, speech against, by Aeschines, 393.

Timesias of Clazomenae, 229.

Timocles, comic poet, 4th century B.C.

Timocrates, 415 : Athenian archon 364–363 B.C. ; 421, archon 324–323 B.C.

Timoleon, 209, 253 : Corinthian who freed the Greek cities of Sicily from tyrants and defeated the Carthaginians, ?–337 B.C. Plutarch wrote his life.

Timothea, wife of Medeius, 407.

Timotheüs, 105, 141, 369, 373, 375, 381 : Athenian general, son of Conon, 4th century B.C.

Tithonus, 127 : husband of Eos (Dawn), granted eternal life, but not eternal youth.

Triptolemus, 323 : instructed by the goddess Demeter, taught mankind agriculture.

Trophonius, a hero whose oracular shrine was at Lebadeia, 5.

Troy, 103.

Trumpeter, a statue, 271.

Twelve Gods, altar of, 429.

Tydeus, 219 : father of Diomedes.

Tyrrhenus, of Sardis, 297.

URANIA, 37 : a Muse.

Utica, 63 : city in Africa.

VESTAL VIRGINS, 141.

WOODEN WALL, 321.

XANTHIPPUS, 361 : father of Pericles.

Xenaenetus, 185 : not clearly identified with any known bearer of this name.

Xenias, wrongly given as Athenian archon, 445.

Xenocrates, 403 : Academic philosopher (Rector of Academy 339–314 B.C.), 396–314 B.C.

Xenophon, 85, 95, 213, 259, 345, 421 : Athenian historian, soldier, historian, and essayist, *circa* 430–354 B.C.

Xerxes, 125 : king of Persia 485–464 B.C. ; defeated at Salamis 480 B.C.

ZENO, 331 : of Citium, founder of the Stoic school of philosophy, *circa* 336–264 B.C.

Zethus, of Amphipolis, 415 : writer of speeches.

Zeus, 5, 61, 105, 111, 129, 135, 175, 177, 269, 329, 333, 385, 427.

PRINTED IN GREAT BRITAIN AT THE UNIVERSITY PRESS, ABERDEEN

THE LOEB CLASSICAL LIBRARY

VOLUMES ALREADY PUBLISHED

LATIN AUTHORS

AMMIANUS MARCELLINUS. J. C. Rolfe. 3 Vols. (Vols. I and II 2nd Imp. revised.)

APULEIUS: THE GOLDEN ASS (METAMORPHOSES). W. Adlington (1566). Revised by S. Gaselee. (7th Imp.)

ST. AUGUSTINE, CONFESSIONS OF. W. Watt (1631). 2 Vols. (Vol. I 6th Imp., Vol. II 5th Imp.)

ST. AUGUSTINE, SELECT LETTERS. J. H. Baxter.

AUSONIUS. H. G. Evelyn White. 2 Vols. (Vol. II 2nd Imp.)

BEDE. J. E. King. 2 Vols.

BOETHIUS: TRACTS AND DE CONSOLATIONE PHILOSOPHIAE. Rev. H. F. Stewart and E. K. Rand. (4th Imp.)

CAESAR: CIVIL WARS. A. G. Peskett. (4th Imp.)

CAESAR: GALLIC WAR. H. J. Edwards. (9th Imp.)

CATO AND VARRO: DE RE RUSTICA. H. B. Ash and W. D. Hooper. (2nd Imp.)

CATULLUS. F. W. Cornish; TIBULLUS. J. B. Postgate; and PERVIGILIUM VENERIS. J. W. Mackail. (11th Imp.)

CELSUS: DE MEDICINA. W. G. Spencer. 3 Vols. (Vol. I 3rd Imp. revised.)

CICERO: BRUTUS AND ORATOR. G. L. Hendrickson and H. M. Hubbell. (2nd Imp.)

CICERO: DE FATO; PARADOXA STOICORUM; DE PARTITIONE ORATORIA. H. Rackham. (With De Oratore, Vol. II.) (2nd Imp.)

1

THE LOEB CLASSICAL LIBRARY

Cicero : De Finibus. H. Rackham. (*3rd Imp. revised.*)

Cicero : De Inventione, etc. H. M. Hubbell.

Cicero : De Natura Deorum and Academica. H. Rackham.

Cicero : De Officiis. Walter Miller. (*4th Imp.*)

Cicero : De Oratore. E. W. Sutton and H. Rackham. 2 Vols. (*2nd Imp.*)

Cicero : De Republica and De Legibus. Clinton W. Keyes. (*3rd Imp.*)

Cicero : De Senectute, De Amicitia, De Divinatione. W. A. Falconer. (*5th Imp.*)

Cicero : In Catilinam, Pro Murena, Pro Sulla, Pro Flacco. Louis E. Lord. (*2nd Imp. revised.*)

Cicero : Letters to Atticus. E. O. Winstedt. 3 Vols. (Vol. I 6*th Imp.*, Vols. II and III 3*rd Imp.*)

Cicero : Letters to his Friends. W. Glynn Williams. 3 Vols. (Vols. I and II 2*nd Imp.*)

Cicero : Philippics. W. C. A. Ker. (*2nd Imp.*)

Cicero : Pro Archia, Post Reditum, De Domo, De Haruspicum Responsis, Pro Plancio. N. H. Watts. (*2nd Imp.*)

Cicero : Pro Caecina, Pro Lege Manilia, Pro Cluentio, Pro Rabirio. H. Grose Hodge. (*2nd Imp.*)

Cicero : Pro Milone, In Pisonem, Pro Scauro, Pro Fonteio, Pro Rabirio Postumo, Pro Marcello, Pro Ligario, Pro Rege Deiotaro. N. H. Watts.

Cicero : Pro Quinctio, Pro Roscio Amerino, Pro Roscio Comoedo, Contra Rullum. J. H. Freese. (*2nd Imp.*)

Cicero : Tusculan Disputations. J. E. King. (*2nd Imp.*)

Cicero : Verrine Orations. L. H. G. Greenwood. 2 Vols. (Vol. I 2*nd Imp.*)

Claudian. M. Platnauer. 2 Vols.

Columella : De Re Rustica. H. B. Ash. 2 Vols. Vol. I. Books I-IV. (*2nd Imp.*)

Curtius, Q. : History of Alexander. J. C. Rolfe. 2 Vols.

Florus. E. S. Forster ; and Cornelius Nepos. J. C. Rolfe. (*2nd Imp.*)

Frontinus : Stratagems and Aqueducts. C. E. Bennett and M. B. McElwain. (*2nd Imp.*)

Fronto : Correspondence. C. R. Haines. 2 Vols.

Gellius. J. C. Rolfe. 3 Vols. (Vols. I and II 2*nd Imp.*)

Horace : Odes and Epodes. C. E. Bennett. (13*th Imp. revised.*)

THE LOEB CLASSICAL LIBRARY

HORACE: SATIRES, EPISTLES, ARS POETICA. H. R. Fairclough. (8th Imp. revised.)

JEROME: SELECT LETTERS. F. A. Wright.

JUVENAL AND PERSIUS. G. G. Ramsay. (6th Imp.)

LIVY. B. O. Foster, F. G. Moore, Evan T. Sage and A. C. Schlesinger. 13 Vols. Vols. I-XII. (Vol. I 3rd Imp., Vols. II-V, VII, IX-XII 2nd Imp. revised.)

LUCAN. J. D. Duff. (2nd Imp.)

LUCRETIUS. W. H. D. Rouse. (6th Imp. revised.)

MARTIAL. W. C. A. Ker. 2 Vols. (Vol. I 5th Imp., Vol. II 3rd Imp. revised.)

MINOR LATIN POETS: from PUBLILIUS SYRUS to RUTILIUS NAMATIANUS, including GRATTIUS, CALPURNIUS SICULUS, NEMESIANUS, AVIANUS, with " Aetna," " Phoenix " and other poems. J. Wight Duff and Arnold M. Duff. (2nd Imp.)

OVID: THE ART OF LOVE AND OTHER POEMS. J. H. Mozley. (3rd Imp.)

OVID: FASTI. Sir James G. Frazer.

OVID: HEROIDES AND AMORES. Grant Showerman. (4th Imp.)

OVID: METAMORPHOSES. F. J. Miller. 2 Vols. (Vol. I 9th Imp., Vol. II 7th Imp.)

OVID: TRISTIA AND EX PONTO. A. L. Wheeler. (2nd Imp.)

PETRONIUS. M. Heseltine; SENECA: APOCOLOCYNTOSIS. W. H. D. Rouse. (7th Imp. revised.)

PLAUTUS. Paul Nixon. 5 Vols. (Vols. I and II 4th Imp., Vol. III 3rd Imp.)

PLINY: LETTERS. Melmoth's translation revised by W. M. L. Hutchinson. 2 Vols. (Vol. I 5th Imp., Vol. II 4th Imp.)

PLINY: NATURAL HISTORY. H. Rackham and W. H. S. Jones. 10 Vols. Vols. I-V. (Vols. I-III 2nd Imp.)

PROPERTIUS. H. E. Butler. (5th Imp.)

PRUDENTIUS. H. J. Thomson. 2 Vols. Vol. I.

QUINTILIAN. H. E. Butler. 4 Vols. (2nd Imp.)

REMAINS OF OLD LATIN. E. H. Warmington. 4 Vols. Vol. I (Ennius and Caecilius). Vol. II (Livius, Naevius, Pacuvius, Accius). Vol. III (Lucilius, Laws of the XII Tables). Vol. IV (Archaic Inscriptions). (Vol. IV 2nd Imp.)

SALLUST. J. C. Rolfe. (3rd Imp. revised.)

THE LOEB CLASSICAL LIBRARY

SCRIPTORES HISTORIAE AUGUSTAE. D. Magie, 3 Vols. (Vol. I *2nd Imp. revised*.)

SENECA: APOCOLOCYNTOSIS. *Cf.* PETRONIUS.

SENECA: EPISTULAE MORALES. R. M. Gummere. 3 Vols. (Vol. I *3rd Imp.*, Vols. II and III *2nd Imp. revised*.)

SENECA: MORAL ESSAYS. J. W. Basore. 3 Vols. (Vol. II *3rd Imp. revised*, Vol. III *2nd Imp. revised*.)

SENECA: TRAGEDIES. F. J. Miller. 2 Vols. (Vol. I *3rd Imp.*, Vol. II *2nd Imp. revised*.)

SIDONIUS: POEMS AND LETTERS. W. B. Anderson. 2 Vols. Vol. I.

SILIUS ITALICUS. J. D. Duff. 2 Vols. (Vol. I *2nd Imp.*, Vol. II *3rd Imp.*)

STATIUS. J. H. Mozley. 2 Vols.

SUETONIUS. J. C. Rolfe. 2 Vols. (Vol. I *6th Imp.*, Vol. II *5th Imp.*)

TACITUS: DIALOGUS. Sir Wm. Peterson; and AGRICOLA AND GERMANIA. Maurice Hutton. (*6th Imp.*)

TACITUS: HISTORIES AND ANNALS. C. H. Moore and J. Jackson. 4 Vols. (Vols. I and II *2nd Imp.*)

TERENCE. John Sargeaunt. 2 Vols. (Vol. I *6th Imp.*, Vol. II *5th Imp.*)

TERTULLIAN: APOLOGIA AND DE SPECTACULIS. T. R. Glover; MINUCIUS FELIX. G. H. Rendall.

VALERIUS FLACCUS. J. H. Mozley. (*2nd Imp. revised*.)

VARRO: DE LINGUA LATINA. R. G. Kent. 2 Vols. (*2nd Imp. revised*.)

VELLEIUS PATERCULUS AND RES GESTAE DIVI AUGUSTI. F. W. Shipley.

VIRGIL. H. R. Fairclough. 2 Vols. (Vol. I *16th Imp.*, Vol. II *13th Imp. revised*.)

VITRUVIUS: DE ARCHITECTURA. F. Granger. 2 Vols. (Vol. I *2nd Imp.*)

GREEK AUTHORS

ACHILLES TATIUS. S. Gaselee. (*2nd Imp.*)

AENEAS TACTICUS, ASCLEPIODOTUS AND ONASANDER. The Illinois Greek Club. (*2nd Imp.*)

AESCHINES. C. D. Adams. (*2nd Imp.*)

THE LOEB CLASSICAL LIBRARY

AESCHYLUS. H. Weir Smyth. 2 Vols. (Vol. I 5th Imp., Vol. II 4th Imp.)

ALCIPHRON, AELIAN AND PHILOSTRATUS: LETTERS. A. R. Benner and F. H. Fobes.

APOLLODORUS. Sir James G. Frazer. 2 Vols. (2nd Imp.)

APOLLONIUS RHODIUS. R. C. Seaton. (4th Imp.)

THE APOSTOLIC FATHERS. Kirsopp Lake. 2 Vols. (Vol. I 7th Imp., Vol. II 6th Imp.)

APPIAN'S ROMAN HISTORY. Horace White. 4 Vols. (Vol. I 3rd Imp., Vols. II, III and IV 2nd Imp.)

ARATUS. Cf. CALLIMACHUS.

ARISTOPHANES. Benjamin Bickley Rogers. 3 Vols. (4th Imp.) Verse trans.

ARISTOTLE: ART OF RHETORIC. J. H. Freese. (3rd Imp.)

ARISTOTLE: ATHENIAN CONSTITUTION, EUDEMIAN ETHICS, VIRTUES AND VICES. H. Rackham. (2nd Imp.)

ARISTOTLE: GENERATION OF ANIMALS. A. L. Peck. (2nd Imp.)

ARISTOTLE: METAPHYSICS. H. Tredennick. 2 Vols. (3rd Imp.)

ARISTOTLE: MINOR WORKS. W. S. Hett. "On Colours," "On Things Heard," "Physiognomics," "On Plants," "On Marvellous Things Heard," "Mechanical Problems," "On Indivisible Lines," "Situations and Names of Winds," "On Melissus, Xenophanes, and Gorgias."

ARISTOTLE: NICOMACHEAN ETHICS. H. Rackham. (5th Imp. revised.)

ARISTOTLE: OECONOMICA AND MAGNA MORALIA. G. C. Armstrong. (With Metaphysics, Vol. II.) (3rd Imp.)

ARISTOTLE: ON THE HEAVENS. W. K. C. Guthrie. (2nd Imp.)

ARISTOTLE: ON THE SOUL, PARVA NATURALIA, ON BREATH. W. S. Hett. (2nd Imp. revised.)

ARISTOTLE: ORGANON. H. P. Cooke and H. Tredennick. 3 Vols. Vol. I. (2nd Imp.)

ARISTOTLE: PARTS OF ANIMALS. A. L. Peck; MOTION AND PROGRESSION OF ANIMALS. E. S. Forster. (2nd Imp.)

ARISTOTLE: PHYSICS. Rev. P. Wicksteed and F. M. Cornford. 2 Vols. (2nd Imp.)

ARISTOTLE: POETICS and LONGINUS. W. Hamilton Fyfe; DEMETRIUS ON STYLE. W. Rhys Roberts. (4th Imp. revised.)

THE LOEB CLASSICAL LIBRARY

ARISTOTLE: POLITICS. H. Rackham. (*3rd Imp.*)

ARISTOTLE: PROBLEMS. W. S. Hett. 2 Vols. (Vol. I *2nd Imp. revised.*)

ARISTOTLE: RHETORICA AD ALEXANDRUM. H. Rackham. (With Problems, Vol. II.)

ARRIAN: HISTORY OF ALEXANDER AND INDICA. Rev. E. Iliffe Robson. 2 Vols. (*2nd Imp.*)

ATHENAEUS: DEIPNOSOPHISTAE. C. B. Gulick. 7 Vols. (Vols. I, V and VI *2nd Imp.*)

ST. BASIL: LETTERS. R. J. Deferrari. 4 Vols. (Vols. I, II and IV *2nd Imp.*)

CALLIMACHUS AND LYCOPHRON. A. W. Mair; ARATUS. G. R. Mair.

CLEMENT OF ALEXANDRIA. Rev. G. W. Butterworth. (*2nd Imp.*)

COLLUTHUS. *Cf.* OPPIAN.

DAPHNIS AND CHLOE. *Cf.* LONGUS.

DEMOSTHENES I: OLYNTHIACS, PHILIPPICS AND MINOR ORATIONS: I-XVII AND XX. J. H. Vince.

DEMOSTHENES II: DE CORONA AND DE FALSA LEGATIONE. C. A. Vince and J. H. Vince. (*2nd Imp. revised.*)

DEMOSTHENES III: MEIDIAS, ANDROTION, ARISTOCRATES, TIMOCRATES, ARISTOGEITON. J. H. Vince.

DEMOSTHENES IV-VI: PRIVATE ORATIONS AND IN NEAERAM. A. T. Murray. (Vol. IV *2nd Imp.*)

DEMOSTHENES VII: FUNERAL SPEECH, EROTIC ESSAY, EXORDIA AND LETTERS. N. W. and N. J. DeWitt.

DIO CASSIUS: ROMAN HISTORY. E. Cary. 9 Vols. (Vols. I and II *2nd Imp.*)

DIO CHRYSOSTOM. 5 Vols. Vols I and II. J. W. Cohoon. Vol. III. J. W. Cohoon and H. Lamar Crosby. Vol. IV. H. Lamar Crosby. (Vols. I and II *2nd Imp.*)

DIODORUS SICULUS. 12 Vols. Vols. I-IV. C. H. Oldfather. Vol. IX. Russel M. Geer. (Vol. I *2nd Imp.*)

DIOGENES LAERTIUS. R. D. Hicks. 2 Vols. (Vol. I *3rd Imp.*, Vol. II *2nd Imp.*)

DIONYSIUS OF HALICARNASSUS: ROMAN ANTIQUITIES. Spelman's translation revised by E. Cary. 7 Vols. Vols. I-VI. (Vol. IV *2nd Imp.*)

EPICTETUS. W. A. Oldfather. 2 Vols. (Vol. I *2nd Imp.*)

EURIPIDES. A. S. Way. 4 Vols. (Vols. I, II and IV *6th Imp.*, Vol. III *5th Imp.*) Verse trans.

EUSEBIUS : ECCLESIASTICAL HISTORY. Kirsopp Lake and J. E. L. Oulton. 2 Vols. (Vol. I *2nd Imp.*, Vol. II *3rd Imp.*)

GALEN: ON THE NATURAL FACULTIES. A. J. Brock. (*3rd Imp.*)

THE GREEK ANTHOLOGY. W. R. Paton. 5 Vols. (Vols. I and II *4th Imp.*, Vols. III and IV *3rd Imp.*)

THE GREEK BUCOLIC POETS (THEOCRITUS, BION, MOSCHUS). J. M. Edmonds. (*6th Imp. revised.*)

GREEK ELEGY AND IAMBUS WITH THE ANACREONTEA. J. M. Edmonds. 2 Vols. (Vol. I *2nd Imp.*)

GREEK MATHEMATICAL WORKS. Ivor Thomas. 2 Vols. (*2nd Imp.*)

HERODES. *Cf.* THEOPHRASTUS : CHARACTERS.

HERODOTUS. A. D. Godley. 4 Vols. (Vol. I *4th Imp.*, Vols. II–IV *3rd Imp.*)

HESIOD AND THE HOMERIC HYMNS. H. G. Evelyn White. (*6th Imp. revised and enlarged.*)

HIPPOCRATES AND THE FRAGMENTS OF HERACLEITUS. W. H. S. Jones and E. T. Withington. 4 Vols. (Vol. I *3rd Imp.*, Vols. II–IV *2nd Imp.*)

HOMER : ILIAD. A. T. Murray. 2 Vols. (*6th Imp.*)

HOMER : ODYSSEY. A. T. Murray. 2 Vols. (*7th Imp.*)

ISAEUS. E. S. Forster. (*2nd Imp.*)

ISOCRATES. George Norlin and LaRue Van Hook. 3 Vols.

ST. JOHN DAMASCENE : BARLAAM AND IOASAPH. Rev. G. R. Woodward and Harold Mattingly. (*2nd Imp. revised.*)

JOSEPHUS. H. St. J. Thackeray and Ralph Marcus. 9 Vols. Vols. I–VII. (Vols. I, V and VI *2nd Imp.*)

JULIAN. Wilmer Cave Wright. 3 Vols. (Vol. I *2nd Imp.*, Vol. II *3rd Imp.*)

LONGUS : DAPHNIS AND CHLOE. Thornley's translation revised by J. M. Edmonds ; and PARTHENIUS. S. Gaselee. (*3rd Imp.*)

LUCIAN. A. M. Harmon. 8 Vols. Vols. I–V. (Vols. I and II *2nd Imp.*, Vol. III *3rd Imp.*)

LYCOPHRON. *Cf.* CALLIMACHUS.

LYRA GRAECA. J. M. Edmonds. 3 Vols. (Vol. I *3rd Imp.*, Vol. II *2nd Ed. revised and enlarged*, Vol. III *3rd Imp. revised.*)

LYSIAS. W. R. M. Lamb. (*2nd Imp.*)

MANETHO. W. G. Waddell. PTOLEMY : TETRABIBLOS. F. E. Robbins. (*2nd Imp.*)

THE LOEB CLASSICAL LIBRARY

MARCUS AURELIUS. C. R. Haines. (3rd Imp. revised.)

MENANDER. F. G. Allinson. (2nd Imp. revised.)

MINOR ATTIC ORATORS. 2 Vols. Vol. I (Antiphon, Andocides). K. J. Maidment.

NONNOS: DIONYSIACA. W. H. D. Rouse. 3 Vols. (Vol.
III 2nd Imp.)

OPPIAN, COLLUTHUS, TRYPHIODORUS. A. W. Mair.

PAPYRI. NON-LITERARY SELECTIONS. A. S. Hunt and C. C.
Edgar. 2 Vols. (Vol. I 2nd Imp.) LITERARY SELECTIONS.
Vol. I (Poetry). D. L. Page. (2nd Imp.)

PARTHENIUS. Cf. LONGUS.

PAUSANIAS: DESCRIPTION OF GREECE. W. H. S. Jones. 5
Vols. and Companion Vol. arranged by R. E. Wycherley.
(Vols. I and III 2nd Imp.)

PHILO. 11 Vols. Vols. I-V. F. H. Colson and Rev. G. H.
Whitaker; Vols. VI-IX. F. H. Colson. (Vols. I, II, V,
VI and VII 2nd Imp., Vol. IV 3rd Imp. revised.)

PHILOSTRATUS: THE LIFE OF APOLLONIUS OF TYANA. F. C.
Conybeare. 2 Vols. (3rd Imp.)

PHILOSTRATUS: IMAGINES; CALLISTRATUS: DESCRIPTIONS.
A. Fairbanks.

PHILOSTRATUS AND EUNAPIUS: LIVES OF THE SOPHISTS.
Wilmer Cave Wright. (2nd Imp.)

PINDAR. Sir J. E. Sandys. (7th Imp. revised.)

PLATO: CHARMIDES, ALCIBIADES, HIPPARCHUS, THE LOVERS,
THEAGES, MINOS AND EPINOMIS. W. R. M. Lamb.

PLATO: CRATYLUS, PARMENIDES, GREATER HIPPIAS, LESSER
HIPPIAS. H. N. Fowler. (3rd Imp.)

PLATO: EUTHYPHRO, APOLOGY, CRITO, PHAEDO, PHAEDRUS.
H. N. Fowler. (9th Imp.)

PLATO: LACHES, PROTAGORAS, MENO, EUTHYDEMUS.
W. R. M. Lamb. (2nd Imp. revised.)

PLATO: LAWS. Rev. R. G. Bury. 2 Vols. (2nd Imp.)

PLATO: LYSIS, SYMPOSIUM, GORGIAS. W. R. M. Lamb.
(4th Imp. revised.)

PLATO: REPUBLIC. Paul Shorey. 2 Vols. (Vol. I 4th Imp.,
Vol. II 3rd Imp.)

PLATO: STATESMAN, PHILEBUS. H. N. Fowler; ION.
W. R. M. Lamb. (3rd Imp.)

PLATO: THEAETETUS AND SOPHIST. H. N. Fowler. (3rd Imp.)

PLATO: TIMAEUS, CRITIAS, CLITOPHO, MENEXENUS, EPI-
STULAE. Rev. R. G. Bury. (2nd Imp.)

THE LOEB CLASSICAL LIBRARY

PLUTARCH : MORALIA. 14 Vols. Vols. I-V. F. C. Babbitt ; Vol. VI. W. C. Helmbold ; Vol. X. H. N. Fowler. (Vols. I, III and X *2nd Imp.*)

PLUTARCH : THE PARALLEL LIVES. B. Perrin. 11 Vols. (Vols. I, II and VII *3rd Imp.*, Vols. III, IV, VI, VIII-XI *2nd Imp.*)

POLYBIUS. W. R. Paton. 6 Vols.

PROCOPIUS : HISTORY OF THE WARS. H. B. Dewing. 7 Vols. (Vol. I *2nd Imp.*)

PTOLEMY : TETRABIBLOS. *Cf.* MANETHO.

QUINTUS SMYRNAEUS. A. S. Way. Verse trans. (*2nd Imp.*)

SEXTUS EMPIRICUS. Rev. R. G. Bury. 4 Vols. (Vols. I and III *2nd Imp.*)

SOPHOCLES. F. Storr. 2 Vols. (Vol. I *8th Imp.*, Vol. II *5th Imp.*) Verse trans.

STRABO : GEOGRAPHY. Horace L. Jones. 8 Vols. (Vols. I and VIII *3rd Imp.*, Vols. II, V and VI *2nd Imp.*)

THEOPHRASTUS : CHARACTERS. J. M. Edmonds ; HERODES, etc. A. D. Knox. (*2nd Imp.*)

THEOPHRASTUS : ENQUIRY INTO PLANTS. Sir Arthur Hort. 2 Vols. (*2nd Imp.*)

THUCYDIDES. C. F. Smith. 4 Vols. (Vol. I *3rd Imp.*, Vols. II-IV *2nd Imp. revised.*)

TRYPHIODORUS. *Cf.* OPPIAN.

XENOPHON : CYROPAEDIA. Walter Miller. 2 Vols. (Vol. I *2nd Imp.*, Vol. II *3rd Imp.*)

XENOPHON : HELLENICA, ANABASIS, APOLOGY, AND SYMPOSIUM. C. L. Brownson and O. J. Todd. 3 Vols. (*3rd Imp.*)

XENOPHON : MEMORABILIA AND OECONOMICUS. E. C. Marchant. (*2nd Imp.*)

XENOPHON : SCRIPTA MINORA. E. C. Marchant. (*2nd Imp.*)

VOLUMES IN PREPARATION

GREEK AUTHORS

ARISTOTLE : DE MUNDO, etc. A. L. Peck and E. S. Forster.
ARISTOTLE : HISTORY OF ANIMALS. A. L. Peck.

THE LOEB CLASSICAL LIBRARY

Aristotle: Meteorologica. H. D. P. Lee.
Plotinus.

LATIN AUTHORS

St. Augustine: City of God.
[Cicero :] Ad Herennium. H. Caplan.
Cicero: Pro Sestio, In Vatinium, Pro Caelio, De Provinciis Consularibus, Pro Balbo. J. H. Freese and R. Gardner.
Phaedrus and other Fabulists. B. E. Perry.

DESCRIPTIVE PROSPECTUS ON APPLICATION

LONDON	CAMBRIDGE, MASS.
WILLIAM HEINEMANN LTD	HARVARD UNIV. PRESS
Cloth 15s.	Cloth $2.50